Talking Art

Talking Art

Interviews with artists since 1976
Edited by Patricia Bickers and Andrew Wilson

Art Monthly | Ridinghouse

Contents

1980–1984

1984–1987

1998–2007

Patricia Bickers

Introduction

In her essay, 'An anatomy of the interview', reprinted here, Iwona Blazwick describes the interview form as 'irresistible'. She is surely right; right, too, when she says that 'the notion of revelation through verbal exchange has emerged from psychoanalysis' and, owing to the inextricable links with the development of recording technology, it is perhaps inevitable that the interview has become 'a quintessentially twentieth-century form of historical narrative'.

And yet there is plenty of evidence to show that in the West, as elsewhere, the thoughts and utterances of artists have always been a source of fascination to fellow artists as well as to non-artists. To satisfy this appetite, artists' letters, writings and sayings have been handed down from generation to generation by word of mouth or recorded in writing in the form of manuals, personal memoirs and histories from Cennini at the beginning of the fifteenth century to Vasari in the mid-sixteenth century. It is arguable that the famous account by collector and art connoisseur, Paul Fréart de Chantelou, of Bernini's visit to France in the summer of 1665, can be seen as a prototype of the interview proper. Bernini, who was sixty-five at the time and still at the height of his powers, had been invited in connection with his (ultimately unsuccessful) plans for the building of the Louvre as well as to execute a portrait bust of King Louis XIV. Chantelou who, on the king's orders, accompanied the great man throughout his visit wrote his account in order 'to preserve some record of what I have heard said by him'. Using the notes he jotted down at the time, it is written almost entirely in the form of reported speech interwoven with direct quotations from Bernini, many of them answers to questions posed by Chantelou himself. The result is extraordinarily vivid, a word Chantelou himself uses to describe Bernini's fluency, 'His enunciation is very beautiful and he has a special talent for explaining things with words and gestures, and for making them vivid as well as the greatest painters have been able to do with their brushes', and, it might be said, as Chantelou was able to do with his pen.[1]

As with interviews, the interest lies in what Bernini says not only about his own practice but also about that of his contemporaries, such as Poussin, as well as the light he sheds on the cultural and social context in which he worked. As Blazwick says, 'the creator and the critic are revealed as subjects, with all the subtle complexities of gender, generation and social interaction that that implies'. In Chantelou's account artistic rivalries as well as cultural and aesthetic differences between Paris and Rome are revealed in Bernini's occasionally acrimonious exchanges with French academicians and aspiring artists, differences that sometimes required all of Chantelou's diplomatic skills to smooth over. Similarly, in *Talking Art*, the encounters between the English critic, Peter Fuller, and American artists, Carl Andre and Jasper Johns, reveal similar cultural and political differences – sometimes with hilarious results as when Fuller asks Andre whether he empathises with the view that British art should be 'less hegemonised' by American art and that it should move towards 'a national art'. Andre replies swiftly, 'In England that would be like demanding a truly national cuisine. I think it would be a disaster'. Things have changed since 1977, and not only in the culinary department, though this does not invalidate Andre's point. On the contrary, the debate about the 'Britishness of British art' was to resurface when it was first proposed to convert the Bankside site into Tate Modern to show international art, and to house the British collection in the old Tate Gallery on Millbank, to be renamed 'Tate Britain'. The issue of which art should be considered 'British' and which 'international' – let alone modern – remains unresolved, as was recently demonstrated by the determination of those most perversely parochial of British artists, Gilbert & George, to stage their retrospective at Tate Modern rather than Tate Britain. Paradoxically, their insistence on being shown in the international context of Tate Modern reflects their desire to be taken seriously at home for, as they complained in the interview with Andrew Wilson in 1989, 'the English will only attend to art that is from wine-growing countries'. English cuisine may have improved since 1977, but England's wine-growing culture is still nascent.

Gilbert & George's remark reveals something of their wilful insularity since it would be truer to say that the English, or at least English artists, were attending rather more closely to art and ideas from America – and not from the wine-growing West Coast but from the East Coast, specifically from New York. Fuller, on the other hand, was well aware of this shift and his concern with a 'national art' was dictated in part by an unabashed anti-Americanism. However, even he could not have imagined that within thirty years – the span of *Talking Art* – London would come to rival New York as a creative centre for the visual arts. Bernini, too, would have thought it inconceivable that Paris would one day eclipse Rome as a cultural centre. Such rivalries can be productive as well as instructive, like that between West Coast and East Coast artists in America. As Ed Ruscha remarks wryly in *Talking Art*, 'Not just artists but writers and very intelligent people feel that unless you have somehow checked into Manhattan at some point or another, or at least have a PO Box there, you are destined for territorial purgatory.' His choice of metaphor deliberately references Catholicism, part of the cultural mix that separates the West Coast from what Joseph Masheck has described as 'the spiritually impoverished Calvinist culture all but legally established in the USA'.[2] Fellow West Coast artist, John Baldessari, speaking to Liam Gillick, recalled that one of the things that used to bother him on his 'forays into New York' was 'the sense that things had to fit into history or they weren't viable.' However, when Clement Greenberg claimed in his interview with Trish Evans and Charles Harrison in 1987 that New York had become by the late fifties and early sixties as provincial as Paris had become 'in the old days', it was an assessment that was more a function of his own inability to come to terms with the art of the time than a reflection of reality. Lucy Lippard, interviewed here by David Coxhead, gives an altogether different, and fascinating, picture of New York in the sixties. However, today it is arguable that the West Coast, and Los Angeles in particular, is a more vibrant creative centre than its old rival in the East.

While purporting to be a true account of Bernini's ideas and observations, as a Frenchman and as an avid collector, Chantelou also had his own agenda. For instance, knowing that an endorsement from Bernini could enhance both his own judgement and the value of his collection, he shamelessly records a conversation about a work by Poussin in the collection of Cardinal Barberini (later Pope Urban VIII), and has Bernini interrupt: 'You should see those M. Chantelou has: they are something different. He has seven representing the Sacraments which I could look at for six months without tiring'. It is probably safe to assume, in modern parlance, that Bernini was not given copy approval of the final text.

Chantelou can be said here to have elided the role of faithful amanuensis with one of the roles or models of the interviewer identified by Blazwick: that of the 'interrogator' who dictates the form of the interview to fit his own 'agenda of enquiry'. There are instances in *Talking Art*, too, when artists either suspect or accuse the interviewer directly of having an agenda of their own. Anthony Caro, for instance, takes Fuller to task for 'trying to use art for something else'. It has to be said that Fuller's aggressive questioning elicited some fascinating responses, but then given the calibre of the interviewees, that is hardly surprising.

Today, however, it is rare to encounter such a confrontational style of interviewing and, whatever the agenda of the interviewer, it is likely to be less overt. This is perhaps because in the pluralist present the lines are no longer so clearly drawn between, for instance, Greenbergians and anti-Greenbergians, formalists and anti-formalists, nor are the distinctions between Pop Art and Minimal Art as absolute as they once seemed. At the same time the elisions between Minimal Art and Conceptual Art – for instance in the work of Sol LeWitt – are more apparent than they previously were. The subtle yet precise ways in which artists themselves define their practice, both independently and in relation to their peers, defy easy categorisation. Where art historians, at least traditionally, may be said to seek continuities, and critics may look for the discontinuities that distinguish one artist's practice from another's, artists frustrate both. Though Greenberg speaks disparagingly of Brice Marden, when interviewed by Bill Furlong, Marden himself is not only sympathetic to some of the critic's views, but says that he considers his work as being closer to Abstract Expressionism rather than to Minimal Art – with which he is usually associated – or Conceptual Art, though he confesses to a certain 'guilt by association' in the case of the latter. Similarly, Agnes Martin, though flattered to have been invited by Andre, Dan Flavin, Donald Judd, LeWitt and Robert Morris to show with them, tells Irving Sandler: 'I considered myself to be an abstract expressionist but they considered me a minimalist. I couldn't do anything about that.' It seems that even artists can be wrong, nominally at least: where the younger artists saw affinities with her work, Martin saw only that they had a certain 'classicism' in common.

The model of the interviewer which is most prevalent today is that of 'collaborator'. Chantelou also adopted this role, identifying with the interests of his subject to the point of promoting Bernini's claims over that of his (ultimately successful) French rival, Claude Perrault, in the matter of the design for the Louvre. Chantelou's instincts served him well, however, since while Perrault's fame has dimmed, that of Bernini has lost nothing of its glow and, as a result, Chantelou himself has been 'inscribed into art history along with the artist'. This, as Blazwick points out, is part of the thrill of the interview, but it is no less true for the readers (or listeners) for whom the interviewer stands as proxy, allowing them the illusion of access to the artist without being present. It is testimony to the irresistibility of the first-person account that Chantelou wrote up his notes of Bernini's visit in response to pressure from his brother, Jean, a fellow art collector and connoisseur. Connoisseurship may now be regarded with suspicion for its negative associations with the market and with outmoded ways of evaluating art – an association that tainted Greenberg perhaps unjustly – but the value of the interview to critics, historians and other specialists, for whom it constitutes primary research material, cannot be overstated.

It is worth asking, however, what value the interview has for the artist. Though some artists are reluctant to be interviewed, the majority have been willing to submit to interview, effectively becoming mediators of their own work. The correspondence between Chantelou and Poussin, in particular a famous letter of November 1647 concerning the painting of *The Ordination*, one of the 'Seven Sacraments' alluded to by Bernini in Chantelou's account of his visit to France, provides one answer. Apparently Chantelou had convinced himself that a painting owned by a rival patron, Jean Pointel, was superior to his own and pestered the painter about it. Eventually, irritated by Chantelou's persistence, Poussin, who was by then living in Rome, wrote a long letter to him explaining patiently that different subjects require different treatments and, drawing from music theory to support his argument, that these treatments or 'modes' excite different feelings in the viewer.[3] To the modern reader the subsequent argument might seem arcane but what comes across clearly despite the distance in time, is the artist's frustration which drove him eventually to respond to Chantelou. In other words, he felt he had to clarify his position – not to explain or justify the particular work but rather to set down the parameters within which his work should be discussed or, more importantly, viewed. This brings to mind the frustration LeWitt experienced in the face of similar misunderstanding or misrepresentation which led him to write his famous 'Paragraphs on Conceptual Art' and 'Sentences on Conceptual Art', published at the instigation of Robert Smithson in *Artforum* in 1967 and

1969 respectively. As he explains in his interview with Andrew Wilson: 'I wanted to counter the current notion of Minimal Art. This was being written about by critics, however I thought it missed the point because it regarded this art in a formal way rather than what I believed was more conceptual.'

The letter, the article, the manifesto, the artist's statement and latterly the recorded interview have long been avenues through which artists have sought to make the case for their art. This was never more true than in the late sixties and seventies, and it had nothing to do with developments in recording technology. Writing in 1974, in the second edition of his anthology, *Artists on Art*, originally published just after the Second World War in 1945, Robert Goldwater attributed the increasing willingness of artists to 'use' the interview to the desire to bridge what he described as the widening 'gap' between themselves and the public.[4] Whereas he saw this move as occurring almost by default, Ellen H Johnson, writing in 1982, more accurately saw the flow of 'writing and talking' by contemporary artists in the seventies as a direct outcome of artists' own perception of their changing role 'in a democratic, industrial, and technological society'.[5] Writing in 1988, Jeanne Siegel goes further, suggesting that in contrast to the abstract expressionists who had 'turned their backs' on a hostile public – with the result that the artist came to be seen, in Ad Reinhardt's words, as 'a bumpkin or Dionysian or dumbbell' – the artist emerged in the mid sixties as 'a truly public figure.'[6] This is paralleled in the trajectory of Dan Graham's work in the sixties. Interviewed by Mark Thomson in 1992, he discusses his transition from inserting works into mainstream magazines, like the *Homes for America* project in 1965, to his direct architectural interventions in the form of mirror-glass pavilions that mediate between the private and public realm, between interior and exterior. From a European perspective, the retreat of artists from the public into the private sphere began with the rise of Romanticism in post-revolutionary France, a consequence in part of the dismantling of the aristocratic system of patronage that led to the gradual isolation of the artist from society. This being so, it is surely no coincidence that one of the most valuable primary sources of the period is in the private form of a diary: the famous *Journal* Eugène Delacroix kept from 1822 to 1863.[7]

In the political turmoil of the sixties – Siegel cites the Vietnam War, political activism in the US and Europe, especially in 1968, the civil rights movement and the emergence of Black Power and feminism, to which could be added in subsequent years the Arab-Israeli conflict, Northern Ireland and Greenham Common – retreat was no longer an option for many artists for whom the notion of the autonomy of art, so dear to Greenberg, was simply untenable. Daniel Buren and Seth Siegelaub, interviewed by Deke Dusinberre and Michel Claura, make this absolutely clear: when asked whether he would like to begin the interview by talking about 'personal moments of inspiration' Siegelaub replies forthrightly, 'No. I would want to talk about the larger political context within which I grew up. The context for me during my early working life in the United States was the Vietnam War, it was an important factor in my growing up. Whether it was an important factor in the art world as such remains to be seen.' Lippard similarly locates herself within the wider cultural and political context in her interview, 'Growing up'.

Against such a background, romantic talk of 'inspiration' seemed impossibly arch and self-indulgent. For Hanne Darboven, interviewed in 1998, the entire twentieth century represents nothing less than 'the disaster of Romanticism'. While it might be acceptable for English artists to flirt with Romanticism (she cites Richard Long among her contemporaries, and it is interesting that Anya Gallaccio, interviewed in 1999, tentatively describes herself as a Romantic), for Darboven, a German born in 1941 in the midst of the Second World War, such an identification would be impossible even, in her view, dangerous.
For artists emerging in the sixties and seventies it was not just a matter of 'writing and talking', but of finding an appropriate language commensurate with their work and intentions – one as far from Romantic rhetoric as possible.

This shift in language can be tracked in the contrasts between generations and cultures in *Talking Art*, though one artist whose language and work connect all three decades covered by the book is Naum Gabo, the first artist interviewed by *Art Monthly* and just a few months before he died. His belief in the constructive principle in art connects him with Caro and Richard Deacon, while his concern with the social context of art and his workmanlike ethic – as well as his aesthetic clarity – finds echoes in Andre and Alan Charlton, for instance.

In the late sixties and seventies, the issue of direct political and social engagement in art – an issue that is once again preoccupying artists against the background of another disastrous war – was a vital concern that artists addressed in different ways both in their work and in interviews. LeWitt, for example, when asked whether art should have a social or moral purpose, replied, 'No. I think artists should have a social or moral purpose'. Richard Serra takes a similar line; though he became 'personally politicised' in the sixties, when it comes to direct political engagement he states clearly: 'I make a division between my work and my language.' For Gustav Metzger, veteran of auto-destructive art in the sixties, on the other hand, it became impossible to make work at all and he announced a three-year moratorium on making art in the seventies. His subsequent return to making work was described by some as a sell-out but as Metzger himself says, 'In my old age I am no longer so radical. I am not saying "Stop it", I am now saying "Change it, please"'. Hans Haacke, regarded by many as the doyen of political artists, has also been accused subsequently of selling out but he robustly rejects the kind of one-dimensional view of his work that tends to relegate the aesthetic aspect while concentrating solely on its overtly political content. Times change and, in many ways art – including his own – that addressed issues surrounding the political and economic underpinnings of the institutions of art could be said to have had some success in opening up that debate. In focusing on different issues in his recent work, therefore, he is not 'selling out'. On the contrary, while it might not be political 'in the immediate sense', it may nevertheless lead people 'to recognise why or how they respond to images and that this has ideological implications and by extension also political consequences'. Barbara Kruger, speaking to John Roberts in 1983, put it succinctly: 'I don't see politics as something out there, it's all one cloth.'

For these artists, interactivity – strictly with a small 'i' – with audiences is a given. However, it is ironic that the advent of the internet, an interactive form of communication designed to give instant global access to people and information, should have given rise to the email which is, in effect, merely another, more rapid epistolary form. Emails, like letters, tend to be more formal in address and are often characterised by longer, albeit more considered questions and answers. This is certainly true of the interview with Jeff Wall in 1994, for instance – though a more formal mode seems somehow appropriate in discussing the work of an artist who has successfully readdressed the grandest academic genre of them all: History Painting. In fact, however, as in the case with Chantelou and Poussin, it was largely a matter of logistics. Similarly, the interview between Sandler and Martin was conducted by telephone because the artist seldom left her desert retreat in Taos, New Mexico, and Sandler, the quintessential urban New Yorker, preferred, as he told her, to 'infer' the vastness of the New Mexican mesas from looking at her paintings rather than to experience them directly.

The majority of interviews in *Talking Art*, however, are transcriptions from recorded conversations conducted face to face. This is for a number of reasons, chief among them being that, since 1992, interviews have focused on new work, particularly in the case of well-established artists, to encourage the possibility of fresh insights into both recent and earlier work, and that they take place during a major showing of the artist's work to offer readers of *Art Monthly* the opportunity to see the work for themselves, and in depth. However, it is also true to say that, like any encounter between two or more people, the recorded interview can throw up the unexpected. There is an intimacy, albeit temporary, between the interviewer and interviewee, as is suggested by the title of one of the interviews with Deacon, 'Between the two of us', taken from the title of one of his works under discussion. This is not to suggest that the recorded transcription is somehow 'truer' than the interview by letter, email or even telephone. On the contrary, as Blazwick says, 'The interview, which seems to promise veracity by giving access to the primary source, is of course a beautiful construct'. Indeed, artists have been known to fake interviews, while Andy Warhol set up *Interview* magazine in 1969, dedicated to celebrities rather than artists, mainly to serve as a channel for his own fascination with fame. For both practical and ethical reasons, all *Art Monthly* interviewees are given full copy approval and, while the sense of immediacy – however illusory – may be reduced as a result, much is gained in terms of trust between interviewee and interviewer.

All histories are constructions to some extent and, like any form of history, those written in the first person can only ever be partial. The interview is by definition a narrative form that unfolds in time; it is revised, edited and structured according to fixed design and layout formats and, as in any editing process, much ends up on the cutting-room floor. It is often forgotten, for instance, that Dan Flavin also took part, with Judd and Frank Stella, in the famous 1964 interview with Bruce Glaser, for WBAI-FM radio. Flavin edited himself out of the broadcast version and was not included in the later printed version that appeared in *Art News*, edited by Lippard. Similarly, the interview with Martin published here was initially a three-way conversation, but I later edited myself out of the printed version since, having introduced Sandler, it seemed appropriate to leave them to enjoy a fascinating conversation uninterrupted.

Narrative is arguably the last bastion of Modernism to fall and it is no coincidence that in recent years many artists have chosen to adopt it as a form, especially in film and video work. Sometimes, as in the case of Douglas Gordon, by appropriating an existing narrative in the form of mainstream movies, famously in *24 Hour Psycho* or, as in some works discussed by Angela Bulloch, by re-editing cult films. Others, like Mike Nelson, relate more to literary forms of narrative. As he explains, 'I think my interest in narrative comes out of the fact that I found it very difficult to absorb theory at college but after I left I would find those same ideas articulated in some lowbrow piece of fiction – it was like going straight to the source.' Though not primarily concerned with narrative, Simon Patterson, interviewed by Ian Hunt, says 'From the beginning I wanted to work with material that was familiar – film, football and so on – but not just to borrow its familiarity, to do something else with it'. For Sophie Calle, the narrative form is crucial. A reluctant interviewee, she sees herself primarily as a storyteller and that, in her view, places her somewhat at odds with the interview process. As she explains to Lynne Cooke, 'Storytelling is very different from an interview. I like to tell stories and it's what I do in my work. I'm not going to tell them again when I speak to you. This is not storytelling, it's a kind of analysing and this is not the language I like to use'. In her recent work Tacita Dean has been drawn increasingly by personal histories, her own and others', while for Jimmie Durham, history and the present are almost indistinguishable from each other. Recalling the harrowing stories his Cherokee grandmother told him of 'The Trail of Tears', he says that it is only when something is resolved that it becomes history, the past: 'Until it's resolved then it is in the present, it's always in the present.'

In another sense, history when written in the form of an interview always reads as if it is in the present. For the reader as for the editor, so many serendipities can occur, too, which link artists and ideas across generations and cultures, and one conversation with another, and this is part of the excitement of gathering them all into one volume. For example, in his interview with Blazwick, Willie Doherty discusses his 1993 video installation, *The Only Good One is a Dead One*, while in the very next issue, Durham explains that he moved to Mexico from New York because it was cheaper but also, as he joked to Mark Gisbourne, because 'There are so many Indians in Mexico, you shall not deny us there, you cannot even say that you haven't met a good one'. On a more sombre note, Doherty said of *The Only Good One is a Dead One*, 'I wanted to try to understand the notion of the terrorist, especially in light of the media ban that exists here and in the Republic of Ireland. This work tries to reinvent that character by suggesting that it's possible for the perpetrator also to be the victim and the victim to be the perpetrator'. While the media ban was eventually lifted, and this year a power-sharing government was at last established in Northern Ireland, Doherty's work remains all too relevant in the context of the so called 'war on terror'. In a terrible sense, it will always be relevant. As Metzger says of his found newspaper series, the 'Historic Photographs', they 'recycle what has been discarded, that is exactly what makes it so relevant. You could say it is always the same newspaper and it is always the same image. In that sense it is eternal.'

1 *A Documentary History of Art*, Vol II, selected and edited by Elizabeth Gilmore Holt, Princeton, 1947, reissued Doubleday Anchor 1958, p 125 and ff.
2 Joseph Masheck, 'Minimalism: NY', *Art Monthly* 277, June 2004, p 6.
3 E Holt, *op. cit.* pp 154–156.
4 *Artists on Art: from the XIV to the XX Century*, compiled and edited by Robert Goldwater and Marco Treves, Pantheon Books, New York, 1945 and 1974, p 18.
5 *American Artists on Art: from 1940 to 1980*, edited by Ellen H Johnson, Icon editions, Harper & Row, New York, 1982, preface p 18.
6 *Artwords: Discourse on the 60s and 70s*, edited by Jeanne Siegel, Da Capo Press, New York, 1988, Introduction p 1.
7 *The Journal of Eugène Delacroix: A Selection*, edited with an introduction by Hubert Wellington, translated from the French by Lucy Norton, Phaidon, London, 1951.

Iwona Blazwick

An anatomy of the interview

From vox pop to celebrity exclusive

Reading dialogues is as irresistible as eavesdropping, and it is the interview as a genre of art criticism which promises to deliver the frisson of listening in on the voice of the creator – the primary voice, concealed behind the image, the text, the work of art.

From vox pops to celebrity exclusives, the proliferation of this genre is inextricably linked with technology, with the speed and sophistication of recording and reprographic techniques which make the interview a quintessentially twentieth-century form of historical narrative. It is a truly modern manifestation of our ever-expanding capacity to translate the temporal into the material, the private into the public and the individual into the icon.

What makes interviews so compelling? In the sixties the Italian feminist art critic, Carla Lonzi, stopped writing structured critical essays and began to record interviews with artists, publishing them with the minimum of editorial intervention. She wrote: 'I felt the work of art as a possibility of meeting, as an invitation by the artists to participate, directed to each one of us. This seemed to me an act to which I could not respond professionally. These last years I have felt doubt about the role of the critic, in which I have seen a coded nature estranged from art as well as an exercise of discriminatory power over artists. Even though it is not automatic that the technique of tape-recording is sufficient to produce a transformation of the critical act... the complete and verifiable act of criticism is only that which partakes of the work of art itself.'[1]

This rejection of critical distance is not only broadly symptomatic of a desire to connect art with lived reality and actively to engage criticism within the procedures of art – for artist and critic to share responsibility, as it were – it also questions the notion of objectivity. The creator and the critic are revealed as subjects, with all the subtle complexities of gender, generation and social interaction that that implies. Christian Boltanski played with this by making a series of interviews with the same person but under the influence of different kinds of alcohol.

Some analogies suggest themselves in relation to the roles meted out within the frame of the interview, most specifically in regard to the interviewer: for example, that of the detective, the prosecutor or the psychoanalyst. Interviewers may play interrogator, asking preset questions following a pattern which does not take into account the artist's responses. Holding back commentary or opinion, the questioner does not allow a dialogue but dictates the form of the interview to fit her own agenda of enquiry, as if the artist might in some way attempt distraction or dissemblance. A different model sees the interviewer talking back, questioning, even challenging an artist's views. This prosecuting role is most often adopted by media journalists, in an attempt to debunk or 'bring to trial' perceived 'excesses' or 'obfuscations', charges regularly levelled at contemporary artists. Most critics, historians or curators, however, are more likely to combine the roles of biographer, researcher, analyst and, of course, collaborator. The interviewer is in the privileged position of having gained access to the artist, to be in the same place, at the same time, engaged in an interactive exchange. The artist – the star – makes a public affirmation of trust in the interlocutor, who is also caught in the glow of reflected glamour. Most crucially, the interviewer is inscribed into art history along with the artist.

The notion of revelation through verbal exchange has emerged from psychoanalysis; the interview can be a process of stripping away layers to reveal an unconscious motive or concept. Maybe it is the promise of the true confession that makes it so seductive. Yet this exchange is a self-conscious performance, edited and reconstructed for the third participant, the reader. Nonetheless, the silent observer may gain an insight that is not discernible to the active participants, by virtue of what they avoid saying.

The interview, which seems to promise veracity by giving access to the primary source, is of course a beautiful construct. It can, nonetheless, represent a formulation and clarification of ideas in progress, albeit refined and reordered through editing. In a conversation with the artist Jessica Stockholder published in *Bomb* in 1992, Stephen Westfall (himself a painter) relates this process to making art: 'the transcription of the interview, and the restructuring of questions to establish a certain compacted continuity, find a corollary in your work process. You talk about the power of your own work coming from overlapping systems. The interview process is a literary version of that.' Despite the consignment of hesitations, repetitions and contradictions to the dustbin of cyberspace, this assemblage can offer concrete insights, not only to an artist's particular and complex imagining of the world, but to the work of art. Descriptions of method and technique ground the work in process. Formal strategies may be situated within an ideological framework, or understood within the context of a *zeitgeist* which expands from the subjective, lived experience of the artist within a cultural and sociopolitical context. We establish, perhaps unconsciously, an empathetic relation with the object of art as its autonomy is inflected with a psychology, a voice.

This process of identification seems to relate to the actual experience of reading dialogues. After scanning the pictures and the ads, most art magazine readers instinctively head straight for the interview. The layout of type on the page is itself seductive. Instead of seamless and impenetrable blocks of type, Q&A transcripts exhibit an inviting textual rhythm, punctuated by white space where the eye can rest. The form invites us to roam between sets of questions and responses, to jettison sequence and dip in. Furthermore, I wonder if we even experience an anthropomorphic impulse of identification, triggered by the incidence of the word 'I'.

The word 'interview' describes a visual, not an aural experience, literally a mutual view. It is an important genre of art history and criticism because it incorporates the primary, the subjective and the contingent. It is based on exchange, contestation and affirmation, and it represents an evolving critical discourse. As a literary genre it is irresistible because it invites a particular kind of participation and most importantly, just as Alice knew, sitting in a meadow on a hot summer's day, it invokes pleasure. 'Alice was beginning to get very tired of sitting by her sister on the bank and of having nothing to do: once or twice she had peeped into the book her sister was reading, but it had no pictures or conversations in it, "and what is the use of a book," thought Alice, "without pictures or conversations?".'[2]

1 Carla Lonzi, extracted from *Autoritratto*, De Donato Editore, Bari, 1969, by Carolyn Christov Bakargiev, in her introduction to *Arte Povera: A Source Book*, Phaidon Press, London, 1997.

2 Lewis Carroll, *Alice in Wonderland*, 1865, Paul Hamlyn edition, London, 1965.

Issue 200, October 1996

1976–1980

Naum Gabo

interviewed by David Thompson

The constructive idea in art will live

NAUM GABO This fountain is really a sculpture or what you call a construction. The first model was done in 1929. Then I made it later on in bronze and this was acquired by the Tate. I had from the beginning an idea that this subject, called *Torsion*, has certain curves outside, that it should be connected with kinetics. This piece changes its image when it turns round. Whenever the models were exhibited they were always exhibited on a plate, on a table, and the water was moving them. Apart from that, I thought the wings of the piece should also have a movement of their own in the form of water jets. Now these water jets should replace lines. At that time I was very much preoccupied with making surfaces with lines, so I connected it with water to make jets, and the jets will give a certain kind of form by themselves. The direction of the water is dictated by the form of the wings of the structure – it goes round and then it becomes like a ball of water, and then it goes down, you know. All these wings are provided with 140 jet holes and the jets go out and round and, when you face the water out more, they become a kind of ball. In ten minutes one movement, so you stay there and look at the whole thing and then you suddenly see a totally different thing in the middle.

DAVID THOMPSON *Is this in some sense the nearest realisation you've done to that original kinetic sculpture in the Tate?*

NG Somebody asked me the other day: you have done the thing in 1929 and it is modern today. But the building of the thing did not succeed. I had nobody to pay for that.

When this piece in bronze was acquired by the Tate, the director knew about my wish that this piece would serve as a model for building it about twelve feet high. One day we were invited for lunch with a young man, Alastair McAlpine, and we started to talk about this piece. And I told him what I want and so on. And he said, 'How much will it cost?', and the very next day he telephones me, 'I am going to do it, to build it'.

DT *The original model is actually in plastic, isn't it? It's already transparent in its original version.*

NG Yes, but I knew I could not do it on a big scale in plastic. So I made it in stainless steel, so it has the same tone as water to a certain extent, but its shadows you can see, and you ought to see, in the water.

DT *Is the fountain a theme which has always attracted you? I remember there is a metal and glass construction of 1925, even earlier than that sculpture of yours called* Fountain, *and there are some other drawings that I remember and of course you did one for the New York World's Fair in 1938. It was not built, but you did designs for it.*

NG I designed it, yes. So I had several. One I had built already. I built this one which you mentioned, a fountain in Dresden. But that was in a private garden, and it is completely ruined now. A fountain is only a kind of accompaniment to any work in the open space where people are, for the streets and parks and so on. Why not also on water? Water in itself is a very agreeable thing to look at when it is in a fountain; it distracts a man from his own thinking and lets him stop a little and look.

DT *In an ideal world would you have liked to develop even more public projects? Your early drawings, the year after Tatlin's model for the Third International, were very close to some of the public ideas. In 1919 there was a project for a radio station, for an observatory, a monument for an airport... Would you like to have developed further into architectural areas?*

NG You know, the whole structure which I am practising is really for a new world, a new city, for the public, for people to see and live with. If you ask yourself what was sculpture for, it was for two things: one was for religion of any kind, and the other was for people so that they live with it. We have no religion now and whatever is done in the Christian religion is done already. It is exhausted and they don't need anything particularly, because the images which they used are there and they are good for that purpose. So, the only thing for sculpture remains the street, the place, the public gardens, or the building.

I had put a construction in the garden in Princeton University and

I gave a lecture to the Science Faculty because they were interested in the scientific implication of it. I was asked why I am not represented in buildings everywhere – they are all doing sculpture. I say it is partly because the people do not yet understand me and partly because the buildings which they do I wouldn't like to have my sculpture in because our architecture is vulgarised more and more.

DT *But in realising some of your own images for public places you have been able to really surprise architects and engineers. I'm thinking of the Rotterdam monument (a three-storey-high sculpture built between 1955 and 1957 for the Bijenkorf building) where your whole structural principle was argued against by all the architects and engineers. And you were proved correct.*

NG It is characteristic, and to me very satisfactory, that it was the architects and the engineers who first reacted to my work, and not the art critics. In all the universities where I have been lecturing, I am not teaching art, I am teaching architecture. You see, it is the architecture faculty which invites me. It is the architects that understand my work, it influences the mind of the students to go somewhere in a different way, you know, making the image of the city. I am very pessimistic about the state of our cities now.

DT *But your art – and I feel the message that comes from that whole extraordinary upheaval in Russia that you were involved in – is one of optimism and it seems to me that is the most important thing we can build on.*

NG My art is optimistic because my art looks forward and has a vision. I do have a vision of how it could be. That does not mean that it will be... What happens with my art in Russia? It is forbidden.

In Russia our disagreements were fundamental from the point of view of philosophy and social consideration. Russia has its own history and development. The idea of anti-art, after all, is nothing but anti-art that was there at that time; this is an old trend in the Russian collective mind. We had a hundred years of it before the Revolution's nihilism. The principle of it was just that: against art. The slogan was: 'a full pot in the oven is much more important than a poem of Pushkin.' Now, this was not just a joke, it was a serious idea, it goes together with the social order of Russia, with this extreme backwardness. And they had chains on them – on the intellect. They wanted European literature, European science – all practical things – not some philosophical preoccupation. The character of Bazarov in Turgenev gives you the type. Now this type of man was reborn in

Russia at the Revolution. He is represented by Mayakovsky as a poet. He was the man who propagated the whole thing, and behind him was a class representing the nihilism of the past, very reactionary. Russia needs a new technique, and new things and so on. Therefore, the young drop art and do pieces of furniture, make settees...

DT *What about the fundamental Russian tradition of folk art?*

NG Folk art was not a matter of concern to the nihilists. It was for Lunacharsky, and what he wanted was to do things for the arts that every man and peasant could understand, and could use in some way, in their home and so on. This was the idea which prevailed in the political parties. But not among the nihilists – Mayakovsky, Brick and all the rest of them, and Tatlin and the others – they were anti-art. No art at all. They did not know, although I warned them about it, that when you do that – deny art – our workmen will cut out pictures from the newspaper and hang them on the wall. And they wouldn't like that. They had an answer to it. Oh, no, we do like it, because that will be photographs and we will make photographs. So they had an answer to everything. I had my own answer, and I said that you cannot deprive the human race of certain kinds of inclination without which it cannot live. In my formative years I lived very near to the people, to the real *Mudjiks*. I was born in a village, and I was very much with the people in my formative years. I knew what was going on, I knew the peasants, I knew the mentality of the workmen. Whereas these advocates did not know the people. I say it in full knowledge of what I am saying, and I can vouch for it, because they were all either born in the cities and had never even been in contact with *Mudjiks*, or they were born in Europe, and came with European ideas, with German philosophy.

DT *You have spent a great part of your creative life in a so-called free society. Have you found that that has liberated or constricted your work?*

NG This is a question I never ask myself. I believe that the arts, like science, like any other ideological development, have their own law of growth. It is a human capacity. They are influenced to a certain extent from outside, by other social situations, but in themselves they have their own way of development. My art can be traced very clearly to both Russia and the West because Russian art was always influenced from outside. Byzantium gave them the art of the icon, Byzantium gave them the religion. Then Byzantium and the icon worked itself out. So there came a new generation by the end of the last century and a man by the name Vrubel who brings into this Byzantine spirit a modern trend, quite new. And when you study it now and study it properly, you will see that it had an influence on our mentality as strong as Cézanne had on the European. I say that the cubists were influenced by Vrubel just as we were, because there are many works of Vrubel where you can find the Cubism trend. At that time, when the Diaghilev ballet was so active in Paris, London, Berlin and so on, he was very much in Paris with the artistic world. There were books on him. He was a friend of Picasso, of Braque. They were doing work for him, you know. It is quite impossible that this young generation of French artists had not seen some of Vrubel's illustrations. There were also many Russian artists there who were influenced by Vrubel. So here comes the history of art, where the East and West have come to the same conclusion.

DT *Do you feel that the full potential of your art has been realised in western society?*

NG Not yet – I'm hoping. Even now I am full of all kinds of ideas. These ideas are there, they congregate and in the end they begin to give one piece or two or three... I don't really believe that western society is so bad as we very often see in vulgar examples. A great search, I feel, is now going on in this so-called rotten western society. I hope I have had a central idea which can develop. The Spheric Theme can give many artists possibilities even if they are already, you know, sympathetic to this kind of thing, not only by copying. It is a structural principle. Then there is the kinetic principle, which is also an open field with great possibilities. It all depends upon what kind of people the young generation will be. The constructive idea in art, I think, will live – it is a product of the human mind.

Abstraction also happens in other fields. Science is also abstract. And yet this abstraction in science has never neglected the laws of nature. So it is in art. And that is perhaps one thing which artists – abstract artists – perhaps don't know. Never forget that this abstraction must never be opposed to the laws of life and nature.

DT *Would you say that in practical terms of making sculpture that the laws of life, of nature, are equivalent to developing your ideas through science, technology, in art materials? What I mean is, a lot of modern sculpture develops its ideas through the manipulation of material. Has this ever been an important thing with you?*

NG Very much.

DT *There is a sense in which transparent materials, plastic and so on, were born at the same time as your ideas.*

NG That doesn't come out of calculations. Some people think my work is a mathematical formula. It is not, ever. Of course you can do anything with mathematics. What you're doing can be done in that formal line in the end. But what I am doing is purely intuitive. It is something which is independent, unrestricted, it is in you. And that is what we call artistic inclination, it's in every artist. It is something in us as human beings. So the material definitely plays a great role, the mere fact that I started to work in glass, use transparent material. Why? Because I felt, how can I get into the image which I am making the feeling of space? I started to feel that space is not around us, space is in us, that we are all, and everything all around us is, transparent. But if you are doing a four-year course in all kinds of scientific things, you know what is going on. It affected the artist, it affected me, no question about it. I was always an artist and always looking, and I feel space very much. So why should I not see the thing? I started to work in glass because I drew the form, but yet the glass is there. And then I started to do these kinds of lines, which are also transparent, the surface is not dead. It does not cover up what is behind it, because I do feel it, you know.

Issue 4, February 1977

Frank Stella

interviewed by Juliet Steyn

Hybrid paintings

JULIET STEYN *I would like to restrict the discussion, as far as it is possible, to the works in the Oxford show. I feel excited by the work but there are a few aspects about which I am uneasy.*

FRANK STELLA There are a few things I feel uneasy about, too.

JS *For instance, are the works paintings or sculpture for you?*

FS I think of them as paintings. I know they are reliefs. They are basically pictorial reliefs. I see them more as paintings because they are really meant to be seen dead-on, and then they work best. They have relief elements. They work as paintings except that they are made up of discrete parts rather than a flat surface. They are probably more like collages than reliefs. Collage can be relief-like. My work is a kind of hybrid, but I don't feel self-conscious of its being a hybrid because it doesn't feel like a hybrid to me. It seems like the way I want to work.

JS *What has this form released for you?*

FS I like the idea of the shapes being all there. You can pick them up. I just couldn't bring myself to paint a French curve. I just couldn't get half-way through it. If the French curve is handed to me and it's as big as I am, then painting on it is rather easy. It seems like fun. But I would never in my wildest dreams think of painting a blue French curve six feet high, so that then I could scribble on it. But if I have someone hand me a blue French curve that I can paint in a few minutes with enamel, then to scribble on it seems like a good idea. I guess it just makes the shapes more accessible in the use of them.

JS *When you use a tool like the French curve it has a form, it has a space.*

FS A lot of the pieces have holes in them, that is true. That's one of the advantages of using relief. I mean something can go on behind something else.

JS *How do you feel about the fact that one approaches the works frontally but that they break down when one gets to the side?*

FS A lot depends on what you mean by break down.

JS *They become the mechanism of how they are held together.*

FS It depends how far round the side you get, but you can say the same about painting. How much can you see of a painting when you get 10 or 15 degrees around the side?

JS *But a painting doesn't demand to be inspected in the same way.*

FS Right. I don't know. I like most of them. It is true that once you get parallel to the wall it's pretty hard to see much of anything. But say you get 180 degrees? I should think that from about 140 degrees it's pretty good. Doing something to hide the mechanisms wouldn't interest me. And as long as they're going to be planar there wouldn't be any particular answer to that. I could build them more but they are basically constructed paintings and I'm not trying to make them into perfect reliefs. That they have relief elements in them – use of relief characteristics is alright with me. That they're not so great from certain angles doesn't bother me, as long as they're real good from some other angle.

JS *What is the hardest problem in making these works?*

FS The metal. It is structurally necessary. It does a lot of things but it is hard to work with, it's unreliable because of the changes in temperature. It's really hard to get the paint to stay on, it inhibits your working. I can't change things. If I paint in a certain way it'll all come off, it's very annoying. There are limits to the machinery that I don't particularly like. I guess I could put it together a little bit better.

JS *What about the pins?*

FS I don't mind the bolting, no matter how crude it is. I don't mind putting the pieces together.

JS *You could weld them, though.*

FS Then they couldn't go anywhere. I actually like taking it apart, because it makes it a lot easier to paint. Instead of painting it as a whole picture I paint the parts individually and then I just put it together. You can't weld aluminium very well. It would be heavy if you work with that. I'm much more worried about the fact that I can't get the paint to stay on the aluminium.

JS *Why didn't you use stainless steel?*

FS Stainless steel is very expensive and incredibly heavy. I've etched on them and I can polish them too.

JS *Why do you use the glitter?*

FS I like it. Ground glass is just another surface. When you paint on it the paint slides on the metal and it catches on the ground glass. The ground glass seemed to be an appropriate ultimate surface to put on the metal.

JS *Are you interested in the transformation of the materials?*

FS I don't care about transforming it so much. I just want to change the pace. If you have a big expanse of something that's exactly the same all the time it gets kind of boring. You can't change the pace of it because it just slides, it's like painting on walls. It's the same painting all over. It is to be able to vary the facture.

JS *It bothers me that you can't have complete control over the work as you send it out to be produced.*

FS I'm willing to take it or leave it at that point, and then in order to change it I make another piece.

JS *Are you surprised when you get the work back?*

FS It comes back pretty different. Usually what I'm surprised by is that they don't do as I've told them!

JS *Are there a lot of failures for you in the show?*

FS There are a couple of things I've got to change, but there's only one piece in the show that I don't like and there's one that's not too red-hot, but the others are okay.

JS *Which one don't you like?*

FS I ain't saying!

JS *Which one do you feel to be the most complete, in your terms?*

FS Well, I think about three of them are the same. They reach the same level.

JS *Why did you put the maquette in the show?*

FS I actually sort of like it for one thing. And I figure it's going to be here once and not ever going to be seen again. Some people come a long way so I figure they might as well see everything I did about the pieces. It is just sort of information. If the show had been in New York I wouldn't have put it in. I don't think it does any harm to see it.

JS *Do you think it's any good?*

FS It looks a little lost there, it is true, but I like the piece. It is another image, so you get to see a little more.

JS *Why didn't you put the full-scale in as well?*

FS I didn't have it. I suppose I could have put in one more big picture. It is quite hard to get people to pay to bring these over. It is a bit expensive.

JS *Now that you've come off the wall in that way, is there anything you wouldn't do?*

FS No, I feel actually – and it's not a bad feeling – I feel I can do anything I want. I can do lots of other things. These are rather straightforward, planar and boxy. I can do a lot of obvious things.

JS *What sort of reaction has there been to the work in New York? Has there been any response from young artists?*

FS No, young artists in New York seem to have their own things to do. They don't seem overly interested in what others do. I would not say there is a great reaction. Some people found them offensive and some people liked them. That's about it. New York is pretty cool about what happens. It is pretty difficult to get anybody interested in what you do.

JS *But as artists they can't afford to ignore what another artist is doing.*

FS Every artist tries to make the best they can, whatever the time. Sometimes the conditions are that they come out not so great or impoverished slightly, but you do the best you can. You keep on moving.

JS *Are you still getting impetus from living in New York?*

FS I can't worry about what other people care about. The visual culture is a small part of the culture to begin with, and the basic culture's a real small part of the society at large – we're talking about a tiny part.

JS *I realise that, but if that's how you feel –*

FS That's the reality. I feel I know basically what I would like and then I try to do that as well as I can.

JS *Can we talk about these works conveying joy, humour, exuberance, etc?*

FS People do, it just doesn't interest me.

JS *But what if the works embody these characteristics?*

FS I try to work on them till they look right to me. Whether they are happy or sad, I have to admit to a kind of honest indifference. If when they were done and if they were all black and dreary, if they worked that might make me very happy. I only care about getting it done.

JS *You sound as if you have a checklist of things to be done.*

FS You have to to get something done. So the next day you worry about getting some more things done. So when you aren't conscious anymore, when you are dead, you don't have to worry anymore.

JS *Are you concerned about your audience?*

FS Not anymore. The public drifts away. The public doesn't do me any good when I have to go to work, they're not very helpful. When I need them, where are they?

JS *Which artists have helped you?*

FS All of them, when I look at them as I'm thumbing through magazines, or something like that.

JS *What are the sources for these works?*

FS The sources are the draughting tools themselves. I mean the arrangement of the tools themselves. Mainly they come from the pieces I've been doing over the past five or six years.

JS *You've talked in the past about your interest in the sort of painting that holds the qualities of Matisse's* The Moroccans. *Do you still feel the same?*

FS I think it represents a nice level that I would like to come up to. Anytime I can get near to it I'll be happy.

JS *What do you mean exactly?*

FS A level of pictorial intensity that you don't see very often, or at least I would like to see and feel it in front of my own painting.

JS *Have you been to any exhibitions since you've been in England?*

FS Well, I haven't been here too long. Although I did see the Bernard Cohen show.

JS *What did you think of it?*

FS I used to like Bernard's paintings about 15 years ago, maybe longer – 20. They're not the end of the world!

JS *They're not the beginning.*

FS Bernard painted a lot of good paintings actually, 'in the olden days', as they say.

JS *Has your attitude towards drawing changed since you embarked on this type of work?*

FS No, my attitude towards drawing has always been the same as far as I know. Drawing's about what you do. It's a gesture – whatever the gesture is, it's appropriate to what you need to make.

JS *What do you think of the Hans Hofmanns downstairs? Have you seen them before?*

FS I've seen some of them. They are all beautiful.

JS *Would you use a figure in a painting?*

FS I don't know how to draw a figure, so it's no problem.

JS *Do you ever draw things that you see around you?*

FS I might make a little notation but I don't make drawings as a sort of compulsion.

JS *Might this be a limitation on your vision?*

FS After a while you have the feeling of inclusiveness. I think as you get older you get a little more exclusive simply because you have less energy and less time. I mean, time runs out and you are forced to be a little more economical with your resources and your time. When you are young you feel as if you have a lot more time to try out a lot more things, but when you are 40 years old you can't indulge your fantasy.

Issue 7, May 1977

David Hockney

interviewed by Peter Fuller

The English disease

PETER FULLER *The remarks you made on Fyfe Robertson's TV programme*[1] *were unusually provocative, for you. Did the* 'Hayward Annual'[2] *make you angry?*

DAVID HOCKNEY In a way, it did. I couldn't understand some of the choices. If they had asked me to choose, I'd have said no. The London art world doesn't interest me particularly. It's a rather boring set of incestuous people. That's my attitude. When I looked through the Hayward catalogue, I thought, my God, it looks as though they've got a lot of boring things.

PF *How would you like to see future* 'Hayward Annuals' *organised?*

DH Well, I was shocked to find out this year they didn't visit any studios. None at all. The three selectors must have just done it by people's names. I assume they bargained about who should be in. It didn't matter to me whether I was in, or not. I've found out some artists are very annoyed they were left out. At first, I wondered why anyone who could show in any other space in London would want to show at the Hayward. Then I realised, it's this English disease. Artists see it as 'official recognition'. It's just like the old Royal Academy of years and years ago.

PF *Maybe if you had less 'official recognition' yourself, you would not be quite so cynical.*

DH I'm not being cynical. I really don't care. I have 'official recognition', and I haven't. The art world's relation to me has always been ambiguous. They never know exactly where to put the pictures.

PF *Whose work would you like to see in the next* 'Annual', *if you were involved in choosing?*

DH I don't teach. I don't really know what's going on in art schools. But I assume that if any artists in London are doing things, it must be outside the official avant gardism. I've even heard that it was a struggle to get a £500 Arts Council grant for Maggi Hambling because she's not an abstract artist. I think that's amazing.

PF *Some critics say that the Tate, and Arts Council exhibitions, should represent painters like Edward Seago, Terence Cuneo and David Shepherd. Do you agree?*

DH Years ago, the Marlborough was putting on a Seago show. He's the Queen Mother's favourite artist. Joe Tilson, and some others, said to them, 'This is going too far. He's a lousy artist.' The gallery was taken aback – it didn't know. So Marlborough asked Francis Bacon if it should show Seago. He said, 'I don't know what you are worried about. It's as good as all the other crap you show.' I agree, in a way. They are not excluding these artists because they say it's bad quality work, they are excluding it because of its ideas. If they excluded things on grounds of quality, they wouldn't show very much at all, would they?

PF *Would you rather look at a Seago or a Cuneo than at a Bob Law?*

DH Certainly I would, most people would.

PF *So do you think the Tate should be buying them?*

DH I've no idea how the Tate collects. I went there yesterday – I was looking at their Picassos and Matisses, and cubist paintings – their collection of pictures like that is piddley, really piddley. What the hell were they doing in 1932 when you could buy a Picasso for £300? At least John Rothenstein had some ideas about painting. He bought pictures by people whose work he liked. Whether you think they are any good or not is irrelevant. He had a clear view. Now, I can't see any clear view. They have no idea how they decide to do things. Absolutely no idea. They miss a lot.

PF *Norman Reid said that the outburst about Carl Andre's bricks was similar to that against Constable in his day. I've seen it compared with the response to Cubism. Do you accept this argument?*

DH No. Cubism appeared to most people to be a distortion of reality. It wasn't, but that's how it appeared. People get passionate about that, especially about distortions of the human figure. They wonder why. They know the human figure, and that its foot isn't twice as big as its head. But people couldn't care less about the bricks, or Bob Law's paintings. There is no passion for or against them, that's the truth. People think a guy's got a ball-point pen, and he tries to get £5,000 for the picture, and, well, if somebody's fool enough to pay it, what can you do? But to try and equate that with the struggles of Modernism 60 years ago is almost a cheap insult.

PF *Barry Flanagan would say that he is involved with the visible, material world, but you seemed dismissive of him, too.*

DH Was I? I can see his work is about the visible world. But the problem with art like this is that once you take it out of the museum, it becomes a bit meaningless. That's not true of everything. Victor Burgin's posters, taken out of the museum, would be more interesting.

PF *You told me that you thought your mother's question, 'Did he make the rope?' was a good one.*

DH Modern art generally ignores skills and crafts, or assumes they are not necessary. But the real world of ordinary people is full of them. So they question things by asking: 'Where is the skill?' I suppose the skill Flanagan knows is that of deciding to do a piece and placing it. But an ordinary person finds that hard to take. They see the skill as making the actual rope. I don't think their question can be just dismissed, unless you think art is just for a few people. Some people do, but I don't think that, at all. Instead of trying to hide behind the struggles of the past, the art world should begin to deal with the questions people are asking.

PF *As soon as there is an attack from outside the art world, artists tend to close ranks.*

DH I'm not a vicious person. I wouldn't say to someone, 'I think your art's absolutely terrible.' One should be reasonably kind in life. On the other hand, I don't see that I have too much connection with some artists. The art world is not monolithic anymore. There always has been an anti-abstract line that's intellectually respectable, that's not philistine. There is a difference between painting that veers towards music, in the sense that it's about itself, and a pleasurable sensation of looking at something that doesn't refer to other sensations from a visible world. Take color field painting, it can be stunningly beautiful. But, for me, that's just one little aspect of art.

PF *In 1975, you said that most people will now acknowledge that there is 'a crisis in the visual arts'. But you added, 'I don't think it's a very serious thing. I know it will be overcome'. Do you think it is more serious now?*

DH Yes, I think it's more serious. Obviously, the rumblings have started. More people can see the crisis, so things will begin to happen. So I am a little optimistic. If you recognise the crisis, something can be done about it. But it is serious.

PF *What real grounds have you for your trace of optimism?*

DH I'm an optimist by nature, and I'm not yet completely disillusioned about things. Time sorts out a lot. The modern movement can't last forever. History tells us that the Renaissance came to an end. It didn't go on and on. The modern movement began about 1870. I assume that it has actually ended. Obviously, it doesn't end at midnight on June 31 of any given year. And it probably takes 25 years to realise what's happened. But I think it's ended.

PF *I think you can see an end in today's grey monochromes.*

DH That's what I see. I often wonder if Picasso saw that – he didn't venture into abstraction much. As he got near it, he withdrew. Could he see it was a cul-de-sac? I don't know.

PF *After Cubism, and markedly by the 1940s, Picasso had a crisis of subject-matter, and kept copying other people's paintings. I feel that you have a similar crisis. Are your recent references to Picasso an acknowledgement of it?*

DH It is difficult to find meaningful subjects. But the Picasso references in the etching were, of course, from a poem, 'The Man with the Blue Guitar', by Wallace Stevens. Nobody reads the poem. But the desire to produce a significant picture, today, is common among a few artists – and I think it's growing. Of course, there are lots of difficulties that have to be overcome. There are going to be many attempts to do it. One shouldn't be afraid of going back a little bit to find things out; the last 130 years are so unclear to us. But this much is clear to me, and it's becoming clearer: when the visible world disappears from a visual art, you really do have problems. You might produce an art that's sublime, that's sort of over and above reality, but it has not been an incredible success in getting that higher reality across to anybody. Human beings don't seem to be interested in it. It is actually there? You might well ask, is it there?

PF *Can you see anyone in England in their early thirties, or younger, whose work begins to show a way through, or even a hint or trace of one, whose work even interests you?*

DH Not really. Although I'm not that well informed, I go and see exhibitions. I believe that if somebody's doing something, somehow you get to hear of it. But it's too glib just to expect that a couple of people are going to start producing something. Probably, it's even more difficult than I think. Then you might not recognise it straightaway.

PF *The only younger painter mentioned in your new book* David Hockney by David Hockney *is Stephen Buckley. Although I respect him, his work shows the problems. In early pieces, he seemed to be pushing towards a new way of representing but now he imitates himself imitating himself.*

DH I've always had a respect for him, too. But he admits that he can't draw. I urged him to take a year off to study drawing. 'Then you could deal with an area that might be very, very meaningful', I said. But this idea of shutting yourself away to study drawing has been lost. When I suggest it to people in art schools, they think, 'It's the old reactionaries again'. The destruction of drawing in the art schools was almost criminal. One of its effects was to downgrade the activity of painting. This, combined with the new academic requirements to enter art schools – you have to have two A-Levels, and be 18 – 60 or 70 per cent of school children don't do GCEs. This is totally insane. It means that you get people going to art schools because it's their second or third choice, whereas a lot of those with a real passion for drawing and painting are excluded automatically. Silly people who have no faith in art are running the art schools.

PF *Your views on art education are already widely known. The weakness in what you say is that you tend to imply that it was just the change in art education that caused things to go wrong. Isn't the real problem the withering of the social need for the artist? Surely the crisis in art education is just a reflection of this?*

DH I think there is still a social need for art, although I'm not saying it's necessarily for painted pictures. A great problem in the last ten years is that people have written about Art – with a capital 'a' – including many other activities apart from painting pictures. Okay. But you cannot say, for instance, that Gilbert & George are art, but that Benny Hill is not art. I remember a Richard Cork piece about some artist doing something in Perivale, 'because Perivale had no art'. That's stupid. Of course the people of Perivale have some art. They have television sets, and so on. The quality of the art is another matter, but to say that there is none is crazy.

PF *But you also say there is a need for picture-making as such.*

DH This need for pictures is so deep and strong in people that to deny it is crazy. It's there all the time. After all, people are always looking at photographs in newspapers. There's a difference between the moving picture and the still picture. The moving picture takes time to look at, the still does not. You can't speed up a movie. If it's one and a half hours long, you've got to sit there for one and a half hours. Four years ago, I got this video, and I quickly got bored with it. People would come in, set up the video, and they'd be doing things for half an hour. The next half hour you spent watching it, so you only had half an hour of experience in each hour. I thought, well, it's halving my life. So I stopped playing with it.

PF *But don't you think the real problem is that, at present, the state believes it should support artists, but nobody knows what they should be doing, or is prepared to tell them what to do. This creates an 'Artists' Reservation' in which artists produce blank canvases.*

DH I have said how I became less and less interested in being involved in modern art, because one saw where it was going. I thought, well, this is not a solution. But I'll say this – people want meaning in life. That's a desperate need, and images can help. They had an Albert Marquet show in Paris. I went to see it. I didn't know much about him, I'd always thought of him as a rather minor artist till then. But I was thrilled by the exhibition, my enjoyment was enormous. He had an uncanny knack of looking at something, simplifying it almost to one colour, and being able to put it down. The reality of it was so great that at times I thought, it's more real than any photograph I've ever seen. Paul Overy reviewed a Marquet exhibition here, and he dismissed him as a minor painter. I nearly wrote a letter saying I had seen this show in Paris, and it was a very, very vivid experience to me. To be able to walk into the street and to see in the most ordinary little things, even a shadow, something that gives you this aesthetic thrill is marvellous. It enriches life. So these paintings do seem to have a purpose. People seem to see it as well – it was a well-attended exhibition. To me, that seems a perfectly good reason for making the pictures.

PF *Do you think that if institutions like the Tate and the Arts Council commissioned artists on specific projects it might provide a way out of the crisis?*

DH It's a good idea. But the problem with institutions is that they are run by people – committees. Your suggestions would need imaginative men.

PF *Even if they weren't that imaginative, we would get something better than the official avant gardism.*

DH True. I certainly think it should be tried. It is only now that the impasse is being acknowledged by more and more people. That's the first step. There are many imaginative ways which can be tried to get out of it. Some of them will be mad, and fail. It doesn't matter. They must be tried, I agree. Unfortunately there is within modern art a contempt for people. You can read it in criticism now, the idea that ordinary people are ignorant, art isn't for them, you need a visually sophisticated group, etc, etc. This is all hogwash as far as I am concerned. That's why the Arts Council is devoted to certain kinds of art, they see it as a continuous struggle. They'll accuse Fyfe Robertson of philistinism, and shelter behind that – which is cheap. I think he has to be answered – there's a real case there.

PF *Who do you paint for, then?*

DH I don't have a conscious concept of an audience. I have problems in painting. I don't really paint very well. I have technical problems. I should sit down and study some things. It seems so sad that one has to spend a lot of time struggling just to make something if one has an idea and a vision. This is my own frustration as an artist. Here one is just talking about things that an art school should have dealt with. You shouldn't really be having to deal with this when you're 40, you should have overcome a lot of it by then. But unfortunately, I haven't.

PF *Don't you think critics are a bit like the blacks? There's a crisis, so people start blaming them for everything that's happened.*

DH I'm not blaming the critics at all. If the art doesn't speak, then it fails, no matter what theories it fits into, no matter what some experts might say. I wouldn't have written a letter like Peter Blake's[3] myself, I wouldn't have done it that way. The battle between artists and critics was sad, it should have been critic against critic. I think, perhaps, it does show that there was something wrong with criticism if they all took the same view. No critic pointed out that there are great differences between the artists. Artists are wrong in wanting to stick together because they are artists. Ten years ago the critical situation was different, you had John Berger with one line; Lawrence Alloway with another, David Sylvester with a third. But now, with the *Times*, the *Guardian* and the *Evening Standard*, you couldn't tell quite what line they were really taking. Without a position, all is lost really. Artists say, 'Well we want to stick together. We adopt the artists' position'. But there's no such thing as the artists' position. Of course, I'm not a writer. But I try to make my position clear in my painting.

PF *In a 1970 interview you called yourself a 'realist' painter but in your recent book you talk about yourself as a 'naturalist', even though you later add, 'naturalism is something that one should be careful about, anyway... it's a kind of trap. And also in the history of painting naturalism has never been that interesting. Realism is interesting, but I don't mean naturalism in that sense.' Why have you changed you mind about which you are?*

DH The terms are not absolutely clear. Cubist painting is about realism, but it's not naturalism. Naturalism is making a representation of a chair as we actually see it. Cubism is making a representation of the chair as we know it as well. Naturalism is opposed to realism. That's the difference. Then of course there are subdivisions.

PF *As someone who painted a* Portrait Surrounded by Artistic Devices, *1965, I think that you realise that 'naturalism' is just another set of conventions – or devices. But sometimes you deny that, and talk about it as painting things 'as we actually see' them.*

DH True. When I talked about naturalism in the book, I was referring to *Mr and Mrs Clark and Percy*, 1970. I spent a lot of time on this picture. It was a struggle. There are always struggles. I never paint very easily. In these struggles, sometimes one gets confused. Sometimes they are about technical things. How do you put on the paint? How do you make them look as if they are in a room? There are these naturalistic conventions which I always seem to keep veering towards. I tend to think that's not a good solution. But that might be because of Modernism, you see. For instance in this painting of Henry Geldzahler, *Looking at Pictures on a screen*, 1977, it's become a problem again. The painting seems to have gone towards a naturalism that I didn't really want. It's not a satisfactory way of getting the feelings across. Naturalism also leads to an overemphasis on skills.

PF *Aren't your difficulties to do with the fact that naturalism is actually not a true representation of the way we see things at all, it's a convention, too.*

DH But it's a convention that's gone on for 400 or 500 years.

PF *But not forever.*

DH True. That's why it's very difficult not to deal with Modernism. You cannot ignore it. The painters who do must be making a mistake. I see my own painting continually as a struggle. I do not think I've found any real solutions yet. Other people might think I have, I don't.

I'm determined to try, but I keep going off on tangents that get nowhere.

PF *I don't think you have found any solutions either, but I can sense the attempt, which I respect.*

DH One problem is, I'm a popular painter – probably for the wrong reasons. My work is misinterpreted a great deal but there's nothing I can do about that. I don't think I should worry about it too much. But I have not been successful at all yet, not even as a glimmer.

PF *You often visually refer to Cubism as a 'style' with ironic references to cubist figures, etc. In fact, it was a supremely important historical moment in painting in which a new mode of representing reality briefly seemed possible. Knowing that, why do you keep looking to a fairly academic naturalism for a solution?*

DH Because I can't help it. It might be the severe weakness of all my ideas, my real weakness as an artist, that I keep falling back on it. It must have been a euphoric moment when the cubists discovered a new way of representing reality. It must have been. You can understand this euphoria. But it faded out because they realised, the leaders first, that it just wasn't the solution they thought it was in 1908. The branch that led off to abstraction does not interest me that much. I ignore that side of painting. The problem is more interesting, harder, much tougher to deal with on the other side. The solution will be found on canvas, not on a piece of paper or a tape. So one has to go on. I obviously have just terrible weaknesses as an artist. The struggle is very hard. Often you give up and fall back on easier solutions. Then you start again, and try to do it again. I assume if one tries hard enough, somehow one might begin to find something.

PF *You once said that Juan Gris was right to revert to 'classicism' because Cubism had been 'exploited and done enough'. Why couldn't that also be said of conventional 'naturalism'?*

DH The truth is, I suppose, that the arguments for naturalism are stronger. After all, our eyes do tell us things. We do know what faces are like. We do know that there's not two noses there. If you paint pictures you are trying to sort it out both in your head and intuitively. I can't work just from a theory. So I do keep coming back to the fact that this is probably closer to how you really see – for us.

PF *You say that, but one of your most recent paintings,* Kerby (after Hogarth): useful knowledge, *1975, simply reverses all pictorial and perspective conventions, and yet it still 'reads'. It is as if you were asking visually, 'Do these conventions really matter? If I do them back-to-front it comes out the same'.* Kerby *seems very much against the idea that there is a truth in naturalism.*

DH Absolutely, absolutely.

PF *And yet you return to painting.*

DH I know. Look, I think that's wrong. It's gone wrong. The *Kerby* one, of course, was fascinating. I found Hogarth's drawing when I was doing the research for that opera. He did it for a book on perspective. It is quite amazing how everything is just made the reverse of what it should be in perspective. And yet it looks convincing. Now you think of Hogarth as a naturalistic artist, drawing the world as he thought he saw it according to the conventions of his time. Hogarth was not a great theorist, but in his own way he was probably saying, you can ignore all these laws and still make a picture. The moment I saw this it appealed to me. I thought, it's fantastic, I must find out something from it. And it does work, even in the painting it works. You still believe a kind of space, though it's all wrong. I don't know how to develop from this yet. In this year's *Self-Portrait with Blue Guitar*, of course, there's no perspective at all – and that was actually done about eight months afterwards.

PF *I have argued that the painter should try to express visually a moment of becoming, and take his standards from the future. But you constantly look back to the conventions of naturalism.*

DH You can't look forward and see a clear thing. That's the problem. If you could, things could be sorted out. So you are forced to keep looking back. You have to look somewhere. This is a very difficult thing. If a solution ever happens, it will be stumbled upon. I don't think it will be consciously planned.

PF *You still think, then, that this third way I have talked about is a possibility? That the solution will be found neither in naturalism, nor in Modernism, but along a third path?*

DH Yes, of course I think that. But how to find it is a very, very difficult problem. Therefore, as a painter, I have abandoned the idea of superficial consistency. I think that's right because underneath, I suppose, there is consistency in the search, the attempt to find it.

PF *Geldzahler wrote, about your painting* Christopher Isherwood and Don Bachardy, *1968, 'Don Bachardy looks at us while Christopher Isherwood, respecting the new spatial development in Hockney's work, keeps his eyes and his glance in their proper zone. The solid three-dimen-*

sionality of their wicker arm-chairs reinforces the spatial complexity of the painting...' And so on. He never talks about the content or meaning of the picture, only its form. I don't believe that you painted Isherwood's glance like that to respect a new 'spatial development'. But is that really how you want your paintings written about?

DH Henry is one of the few people I talk to about art a lot. I often deliberately shock him. Of course, he's very devoted to Modernism. I think I have had a little influence, and broken down some things – but his way of writing about the pictures is too formalistic. Henry refuses, and Modernism itself refuses, to take sentiment into account. I do take sentiment into account. The problem with Henry and with formalist critics is there is this whole area they don't deal with.

PF *The way you arranged the figures, their glances too, seemed to be saying something about their relationship. Don't you feel that should be discussed in any critical commentary?*

DH Yes, of course it should. I talked to Henry about it, but critics are reluctant to do that. If a picture has a person, or two people in it, there's a human drama that's meant to be talked about. It's not just some lines.

PF *You've taken your stance as a figurative painter, a painter of the visible world, but in any meaningful sense of the word you were not involved with the figure until very late, were you?*

DH That's true. My Royal College paintings were certainly about fantasy, my own fantasy. They didn't deal at all with what we saw. You looked at American Abstract Expressionism and it wasn't dealing at all with what we saw, or the visible world, or real things. So I thought, this is it! This is modern art. At the Royal College, dealing with the figure was considered very unmodern. It still is now with a whole group of people. But that was a dominant idea then.

PF *There was a well-known incident when you complained about the ugliness of the Royal College's models.*

DH Yes. They said it shouldn't matter what the model was like. I told them surely there might be something like inspiration, or something. So I was allowed to bring in my own model, Mo.

PF Painting for Myself, *1962, is one of the paintings you produced from Mo. But the model had no importance. It's just a fantasy. So your point was a false one?*

DH Yes it was. I concede. In a way most of my early paintings are all about ideas. None of the pictures at the Royal College were really about the visible world, even though some people said they were.

PF *Describing working on* The Room, Tarzana, *1967, you say, 'for the first time it became an interesting thing for me, light. I remember being struck by it as I was painting it; real light; this is the first time I'm taking any notice of shadows and light'. I found this a staggering admission. Light and shadow are what reveal the visible world, yet you say you didn't take any notice of them until 1966.*

DH Until 1964 I wasn't painting the specific visible world that was just sat in front of me. I meant that in this picture, I was very conscious of light. A lot of things you do without being absolutely conscious of them. The picture was painted from a little newspaper ad – it attracted me. The strength of the bed and the room seemed clear and solid. I had to superimpose a figure on the bed. I realised I couldn't just put him anywhere because, to make it look real, I had to remember the light was coming from a single source, through this window. So my remark was that I became very conscious that I had to place my model, who wasn't in the room, carefully to fit in with it. The paintings done before that are mostly out of doors so the effects are different. Shadows go all over the place out of doors.

PF *But your very early works – at Bradford Art School, and before – show that you were interested in the way light revealed objects. At the college, you lost that interest, returning to it only in the late sixties.*

DH Yes. When I first went to California, my paintings were still imaginary. I made them up. The woman sat in the garden with sculptures is not a real scene in front of me. So the problems of light were not that important. Suddenly, things began to get more and more specific. I started painting real places that I could see, and I began to get involved with light sources again.

PF *Something which is still absent from your work is any reference to class. In your book you say, 'I think you can ignore this conservatism in England if you want to. I just smile at it. I'm from an English working-class background.' When you paint now you do ignore a large part of your background and experience. You haven't engaged, for example, with the working-class reality of Bradford since your very early works.*

DH In Bradford one painted what one saw – a city full of dark streets. There is a painting I did – it's never been reproduced anywhere – called *A View of Bradford from Earls Court*. It's abstraction, but it's got lots of frontals of little men on it and it has the Bradford motto, which is on every Bradford bus, *labor omnia vincit*: work conquers all. At least it was an attempt to make a link. The moment you put 'from Earls Court' you realise it can't be a visible view.

PF *We've talked about art being shut in on itself. One way of working towards a solution might be to choose subjects that relate to the lives of a greater number of people.*

DH I agree, of course. That's why I am always painting the figure. You can interest people who don't know much about painting. The figure is the most important thing in people's lives, they get more interested in paintings of the figure.

PF *Long before there was a problem of Modernism, people painted the figure. But, as you have pointed out, English art remained conservative. Much of it related only to middle-class experience. Now you recognise that, but you don't try and break it down. Painting the figure is not, in itself, enough.*

DH Of course, there were exceptions in English art, like Hogarth. But, in the sixties, I and a lot of other people believed that there had been a breakdown of class in England. Now I see it wasn't a breakdown at all. I've changed my view on this. But from 1962 to 1965, this breakdown of class was talked about, wasn't it? Something changed, but it didn't change anything like as much as people thought. I remember being shocked as a boy in Bradford when I first read Orwell's *Road to Wigan Pier*. He says that the middle classes all thought that the working classes smelled. I couldn't believe that when I read it. I thought, why would they think that? Now, obviously, things have changed from 30 or 40 years ago. But the divisions are still very much there. That's why you have problems with the Arts Council. The official art world in England is run by middle-class people who have a certain view of art. That's why they side with a certain view of Modernism, because it covers things up. I now realise that, but I've only just begun to see it in that way.

PF *The very conventions, which you call naturalism, seem to me to have been class conventions. they were part and parcel of the middle classes' way of seeing the world.*

DH Perhaps. But one has to remember that the middle classes were the only people, in a sense, who did view the world. The peasant, after all, does not view the world at all, so you cannot just say that it's that. It's a bit more complicated. After all, there are some exceptions. Hogarth was a better artist than most.

PF *He escaped from the aristocratic patrons by publishing engravings. This gave him a much wider audience, and greater freedom. You have sought a bigger audience than that which painting alone offers, too, haven't you?*

DH Now you don't get the increased audience through engravings, but through reproduction. I'm aware that I reached a rather large audience through the book. Any artist wants an audience. But I have a conflict about this. I lock myself in here. I don't go out much. The silly art world I try and ignore. Hogarth had it easier. In his day the conventions were accepted. There was no tradition of a counter-conception that he had to deal with. It's more difficult now, because you have to deal with that as well.

PF *Don't you think you could make a much wider breakthrough if, instead of painting Californian swimming pools, art devices and your friends, you tried to deal with more ambitious subject-matter?*

DH I hope to one day. But there are vast problems to deal with. It's complex and difficult. Sometimes I feel like putting off dealing with a great big subject. But sometimes subjects are deceptive. You see a swimming pool in England is a complete luxury thing. In California, it's not. If England had a hot climate, the attitude would be quite different. Its content is not quite what it appears in Bradford. A swimming pool in Bradford would be foolish.

PF *I'm not criticising you because you paint swimming pools. When Courbet tried to find a way through to realism, in his day, he painted stone-breakers and peasants. You talk about how hard it is for working-class people even to enter art schools.*

DH Personally, I think that's criminal. Really criminal.

PF *You are in a position to bring the experience of those people to the centre of the concerns of art. But you don't.*

DH I have spoken about that many times, though.

PF *You've spoken about it. But I'm talking about what you paint.*

DH On the canvas the subject – the problems are always immense – one thing you have to guard against is that if you let the subject completely dominate everything, you might finish up with illustration, with something that had just a temporary meaning.

PF *I'm not saying you should let the subject 'completely dominate'.*

DH I know what you are saying. I understand the issue completely. I do want to make a picture that has meaning for a lot of people. I think the idea of making pictures for twenty-five people in the art world is crazy and ridiculous. It should be stopped. In some way it should be pointed out that it can't go on. In his way old Fyfe Robertson was trying to say that.

PF *R B Kitaj has said that he would like to be 'A Painter of the People'. He got the phrase from Courbet. Presumably you wouldn't want it that way?*

DH I would, actually. But why have you said that you are not interested in Kitaj's solutions?

PF *One reason is that when all this has been said about how art should break out, acquire a new subject-matter, and all the rest, what does he paint? Portraits of John Golding, painter and art historian, and* The Orientalist, *1975–76, a fantastic imaginary figure, superimposed with literary and art references. He makes the same mistake as those he opposes himself to. You, in a different way, suffer from this same closure. If something is to emerge from this Kitaj-Hockney alternative, you'll have to begin by breaking through that.*

DH I know what you mean. But, for instance, Geldzahler over there, now I've painted him before, I'm painting him again. He's one of the few people I talk to a great deal about art, even though we don't agree about it. I've had some effect – he was once completely devoted to formalism. Personally, he's a friend, a rather amusing person, warm in his way, quite serious. A bit lazy. To paint him in his predicaments fits in with a few other things.

PF *The painting you have recently finished shows a screen covered with reproductions of paintings, and he's looking at them. He's a formalist art expert looking at images of images of other paintings. Formalist painting is painting about painting in one sense, this is painting about painting in another. I feel you are trapped. You want to get through to reality, what's behind the art screen, the real world – but you can't, or you won't, go through.*

DH The painting is called *Looking at pictures on a screen*. This means that the spectator is having the same experience as the subject of the painting. If you've got yourself to here, in front of the canvas, whoever you are, then he is looking at pictures on a screen, but so are you. You are even looking at them on your screen as well as his. It's true, it's meant to be enclosed, all closed in. I was going to put a camera here, behind the screen, as a slight escape. But I haven't got round to it. Now that painting is not just about art. I know that it has hundreds of shortcomings, but I cannot make up my mind what they are. You're saying, probably it's the subject-matter that really starts the problem. I'm not that sure. I think the subject-matter can actually lead outwards.

PF *But your paintings often seem shut within the ghettoism of the art world.*

DH Yes, all right. I painted Henry. I painted John Kasmin. But I've painted other people, too. Celia Birtwell and Ossie Clark have nothing to do with the art world, they happen to be friends. They are no longer together. They've split up. The picture, *Mr and Mrs Clark and Percy*, probably caused it. There's a real example of working-class people both of whom have been, in a sense, really exploited. Ossie's now in a terrible mess.

PF *You can oppose realism to idealism but, in another sense, you can also oppose it to narcissism. There is a strong narcissistic element in you work, which tends to close in on yourself and your intimate friends.*

DH Well, that was why the painting of my parents meant a lot to me, why it had to be done. Frankly, I had so many problems with that painting that if it hadn't been my parents, I would almost have given up as I gave up on George Lawson and Wayne Sleep. I understand your criticism, but I'm not totally convinced of it. Five or six years ago Jackie Kennedy's sister asked me if I would paint her. I said no, I don't do commissioned portraits. I'm not interested. She said, well, will you make a drawing of me? I said I would have a go. It was terrible. She looked like a Hungarian peasant, or something. It was all wrong. But I went to her house in Henley – it was unbelievable. A luxury house that anybody would think, this is how people should live. But I could see she was really, really bored – and sad. I thought, in some ways, there is a subject there, actually. But I didn't do it, I didn't want to. I realised, of course, she wouldn't have liked the subject. I say this because the idea of making a picture of her makes you think you must make her like Sargent would paint some society lady. But in fact subjects are often the opposite of what on paper they might appear to be.

PF *I'm not saying it's as simple as just rushing out and painting ordinary working people.*

DH I think if you are going to paint people you have to know a bit about them. After all, Courbet is the spectator in a lot of his paintings. There is a distance.

PF *Perhaps these spectator-type, 'naturalist' conventions are incapable of expressing working-class experience. There is always a narcissistic limitation in your view of the world. You travel – you've painted in Egypt, Italy, California, France. But somehow there is always something that comes between yourself and reality – your projection of yourself. The world is always your own world, like a child's. This comes out in images like screens, mirrors and reflections, and the visual games. But, in some later paintings, I sense a desire to break through all that.*

DH That's true. But of course that's not just a problem of the paintings. For me it's a psychological problem, it's outside of the paintings as well, really.

PF *You talked about your early painting, in your book, as being in part conscious propaganda for acceptance of homosexuality. What seems to me fundamental about your work – and it is something the critics always avoid – is that it is painted from a specifically homosexual viewpoint.*

DH Well, I think I gave up homosexual propaganda a long time ago. I'm not sure about what you are saying. I really don't know. I am homosexual. I've never had an erotic thought, or an erotic experience, with a female. A lot of people like to make out that it dominates one's life. Sections of the media are always focusing on it. Three years ago, Jack Hazan, in his film, *A Bigger Splash*, tried to make out it was a dominant thing. Whereas I look at it in quite a different way. I don't think it's that dominant at all. It's important, of course. Sex is an important motivation in everybody's life. Perhaps you are right. In the art world context, it's underplayed, in the context of the other media, they overdo it. Nobody seems to have got the true balance.

PF *John Berger's thesis seems right about how most European paintings of women have been produced by men who desire women to be passive, as a result, in many such paintings, women have no personality or sexuality of their own. The woman is commonly represented as available and supine. Now this was a limitation introduced into vision and representation by a sexual mode. One of the things that makes your painting distinctive is that it indicates another way of seeing the figure and the world, because your sexuality is also distinct.*

DH And that's where the art world does not deal with it. I agree with what you've just said. Yes. But really, I've hardly done any male nudes. I do only very few. Somebody pointed out that the tradition of the male nude in art is of strength, a symbol of strength and power, and not one of sensuous eroticism. To make the male nude in that way was, of course, entirely against the tradition. I read that about my painting somewhere, once. But the only thing is there's only two or three pictures on that – it's not a recurring theme.

PF *It comes out in the drawings, particularly, perhaps.*

DH Yes, true. I'm forgetting the drawings. There's not that many paintings. I can flick back through them in my mind. But drawings, you tend to forget.

PF *Your many double portraits seem to amount to a fairly consistent exploration of the doubts and possibilities of two people trying to relate to each other. Is that fair?*

DH Well, about the portrait of my parents, my father said he thought that the portrait – in his words, 'It shows I concentrate', because he is reading the book. My mother, who is a little bit more aware, sensed it was about something else. He's in his own world. My mother is sat there, rather patiently, doing what I say. My father cannot do that. He finally picks up a book to look at the pictures. Now that's quite obvious, not a hidden thing. Many people would read it that way. The problem is that when you look at a picture of two people, you are going to read many, many things into it. You are forced to. Formalist criticism tries to avoid this. I think that's a real criticism of its criticisms.

PF *But in so many of these double portraits, the subjects just miss relating to each other. Recently, it is becoming harder and harder for your figures even to look at each other. Do you take a pessimistic view not just about people getting in touch with their visible world, but about their capacity to relate to each other?*

DH I'm not sure if it's a pessimistic view. It probably reflects my own. Maybe it's just a personal view. It reflects my own failures to really, really, connect with another person. I'm sure it's that.

PF *But, through the paintings, it becomes public. It may account for a lot of the popular interest in them, rather than the formal reasons often given.*

DH Sure. Take the picture of Ossie and Celia, *Mr and Mrs Clark and Percy*. Somebody at the Tate told me that a lot of people complain if it's not there. They don't do that because they think it's like a Degas, or something. The painting must have something people can identify with in some way. There are certainly things that recur in my work. Once, I said I thought it could be divided into two – the dramas and the technical pictures. The technical pictures were essentially about form, and how we should get the picture together. They were things I've needed to help me make the other pictures. I think that's still true. The form of a painting has to be dealt with. It's very complex. That's where Modernism has to be taken into account. If you could find that synthesis, then you could fuse it into something that would be really worthwhile. That's a struggle still.

PF *I feel there are two opposing tendencies in your recent work. On the one hand, the breakthrough in the painting of your parents, and on the other works like the Louvre's windows. The former is becoming more concrete – you are looking for ways of grasping real people in an image. But in the later works, which seem to descend from* A Bigger Splash, *the figure has vanished altogether, or is at best an absent presence, and the visible world itself again seems threatened. On the one hand, you have this reflective, narcissistic, art screen, on the other, a very definite attempt to break through. Do you feel that's true?*

DH Yes. I think that when the work is misinterpreted, it is this which is misinterpreted. Collectively, people don't see the essential struggle. But I admit that at times perhaps it's not very clear. I still think that perhaps that's because of my own failings. I don't make it that clear. The lay audience is less interested in formal problems but the non-lay audience is interested in them, and criticises them. So I'm wedged in between. I don't care really. One just goes on pursuing it, anyway. One can't really stop. Some things just have to be done.

PF *I've been looking at your drawings of Celia, and asking myself how close they get to her. I came to the conclusion that you were still painting a representation in your mind, which Celia stood for. I felt that you weren't that interested in Celia, or in the other people you paint. What you paint is a reflection of them. But there are moments when that begins to burst open, as in the painting of your parents. Do you think that's true?*

DH Yes, but after all, when you paint your parents you paint an idea of them as well. They exist in your mind, even though they are not in front of you. They exist in your head, all the time. William Coldstream's thing is that you sit the model there, you look at him, you do this and that. Well, I can't do that! That's not a solution, at all, to me. Of course, you are dealing with an idea of them as well. And the problem always is, is that part of the reality?

1 Fyfe Robertson, journalist and presenter on the BBC 'Tonight' programme.

2 The 1977 'Hayward Annual' was the first of a series of annual surveys of British art mounted at the Hayward Gallery, London. The first Annual was divided into two parts; Part 2 featured work by Hockney as well as Peter Blake, Stuart Brisley, Victor

Burgin, Michael Craig-Martin, Robyn Denny, Barry Flanagan, John Hilliard, R B Kitaj, Bob Law, Eduardo Paolozzi and the Theatre of Mistakes. This section of the Annual was subjected to an issue of Fyfe Robertson's popular TV programme in which, aided by Hockney, he attacked Conceptual art, Minimal art and difficult-to-read art criticism as being so much pseudery. Targets for 'Robbie' were the works of Brisley, Craig-Martin, Law and also Carl Andre's 'bricks': *Equivalent VIII*, 1966.

3 In Part 2 of the 1977 'Hayward Annual' Blake exhibited a letter to three critics who had attacked Part 1 of the exhibition.

Issues 12 and 13, November and December–January 1977–78

Robert Motherwell

interviewed by Duncan Macmillan

Coonskins and Redcoats

ROBERT MOTHERWELL I remember an interview with Robert Hughes. It took several hours and it struck me at the time that they were never photographing him, they were only photographing me, and at a certain moment they said 'You're through'. I live above the studios, so I went down to the studios to see what was going on, and an hour and a half later I came back to get a Coke or something, and to my amusement the director was sitting where I had been sitting, and they were photographing Hughes, and he was completely rephrasing his questions so that my remarks would seem to be answers; that is characteristic of me.

DUNCAN MACMILLAN *I think you sound very clear.*

RM In one sense falsely clear. Scotland is the most like America of any foreign country that I have been in, in that somehow we are all obsessed with educating, which means in turn translating into ABC, which is kind of falsification. One becomes glib at it willy-nilly, because it happens all the time. Many times I regret that I am not more obscure, because actually my mind works in a much more obscure way. You know I admire John Russell's lucidity but at the same time it often borders on superficiality.

DM *You said something about modernity when you were talking about the forties. You talked about the relationship between what happened then and the circumstances in which it happened.*

RM I used 'modernity' in the sense the French symbolists did and the word certainly came into existence, as so many words do, in relation to an opposition, which is to say, bad painting. When Baudelaire began to use the word 'modernity', it was history and religious painting of a false order. Modernity then meant that which originates in one's own being and not a fantasy about the past and was valid in my generation still. Maybe it's at its last gasp. I don't know if you have any idea of how ubiquitous television, drugs, rock and roll and so on are in the US, but you might say to 20-year-olds in the US I am as remote as Pissarro, and in that sense modernity has no opponent and ceases really to be a battle cry. I would almost now become a traditionalist, not in the normal sense that one is radical when one is young and becomes conservative when one is old, but through sheer history – what was a crucial issue has ceased to be an issue, from one point of view. From another point of view I would use it, again as the French do, simply to denote the people that we would regard as consequential painters since the Romantics, and then I think it splits into various subdivisions – you know, the impressionist, constructivist and the surrealist traditions etc, including some that I think are rather eccentric, such as Viennese decadence.

DM *I was thinking of an analogy – it seems almost a coincidence that Cubism, Einstein, twelve-tone music, Bergson all happened at once as though all these were responding to a shift in ideas. Was this the same way in which you understood modernity in the forties? Did it respond to something which was there?*

RM No. For us, to use a word I dislike, the effort was to enter the mainstream or a world standard which we took to be the impressionist and then cubist-fauve line. I think to some it appeared to be German Expressionism. My own belief is that German Expressionism, given differences in culture and temperament, is really another version of Fauvism. I would say we all took it for granted that Picasso and Matisse were central, as fathers or grandfathers, let's say as grandfathers, and that Miró was the father – and Klee. In 1944 the dealer Sidney Janis wrote a book called *Abstract and Surrealist Art in America* – I think there were 42 people included in it – he ransacked America and found, say, 42 or 32 artists. I was the last he came to because I was the youngest, I think I was 27 then, and so I said, 'What did you find out in all your travels?', and he told me several things only one of which I remember – that if one had to say that there was one artist whose name occurred more often than anyone else's in this, in a sense contradictory, group of abstractionists and surrealists, it was Paul Klee. At that particular moment there were hundreds of Paul Klees in New York because of German refugees, the ones who came off best were the ones who got out works of art or jewellery – and Klees of course are small, so that they were able to get a great many out.

Now this all has to be counterbalanced. Something I have never read anything of in the literature of modern art, but which I think is true of all the English-speaking world – certainly of America – everybody had read *The Golden Bough*. Americans, and New York much more than any other city in the world, are psychoanalytically oriented. Everybody knew Freud and Jung. Anthropology is again a very powerful force in America. All Americans, as Europeans in a more exotic way, are very aware of our Indian history so that one has to couple with the notion of modernity the notion of the shaman, the primitive, the virgin primeval. If you get those things together then you begin to get what an American in 1940 of artistic ambition would begin to be oriented towards, and that the French totally lack. I think that is one of several causes for the collapse of French art after the war.

DM *One of the very interesting passages in our discussion yesterday was when you were talking about the Americanness of American art. We have here a view of American art which I am sure, without intending to, distorts it by seeing continuity with European art as its most important feature.*

RM I would say all of my colleagues were in many ways extremely hostile towards European art – I mean it was a standard, but a standard to be altered and if possible surpassed. Harold Rosenberg wrote once an essay called 'Coonskins and Redcoats' (meaning early Americans and the British Army), and in that sense I was the Redcoat among the Americans, not out of any deliberate choice, simply by background, being the most cosmopolitan, maybe the most consciously anti-provincial, in that sense most alienated. But it was ironic, for example, if one phrases it with that image that one of the strongest Coonskins would be Willem de Kooning, who speaks English with an accent so thick that you can hardly understand it.

DM *Do you think that the way you came to painting, with a background in French nineteenth-century literary and artistic thought, gave you a kind of lead, a prior start in coming to terms with the European influence?*

RM Two things gave me a head start. One day I was playing tennis with a stranger, and afterwards he said 'I am going to have drinks somewhere, would you like to come along?' I said 'No'. And he said, 'I have heard somewhere that you are interested in pictures and I think these people have some pictures.' And I said, 'In that case, I'll go', and it turned out to be the Michael Steins. I saw my first Matisses in the flesh and they went through me with what I can only say was a shock of recognition. I had one of the great intuitions of my life. I was 17 or 18. This was not merely personal genius or talent, it came out of a specific context. Hence, in trying to discover the context, I discovered that it was the French poets (this was in the early 1930s), not the French painters, who had described the context and that is how I got to it. So that all the things that are said about me put the cart before the horse. From the beginning all this other business was in a way to find a point of orientation so that the beginning of the painting would be authentic. It was not possible for me to encounter a painter who had an authentic point of orientation.

Secondly, my father point blank refused to allow me to be a painter. I was totally incompetent to be on my own so finally to end the cold war we made a gentlemen's agreement that if I would get a PhD then he would give me a modest allowance for the rest of my life or, if I didn't want that, he would get me a very good, high-paying, nine to five job. I said I'll take the PhD, and that is how I became educated. It was really a stall for seven or eight years, to slow it, and it was only when I came to New York, through the luck of the war's exiles, that I then came into contact with real artists and particularly the surrealists whose work I didn't particularly like but who were the sixth generation. Surrealism in many ways was more a literary movement than a painting movement – they were a sixth generation or whatever it is of the symbolist movement. Then it all made total sense.

DM *You said that when you were in France you found the response to your painting was very good – people felt this or saw this somehow.*

RM Absolutely, and you see France can't accept anything that is not part of their cultural empire unless it is totally barbaric – folk dancers of the Ukraine or Sinhalese or something. I would think of France as a woman, it has to be in the queen's domaine.

DM *How is this present in your painting now? What was it that they were responding to?*

RM Well, for example, you know the very large red painting called *A La Pintura*, 1971? There is a much larger red painting with a few Phoenician letters at the top, it's called *The Phoenician Red Studio*, 1977. It is what nowadays is called a color field painting, and is what in my estimation is the next step in relation to Matisse's *Red Studio*, which is one of the monuments in New York City, one of the icons that is in everyone's consciousness because it is there all the time, so in that sense it still relates. The other day I read Edward Lucie-Smith's new book, *Art Today: From Abstract Expressionism to Surrealism* – he's always been very down on me, he thinks I am slick or clever – he was pointing out that De Kooning is really the essence of Abstract Expressionism. I don't know what word he used but in effect he means energy and so on. I was one of the founders of Abstract Expressionism but energy, or activity, let's say, in a picture is not a necessary ingredient of Abstract Expressionism. I would say that Mark Rothko's paintings, for example (and in some ways I think that he is the greatest), are not expressionist in the normal sense at all, certainly Barnett Newman's are not, certainly Adolph Gottlieb's are not, but the term 'action painting' was a deliberate political device to put De Kooning and Jackson Pollock at the essence of it, and they are the essence of one aspect of it. I think that there is hardly a single thing, except maybe the depth of commitment which is ambiguous and slippery, that could be called the essence, if you think of all the people involved.

DM *There is something I was reading that Frank O'Hara said when he was talking about conviction rather than style, and I have noted it down: 'They had a kind of conviction, more ethical than visual, each has chosen on several occasions to make moral statements in relation to his art rather than aesthetic ones.' Does that have meaning for you?*

RM Frank was not an intellectual. He was a lyric poet and a sort of latter-day Apollinaire, a poet of the romance of everyday life and friendships. The concept actually comes from Kierkegaard who defines, and I would agree, the aesthetic as a discrimination of sensuous qualities, as the skin of the world, so that for him an important concept is what he calls the despair of the aesthetic: if blue and red and yellow and green – or four girls, let's say – are equally beautiful, why does one choose one rather than another? I think that many of Clement Greenberg's followers are involved in the despair of the aesthetic in the sense that when they choose to put green and purple together rather than red and blue, it is basically an arbitrary decision. Kierkegaard's notion is that in the end one makes the choice not merely on aesthetic grounds because there is, in that sense there can be, no choice if they are aesthetic by definition, but on ethical grounds. It had to do with character, or with one's own felt response, and so on, and for Kierkegaard the ultimate step is always that the ethical in turn is transcended by faith in God, and I stop short of that. But it is in that sense that it is meant to be an ethical choice.

DM *Is this your definition or analysis of ethical against aesthetic? Does this mean a kind of moral dimension is possible in your painting?*

RM I think that ethical and moral mean two different things. I think moral has to do with social relations and the ethical has to do with a solitary individual's sense of what is right and wrong. So that a terrorist, for example, or a heretic, could be ethical but immoral.

DM *You were saying things about the sources of your own imagery and the nature of your own imagery with relationship to the unconscious. There are particular kinds of imagery which you have returned to are there not? How do you understand them?*

RM That is more difficult to answer. I think one would have to set up half a dozen dichotomies to talk about it. For example, one would set up the dichotomy of the sacred and the secular. I am speaking of Abstract Expressionism in general, and then I would say that the main thrust of Rothko and Clyfford Still – and the main hope of Newman – is to deal with the sacred. With me it is in certain works, maybe my more important works. If you take the secular side, then I would say that De Kooning is wholly secular, Pollock is wholly secular, and a lot of my works, especially my collages, are secular. There could be many dichotomies that I think would have to be brought into play in order to answer your question accurately, to individualise the answer to your question.

DM *I have been reading some of the remarks you have made about the sublime in Longinus. Is that something to do with what you meant by sacred?*

RM Yes, but I should also say that somebody concocted the idea that we think about it – and we did – and I wrote what I thought at the time. By the way, as an art historian's footnote, when it appeared Newman (who was not a generous man) embraced me and said 'you are right much more than I am in how you approach it', and I think actually that one takes the last paragraph of what I wrote, which I now think was mistaken, because of the extraordinary selectivity of French art in New York at the time. You know, the silence, the nobility – the whatever – of the masters of the École de Paris. I think Newman took that quite literally. I mean, that paragraph fits better with what his painting actually looks like than anything he himself ever wrote.

DM *Do you know Burke's theory of the sublime, the idea that it is based in the distancing of terror, of fear? There is sometimes a darkness in your pictures which is combined with scale. Scale is something he speaks about in this context.*

RM The thing I can say off the top of my head is I detest the Alps and raw nature and the sublime in that sense. On the other hand, when I listen to music a lot, it tends to be the last Beethoven quartets or Mozart's Requiem Mass, or things that I suppose to a lot of people would seem terrible work, and they fill me not at all with terror but with recognition. You see the difficulty with English criticism right down to Kenneth Clark is that the ultimate metaphysic of an Englishman is the values of a gentleman. That can be very penetrating, graceful, lovely, but when one comes to ultimate concerns such as death or art it is inadequate or distorts. Your friends William Blake and William Hogarth and J M W Turner understood that very clearly.

DM *They weren't gentlemen of course. I suppose you don't know much about the contemporary state of English criticism. The critics are, I think, reacting against the influence of American painting.*

RM I think the English, heroically perhaps – it is never clear to me whether Britain is closer or further from the Continent than the US, most of the time I think that it is further really and then it would not be so heroic – but nevertheless bravely decided after the war, on every level of society including art, to form an alliance with America rather than with Paris, and somewhere along the line in England it didn't get very far. I mean England is strewn with broken artists who did that. I think it is also strewn with broken artists who followed Paris. It is strewn with artists who did neither.

DM *The England-America alliance was obviously a political necessity in that Britain was cut off from Europe. It was right, too, artistically, in that by that time Paris had ceased to signify. It was almost artistically simply following the centre of gravity and shifting over, in fact seeing where it had gone.*

RM The English made a fundamental error. They supposed that the Americans like the English, and the people the Americans really like are the Scots, and particularly the Irish, and not the English. Most Americans feel much more at home – if one discounts the language barrier – in Paris or Rome than they do in London, but any American would also feel at home in Edinburgh or Dublin. Because Americans have a built-in antagonism towards frozen class structure, as I think Scots do too. The English have the most devilish device to enforce it, which is how one speaks. It is almost as though one is branded at birth. Whereas in Scotland you can't tell except when one encounters the brogue – and even then it can be a very sophisticated man – but in general one has no idea any more than one does in America by how one speaks what class one comes from. Not only that, in America one can very easily move from one class to another, in fact practically every American has at one moment or another.

Issue 14, February 1978

Carl Andre

interviewed by Peter Fuller

I'm a kind of anarchist

PETER FULLER *The row over the Tate's acquisition of* Equivalent VIII, *'the bricks affair', took place two years ago. It served as the catalyst for an outburst against late Modernism in Britain. How do you feel about all this now?*

CARL ANDRE It had little to do with art and much to do with authority. Auberon Waugh wrote that the English middle classes were choosing my work as the barricade upon which they were going to fight to gain control of English cultural and political life.

PF *Has this episode changed your way of working, or your attitude to your work, in any way?*

CA Absolutely not. I'm glad I wasn't in England at the time because the temptation to make a fool of myself would have been enormous. Mass media exposure like that is absolutely no use to an artist. It doesn't even help commercially. You don't have 100,000 brick pieces in a warehouse, like a rock and roll group's albums. I don't think I've sold a work in England since then.

PF *You were involved in a similar controversy over here in the US when you made* Stone Field Sculpture, *1977, a permanent site sculpture in downtown Hartford, Connecticut, consisting of 36 boulders, weighing from 1,000 lbs to 11 tons, laid out in eight progressively smaller rows, weren't you?*

CA There was a lot of media attention again. But this does not have much to do with art. Then there was an initial reaction. I spent a week in August directing the placement of the boulders from large trucks, with a large crane. People came up and screamed at me that art couldn't be made from boulders, and if it could, I wasn't making it in any sensible way, and that I had no right to do this. I now believe that initial reaction of waves of vibrating, screaming rage had more to do with the fact that, like many cities of its size in America, Hartford has been gutted through bureaucratic decisions made by people who are remote from the general population, people who work in air-conditioned penthouses at the top of skyscrapers, and ride to their houses in the suburbs in limousines. The common population never meets these people at all. At last, they were seeing someone who was changing the face of their city. He was not just a crew member who could say, 'Well, lady, I can't do anything about this. I just work here.' I was responsible for what I was doing. But I believe that the rage of working men and women who went by was just initial. It occurred while I was working, and dissipated.

PF *Who in Hartford benefits from the presence of your work, and how?*

CA I hope the people of Hartford who pass that way benefit. What was formerly just a bleak stretch of lawn is now a place which invites loitering, standing about, taking of lunch, leaning against stones and talking to your neighbour. I hope it's helped to civilise that small section of Hartford. A park is a civilising influence. It improves the aesthetic surround and raises the level of cultural expectation. The piece was commissioned by the Hartford Foundation for Public Giving, a private philanthropic trust which was celebrating its 50th birthday. They wanted to give a large sculpture to Hartford, and I was called upon to make proposals. Once the project had been originated, the National Endowment for the Arts put up half the cost. Thus, in a tactical sense it is a monument to the Hartford Foundation for Public Giving, and in the larger sense it is a gift to the people of Hartford.

PF *Many left social critics in Britain, myself included, criticise the Tate for pursuing an acquisition policy which treats art solely as the logical development of an autonomous continuum of art history set apart from the material and social conditions of life. We regarded the acquisition of your bricks as a typical instance of this policy.*

CA You are describing a formalist attitude on the part of museum people, but I don't think they are that formalist. Certainly, I think that as a doctrine, formalism has done damage by leaving out the personal histories of artists. It relates one object to another object, but objects do not relate to each other like that. Objects relate to each other only through people, their makers and their audience. This is an almost apolitical objection to formalism, although it has political implications. My work really reflects my earliest experiences, an attempt to recapture the vividness of them. Artworks don't make artworks, people make artworks.

PF *Do you accept that, apart from the wrath of Auberon Waugh, there was also a legitimate left criticism of the Tate's acquisition of the bricks?*

CA I would hope that after the revolution my work would be deemed worthy, as before. There are some things that are going to be, I hope, preserved by the revolution. I do not believe that progressive social change means the destruction of everything that is valued in the present society. I don't think that's a Marxist point of view either.

PF *Andrew Brighton has recently argued that the way in which the Tate collects excludes virtually all contemporary artists whose work explicitly 'services or evokes the emotional lives or beliefs of any section of the general public'. Does your work service or evoke the emotional lives or beliefs of any section of the British public?*

CA The British public doesn't have much to do with art. That's because of the economically determined conditions of society. There's no money for the great capitalists in having people interested in art. There's money in having them interested in television. Television can be used as an art medium, but the television we watch night after night is not art. It is the antithesis of art. So I think the general public is discouraged by all kinds of conscious and unconscious means from having a real, central relationship with art of any kind.

PF *Do you agree that your work is a typical example of an 'international style' in modern art?*

CA There are indeed stylistic bonds between my work and William Turnbull's, for instance. He is an older artist, and a fine one. When I saw his work for the first time I recognised a kindred spirit. Richard Long is also an artist whom I admire enormously. There is an international art community. Actually, it's a NATO art community, because it covers western Europe and North America.

PF *Don't you think that this 'NATO art' might be at the service of international capital?*

CA During the Roman Empire there was Roman Imperial art. Whenever you get a large, cosmopolitan exchange of information, with a centre of dominance – and certainly New York City could have been thought of as the financial and economic capital of this NATO empire – this is bound to happen. Today, it's changing. America is slowly sinking back into a fairly normal country, rather than Number One.

But art follows the surplus value. The reason why contemporary art flourished in New York was because all the surplus value had to go through New York.

PF *Is it reasonable that the Tate should be acquiring your work, and Sol LeWitt's, when, for example, it has no picture by Edward Hopper?*

CA I absolutely agree that they should have an Edward Hopper.

PF *What's your view of Hopper?*

CA It has changed over the years. When I was very much younger, I admired Hopper. But for most of my adult life I just was not interested in his concerns. In 1960, I honestly believed abstract art was morally superior to representational art, because so much representational art was kitsch. Some of the work with the strongest commitment which I see is representational. Hopper is of this kind. Robert Rosenblum was once asked who was the most overvalued, and who was the most undervalued artist – he answered 'Andrew Wyeth' to both questions. Wyeth is very popular with the general public. Hopper much less so. But if you compare their paintings, I agree with you, Hopper is a profoundly more valuable artist.

PF *Hopper was concerned with the material world, and the sensuous world, as you claim to be. He was also interested in the social world and the specific experience of alienation within it. But he was interested in a popular accessibility which you are not, surely?*

CA I'm certain that Hopper was not interested in it, either. He said he was interested in light on the side of the barn. Artists follow their concerns rather obsessively, and their work, if it is valid, or done with energy, strength and quality, cannot help but touch upon ordinary, popular experience. That's what I feel about my own work. If my efforts are so eccentric that they do not touch on concerns which will be valued by any human being, then my work is indeed defective. It may prove, in the long run, that my work does lack that quality, but for me, now, it does not because my work is from the sum of my own experience. I don't feel it as an abstract exercise in design, or mental gymnastics. But I would accept your test that if, eventually, my work fails to awaken some unprejudiced interest, then it has failed. The Tate got my work because they considered it representative of a certain style of practice that emerged because of certain objective conditions in the 1960s, one of which was, in New York, that the so-called New York School, the abstract expressionists, were really the first group of artists from America of world historical importance.

The American imperial assertion was made through NATO, and the victories of the Second World War, and so on. The assertion of this art followed the surplus value and the capital of empire. It definitely happened that way. Now I came to New York in 1957. My work has never been a reaction against Abstract Expressionism, nor was that of Frank Stella whom I knew very well and who was painting his black stripe paintings. It was rather an attempt to keep the aspiration of the older artists, and somehow to approach the power of their work through different means. We had seen the fiasco of the second generation of abstract expressionists – people were painting portraits of paintings by Willem de Kooning, and portraits of other people's paintings. From Frank Stella I learned that you have to make art as strong as the art you admire, but you can't make it like the art you admire.

PF *Don't you think that the abstract expressionist movement was abused by the agencies of imperialism, and pushed throughout Europe as part of America's imperial, cultural policy?*

CA Absolutely. It is documented in the historical archives. During the Second World War the OSS, the secret operations branch of US intelligence, was set up. One of the arguments for continuing the OSS as the CIA after the end of the war was the fact that cultural campaign money, imperial campaign money, could not be gotten through Congress because those who were interested in founding the CIA recognised that, whether they personally liked it or not, Abstract Expressionism would be seen in Europe as the dominant art of the time, and they wanted it to be shown. The US Congress, however, almost to a man, thought that abstract art was a communist plot, and therefore did not want to give any money to it. So you had to form a secret organisation that would propagate the American art image – a wonderful contradiction.

PF *It is sometimes said that your work constitutes a decisive rupture in the fine art tradition, but Richard Morphet's apologia for the Tate's purchase of the bricks claimed they should be valued for classical sculptural qualities. Where do you stand on this?*

CA I may be absolutely mad, but I see my work in the line of Bernini, Rodin, Brancusi, and then I would put my name at the end of that line. Perhaps I am utterly deluded, but the urge in my work does come from the work of the past, and I do not consciously wish to destroy or rupture my continuity with it. There is a principle in science that, when any theory succeeds another theory, it must preserve the previous theory – Einstein does not overthrow Newton, Newton's becomes a smaller, specialised theory in Einstein's general theory of relativity. Not that I believe the work of Bernini, Rodin and Brancusi is diminished because of the work of Carl Andre, rather I think that it is continued. I hope that in my work I preserve the interest people ought to have in Bernini, Rodin and Brancusi. I'm not in favour of destroying museums at all, although I think a lot of the treasures in museums should be returned to the places from which they were stolen.

PF *In 1970 you said, 'To say that art has meaning is mistaken, because then you believe that there is some message which art is carrying like the telegraph, as Noel Coward said. Yes, art is expressive, but it is expressive of that which can be expressed in no other way'. But what is expressed through, say,* Equivalent VIII*?*

CA It's like a poem. If you can succeed in successfully paraphrasing a poem, that is a sign that the poem fails. This is even more true in a painting or a sculpture – if there was another way of doing it, it should have been done in another way. Art does not function merely in the domain of language.

PF *But you should be able to indicate directions in which I, or anyone else, could derive something, whether perceptually, affectively, or intellectually, from your work.*

CA I absolutely agree. I am not saying that nothing at all of value can be said about a work of art, but I'm too subjectively bound up with the work. I could only answer by sitting down and telling you the story of my life. But that's beside the point, too. I can relate to you things in my conscious memory which I think were combined. Perhaps under analysis I could present unconscious things which were there, too. But sculpture is a mediation between one's own consciousness and the inanimate world which is after all what life and death are about. The making of art requires that this mediation between the self and the inanimate world must be of some significance to another consciousness. But, to me, it's not communication. It is as if a beautiful woman invites you to dinner at her flat, and the food is very good, you eat the food, and take pleasure from it, but this woman is not also necessarily telling you something that can be told in any other way.

PF *The fact is that in Britain most of those who saw the bricks, of both left and right, working class and middle class, either failed to respond, or responded negatively – without pleasure. How should they look at* Equivalent VIII *differently to experience a positive response?*

CA The bricks were presented to the British public by the media, as one point. Nothing else was provided – just one point. Given one point you don't know whether you've got a circle, a straight line, or what. If you have only one member of a category, then the category does not make any sense.

PF *Whatever your intentions, many cultural meanings now attach to the bricks. But you tend to deny them and say they have nothing to do with your art.*

CA Years ago, I was quoted as saying art is what we do and culture is what is done to us and our art. Works of art, any human concern that's shared by many people, becomes enriched by the sum of those concerns which can never be identical with each other. But everyone says the bricks cannot stand by themselves, they need an argument, or line of work, to surround them. I absolutely agree. But the *Venus de Milo* would just be a stone woman if nobody knew about sculpture. It would seem a very odd thing to do. It may be true that the line of works that I've done, and even what is called 'abstract art', may prove historically to be worthless, or a great cultural desert. I'm not denying that possibility. The judgement of history will finally emerge.

PF *Since 'culture-free' art is manifestly impossible, shouldn't the anticipation of the cultural response to your work be taken into account in your project?*

CA The only way I could think of trying to do that would be trying to flatter the taste of people whom I thought might otherwise dislike the work. That's verified in portrait painting. Wasn't it wonderful what happened to the portrait of Churchill?[1] I think that was an intimation of what's going to happen to my work. I wish I could say, however, that out of pure motives you make great art, and out of corrupt motives you make poor art. But that's simply not true.

PF *So perhaps you could produce more popular and accessible art without compromise?*

CA If I wanted to do that I would go into one of the mass-orientated arts. I'm not saying that mass-orientated art must flatter its audience, but it may flatter it and still be very strong. The strongest twentieth-century art is film, without question. I love film, but I feel no calling in it, no vocation. I have probably enjoyed film more than sculpture, but I have the calling, or urge, to work in sculpture. The age of film was probably over by 1950 – think of those Hollywood studios which did turn out some extraordinarily great films for the most crass and commercial reasons.

PF *What sort of response are you expecting to your Whitechapel retrospective?*

CA I hope the English public will realise that they have placed much too great importance on my work. After all, it is only art. The fine arts have been called elitist, but 'elitism' seems to me to refer to some degree of power. Few people of any kind are interested in the fine arts today because they are not present in people's homes. There is not an original artwork in the house where I grew up. Perhaps we are seeing the withering away of the so-called fine arts, painting and sculpture. I don't know. If that is so, I hope I'm not accelerating the process.

PF *Who do you expect to come to your Whitechapel exhibition and enjoy it?*

CA It's impossible for me to tell. Perhaps people who are waiting for a bus who come in out of the rain. That's fine if they get some shelter. I hope that the Whitechapel show will provide enough to determine the 'polygon' of my work. There is no reason why the reaction to my work now cannot be informed. It will be easier to sort out just what is blind prejudice, what is informed dissent, and what is informed appreciation.

PF *You once said, 'My works are in a constant state of change. I'm not interested in reaching an ideal state with my work. As people walk on them, as the steel rusts, as the brick crumbles, the materials weather and the work becomes its own record of everything that's happened to it'. Do you therefore disapprove of the Tate's decision to remove the ink-stain from the bricks?*

CA I approve their removal of it. That statement was not meant to refer to vandalism, but to the fact that I do not polish metal plates. As a boy, I had to shine my father's shoes. The idea that somebody would have to shine my sculpture is offensive to me. It certainly would not be the rich collector who did it, but some poor chambermaid, or butler, on their hands and knees. You can't walk on the bricks or timber pieces, but the metal pieces are kept much in the best condition by being out where people walk on them.

PF *Isn't vandalism part of history, too?*

CA Vandalism is part of history, but then so is Auschwitz. That does not mean we should approve and continue the practice.

PF *Although you reject the term 'conceptual artist', you have always agreed that you are a minimalist. What do you mean by 'Minimalism'?*

CA I think it applies less to the work than the person. I found that at that time in order to make work of strength and conviction you could not do a scatter shot. You had to narrow your operations. That's not true of every artist, but it was true for me and some others. I'm a minimalist because I had to shut down a lot of pointless art production to concentrate on a line which was worthwhile. You could say that Minimalism means tightening up ship, for me.

PF *David Hockney has said that he believes that Modernism is dead. Do you see yourself as a defender of late-modernist values?*

CA Certainly not. Abstract art can produce as much trash or kitsch as representational art. R B Kitaj and Hockney, however, have said that their objection to Modernism is that all art springs from drawing the figure. Their art does. But you could not describe Stonehenge, or much other art, as drawing the figure. In debates like that, I can only be correct – they believe that art other than their own isn't valid. Well, if they are right, I'm wrong. But if I am right, then their art has its validity, and my art has its validity. If I am right, they're right too.

PF *Are you a pluralist then?*

CA I'm a kind of anarchist, I suppose. I don't think anybody should tell an artist what he should do, or what he shouldn't do.

PF *Do you have any empathy with the view that British art should become less hegemonised by American styles, that it should move in the direction of a national art?*

CA In England that would be like demanding a truly national cuisine. I think it would be a disaster.

PF *In 1970, you spoke of your attempt 'to make sculpture without a strong economic factor'. You said, 'I find that it's necessary for me to return to this state and make sculpture as if I had no resources at all, except what I could scavenge, or beg, or borrow, or steal.' Do you still feel the same way?*

CA Yes. I think there's a tendency, with our prosperity, to go for ever grander projects, ever more stupendous earthworks, if you can raise the money. Scavenging the streets, industrial sites and vacant lots is perhaps similar, for me, to what drawing from the figure is for Hockney. When I started making sculpture I had no resources except what I could scavenge, borrow or beg. That was how my practice evolved. If I become too remote from that I think my work will lose whatever vitality it might have.

PF *In the catalogue to your Guggenheim exhibition, Diane Waldman wrote, 'the conventional role of sculpture as a precious object, and its ownership, has been vigorously attacked by (Andre's) oeuvre which refuses, by definition, to make such accommodations.' Do you agree?*

CA No, of course not. It is the genius of the bourgeoisie that they can buy anything – collectors buy ideas and goldfish in bowls, all kinds of things. That is the genius of the capitalist system. If they set out to make a commodity out of you, there's absolutely no way you can prevent it. There's nothing wrong with precious objects. There are a lot of objects which I find precious. Other people do not find them precious. The question is whether their only legitimacy is that they are articles in trade.

PF *Would you call yourself a Marxist?*

CA Yes, Karl Marx is the only philosopher I have read who made sense to me of the common life everyone lived. There is no better definition of freedom than Marx's 'the recognition of necessity'. I wish that in the US there was a Marxist political party, but there is not. There's all kinds of infantile Marxist insanity, which is fractionating and divisive. I am absolutely inert and inactive politically now, because by vocation I'm not a politician, but there is no group which I can attach myself to.

PF *As a Marxist you are presumably aware of the labour theory of value?*

CA Yes, indeed.

PF *Where do you think the exchange-value of your works comes from?*

CA Both Marx and Engels separately explained why art was the one commodity that seemed not to reflect the labour theory of value. They wrote that they had seen works on which many hours had been spent which were in their opinion without value, and others that seemed to have been dashed off in seconds that were of great value.

PF *But how are the exchange-values of your works created?*

CA These values are official, but, as we know, they are not scientific. The values the marketplace creates are objective in the sense that they are exchangeable, but they are not objective in the terms of science.

PF *You have spoken a lot about the 'immanence' of your sculpture. Do you mean by this that its value resides inherently in its material existence in the world?*

CA Absolutely. I think that is the essence of materialist philosophy.

PF *Don't you think that exchange-value is something that's projected on to the work by dealers, critics and museum men, and that it contradicts what you call 'immanent value'?*

CA In *Das Kapital*, Marx describes the exchange-value, or commodity value, as something like a ghost which travels alongside the real productive value. But my Marxism has never been a formal, organised study. You may say I admire the sentiments of Marx, and his organisation of a philosophical point of view. But in no way am I a politically effective person.

PF *Much of the popular resentment against your work seems to me to arise from the fact that it comes to signify the high price attaching even to relatively unworked and worthless material if it is legitimised by art institutions as art.*

CA I can give you a perfect example of that. When I was working in Hartford, a man came up to me and delivered a tirade. He was so furious I thought he would have apoplexy. He ended saying, 'There's no art. There's no craft. There's nothing. Art is craft'. I asked him what his work was. He told me that he was a propeller maker. Now that is a doomed trade if ever there was one: in ten or 20 years I don't think there will be many propellers in the world. He was a man who possessed great skill, yet who was rapidly becoming obsolete. I think it was his own lack of significance in the world of production that he was getting at. Productive activity arose in the neolithic age when there was also a great outburst of abstraction, with the megalithic monuments and so on. I'm not saying that abstraction is more advanced, but perhaps abstract art has occurred in human history every time there has been a total technological change in the organisation of society. Perhaps abstract art is just catching up with the industrial revolution. My work reflects the conditions of industrial production, it is without any hand-manufacture whatsoever. My things are made by machine. They were never hand-worked, because they come from furnaces, rolling mills, cranes and cutting machines. I'm the only one who handles these things by hand when I take them off the stack and put them on the floor. I'm not claiming that as any kind of craft. But is it possible to make art, which is a branch of productive activity, in which the hand does not enter into the production of the materials of which it is made? Perhaps my work poses the question as to whether it is possible to make art that parallels the present organisation of production, technologically and economically.

PF *How much did the Tate pay for* Equivalent VIII*?*

CA I think it was £4,000. Something like that. They couldn't have got that Andre for less. That's what is ridiculous about this.

PF *For the Hartford piece you were paid $87,000, of which you spent $7,000 on materials, and expenses.*

CA I would say that I spent roughly $10,000 or $12,000 – it was largely expenses.

PF *Don't you think this sort of pricing increases the anger against your work? If you took a reasonable fee you might get more acceptance for what you claim to be your real concerns.*

CA The economic system tries to drive the artist out of his position as the primitive capitalist to make him another employee. I don't want to be forced to be someone's employee. I have my primitive capital interest in my work, and that is what you are buying – not my labour time. The advanced capitalist wants to drive the primitive capitalist out of business, he doesn't want to drive the worker out of business.

PF *I was in the gallery when Angela Westwater telephoned and ordered the steel plates which you later laid out on the floor to form your current New York exhibition. When they were in the factory stock-room these plates were worth so much, when you arranged them on the gallery floor without working them in any way, a few days later, they became worth a hundred times as much. A six-by-six plate-piece in your gallery now costs $22,000. Aren't these magical values bound to be the most striking thing about the work?*

CA The difference in value between, say, a Morris Louis painting and the value of its canvas and pigment is even greater. Sculptors have to bear the burden, and painters do not, because the material value of the basic supply is so much greater in sculpture. The material cost is a relatively large proportion of the sculptor's cost. I very much resist this thing of turning my relationship to my work into that of an architect who accepts a fee for a large capital project. I am making capital goods and selling them as capital goods, in a primitive capitalist way. I don't deny that.

PF *But why should people value this specific pile of bricks, or arrangement of steel plates, more than any other?*

CA Because that pile of bricks is my work, and if you want to get the authentic example or specimen of the work of Carl Andre then you must go to Carl Andre and buy it. I have a monopoly supply. Now this supply can be forged or plagiarised, but then one would be dealing with the work of a forger or plagiarist. This is very simple. There is less startling matter there than meets the eye. But we generally tend to overvalue money and undervalue art.

PF Equivalent VIII *was a reconstruction, not an original, wasn't it?*

CA Yes. The original has been destroyed. At the time I made these pieces I did not have the money or the space to store the bricks, so I had to return them to the brick supplier. When I wanted to reconstruct the works the plant that had produced the bricks was no longer in existence. In the case of works which have been destroyed, and this is also true of the *Pyramids*, 1959, because I was subject to economic deprivation, I reserved the right to reconstruct them. But I'm not interested in reproducing or adding to the number of works of a given kind that exist. But if others attempt to produce reconstructions, then these would not be art because art is not plagiarism.

PF *What is this factor 'art' which seems to be the component which confers value?*

CA It is a connection we supply between objects. Certainly, it is not scientific or objective. If the human race should be annihilated suddenly art would go with it. The objects might remain, but the relationship between them would be gone. Art is definitely an unofficial system of value created by people.

PF *So art, for you, is a special kind of exchange-value that attaches to arrangements of certain common-or-garden units, or objects, in certain circumstances?*

CA I would hope it was production value, not exchange-value.

PF *Much peasant art is expressed through piles of materials which are used and used up, like log piles, in the South of France.*

CA Or hay bales in Belgium – they are magnificent sculptural arrangements. The only difference is my self-conscious intent to have made it art. In the work of Brancusi, the remaining endless column is the gate-post of a peasant farm. I don't think that's a sign of the debility of a work, but rather of its strength.

PF *You came from a middle-class background, didn't you?*

CA Not really. Not a bourgeois background. My father's father was an immigrant Swedish bricklayer. In the US he met with some success and became a small building contractor and bricklayer. He was a very small entrepreneur, basically a skilled worker. My father worked as a draughtsman in a shipyard, again essentially a skilled worker, but he was no capitalist of any kind. The class structures of England and America are quite different. In Britain, the constitutional monarch is the Queen, in the US the constitutional monarch is the dollar. Not really – obviously economic forces rule. But in England the Queen can knight her horse trainer or the Beatles, and that's one way of conveying value. In the US there is no way of conveying value except with money. I think this is why British artists get less for their work than American artists. Americans are used to conveying value with money.

In a way it makes American society more vulgar, simple and clear. How much money you have determines your social position. It's much less ambiguous. I find it extraordinarily difficult to follow the intra-class wars that go on in English drawing rooms.

PF *You went to an expensive private school though?*

CA I was a scholarship student. My mother was naively socially ambitious. She's despaired ever since because I discovered my vocation in art there. Late at night my mother cries and says that I was ruined at Andover. I found an art studio there, and from the first time I worked in one it was my greatest material pleasure. That's what set me out consciously to make art. Without that experience, I don't think that it would ever have happened.

PF *Barbara Rose wrote that in the early 1960s you walked into her house and announced that you had 'resigned from the middle classes'. Is this true?*

CA Yes, what that really meant was that I had already 'dropped out'. I had abandoned the fantasy of upward social mobility, of having a suit and tie, which I have not worn. My family expected me to do better than my father, to go into a profession, perhaps. I realised that I was not following any course that might lead in that direction.

PF *Do you identify with the working class then?*

CA I identify with the productive class and the production class, too. That must include managers and even imaginative capitalists. The trouble is that there are so few imaginative capitalists any more. That's what is really humiliating. It's annoying to be ruled, but doubly humiliating to be ruled by incompetent people.

PF *Would you accept the criticism that you are an* ouvrier*? You carry out work like working-class work, but you wear clean overalls. Your identification is formal, it does not go beyond the level of appurtenances.*

CA It is formal rather than practical because I don't hang out at the factory, and I don't live in the working-class district of the city. I cannot deny that, but I don't think this formal connection is false.

PF *Between 1960 and 1964 you worked on the Pennsylvania Railway as a freight brakeman and freight conductor. What did that mean to you?*

CA Quincy, where I was born, is an industrial suburb of Boston, so I was with working people all my life. It wasn't a matter of descending into the working class, or any such thing. It was a way of surviving and earning my living. I never expected to earn my living as an artist. My compulsion to make art was not economically ambitious, it was not making me a penny. I had to support myself and my wife. It was outdoor work, and fairly healthy. There are no minor injuries on the railroad. You get cut in half, but you don't cut your thumb. I learned a hell of a lot about sculpture on the railroads.

PF *Is that echoed in things like the timber blocks arranged in a long line?*

CA Yes. My work was taking long trains of cars that had come in from another city and drilling them – that is, hauling them up in bands and drilling them into different tracks. I'd have to draw up new bands and take them all over the place. It was essentially filing cars, a matter of moving largely identical particles from one place to another; then there was the whole terrain-following business which I like very much in my work – a band of cars segments and follows a terrain – it's not rigid.

PF *You once said, 'I'd like to reduce the image-making function of my art to the least degree.' Is that still true?*

CA Yes, it is. But in a way I've realised that it's a futile job. You cannot absolutely remove the image.

PF *The work itself becomes an image of late Modernism, doesn't it?*

CA Yes, it did. But I once said that the earthwork people were taking the concerns of Modernism and putting them in wild and distant places away from the museum and gallery scene. But if my work had any significance, I was introducing into Modernism concerns which had escaped it, like industrial materials. There had been the Bauhaus, and so forth. But I thought the Bauhaus was backward. The stuff students produced in the first year always seemed much sounder than what they produced in their last year.

PF *Hollis Frampton once wrote of your 'utter concern for the root, and the fundamental nature of art'. Would you accept that?*

CA The appearance of art is not usually of interest to an artist – it shouldn't be of interest. Aristotle said that all art was representational but that it must not represent the appearance but the process of nature. I think works of art should reflect the process rather than the appearance of art.

PF *Wouldn't you agree that part of the root, the fundamental nature of art, is image-making?*

CA Which came first, sculpture or painting? Probably painting. The first savage who smeared himself or herself with red mud and was delighted. I think the urge to sculpt is closely related to a sense of mortality. People began to sense that they physically and temporally passed through this world, and started setting up markers to indicate where they had been, almost like tracks, evidence of existence. Fundamentally, primitive art had more to do with this than communication. The evidence of existence could start to be used to communicate. Art can be used to communicate and to facilitate communication. But that is not its fundamental essence.

PF *Although the work of sculpture must exist as a thing in the world, its* raison d'être *as sculpture is surely its ability to refer to areas of experience beyond itself?*

CA It must have a demonstrable relationship with other works that we call sculpture. That's one relationship.

PF *You once said, 'I want wood as wood, steel as steel, aluminium as aluminium, and a bale of hay as a bale of hay.' Then you say you want a bale of hay as art. But there is a contradiction here. In order to become art, you must present the bale of hay as something other than itself.*

CA I almost never have used a single bale of hay – that, to me, is not a work of art. The urinal is not a work of art, to me. Perhaps to Duchamp. But the relationship among 12, 30 or 50 bales of hay or plates, the will and the desire to make combinations like that is, to me, the desire of art. A metallurgist might be interested in one plate or even a chip of steel. My early pronouncements on these matters were very much overdrawn. I was a young man trying to clarify for myself what my work had to be. Now I hope I am as stern with myself, but I also hope that I have a better understanding. But one has to narrow one's understanding to a certain degree to get something done.

PF *Would you agree now that the thing-in-the-world is only realised as a sculpture when it is seen, through perception, as a meaningful sign?*

CA No, no. It could be an empty sign, and that may be valuable.

PF *But certainly a sign.*

CA No, no. As evidence, you may say you wish to stop the traffic on a road. You can put up a 'STOP' sign, or a red light, or you can put a landmine there. I think the first form is a sign, but the second is not. It is a phenomenon. Works of art are fundamentally in the class of landmines rather than signs. That's my own deep feeling. The linguistic aspect of art is tremendously overstressed, especially in the conceptual thing. It is part of the vulgarism of our culture, 'What does it mean?' and all that. Ten years ago I would have argued this point with you about the cultural matrix that makes a work of art sensible. But now I realise that without the matrix of art, of sculpture, or of the general culture, there would be no reason to value the work.

PF *You reduce sculptures to the role of signifiers which you say signify nothing. These are then released into the cultural world where they signify things external to yourself, like late Modernism. And this is what is constituting them as works of art, whatever your intentions may have been.*

CA This may be what is happening, but it is not part of my conscious design. I think in our society we constantly confuse the information and the experience. Certainly Conceptual Art is really about information. It is not about thought processes and the body operating in its own luxury and pleasure and so forth.

PF *Would you agree that Pop Art was essentially a superficial art which attempted to put in brackets the substantial signifier, whereas you set out to produce the obverse of Pop, signifiers completely devoid of signs?*

CA To a certain degree my work is the antithesis of Pop Art. Many of the Pop artists had attempted second-generation Abstract Expressionism and, disappointed with their results, wanted to find some other thing to do. But Pop Art has always seemed to me to be about a world that was already formed, its images were already present, whereas my materials have not yet reached their cultural destiny. The bricks are not joined together; the plates are not stamped, or deformed. They represent the unrealised material possibilities of the culture. This may be fanciful, but it is the exact opposite of Pop Art, which generally represents something finished, whose destiny is totally determined. Perhaps one thing my work is about is the fundamental innocence of matter – I don't think matter is guilty of all the transgressions of which we are always accusing it. Advocates of gun control think that by keeping these tools of death out of people's hands there will be less murder. That may be true, but it is not the problem. The problem is the values of a society where guns are lusted after in the first place. Matter is not guilty of the material conditions with which we surround ourselves. You cannot blame the bricks for my art – you must blame it on me.

PF *Is it true that in 1965 you were canoeing on a lake in New Hampshire when you suddenly realised your work had to be flat as water?*

CA I had found a brick in the street, a beautiful white brick made of synthetic limestone. Sand and lime are mixed and run through a super-heated steam oven. Chemically, it is almost identical to limestone. It's a very nice material, and I wanted to use it in my next show, although I was not sure how. I think I already had the 'equivalent' idea, that all the pieces should have the same number of blocks. But I was wondering whether they should be of different heights or not. In a canoe, the centre of gravity is below the surface of the water. I looked out at absolute water seeking its own level. The surface had a perfection you never got on land. There is no grade on water. From that, I decided I wanted them all two tiers high.

PF *Wasn't this close to the kind of flatness Greenberg was talking about at the same time?*

CA My practice is so remote from painting that I would not even have thought of the connection. At high school, I never could do anything but a flat painting. Whenever I tried to achieve some idea of space, I failed. Finally, I did a monochrome painting, not as a revolutionary art form, but because that was all I was painting even when I used colour.

PF *When you were seeking flatness, there was also Greenberg's flatness, and the literal superficiality of Pop. Do you deny any relationship between these three apparently similar phenomena?*

CA The objective conditions under which these works were produced were the same. But there was much less interchange among all these people than is usually assumed. They didn't really know each other – I didn't know Donald Judd, or Robert Morris, and they did not know the timber pieces using units which I made before 1960. Although I agree that the objective conditions for Minimalism were essentially the same for the Pop artists and colour-stain painters, 'flat' in sculpture is not fundamentally about illusion at all, but about entry. I wanted to make sculpture the space of which you could somehow enter into. You can enter the horizontal plane in a way that you cannot enter the vertical unless you are Simon Stylites. But also as Lucy Lippard and I have agreed in conversation, works like my metal pieces could not have arisen without air travel. There is an analogy between looking out of an airplane at the ground, and looking down at the work.

PF *I think that the emergence of 'flatness' as a credo in the fine arts reflected a certain urban experience which emphasised the superficial rather than the physical, which denied interiority. Despite many of your claims, I feel that the floor pieces express this experience without transcending it.*

CA I would hope that they do. But, if the works do not convince you otherwise, I cannot. But I would say this. The one single characteristic of matter that draws me to sculpture is its mass. It is flat because that is the most efficient use of mass one can arrive at. I've never made the prototypical minimalist work, the box. I have never been interested in volume at all. The way to achieve mass effects economically, of course, is through flatness because the three-eighths-inch, foot-square plate is a much more efficient unit of sculptural mass than the cube made from the same amount of steel.

PF *But why does 'flatness', or efficiency, matter in a sculpture?*

CA I was once quoted as saying that sculpture was a matter of seizing and holding space. Given the resources available, using plates rather than cubes or boxes was the most efficient way of working. I think aesthetic efficiency is one of the signs of a strong work of art. I don't mean simplicity, because a complex work of art can pack aesthetic efficiency too. The struggle is not between simplicity and complexity but between efficiency and inefficiency.

PF *You once wrote, 'There is no symbolic content in my work.' But a pile of bricks, say, is a very personal symbol, surely?*

CA Almost a personal emblem, or a psychological emblem, that relates to earliest experiences.

PF *A symbol in the psychoanalytical sense?*

CA Yes.

PF *You are modifying your view about symbolic content then?*

CA When I made that statement I was both naive and being polemical. In polemic one caricatures – one must. I now realise that one cannot purge the human environment from the significance we give it. But I have a theory that abstraction arose in neolithic times, after paleolithic representation, for the same reason that we are doing it now. The culture requires significant blankness because the emblems, symbols and signs which were adequate for the former method of organising production are no longer efficient in carrying out the cultural roles that we assign to them. You just need some *tabula rasa*, or a sense that there is a space to add significance. There must be some space that suggests there is a significant exhaustion. When signs occupy every surface, then there is no place for the new signs.

PF *But what would you say to the view that your obsession with materials which have been 'digested' into similar units, but not fully refined by industrial production, can be correlated with a fascination with shit?*

CA Yes, of course. Absolutely.

PF *Would you also accept that the obsessional ordering and arranging of materials which plays an important part in your work correlates with the ego-defence mechanisms holding back the dangerous instinctual desire to play with your own shit?*

CA Yes, but some infants would rather smear on the wall, and others were drawn to play on the floor with it. And that's only to divide painters from sculptors. I don't think that I could be accused of being a painter, even as an infant.

PF *Perhaps one reason why your work interests some people is because it closely reflects anal-erotism, which has been thinly sublimated through classical, middle class, obsessional modes of ordering, close to those of the miser or the accountant.*

CA Exactly, although the same thing is true, but cannot have the same class connotations, for Zen gardens in Japan. That's a different class, but also human beings. William Carlos Williams once answered that question beautifully when he was asked if all artists and poets were neurotics who had never left a primitive state of sexual development and therefore were obsessed. He said, 'Yes, that's true of anybody who does anything remarkable.'

PF *You wear industrial overalls, but they are always immaculately clean. Here again is this association with dirt, manual labour, physical smearing, and so on, and its immediate denial in their cleanliness.*

CA If you are really interested in dealing with dirt, you have to be very fastidious. You can't afford to be sloppy. Here's another of these parallels. When he was a draughtsman out on the ships, my father pragmatically and empirically built up his knowledge of a very strange speciality which was not taught: the sanitary and freshwater plumbing of ships. His great ambition for me when I was a little boy was that I should grow up to be a sanitary engineer, planning the great plumbing and civic engineering works of the city.

PF *A new Haussmann!*

CA Not so much the streets as the sewers.

PF *Haussmann made a sewer which was his joy and pride. He took people on tours round it.*

CA Ah! The municipal sewer of Boston was indeed right by my house in which I lived as a child. The house was on a kind of peninsula in a marsh, and on either side of it were two gigantic dykes. When the enormous sewer, it was so big you could drive teams of horses through it, could be underground, it was. But they had to keep a certain grade, so that when it went over lowlands they had to build these enormous dykes. My boyhood experience with these great earthworks, and the idea that the excrement of the whole metropolis of Boston was pulsing by my house, was undoubtedly important.

PF *Sometimes the instinctual impulses break through in your work, as in your dog-shit cement pieces of 1962.*

CA Absolutely.

PF *Do you agree that the particular infantile experience that you are recreating as an artist is the productive one of shitting?*

CA It is more complex than that. It starts with that. It is a vision in which excrement is necessary, and can be satisfying in certain ways, but it also has to be accounted for in another way. In the West there is an over-developed system: we do not know how to get rid of our industrial excrement. And we have a crisis, indeed almost an anal crisis, in the culture.

PF *The infant values his own shit very highly, and the family, particularly the middle-class family, tends to value it not at all. Your work is involved with this same paradox: is this thing to be valued highly, or not at all?*

CA In a certain way. It is a kind of primal scene of its own, isn't it? I think this cannot be denied.

PF *In the Freudian conception, the obsessional is also usually preoccupied with the contradiction between the idea and the thing, and so on. Your denial that you are a conceptualist and your preoccupation with 'immanence' and stuff can be seen in these terms too.*

CA Absolutely, yes.

PF *Is your work a symptom of an obsessional neurosis which it does not transcend?*

CA I hope that it does not transcend it, but provides catharsis for it and goes beyond it. Henry Moore said, and I'm paraphrasing now, that all art is an attempt to regain the vividness of first expressions or experiences. I think he meant conscious experiences: at least it goes beyond the instinctual, beyond the infantile omnipotent state, when we begin to be aware of ourselves in the world. The omnipotent infant does not require any art because he is god.

PF *When you create value as if by magic, by laying out those steel plates, that seems to me an immediate gratification of early feelings of infantile omnipotence.*

CA But I started placing them there when they weren't worth anything.

PF *But the situation changed. At last the world recognised the value of your shit! Don't you acknowledge that there is an element of magic-*

making, of infantile omnipotence in your work?

CA Well, not omnipotence. But I used to dream when I was a little boy that I was a great general leading a great army into battle. And then somebody would come up to me and say, 'You can't do this. You're just a little boy.' And then I would be sent home.

PF *Are you still waiting to be sent home?*

CA I hope I'm not sent home when I go to the Whitechapel.

1 Graham Sutherland's portrait of Winston Churchill, 1954, was destroyed on the orders of Lady Churchill.

Issues 16 and 17, May and June 1978

Jasper Johns

interviewed by Peter Fuller

Between thinking, seeing, saying and nothing

PETER FULLER *Michael Crichton, who wrote the catalogue, was previously best known for sci-fi,* The Andromeda Strain, *and so on. Why was he chosen?*

JASPER JOHNS The museum asked me what I felt about the catalogue, and I said I would like someone who was a writer rather than an art critic. People who are used to studying my work have such a layered kind of knowledge about it. There are so many references they make, that I thought it might be more interesting to have someone outside that kind of training, or business, to see if such a person could see anything in my work.

PF *In the catalogue, Crichton describes creativity as a product of the neurochemical serotonin, and speculates that your 'serotonin-mediated inhibitory mechanisms are more finely adjusted that those of many other people', thus allowing you to produce the kind of work you do. What do you feel about this?*

JJ That's an amusing kind of speculation. Beyond that, one would have to test it. I don't know how those tests are made, and I don't know if I'd be willing to submit to them.

PF *Just before the show, you were quoted as saying, 'I'll go on painting unless seeing all the work together changes things.' Did it change things?*

JJ Not consciously, I think. I'm sure there's some effect I can't reckon with. But not as far as I know. But my painting has been inhibited by the kinds of activity this sort of exhibition entails – such as talking with you. There's a constant barrage of stuff that keeps one from concentrating strongly on any one thing. So I haven't done much painting in the last year.

PF *You have been quoted as saying, 'I've always thought that my work is too much of a piece.' Do you still feel that after the show?*

JJ Yes, I always feel it. I don't know whether that's an intellectual response. I don't know where one feels it. But I do feel I would like my work to be more varied than it is.

PF *Hilton Kramer wrote about your exhibition that Johns 'repeats, and endlessly, the same themes, devices and mannerisms but very quickly wears them out'. That is close to saying your work is 'too much of a piece', isn't it?*

JJ No, no. I'm not talking about repetition. He seems to consider that there should be novelty within the work. I'm not talking about that. My experience of life is that it's very fragmented. In one place, certain kinds of things occur, and in another place, a different kind of thing occurs. I would like my work to have some vivid indication of those differences. I guess, in painting, it would amount to different kinds of space being represented in it. But when I look at what I've done, I find it too easy to see the connections between one thing and another thing. It may just be that I know how I come to make a work – I know how hard it is to discard ideas or involvements that you already have, to come up with a different approach. Even if you succeed in altering your way of thinking, you very easily attach that to the past in your own life, even though you may have changed a good deal.

PF *What did you feel about the critical response, in general? Even your supporters like Robert Hughes, in* Time *magazine, were writing that the show revealed you as 'not the Leonardesque genius we have all been conditioned to expect'.*

JJ How many artists are criticised in that way? For not being Leonardesque! Hilton Kramer certainly didn't think my work was as interesting as Cézanne's, yet he bothered to point out that it wasn't. I find that an astonishing attitude to bring to that kind of exhibition.

PF *Hughes also called you 'the intelligent person's Andy Warhol'. What does that description mean to you?*

JJ It means nothing at all.

PF *You once said, 'whatever I do seems artificial and false to me'. What did you mean by that?*

JJ I don't know.

PF *You don't just get bizarre negative criticisms, the positive ones are often just as strange. Barbara Rose once wrote of you, 'He is among those artists for whom the activity on the canvas is the exemplar of his under-*

standing of right human conduct.' Do you accept that kind of judgement? If so, how do your works exemplify 'right human conduct'?

JJ I don't read criticism in that way, to see if it's true. What one is touched by is the fact that anyone has anything to say about one's work. When I think how hard it is for me to say anything – and I know my work fairly well – I find it quite marvellous if other people can come up with something to say about it. It seems perfectly acceptable to me that it be rather outlandish.

PF *She also wrote of you, 'Out of negation and a refusal to compromise or to conform has come a heroic affirmation of creativity in the face of all forms of entropy, demoralisation, nihilism and despair.' Do you feel your work to be a heroic affirmation of this kind?*

JJ I tend to think that all artwork is heroic. I think it's a heroic enterprise from childhood, from the very beginning, whenever it begins.

PF *So there's nothing especially heroic about yours?*

JJ Certainly not from my point of view. It's just what I do.

PF *Why do you think your work attracts this sort of exaggerated claim, not just from specialist critics, but even from popular magazines like* Time *and* Newsweek*? Probably no other artist is treated like this.*

JJ I don't know. I tend only to read criticism of my own work, or of people I am very interested in. But I don't have any sense of what criticism is in terms of living people.

PF *Do you think these kinds of estimations have anything to do with your success in the market?*

JJ How? In what way? Do you mean that one causes the other? Which being the cause? And which being the effect?

PF *I am suggesting you attract such critical claims because of your market success. I find it difficult to relate them to what seem to me to be the concrete concerns of your work. Questions of 'heroic affirmation' and of 'right human conduct' don't seem to me to be issues which you are actually concerned with.*

JJ In painting, human conduct is the act of painting. That would seem quite reasonable from my point of view.

PF *You once said that you preferred the work of Willem de Kooning, Philip Guston, Jack Tworkov and Cy Twombly. That's Abstract Expressionism, primarily. What is your view of Abstract Expressionism as a movement now?*

JJ I don't have a strong sense of it as a movement, really. I have some sense of individual artists who were part of that movement.

It's certainly not the idea of the movement that interests me.

PF *Well, take De Kooning specifically. Why do you admire him so much? What did you learn from him?*

JJ I think more interesting is what I have not learned from him. De Kooning is a wonderful painter. But I don't know how to describe or justify the value one gives an artist's work. One tends to use clichés: 'energy', 'technical mastery'.

PF *Do you think that the claims made for Abstract Expressionism in the fifties were excessive?*

JJ What claims?

PF *Claims made by critics, especially Clement Greenberg, American art institutions and museums.*

JJ I don't know what you are talking about when you make a statement like that. When I came to New York in the fifties, Abstract Expressionism was rampant. Everyone was concerned with it, and that made a very nice kind of screen. One felt that it was in very good hands and one did not have to be concerned with it. Because everyone was concerned with it, it made it seem very lively even though one was not going to join it.

PF *Many British critics believe there was a concerted attempt to manufacture an exportable, international, modernist style emanating from New York. And that unprecedented financial and institutional support was put behind American Abstract Expressionism. Are you aware of this view?*

JJ I am not really aware of it, and I think I would not credit it were it brought to my attention. The configuration could be described differently. A new kind of activity which attracts attention from outside, and which is supported, could be described in a very different way from the way you have just proposed.

PF *The rise of Abstract Expressionism did coincide with the expansion of American markets after the war, with the outflowing of American culture throughout Europe, didn't it?*

JJ I don't know enough to propose that those things would often coincide. But it would not seem unlikely. When one kind of energy is very strong another, attached energy, is also apt to be strong.

PF *By the late fifties, Abstract Expressionism was looking more than a little tired, wasn't it?*

JJ Any 'ism will expire. By having an 'ism you are separating it from other things. Your attention has to deal with the entire field. Things displace one another in one's interest.

PF *In 1958, you had your first one-man show at Castelli's. You were 28, and unknown. But you got incredible critical attention – almost all your work sold. Alfred Barr bought three pictures for MoMA. Why do you think you had this sudden success?*

JJ A number of reasons. My work was unknown generally by the art world and particularly by other artists. There were very, very few people feeding information about my work to other people. At that time, in New York, most young artists worked in a social setting where everyone knew what everyone else was doing. But my work took shape without many people knowing about it. Also, Castelli had just begun his gallery, it had no habits, and that was important. Then there was the obvious novelty of my work in relation to what was generally being shown. Fairfield Porter came to my studio before the show opened, and did a criticism for *Art News*. Tom Hess, who was then the editor, decided on the basis of that, I believe, to put a painting of mine on the cover. That again was something quite unprecedented – that someone no one had ever heard of had a picture on the cover of *Art News* – especially as Tom's primary interest was abstract expressionist painting.

PF *In 1959, Ben Heller wrote, 'Johns has been as much a pawn in the current art world game of power politics as the bearer of a new or individual image.' Do you think that was true?*

JJ I am not sure that I understand.

PF *Well, in 1958 you expressed surprise at the interest in your work. You said you thought anything that you made could only be of interest to yourself. Do you then think that Leo Castelli, Alfred Barr, Tom Hess, etc saw a cultural function for your work, which you did not see, which they then exploited?*

JJ Not in any sinister sense. Art in the mid fifties took on a value it had not had previously. Just look at the change in the number of publications, galleries and artists between, say, 1955 and 1965. It's not that someone made something happen. Something was happening and people were making things. It is difficult to come up with a cause and effect. You had a complex in which many things were affecting one another. The fact that Leo was just forming his gallery was very important. All the other New York galleries that I know existed then had an attitude towards work into which my work could not comfortably have fitted. I think my work would have been seen in a very different way if I had shown at, say, the Stable Gallery. I don't think any of those dealers would have shown my work but if they had I think it would have been treated in a very different way. The only dealer

I wanted to show my work was Betty Parsons. I felt her artists were not of one kind. But that didn't work, so the fact that Leo appeared was interesting and a marvellous coincidence from my point of view, the fact that my work existed was a marvellous thing for him. Instead of putting him in competition with other galleries with the same kind of interests, it made a very clear difference between what he was doing and what other people were doing. That kind of clarity perhaps brings a sharpness to the situation. It demands either that the new work be deliberately ostracised or paid attention to.

PF *In 1964, Sidney Tillim wrote that your work provided 'an alternative to abstraction that would nonetheless preserve its principal formal characteristic – the flat picture plane'. Did you ever see your work that way?*

JJ No, of course not.

PF *Yet surely it was because that kind of claim could be made about it that you received so much art world support in 1958.*

JJ Why couldn't you believe that aspects of my work emphasised certain things that painting at that time generally did not emphasise, and that this change of emphasis was useful in the society, as well as having a novelty which engaged people?

PF *But in what ways was it useful, useful to whom, for what, and why? Are you saying that those who wrote like Tillim about you misunderstood your work?*

JJ I don't think work can be understood, if you mean by that it is to be one thing. I don't feel that. I don't even understand my own work in that sense.

PF *The standard art historical view of your work is that you provided a link between Abstract Expressionism and Pop Art. You've dismissed this as mere 'sociology'. Don't you accept that much of the enthusiasm for your work at the time of your first show arose because it found a way through for Abstract Expressionism, or American-style painting, at a time when this national art looked very much in crisis?*

JJ I don't follow you. My work expressed ideas that were not being expressed in painting that needed expressing, but it isn't clear to me. Are you trying to give it some political significance?

PF *It is more a cultural question. Greenberg once wrote that the 'abiding significance' of your art 'lies mostly in the area of the formal or plastic'. Do you agree?*

JJ Isn't that where he wants the abiding significance of all work to lie? I would doubt that work has 'abiding significance'.

PF *Nevertheless, from the point of view of the formalists, you introduced the appurtenances of representation into what was essentially an abstract aesthetic.*

JJ I wouldn't agree with that if you mean to give me that responsibility within the large field of art in America. I think my work drew attention to that, but it was in the air. It was also a strong aspect of Robert Rauschenberg's work from the period of his red pictures on. Almost all the elements of his work conveyed themselves as well as some other kind of information – written, photographed, or whatever. But perhaps the superficial simplicity and blatancy of the images that I used suggests the kind of remark you just made.

PF *But Greenberg also said about your work, 'everything that used to serve representation and illusion is left to serve nothing but itself, that is abstraction; while everything that usually connotes the abstract or the decorative – flatness, bare outlines, all-over or symmetrical design – is put to the service of representation'. Was that true?*

JJ In a sense it is true. It's a smart thing to say – by 'smart' I mean 'not stupid', I don't mean 'cute'.

PF *In the work which you have been making since 1972, the cross-hatching series, you have even abandoned these appurtenances of representation. This could be taken as indicating how little you ever moved from a classically abstract expressionist aesthetic, couldn't it?*

JJ You could take that point of view, yes. But I am not sure of the degree to which I make the distinction between abstract and whatever it was we were opposing it to.

PF *With the abandonment of even the appurtenances of representation, I am suggesting you are lapsing into classically abstract expressionist pictorial concerns.*

JJ You can take that point of view, but I don't see it that way, I must say. You are making a point, but it is not a point of mine.

PF *Recently, Suzi Gablik, a friend and admirer of your work, wrote about the recent paintings, 'with these pictures Johns emerges as an "all-over" painter in the sense defined by Clement Greenberg'. Does the fact that you are being read in this way even by your most sympathetic viewers worry you?*

JJ No, because I think it is very hard to have an idea about a picture. Any picture carries such a dead weight. It is very hard to tell what is interesting about a picture, and then to state it is even more difficult. But I don't think that my pictures are interesting because they are like abstracts.

PF *In 1970, Hilton Kramer described your work as 'De Kooning plus Duchamp'. He wrote, 'The De Kooning-Duchamp synthesis was a winning combination. Its large debt to Abstract Expressionism offered just the right obeisance to established taste, and its debt to Dada – a Dada now cleansed of any political overtones – just the right degree of innovation and surprise.' Was your work 'De Kooning plus Duchamp'?*

JJ It does not make sense as a formula for doing my work, but I understand that someone could see relationships between my work and that of those two artists.

PF *You saw quite a lot of Duchamp just before his death, didn't you?*

JJ Not really.

PF *Why do you always play down your relationship with him?*

JJ Only because people have assumed I was very close friends with Marcel, and I was not. I saw him perhaps a dozen times in my life. The first time, I saw him at a party. I did not speak to him. Then someone brought him to my studio. Once, I went to a Christmas dinner which he was at in Chinatown. Then I saw him again at a party. After that I did not see him for years. Then John Cage began to study chess with him and around that time I saw him perhaps eight or ten times. These were very modest encounters. They did not involve much exchange of ideas. There was a set for Merce Cunningham based on the *Large Glass*, I saw him around that a few times.

PF *Are you saying he was not a significant influence on you?*

JJ No, I never said that. I first went to see his work in the Arensberg Collection when someone referred to me as 'Neo-Dada', and I did not know what Dada was. Then I read the Robert Motherwell book on Dada and Surrealism. The Robert Lebel book on Marcel appeared about that time – I got it when it was remaindered. Then someone gave me the *Valise* and a year or two after that I knew that Marcel had a copy of the *Green Box* and I wanted it. But it was all in French, and I can't read French, so I decided not to get it. About that time, the translation which Richard Hamilton did the typography for appeared. So then I went back to Marcel and asked if I could buy the facsimile thing, which I did. So I was very inquisitive about his work and ideas. But he was not a person that I would ever have bothered asking too much. Actually I asked very little. He was not terribly generous about exposing himself.

PF *But did you consciously try to keep politics out of your painting, as Kramer suggests?*

JJ I don't think politics was ever a concern of mine, to keep out or to bring in.

PF *Hughes wrote, 'Just as Marx is said to have stood Hegel on his head, so Johns has inverted Duchamp's assault on painting. He has embraced these attempts to undermine the foundations of traditional painting and made them serve his own artistic ambitions.' Is that a fair description of your relationship to Duchamp?*

JJ What was negative in Marcel, for himself, became positive in my work, certainly. He said that he wanted to kill art, or to destroy art, himself. Then of course he said that he was nothing but an artist. My interest in his work is not from the point of view of killing art. I know one's not supposed to say this, it's not quite proper, but I regard his work as art of a positive nature. I see it as art.

PF *You once said you were brought up with the idea that the artist had to be socially useful, adding, 'I think artists are the elite of the servant class'. Do you think it is wrong for artists to challenge the way things are in the world?*

JJ Not at all.

PF *Kramer once wrote, 'Johns like Rauschenberg aims to please and confirm the decadent periphery of bourgeois taste.' Is that a suitable function for 'the elite of the servant class'?*

JJ I have no interest in that remark. Most of what Kramer says means nothing to me. I don't want to criticise Kramer.

PF *Asked about how the state should choose artists for support, you suggested using a lottery. But you added, 'We are in a funny, broken society. It is not easy to know what is to be done.' What is your view of the world beyond art? What are your politics?*

JJ I am very stupid politically, actually.

PF *In 1954, you had a dream in which you saw yourself painting a large American flag, and the next day you began painting one. People dream of many things. Why did you decide to make the flag?*

JJ I don't know. I have not dreamed of any other paintings. I must be grateful for such a dream. The unconscious thought was accepted by my consciousness gracefully.

PF *You tended to talk as if the flag was a neutral, given, image. Is that really what you felt?*

JJ That was my feeling at the time, but I think that has shifted. It is hard to recover the original feeling.

PF *Flags, targets, maps and so on belong very much to the iconography of American imperialism. Certainly, during the sixties, such images were anything but neutral. They took on very charged connotations, didn't they?*

JJ I never thought of that. I don't know whether it is true or not. I think that in the art world people have learned to look at kinds of images which they did not look at at that time, and so things now are visible that may not have been visible at that time. I remember once I had a painting of a flag in white – a large one – and someone leaned against it. That sort of thing is much less likely to happen now. I don't think that is a change in the picture; I think it is a change in, well, people.

PF *But in 1958, weren't you just hoisting the flag in Abstract Expressionism? You identified the next step in Modernism with peculiarly American signs and symbols.*

JJ My training as an artist is very modest, and my exposure to painting at that time – well, even now, but certainly then – was really very slight.

PF *Last week in Washington I discovered that Senator Javits, a Republican, has a Jasper Johns flag in his office. Everyone knows what sort of people fly the American flag at the bottom of their gardens. Wasn't the flag series, whatever you may have intended it to be, treated as a manifestation of Modernism made acceptable to this element in American society? This sort of Abstract Expressionism could not be seen as a communist plot.*

JJ You can see it that way, I suppose. Let me think a little more about that. I'll tell you an anecdote. Once, I made a kind of sculpture of a flag in bronze – it was an edition of three, I think. One of them was given on some occasion to President Kennedy. I became very upset that this was happening. It was given on Flag Day! It seemed to me to be such a terrible thing to happen. I complained bitterly to my very good friend, John Cage. He said, 'Don't let it worry you. Just consider it a pun on your work!'

PF *Was that the sort of thing you had in mind when you said, 'I have no idea about what the paintings imply about the world. I don't think that's a painter's business.'?*

JJ In working, one doesn't set out to make a work which will have a certain effect in the society. I don't think I have that kind of large grasp of society to begin with. I tend to relate to a smaller thing, like theatre, where you have an audience. That's my image of society. And one knows that the audience is always changing. So by the time you've imagined what the audience is, and formed your ideas, it is going to be something else. It's very tricky. As well as I can tell, I am concerned with space. With some idea about space. And then as soon as you break space, then you have things.

PF *You cannot avoid the meanings of the signs you make. Javits can happily hang a Johns flag in his office, but it could not hang, say, in an office in Vietnam as a statement about 'space', could it?*

JJ My concerns are probably largely invisible in Javits's office. Anything can be used in some other way. That's an interesting point about our experience of the world. Things aren't necessarily what we say they are or what we want them to be. Anything, from some point of view, can be abused or can become invisible.

PF *Do you agree that Modernism, as defined by critics, dealers and art institutions, has tended to see art as a self-evolving continuum, and that this has led to the underestimation of many artists whose primary concerns are with the experience of the world rather than with the experience of art?*

JJ At all times, when you look at one thing, you don't look at another. So, at any time in the society, some things have a kind of prominence that other things don't have. What is one to do? At a certain point everyone wants to live his own life. Part of that life is to attract attention – everyone wants to attract attention to what he is doing – that is part of it.

PF *But you were almost a victim of modernist historicism. In fact, it turned out that you weren't because you provided a 'missing link'. But, in 1963, Michael Fried wrote about you, 'The historical moment to which his style belongs is past and in effect was past by the time he came on the scene. Already Barnett Newman and Clyfford Still have pointed the way past the de Kooning problem. He didn't see the connection you provided into Pop Art and everything that came after.*

JJ But look at how Michael sees the world – I don't think that he believes that what came after ever happened. But whether or not I was of any importance, that's what happened.

PF *You agree it is an incredible view of art, his style 'belongs to the past' because the 'De Kooning problem' is already solved?*

JJ Yes.

PF *Nevertheless, I am saying it is the dominant attitude among museum men, from which – despite this specific instance – you have benefited a lot.*

JJ I don't know how to reply to that.

PF *It is often said that you became an 'Old Master' within two years because of the emergence of Pop in the early sixties. What was your view of Pop?*

JJ In the press, everyone is put together and called something. But that unit of thought is of no interest to me. Some artists who fall within that have done works that have been interesting to me. And then one has friends who are artists in such an area. The meaning of one's life is different from a judgement of something like that.

PF *But your preoccupation with the given was certainly shared by some Pop artists. It is also apparent in Minimalism, for example in Carl Andre's use of given industrial elements, and in 'new Realism' – in Duane Hanson there is a concern with the appearance of the other as a given, a cast. This seems quite close to, say, the use of flagstones in some of your recent work. Would you agree that this preoccupation with the given runs through all these tendencies which are often thought of as being opposed to each other?*

JJ One has to agree with that.

PF *Why are you interested in things which are, as you say, 'not mine', things which have been designed, but are taken from the world, not made by you?*

JJ I was interested in what was seen, and what was not seen. One wanted to avoid the idea of an interpretation – I know how simple-minded it is – but nevertheless those sorts of images gave a sense of objectivity rather than of subjectivity. And then one could deal with the question of when you see it, when you don't see it, what do you see, what do you think it is, how do you change what you see, and what differences do these changes make to what you see and to what you think. It's a rich area for nuance there. It's a pretty limited area if you are going to make any strong point. But I was interested in the kind of nuance, modulation, play between thinking, seeing, saying and nothing.

PF *Don't you think that this preoccupation with the given, common to so many American artists, can be correlated with a culturally widespread imaginative failure among artists, a refusal to imaginatively grasp their world and to recreate it through their art?*

JJ I don't believe that. Do you believe it about other art? I don't know what to say. I don't feel that. My problem is to relate myself to the other artists that you have mentioned. I see that you can see what you say, but I don't think that I would see it that way.

PF *David Hockney has said that he believes Modernism is dead. Many critics in Britain would agree that it is dying. In England it does seem to be almost over. In America, largely because of the buoyancy of the market, and the presence of collectors, it has not run down completely, but has stopped at this idea of simply representing the given. The imaginative function of the artist, his capacity to depict experience, seems to have withered.*

JJ Well, I don't believe that's true, unless you are making the same sort of point that you made earlier about Abstract Expressionism losing its strength, and becoming repetitious. If you are suggesting that because, numerically, there is this concern with the given this constitutes a 'lack of imaginative function' among artists, I don't agree. If you take say an extreme example – Duchamp's readymades. Now they, in themselves, do not mean what you say. They don't point to this kind of inertia. But I have never thought about this in this way, and I don't know what to think, or what to say.

PF *Which living British artists do you respect?*

JJ Much of my thought is affected by people I see, or meet, or whatever, socially. The people I think of immediately are, of course, Francis Bacon and then Richard Hamilton and Bridget Riley – those immediately.

PF *Stephen Buckley's work has sometimes been related to yours. Are you aware of his work?*

JJ Yes, but not in an elaborate way. I saw his last show here whenever it was. I know Stephen. Before that I had seen photographs of some other pieces. I don't think I had seen works.

PF *He is one of the few painters under 35 who have made a profession of it in England. Barbara Rose said, your 'courageous refusal to abandon the painter's craft has given all painters new hope'. Are you hopeful about the future of painting?*

JJ I am neither hopeful nor not hopeful about the future of painting.

PF *Hughes described your work as 'a particularly knotty kind of conceptual art'. But don't you think the ideational content of your work is often exaggerated? Or do you see yourself as an artist primarily concerned with ideas?*

JJ That's a critical thought that is often repeated. Now this sounds an awful thing to say, but I still think it's based on people's experience of abstract expressionist painting, and the kind of subjectivity indicated in much of it, even in the very finest abstract expressionist painting. The artificial construction people make is that painting is not intellectual, and does not involve much thinking, but involves psychic or subconscious pressures which are released through the act of painting. But I think painting like mine shows obvious kinds of hesitation and reworking which people associate with thought.

PF *Pieces like* The Critic Smiles, *1969, and* The Critic Sees, *1961, strike me as amusing, but hardly to be taken seriously at the level of ideas...*

JJ I think of them as cartoons.

PF *Exactly. They are the kind of ideas a good cartoonist has a dozen times a week.*

JJ Of course. I hope so.

PF *Don't you think that the extraordinary outpouring of critical attention such pieces have attracted is exaggerated? Max Kozloff, for example, once said that to engage with your paintings was to engage not so much with a personality as with a way of thinking, a philosophy almost.*

JJ As for *The Critic Sees*, and *The Critic Smiles*, I think it is because critics write about them that they take them so seriously. And because they are aimed at critics.

PF *You read Wittgenstein in the sixties. Whom have you read since who has been a major influence on your ideas?*

JJ I'm trying to think about whom I've read. I'm reading Céline right now.

PF *Have you read Sartre, for example?*

JJ Not since college.

PF *But you read him then?*

JJ Bits, bits.

PF *Did you read much existentialist literature?*

JJ Not much. I formed some kind of cheap idea about what it was.

PF *Did you recognise its concern with the given, with what Sartre calls* facticity, *or being-in-itself?*

JJ I don't know. It's very hard for me to remember what my thoughts were.

PF *Is it true to say that rather than being 'intellectual', your subject-matter is often about the nature of perception?*

JJ I don't think it quite makes it on that level.

PF *Are you getting tired?*

JJ No. I don't think so, I just don't seem to have many ideas. In this sense, it's not about the nature of perception because it's too tied, in the making of it, it's too tied to the nature of – I don't know how to say it.

PF *It can't be about perception, because it's tied to the nature of perception. It is that what you are saying?*

JJ Yes.

PF *There's a painting of yours in which the word red is rendered in blue and yellow paint. A critic wrote about this, 'such works do more to force the viewer to think about representation and what it entails than almost any painting since Cubism'. But the idea you were making use of is just a commonplace, a given among ideas for anyone who thinks for half-an-hour about words, colour and representation. Did you consider it a major statement about representation?*

JJ No. The importance that things have obviously is not the importance that one has assigned to them, or intends them to have. I don't think that one paints to do something important in that way.

PF *Your work often has an extremely sensuous, sometimes almost pretty kind of quality, doesn't it?*

JJ The physical facts of painting are very important to me.

PF *But once you said you weren't a colourist, that you could barely differentiate between colours.*

JJ My painting of the last few years has improved my colour. I think I'm better at colour than I used to be.

PF *The explorations with colours and words – were they investigations of colour for yourself because you knew this was a weakness of yours?*

JJ You are talking about *False Start*, 1959. Well, no. For me, that was more an attempt to get rid of predetermined boundaries which had existed in the images which preceded those pictures; painting within lines, basically.

PF *David Bourdon once asked you, 'At what point did you realise you are what society regards as a successful artist?' You replied, 'It hasn't happened quite yet.' What has to happen before you will feel that society regards you as a successful artist?*

JJ Oh I think society regards me as a successful artist. I think society regards any artist who makes a living from his work as successful. I probably meant my own sense of myself. I would certainly think that if the society thought of anyone as a successful artist, they would include me. I would hate to be left out.

PF *You have been quoted as saying you wanted to sell a painting for $1m. Would that make you feel more successful?*

JJ No, I think it would make me feel a lot richer. That's just the kind of remark one makes on some occasion.

PF *But the prices reached by your works are extraordinary. In 1971,* Map *sold for $200,000, in 1973,* Two White Maps *for $240,000. Early works have reached $270,000. The beer cans passed through auction at $90,000. What kind of effect have these high market figures had on you as a painter?*

JJ I would say none, but I would doubt that. Those things have unconscious effects that one can't determine. I don't know. I really don't know how to answer the question. New works are fetching between $80,000 and $120,000.

PF *Don't you fear the effects of overpricing?*

JJ I don't have anything to do with pricing. Pricing is determined by other people.

PF *It is sometimes said there's a connection between your low production and these high prices.*

JJ I think that's a lot of nonsense. I believe it's nonsense.

PF *You have never held back works to maintain market prices?*

JJ No. I've held back work because I wanted to hold it, and I've often sold because I had to sell because I needed the money.

PF *Has your dealer ever advised you not to produce too much?*

JJ No, I assure you he has not – I wish Leo could hear that.

PF *Is there a long waiting list for your works?*

JJ I don't know that there's a waiting list. I think there are people who would like works, who don't own them. I don't really know that. It's a guess.

PF *Doesn't the knowledge of the kind of exchange-value you are creating inhibit you when you sit down in front of a canvas?*

JJ I often find it difficult to make a picture. That has always been true. It has nothing to do with the price of a picture. I don't think that scale has much meaning. I think that one thinks as one always thinks, that one may be making a picture that no one will be interested in.

PF *In one passage, Crichton compared you to Adlai Stevenson, and wrote that you 'perpetually risk frozen indecision'. He said that you had been viewed as 'a limited, inhibited artist entangled in your own past'. You seem to be saying that painting is so difficult for you that you really do 'risk frozen indecision'.*

JJ I think that's true.

PF *So every time, even now, it is hard to paint?*

JJ I would not say every time. I would say often.

PF *I once read something by you where you said you tried to make your work 'not me'; you explained that you didn't want to 'confuse my feelings with what I produced'. Why are you so concerned about not letting feelings through?*

JJ I think that I either made that quote some time ago, or I intended it to refer to earlier work. Let me put it this way – my feeling about myself on the subjective level is that I'm a highly flawed person. The concerns that I have always dealt with in picture-making didn't have to do with expressing my flawed nature, or my self. I wanted to have an idea, or an image, or whatever you please, that was not I. I don't know how to put it. I don't know what supports what. I wanted something that wouldn't have to carry my nature as part of its message. I think that's less true now. I don't know whether my work now has bypassed that concern, or includes it, or what. But I don't think I'd express that thought now.

PF *You said once that you disliked psychology because you had such a bad one yourself.*

JJ Yes, that's right.

PF *Have you read Freud, or any psychoanalytical literature?*

JJ I love Freud's writing. I still read it.

PF *Why do you dislike talking about your early life?*

JJ It wasn't especially cheerful.

PF *Henry Moore once said that art was invariably an attempt to regain the intensity of earliest experience. Do you think that?*

JJ I certainly believe that everything I do is attached to my childhood, but I would not make the statement that you just said he had made.

PF *Despite your statements about 'objectivity', and your desire to exclude feelings from your work, quite a lot of your unconscious does, and indeed, did, come through. Your obsession about things and their representations, the denial of affect itself, your interest in the sensual surface can all be seen in these terms. But most remarkable are images like that of a shattered body. This was in your earliest works, and it recurs explicitly in* Untitled, *1972, and 'The Corpse and the Mirror' series of 1974. These pieces seem to have very private, personal subjective meanings.*

JJ I certainly agree with you.

PF *Were you exaggerating the 'objectivity' of your work, its separateness from your feelings, then, say 20 years ago?*

JJ What can you say? Obviously, the idea of objectivity itself exaggerates the absence of subjectivity so that, at best, one can say that one's intention is so and so, and obviously one does not do exactly what one intends. One does more, usually, and often less, also. Or you could just say one does other.

PF *Crichton wrote that, like Rauschenberg, you shared a belief that art sprang from life experiences. Would you agree with that?*

JJ Yes.

PF *What life experiences do images like the shattered body spring from? It haunts so much of your work.*

JJ I don't think that I would want to propose an answer on the level of subjective experience. I can come up with a substitute.

PF *But the body in several parts, which occurs in* Target with plaster casts, *1955, and later works, can only be derived from your earliest fantasies, if art springs from life experience, surely. You have presumably only experienced such things at the level of fantasy?*

JJ I don't know that it can only be that. I would not take that point of view. I think any concept of wholeness, regardless of where you place it, is... Well, take the *Target with plaster casts*, the first one. Some of the casts were in my studio. They were things among other things. Then, of course, they were chosen again for use in that way. But I don't feel qualified to discuss it on that level, I must say. I've not been in analysis, and I wouldn't want to give it that meaning in such a specific way as you have done. I believe that the question of what is a part, and what is a whole, is a very interesting problem on the infantile level, yes, on the psychological level, but also in ordinary, objective space.

Issues 18 and 19, July–August and September 1978

Anthony Caro

interviewed by Peter Fuller

Look at the work – that's where nothing is hidden

PETER FULLER *You went to Charterhouse, a public school, and then to Cambridge where you read engineering. Why did you choose this subject? Did you want to make functional objects?*

ANTHONY CARO My father was a stockbroker. He wanted me to be a stockbroker and join his firm. I did not want to do that, I liked drawing. I was better at mathematics than other subjects. Once, in desperation, my father got me to work for a few weeks in an architect's office. I was bored stiff. I spent most of the time in the lavatory reading. Later my father suggested engineering since it involved drawing and maths.

PF *Did you think about becoming a professional artist?*

AC I wanted to be an artist, yes. When you are young you dream about all sorts of things. Such dreams are the basis on which you later structure your life. The room I made art in was the one place that I felt free and able to do exactly what I wanted.

PF *Did your father resist this ambition?*

AC Very much so, although later on when I did become a sculpture student he was supportive. I was very bad indeed at engineering. I had vague thoughts of bridge-building but what I had to study had nothing to do with that. I learned things like heat theory and what went on inside a boiler. I just scraped through my exams.

PF *Your early, 'post-student' works were figurative and expressionistic. In a 1972 interview you said, 'My figurative sculptures were to do with what it is like to be inside the body.' What do you feel about them now?*

AC I don't look at them much. They were honest. I was searching to find a way to say what I had to.

PF *They were theatrical and humanist, weren't they?*

AC Humanist, yes. All my work is humanist. The figurative ones were expressionistic, not theatrical.

PF *Michael Fried thinks that your later, abstract works, too, are almost metaphors for bodily experience. He refers to their 'rootedness in certain basic facts about being in the world, in particular about possessing a body', and argues 'the changes that took place in (Caro's) art in late 1959 and early 1960... were not the result of any shift of fundamental aspirations'. Another major commentator on your work, William Rubin, dismisses this as 'purely speculative'. Who is right?*

AC The critics who have influenced me the most by coming to the studio and talking about my work are Clement Greenberg and Fried, not Rubin and Fried. I am not responsible for what any critics write. However, in this case, Fried is right. The changes took place because I had reached a sculptural impasse. My aspirations and beliefs about being in the world or the value of human life have not undergone fundamental changes since I was an undergraduate and spent time sorting these things out for myself.

PF *Fried is sometimes self-contradictory but at one point he insists that the value of all your sculptures resides in their relationship to the body. 'Not only is the radical abstractness of Caro's art not a denial of our bodies and the world', he writes, 'it is the only way in which they can be saved for high art today, in which they can be made present to us other than as theatre.' Thus Fried argues your sculptures stand for the body, though not by reproducing its external appearance. Is that true?*

AC Let's leave the critics out of it. In my beliefs about sculpture I am very conscious that it has to do with physicality. I don't think it is possible to divorce sculpture from the making of objects. Back in the sixties I found certain materials, like plaster and plastics, difficult and unpleasant to cope with simply because they do not have enough physical reality. It is not clear enough where the skin of them – not the skin, the surface of them – resides. They are flat-white in that kind of unreal way that you can't tell exactly where they are. The appearance of them also gives no indication of their mass or weight. I needed to use a material that you could identify that it was there. I do not believe that the 'otherness' of a sculpture – and by that I mean what differentiates a sculpture from an object – should reside just within the material itself. I find that insufficiently significant: there's a tremendous 'otherness' in a looking-glass for example. 'Otherness' should be born in relationships.

PF *But do you think that insofar as your work has relations beyond sculpture itself then those refer to not just physicality but also, as Fried put it, to what it means to possess a body?*

AC Certain things about the physical world and certain things about what it is like to be in a body are tied up together. Verticality, horizontality, gravity, all of these pertain both to the outside physical world and to the fact that we have bodies, as evidently does the size of a sculpture. These things are of importance in both my early figurative and the later abstract sculpture. In the abstract sculptures they are crucial.

PF *You recently said that the artists you sympathised with least were those 'who use painting or sculpture as a means to something else'. You said art of 'the very highest class' was first and foremost 'about art'. You were even derogatory about Franz Kline and Mark Rothko whom you called 'high class illustrators'.*

AC I stand by that. After seeing the Rothko retrospective at the Guggenheim I'd say his best paintings are very high-class illustration, in much the same way as Bernard Berenson might have used that word in comparing Uccello with Giotto.

PF *Your complaint was that their work was not just about art but illustrated 'states of mind'. Fried argues that your work too is about something other than art – about 'states of body', if you like. Do you really think that the 'highest art' is 'about art'? I value Rothko for the way in which his forms express experience.*

AC Art, music and poetry are about what it is like to be alive. That almost goes without saying; depth of human content is what raises art to its most profound level. But that human content resides and finds expression within the language of the medium. The language artists use has to be the language of the subject – that is not the language of everyday life. The language we use in sculpture is the language of sculpture – that has to do with materials, shapes, intervals and so on.

PF *Your use of an analogy with language is very doubtful. Sculpture lacks anything like an agreed grammar. Language always points beyond itself to signify something other than itself. Now you have said that art of 'the very highest class' is first and foremost 'about art'.*

AC You are jumping feet foremost into philosophy. I think what I said was clear enough. Concentrating on the niceties of verbal expression is not my subject. I am a sculptor. I try to form meaning out of bits of steel.

PF *Exactly, and I am trying to discover what sort of meaning you attempt to form.*

AC The meaning of 'me'. The question you ask is literary and philosophical. Your next question could well be 'What is art?' I can't tell you what art, or music, or poetry is. If I could answer that I would be much cleverer than I am. I probably wouldn't even have to make it.

PF *My next question is in fact not 'What is art?' but 'What is sculpture?'. You talk as if your only concern is with an object in the world, a physical thing. Evidently, a sculpture must exist as an object in the world but the sculpture as sculpture can only come into full existence when it is completed as an image in the consciousness of a human observer. This is not just empty philosophising. My quarrel with formalists is about the nature of sculpture itself. You focus on sculpture's physical existence to the degree that its meaning as an image seems barely to concern you. This sort of emphasis accounts for the vacuousness of much sculpture. So my questions about the nature of your images and meanings strike me as being very practical. Surely you are concerned with the signified as well as the signifier?*

AC Absolutely. To the spectator a sculpture or a painting for that matter is essentially a surrogate for another person. Therefore it has to be expressive. Abstract art which is not expressive becomes arbitrary or decorative. Sculptures or paintings which are figurative and not expressive are at least about figures, but abstract sculpture which is not expressive is just itself, the metal or stone or wood it is made of, and it is for this reason that so much bad, inexpressive abstract sculpture is more vacuous than its realistic counterpart, which at least portrays something.

I most certainly do not deny meaning or intent in a sculpture but I doubt if I go along with your interpretations of the words. As I said, the value of an artwork lies in its depth of introspective and emotional content expressed through and enmeshed with the fullest understanding of the medium.

PF *You often seem to me to be producing works which are not first and foremost 'about art' but about experience beyond art. These are the works I respond to most strongly and those which differentiate you from your many imitators. For me, your weakest sculptures are those most manifestly 'about art'.*

AC Give me an example of one which is about art and one which is to do with experience.

PF *Often it is moments within the same work, but* Twenty-four Hours, *1960, with its references to Kenneth Noland's targets and Greenberg's theories, seems first and foremost 'about art'.* Orangerie, *1969, a light-hearted enough piece, nonetheless immediately transcends such concerns – its energy and vitality seem to come from the lived experience of movement. I value Rothko more highly than Hans Hofmannn because Rothko's work was first and foremost 'about experience' whereas Hofmannn's mature painting was painting about painting. But that is not to say that Rothko was not also formally accomplished or that there is no residue of experience, beyond painterly experience, in Hofmannn.*

AC I do not think you have really come to terms with abstraction. In abstract art its subject-matter, not its content, is art. But if you want to talk about content, don't miss the affirmation, the joy, even ecstasy of life lived, in Hofmann's late abstractions. Art comes from art. I remember going to the Matisse show and seeing how Matisse had taken one of his own paintings, worked from it and transformed it, and that had led on to the next one and the next.

PF *In your early period did you ever think your engineering knowledge would be of use to you as a sculptor?*

AC No.

PF *Between 1951 and 1953 you worked as Henry Moore's assistant. In 1960 you praised him, 'Doors of a whole world of art which I had not known as a student, he opened for me.' Then you were sculpturally rejecting much of what he stood for. You have already said your father opposed your wish to become a sculptor. Do you think that – in terms of sculpture – Moore was a father figure for you?*

AC That's right – Moore and David Smith, ten years later, were, in different ways, my fathers in sculpture. I suppose I felt something of a love-hate relationship for both of them, particularly Henry who taught me a great deal at a very important time of my development. David Smith was killed in 1965. I was never really close to him personally, he was 18 years older than me. They were both father figures. One's feelings are so mixed in these situations. You're immensely grateful for what you learned from them, at the same time...

PF *People both love their fathers and seek to destroy them completely.*

AC Something like that. Something like that.

PF *Have you maintained personal relations with Moore since 1960?*

AC Yes, but I don't see much of him. He's out of London and he's busy. I saw him at his 80th birthday and felt a surge of affection and respect for him. I took my younger son to see him at his place two or three years ago. It was a very good visit. But Henry and I belong to very different generations. I don't think there is a great deal in common in terms of sculpture. Since I worked for him I have not had close contact sculpturally. But then David Smith and I never got down to talking about sculpture.

PF *What were these 'doors of a whole world of art' he opened then?*

AC I had been at the Royal Academy schools. My first knowledge of negro art, Surrealism, Cubism, of the whole modern movement, came from Moore. You can scarcely conceive what a closed world it was then for a student in the Academy schools. We were expected to look either at casts of Greek sculpture in the school corridors or else go upstairs to the Royal Academy Summer Exhibition. Our education was very bad, very incomplete. But all the time I worked at Moore's I would take two books at a time out of his library, he would show them to me and talk about art. He was a most generous teacher. All sorts of possibilities began to open up then that changed my perspectives a great deal. It was as if I had been in a monastery before that.

PF *The essence of Moore's sculpture is his experience of nature and natural forms – shells, bones, pebbles and especially the human body, isn't it?*

AC Yes, there is a big difference between his art and that of people of my generation. It is misleading to call our art 'urban' but if his art is to do with the countryside and nature then ours could certainly be said to be more urban than his.

PF *Did you see* Sheep Piece, *1971–72?*

AC I thought *Sheep Piece* was terrific.

PF *What did you admire about it?*

AC It is undeclaratory. It is not too big for itself, and that has not been true of all Moore's sculptures in recent years. *Sheep Piece* is the right size for its feeling. It is a grand sculpture. I first saw it at his farm when I went there with my son and I thought, 'that is a really felt piece'. I would be happy to have made it.

PF *Do you know what Moore's view of your achievement is?*

AC I doubt if he would have any comment to make publicly. I think he realises that I am a very serious sculptor and that I have the welfare of sculpture at heart. But I would guess that certain things about my work he would regard as inadmissible. Probably I may find the next person who comes along and makes new, good sculpture of a very different sort from mine hard to take. The area of sculpture that is legitimate keeps moving a bit. Certain things in Moore's credo, such as his internal structure, are denied in the sort of work I do. Perhaps that would bother him.

PF *In 1959 you went to America for the first time. What were your impressions then?*

AC No doubt one could give a pat answer about what happened 20 years ago – naturally there's some distortion by the lapse of time. I was certainly impressed by the hope then, the freedom from rules, the determination to achieve the best. And, of course, I was very excited by a lot of the art I saw.

PF *Were you aware of the great influence which America had on many aspects of British cultural life at that time?*

AC You bet! But a lot of what I thought America was like before I went was blasted by my trip. I had been fed on Lawrence Alloway's concept of America that was a very Madison Avenue, advertising kind of version. I remember talking to a photographer who wanted to go to the States to be 'planed smooth as a board'. That was the expression he used. When I got there I found it wasn't a bit like that. It wasn't a slick, whizz-kid culture at all.

PF *Had you met Clement Greenberg before you went over?*

AC Yes, but it was after I had applied for my Ford Scholarship.

PF *The changes in your work after your American trip are well-known. But what was influencing you? How far was Greenberg involved in your sculptural conversion?*

AC Greenberg was totally involved. He more or less told me my art wasn't up to the mark. He came to see me in my London studio. He spent all day with me talking about art and at the end of the day he had said a lot of things that I had not heard before. I had wanted him to see my work because I had never had a really good criticism of it, a really clear eye looking at it. A lot of what he said hit home, but he also left me with a great deal of hope. I had come to the end of a certain way of working. I didn't know where to go. He offered some sort of pointer.

PF *It could be said that by stripping you of your expressionism he 'planed you smooth as a board'.*

AC No, he clarified things for me. And thanks to him I began to learn to trust my feelings in art.

PF *Apart from Greenberg who had the most influence on this change?*

AC Noland, he was my age. I saw one of his first target shows in New York and I thought very highly of it. I liked him as a human being. I talked to him about art and about life one night till six in the morning when his train left for Washington. Noland was an ordinary guy – his clothes, the way he talked, were not extravagant in any way, and yet I had evidence he was also a very good artist. For me this was something unexpected. I had learned to expect artists of my age to express themselves well verbally or be poetic or look the right sort of character. This sort of charisma was, and doubtless in some circles still is, the sign by which one recognised the artist. Noland reaffirmed for me that you put your poetry or your feeling into your work, not into your lifestyle.

PF *Wasn't Smith involved in your conversion?*

AC I had detected Smith was a pretty good artist from the few photographs of his work I had seen. When I got to America in 1959 I did not go to his place but I did see one or two works by him and I met him twice. But the influence of Smith did not really hit me until 1963 to 1965 when I went to Bolton Landing and saw perhaps 80 of his sculptures in his field and made many visits to his studio.

PF *What did you value in Smith's sculpture?*

AC Character, personal expressiveness, delicacy of touch, sculptural intelligence, immense sculptural intelligence!

PF *I admire Smith but I suspect I see him differently. He once said, 'I know workmen, their vision, because... with the proletariat and their struggles.' He believed, perhaps wrongly but passionately, that 'art is always an expression of revolt and struggle' and that since 'freedom and equality are yet to be born' art should relate itself to that future birth.*

AC Is that what you admire in him?

PF *He wanted his sculpture to relate to historical becoming not through naive 'social comment' but through the creation of radically new expressive forms. Did none of that side of him matter to you at all?*

AC Of course his 'creation of radically new expressive forms' mattered to me. The rest of your question I find rhetorical hocus-pocus. Anyhow the socialist bit was David's spiel. He intentionally took up a simplistic position in his conversation. 'I'm just a welder', he used to say. He consistently made the most intelligent decisions in his sculpture and yet he hated art-talk. He stressed his role as a maker perhaps because he was embarrassed by his own artistry – saying he was just a welder was his defence. He liked to go into Bolton Landing for relaxation and there was even talk about him running for mayor. His place was very isolated and it must have been very lonely there. He used to go down to Lake George and drink with loggers and local people. Since David died I have talked to some old friends in whom he confided, and they have confirmed what I suspected; although David never showed what went on in his mind, he was paying attention to every sculptural or artistic thing that was happening. But publicly he never let on. He talked instead about 'being a welder'. What a smoke-screen! He was a highly sophisticated man.

PF *What I quoted from Smith was not simplistic. His socialism and his aesthetics in the first part of his life at least were inseparable. This profoundly affected the sculptural forms he produced.*

AC This is basically where we differ. I think one should pay attention to the work as that is the only real evidence one has. Artists are just as likely to be hiding their real feelings as other people when they talk, especially when they talk big. That is why you look at the work – that's where nothing is hidden.

PF *Because a sculpture is not just an object, attending to the work includes attending to its meaning as an image, to its relationship to history – and not just art history. Moore transformed natural forms. Smith confronted and transformed the forms of men and women engaged in productive labour.*

AC Does Smith have more to do with the production of labour, or whatever you are talking about, than someone grinding or welding a piece of bronze?

PF *Smith's factory techniques, his use of industrial materials and components, certainly refer to a specific form of labour to which Moore makes no reference. Smith was quite conscious of this.*

AC I don't think that is the difference between Moore and Smith.

PF *Why did you decide to make Smith rather than Moore your 'father figure' in sculpture in the sixties?*

AC It was not so much a decision as a question of growth. When I was at Moore's studio I was still a student, and in the figurative sculptures I made in the years after I worked for Moore I strove to find a voice of my own. When I turned to making abstract welded steel sculptures it is true that I used many of the same materials as Smith but I was not so much directly influenced by him in the early sixties as trying to do something very different from him.

PF *It seems strange that you seek to minimise the influence of two great sculptors, Moore and Smith on your work, while stressing that of Noland, a painter, and Greenberg, a critic and apostle of flatness.*

AC Moore was enormously influential to me as a very young sculptor and I am in no way seeking to limit my debt to Smith. But it is true that in 1959 when I first went to America, Greenberg and Noland had more influence on me, one gets more from talking to and thrashing out ideas from one's contemporaries. I lived near to Olitski and Noland, they were my neighbours. We saw each other almost every day. We talked a lot of art-talk, ideas, possibilities, that sort of thing. Greenberg came in with a clear eye and a clear mind. He is terrific in the studio. He is very direct and he cuts right through to the meaning.

PF *The 'meaning'? I didn't think that interested him at all.*

AC Certainly it does – insofar as whether the art is true and felt, or whether the artist is performing or using his art dishonestly. Whether the artist is discovering something and can go on developing it, even if at the time he is not fully aware of what he has done.

PF *You introduced a new set of sculptural conventions, including emphasis on horizontality rather than verticality, apparent 'dematerialisation' of the stuff you used, and absence of an illusionary interior paint, welding, an absence of a pedestal, and so on. Why do you think these things were significant?*

AC Look at history. Sculpture was bogged down by its adherence to the monumental and the monolith, by its own self-importance. To release sculpture from the totem, to try to cut away some of its rhetoric and bring it into a more direct relation to the spectator has helped free it a bit. Its physicality is less underlined than it used to be. All that is what I would like to think I have been a part of.

PF *You said earlier that you were always conscious that sculpture had to do with physicality. Now you seem to be claiming that your most significant contribution was that you freed it from just that.*

AC Provided that a sculpture is made with a true understanding of the nature of the medium it can take to itself a great deal of pictoriality and vice versa. For example, see how sculptural is Piero's painting *The Flagellation of Christ*, and how pictorial Donatello's *Banquet of Herod* in Siena.

PF *When John Berger went to New York for the first time he wrote that what impressed him was the absence of a sense of interiority in the city. Buildings, faces, everything seems to lack an intimate inside. Your later sculptures similarly are divested of an interior. Was your experience of America a determinant of this particular convention?*

AC No, that's your theory. You are entitled to it.

PF *You talked about the alleged burden of physicality which sculpture had been suffering under. If you go to Times Square in Manhattan, or drive along almost any American highway, you see a constant stream of advertising images which, as Susan Sontag has suggested, appear almost more real than reality itself. You have the impression of a physical world where things have been dematerialised or reduced to surfaces, don't you?*

AC I haven't the faintest idea.

PF *If you look up at a building and see a 50-foot truck floating as an image as many feet above the ground, you are experiencing something peculiar to those cultures in which there is a proliferation of advertising. Don't you think that your intention to 'dematerialise', to render less physical, had anything to do with such experiences?*

AC No, I don't think so at all. But I will agree that the experience of going to America changed me. I doubt it was in this way. However, you are entitled to speculate if that amuses you. I find all this is high-falutin' theory.

PF *I have just finished working with Berger on a book about the peasant sculptor, Ferdinand Cheval. His forms emphasise physicality, growth and interiority, they are pervaded by a sense of the mystery of the inner. The peasant is necessarily conscious of the physical. He always has to imagine the inner, whether of a grain of wheat, the soil, a rabbit, or a cow. He is preoccupied with what goes in and what comes out of those unseen regions. In the city, however, one tends to live in a world of surfaces, flat illusions, and constructed rather than growing forms. Don't you think your emphasis on a lack of an interior, dematerialisation and constructed forms is expressive of a mode of being within the modern city?*

AC If you want to talk about lack of interiority why not talk about minimal sculpture which is made of hollow boxes? I always felt that they were not sufficiently physical, that their thickness was not apparent, and I have wished I could cut a hole in them to make them more real.

PF *You have abolished interiority even more thoroughly. Beyond the thickness of the steel your works have no insides. They could only have been made in a culture where concepts of dematerialisation and lack of interiority meant something.*

AC Your questions contain so much speculating and theorising about the sort of society we have that it seems we are getting really far away from the point of either my sculpture or my attitude. Like Berger, you are trying to use art as a handle for something else. And your interview with me becomes a vehicle for propagating your views of society.

PF *Nonsense. Your sculptures aren't just things but also potentially meaningful images realised in a particular time and place. Greenberg himself said, 'It ought to be unnecessary to say that Caro's originality is more than a question of stylistic or formal ingenuity.' But he does not say why it is unnecessary to say that. I think this is a necessary question.*

AC It is unnecessary because worthwhile art includes human passions, intense feelings and imagination and the highest human aspiration. I would have thought, as Greenberg obviously did, that it was unnecessary to add that.

PF *In contrast to, say, the early Smith, you appear neither aware nor critical of the historical phenomena reflected in your work. You accept them with passivity.*

AC My job is making sculpture, and by that I mean using visual means to say what I, a man living now, in 1978, feel like. And that can incorporate, as well as my emotional life, my living in London, and visiting the US and any other experiences that have gone to enrich or delete from the sum total of being a human person. Add to that the practical logic of my trade – my tools, the steel I work with sometimes too heavy to manhandle, the need for triangulation to make things stand up; also my knowledge of the history of and my experience of sculpture. In the same way Matisse's art was to do with his women, flowers, colour, paint – all of these things – and to do with when and where he lived. People have asked me, 'What does your sculpture mean?' It is an expression of my feeling. The meaning in art is implicit, not explicit, and to require explanations suggests a real discomfort with the visual. I wish people would trust their feelings more when making or looking at art, then the programmed and literary approach and response would begin to disappear from painting and sculpture and their interpretation. Of course I realise there are more important things than my feelings and by the same token more important things than art: whether people have enough to eat, war and death, love, the life of a single human being. I am not denying the importance of the quality of life for everyone. But in my art my job is not the discussion of social problems.

PF *What is your job?*

AC My job is to make the best sculpture I can. By doing this, rather than by being a member of committees, or trying to exert influence in art politics or even taking part in the never-ending debate about what is wrong with the art scene in England, I believe I can help to keep sculpture alive and kicking and keep art moving. My job is to do with art, with pure delight, with the communication of feeling, with the enrichment for a short time of those who look at it, just as I myself am enriched for a while when I read a sonnet of Shakespeare's. I cannot hope for more. I cannot hope to change the injustice in the world, and in my art I am not overtly concerned with that or with anything like it.

PF *You say people ask you what your sculpture means. You were once quoted as replying, 'What does your breakfast mean?' But people ask because they believe that, unlike their breakfast, a sculpture is among other things a signifying object, and so do I.*

AC Food feeds and sustains one part of you, art another.

PF *But I have never suggested that artists can directly change or should explicitly refer to injustice in the world. What I am saying is that because of your indifference to history you are peculiarly vulnerable to the prevalent ideology.*

AC Your questions are to do with 1978. Do you realise how in line with current fashion your questions are? They are to do with the social questioning which is the prevalent ideology.

PF *I am not interested in whether a view is fashionable but in whether it is true.*

AC I am sincerely delighted to hear you say that.

PF *American influences aside, the Englishness of your work is often stressed. Greenberg related it to 'Perpendicular Gothic', John Russell wrote, rather absurdly, of 'the element of English discretion in the work, English tolerance'. I perceive an emphasis on linearity and flattened forms characteristic of the British fine art tradition. Do you recognise this?*

AC You are so consistently referring back to criticism that it strikes me that you are more at home with a book than with a sculpture. That is bad in a critic. I can't say whether my work is English or not. One doesn't notice one's own accent. People don't talk about my Jewishness, but I am a Jew, or the fact that I was born in New Malden, although I was, or even the shape of the studio I work in.

PF *My point is not literary. When I look at your sculptures they manifest visually the flattened, planar forms which I see also in, say, medieval manuscript illumination, or a Edward Burne-Jones window. The prevalence of such forms may relate to the persistence of feudal components in so many aspects of British society. When, with my eyes, I see such forms in your work it affects what I think of it, how I evaluate it.*

AC I do find the point you've made is really very literary. I will say that I have worked in different countries at various times and the work I have done in different places often does look different. I don't know why. When I exhibited some work I had made in America in England some English sculptors whose opinions I respect did not like it very much. They found it rather stark. When I worked in Italy people said, 'Your work looks Italian.' I have no idea why but that does seem to happen. Maybe it's something to do with the air we breathe.

PF *Perhaps you are influenced by cultural forces to a greater extent than you realise.*

AC And visual forces too. Perhaps.

PF *You got back from America in 1959. You had a one-man show at the Whitechapel Art Gallery in 1963. That was a moment of cultural, political and social change in Britain. A vision of a new world emerged in many areas other than sculpture.*

AC In the period 1960 to 1963, in fact right up until about 1967, the real effect of my work was nil. Don't be misled by the fact that John Russell wrote a good review. People who were in the art world in the years between 1959 and the Whitechapel show, and even after that, came to the courtyard by my house where my finished work was and thought what I was making was junk, scrap. It had no impact except with a small group of people, some sculptors at St Martin's, and some painters in the 'Situation' group. And these people were working outside the given, accepted norm of what artists were making. My dealers, Gimpels, did not want to handle my work any more. In the Battersea show in 1963 where my sculpture, *Midday*, was shown it was placed among some bushes – it looked completely out of key with all the other works. Believe me, the effect was a small one.

PF *That surely was not the case after the Whitechapel show. Some people may have ignored or resisted your innovations but, from 1963, others acclaimed them as something new, original, radical and important. Look at the headlines to the Whitechapel reviews. One* Times *article was headed, 'Mr Caro's new and original sculpture', another 'Out-and-out originality in our contemporary sculpture'. Russell wrote of 'new areas of awareness'. Even the* Telegraph *headed its review, 'The time of the modern'. No British sculpture exhibition since then has attracted similar attention. The critics were attracted by a sense of newness, dynamism and radicalism.*

AC Yes, but it didn't have much to do with people's consciousness of art, rather with their sense that something new and 'swinging' was happening. I was working in quite a solitary way – or rather in a small arena I shared with half a dozen other young artists. At that time our only real audience was ourselves.

PF *1963 was a key year – with the Profumo affair, the old men of politics were toppled from their pedestals. Harold Wilson, on the threshold of his victorious election, spoke of the 'white heat of the technological revolution'. With talk of nationalisation, steel was in the news. The Beatles emerged with their new sound. You effected a parallel change within sculpture, didn't you?*

AC I am not like The Beatles. They were much more important. Also they were much more fun. Newness is what the reviewers hit on. But as far as I was concerned, I wasn't so much trying to be new as to say something more clearly and more exactly.

PF *1963 was the year of the 'Honest to God' controversy. The Bishop of Woolwich provoked a national debate by claiming God was not an anthropomorphic 'Daddy in the sky' but rather 'the ground of our being'. In this new theological space God was radically abstracted, rendered horizontal rather than vertical, private rather than public. This theology was locked into that moment of history – unwittingly, it was permeated by the ideology of its time. You say social trends do not affect you much but your sculptural space, the imagery of your work, is very close to, say, this theology. Your sculpture, too, was bound up with this moment.*

AC What I remember about 1963 was learning to ski and breaking my leg. Come on. You are like the man who says 'Cubism was the result of the discovery of quantum physics'. I think Cubism came out of Cézanne.

PF *The two are not exclusive. I'm not saying Honest to God theology determined your sculpture, but that it shared the same determinants.*

AC They are not exclusive but if I were a cubist I'd certainly be thinking and talking more about Cézanne than about quantum physics. What you are saying is really nothing whatever to do with my pursuit. We are all necessarily involved with our time – the clothes we wear, the way we travel, the tone of our thought, are all part and parcel of living nowadays. Only the naive, primitive artist is unaware of these things – and oddly enough the work of all of them has a sort of similarity.

PF *Those who are fully conscious of history can prevent themselves from being history's victims. Smith's work shows that with all his contradictions he was conscious of it, yours does not.*

AC Stuff and nonsense. Was Picasso after the Spanish Civil War less of history's victim or a better artist because he was more conscious of history, or Matisse or Cézanne worse because they were less? Cézanne's greatness lies in his consciousness of the art problems, not the social problems of his time, and in the dedication with which he set about solving those.

PF *Why did you revert to raw metal and more jagged forms in the seventies?*

AC That was in 1972. I found soft ends of steel rollings in a scrapyard near Milan. I worked in Italy in a factory using these pieces. In England I had to go to the steel mills in Durham and Consett to get similar pieces. For the last couple of years I have not been working in that way but that is not to say that I may not go back to it.

PF *Your high abstraction coincided with the economic boom. You turned to a brute, raw look during the recent recession. Now, as the economy picks up, you are abandoning that too. Sculptors I really admire, like Ernst Niezvestny who recently left the USSR, struggle for a vision which does not belong to the immediate ideology of the culture in which they live. This is my point about Smith in America too.*

AC What is admirable about Niezvestny is his struggle for the freedom to work how and where he chooses and I believe that you, like decent people everywhere, are responding to that. It's not his art that commands respect. That's an important distinction.

I detect a film of socialist prejudice over your eyes which in other critics of the Left has developed into total blindness. However, you do not jettison the disciplines of sculpture or the quest for quality. We also agree that there are a great many factors involved in the making of art. Your interest is with the social, psychological and cultural influences on an artist and his response to them, whereas I believe that, although the artist should monitor and control his life and his art, it is his art only that is a pertinent subject for discussion and criticism. Your focus is on art in a more socialist society, mine is on making better sculpture and the 'onward march of art'. And this I believe will endure whatever the society one lives in.

PF *Niezvestny's sculpture commands my respect. But the difference between us, in the first instance, concerns what a work of art is. I cannot accept it is anything like a thing-in-itself. I believe that the social, psychological and cultural relations of the work, its relationship to experience, are not optional extras but in the most literal sense part of the work. If you do not attend to them you are not attending to the art.*

You have said that all your work is 'humanist'. You apparently reject socialism. For me, the struggle for true socialism is inseparable from the struggle for the full realisation of human potentialities. Although I recognise the relative autonomy of the sculptural tradition, I cannot erect sculptural values, or any other kind of values, nor can I search for 'quality' without taking this struggle into account.

Your position differs from mine in some respects but you certainly differ from some of the formalists who have written about you. Rubin, for example, describes your sculpture 'objectively', perhaps cautiously relating it to other works of art, but he never hints at why your forms are to be valued. Why do you think there has been so much formalist writing about you in America and so little in Britain?

AC In this country in the last 30 years the social climate has undergone big changes. The status quo is more steady in America and people have become accustomed to looking at art and testing it solely by their visual responses, talking about art in art rather than social terms, sculpture in terms of sculpture, painting in terms of painting. Throughout my working life at any rate there has been a tendency towards literary and theatrical interpretations of art in England.

PF *We discussed how Fried once suggested your work should be seen as being about the body. But he, like almost all your other commentators, elsewhere says that it is only the syntax, or internal relations of pieces, which matter. Surprisingly, given his bodily interpretation, Fried wrote, 'all the relationships that count are to be found in the sculptures themselves and nowhere else'. Which view is correct?*

AC Fried has made some very penetrating and useful comments about my work. I don't think 'the rootedness of my sculpture in bodily experience' contradicts an emphasis on the internal syntax. However it is not up to me to influence the readings of my work. I want people to feel moved when they look at my art. I want to touch their deepest feelings, but I cannot twist their arms. When I am in my studio working, I go on until I can say, 'That's it. Yes, it's right. That works'. To tell the truth, I don't read articles about myself that closely, I tend to zip through them. Look what I brought along to read on the way here, Lawrence Sanders' 1973 thriller *The First Deadly Sin*.

PF *Writing about you has affected the way your work has been seen by others. You talk as if you had no authority about your own work.*

AC You bet I have authority about my work – I make the stuff. It is certainly sad that so many people would rather read about art than look at it. I have the sort of authority that a football player has about his game. But I don't have the sort of authority that the commentator on TV has about the football game.

PF *Although your cultural reputation has been predominantly in America, you have had a strong influence on a generation of sculptors as a teacher here. Have you used your position as a teacher to perpetuate your style?*

AC Of course not. I have treated the people I have taught as adults and equals and helped them question the assumptions on which they make their sculptures. I wanted them to feel it wasn't just a career that they could go ahead with and end up by just doing like a nine-to-five job or like becoming, say, an accountant or a carpenter. A lot of former St Martin's students who have been quite successful artists in a conceptual way have ended up with a completely different view of art from mine, yet they all take themselves seriously as artists and have questioned the justifications for what they make. They haven't ended up making an Adam and Eve for the local church. The best artists have queried my style – the fact that several of them work in steel is not at all to the point. The use of steel, or rather of collage, is a way of working that wasn't possible before this century, just as with the discovery of oil paint and canvas painters found they had the freedom not to use fresco and walls any more. People just don't look closely enough – they say, 'They're all working in the same style' – in fact sculptors happen to be doing things in steel which are actually very different. One might as well say, 'All Greek sculpture is made of stone, what a bore, it's all the same style.'

PF *Bryan Robertson once wrote, 'Partisans of St Martin's claimed the road to or from St Martin's was the one and only true path… a prevailing orthodoxy had turned into a new gospel narrowly interpreted… For everyone outside St Martin's the school had turned into a tediously exclusive club; for those inside, the world of other sculptors did not exist.' He described a closed, dogmatic institution rather like the old Royal Academy but with different conventions.*

AC Yes, it is rather a closed system, despite encouragement that's given to students to work naturalistically, if that's their bent. But take a look at other closed systems and how strong they have been. Look at Cubism, Fauvism, Impressionism – they have all been closed systems. When one attempts to get at the core of a subject one sometimes has to narrow one's vision in order to see clearly. If you get a nice, open, tolerant system like you have in many art colleges, you get a very weak, watered-down form. St Martin's sculpture school has never been invulnerable. Indeed, the piece you have quoted is precisely the point of view that has been held and acted on by successive administrative officers who controlled the destinies of the department. St Martin's sculpture has been well enough known inside and outside this country to attract mature and serious students from all over the world and yet it has never been recognised as a postgraduate centre. It is exceptional in that it's a department with a point of view. It demands a great deal from its students, not least that they push themselves and ask fundamental questions. Yet despite everything that Frank Martin has done to build up and strengthen the department its future is shaky. I find that very difficult to understand or to accept.

PF *Recently I received a letter from an American student who had come to St Martin's because 'in the past' the school 'enjoyed quite a considerable progressive reputation'. But he had abandoned his course because he felt the sculpture department had 'degenerated' into a closed shop which silences healthy dialogue on all general issues in art not catered for in the strict Caro Geenberg housestyle. He called this 'the antithesis of the satisfactory learning situation'. It certainly seems a long way from the 'whole world of art' to which Moore introduced you. I have seen your teachers in action myself and I was appalled at how they coerced students towards your stylistic tendencies.*

AC One of the distinguishing marks of St Martin's teachers is their total dedication to sculpture and the future of sculpture. But don't say 'my teachers', the school is not mine. Something of the tone of the place has been set by attitudes which Martin and I fostered about taking responsibility for one's art, taking sculpture seriously, being prepared to subject one's work to tough, rigorous criticism. Certain people cracked under that and it sounds as if the letter you quote was from one of them. But the hard criticism is not ever levelled at cracking or breaking people. A school can never necessarily produce radical ideas that instigate change and growth. But students get the message: 'It's up to you. If sculpture is going to go on being good and going to get better, it is you who are going to do it.' I think this is a very responsible attitude. It gives people the feeling they are in the driver's seat and, by and large, they respond.

PF *Nobody has challenged you radically as you challenged Moore and got away with it have they?*

AC The time has not been right for that.

PF *You have become the authoritarian father you rebelled against, haven't you?*

AC No. And I would certainly welcome a challenge. But that doesn't mean I am going to say jolly good to anybody or everybody who is doing things I think are not good. After all, some conceptual sculptors did challenge me frontally, but I never found their work was up to scratch.

PF *Let me talk formally. The new conventions you introduced and taught were fundamentally unsculptural. They were derived from painting and criticism, not sculpture. Your work in the sixties consisted largely of painted, often flat, surfaces. You got rid of volume or mass and introduced an illusion of dematerialisation. Although you protested, 'I never wanted to take sculpture right out of reality into the realm of illusion, out of thingness, weight or physicality', you have also claimed that your contribution was freeing sculpture somewhat from physicality. You thus not only impoverished the image but also eroded sculpture's formal conventions. You object to the efflorescence of non-sculptural and conceptual activities. Broadly, I agree with your estimate of them. But these artists were simply reducing your conventions as you had done Moore's. They had less to 'dematerialise'. You allowed your students no choice but to imitate you or go beyond sculpture altogether.*

AC In 1960 I said, 'Let's look afresh. Sculpture can be anything. It doesn't have to be bronze and stone.' Well, it is not my fault if people have been so literal as to go and call walking or breathing sculpture. I don't feel I can be held responsible for that idiocy. It is possible to challenge sculpture's present conventions and stay within the realm of sculpture, just as Cézanne challenged the lack of physicality in Impressionism. Some of the younger sculptors are doing just that. Some of them are quite validly pushing well away from what up to now has interested me. I think it is not unlikely that a new sort of sculptural volume may turn up and that's a healthy resurgence.

PF *How many of your students have you encouraged to look at Moore's work which might help towards a new conception of mass and volume?*

AC None, recently.

PF *Even though he is the major living sculptor in this country?*

AC I have not encouraged them to look at Brancusi either.

PF *One sees this narrow, restrictive approach elsewhere too. Andrew Brighton has pointed out that because of the Tate's predilection for a certain type of modernist work it tends to acquire paintings and sculptures which are of interest only to a small number of art world people. Do you think the Tate should acquire a David Wynne?*

AC Certainly not. Purchasing should always be done by people whose minds are open to new things, but who have complete conviction about their taste. The fashion now is that there should be a little bit for everyone, and the Tate, like modern art museums throughout the world, has become too influenced by fashion. This gets it a bad name. I think they should acquire works on the grounds of quality alone. And by this I don't necessarily mean only abstract art. Incidentally, the fear of being out of step with the latest thing permeates most public bodies in art.

PF *How do you see your own work developing in the future?*

AC At this stage in my life I am interested in trying a lot of new things and going into areas I have not attempted before. I have been thinking about making some sculptures in paper. I have been trying to weld cast and sheet bronze. I have also been working on some pieces in wax for casting. I have had problems with this but I am hoping to find a way through. I still want to make sculpture in steel because that's where I feel most at home. In some new way I foresee it becoming more rather than less abstract. That at any rate is my intention and that is what I see as my struggle.

Issue 23, February 1979

Lucy Lippard

interviewed by David Coxhead

Growing up

DAVID COXHEAD *How have your attitudes to art and artists changed since you first came in contact with the art world?*

LUCY LIPPARD When I first came to New York, I was starry-eyed about artists. It was the first time I'd seen intelligent people who weren't polished and pompous like in academia, people who talked about ideas and their work with that kind of intensity. What passed for freedom in those days – this was 1959–60 – was a revelation. At first I was living with a Bowery pan-handler, hanging out literally with bums, on the far fringes of the art world – we went to tenth Street openings, Cooper Union free lectures and the Amato Opera. But I was also working as a page in the library at the Museum of Modern Art, where Bob Ryman, Sol LeWitt and Dan Flavin were guards, night watchmen etc. I couldn't get over the fact that the artists I met knew so much more about writing and music and everything, than the writers I met knew about art and music, and the musicians I met knew about art and writing. I was very impressed by the artists' breadth of knowledge and the literateness and especially the articulateness. Plus of course the dedication to their own work, although nobody else was paying any attention to them then.

DC *What about your attitudes to art in a more general sense?*

LL Well, I thought that I'd always be able to support all kinds of art, even though of course I didn't like everything I saw in any so-called movement. I grew up aesthetically with late Abstract Expressionism and the shoots it was putting out, some of which became hard-edge abstraction, Pop Art and so-called Minimal Art. When I first came to New York, Dore Ashton was a kind of role model for me. She was the most visible woman critic. I liked how she wrote and how she looked, and she was married to an artist. Then when Minimalism came along, she absolutely put it down from start to finish and I remember telling myself, I'm never going to get to the point where a whole movement is just anathema to me. At that point, you know you'd better quit. Then around 1970, when I'd only been writing for five years or so, it hit – with 'lyrical abstraction', which wasn't a real movement, but the fact remains I never saw one woozy 'lyrical' painting I liked at all. And I thought, 'Oh my god, it's happening to me. It's already happening.' But I wasn't ready to give up yet, so I decided someone else can deal with that stuff. There's still a lot of other art I'm interested in.

Maybe that was the beginning of what I can only call my present jadedness. Something does happen to you when you do almost nothing but look at art for 20 years. You get less open in spite of yourself. Openness, pluralism, has always meant a great deal to me. I always prided myself that I was as open to one thing as to the next. Feminist art, for instance, has had that effect on artists – a kind of tolerance for all kinds of experience brought into art, and to hell with stylistic restrictions and fashions imposed by the market.

DC *Do you feel guilty for not being as open as you used to be?*

LL I simply have to admit that now I not only know what I like, but what I don't like, and there's no use pretending to anyone, much less myself, that I'm interested in seeing everything that's done, because I'm not. Nor am I interested in everybody's career any more. At one point I was a great crusader for all the kind of third stream art that's been called Conceptual Art. Then I insisted on women's art, helping to force it into the mainstream too. There were so few women artists visible in the early seventies that it wasn't difficult to go to virtually everybody's show or studio. Now, happily, it's different. No way any one person could cover it all. I find myself getting cranky when it's suggested that I have some sort of obligation to go to everyone's studio or show, even when I know I don't like their work and it has nothing to do with things I'm writing at the moment. At the same time, I do feel guilty for this crankiness because I'm well aware that everything I know about art I learned from artists. After all, what is a critic without art?

DC *Your early contact with the art world came out of your relationships with friends and neighbours?*

LL Yes, I was living with Ryman and later married him. LeWitt was around the corner. Bob and Sylvia Mangold lived in our building. Bob M had taken my page job at the Modern when I left. Eva Hesse, Tom Doyle and Ray Donarski were living down the street. Jim Rosenquist was around a lot, and Alice Adams (then his sister-in-law) and Frank Lincoln Viner. It was a very mixed group stylistically.

Sol was also a literary influence for me. He used to get books out of the Donnel Library across the street from the Museum and read them all night at his desk. We'd share them, trade back and forth, talk about them – especially about the French New Wave stuff – Butor and Sarraute and Robbe-Grillet and Pinget. Sol also took women seriously all along. He's helped a lot of women artists to find themselves by just naturally respecting them and treating them like equals – sadly, a rare thing among men in the art world, even the 'good guys'.

DC *How long were you writing art criticism before you started living with Ryman?*

LL Not at all. I didn't actually start writing – or rather, publishing – till late 1964 and Bob and I were together in 1960. When I first came to New York in September 1958, I'd bombed right in to see Hilton Kramer, who was editor of *Arts* then. I wanted to be a reviewer and I did some samples for him. He was very kind about it. He wrote me a really nice letter about these truly awful reviews – I knew nothing, but I said things like so-and-so uses colour quite well, and was appallingly matronising about the art. Anyway he said they were well written but I needed to live through a showing season to understand more about how it all worked, and come back in the spring and he could probably use me. But I felt so hideously rejected I never went back – which I think is a typically female and insecure response to such an experience. It was about six years before I submitted another thing for publication, with one exception, an art historical piece that came out of my thesis on Max Ernst and was published in the *Art Journal*. I kept on writing fiction and fiddled around with several long articles about art I never showed to anybody. I worked as a freelance researcher/indexer/bibliographer/translator, and got a graduate degree in history of art at night so I could get $3 instead of $2 per hour. I earned most of Bob's and my, and then Ethan's, living the seven years we were together.

DC *How did you feel about supporting a male artist?*

LL I wanted to work. I was just out of college and determined to support myself and I loved Bob's painting. He'd been working full-time and making art part-time for years by then, and he desperately needed to paint full-time. Eventually, I was going to have my turn and write fiction while he worked, but by the time that could have happened, we'd split up. It's always been very important to me to be able to support myself, and I always have. I suspect that's some sort of fear of going under in the traditional female role.

DC *The significance of people being able to support themselves by their work is major, I think. Particularly for women. How do you reconcile this with your encouragement to artists to show in public spaces instead of being both exploited by and exploiting the commercial gallery system?*

LL That's the conflict. I don't make much sense here. Basically, I wish art were simply considered work like all other work. Society needs art in one degree or another. Certainly as much as society needs, say, cosmetics, toys, sports equipment – what have you. It's because I do believe in art, and even in the effectiveness of the image as a provocation to action or change in some instances, that I expect artists to get it together and see their work as more than a football in the fashion field. Or more than something done simply for self-satisfaction. It's very hard to watch artists you know and love become successful. Few seem to survive it happily. Because the goodies and the miseries are both out of their control. Why does exploitation have to be the norm? But at the same time I know, and the artists know, that in a capitalist system you can move only so far to left or to right. There are degrees of control available to an artist, but only degrees. You still depend fundamentally on the economic system that supports you and psychologically restrains you from unionising or organising a support system for art that bypasses the endless middle-people. But obviously I can't run around telling artists not to make a living when I'm able to make a living off of their art. And it doesn't make much sense to tell people, hold yourself back for ten years, 15 years, whatever, the way I have with my fiction. I've always been pissed off at myself for not having the nerve to come right out of college and start writing fiction full-time, because the artists I knew just started making art and took their lumps. Why did I have to find a way of making a living? I've never really made much money. It is just that fetish about supporting myself.

DC *Because you're a woman!*

LL Well, yeah. But I didn't know that then! I found that out the hard way.

DC *Even though criticism was something you started doing instead of going off and writing fiction like you wanted to do, you don't downgrade the art of criticism.*

LL Actually, I do, sort of. I don't think criticism is an art. I've always said that and it's not very popular with other critics. The fact remains that the difference between writing your own work and writing criticism is gigantic. I don't see how anyone can pretend that they're the same thing. It's much harder to sit down in front of a blank piece of paper and do your own art. I mean, even if I'm half-dead and depressed and not writing very well that day, I usually can come up with some damn criticism. Because I have the other person's work to lean on.

What I do like about writing criticism is the impossibility. That gap between writing and seeing, knowing you'll never really be able to capture the visual experience verbally. I like that challenge. I got into writing about art ass backwards, anyway. I majored in art history in college because I knew I was going to write and I didn't want anybody telling me about the things I cared most about, so I stayed out of the English department. I thought I knew it all already. Then when I got to New York, criticism seemed an honourable way out of the same bind. I'd be writing, but not selling my precious soul. Ha! I wonder now if I didn't, unconsciously, understand that to be a writer in the art world was to be different, and to have some automatic clout. I certainly wasn't aware of this, but it was obviously easier to write criticism, to be the only writer among artists, than to go out and compete with the real writers.

DC *What did you think real writing was, at that time?*

LL I thought I was going to write novels. I kept starting but not finishing them.

DC *Like what?*

LL Samuel Beckett, and William Faulkner, and mainly James Joyce. Not Gertrude Stein or Virginia Woolf, oddly enough – or maybe not so oddly. I don't remember courses on them being offered in college, and I had to find Beckett for myself, in Paris and not at Smith College. D H Lawrence had always been a favourite too. Then when I came to New York I got involved in the Beat Generation, Zen, Indian philosophy, all that. Then the *nouvelle vague* and new art – the real influences on the fiction.

DC *Whether you were conscious of it or not, Lawrence and Beckett in different ways were very much male models, and there's always a problem for women writers, that if you attempt to speak 'for humanity' you're being inauthentic, whereas if you speak 'as a woman' you're being trivial. I wonder if you had this particular conflict at the time, and if movements like Minimalism and early Conceptual Art – whose work seems to me not to be obviously either male or female – allowed you to avoid or perhaps to solve this conflict?*

LL That's an interesting idea. It would have had to be unconscious, though, because I was completely unaware of these problems. I was trying to be superwoman for most of the sixties. Dressing up and having a baby and giving big dinner parties to show I could be a writer and a woman too. Then later, when I had started writing fiction seriously again, in the late sixties, it was very free-flowing, formless. I don't have a structural or logical or analytical mind. Maybe one reason I could identify so much with Eva Hesse's work was that at first she had no armature, either. She was good at making images, but couldn't find a place to put them, how to frame them. That was in the heyday of the grid, and Minimalism – especially Sol's work – provided her with that structure. The same thing happened to me later, when I was writing the original version of *I See/You Mean* in dribs and drabs and it kept changing with all the new art I liked because I never had time to work consistently on it.

DC *But the book is very different from the cool tone of most of that art.*

LL Yes, because when I got to Spain alone, away from all the art, and just started rewriting it from scratch, it became a completely different book. That amazed me. Just before I left New York, the novel consisted of nothing but descriptions of photographs and there was an index that gave clues to the entire plot, which happened in the changes of position, glance, relationship, etc within the group photographs. A brilliant conceptual idea that would have been deadly dull. When I realised that if I were really going to finish this book, I'd have to go off and do it alone, away from the art world, I destroyed the manuscript and went off to Spain with nothing, to start from scratch. Spain was a great place for a radical writer to go in 1970, but the house was free for four winter months and I was desperate. There I got away from that image of cold, hard, Minimalism – which was its public image, and people thought that since I wrote about that kind of art I must be that way, too. Anyway, the book changed drastically, and that was when I had to confront the whole feminist issue. I'd been political before, but not a feminist.

DC *When you say political, do you mean radical politics, the New Left?*

LL Yes, radical politics, the anti-war movement. I'd always considered myself political but I knew absolutely no theory. I was brought up within the civil rights movement, or Race Relations, as it was called in those days, because my grandfather was a Congregational minister and was president of a black college in Mississippi, and my mother worked as a volunteer on civil rights and housing. My own political eye-opening was when I worked in a very poor Mexican village with the American Friends Service Committee – Quakers – just after graduation from college. But it wasn't until ten years later, when I went to Argentina and got caught in a political situation where I had my first taste of public rebellion and got virtually kicked out of Buenos Aires, that I really started to do anything. (I've always hated being told what to do. I have a real authority problem that has provided me with some of my finest moments.) Then I got involved with the beginning of the Art Workers' Coalition, protesting the political use of art by the 'apolitical' powers that be. Then some of the women in the AWC formed a group called WAR – Women Artists in Revolution. I didn't even know the feminist movement was happening then. They started raising hell about women's issues and I was sort of embarrassed by it. I thought – ugh, yet another faction. But I realised that, given my politics, I couldn't reject them. I supported them in a half-hearted way but I resisted joining them. They kept saying what are you doing not with us? And I kept saying, 'I made it as a person, not as a woman', tra la.

DC *What year was this?*

LL 1969, because the art world always gets everything late anyway. At this point I was already going through this personal thing of trying to free myself to some extent from criticism. I'd realised I was 32 and if I was really going to write fiction I'd better get hot. Then when I did leave and start writing, I finally understood that for all my identifying with various underdogs, I hadn't been willing to admit I was one myself. I found I'd have to start identifying with women because I was denying this huge chunk of myself.

DC *When you can say things like, 'The art world always gets things late anyway', you are already standing apart from it.*

LL But that was also the politicisation – beginning to understand that all was not sweetness and light in and around art and artists. The beginning of a basic disillusionment, I guess. Idealism foundering on reality.

DC *You've been able to integrate your feminism with your art criticism. Was that a conscious decision? For example, when did you decide to write only about women artists?*

LL In fact, I do write about men now and then, but I mostly write about women because that's the work I like best. When I became a feminist, I realised that somebody had to write about all this women's art that was out there ignored, and it was going to be me. And of course the ideas were particularly interesting to me, and the discoveries about what women's art was and could be. I often say I'm more interested in mediocre art by women than in mediocre art by men – which is interpreted as I only like mediocre art or women only do mediocre art – all that shit. I don't write about mediocre art but I look at it and it does interest me for the information it gives me about women's imagery, women's psyches, women's lives, women's experience.

DC *After you decided to become an apologist/critic for feminism, to what extent do you think you succeeded in integrating women's art and feminist art into the art world in general? And to what extent has it got stuck out on the sidelines as a genre?*

LL Well, I've always been an apologist if we have to use that word. I've always identified with artists. I was an artists' advocate all along. That was my point of view and I never questioned it. In fact I'm often criticised for not criticising artists enough. Because I never write about things I don't like. Life's too short. Why should I waste my time on something that doesn't involve me? I'm not answering your question. Okay, I think we've succeeded all too well on some levels in integrating feminist art into the art world. All too well for my taste, that is. I've always got this idealistic notion that the next attempt to 'get out of the art world', 'reach a broad audience', 'rehumanise or resocialise art' is going to work, knowing all the time that it can't until the basic system changes. By thinking that, by hanging on to at least some of my illusions, I'm doing just what the 'opposition' is doing – thinking of the art world as separate from the real world, art as separate from life and from work, all that stuff. When in fact demystification or a kind of economic and aesthetic detoxification of art depends almost entirely, it seems to me, on artists being able to work in both places and – more important – gain satisfaction from working in both places. I've been mumbling for years about a 'trialectic' for women artists, their work existing and actually working not only in the art world, but in the 'real' world and in the feminist world – the separatist world, if you like, though some prefer the word 'autonomy' since separatism is interpreted, in socialist circles, as 'man-hating'. The kind of separatism I'm committed to is the kind that permits women to work together and find themselves without all the pressure and tensions of the other two worlds, but it doesn't exclude the other two. My personal 'separatist' life is led within *Heresies* – doing collective work to publish a magazine and at the same time working with totally different collectives on different theme issues of the magazine.

DC *Is the feminist art that has been integrated – to whatever extent – less feminist than the art that hasn't?*

LL The 'too well integrated' women's art tends, of course, to be less feminist – but then none of us really knows what feminist art is or could be yet. So far the best definition of feminist art is sort of Duchampian: art made by a feminist who is trying to make feminist art from a feminist consciousness – as opposed to art made by a feminist who is consciously making androgynous, art world, neutralised art. That's the art that's been most easily assimilated – the latter. And a great many feminist ideas have been both effective in the art world and effectively absorbed by it and by male artists.

The feminist notion 'the personal is political' – though it does often get misinterpreted as pure self-indulgence – has made it easier for feminists to deal with material that has been suspect in the modernist art world. Autobiographical stuff – and I don't mean the contrived wise-ass autobiographical stuff that makes up most of what is called 'narrative art', but art that honestly looks at, reflects, provokes thought about a person's place in the world, her relationships, his values. Anyway, the feminist art that, as you put it, gets stuck on the sidelines, is often by artists who want to be on the sidelines, who are committed to making the sidelines a valid place to be working, who get pleasure out of bypassing the mainstream. Other women have tried to make it into the mainstream, found the art world still so heavily threatened by feminist ideas that it won't touch them, and have then very courageously, I think, set out to create their own audience, their own market, their own respect and authenticity networks, to a point where the mainstream has to eventually acknowledge them.

A current case of this is Judy Chicago's *The Dinner Party* project – a huge sculpture or environment that she and several hundred other people, mostly women, have been working on for five years. It's a huge triangle, 50 feet on each side – a table with place settings for 39 women, sculptured, painted plates and embroidered runners. Another 999 women are commemorated on floor tiles and the biographies of all 1,038 are included in the documentation and the books. It's a wildly ambitious project. Judy compares it to the Sistine Chapel, which is a bit much for me, but she has done something enormously important. Although I didn't like every individual part of the piece, I was immensely moved by the whole, by its visual richness, the combination of what it wants to be and what it is, by the breadth of vision. I love the fact that it wants to be bigger and better than anything a twentieth-century artist has done, and to bring all of women's history along with it. I don't know of any man who's even tried to do anything comparable or would be able to work with other people co-operatively that way. Yet after a huge financial and popular success and nationwide media coverage at the San Francisco Museum, no other museum will touch it. Its content is apparently still too threatening to the art establishment, though not to the audience. There is neither money nor support for a work of that scope that appeals to people outside the art world. So the feminist community is, yet again, going to have to raise the money to travel the piece, to keep it visible, to house it permanently, so it won't disappear like the rest of women's history, while the most superficial art by men, costing far more to transport and install, continues to fill the museums whether the audience likes it or not.

I for one have lost interest in dragging people into the art world. I know when I write about someone it helps her to 'make it'. At one point that was one of my major goals, but it just isn't any longer. I certainly don't try to keep people from moving where they want, and there's no reason why women can't want what everyone else has. But I don't feel obliged any more to spend my energy on that except in the most general ways. I don't want to be an agent. I've never liked dragging women into the art world because I've seen what it's done to the men and I'm not happy with that. Now the mechanisms for getting women into the art world exist. Channels have been set up and women squeezed into them. A lot of work has been done and will continue to be done. Originally there was this terrible prejudice against women artists. You had to stand on your head to even get anyone to look at women's art. That happens rarely in America now, though it's still a problem here in England, and elsewhere.

DC *How else do you see things in England as being different from the US?*

LL I don't really know the London art scene at all, except from hearsay. I've never been to the Bond Street galleries, and only rarely to Acme, Art Net, Hester van Royen, Lisson, and of course to the Women's Free Arts Alliance. I've never been to an opening, a private view in London. From what I hear there really isn't a market in London. Nobody's buying art and – something I didn't like to admit for years – art is dependent on the market. The stimulus happens around the markets and the magazines. A London artist told me something very frightening last year – that she didn't know a 'successful' English artist who didn't have private means – money from outside of selling art. When people in New York asked me about the art world in London, I kept coming back to one word – muffled. I don't know quite why that is, since the artists I've met have been very articulate and actively trying to change things. (Of course, I've met mostly feminists and socialists – that may have something to do with that.) The issues seem clear-cut, but the response somehow gets muffled. But this is hardly an expert's opinion. I came here to do my own work, to escape from art, so I haven't given myself to finding out about the broad art scene here on the level I'm accustomed to doing at home.

DC *You've mentioned the power that critics have and you've touched on the art market. I'd like to talk about vested and commercial use. Were you given work by people you wrote about?*

LL Yes, I do have small things by people I've written about, and now and then I buy something – rarely, because I don't usually have the money and also it's so hard to choose from all my friends whose work I like. Sometimes I buy something when somebody can't pay the rent and I can. Sometimes I just make a loan instead. I think I have more art by people I haven't written about than by those I have. I've never sold anything that was given to me, although things I'd bought financed both of the times I went off to write fiction for any extended period. I like Carl Andre's idea that he gave his 'valuable' art to a lot of artist friends and if they could sell it so they could make more art, that was a proper use of his gift. But because of Clement Greenberg's alleged misuse of works artists gave him – no, that's not true, artists supposedly gave him work to support him – anyway that's not what I think the relationship between critic and artist should be. I make my living from writing about their work – not from selling it. It gets very complex though, where the lines are drawn. Ree Morton said she wanted to give me a drawing and I always got embarrassed and humhummed, and she thought I didn't want it and was hurt and never gave it to me. And then Bob Huot, years ago, gave me a painting – I'd never written anything on him, but he was a very close friend – and I went into my little act about how I didn't really like to accept things from artists and morality and tralalala, and he got just furious and said you're my fucking friend and if I want to give you a painting it's because it's something I love being offered to someone I love and screw you if you think I'm trying to buy you off. And I was terribly ashamed and thought how pretentious of me, and didn't pull that number again. The classic one was with Ad Reinhardt, though. After I wrote the catalogue for his Jewish Museum show, he had given the show's director a small painting and said I should get one too, and I said 'oh no I couldn't' and we went on for months, having a lovely time endlessly discussing the morality of our superior moral positions in an immoral world, knowing perfectly well that I was dying to have a little black painting and eventually I would. But then he died, and that was that, which was just as well, since I'm a slob and don't take very good care of the art that's given me no matter how much I love it.

DC *When you talked about* The Dinner Party, *you talked mainly about its social aspirations and ramifications.*

LL That's where I am. I don't relate to art in the totally affective way I used to. I've also rejected the whole notion of what a great artist is, although the residue of that notion comes out in the way I seem to talk (rather nostalgically) about LeWitt and Ryman, who were the two artists I knew when nobody else thought they were even any good and who I thought were very good. So that's a funny build-up, a psychological commitment to people who are – I won't use the word 'great' – but who made damn good art before anyone made anything of it, and art that came from inside not from outside trends. But I wasn't even writing about art when I was falling for Ryman's and LeWitt's art, so my relation to it was very different.

DC *You say, 'falling for their art'. That's a curious expression.*

LL No, that's what I did. I was really knocked out by things in those days.

DC *Are you saying you don't 'fall for' art any more in that way? 'fall for' is a very innocent thing, isn't it?*

LL I can still get pretty excited about things! – all these terms of endearment – I still thrive on the kind of constant stimulus that made me a perfect avant-garde critic for a while. But now I measure things against other things much more – the result, I suppose, of trying to make myself think more theoretically. That need for a framework again. I don't really think in depth, and I'm not apologising for it. It's something I've gotten very interested in and my fiction is about scanning, skimming, fragmentation, juxtaposition, falling into the gaps, the reader participating in making the 'plot'.

I like a sort of point-to-point stimulus. I think most people who get involved with the Avant Garde are that kind of person. Maybe we've been created by a consumer society. Or maybe it's a way of seeing and thinking that is simply more like real life. The tension between art and politics provides that kind of stimulus too. I'm finally getting down to the two areas of art that interest me most – and make me most schizophrenic. That's art that is socially aware and outreaching, and art that has to do with nature, ritual, ancient symbols and images – especially art outdoors. I know they sound politically opposed, like cultural feminism and socialist feminism, but I'm committed at the moment to closing that gap – at least for myself.

But now I think I'm also finally weaning myself from my identification with and dependence on visual artists. I really want to mostly write fiction. But I'm only creeping towards that point.

DC *Do you think you'll ever be able to live by writing fiction? Or will you continue to lecture and write criticism part-time?*

LL It seems very unlikely I'll ever be able to live on fiction, and since I resist teaching, I'm stuck with the lecturing because writing fees have stayed put while the cost of living has done its spiralling number. The maddening part of it is that as long as I am making my living from criticism and lecturing, I feel that tremendous obligation to see all the art I can possibly see, even if I will never write about nine-tenths of it – or even think about it ever again. That's valuable time spent trudging round the galleries that I'd rather put into my own writing. I'd love to have my cake and eat it too – just see what I know I'm interested in, and write and talk about that and simply miss the rest of it. When I lived in Devon for ten months last year, I was kind of practising for that. I missed a whole art season and it really didn't make any difference to anybody. Same with the organisational work I do. People said: 'What do you mean you're going away for a year? What will happen to this and this and that?' And of course, it all survived without me.

DC *If there were another feminist art critic, could you really pull out, personally? Even if their viewpoint within feminism were completely different from your own?*

LL Yeah. I think so. I mean I know that person won't be me and they wouldn't want to be anyway. And I could continue to support her or them. But I wouldn't feel as I do now that if I don't do it nobody else will. Which of course is rather conceited of me. There are other women writing about women's art, but just not as a full-time commitment. And of course my own commitment is getting less full-time, which scares me. We've worked so hard, and the backlash is getting heavy. I'd hate to see it all going down the drain, to have to start again from scratch years later.

Issue 32, December–January 1979–80

1980–1984

Stuart Brisley

interviewed by John Roberts

The dynamics of performance

JOHN ROBERTS *Why did you stop making objects?*

STUART BRISLEY I needed to change the framework in which I was working to coincide with certain developing political ideas I had about my position as an artist.

JR *What was this?*

SB It was to do with the use of art in the market; my feelings about being with a private gallery. I was under the impression that this was the most realistic way of operating as an artist. I was unhappy with the limitations of the gallery system, the fact that commercial galleries can only deal with material formed in such a way that it is amenable for sale. It was also to do with education. My own assumptions were being brought into question through the teaching I was doing – this was at Hornsey. I began to think about other means of working which weren't specifically related to the making of objects. I believe that what constitutes art is like a kind of unspecified consensus. With any individual, whatever ideas he has and whatever he might want to do as an artist, it is only his assumption that he is an artist. So it is an individual concern. Art is always a speculation which deals with social conditions. For an activity to be considered as art it has to fall within that unspecified consensus. It's useless for me to say 'this is art' if in fact it is not related to a broader notion of what art might be.

JR *How much had the dematerialisation of the object been prepared by a knowledge of what had been going on, on the continent?*

SB Very little. In 1966 there was DIAS (the Destruction in Art Symposium) in London organised by Gustav Metzger.

JR *That was your first contact with European performance?*

SB I went to very few of the things.

JR *Did it confirm what you were thinking?*

SB No. I tended to see the films. I don't think the events had a particularly strong influence on me or the people I was involved with at the time.

JR *Your work at the time was acknowledged to be quite theatrical.*

SB No, it wasn't. There were certain theatrical aspects but these came later as part of an investigation into what could be done in this area. These aspects were used in a naive way. They weren't taken directly from the theatre but came up out of the work itself. I had worked in the theatre as a stagehand – I really disliked the theatre at the time. I disliked the illusion of it. We weren't actually concerned with the form – whether it had theatrical elements or not – we were much more concerned with doing things. All the problems of categorisation came much later.

JR *Can performance still make claims to being an 'interventionist' activity?*

SB Yes I'm sure it can but it is more difficult than ever to break out of the constraints of high-cultural entrepreneurialism. What do we mean by performance? It seems to me that performance stands for a whole range of activities which are all in some way related to what we understand as traditional activities. It's related to those forms of creative activity which have some limited history, for example painting and sculpture. Its value lies in the fact that it presupposes a dynamic relation with society, unlike, say, painting.

JR *You believe your work has a direct grasp on history, that it anticipates a time when art will come to reroute itself through relations rather than objects, then art will 'collapse into life'. Isn't this the kind of idealism which misdirected so much art in the seventies?*

SB It probably is. It is obviously unlikely that art, as you say, will 'collapse into life', but I think it is only a form of idealism if one assumes that society can't change to that extent, where the material conditions become such that art must become part of life. It remains idealistic if one can't really believe it could happen. I think it could happen, but it demands an extraordinary change in society. The fact remains that it has been an authentic aim. I don't think it is spurious in any way. My activity exists as a kind of gesture which is in recognition of the possibility of change.

JR *By that are you saying all traditional practices are functionless?*

SB One could say that the social and political structure is a reactionary one, and part of the effect of that would be an art which materially is in a disjunctive position. So when I talk about a gesture, the gesture that is made is an attempt at direct communication, this is in recognition of that problem.

JR *Your work could be described as a process of meeting yourself anew, a learning process. The psychodrama of Jerzy Grotowski would seem quite pertinent here. I don't want to openly confuse your work with his theatre but there are striking similarities. Grotowski's theatre is essentially sculptural. It focuses on body and self-expression in place of textural narration and interpretation and technical resources. This process of self-confrontation is central to your work.*

SB That's a very eloquent statement which I would be flattered to find a relation with. I see certain connections. Although I know of Grotowski I am not conversant with his views. But certainly in my way one of the things I've really been concerned with is to work economically, to use as few material resources as possible in order that I use myself, and also to try not to deny aspects of myself, to really take a risk with myself.

JR *Technical apparatus gets in the way?*

SB I have resisted using mediating devices precisely to put myself on the line. This is one of the essential stances that I have taken. Whether one ever really does that is another matter, but that has been the attempt. Mediating devices tend to get in the way of that challenge. At the same time it does throw up all kinds of problems of how one relates to the kind of activity where the artist is present, engaged in an activity over a period of time. Some people misunderstand the situation precisely because the artist is present in the work. That misunderstanding refers often as not to the predominant behaviour in our society, which is individualistic and competitive. Therefore if the artist is seen in the work it's seen as being very individualistic. The signification on my part is about something beyond the individual. It's an interesting paradox that the attempt throws up issues such as narcissism, which refer much more to common social behaviour than the concept behind the work, which often incorporated criticism of conspicuous competitive individualism.

JR *How important are audiences for you?*

SB They are vital. But it's not so much size – I can't talk about quality of audience – it's to do with the presence of other individuals.

JR *How do you gauge the success of the work?*

SB It's like watching a film. There is a series of sequences which take place in time where the conjunction of one sequence in relation to another begins to operate beyond the sum of its parts. When that happens I would describe it as being productive.

JR *And this process produces what? Moments of insight?*

SB Yes. But one can't specify those moments. They can't be sustained. They arise out of the culmination of circumstances. One may intend this to occur but it is not something one can consciously make happen. I suspect if one did try to sustain those moments one is into the game of acting. The work is anarchic in the sense that these moments cannot be specified to happen at a given moment in time.

JR *Could we expand this reference to film? The unity of the pictorial and sculptural in your work shows a keen regard for location. Your body is invariably framed by a structure, object or wall. It has to be said you're quite good at posing.*

SB That may well be the case.

JR *For example* Moments of Decision/Indecision, *in Warsaw in 1975, in which naked and blinded by paint you moved around the space in relation to where you felt Leslie Haslem, your photographer-collaborator, was standing.*

SB I was trying to make some sense of how a work is reproduced. I took a fairly limited but strict view as to how it should be reproduced, to the point where the position of the camera was determined – now that still happens but in a different way. I'm less interested in sequences in terms of reproduction because it tends to produce a form of reproduction of the work which is no longer convincing to me, for example a single image might represent the work in a more dynamic way than a sequence. In the realisation of the work – to separate the reproduction of the work from the doing of the work – I think in terms of sequence. These sequences vary as the work progresses. Elements are discovered, celebrated and die. It is up to me to take risks. To say: 'Look at that thing which was very successful ten times now no longer means anything, it's dead.' I'm not always clear enough to do that but what happens is, if I tend to rely on those things knowing that ten times they worked and I try it the 11th time already knowing it is dead, I will have lost touch with the work. I think this occurs in creative activity where one is relying on an intuitive evolution in the work. Hence what one would find in any piece of work that I did – if anybody could bear to be there long enough – would be periods of evolution. A tension is given to the work by the people coming to it because they also intuitively recognise that something is happening. There are other moments when the whole thing is absolutely flat. Depending on the length of the work, the circumstances, the people coming to it, the kind of sympathy there is for it, one gets a richer mix of these things or a relatively thin mix. For example, the piece I did at the IKON, *Approaches to Learning*, 1980, was a fairly thin mix because there weren't enough people coming to it, so that when Iain Robertson and I were developing the work, we could not lift ourselves to sustain the work for its specified 48 hours.

JR *I think you're placing too much emphasis on the audience. I think the work was unsuccessful because the context wasn't particularly interesting. I think you realised that early on.*

SB Yes it may well be.

JR *Your work is physically challenging, there's not much pleasure involved in it for either you or the audience. The images you deal with have always been concerned with things 'on the edge'. Would you say the only authentic pleasure today is a pleasure of the horrid?*

SB That's difficult to answer.

JR *Your work at times, especially the early life-situations, is quite brutal.*

SB It has got to do with how one senses life. I'm very conscious of the fragility of it all, the artificiality of civilised behaviour. So much of social life is articulated by basic, animalistic drives. Work is an attempt to reveal the more brutal – not the more brutal in the sense of how badly we treat each other – but the more brutal aspects of what it means to be alive. We do anaesthetise things in order to make them acceptable. I am pointing towards the inhuman aspects of how it is to be a human being. The earlier works were very direct in that respect. They were also limited because of that, like *And for Today Nothing*, from 1972 – the figure in the bath. At the same time there was an implied political commentary attached to it.

JR *They struck many people at the time as like live Duane Hansons.*

SB When I was making those pieces I wasn't aware of Duane Hanson. It was only when I went to Berlin in 1973 that I met him. I knew of Ed Kienholz. I rejected Kienholz because of the fact that they were tableaux. But at the same time I recognised the validity of the arguments he was using at the time.

JR *Your later work has become more complex, discursive, particularly* 180 hours – Work for two people, *1978. Could you talk about this development?*

SB I tend to make a distinction between work done in this country and work done abroad, and I would make it on grounds that it is the social circumstances in which one lives that provide the sources for the work. The work that I've done in England, which is fairly infrequent, has been more conscious in its attempts to deal with social issues precisely because when you live in a place you contribute to it, understand it and are anti-social within it. The work done abroad, precisely because one is visiting and therefore usually working in art contexts which appear to be neutral, tends to become more general, more abstracted and alienated.

JR *You mean you're more diplomatic?*

SB No, I can't be in a position to understand what it is really like to live in Poland, for example. I have no experience of it. Whereas in England a lot of the work I've done – and it's fairly well spaced out – attempts to come to terms with more complex social issues. The earlier work was more direct and therefore apparently more aggressive. The last piece I did like that in this country was in 1973. Then I lived abroad for a while. The next major work I did in Britain was in 1977–78, and then came *Work for two people*, so there was quite a jump from the earlier work to the later work. I was trying to deal with the same issues but in a much more complex way. Rather than presenting images I was trying to deal with dialogue to allow the ideas behind the work to be expressed more directly as part of the work and questioning what an audience could be through audience discussion becoming part of the work. I understand 'audience' to be a condition in which one may receive something by giving one's attention to what one has chosen to witness. The audience as witness, given the form of what is witnessed and the context in which it takes place, is never static. When context and form are changed then self-evidently the form of the audience as witness also changes. The earlier work was to do with presenting images and the later work was about opening up and articulating the arguments that were represented by those images.

JR *Is this something that has developed gradually or did you reach a point where the old methods were just not working?*

SB I think it goes back a long way – I think it was there but it was underdeveloped. I'm thinking of the thing I did in Brighton in 1969 which was an ambitious project involving lots of people which relates to *10 Days*, 1978. The problem is to find the right context in order to allow those sorts of investigations to occur. It is difficult because it has a lot to do with creating opportunities. Those kinds of ideas like *10 Days* come to me slowly, so they tend to be the major works, but since they're the major works they can also be really bad works because they are ambitious. Ambition is quite often a bad thing to have when working. The ambition sometimes destroys the work. To look at the Hayward piece is to see this piece quite clearly. It was an attempt at a major work which was in a way false. I wouldn't say that about *10 Days* and I wouldn't say that about *Work for two people*. I think that you can see that in the Hayward piece in relation to the imagery. It was unspecific. That may have had something to do with the fact that I was working in a place like the Hayward – it was very difficult to find a live connection. A different problem occurred in the '*Un Certain Art Anglais*' exhibition in Paris. The work disappeared as any kind of manifestation within the terms of the exhibition but became effective underground with all the tramps. When I say effective I mean there was a live connection. The live connection appeared in an anti-social context. That is the kind of problem I have – how to find within these big institutions a point where one can be specific and authentic, where the ambition isn't realised in an elephantine gesture, as it was at the Hayward.

JR *How far was the dialogue between A and B in* Work for two people *a dialogue between opposing operations in yourself?*

SB Very much so.

JR *How much of it was role playing? Playing A against B and then playing B against A?*

SB I could never play A because A was the person who in a way conceived the whole of the work. So A was in part an imaginative representation of myself, B was another aspect of me – my work in art institutions. B is the figure with the power, A is the anarchist, the 'feeling' person, the more feminine aspect of one personality. B was the person with will, the one who acts against other people – as I do quite often. I found that the work was set up in such a way – I didn't realise this before I started because it was an investigation – that I could only play B and by implication A would develop. I did try to articulate the role of A for three days. But then I realised it was a waste of time. The only way A could evolve was through B's role becoming more and more explicit. I had no idea how B was going to evolve but in discussion with people, which was an important part of the work, B demonstrated his schizophrenic tendencies. Initially he was in a position of power over A who was posed beneath him, then his position became contradictory. B described it as a love of order and the preservation of what is a hatred of nature and an acceptance and indulgence in the processes of decay. When this evolved and was clearly expressed he began to break up. A's position, which at first appeared to be negative, became much more positive. In a way it was an interpenetration of me as an artist conceiving the work – that was A's role – and me as a wage earner, B's role. I couldn't step out of the work which A had conceived in order to get back into it and play A. I could only play B and allow A to rise up within it.

JR *What of the wider implications of this division? Was class conflict uppermost in your mind?*

SB Very much so. Part of the idea for the work was from reading a small section of Marx which makes an analysis of bureaucracy. It was also that which I experience all the time which set the work in motion. At the back of it was a power struggle, a class struggle, where people in positions of power assume superiority over the majority. I saw A not only as the artist, but as the private individual, the civil person. The individual who walks freely down the street. B was a figure of authority corrupted by his own power. I gave to B the simplistic idea of being opposed to anything organic, because I was making that relation between the free, private individual having his own feelings and intuitions and the individual who suppresses all that in himself and others.

JR *You haven't used video as a means to record or visualise work – why is that?*

SB I haven't enough feeling or understanding of the medium. Obviously working live one thinks of using video to document with, but in my experience video documentation of live work is ineffective. I don't think I can fully understand and use video because access to it is denied in its socially dynamic form – TV. It has a limited value as a tool, like a sketchbook, but I can't envisage video without taking into account its potential as a socially dynamic medium. But with advances in video recorders and receivers and their present commercial marketing the situation will change. Tapes could well be marketed to private individuals. This doesn't immediately interest me, but the effect it might have on centralised media control does.

JR *Would you ever produce work solely for film?*

SB Yes. I've been involved with film in order to grasp qualities of a work which remain hidden in live work. I find that film is an effective medium to use but not as documentation. I don't like the notion of the kind of documentation which seeks to present an objective view. What I've tried to do is use film-as-film, use live work as script in order to produce filmic statements. So much of what is important in live work has to be dropped in order to make it work as film. That was difficult when I first started using film. I felt the value of putting something on film was directly related to what I thought was valuable in the live work. There is a certain kind of atmosphere or tension in live work which only exists in isolation from other events. Film breaks that. One has to become more alienated in order to produce film – the film becomes dominant. Something has to be produced within a given period of time which doesn't happen in live work. I consider work for film when I've done most of the investigation in live work. I can look back and select sequences for development as film. It then becomes economical to film as well. I like what Sally Potter has done with *Thriller*, which is to use a traditional performance form, opera, and then subjected it to analysis and in the process brought up certain aspects of live work to illuminate it. The basis of the film was the structure of the opera, and that seemed to be an effective way of overcoming the problem I have at the moment, which is to find the relevant structure on which to conceive a film. I need to find something which allows me to conceive of performances in relation to film. If I could do that the necessity to work live would probably diminish, then again maybe not.

Issue 46, May 1981

David Salle

interviewed by John Roberts

Painting by default

JOHN ROBERTS *What were you doing between 1979 – the time of your* Cover *article on your painting – and 1981, the year your work came to the attention of a wider audience through Tom Lawson's* Artforum *article 'Last Exit: Painting'?*

DAVID SALLE At that time I was working on a series of paintings which, as far as I know, have never been shown. The paintings were canvases stained a single colour with various images drawn on top in charcoal. The images tended to be fairly consistent groupings of things, more or less hovering near each other, but not touching or overlapping.

JR *This was after a period of minimalist/conceptual work?*

DS Well, that's what often is assumed. Conceptual work has the ring of a specific kind of investigation and a specific historical time frame and it is something I don't feel I shared or participated in. I feel in a sense that it was all over by the time I started to make my work. I don't feel my concerns were those concerns. My interests have always been imagistic, and that didn't seem to me to be the concern of conceptualism at all. As far as Minimalism is concerned I have even more of a remote connection. I see Minimal and Conceptual Art obviously as very closely linked – maybe one is just a further point on an evolutionary scale of a primarily American formalist way of thinking about art – but this was not only something I was not sympathetic with, historically it was not of my time. It was a completely different generation, a completely different set of *a priori* rules and desires. The kind of journalistic assumption is that first he was a conceptual artist then he started to paint.

JR *But all the same there was a certain conceptual input into the work.*

DS Painting is not monolithic. There has always been in my frame of reference a kind of painting that has a self-reflexive nature, which conceptualism shared. There is a way in which painting embodied or projected a kind of questioning, first of all the identity of the object itself and second, more interestingly, of the relationship between the viewer and the object, how that relationship could be changed, making visible the inherent subversiveness of the act of looking at a picture and having a picture looking back. This was something I was thinking about from the time I started thinking seriously about art. The other thing I was thinking about was the idea of a presentational mode of address and the way images become visible. I think the thing I've always been concerned with is visibility, how a thing acquires visibility. Which is perhaps another way of saying, why is it that we notice what we notice? Whether the work took the form of a video or a set of photographs, this is what interested me. In 1974 I started making very large works on paper – images were painted with a brush on flat rectilinear surfaces. The orientation was always to painting space, pictorial space, as opposed to sculptural space or purely mental space. Actually this so-called mental space turned out to be another kind of formalism. So I don't feel as if any break or shift has taken place in the work – it ranged around, tried out different guises, meandered for a while. Around 1976 I started making the first works on canvas that physically resembled paintings.

JR *Where were you making these?*

DS In New York. It wasn't necessarily my intention to quote start painting again unquote, or to continue to avoid painting again. But I had been making these works on paper, they were getting destroyed because I was moving around a lot – every time you put them up on the wall they got ripped – so I made works on canvas, and then thought making works on canvas without stretching them made a statement about materiality which wasn't really interesting to me. When I stretched them I realised almost by default that I had in fact made a painting, I had almost 'backed' into it. They were paintings in a very provisional way, which was a way of thinking about what a painting is or isn't. Now I would think that really isn't what makes a painting anyway. And yet at the same time that is an essential ingredient, it is the kind of thing I've always tried to keep in focus even if it's sometimes in the background. The simple fact of the thing's existence as a thing was inherently mysterious to me or inherently problematic or self-reflexive. But to me that was not theoretically different from my earlier works which involved tearing pages out of a magazine and putting them on the wall, somehow that alone had resonance.

JR *Did the fact that these objects didn't look like paintings present a problem for you?*

DS The non-paintings?

JR *Yes.*

DS No. There was no possibility of the work being confused with so-called 'painting concerns' about immateriality or surface or gesture. You have to understand this was all taking place in the context of mid-seventies New York in which what passed for art was primarily an exercise in craft or an exercise in private mythology or hero worship, or all three combined. There was nothing in that which was holding my attention.

JR *Who were you associating with at the time? Did you consider yourself as part of an emergent group then?*

DS I was close with people who I went to Cal Arts with, most of whom had either individually or in small bands migrated by 1976 to New York. It wasn't such a homogeneous group, people were doing different things because they were different and distinct personalities. At that time I met Julian Schnabel whose work was probably about as far from mine as anybody I was close with at the time, his concerns were largely material, mythological, heroic – mine just weren't. People that I was intellectually closer to were James Welling, Sherrie Levine, Tom Lawson, Ross Bleckner, Barbara Kruger, Matt Mulligan. I think everybody was pretty depressed at that moment. There was very little recognition that anything that we were thinking about even existed. The stuff that we thought was real and interesting and provocative truly just did not exist for anybody else, it was like making invisible art. What is funny, what is interesting is how certain things have become highly visible, while other things have persisted in being largely invisible. Well, actually none of that stuff has persisted in being invisible, even the most stubbornly invisible art. Levine's has in fact become quite visibly controversial, at least in New York. However, I feel that something essential about our work, including Julian's, is still largely invisible.

JR *How equivocal are you about your images? You have referred to them simply as 'presentations'. Is this as neutral as it sounds in view of what you said in the* Cover *magazine article: 'I am interested in infiltration'? Tom Lawson emphasised this line in his article 'Last Exit Painting', placing you, albeit tentatively, in the 'deconstructionist' bracket. On the other hand, Donald Kuspit wrote recently: 'Salle's message is that there is no longer any inner necessity for criticality.' Has something happened along the way or are things as deterministic as Kuspit makes out?*

DS Neither what I said in 1977 nor what Tom said a year ago nor what Kuspit said six months ago, sums it up, I hope. I don't feel any particular allegiance to something I might have published that was clearly, deliberately polemical. So, I'm not sure what you're asking me. Are you asking me if something in the work has changed to allow people to be able to use different metaphors to talk about it?

JR *I'm asking you have your strategies changed?*

DS I don't think I ever had any strategies and I don't think I have any now. It depends on what you mean by strategy. I have nine million little strategies, but you might substitute for the word 'strategies' the word 'ideas' or 'desires' to use a certain thing or do a certain thing. If that is what you mean by strategies then those change constantly.

JR *But when you use the word 'infiltration' it implies a certain didacticism, a certain aggression.*

DS Yes, but all of those statements, and particularly that one, are really to be understood in the most metaphoric way. I think this applies not just to my writing but to most writing produced by artists in the history of modern art. Usually the statements exist in advance of the work, they are much more shrill than the work itself. The futurist manifestos don't have a lot to do with the painting. The same is true of Sol LeWitt's statements about Conceptual Art. It's a kind of tradition. That is something to keep in mind. Now more specifically has the idea of infiltration changed? I don't think so. I could still make that statement today – that I'm interested in usurpation and beating people at their own game – because what I mean by that is what happens when you look at pictures, which to me is fairly constant and part of my life, and has nothing to do with market acceptance or market rejection. That just doesn't apply. What has been implied in certain criticism is that market acceptance, and the kind of criticality which the idea of usurpation implies, are mutually exclusive, and I don't think that is true at all, I think that is really presumptuous. And anyway that is not what usurpation means, for two reasons: first it's not terribly interesting to usurp the power of the art market to begin with, because who wants it and what would you do with it if you had it? Second, the usurpation I'm talking about is really psychological. That's not so easily done anyway, and if it is done it is probably done for about six people at a time. It is the beauty of that which interests me and not the polemics of that. Disappointingly to some people, my usefulness as a political critique of things doesn't go very far. My meanings are primarily aesthetic, which is to me not in any way having to settle for something. It's one thing to talk about the relationship between the political and the aesthetic, but it's not political in the sense that Dada was. My ideas aren't as simple as *épater la bourgeoisie* – it never was about that in my mind, and if other people wanted to make it into that it's their prerogative but then they shouldn't be disappointed if it turns out years later that it didn't fulfil any programme. I feel that my work contrives to deal with ideas of authority or agency in ways that most art doesn't and couldn't. It's quite complicated and not unspiritual.

JR *Your references are pan-cultural, anything is worth taking and re-using. But these are not indiscriminate or reflexive. You enjoy playing with certain codes, genres. What process of selection goes on?*

DS The pictures may give an illusion of being pan-cultural, but in fact I think they are quite culture-specific in terms of most of the images and most of the material. I've used Japanese calligraphy in my painting – I've gone totally oriental – but that's just Orientalism as it appears in the West in 1982. It is the way things appear in reproduction, the way things appear through various forms of presentation, that's what is interesting to me. The original source is never really very interesting to me. What I've recently refused to do is to identify all the different sources. The point is all the images come from somewhere: sometimes they come directly from things I've drawn or observed, some of them are drawn from life and some of them are invented images – so-called imaginary images, which is a hilarious term in so far as what it discriminates against. It's not the case that they come from anywhere. To focus on where they come from is I think to make at this point a distortion about what it is they are all doing together. Basically, I am attracted to images which are either self-effacing or self-conscious or both. The way I used to experience it was: images which seem to understand us.

JR *They're not surreal, they bear no relation to Lautréamont's umbrella on a dissecting table.*

DS They are not cathetic in that hocus-pocusy sense. But it is interesting just as an aside that I've started to become very attracted to surrealist imagery. The most recent painting has some quotations from surrealist imagery. Ultimately I am not sure how I can answer the original question because even though the collecting or filtering of the images isn't automatic writing it is primarily intuitive.

JR *But all the same there is a recurrence of certain sets of images: the figures in bed, the nudes, the animals.*

DS Actually there are very few animals in the pictures. There is sometimes cartooning in the pictures. And cartooning takes as its subject almost always animals, because cartooning is about personification, it's about making personification visible. That interests me, so cartooning interests me. So sometimes there are animal images in the paintings, but that doesn't have much to do with animals it has to do with characterisation, personification. Anyway, I think the consistent ingredient about the selection of images and what I do with them once selected is a certain kind of erotic poetry. That's probably the only consistent thing I can focus on. Now what I mean by erotic has a direct relationship with the presentational. That probably is what makes my work, my work.

JR *So the images are not as cold as some commentators have made out.*

DS Not in my mind. I'm not saying they don't appear that way, that the paintings ultimately don't have that attitude, but that's not the way the images appear for me to want to use them. The images are about empathy. A lot of people are horrified to hear that. Because the images sometimes have a public source they consider them to be *a priori* debased or banal. I wish people could stop using that word. Probably one of the reasons why some people have difficulty with my work is because of that assumption which doesn't exist for me. It may exist for other images I don't use, but it seems to exist for a lot of people concerning any image that doesn't spring full-blown from the so-called imagination or which is somehow derived from what might be called close observation. But I'm not using images from either of those sources. I'm using images that exist on some level already. The distinctions I make are between some images that exist already and other images that exist already. Historically that is not so different from what artists have done for a long time.

JR *It has taken on a polemical force, whether you call it Postmodernism or not.*

DS Not just because of its use for the postmodernist but because of this other thing that you touched on which is that people see it as cool or detached or distanced. Which is not a contradiction – I'm not saying it couldn't be both, or couldn't be somewhere in between the two or couldn't be about those things being the flip side of the same coin. But in my mind it is about the process by which something transforms itself from a point of empathy to a point of detachment and vice versa. It's that kind of reciprocity in one's emotional life which I am interested in. I'm not interested in making a statement about alienation, or any of that nonsense. What is interesting about that is that empathy by nature is very humble and very humbling and yet the depiction and presentation of it is somewhat arrogant. That is another polarity between which the work seems to run back and forth. I don't think it is something one would be even momentarily puzzled by in poetry. Yet in painting it is seen as something very unpainterly, almost unmanly. The reaction to it is very revealing in itself.

JR *What you borrow, what you reuse is imaginative, it becomes a product of the mind.*

DS That is certainly one of the ideas the work insists on. Yes, that's true. I think that too much emphasis – and it might be a fault of the work that this has occurred – is placed on the fact that these images have sources outside of the painting. As you say, ultimately it is imaginative. The other thing to say though is that when something is drawn naturalistically it also has a source outside its own existence. The desire to do that is cultural and, more importantly, the way the patterns of meaning and communication that almost inevitably it will fall into are totally cultural. Anyway it is always the imagination that activates something – whether it's found in this pile or that.

JR *It's a false distinction.*

DS Yes, but it is not a totally false distinction. The distinction is only useful in a stylistic sense, not in a philosophical sense, and yet somehow the distinction has been made philosophically and not even stylistically and that's the point.

JR *It is interesting that a critic like Craig Owens has got a lot of mileage out of this. But he's never written about your work.*

DS He isn't smart enough to think about my work or anybody else's work. He doesn't really write about art in a very convincing way.

JR *Your relationship with popular culture seems to be highly ambiguous.*

You don't celebrate it, you don't criticise it. It just seems to be simultaneously there, ubiquitous, unavoidable.

DS Consider someone who paints landscapes. Somebody who had recently been to Anselm Kiefer's studio told me that the view outside his studio window actually looks like one of his pictures. He's basically painting what he sees outside of his window.

JR *That implies a certain passivity in relation to your material.*

DS I'm not sure that my relationship with things isn't in part passive. I think that a starting point is a certain passivity. We tend to use the word pejoratively, but I don't think that has to be the case. But the other thing I was going to say, which is actually the opposite, is that in a seemingly passive landscape there is a heavy amount of interpretation going on. Then again the interpretation is largely painterly, aesthetic information, what's left out, what's included, what's emphasised. Which my work also does. It's interesting – an artist interprets a classical theme like landscape but is either passive or manipulative. This is a very old controversy. It is easy to look at Edward Hopper's paintings and say: 'look at those bleak desolate American landscapes'. But maybe Hopper found them very beautiful, very moving. Is that passive? Is that highly interpretative? Is it both?

JR *Your work has been accused of being solipsistic. How would you react to that?*

DS I have no objections. The thinking in my work in some ways might be a meditation on solipsism. I'm not going to sit here and say solipsism is the issue of our time. The notion of solipsism does have a hard-bitten resonance, just as the idea of inevitability appeals to me intellectually and emotionally.

JR *Isn't that a very New York credo?*

DS Well, isn't it very European to want to make it into an ideological issue? But you meant something else I think? What was it you were saying about my relationship with popular culture? It was ambiguous?

JR *Well, that really you didn't have room for it, that it didn't impinge upon you – it was there, but you couldn't take it or leave it.*

DS I don't have much relationship to it really. I'm seldom sure what people mean when they talk about it, which perhaps says something about my relationship to it.

JR *I now have a very long question, which hopefully will put into perspective, and to a certain extent tie up, some of the things we've been talking about.*

I have always felt that the determinism and pessimism of recent American art has much to do with the crippling nature of the American mass media, a sense of estrangement that just hasn't taken root here. You once said you never watch television. Cindy Sherman reputedly watches television all the time. That polarity of response has no equivalent here. There was a show recently at Riverside Studios of the work of John Wilkins, John Stezaker, Jan Wanjda and Jonathan Miles, four artists who have been closely associated with the magazine ZG. *As a British response to the found image, popular culture and the mass media, it is quite different from recent American work. The interaction with the city, its confusion, its energy, is less marked, if not at all. The artists in a sense live with their images longer. There isn't the same sense of pressure, of pushing, of profligacy. What I'm getting at here is this question of productivity, of finding a language and mode adequate to the density and variegation of images and forms in contemporary culture. Like most young American artists using media images – no matter how indifferent you are to them in the end – you use what is essentially a 'democratic' process. Images are transferred from source with the minimum amount of fuss. The painting is done quickly. This may have once been motivated by a desire for a disposable urban art, but now the market has stepped in – and you are a conspicuous success – how has this affected the terms of your productivity?*

DS Why push and profligacy? They contain very different implications. There is enormous push in Barnett Newman and enormous profligacy in Ellsworth Kelly. You could say those are two qualities of American painting.

JR *What I'm trying to get at is, do you find any conflict between your methods – the 'quick' painting – and the increasing demands of the market?*

DS The way my work is used culturally – that is to say what it will come to mean for any given generation, and this needs to be said in response to the last question and the question before – bears directly on the conflict between this generation and the generation of conceptualists and political literalists like Owens. I don't feel necessarily that the life of my work in my mind is how it's going to be used in the culture. It goes without saying that I don't feel like a sloganeer or a pamphleteer. I feel that there is something about making art which is more complex and interesting than that. If you want to say that [*places box of matches on the table*], then the chances are the way to say that is not to put that there. Maybe the way to say that is to put that there [*puts cigarette packet on table*]. All kinds of other meanings enter the work than the one originally intended. What I attempt to do in my work is really to control what it means and not just have it mean nothing in particular. You do not solve the question of what is the nature of art by going up to art and asking, what is your nature? That is a category-mistake that has generated an enormous amount of bad art and bad criticism. If I had to get up in the morning and define my relationship with contemporary culture because I thought that that was what my work was about – I wouldn't be an artist. And it doesn't matter if it is a slow, plodding British artist or a fast, productive American artist. I don't think artists go about representing their culture by necessarily intending to do so. Culture doesn't submit to critique quite so passively anyway. If culture is anything worth thinking about it doesn't even hold still long enough for you to subject it to the tools of criticality such as they have been developed in the graduate centre of City University, New York. By the time they have applied their critical tools to it, it's not even there any more, it's further down the road. The confusion is a misapplication of means to ends, because of a confusion about what the ends are. The other thing is that the ends aren't the ends anyway.

JR *What are your ends? Would you accept the label that others have given you that you really aren't a painter?*

DS Well, if those people would also accept that neither is Frank Stella, if they would say that about him then I would accept them saying that about me. Stella never really painted a picture, although he covered a lot of surfaces with paint. He just changed the terms of what painting he wanted to make.

JR *Do you see yourself painting over the next five years? Because the feeling I get from following your work over the last two years is that you may stop altogether soon and move on to something else.*

DS The idea of stopping has had a functional seductiveness to it for a long time. It lies within a certain idea of making art. The last picture – not needing or being able to do that any more – has fuelled some great work. But what we feel in our heads, in terms of possibility and potential, is sometimes a way of thinking about the variety of life, wishing your life had more variety. If I sit here and fantasise I can imagine doing a lot of different things, one of which would be making paintings in a naturalistic mode, it's something I think about all the time. Painting what I see, which I did as a kid. I think about film and writing projects. And I also think about drying up and not having any creative impulses left any more and just trying to have a nice life or being a libertine. But in reality the work is probably going to continue along the trajectory that it has been continuing along for some time, to work in a relatively two-dimensional way with the complex juxtaposition of images. It depends on how you want to talk about yourself to yourself. You can say starting tomorrow I'm going to turn over a new leaf and be a good person, although chances are when you get up tomorrow you are going to continue being the way you were today.

Issue 64, March 1983

Anthony Hill

interviewed by Stephen Bann

A rather special historical view

STEPHEN BANN *Your retrospective exhibition opens at the Hayward Gallery in mid-May. How complete a record is it?*

ANTHONY HILL My exhibition isn't a retrospective in the usual sense of the word. It is very much a selection from works in England. The Arts Council was not able to pay for the transport of works which are in the US or Europe. I read recently Aleksandr Rodchenko's avowal that you put everything in an exhibition, the good and the bad, to show a true picture of your development. That sounds okay, but what about the things which are deliberately destroyed, cancelled as it were? My output has been quite large, and a fair proportion of the total has been either cancelled or thrown out through lack of space – especially lots of studies. However, I have documented nearly all of it – very little wasn't either documented or photographed.

I have taken the opportunity to have some paintings remade, either in the same size or smaller. But I've not attempted to recreate something enormous like the relief commissioned for the International Union of Architects Congress in 1961, or to make anything that appeared unrealisable in the past – I've made two reliefs where in fact the pieces have been in the studio, carried from place to place as it were, so that they bear funny-looking dates.

SB *Moholy-Nagy once said: 'There is nothing more important to me than seeing my whole development in retrospect.' He also commented on an exhibition of his work held in 1934: 'The real purpose of exhibiting my pictures is to make the spectator grow slowly as I grew in painting them. What a long way to go!' How important to you as an artist is this opportunity to see, if not all, at least a good proportion of your works exhibited in one space? And what impression of 'development' would you expect the spectator to gain from it?*

AH The catalogue probably gives a better view of my 'development', such as it has been, although I don't look for a linear progression, the unfolding of a programmatic accretion. Somewhere, there is a plateau of about ten years when I was 'militant'– about 70 per cent commitment – so it is interesting to see if that shows up against works made just before and after. I don't believe there is any important break or crucial volte-face. I have been in the same territory since 1954. I suppose in one sense it is an exhibition about that.

People may have a good nose for where it starts to wobble a bit, the moments when an artist turns off one switch and flips another – so there is a discernible change. Sometimes this comes about on a very small scale, and is imperceptible to the non-specialist audience. On other occasions it is 'the big change' and this might well cause some reaction: 'he used to do "*a* things", now he's doing "*g* things", or even "*z* things".' These 'morphological phenomena' in an artist's oeuvre indeed make for a response, as if, for example – and this seldom happens – a 12-tone composer has a work which all of a sudden breaks out with the recognisable strains of the '*Marseillaise*'.

SB *When you wrote a short piece for Kenneth Martin's retrospective catalogue, you suggested that 'he may have had a profound advantage over artists like myself by having opted for abstract art when he was 40 years old (and abstract art 50 years old)'. But you also pointed out that the same exhibition gave no hint of Martin's earlier, figurative work. How does your exhibition relate to the question of 'opting for abstract art'? Could you say something about your work immediately before that?*

AH Everything in the exhibition is 'abstract' – it's an exhibition of abstract works: paintings, reliefs and free-standing pieces. The largest informal work I made had to be destroyed, like a later formal painting on a wood panel, because of wood-worm. I haven't too much of the informal work left, though there are quite a lot of early things which you could call dadaist or surrealist in spirit, and they aren't abstract. There's nothing left that I really started with – none of the still-lifes, which as I remember were not done from life. There's nothing which resembles what one is supposed to have put time into doing – painting from life. At my first boarding school, we were taught sculpture by Willi Soukop, but I was very keen to make 'copies' of the Sphinx (at Gaza) and the *Venus de Milo*, which I had seen in the Louvre when

I was six years old.

SB *What about your experience at art school?*

AH I left St Martin's after only a few terms, hearing that Victor Pasmore and Robert Adams were teaching at the Central School. I took my portfolio along. It turned out that Pasmore and Adams were only 'licensed' by William Johnstone, the principal, to do 'Bauhaus' classes and these were for people doing interior and industrial design. So I joined the interior design course!

SB *How did the connection with Pasmore develop?*

AH In 1950, Pasmore received a commission from Misha Black to do a mural for the Regatta Restaurant on the South Bank for the 1951 'Festival of Britain'. The mural department dissolved away, Victor occupied the vast space, and I became his assistant while he planned his tile mural. But my art school studies came to an abrupt end as I had registered as a conscientious objector, and my time was up.

SB *How did that affect your work?*

AH The judge took the view that while I was educated, I didn't have any qualifications. So I was told to fix myself up with work of 'national importance'. The labour exchange, now in charge of me, decreed that they had found the work – washing up at Lyon's Corner House, Coventry Street, and that 'induction' (sic) was on such and such a day and don't be late. I had no intention of washing up for two-and-a-half years, and so took matters into my own hands and obtained a job as an 'art therapist'.

For the next three years I had an interesting task. I was a short order visitor at a TB sanatorium and two mental hospitals, running art classes. During that period I was able to 'scrape a living', and this included visits to Paris. Sitting in my 'office' at Belmont Hospital, when not attending to the assembled class, I planned works, read books and made decisions about a variety of important matters for an artist who, at 21, had the message in his heart, namely abstract art.

SB *What kind of books were you reading at this time?*

AH It was at Belmont that I received the clue to Charles Biederman, and discovered L E J Brouwer. This happened as follows: a patient approached me and said, 'I have a book for you to read, it's called *Signs of Insanity*.' 'But I am not really interested in insanity', I replied. It turned out that the book she was pressing on me – she had rejected it – was Count Alfred Korzybsky's *Science and Sanity*. A few months before, another book had reached us, it was Biederman's *Art as the*

Evolution of Visual Knowledge. Biederman had been inspired to write it after attending some classes by Korzybsky.

SB *Biederman's book was clearly a great stimulus to Pasmore and to the whole group of English abstract artists which was rising in the fifties. Pasmore later spoke of him as having reorientated the 'cubist-constructive outlook'. Yet none of those artists accepted his procedure of abstracting from 'the structural process level of nature'. You made your own position quite clear in the article 'On Constructions, Nature and Structure' which you published in 1959. Why do you think that English artists remained so resistant to his basic outlook, while acknowledging his importance?*

AH In the end, what Biederman required one to acknowledge was tantamount to a view of art history which rejected everybody since Cézanne, while recognising the importance of abstract art. He wanted to put abstract art on a radical course which turns out to be acceptable only to himself and some Canadians who ironically claim to have arrived at the same view, via only a 'glancing off' influence from Biederman. Of course he is respected here, his work from the middle fifties onwards is a paradigm, just as Wagner's music is. I personally don't listen to Wagner, but I am aware of his importance – and remember, Mahler is supposed to have said: 'There is only Beethoven and Wagner and after that nobody!' Biederman, need one say, represents the very opposite of Wagner. But they share this: each wrote extensively about the relationship of art to life, and few read either of them – at least as much as you might expect.

SB *It has often seemed to me that the basic difference between you and many other artists working in the same broad tradition is that you are maintaining a rather special historical view of abstraction. For example, Frantisek Kupka is an important point of reference for you – the Theo van Doesburg of the Concrete Art manifesto perhaps less so. In particular, you stress the link between abstraction with prevalent modernist styles in architecture and the decorative arts. Could you explain this?*

AH Rodchenko was an exhibitor at the great exhibition which gave birth to the term 'Art Deco'. Mondrian had also wanted to participate, but Van Doesburg said 'no'. In 1970, in discussion with Gillian Wise Ciobotaru, we arrived at the idea that the best of abstract art was in fact the triumph of 'High Art Deco'. Soon afterwards, I took the thing a stage further. It seemed clear that the formula was incomplete. The pinnacles of abstract art are: High Art Deco plus 'linguistics' – eye plus mind. Of course this is a misleading formula if you are:

(1) against formalist abstract art (and most people are), and (2) against the encroachment of 'scientific methodology' in art (and nearly everybody is). It is thought that taking such a stand in art cuts out the irrational and poetic in art – in short the art (and this is the prevailing view).

SB *What do you think of the prevailing tendencies of 'high culture', as far as the arts are concerned? As you put it, they could be seen as the other side of the coin to what you are doing, or as a bent version of it.*

AH I have nothing against them. What I react against is the mindless promotionalism which succeeds in convincing the vast majority of the 'Bohogeoisie' and the intelligentsia that such art is to be viewed as a monumental achievement: that Pollock = Van Gogh; De Kooning = Rembrandt; Newman = Poussin; Noland = Ingres etc. I cite the Americans because it is they who are the worst offenders. It is easy to see why they do it. During the making of modern art, America produced practically no one to compare with the Europeans. A Calder doesn't make for a golden summer. Along with Calder they had artists who certainly strove – and in a society which was quick to accept modern art. But architecture, cinema and popular music were the only things the Americans knew were making an impact on Europe vis-à-vis culture – apart from writing.

SB *What about the same period in England?*

AH In England there emerged Henry Moore and Ben Nicholson, and these of course were to be the only substantial artists, because the vorticists turned out to be a false dawn. Moore and Nicholson were artists who responded to modern art, and they stayed that way until the outbreak of war in 1939. Of course Moore and Nicholson matured into quasi-modern artists. As far as I am concerned, modernising traditional values is not being a modern artist. As Marcel Duchamp pointed out in an interview, the pre-Raphaelites remain no less radical than the impressionists. They remain as important a point in art as Moore and Nicholson, paradoxical though that might seem.

SB *I have the impression that for you Duchamp is virtually the most important of modern artists and theorists, and Kenneth Frampton has drawn a light-hearted analogy between Duchamp taking up chess and you yourself taking up mathematics. Do you see Duchamp's view of the modern work of art as a 'brain-fact', a* 'cervellité'*, as being absolutely inescapable?*

AH I can't think of Duchamp as an artist in total isolation. The disengagement people speak of is only one of many strands in Duchamp.

I see Duchamp as one of a number of important artists of that generation, no one of whom is completely overshadowing the others. His contribution does involve many things which opened up a lot – nobody doubts that. What they don't like about him is the consequences, what they see as the benign Savonarola influence. And remember it is only an influence. He had no intention to dictate, to change the course of art.

SB *What do you think of the immensely increased activity of national organisations and museums in promoting the arts today?*

AH Chauvinistic promotionalism is simply a primitive phenomenon – a trick exercised to prove the power of the say-so man. The support-system of an artist today is a corporate affair, and the 'corp' men are almost more important than their properties. I don't subscribe to this – it is something the Americans have decided on in order to succeed and outclass all other comers!

The key word is curatorial – it combines culturological imperatives and the financial/promotional element. Above or below that razzmatazz, the voice of the artist – *sui generis* and disinterested – is something barely heard. Yet modern art was primarily the voice of the artist – promotionalism at the *ad hominem* level was, as it were, tumescent. Since then, there has been a total polarisation, the artist speaks his line(s) through the machine, in harmony with it, as if this symbiosis was a *sine qua non* for the production of creative art. I am totally against this. And I would go so far as to predict that Monsieur Boulez, in his Pompidou bunker, has paid the Faustian dues. He may never again make musical compositions which have germinated from the essentially interior and private realm.

SB *Your thoughts on the present and the future?*

AH One's own future is not entirely independent from the mass directions, the continuous acts of the world art drama. There seem to be both positive and negative aspects of what has been taking place in the last ten years or so. You yourself have written of the overall tendency of entropy, and I think that is indeed evident – much done in the way of support, writing is trying to ignore or stem this factor. The dawn of a true culturology is as far away as ever. People will rewrite the instant and definitive authorised versions of modern art's history but probably make as many mistakes as before.

Issue 66, May 1983

Barbara Kruger

interviewed by John Roberts

The real change has not even begun

JOHN ROBERTS *The fashionable designation 'postfeminism' has been applied to your work. How do you react to that?*

BARBARA KRUGER The 'postfeminist' thing is the most superficial, unthought kind of journalism. It's like a *New York Times* fluff piece. There was an article in the magazine section two years ago on 'postfeminism', which was just a secular extension of Clare Sterling-ism – it's crazy, it's stupid. The idea first of all that there is a singular feminism is indicative of that very phallic univocality that the *Times* and *Time Magazine* and *Newsweek* want to put feminism in. I hope for the idea that there are feminisms, that there is a multiplicity of readings of what constitutes feminism, and I think we have barely begun to enter it. The whole idea of a 'post' is to say that we have 'done that' – it's soiled and full of women in denims and ponchos – we've been through that, we're 'postfeminist' now. It's just airhead. The real change has not even begun.

JR *Do you think the reason that the term has gained currency is that despite the feminism of the work, the spectator you address is not gender-specific?*

BK Let's just say that I'm interested in ruining certain representations and welcoming the female spectator into the audience of men, which doesn't mean a female audience, it means mixing that audience. I think that the interesting thing that I would hope for is that a spectator can choose to decline or accept the address. In many cases there are specific gender proclivities that I would say I engage in, in terms of the viewer, but it's really a free field. The last thing I want to be is correct in terms of a reading of my work. The last thing I want is a singular reading.

JR *You are currently having a show with Robert Mapplethorpe at the ICA. Mapplethorpe's ironic use of the stereotype and your sharp displacement of it is quite a productive conjunction. Do you relish that difference?*

BK Why do you think it's productive? I am not interested in binary oppositions. I really like the idea of a free field. I would say, without wanting to get involved in that opposition, that Robert's work is more about desire and mine's more about pleasure. Desire only exists where there's absence. And I'm not interested in the desire of the image.

JR *But like Mapplethorpe you are interested in challenging gender images.*

BK I'm basically interested in suggesting that we needn't destroy difference.

JR *Jane Weinstock has called you a 'guerrilla semiologist'. That has strong overtones of Situationism. Does Situationism play a part in your thinking?*

BK I think there's something to be said for the resuscitation of that writing now. I think some of it is quite interesting in that it acknowledges a broad field of spectatorship for all of us, how what we see dictates so much of what we look like and what we do. But I think that, like similar and much more ambitious writing such as Art & Language's work, there's an incredibly mean didacticism to it all, an incredible disallowance of difference. There was a film I wrote about called *Call it Sleep*. Basically it was a film about spectacle, a collage film of found footage, combined with shot narrative. Over this footage was this insistent, unrelenting male voice dictating our histories to us, dictating the specific directions for change. Now I found that unbearable and I feel that in much of that – very similar to Art & Language again – is a total absence of women, if not contempt towards any analysis of gender. So I'm not interested in situationist theory on that level because it doesn't allow for me as a subject, it doesn't construct me as a subject: don't worry girls when the dictatorship of the proletariat comes we'll get you washing machines.

JR *So you don't see works as strictly interventionist?*

BK I see them as such, but I think that there are some situations where they would function more powerfully than others. Again, I see my work as a series of attempts.

JR *In an odd way I was reminded of Daniel Buren in your work, there's the same assertiveness through repetition.*

BK Perhaps. I think that you can say something a million times before you can actually intervene. Or you can intervene stultifyingly once and it's forgotten. So in many ways I agree with that. And also the notion of 'originality' is one that is strained and ridiculous just like the notion of the 'authentic' and the 'genuine'.

JR *Like Buren do you see yourself ostensibly as a poster-artist?*

BK Sure.

JR *Are you involved in any poster campaigns at the moment?*

BK It's interesting because with the gentrification of SoHo and Tribeca there are fewer and fewer buildings that you can post. Last year when I was here I went to the Cockpit Gallery and saw a show by the Poster Collective and was really impressed, and the fact that they were used as teaching aids in schools as well as posters would just be unheard of in the US. We're just 25 years out of McCarthy. Our tradition of political posters, art posters, is very small. In Los Angeles there was a mural tradition in the sixties and seventies that is much less active now. In New York, rather than a community effort to say something about a particular topic, to engage in a view or particular issue, what we have is the reduction of writing into one's name. The call has been diminished to a yelp. I put my name on a piece of property, that's what has become of poster work. There's little, almost none. I wish there was more. I did some posters in Europe last year and I'd like to do more in New York. I'm doing the spectre-colour sign in Times Square. It's really important for me to do work which concretely addresses the issues of my social life. I don't see politics as something out there, it's all one cloth. As far as making films, for instance, it takes two years to make enough money to make a film. So while I'm doing that I can try and get teaching jobs where I am able to address a room full of people as a woman writing criticism. I don't consider myself a theorist, I'm writing journalism – and this is also important, I want to make myself accessible to people. Which doesn't mean I'm against theory, I totally support theoretical writing. It's been very important to me, that's part of my work too. Because the art world is a cottage industry, I can still borrow enough money to make work that can be shown in a white room and thus enter the discourse of benighted and exalted male art historians. They talk about you because you have entered the market to some degree.

JR *So the market provides an enabling function for you?*

BK Sure. I don't know how long it's going to last though, it's so cyclical. Unlike most men I know, recently it's been very good for me in New York getting a lot of press. The *Voice* did this Power of Art/Art

Power thing, so I was on the cover and did a full page. Never under any situation would I consider myself a phenomenon. The phenomenon is the structure that needs the phenomenon. I think people get so easily deluded about their own elevation for 60 seconds or 15 minutes, as Andy Warhol would say. And to me it's that system which needs that celebratory mystique. And I will use it, if that gets a particular message across.

JR *Do you see your work ever becoming issue-specific, in the way, say for example, Peter Kennard's work is?*

BK I did a number of pieces, in particular one – *Your Manias become Science* – which was in an anti-nuclear show going across America. Certainly my appearance on panels has been issue-specific – The Artists Call for Art in Central America. I certainly haven't fudged that, that's very important to me.

JR *Is it worse for women artists now than it has ever been?*

BK Yes, I think it's pretty bad. My wish is that more women and men did work which addressed social issues. Now of course there are a lot of women who are going to get into galleries who are doing color field painting. I will support the effort of any woman to define herself through her production because I know how much more difficult it is. But I cannot support all work because a woman did it. People say to me there aren't any more big star women artists. If I had a choice – and most women in the art world are appalled when I say this – between having three more women art stars who spend all their money at Georgette Clinger and Bloomingdales, and health care for 400 women in the South Bronx, I would pick the latter. What's appalling to me is the idea of women getting an audience within the art world, entering the market, doing work and not being concerned with what we are and how we have had to struggle. I don't care about these people. That's reprehensible to me. What does give me some pleasure is when women do get some audience, and do make certain inroads. I'm not interested in buying a beautiful loft, in buying a beautiful man, in buying a beautiful car, all the things that most men I know are engaged with. And I can name a few women in similar situations who would agree. I'm not trying to pass for white. That's what puts me off here. America's certainly not a classless society but compared to here – at least our traditions are not carved in the great oaks of history.

JR *So there's still room for struggle within the art world?*

BK Of course. I am working with representations, with pictures, pictures we have all grown up with in some ways, pictures that have dictated our desires, that have dictated our appearances. If one of the extensions of my work is within this white room, I hope that seeing the work and its reproduction – it's very important that the work be reproduced – can change things a little bit perhaps. I'm not interested in any of this complicit subversion trip that people talk about. The critique in my work is fairly explicit, you don't have to have read three essays by Doug Crimp to understand what my work is saying. I'm not interested in an implicit critique that's available to ten people who go into a gallery and know what the line of the gallery is. I really want to reach more people. You don't have to have an understanding of the meandering phantasms of the resonance of graphite on paper to understand my work. I want to make it more secular.

JR *There's a negativity to your work, a stripping away, a disabling of categories, do you think this puts the idea of a positive image in jeopardy?*

BK When I say I'm interested in coupling the ingratiation of wishful thinking with the criticality of knowing better, I think that there's this kind of flux that's part of the seduction. I am making something to be looked at, there's a retinal address. You make something people want to look at and then you deliver a message. There is a negativity involved but I think that negativity is balanced, hopefully, by the construction of another kind of subject. For one spectator the work is negative but perhaps for another it's very positive.

JR *Where are your images appropriated from? Film stills, magazines?*

BK Many different places. I'll see an image and I'll know right away whether I can use it. Again there's a lot of radical cropping going on. What I'll do is find an image first. Almost none of these are film stills though. I don't like the idea of nostalgia. I try to make them as generic as possible.

JR *What were you doing at Condé Nast?*

BK I was a designer, laying out pages exactly the size of the pages that I use to blow up to this size.

JR *What kind of projects were you working on?*

BK I worked at *Mademoiselle* for four years, I worked at *Vogue* and *House and Gardens* as a designer and picture editor.

JR *Were you politicised through this world?*

BK See your notion of politics here is so different from that in America, especially as regards somebody like me who was out of college by the time she was 19. There wasn't any women's movement, there was nothing, I was on my own. I was totally in limbo really, I didn't belong to the hippie movement, I wasn't a masochist. I don't know one woman who can think back to that movement today and not think that it was the most oppressive experience of her life. I believe that any discourse, any political movement, which doesn't take considerations of gender into account is complicit, that's all.

JR *It is interesting – though not surprising – that there should be a so-called explosion of political work in the US given the current climate.*

BK What? Where's this explosion?

JR *Your work, Dara Birnbaum, Martha Rosler –*

BK Three people who have been peripheral for years – hardly an explosion. One must see it within the picture of the American art market, which would not define Dara, Martha and myself as an explosion.

JR *But there's a sense of things being taken into account. Politics is suddenly an issue again. It's there in the pages of* Artforum, *it's there at* Art in America *since Craig Owens and Hal Foster joined.*

BK Most people who write art criticism are airheads, all they want to do is lick the arse of some artist who is parading up and down West Broadway. What can you say? Most artists who the Brits might construe as doing media-conscious work see their role as being the guardians of culture. They're not taking a critical position, the critique is implicit, 'get it'?

JR *So you don't think things have changed?*

BK There have been cycles of work which have pushed towards a more secular reading which connects more concretely with one's life, sure, sure. I can't see it in terms of progress though. We have to define the notion of progress too. I think that there are certain works – mine included along with Sherrie's and Jenny's and Dara's and Martha's – I wish I could name some men. Michael Glier's work – Mike is somebody who thinks about these things also.

JR *Do you sense that the energy and excitement that has taken hold of the New York art world over the last few years is now dissipated? Or was it all a myth anyway?*

BK I never felt any energy or excitement because I can't get excited about the art world. I think things are better in some ways. They're certainly better for me, they're certainly better for Jenny and Martha. If I feel excited about something it's very seldom it's going to be in the art world, it will be in film. That's why I don't write about art,

I write about film. But I'm not saying that the art world is ours to cede to the great expressionists because it's not even ours to cede. But do we give up one venue? I say it's silly to. If those pictures can make an intervention into the seamlessness of representations in that space, why not? But then there is an insistence in certain critics like Benjamin Buchloh, for instance, to just look at my work as an example of montage theory, and never think about gender, never think about a reception or a response or a spectator, because he feels that doesn't constitute a political view. Hans Haacke agrees. They see it as frivolous and trivial.

JR *In the piece Buchloh wrote on allegory in* Artforum *recently he mentioned your name at the beginning and then failed to discuss the work.*

BK That's right – because he was afraid to come out against feminist art. He was afraid he would be attacked. Jonathan Caplan, the American director who did *Heart Like a Wheel*, made this statement that most Hollywood films with a feminist slant are about women deciding which town house to live in in New York, and I totally support that view. Because I think the problem with so much American bootstrap *Ms* magazine feminism – and with French theoretical feminism which has meant a lot to me – is that it is always discussed in some Café de Bourgeoisie. Class just does not become an issue. And I think that's something that bothers Benjamin. But if he had troubled to talk to me about it, it bothers me also. I am not concerned with issues if they are not going to be anchored by some kind of analysis or consideration of class. Any questioning or displacement of the subject within patriarchy that is going to change the strictures of that construction is going to be an attack on class. To change the dominant position of the subject is to change class.

Issue 72, December–January 1983–84

Clement Greenberg

interviewed by Trish Evans and Charles Harrison

Major to minor

CLEMENT GREENBERG I was brought up in a family where socialism was the only religion. My father's and mother's culture was Italian opera and Russian novels, and being an intellectual was supposed to be the height. The conversion came after my first year and a half at college. I had just wanted to have a good time. I got good marks and all that, no trouble, but I wasn't in it. And one afternoon I took a nap in the fraternity house – that awful place – and woke up. I had an anthology of English Romantic Poets on the floor and I opened it by chance at the 'Ode to a Nightingale':

Darkling I listen; and, for many a time
I have been half in love with easeful Death.
Called him soft names in many a mused rhyme.

And I thought, good God, this is something. It sounds too dramatic, that's the trouble. It sounds like one of those things made up afterwards. But it was just like that. And from then on I became damned interested. I left the fraternity house that year and became a greasy grinder. And from then on – I was a bad swimmer on the swimming team, but I hung on until I graduated – I got more interested in literature than in anything else. I'd already learned French at high school, and I learned German and Italian.

TRISH EVANS *So how did you move on to art?*

CC I'd been a child prodigy. I could draw from nature photographically from about five. At home they didn't take me seriously because they didn't think anything their children did amounted to much.

But finally my father showed some of my drawings to a fellow who did designing for him, and he said, 'You ought to send the boy to the Art Students League', and he named the teacher, Richard Lahey. I was 16 then and went to the Art Students League three nights a week after high school – a long haul from Brooklyn. And there I saw naked women for the first time in my life. Afterwards my father said, 'If I had known you were going to draw from naked women I wouldn't have let you go. It's too late now.' This wonderful teacher Lahey, who was a pretty fair landscape painter, looked at my stuff and once he asked me, 'What do you intend to do?' and I said I was going to college afterwards, 'I'm not going to art school'. And I remember his saying, 'Well, George Bellows went to college and it didn't hurt him.' I went to college the next year when I was 17 and stopped going to the Art Students League though I still drew obsessively. And finally it was all literature. I paid relatively little attention to art though Syracuse, where I went, had at that time the best studio art department in the country. It was the first university to give you academic credit for painting and sculpture. After college I worked for my father for a while and finally got a job in the Civil Service and from Civil Service to Customs Service, as a clerk in the department of wines and liquors.

I started writing there because I had an office of my own and a lot of free time. I published in *Partisan Review* in 1939. It was a piece on Bert Brecht's novel, the one he made out of the *Dreigroschenoper*. The next thing, I wrote a piece called 'Avant-Garde and Kitsch' and in 1940 I became one of the editors of *Partisan Review* – there were five of us. I could write my own ticket in *Partisan Review* and get printed. I published art criticism in the *Nation*. I knew the lady, Margaret Marshall, who ran the 'back of the book' – I dedicated *Art & Culture* to her. The art critic of the *Nation* had gone on vacation and I said I'd like to take a shot at it. And then I stayed on and except for a year in the army I wrote for the *Nation* until 1949 and I wrote for *Partisan Review* off and on until 1955. I resigned from the latter in 1942.

CHARLES HARRISON *'Avant-Garde & Kitsch' reads like the fruits of some deliberations. It says some very specific things about what art is like.*

CG I'd started looking again really about 1936. I began thinking about 'Avant-Garde & Kitsch' on account of Brecht and the business of making high art that a broad public could get and why that wasn't being done and couldn't be done at that time. An emigré German magazine touched something off. I've got the magazine somewhere and I find it every five years or so. But it was Brecht most of all. I didn't hear of Walter Benjamin till Hannah Arendt was over here in the late forties. He didn't give me much – much as I admire him. I went on to review T S Eliot's *Notes Towards a Definition of Culture* then dropped the subject. I didn't have anything more to say about it – the question of culture and the masses – I hate that term 'the masses'. 'Avant-Garde and Kitsch' was the fruit of three or more years thinking about the subject.

TE *At what stage were you in direct contact with the artists? Early forties?*

CG I'd known Lee Krasner. I'd known Harold Rosenberg and May Rosenberg. I'd met Willem de Kooning, I knew Arshile Gorky and some others. I hung around Hans Hofmannn's school. It was the only place to be if you wanted to talk about art in 1937–39. I'd gone to WPA (Works Progress Administration) art classes around 1936–37. You got a model for free. I went about twice a week, I went back to drawing from the figure.

I met Jackson Pollock outside the Appraiser's Stores of the Customs Service. There on the sidewalk was Lee with this gentleman wearing a grey fedora hat of all things and a nice, proper grey topcoat. She introduced me and said, 'This guy's going to be a great painter.' He had this open face. It was the only time I ever saw him wear a hat. He looked even more respectable than I did. Then I was in the army for a year. After I came out I saw Jackson's first show in 1943. I was impressed by it and I wrote about it in the *Nation*, but I didn't glow about it. A while later he painted this picture, the end of 1943, a portable mural for the foyer of Peggy Guggenheim's apartment. It's now at the University of Iowa. It went on and on repeating itself and I thought it was great. We got much closer friends after that.

I quit the *Nation*, not for political reasons as so many people have it. I felt I'd had enough of reviewing. From then on I did occasional reviews for *Partisan Review*. In the course of time I stopped reviewing. In 1945 I got a job with a magazine published by the American Jewish Committee called *The Contemporary Jewish Record* which turned into *Commentary*. I worked for *Commentary* till 1957 when I got fired. The reasons for that are beside the point. I haven't worked for anybody since then. I got married in 1956, second marriage.

CH *Was there a certain point at which you thought of yourself as a critic?*

CG From the very beginning I think. Or rather I didn't think of myself as a critic. I felt a certain confidence as a critic because I felt I could do the same thing as artists. Not as good, not at all. But I knew what it was about from the inside.

TE *Do you feel that an art critic should –*

CG No 'shoulds' here. An art critic should have an eye and I can't say any more.

TE *But do you think it's helpful for an art critic to have some idea of the practice of painting?*

CG I can't really say because a great critic like Julius Meier-Graefe didn't paint at all. On the other hand a great art critic like Roger Fry did paint and, as I think, better than most people realise.

TE *But you think it helped you?*

CG It gave me a certain confidence that I might not have had otherwise.

CH *If the art critic should have an 'eye' and you felt confidence as a critic, there must have been a point at which you became significantly confident that you did have an eye.*

CG Enough of an eye – it was after getting the hook of abstract art, which I couldn't see until 1937. I'd been round these abstract artists but I couldn't see abstract painting till 1937.

CH *What made that possible?*

CG Looking enough. And coming across something like Paul Klee's *Twittering Machine*, 1922, in the Museum of Modern Art. Good God, you know, it just sat there. I tried to paint like that but I gave up on abstract art. It's no fun, for me. Landscapes, the figure – not that I went about it seriously – that was fun. But abstract painting – no fun. But I realised I could see abstract art, tell the difference between good and bad, get a bang out of what's good. It's the same for non-abstract art, just the same – you look enough. People ask me, 'How do you tell the difference between good and bad in abstract art?' and I say, 'The same way you tell the difference between good and bad in Raphael.' It's the same in essence, of course.

TE *How did you see the relation between art criticism and literary criticism?*

CG I didn't think about it. I thought art criticism was tougher. Tougher to write. Whether literary criticism is really easier than art criticism? I think, no. It's just easier to be plausible.

TE *How do you see the function of the art critic in the art world?*

CG That damn question – it gets asked all the time and it isn't worth asking. He points, okay, he points.

TE *So what's the difference between the critic's pointing and anyone else's pointing?*

CG The critic supposedly tries harder, sees more – supposedly. And maybe reflects more – supposedly. And the critic makes his pointing public. Somebody else doesn't have to.

TE *In making his pointing public, in print, the critic needs to justify it to some degree.*

CG Well, you know you can't demonstrate aesthetic judgements as Kant pointed out. You can't prove them. You can't prove anything when it comes to art, literature, music, so far as value judgement is concerned.

TE *You can't prove anything, but you might need to justify it.*

CG You spend some adjectives and thus implicitly you say, 'Go and see for yourself'. Now it's true that people in Peoria can't come to New York so easily, and that's frustrating. In the case of literature and music, which are reproducible, you can ask that the reader read for himself, the listener hear for himself. But since I don't believe in reproductions of the visual arts and have no faith in them, I feel in a bind.

TE *When the critic writes about art he must write about it in relation to other art and that's how he justifies.*

CG 'Justifies' is a questionable word here. He tries to back up his seeing, not to justify. All I can say is it's something I wrestle with all the time and I read my stuff and see how I go about it. What I prefer to do is to say 'this is good', 'that's not so good', to walk through a gallery with somebody.

TE *But is something good in relation to the art that preceded it? It can't just be good in isolation can it?*

CG You're asking a question that's answerable but it takes a lot of words. I think even cave painting had to have some kind of tradition behind it. You can say the first art might have been handprints or whatever, we don't know about that. All we know is that the best art always hooks on to previous art, even among non-urban people. That's a matter of record. There seems to be no exception, nothing that comes out of the blue, in urban art and as far as we can tell not in non-urban art either – I won't call it primitive art because that's the wrong term. West African sculpture comes out of life – I finally found out when they had a show of life heads in the Met. I'd seen them in reproduction but it wasn't till I saw them in the flesh here that I realised how much of West African art comes out of life. Where life comes from is a great mystery.

TE *But is the goodness or badness of the art in relation to its antecedents?*

CG It's absolute. The production depends on its hooking on to tradition, but its quality doesn't. Otherwise how could we appreciate Japanese or Hindu or Persian art? Sometimes you don't know the tradition at all. It helps to bathe yourself in Japanese or Hindu art – to find your eye some. But there've been times for me in the past when those prints – Hokusai and Hiroshige – looked so good to me, and this goes back 40 or 50 years when I knew nothing about Japanese or Chinese art.

TE *So it would be possible to hypothesise a good piece of art which didn't hook on to a tradition?*

CG It is possible, but on record everything does.

TE *But you would allow for that possibility?*

CG Yes. In art you allow for anything. There are no rules in art, either in the seeing of it or the making of it, the hearing of it or the reading of it. You're asking me questions which have troubled the philosophers of aesthetics a great deal. Better minds than mine. And these questions can't be coped with in an interview. The other big question is: are judgements of taste objective? Or are they just subjective – you like what you like and so on? Even someone as great as Benedetto Croce dodged that. And he also dodged the question of whether bad art is art at all. He just said bad art was not art, which is a cop-out. What do we do with bad art? Given the human mind we have to classify it. What do we say it is? In this damned book I'm trying to write I want one final chapter towards the end about bad art and where you put it. I haven't gotten the answer yet. Kant was the only one, the first one, who really tried to wrestle with the question of whether taste is just subjective. I don't think he really came up with enough of an answer, but he came up with half an answer in his *Critique of Aesthetic Judgement*, but you have to read the *Critique of Pure Reason* in order to be able to understand it.

CH *The question of disinterestedness of aesthetic judgements is an open question.*

CG It's partly closed I think. But I won't go into how closed it is or how open because it has to do with intuitive experience. All the evidence of experimental psychology shows that no one has gotten inside intuitive experience or been able to analyse it. Why do we see the sky as blue? We know the wave lengths are 'blue', but that still doesn't do the job. You can't tell a colourblind man what red is like. Incidentally, women can name colours better than men can, which is not the same as recognising.

CH *Causal theories of reference suggest that the uses of different names are to a certain extent matters of different histories, different contexts of learning, let's say. Let's go back to the matter of 'spending some adjectives' to back up one's seeing. The adjectives you spend will not be the same as the adjectives I spend and that's partly by virtue of different causal histories to our respective terms of reference.*

CC And a temperamental difference comes in.

CH *You've also said you re-read your writing.*

CC You do that before you send the copy to the printer.

CH *But what happens when you re-read and you decide you pointed at the wrong thing or spent the wrong adjectives?*

CC You change it.

CH *What if it's something you wrote five years ago?*

CC Oh, then I squirm. There's plenty. Oh man, there's plenty!

CH *But do you ask why?*

CC I ask why and usually it is aesthetic. I get no satisfactory answer. People quote me and show I've changed my mind sometimes. They want to nail me on that and know why I've changed my mind. Greater experience, that's all. It's all about educating oneself in public. I've said that in the foreword to my selected essays. I did educate myself in public. I'll add that if you don't change your mind you're lost. The fun has gone out of it.

CH *Could you ever look back on anything you've changed your mind about and say it wasn't so much lack of experience but because some mechanism was in the way?*

CC My eye was off.

CH *What sets it off?*

CC I don't know. Let the experimental psychologists find that out. My eye was off. Your eye goes off. As I get older my taste gets more and more catholic. I maintain that it's evidence that your eye is still developing – as you like more and more art instead of less. That's my experience and I set my experience up in this respect as final court of appeal.

CH *Does this make you more open to what you were previously closed to?*

CC Yes.

CH *Can you identify the closures?*

CC Yes, but not the reasons for them. I didn't have enough of an eye then. My eye's got better. That's the best I can say.

CH *Do you equate 'more catholic' with 'better'?*

CG It means you've got a better eye – according to my experience. And it doesn't mean that you need experience of more exotic art either in order for expansion of taste to take place. I don't think it's necessary to see what China or Japan or Persia have produced. You just keep on looking. I'd like to go back to myself. I have a knack of getting myself misunderstood and twice lately it's been said that I'm for abstract art. Things I've written get quoted back at me, always a little off. One case is a sheet called *Art World*, the other case is the *New Criterion*, quoting things said by Fairfield Porter in an interview for the *Archives of American Art*. 'Towards a Newer Laocoon' was quoted back at me in a letter protesting at what I'd said in a previous letter. That thing was published in 1942. The writer didn't allow for the fact that I might have changed my mind. But that's beside the point. I was very rigid then in a Marxist way, I failed to make a distinction between major and minor art. That hadn't come up for me as that important in 1942. It was only with the abstract expressionists that that came up. We'd had some wonderful American painters in the nineteenth century, so had the Germans and the Italians. I had not yet made that distinction between major and minor art. The quotation you'll find in the *New Criterion*. Someone called Rackstraw Downes wrote the rejoinder to my letter. Every word he quoted needs qualifying in terms of the difference between major and minor. I said that abstract art was inevitable given the conditions of history. I should have said that abstract art as a major way of painting was inevitable, but that this didn't exclude the representational.

CH *I've always felt the soft spot in your more general theoretical arguments, for instance in 'Modernist Painting', is the claim for necessity in the tendencies you describe. That seems to lay you open to criticisms of historicism.*

CG I did a postscript to that piece when it was included in Richard Kostelanetz's anthology called *Contemporary Aesthetics* – I said it was the fault of my rhetoric not to spell out the fact that I wasn't prescribing but describing the internal logic of Modernism. It was taken as prescription and I must say I was shocked.

CH *To call it logic is to close an open system.*

CG But there are logical set-ups all over the place. There's a logical development of carpentry. The word 'logical' is open, that's the trouble. And I did say in the postscript that I didn't imply it had had to be this way but that this was the way it had been in fact and that there was a logic to it. It wasn't supposed to be prescriptive, but it was taken as that and that was the fault of my rhetoric. And I am careless. I sounded as though I was laying down the law.

CH *I would want to criticise what you wrote not so much on the grounds that it is prescriptive of the future of art, but because it turns the open systems of history into a closed logic of development which produces the present – or the present according to a specific view.*

CG In the different disciplines it looks that way in retrospect. It need not have been that way. But if you're going to deal with the past you have to see some logic in the way one event follows another. You can't say it's random. There's free choice I'm sure, but somehow as it happens you can see some inexorabilities, and a series. It's the way to make sense of the hint.

CH *It sounds to me like a way to make sense of the present.*

CG I don't see the difference. Or rather I do see the difference because the present's too present. When I talked about the purity of art, about pure art in that article, I didn't point out that it was an illusion – a useful one. It was a useful illusion for Mallarmé, even for Picasso. I don't believe in purity at all. It acts as some kind of beacon. It's there but it's not possible. It has no ultimate reality.

CH *You accord a disinterested and involuntary status to the immediate aesthetic response.*

CG I do indeed.

CH *The aesthetic response is what informs you that you have the logic right.*

CG True.

CH *So what we have is a circularity where the disinterestedness of taste and consensus in response and the inevitability of the development impose a logical necessity upon each other.*

CG No. Experience decides that. Consensus of taste decides. Kant had some inkling of it. There hadn't been enough art criticism before him or something. What the people who've seen most, read most, heard most – and who've worked most on what they've seen, read, heard – decide in the way of value judgements proves in the long run to be right. How do you test that? You go to Italy and there's this Milanese fresco painter you've never heard of, Borgognone, pieces of fresco in the Brera, and you think 'Wow, they're good!' And you re-read Bernard

Berenson and he refers to this guy as a great painter. And you think, good God you've made this discovery and Berenson's been there ahead of you. There's consensus. Berenson was good. He's not so hot about the Sistine ceiling. The consensus slips sometimes, or for a long while it operates without including someone like Georges de la Tour. They hadn't identified Vermeer, so they waited for Thoré-Burger to come along in the nineteenth century and isolate him. But those are the fringes of the consensus – not of art itself.

CH *Have you had the experience with the art of the past of seeing someone who's not incorporated in the canon, and seeking validation (as with the case of Berenson) but not finding it?*

CC I didn't feel validated there. Not even confirmed. Beaten to the point rather. I didn't need confirmation. I'm that arrogant. I can't remember. There are these fifteenth-century Flemish paintings in the Wallraf-Richartz Museum in Cologne by unknown artists, and they're great. But the curators had already beaten me to it. Incidentally, the Europeans criticise us Americans for going by names so much. We haven't got enough 'ignoti' or 'Unbekannte' hanging in our museums. I can't remember discovering anything for myself that was outside the canon. I may find some late nineteenth-century German painter, but that's a local issue. It's a matter of the work being underrated outside Germany. Willem Trübner, Hans Liebl, for instance. Or Pieter Stobbaerts in Belgium. I find all along artists who are underrated. There's a mid-nineteenth century American sculptor called Thomas Ball. He turned me on and I found he'd no name at all. I came across a work in the Louisville museum and they included him in the Whitney American sculpture show a couple of years back. They had one Ball, solely for historical reasons. And lo and behold Kenworth Moffet, who'd never heard of him – and I'd never mentioned Ball's name to him – came back and said, 'Hey, there's a new sculptor there.' That shows how good Ken's eye is. These bronzes aren't supposed to be good, they're too literally realistic. They are good, but these artists are never major. The major ones hardly ever get overlooked – De la Tour and Vermeer were exceptions.

TE *What do you mean by that distinction between major and minor?*

CC Aesthetic judgement. A major artist gives you more punch. Though sometimes a minor artist can be major in one work.

TE *And a major artist is one who sustains it?*

CC More or less. It's tough, like good and bad – what do you mean by good and what do you mean by bad.

TE *Is the aesthetic response gradable?*

CC Judgement is gradable. There are degrees, in my experience.

TE *That seems to conflict with the idea of its being absolute.*

CC The degrees are absolute. Why not? When the temperature is 50 degrees, it's absolute – for our experience it's absolute. It's there and you can't get underneath aesthetic experience, at least not yet. It's not something you can change by circumstance, 50 degrees of temperature are not changed by circumstance.

CH *By absolute do you mean mind-independent?*

CC I hesitate to say that. I go along a little bit with Bishop Berkeley. The instruments we have for measuring temperature are human. And they're not mind-independent. We establish the gradations in relation to other mind-dependent facts.

TE *So what is the 'instrument' for measuring aesthetic quality?*

CC Sensibility, which is all we have when it comes to art.

TE *And that's something we develop?*

CC All people are born with the faculty but I don't think anyone is born with taste. I can't say you're born 'musisch'. I have to believe all people are born with the faculty, the capacity.

TE *So how would you describe its development? How much is sensibility developed through education, through spending one's time in the company of people with taste and so on?*

CC That's an open question. In our culture it does seem to be the case that females tend to be more readily 'musisch' than men. But there may be social reasons for that. It may have nothing to do with hormones. I don't know. I'm so happy to be able to say I don't know. It's such a relief.

CH *How far do you go with Bishop Berkeley? Do you withhold assent from scientific realism altogether?*

CC No. Only in certain contexts.

CH *The big question seems to be, to what extent is aesthetic response a response to some mind-independent property of the work of art?*

CC To no extent whatsoever. Aesthetic experience is outside material circumstance or consequence. Hard to explain that, but that's my experience. I'm ready for some subtler philosophic mind to come along and correct me.

CH *The work of art is identified for you in terms of your response to it. That response is supposedly involuntary and disinterested. It is a special kind of experience. What sets the conditions of relevance to the response? What decides its status as aesthetic?*

CG When it comes to aesthetic experience you're all alone to start and end with. Other people's responses may put you under pressure but what you then have to do is go back and look again, listen again, read again. You can only modify your judgement by re-experiencing. You don't change your mind on reflection. You may get doubts but you have to go back and check again. It's not a matter of probative demonstration. When you can demonstrate an aesthetic judgement probatively art will cease – art as we've known it so far.

CH *Can you recall any really decisive instances of re-experiencing?*

CG Too many to remember. I'll have a stab at it, though this may not be to the point. Clyfford Still gave me trouble when I first saw his art. There were so many who admired him who didn't admire Pollock's all-over art. So I'm given pause. I go look again. In Still's case I did see a small picture at Alfonso Ossorio's that I got the point of. Then some more. I found myself taking him too much on blind faith. I'm talking now about the end of the fifties. Two years ago there was a huge show at the Met. It was largely a dud. There were two or three smallish early paintings which were okay. I decided to write about it and see. In my original failure to see Still there had been the seed of something. Then there was Diebenkorn's first New York show in 1954. It was the first show of Abstract Expressionism that sold in New York. I liked every picture – it was too good to be true. I could see why it sold out. Diebenkorn had a retrospective ten years ago at the Jewish Museum – those early works had gone to pieces – I wondered about my eye at that time. Charles Hinman – someone I like enormously personally – had a show of sculptured canvases. This was a dozen years ago. I thought every one of them was right there. That show sold out too. I saw some of those three-dimensional canvases three to four years later – they'd gone away. Since that time I've gotten suspicious. Now when I like everything an artist does, I suspect I'm wrong. I want to see failed paintings, failed sculptures. I don't want to make that a rule though.

CH *Have you seen an interesting mixture of significant failure and significant success in anything done over the last few years?*

CG I'd have to go back to be sure of what I say. In David Smith's case and in Hans Hofmann's case they could fall on their faces so often and then come up. And it was as if it were necessary for them to fall on their faces in order to come up. Only, as I've said before about Smith, no matter how bad the piece was it always got better with time. It never got worse. And the same for Jack Bush the Canadian painter whose picture is hanging over there. Bush usually looked worst the first time. That says more about the artist than about my eye. And in Smith's case and Hofmannn's case there was no falling off with age as there has been with so many artists. They have that ten-year run. A 20-year run for Picasso and then the slope downhill, though with interruptions always. As there were with Rothko during his post-1955 decline. Hofmannn and Smith were going to be as good as they'd ever been had they lived to a hundred. There are ups and downs. Again that's not a rule, it's just something I've noticed, just as I've noticed that neither Titian nor Rembrandt could bring off group compositions after middle-age. Again with exceptions. What goes on I don't know. Why do poets fall off? Wordsworth fell off, so did Auden.

CH *Kenneth Noland seems like someone who has a wide range between success and failure.*

CG Noland will keep going till a hundred. The difference isn't as glaring as in Smith's case or Hofmann's. Someone else who'll keep going is Jules Olitski. He's like Smith. He doesn't give a damn. His failures don't trouble him. Hofmann was troubled by his misses, or rather by their being identified as misses. Nobody could tell him anything. I wrote a little book about Hofmann and talked about his bad pictures and he complained, 'I never painted any bad pictures.' European hot air. And I thought Hofmann at his best was a very great painter. And sometimes his mediocre pictures, in group shows with Pollock and company, would in a curious way beat them all – in a curious way that I can't put my finger on.

CH *How about Europeans over the last ten years or so?*

CG About Europeans – I made the distinction between Europeans and Americans only in the early 1950s when I thought our painters were getting better. Saying that was a reaction to circumstance, because the Museum of Modern Art was then readier to buy a Mathieu than it was a De Kooning. And I think Mathieu is good by the way, and underrated. He's fallen off lately, I know, but he was damn good when he was good. But there was this tendency at the Museum of Modern Art for a while to accept a European quicker than an American and I was reacting to that. Otherwise – I've written this – the French tradition was being maintained in this country better than it was in France itself.

And none of the abstract expressionists denied their debt to France, though people like Rothko and Gottlieb would murmur way back then and say, 'Oh, you're buying French paintings instead of ours and we're just as good or better.' But nobody denied his debt to Paris. That only came with the minimalists. They said, 'We're American, nothing but American.' There was a show, 'Twenty Years of American Painting', organised by the International Council of the Museum of Modern Art and sent to Tokyo, Kyoto, New Delhi and Sydney, and the State Department decided to send me along with the show – half of which I thought was bad. And I went to the opening in Tokyo with this wonderful Japanese the USIS had assigned me as an escort. And he came into the first room of the show and there was a Gorky and a Pollock and I forget what else, and he said, 'Oh, how French!' Those artists, had they been alive, would have loved to hear him say that. It's only the likes of younger Americans, brash ones, who say, 'We're American, we don't do things the European way' – which is nonsense. Pollock, when interviewed, didn't go on about being American. He knew better. We came out of Europe, we're tied to Europe and that's all there is to it, and we're no more non-European than the Germans are or the Portuguese.

CH *Do you feel that now? Do you feel that moment of the mid-sixties, when Judd and Co turned their backs on European art, is now over?*

CG I don't know whether it's over or not. I dare say there are plenty of American artists shooting their mouths off about how we're American, not European.

CH *There's clearly plenty of hostility now, which I've heard expressed informally, to what seems like a European invasion – to put it in vulgar terms – a European invasion of the market.*

CG No. That's literal. That's the truth. It's there. But New York had become, as the fifties wore on and more so in the sixties, as parochial as Paris had been in the old days. European art was given less of a chance until just lately with the Neue Wilden and the Italians. I like that, except that the European art that's broken into New York isn't so hot. But I like the breaking of the parochialism.

CH *The impression I get, walking around SoHo, is something very like what it was like walking around the Left Bank of Paris in the early sixties, when what you had was the sense of a market based on the idea that Paris was the centre, while what it was really was just the centre of the market. So you had a lot of stuff produced to feed this market – which could swallow a lot of bad art. The argument I had with Michael Steiner the other night was over his suggestion that a wave of what he called non-art from Europe was destroying and impairing the conditions for the production of art. I see it differently. I see the academicism of the market and the capacity of the market to swallow everything as being what destroys the critical conditions.*

CG I disagree 100 per cent. The market is a handy factor to bring in – a handy explanation. There was a Bob Hughes piece in *New York Review of Books* about what has happened in New York art – all about dealers, dealers, dealers. In my 40 years around art that's not borne out. There's art opinion, whose moves are mysterious to me. I haven't seen the market or the dealers interfering with the production of good art – yet. Any more than market conditions in the 1890s, when Bouguereau was on top, interfered with the production of art by Cézanne or by Signac for that matter, or by Bonnard or Vuillard, who were maybe doing their best things then. Market conditions in the early 1900s in Paris – who was the great international star in painting in those days? Eugène Carrière – who wasn't a bad painter incidentally. He was world famous. He wasn't a great painter. He had a big influence on photography, with the soft focus and sepia. Again, he wasn't a bad painter. The Museum of Modern Art finally brought itself to acquire a Carrière a while ago. We want to find an agency for whatever happens – somebody's engineered something. We prefer most of all conspiracies – things have been arranged, that explains it. And of course dealers and commercialism are always the bad boys. Everything's contrived and so forth. I say nonsense – in my experience. When Leslie Waddington puts on a show of Julian Schnabel in London he's not furthering Schnabel's reputation. What's happened is that Schnabel's reputation has forced Leslie to show him. The agent is art opinion, not Leslie's venality or whatever.

CH *So what happens if art opinion goes off?*

CG Well, it's gone off ever since Manet's day. Ingres was opposed early on. New art became controversial with David even before Ingres.

CH *I wasn't trying to describe a conspiracy.*

CG No, I know you weren't. I was just scotching the notion.

CH *I was trying to identify a tendency, just as you yourself have tried to identify a tendency.*

CG I haven't seen commercialism interfere with art in my time – with the production of art. Contemporary art fares, in scheme, the way it has since Manet's time. The best art starts off in the background. It comes foreground after ten or 20 years. Then another, later kind of 'new' art comes foreground. We saw that in this country. Abstract Expressionism was the top thing – but not on the market until the later 1950s. Then there came a stock market decline from February to May 1962 and Abstract Expressionism went out, stopped selling. The second-generation abstract expressionists disappeared the way flies do in the fall. Pop Art came in the fall of 1962. Meanwhile – this is part of the ecology – the first-generation abstract expressionists rose again. There was Pop Art occupying the foreground but there was also first-generation Abstract Expressionism becoming consecrated, and bought and valued and so forth, and the two things went together.

CH *Would you see the enormous early success of Jasper Johns, and to a lesser extent Robert Rauschenberg, as a reflection of that tendency for the market in second-generation Abstract Expressionism to collapse?*

CG It coincided. All I can say is that Johns and Rauschenberg – as bad as Rauschenberg could be – looked refreshing by comparison with the second-generation abstract expressionists – by comparison with 10th-Street Abstract Expressionism. Cause and effect here – I don't know enough. Somebody ought to do a dissertation on that. Another dissertation ought to be done on the ups and downs of art opinion in the second half of the nineteenth century and right up to the twenties, and still another on taste in the twenties and thirties.

CH *You puzzled at Johns in that 'After Abstract Expressionism' article in 1962.*

CG Yes, because I liked him, but he wasn't good enough. He wasn't major.

CH *So why did you feel you had to puzzle over him?*

CG It was a premonition, I guess. When he had his retrospective at the Whitney three to four years ago everything that I'd liked fell off. Not only the 'number' and the 'flag' paintings – I'd liked more than that. They all fell off. The record shows early success has been fatal since the 1850s in any art. Didn't T S Eliot write that when a book of new poems goes over fast we have every reason to suspect it's not so new? Eliot didn't specify at that time that 'new' was not such a value. He knew better.

CH *Do you think the 'disaster' of early success is something it's possible to recover from?*

CG Sure. Anything is possible in art. So far it hasn't happened but

I want to see it happen.

CH *I tend to see the best of Johns's cross-hatched paintings as showing a kind of recovery.*

CG The colour isn't good enough, and it shows he doesn't know how good Olitski is. Not that he's got to paint like him. If right now you're an ambitious painter with major aspirations you've got to see how good Olitski is. Just as in the twenties if you wanted to be major you had to see how good Picasso was, and Leger. Later on, Matisse, who came to the rescue as it were. That seems to be another constant: you'd better recognise who the best artists just before you are, in order to take off – not in order to paint like them – but in order to get enough pressure on yourself.

CH *Would you agree that they are also in a sense your door of entry to what's good in the past?*

CG No, I wouldn't. There are painters who I don't see as major but who've seen the past damn well.

CH *What I mean is that the capacity to identify what is most important in the art of the recent past may be a necessary condition for getting further back, practically.*

CG Possibly. I won't say yes or no. Manet's a special case. He says how good Courbet and Corot were, but he jumped back to Velazquez and Goya. Special case.

CH *I have a personal axe to grind perhaps. I think that for Art & Language the recognition of Pollock – of the necessity of Pollock – has been very much a means of getting access to aspects of Manet, to Courbet perhaps accidentally.*

CG Well I'll be damned. I wish you'd go on record saying that. It pleases me, I don't know for what reason.

CH *It's paradoxically so, perhaps, in ways one certainly couldn't have predicted. That may be to say that it's a practical point of entry, not a theoretical one.*

CG There's no theory here. Come on. Accept your eye and nothing else. What's theory? What has theory got to do with art?

CH *I think it's true that, however much you may admire let's say a painting by Manet or Courbet, you can't use it – you can't make anything practically of that interest – without some confrontation with something more recent.*

CG I'll grant you that without knowing it. Pollock refused after a while to visit the Old Masters. Once at my place, in the early fifties,

I had a book of reproductions of Rubens landscapes. He slammed the book shut and said, 'We paint better nowadays.' I won't repeat what I said, it's too obscene. Now in a funny way he was borne out because I hadn't yet seen any of the Rubens landscapes in the flesh and then I saw them – and Rubens wasn't such a good landscape painter. But that's not what Jackson meant. And Rubens was otherwise a great, great painter (as long as his shop didn't work on his pictures). Morris Louis, when I visited him in Washington, would drive me to the National Gallery and then leave. I'd go in and he'd go home, then come back and pick me up. I asked him why and Louis replied, 'They might get into my blood.'

CH *I have the intuition that in late 1950 or 1951 Pollock let them get into his blood a bit more.*

CC It wasn't because of going to museums, that's for sure. 1952 he began to lose, waver. He painted some all right pictures but –

CH *I don't mean all that rubbishy stuff about how the black-and-white paintings are all depositions and lamentations and so on. But what I get is a sense of engagement, not exactly with the grand historical subjects of European art but with something which is contained in those subjects.*

CC There was something that happened to Pollock in the ten years during which he didn't go near nature – from 1941–42 say to 1952. He learned how to handle paint in an accepted way. And his drawing became way better. He hadn't drawn from life at all during that time. But in 1953 he began to draw with facility, and paint with accomplishedness. All this was like taking place underground in those ten to 12 years. Jackson had been painting great pictures since 1947, and before, and then those 1950 pictures.

CH *Yes, but the works of 1950 are superbly achieved paintings. One of the great things in the early all-over paintings is the sense of something being powerfully practised and learned.*

CC The usual Pollock show would have five first-class pictures and then the other 15 would be so-so. They got better with time – some of them. Some of them didn't. Those *Eyes in the Heat* pictures which just preceded the drip paintings I always thought were good pictures. In 1953 Jackson showed he could paint the way you were supposed to paint, handle paint according to tradition. But that didn't stop the 1953 picture in the recent Acquavella show from being bad.

CH *But it's 1950 to 1951 that fascinates me.* Echo, No. 14 *– it seems to me there's an engagement – there's a marvellously practised and articulate* *technique which has its accomplishment in that 1950 show. And then –*

CC God, you're so intellectual! You're fancying it up. You may be on to something, but in 1948, 1949 he'd been doing terrific painting.

CH *Yes sure. I'm not talking about quality. I'm not talking about what you mean by quality.*

CC Oh, I beg your pardon. You're talking about the practised bit.

CH *I'm talking partly about what must have been his problems as regards what he was in a position to work with and go on with.*

CC Ah. I'm too intolerant. Okay, go ahead.

CH *That Lee Krasner quote, 'What do you do after the 1950 show?' That is a practical problem.*

CC That's a bit of hindsight. What went on was that Jackson went back to booze just before that great 1950 show. There were wrangles. That's why I'll never write a book about Pollock. I was there.

CH *I'm trying to think practically what it must have been like to have that 1950 show and see the work on the walls. There's a certain sense in which the very quality of the work cuts off the possibility of just that being developed. He wrote to Ossorio in 1951 that he was drawing on canvas 'with some of my early images coming through'. The early imagery refers to the 1938–41 drawings – that's Picasso, there's a lot of Picasso in them. It's a kind of re-engagement or re-entry.*

CC He liked Picasso even when he was bad.

CH *I feel that, in thinking again about Picasso, he had to let back in a bit of what came with Picasso – Picasso's interest in Rembrandt, for instance. The kinds of themes that come up in those mid-forties etchings when Pollock must have looked at Picasso's graphics – reclining figures, self-portraits. Those black-and-white paintings are full not so much of reclining figures and portraits but of what was dealt with in dealing with those themes.*

CC Maybe. You know I don't like this kind of talk because I was there. That entitles me to nothing, my being there. Jackson always longed for the third dimension. Unnatural painter though he was, with no gift for nature, he always longed to go back to modelling, just as Gorky did, and just as De Kooning did. But abstraction – I hate that word – abstractedness was liberating for Jackson. It wasn't for Gorky or De Kooning. You long to model when you paint. You not only long to do something from nature, you long to go into the third dimension. Man, that generation – I won't compare myself – but I know when I tried to paint abstract, Oh God, I yearned to be back carving around the figure. I fudged by going into landscape. Sure Jackson always was nostalgic for the figure.

CH *But could it possibly be the priority of your 'logic', your necessity –*

CG No.

CH *– that would lead you to see it as nostalgia, as a kind of backwardness?*

CG When Pollock went back into modelling it didn't look good enough. He was guided by that. That's all. It didn't look good enough, or let's say 'major'. So he had to stay flatter. That's the way it works. Manet flattened art, for God's sake. It didn't look strong enough otherwise. That's all. That forced your hand. Hell, you wanted to do the figure, get involved with the female body and model it – you wanted to do apples or what not, model, model, model. But you couldn't any more. It didn't come out good enough. Somebody had always done it a bit better.

Gorky longed to be able to paint from nature. De Kooning said to me he didn't like any damned abstract painting except Rothko's. That showed what was wrong with Bill's eye. Rothko was a great painter for a while, but all the same De Kooning should have mentioned Pollock, but he couldn't see Pollock. Nor could Hofmann. Nor could hardly any of Pollock's painter contemporaries in New York, as he found out when he visited the Cedar Street Tavern. But sure, even in the black-and-white paintings he couldn't let himself model.

CH *I'm intrigued by that tension between the desire to model as you call it, the instinct –*

CG Or shade, let's get it right down to shade.

CH *– and the impossibility of making a plausible painting by doing that, which I accept.*

CG Plausible yes. No come on, we choose our terms: not good enough. Plausible yes, but not good enough – the difference between major and minor.

CH *Okay, but that sense of 'not good enough' becomes what feeds back into the practice as a working problem at some level – some intuitive level.*

CG That's the whole thing. That's what drove these people to go flat.

CH *Now I'm suggesting that that tension, which is a grand tension, an historical tension, becomes a productive one.*

CG You should write that. Because I've maintained for a long time that if you didn't know western art of the past you couldn't see abstract paintings in the present, and I didn't know how to put it.

CH *You would misread it.*

CG That's right, you don't see enough of the picture.

CH *And you don't see why it's difficult.*

CG Yes, that tension. I hate the word 'tension', but I don't know what to put in place of it. You write it, that's fine. It's true that the Japanese and Indians now have seen the point of western abstract painting. I witnessed that in the sixties in Japan and in India. They'd gotten the point. I kept wondering why because I felt, before, that you had to know Rubens and Rembrandt and Titian and Raphael, and so on, in order to see how good Pollock was – if you could see how good he was, or as far as anyone could or still can.

CH *I think a lot of the best modern art is born out of the encounter with what can't be done – with what's impossible.*

CG Well, it's not impossible because it comes out in good pictures.

CH *No, when I say impossible I'm talking about the sort of thing you mean by shading.*

CG But you can't do it any more. You're lost if you do it, so you do what? You just say goodbye to it for the purposes of major art.

CH *But that hanging on to, and longing in respect of these people, your sense of respect for the achievement of doing it in the past –*

CG You want to do it yourself, but you can't because it won't come out good enough. The main thing for artists is to be able to make it good, and it's nothing to do with expressing yourself. Sometimes your vision comes in, yes, you've got a vision, but in order to be able to make it good – major rather – you have to go flat. Just as in Italy by the fourteenth century you could no longer stay Byzantine flat and make good enough painting.

CH *Yes. But bad abstract painting, it seems to me, is produced out of the acceptance of the necessity of that flatness, abstraction. That's what produces bad art.*

CG No, that's too easy. What produces bad art in any time? If you go to the new André Meyer wing at the Met you see this delicious small Meissonier, delicious small Gérôme, and elsewhere good smaller Landseers, and then when they had to go bigger they couldn't put the picture together. You see this larger-size Meissonier, *The Battle of Friedland*, and the thing's dull. Degas said of that picture that everything in it was made of steel except the armour. In order to paint bigger pictures from the 1860s onwards – I mean pictures, say, at least three by four – you had to go flatter, inexorably. That's what hindsight shows. So Manet did it and then the impressionists did it. But the

Salon virtuosi – and they were good – they couldn't bring it off. This is Schnabel today, painting big pictures. He can't bring them off, though he can put paint on. It's the business of putting a picture together.

I feel uncomfortable in talking about the necessity of flatness. I mean that only with regard to major pictorial art in this time. There's still so much good minor art that embraces illusion and modelling and shading. And I value minor art, I'm not just for big names. The nineteenth century is strewn with so much good, good minor art. The trouble is I grew up into art insisting on the 'major' for American painting and sculpture. And in an article like 'Towards a Newer Laocoon', which I did very early on and have been embarrassed by ever since, I was too short and dogmatic in my apotheosising of the abstract without emphasising that I was focusing on the major alone. I was so callow back then, with my quasi-Marxist rhetoric. At the same time, reviewing in the *Nation* and *Partisan Review*, I praised painters like Edward Hopper and Arnold Friedman, who loathed abstract art, and still others who were far from abstract.

CH *Do you see any figurative painting today which is large-scale and which sustains itself?*

CG Balthus, when he's good. I think he's fallen off some, but he's good. But it's not major, dammit. There are others, Lucian Freud in your country, Peter Blake and William Thomson – especially Thomson, who should be better known. And Blake I've long had a special fondness for, though I haven't seen anything of his for maybe ten years now. Still others, but none of them major.

CH *And younger? You mentioned Schnabel earlier. There are a lot of people Schnabel has been lumped with. Do you discriminate between them – Germans and Italians?*

CG I've only seen reproductions of Anselm Kiefer, but he always looks better to me than the other Germans. Except the other day I saw a big A R Penck – and I always thought better of Penck, too, than the other Germans – a real try, though if you compare him with Olitski or Noland he looks on a lower level. Mike Steiner told me you don't like Olitski. That's your challenge. You'd better like him.

CH *I don't like Penck or Kiefer either.*

CG Well, maybe I've got you wrong.

CH *I've seen Pencks that look good in reproduction.*

CG They reproduce very well. Why shouldn't they? There was this tall one – I'd never seen one that big and I had to ask who painted it because I couldn't believe it was Penck.

CH *Sandro Chia, Enzo Cucchi, Francesco Clemente?*

CC I've told you about Clemente, that show in New York that had one sweet – and better – picture that was a giveaway. It's not because of that. The pictures are not much good, that's all. And the 'bad painting' stuff must play a part: the tendency to say 'Let's paint bad'. The explanation would take too long and I'd have to qualify too much.

CH *Have a go.*

CC Okay. You've already heard me say this. In the early sixties a new generation of artists and art lovers came up. It seemed that the reputedly best art of the previous 100-odd years had always been far out, had always created scandal – Manet, the impressionists, and so forth. The categorical imperative became 'far out'. And Pollock was the key example. Didn't the painters in downtown New York in the fifties use to say Pollock was a freak painter, not a real painter, not like De Kooning and not like Kline and not like Milton Resnick? And then it was like someone had bugle-called you up in the morning: 'Okay, now we know art. This is it. Far out, far out.' The Pop artists sensed it, and the minimalists and the conceptualists knew it.

CH *I'd like to say something about that moment in the early sixties in relation to what came after. I remember you said something about it in an article called 'Avant-Garde Attitudes' – it was a lecture you'd given in Sydney. It seems to me that that reading of Pollock was to do with mistaking the means of addressing the problem for the problem itself.*

CC That they misunderstood Pollock was beside the point in this context. I still want to meet some people who can tell the difference between a good and a bad all-over Pollock.

CH *It seems to be an endemic weakness in American culture that a change of medium – a new medium – is mistaken for a new meaning.*

CC It's spread all over western Europe too. Come on now, don't just pin it on us poor Americans. It's spread all over the western world.

CH *I'd like to try to defend my own history a bit. I'd like to defend what went on in the later sixties, early seventies. We suffered – by we, I'm talking about Art & Language now, and I'm speaking largely for others rather than myself – we suffered people making precisely the same confusion of how we were doing what we were doing, with why we were doing it.*

CC Now you've gotten into art history I bring it down to that. I don't think it was all that conscious about getting down to, referring to art history of the recent past – I'm simplifying – but at any rate far-outness has become by now official art in this country, and elsewhere.

CH *But that was a terrible condition, and I think what we were trying to do was to work through that condition. to work through Minimal Art and what that did to art, to work through Duchamp and what he did to art, and so on. This is hindsight.*

CG Okay. I want you to write those 2,000 words or more to explain. Because I don't get the prose.

CH *It interests me – and I could never have foreseen it – that what seems to have happened, more or less accidentally, was that we'd worked ourselves to Pollock and to Manet, to Courbet and to Picasso. It was the last thing I could have foreseen.*

CG Well, that showed there was something real going on.

CH *There was.*

CG Which I doubted when I saw those pastiches of Pollock in magazines. I didn't draw any conclusions from them but I was given pause.

CH *They were serious.*

CG Yes I was given pause. So poor Jackson is the culprit! He wouldn't have known what to make of it.

CH *But he was also serious.*

CG Jackson was as serious an artist as there ever was.

CH *I find it very hard to find anything more recent which is serious like that.*

CG Oh look. All these paintings around here – not because I've got them – they're serious.

CH *The long Noland over the bookshelf.*

CG That's not serious?

CH *No, I guess it is.*

CG It sure is. Again about Pollock, Pollock was the first one to fool around with the shape, the format. And I remember seeing those first paintings in which he did that – and I wouldn't call them pictures I called them 'friezes' – and they're some of the best things he ever did.

CH *And some of the worst.*

CG Until that second show in 1950 he always had shows with two-thirds failed pictures and one third successes. That was taken as a matter of course, by me, and you know I think by his wife too, who had a better eye than I did back then. I learned a hell of a lot from her, just as Jackson did. Well, so the far-outness is here. You change that. You change that. This is the foreground. The foreground is official art, it's middle-brow art. Pop Art is middlebrow. And some of the guys could paint. Jim Dine could paint, though he's dumb as the day is long, and Lichtenstein can paint. And Warhol had his moments, but when he did a show of all-abstract pictures you saw that he didn't have much at bottom. And Johns's cross-hatching pictures – he doesn't know what it's about. He hits the right colour by accident, you can see that. When he hits the right colour he's good, but –

CH *Ah, but your theory must rule out –*

CG There's no theory.

CH *Okay, your aesthetic protocols, your morality must rule out.*

CG No morality. Don't bring that word in. Morality has nothing to do with the aesthetic. Rule out what?

CH *Well, if you are told by your response and your response is a response to quality – how can you justify saying that he hits it by accident?*

CG Because it looks like accident. That I say 'by accident' is of no importance. It's not important that I said that. That's beside the point. That's journalism.

CH *Journalistic denigration.*

CG Denigration's right. But when you see the other pictures you realise Johns is on to something, maybe it's serious and all that, but that someone like Olitski, who can draw better than he, would spurn it. That doesn't matter. That doesn't pertain either. But how do you know it's colour? In this case the choice of one colour is going to make a Johns picture, and so it seems. Since so many of them fail when only one or two of them succeed, the successes must be by accident, otherwise he'd be closer in the other pictures.

CH *But you said before that what you look for is a measure of success and failure.*

CG Yes. But there are failures and failures. If Johns in the last cross-hatching show of his I saw had had four good pictures, I'd think that's enough to do it. But he only had one. That was it.

CH *Four's enough, but one isn't.*

CG It's like Brice Marden, who is so ungifted, so untalented, but I've seen two good pictures by him – and they were accidents.

CH *That's two more than I have.*

CG And one of them was a giveaway because it was pretty. He had to go to prettiness like Clemente did. When I use the word pretty I get flayed. People objected to Monet's water-lily paintings because they were pretty. They didn't know what they meant by pretty. They objected to Olitskis because they thought they were pretty, and they didn't know what they were talking about. Iridescence is pretty? No. Iridescence can be great. Thank God iridescence came in in the late-nineteenth century to relieve Victorian mud and darkness. At the Carnegie Biennial I remember the public going for Jack Smith, an English artist, because he was the most iridescent.

CH *Yes. He suddenly won a prize. He was best when he was what was called a 'Kitchen Sink' painter in the early fifties.*

CG Yes. I remember Bratby too. Bratby's character is something else. Bratby had something but he wasn't doing it.

CH *I want to go back to this question of whether or not good art can be made by modelling. You want to do it but you can't.*

CG It doesn't turn out. It turns out – oh – all right, but it's not big, it's not the most.

CH *Okay. We – I don't know quite whether to say 'we' or 'my friends', because we have such funny relations of production – they're trying to make a painting at the moment. The idea is to set up the sense of drama. Always go back, go back, have a point of reference. The person they found was Delacroix. There's a sort of nightmare subject derived from Delacroix's* Hercules Feeding Diomedes to his Mares. *The idea was to snow on top of it – the snow as a surface which would make recognition of the dream or nightmare implausible. What they found is that there is no way you can paint snow as a surface without its looking naturalistic, whether you drip the paint, whether you make brushstrokes look like brushstrokes or whatever – absolutely no way.*

CG I can see that.

CH *So they had again to have another point of reference, to have another configuration. There's a funny conjunction in what they found as reference points: Leonardo's* Deluge *and Van Gogh's* Starry Night. *You take the rhythm and make the snow conform to it. Now that's the intellectual bit –*

CG – it's not intellectual, it's something else. It's not intellectual.

CH *It's sort of systematic. But what seems to be necessary is that a problem should be generated, or something should happen that the system was not designed to take care of.*

CG What's my reaction to all this? God, it's a supercilious one. That's a desperate way of making art. Desperate, desperate, desperate.

CH *Absolutely right.*

CG It still could come out great in spite of it being desperate.

CH *I think the conditions are desperate. What we do have is a culture of ruins and fragments.*

CG Journalism. We've got maybe a culture threatened by decadence, but otherwise. I think how good mosaic art became in the throes of Roman decadence in the sixth century. I'd say that someone like this kid Daryl Hughto, he paints bad, he paints good, but it's got nothing to do with decadence. It's not desperate.

CH *I'd see that painting as highly unsophisticated.*

CG Hey look, if you can't see Olitski you're not where the best contemporary painting is at –

CH *I had my 'crisis' with Olitski in 1968 I wrote a piece about Olitski which he actually liked – whether that was quixotic or not I don't know. The dilemma I was caught on the horns of then was that the invitation – I'm using terms you won't like at all –*

CG Of course not.

CH *– the invitation to assent to the pictures was very seductive. I couldn't divorce the pictures from the conditions which that assent seemed to require of me.*

CG You have to explain when you talk about conditions.

CH *I think I felt that I didn't want a culture in which that was 'good painting' – that's playing into your hands.*

CG It sure is. Good God, is it playing into my hands!

CH *Now what I would say – I'll play English and say I can see why you and others would want to see that as good painting.*

CG We don't want to, we're forced to. Do you think we choose?

CH *It doesn't force me.*

CG I know, that's too bad for you. That's aggressive on my part. I don't want to get aggressive. I want to add to the sum total of human happiness. A lot of people can see Noland. A lot of people can't see Olitski. He meets more resistance in Europe than over here. The resistance is so close and hard and it's promising for Olitski's future.

CH *That could be romanticised.*

CG It can be, but I'm not romanticising, I'm not. I have my own take on Olitski's stuff so I can't romanticise him. I don't think he's better than Noland, but he's where painting's at. Olitski's where painting's at, but it's not where painting has to go.

CH *I wondered whether Noland's tendency to use higher-keyed colours in the late sixties and 1970, might have had something to do with Olitski. If so I'd see it as a bad influence.*

CG Olitski can't use a red and only seldom a blue. He can use a yellow, he can use ochre. That came out 15 years ago. He can't use saturated colour except when staining back in the early sixties.

CH *There was a painting at Kasmin's in London, back in 1968 I think, which I tried to come to terms with, a big yellow one.*

CG He can fail when the canvas shape goes too high. It depends on the format, its proportions.

CH *There seems to have been an attempt in the late sixties to get away from tone, to lighten painting.*

CG You mean values: dark and light. We take the French term, 'value'.

CH *Yes, and I think that was not like the need in the forties and fifties to do away with shading. It was something different, and I think that no good painting yet has got away from tonal values.*

CG Painting can go anywhere. Vuillard in the early 1900s is a good example. He did some landscapes where the values are so close.

CH *One suggestion that I want to make is that if you keep going, persist, and if that persisting is let's say serious, for want of a better word, you can't help at some point running up against what you would call the logic, the necessity. You must engage with problems which are historical, historically real, or you might as well not bother.*

CG 'Historical' is a real problem. I want to know what you mean by that. What came up with Modernism was that in order to make better art, art which measured up to the standards of the past, your hand was forced.

CH *But surely what you must do is to work to get into that position where your hand is forced.*

CG Yes that's right. It's by seeing how good the best art was or is, and especially how good the best art just before you was.

CH *But what you can't predict is how to get into that position where your hand is forced.*

CG Of course you can't predict. You have to see first.

CH *But also the procedures by which artists have got into that position must at times seem ludicrous, accidental.*

CG I don't know. It depends on where you live. You had to live in Paris from the 1840s on to get position. It's always mattered a lot where painters and sculptors lived.

CH *One of the reasons why the notion of avantgardism predicated on Pollock is so weak is because what it does is to take the accidental means of getting into that situation for the means of getting into a similar situation. That's the Robert Morris approach, that what's interesting about Pollock is that you can recover the procedure directly from the work, so what you do is produce stuff which you call 'Process Art', which is all about recovering the procedure. That's a nonsense.*

CG Morris wasn't even that much interested. That's a judgement. What he did before he went – what? I won't call him conceptual, no. When you saw Morris's first plaques at the Green Gallery you saw conventional good taste. They were nice and they weren't good enough. In order to escape his good taste he had to go far out. That's a way of escaping conventionality. The same thing for Carl Andre. So you go far out. Also you know that going far out is the way that art history, art history in terms of Pollock and so on, is supposed to be made.

CH *But that's to mistake the tension in the procedures for what you call the logic of development.*

CG Of course. It's the way to score instead of making good art. And you've kept your conventional sensibility. The giveaway on Donald Judd was the paintings he did. He hadn't got the point of good painting. He'd got the look of what good painting is supposed to look like, but he hadn't got good painting. In Judd's case his boxes were always too high for their bases. If he'd really had it the boxes would always have been lower. That's the way I saw it, I could always make his boxes better.

CH *What was good about Judd though, from a European point of view, was that some of the things he had to say about European art were effective.*

CG Did it help? With what artists?

CH *I suppose I'm talking about some of my friends who would see Judd now as ludicrous.*

CG He's never ludicrous. He's not laughable. He's not so hot that's all. I'm tempted now to diagnose you, which is the most aggressive thing you can do to another human being – that is unless somebody comes to you and says, 'Look, I'm paying you to diagnose me.'

TE *He won't mind. He likes it.*

CG Okay. There's a certain way in which you're literal. In my book it's the wrong way. It means you're being serious in the wrong direction. You've asked so I've got to say why, which is even more aggressive. You don't look hard enough. You think too much. There's too much thinking going on. You can think about politics and you can think about personal relationships, which is the most important thing in life – though you have to do more feeling there than thinking – but when it comes to art, watch out for thinking. Let your eye or your ear, your taste, take over. Don't think too much. I think Leavis and Eliot – I've read French and I've read German literary criticism – but in my book they're the two greatest literary critics, and I would correct them by saying that where they go wrong is in thinking. When Leavis brought morality in – he didn't need to – he went a little wrong. Eliot had read philosophy and goddammit he's good when he's good. But it's still a sickly cast of thought that tricks him. I'd say you've got to be readier to just go with your eye and not decorate it. I sound American primitive. Just your eye – good and bad, good and bad, let's start from there – the hell with thinking. Let that come later, and the historical questions. History's there in our bones. It's there. You want to fantasticate things with all this culture. The culture's there and we can't get it out of our flesh. 'Penetrated' is too weak a word, it's part of our warp and woof. We don't need to bring it in. It's there – to use that awful word – inexorably. And so you go honest. If you want to make a career as an art writer you'd better do more than that, but we're not talking about careers now, we're talking about the truth.

CH *When I went in to lecture at the Fogg Art Museum there was this big building and over the door was written the word 'Veritas'.*

CG That's not Harvard's motto.

CH *No, it's the Fogg's.*

CG Well there is nothing better. St John said, 'The truth shall make you free', and was he right. There's nothing like the truth. The truth is delicious. You can eat the truth, you can drink it and you can sleep with it. There's nothing like the truth. And sometimes, when it's about yourself it hurts. It hurts, but it still makes you free. Alas, the truth can also be a weapon, a means of punishment instead of correction. But we're away from art now.

Issues 73, 74 and 75, February, March and April 1984

Kenneth Martin

interviewed by Alastair Grieve

Relationships of intervals

KENNETH MARTIN My own work is based on the study of the relationships of intervals, in the European tradition of painting, this interest is in all my works.

ALASTAIR GRIEVE *Is this back to the Dutch, to De Hooch?*

KM It's back to how I learnt it at the very start, copying at the National Gallery. This use of interval came from my interest in European art, from Poussin and the great masters. That was the theory that sustained me. I could not eternally do screw mobiles because there was this thing behind me. Mary (Kenneth Martin's wife, d. 1969) started it pretty well straight away, it's architectural. It goes right up, we see it in Renaissance painting, in Ingres, in Degas, and Seurat, and it goes right up, which is not really understood, and actually the interval in Kasimir Malevich is something different really, some of his compositions look like aeroplanes.

AG *He was interested in flight.*

KM Yes. It is the first ones which are most remarkable. He was a sort of religious artist.

AG *You say in your 1979 Townsend lecture: 'The development of abstract art is most powerful when it goes towards the symbolic structure rather than the decorative composition.' And in another place you talk of your own work as 'life in epitome'. Is your interest in interval concerned with life?*

KM Now, I'd like to see the whole of that lecture again because I've moved further than that really. It is 'life in epitome'. In the essay 'On Construction', I use 'reality'. I vary the meaning of the word 'reality' I find but, the thing is, each work is in a world of its own and each work of art, no matter how realistic it is, is conventional, because you have to have a convention to put it down. So you are making something which is 'life in epitome'. I'm interested in this thing with regard to the sinusoid, this relationship of art and nature. You really go to bigger things, not bigger things but things that happen most powerfully. I mean a flower does not have any power over you but the sun rising and the sun setting does. Now, I look out of this window: I don't see the sun until getting on towards midday, and then I only see it for a little while because, only for a week or two now, it goes behind this towerblock. If I sit here and look there and keep looking, at the same time every day, I can see the sun either coming down or going up and then also as it gets higher, it goes more round that way, and then there's a time when the sun comes in this window round about seven o'clock in the morning. I mean, I live in a world of nature. People think of nature as green fields, I live in a world of nature. You want to express that, it's always occurring. I mean anything's the use of a sinusoid – and the arabesque – it's always occurring. Another thing I've been interested in, through these recent paintings, is where things affect one another. When one line crosses another line it's affected by it and so you're beginning to get these bends, lines changing their colour or changing their direction.

AC *The lines bend when they cross another line. Do they shift 10 degrees or switch onto the next point at the edge or what?*

KM The next point, there are points all round. In a sense they're like a Vantongerloo piece of solid perspex which comes to a knot and then another piece. Or it's like a thing that affected me a great deal, this figure of Matisse's *La Serpentine*. This had a terrific effect on me when I saw it in the Moderna Museet in Stockholm [seen on a recent visit for an exhibition of his work at the Galerie Blanche]. I nearly cried I was so excited. You see you've got the top part which is terrific and then the legs right at the bottom which are also terrific. That relationship of one leg with the other is absolutely marvellous. They are both remarkably felt, all the way through, but the top and the bottom make you weep they are so marvellously done. There was a Vantongerloo as well that did something and those two really made my trip to Sweden.

AC *I was wondering about the start of the 'Chance and Order' paintings in 1969 and your use of a numbered pack of cards, drawn at random, to fix the points for the lines. You talk, in your Townsend lecture, about some artists who carry through systematic permutations exhaustively, and I suppose an example might be Richard Paul Lohse, but your use of chance, of the numbered pack drawn at random, makes you very different. What gave you the idea?*

KM Actually they're just done with numbers, often written on the back of pieces of paper. That's really as far as I've taken chance. I've not done any *I Ching* or anything like that because I have not wanted to, I've used the ordinary methods of European construction I suppose. I mean I draw the numbers out and it gives me an order straight away and I can use that order and I can turn it around. The order is changed by the event of the one meeting the other, but it gives me that order. Chance gives me an order. It's almost like using a landscape. It gives me a motif. I realise what I haven't done when I look at John Cage, those things with *Finnegans Wake* where he goes through it and the change is going on right the way through and gets delightful, sort of scintillating. The way he does it is much deeper and more profound in a way. I'm told that I'm like François Morellet but that disturbs me because I'm not in the least.

AC *How does Morellet use chance? Doesn't he get numbers out of a telephone book?*

KM Oh yes – he's quite a different thing. In a sense he's less academic than I am and in a sense he's more academic. I'm using the academic methods of art but he's making an academy. One of the difficulties of my work is that I approached construction through composition. But other people like Lohse, Max Bill, and later people like Morellet, they are starting from scratch. I, in a sense, stumbled my way along. Morellet's more outward, I'm more ingoing. With my work the line is real, when it goes down, it's real. It's painted and it gets more real as I work. Its realness then affects others. I've used that quite a lot, by changing of colour. Now, what could I use? I've got the character of a line. How can I develop that character within the simple convention of drawing, of painting? How can I develop it? Well, to begin with the line has two ends, it comes from one place and goes to another place, so then it can be said to have a direction. Then the thickness can be placed on one side of the line or the other, so then I have an emphasis on right or on left, so I've got two characters. I don't alter the lines arbitrarily, I don't give them a hierarchy as regards character. I find that is far too complex. I find with all these things that you're really in a sense out of your depth in a moment. These paintings I've been doing for this exhibition, they're complex but I've gone into it because I want to see what would happen: 'Mozart has written of how in prolonged inactivity, on a coach journey for instance, he was able to build a piece of music in his mind so that at the end he could remember it completely. And not only this, he was able to imagine it clearly as an edifice altogether in one and the same time.' (From the essay 'On Construction'.)

AC *You say you don't know the way something is going to end up. You are not able to forecast it?*

KM I think that somebody who plays chess could work it out in their mind. I can do it a little way, but not very far and then I forget what I've worked out because if I think of what I'll do tomorrow or something and then I forget.

AC *You talk in your Townsend lecture about the difference between your drawings and your paintings, how your drawings show the method being worked out while your paintings are more contemplative. But do you want people who look at your paintings to be able to work out the method you have used, or is that not important?*

KM You see, I'm really not all that concerned with people. I suppose I am, but I'm not really concerned with explaining life to people or anything like that. I'm not a preacher. I'm not a preacher at all. The things are done mainly for myself.

AC *But, as you say, there is a difference between your drawings and your paintings. In the drawings you give a key of numbers at the side so that the order can be followed. The paintings don't have that. I suppose this means the paintings are more contemplative, as you say.*

KM Yes, contemplative in being made, in being made. I can go to sleep over them. I could put the numbers on the drawings in pencil and then rub them out. But if I can't see the numbers I make mistakes, so I have to do them in ink. If I have an exhibition and sell them, they are photographed and I can use the photographs. I did one or two which have an overlay to them, the printer made these overlays. I was quite interested in them but the tendency is to show them and have them with the overlay on top and it destroys the colour, it is not necessary. I don't like it. I've done lithographs with printed keys.

AC *Yes,* Metamorphoses, *1976, and* Rotation, *1977.*

KM Yes, there are these two things. I want to do a 48 by 48-inch painting. It's going to take a year. It's a nice size.

AC *What makes you select a particular drawing to be painted? There are many drawings that aren't painted, aren't there?*

KM There are various reasons. When I've done lots and lots of drawings I have almost picked one out at random. I have done drawings where the first drawing done was chosen immediately as the one I'm going to paint. I tend to pick the ones for painting that don't seem to make a figure, not in the sense of figurative but where you see a definite shape, well it could be like that Malevich, a square or something. I've done one or two drawings where I've liked the line which makes a spiral but I wouldn't paint it because it's too definite. It's very, very difficult. When I work on my paintings sometimes, I come back the next morning and the thing looks daft. But as soon as ever I start working with the intervals again, hardly altering them at all, I can see these happenings and I forget all about how bad I thought the painting was because I get interested in the happenings and I think: 'What a clever fellow you are Kenneth Martin.' What is happening with the new ones, where you get the lines changing direction, is that they have less depth. The 'Milton Park' paintings have a great deal of depth but these recent paintings are flat. The surface is a real surface, that's interesting.

AC *What about these 'double' works? They are a recent development, the long format with two images side-by-side. You've always been interested in oppositions, in relations, are the 'double' works an extension of this?*

KM You've got these opposites together. One turns into the other. That's very important. For a long time it was just two drawings, perhaps unrelated to each other, on a sheet of paper which took two squares. Then I wanted to work with translation, turning one into the other, and so I began to work like that. I began to pull one actually touching the other, so I have I now got a space made in between. I've now got three characters, with this space in between – it's a gift, this space: 'By the use of these movements – translation, reflection, rotation, twist – I have been able to produce drawings from the same source which are the complementary or the opposite of each other. I have worked to go further on in these with the ideas that have produced the "Chain Systems" and "Screw Mobiles".' (From Kenneth Martin's Ruskin School lecture of May 1982.)

Issue 74, March 1984

1984–1987

Howard Hodgkin and Patrick Caulfield

in conversation

The edge is important

PATRICK CAULFIELD *The first time I saw your work was a painting,* The Interior of a Museum.

HOWARD HODGKIN In the London Group.

PC *It really stuck in my mind. I think there were two paintings, weren't there? One was of Jack Smith.*

HH That's an incredible memory. Yes, one was of Jack and Susan Smith.

PC *Well of course Jack was teaching me about that time, or had been, I can't remember quite.*

HH Well, it would've been about that time. How does that relate in date to the first time I saw a picture of yours which was in 1959 was it? Which I remember also seeing in the RBA Galleries.

PC *But, just looking through this catalogue, your work has changed quite a lot since I've known you. What's good about this one is it has got a sort of rawness and also dryness that you've developed into a much lusher –*

HH Yes, I tried quite hard to get rid of that. I don't think the way I paint has fundamentally changed very much, it's just that I've managed to join the bits together a bit more.

PC *It's more sort of overlapping in a way isn't it?*

HH Yes, yes.

PC *I think your painting has changed in two dramatic ways since I've known it – becoming more lush, and more complex and intense – but still you've got this autobiographical element haven't you?*

HH Yes, they are always autobiographical. But your pictures are always autobiographical.

PC *Well not in a way as explicit as the titles of your paintings suggest when you name actual friends of yours as though they were – well they are double portraits aren't they?*

HH Yes, or they were.

PC *But the way everything has changed again is that they seem to be less subjective, less about your friends and that sort of more public life, and much more intimate really. I think these are more personal.*

HH Yes. I think that is true and I think that has perhaps made them both more and less explicit. My most recent pictures are probably among the most figurative I've done for a long time. Looking at the early pictures – no they're not as figurative as those.

PC *No. The very early pictures are quite readable for anybody first coming to your work. But what I feel is that with the later work you've pulled out a lot of stops where you've been holding back and it's as though you've got some vision of the limitations of your life and the time you'll be able to produce work.*

HH That's absolutely true, I have. Obviously I'm getting old, and I want to do as much as possible in the time that's left.

PC *Yes. You never indulged in quite such baroqueness and lusciousness before. It's become quite sensual.*

HH No, I don't think I was able to. I think I had great trouble making pictures for a long time and I think that a lot of the baroque sensuality has come from learning by painting. It's not a decision – it's not just by saying I'll do this or I'll do that instead of what I used to do.

PC *Well it's not a dramatic change anyway. It's all very interrelated – a gradual change. But if anything it's even more of a tightrope walk than before. And you're using more variety of devices such as the use of the painted frame. I don't know when you first did that.*

HH A long time ago, but that has gradually increased more and more, I think for a very simple reason, and that is that I think my pictures have become much more illusionistic, the sort of depth of space in them is much greater than it used to be. There's much more *trompe l'œil* than there was, and of course the painted frame makes that increasingly possible.

PC *Yes. Has it got a sort of theatrical theme?*

HH Well, lots of people have said that but I don't think of the theatre when I'm doing it. I'm just trying to place the viewer in a particular relation to the subject, which is what a frame does. It frames what you're looking at and directs your gaze. But I try from time to time to paint pictures that have a sort of multiple viewpoint, but I've never really succeeded; I'm trying to paint one at the moment but I'm having terrible trouble because it's nine feet wide. It's very difficult to make a picture which exists all the way across the surface and I've found willy-nilly it has become centralised even though the subject was meant to have various… It was a sort of interior, so that you got views of the different rooms, but eventually, of course, it has become really like all my other pictures in the sense that there is the centre and there are two sides. It's a symmetrical composition all over again.

PC *But is it an interior?*

HH Yes. It's the largest interior I've ever painted.

PC *One thinks of that shape commonly as a landscape.*

HH It is the sort of shape which is called landscape, but perhaps to paint an interior in that shape is asking for trouble, but I've often – not out of perversity – used funny shapes as supports, which makes life more difficult but in the end perhaps it makes it easier because their identity is so strong. Anyway using a shape that has such a violently impossible identity is I think most difficult. A square runs it very close. I think it's impossible to paint a square picture without having to make a great effort to make it appear not square.

PC *There's this border thing – is it irrelevant to think of it in relation to the borders around Indian miniatures which do seem to be often a part of the image?*

HH That's much easier for other people to say than for me. I've been working with Indian pictures hanging on the walls which have borders so I must become aware of them sort of unconsciously. I'm very concerned about the edges of paintings anyway. It infuriates me to see the edges of even old pictures in the National Gallery covered up by frames. It seems to me that the very edge of the panel or the edge of the paper should be seen.

PC *You did that at the National Gallery. You took the Velazquez out of its frame, which was quite remarkable, to see a painting of that period in the raw, so to speak.*

HH It had a terrible frame. But I've always been fascinated by picture frames. I used to collect them at one time. I started buying picture frames in junk shops, antique picture frames, and selling them to augment my income as a student and I became completely obsessed by them. That's never really gone. I've bought a lot of frames lately, but there aren't any pictures to go in them.

PC *Actually one of the images here I thought could nearly go in a frame like that. This one.* Anecdotes. *It's got a frame round it hasn't it?*

HH No, it's a *trompe l'œil* frame. The difficulty is then to add another frame, a real one on to a *trompe l'œil* frame.

PC *And the edge is very important.*

HH Oh the little bits that show, yes they're essential.

PC *But you often paint on bits of wood that you find. You don't work on shapes for perverse reasons but often because you find bits of wood that are a particular shape.*

HH That are suitable, are suitable for a particular thing. But I couldn't – like Frank Stella did when he did his 'Protractor Series' – sit down and make drawings of all those different geometric shapes and then have them made and then work on them.

PC *How long have you worked on wood?*

HH For at least ten years I should think, probably longer.

PC *I once tried to paint on coconut matting.*

HH Oh well, that's even better than Olitski painting on Wilton carpet.

PC *I mounted it on a hardboard panel which made it incredibly heavy and then I couldn't get the paint in the coconut matting. I should've sprayed it of course but it was the pre-graffiti time, before spray cans were commonly used.*

HH It was in the Bernard and Harold Cohen period of spray painting then.

PC *The Cohens? Did they spray paintings?*

HH Yes. Well, what happened to the coconut matting picture?

PC *Oh it never worked so I abandoned it. I've actually never witnessed you working except on film and I notice the way you attack the canvas with a big brush and sort of hit it at the surface as though you're trying to get some mad temper out of your system. In a way it's surprising that you choose wood and attack it in that way because canvas has this kind of trampoline quality where you can bounce off it. Perhaps more satisfying to attack in that way.*

HH Yes. but I want to be able to attack again and again and again, and the trouble with canvas is that if you attack it more than once or twice there's nothing left. Or else a piece of sort of distressed linoleum.

PC *Oh yes. I know that quality. Both acrylic and oil have that quality if you labour them.*

HH But you see at least on wood you've got endless opportunities of scraping off. Well, not scraping off, but just putting more on. Sometimes I put so much on that if it was on canvas it would just drop off the wall. But I think also that wood has such character of its own. In a piece of wood with grain, particularly a piece of plywood, you get these beautiful wave patterns and things like that which I don't use specifically, but there is already something to work with – either with or against. It has an identity already. Whereas a white canvas is just a piece of white canvas, it hasn't any identity of its own at all.

PC *No. It's very daunting. I can see why people like John Hoyland paint the raw canvas, he doesn't prime the canvas, he just puts a colour on it. He may not show that colour at all, but it gives him something to work to.*

HH Work against, or with or for or on. I remember someone saying that he couldn't start a picture without making a mess on the canvas first. Some people thought that was what he ended up with too, but I did sympathise nevertheless.

PC *The trouble is if you stretch and prime your own canvases, by the time you've done that, I feel that's so much of an achievement that to actually ask to paint a painting on it –*

HH – is asking too much. No, I used to do that, and I used to mix my own grounds, all according to the book. That's how I learnt to make mayonnaise, by adding linseed oil to the emulsion, drop by drop. But I agree with you, I couldn't go near the canvases again for quite a time.

PC *It's rather like when people make handmade paper. If I made beautiful handmade paper I'd feel that that was enough achievement in one lifetime. But you had that wonderful experience in India of having the paper made for you when you had to work on it, or you chose to work on it while it was wet, I'm not sure. Which way was it? But they were a very successful series; they were very much tightrope walking.*

HH Oh they were, and they could've easily become, as I think they sometimes did, either simplistic or banal.

PC *Well, I didn't think they were all 100 per cent successful, but the ones that made it were remarkable.*

HH No, of course they weren't. And there were some far worse ones that were never shown. But it was very hit and miss. But then to me all painting is still very hit and miss. I once long ago described my pictures as anxious improvisations. They've been called that by other people since and I think it's still true. I wish it wasn't. I don't hold any sort of brief for that. It's funny because with age virtuosity creeps in in a rather alarming way. You find that there were so many things that were once very difficult for you to do you can now do quite easily. But the fact that you can do them more easily doesn't immediately give them meaning. In fact it can often make it more difficult to give them meaning. Don't you find that there are lots of things that come more easily? It's bound to happen simply because one has gone on working.

PC *Well, I suppose maybe in a similar way I have pulled out a lot of techniques that have lain dormant.*

HH And you also use far more than you used to. But I do wonder sometimes if people looking at my pictures see what I see.

PC *Well, you started to wear glasses.*

HH But not for working in, to read menus and things.

PC *Well, that's quite hard work. But one wonders what one should see. I mean if you look through a very powerful microscope you can see atoms or whatever. So that is the question, where do you limit your sight?*

HH It is the most horrible thing, wearing glasses which I still do with great difficulty. I find it traumatic. Not from vanity as everyone imagines but because it changes one's vision so much. You said that you found it difficult to wear glasses because you could see better but it made your vision less – and I find that. As soon as I put on the glasses that I wear to read and look through them at anything further than quite close to, all the lines begin to curve and I get these appalling sort of changes of focus. It is probably just the sort of glasses I wear, but it is unnerving when one is so used to seeing in a specific sort of way to have it completely changed.

PC *But if you think of the past when there weren't opticians at every street corner, how did artists work then as they got older?*

HH I think rather like composers who go deaf: they often seem to compose their greatest works when they can't really hear very well, and certainly there are many examples of painters who clearly couldn't see very well any more when they painted some of their greatest pictures. It must have a very liberating effect on the right person.

PC *I suppose Monet is quite a good example.*

HH He couldn't see very well for a very long time. It works in different ways. Matisse couldn't see terribly well or even move very easily when he made his cut-outs which I think would have been impossible for anyone to make had they been able to see well because the impact of these brilliant colours, with edges cut with scissors, would have been too much. Sighted people can stand 100 feet away and think how beautiful.

PC *I suppose one could employ an assistant.*

HH I've always wanted to be able to employ an assistant to do my work for me. So maybe beginning to lose my sight will bring that nearer.

PC *This is a very middle-aged conversation.*

HH Yes. I feel increasingly that there isn't very much time left and that with luck I will have probably another 15 years in which to work. I'm sure that after these next two years when I'm going to have all these exhibitions and so on, I shall paint in a very different way in that I want to rationalise everything and paint pictures that have much more similar dimensions. Because at the moment I paint big pictures and tiny little pictures.

PC *But you've always done that, not just at the moment, but I never think of your pictures as being any particular dimension, except never very large, I suppose.*

HH No. But they actually really fall into amazingly few catagories – quite accidentally – of perhaps four specific sizes. So if I buy a frame in a junk shop and think that I'd like to paint a picture to go in it and I lean it against the wall, I find there's a picture I've already worked on, of almost the same proportions.

PC *I admire you for actually not jumping on the big canvas bandwagon which was, it seemed, a necessity at one time.*

HH Well I remember many years ago, and I think he's a great man and a great critic, but being nonetheless astounded when David Sylvester said that it would be hard nowadays to take a small picture seriously. That bit deep.

PC *But small pictures are very, very difficult to paint.*

HH They're very difficult to paint and yet they grab you, and grab the spectator.

Issue 78, July–August 1984

Leon Golub

interviewed by Jon Bird

The imag(in)ing of power

JON BIRD *Reading through the catalogues and early reviews of your work, I was struck by the persistence of certain themes and the fact that the image of the mutilated body is present over a 30-year period.*

LEON GOLUB It must be a really deep imprint on my unconscious, or call it what you will, I mean, really deeply imprinted. I have always dealt with victims. I had the victims and then I had the priests and the shamans, who were the interveners in society – they weren't victims. Now I still have victims but on another order, another scale, and I have these other external forces who are much more irregular because, if you think of the shamans or priests, they are central to the culture. I no longer believe that I can represent the central figures. I can't show the president, or the prime minister, and show how they affect policy because it's too indirect – they sit around the conference table and make policies. If I make a painting of that it's not going to mean anything much. A shaman waving his arms and making the spirits obey is a gesture we can comprehend in a visual sense. In a way, I'm still doing the same thing but I've caught up with the media, in part anyway. I've been running after media all these years, taking my imagery and locating it in media to make it more relevant. Another aspect which I found looking through my old work, like the *Damaged Man*, 1955, or any of the work in the New Museum show, is that they're very frontal – they're pushed to the forward plane. So my notion of space, of two-dimensional overlay – pushing it forward is what I'm still doing today. I still have what I would call a presentational attitude.

JB *During the fifties and sixties, you were producing semi-figurative imagery with classical references at a time when most work was purely or predominantly abstract. Consequently, you were working very much against the grain of the dominant iconography. To what extent did you feel consciously alienated from that kind of imagery?*

LC I didn't have any connection to what I felt were the dominant visual attitudes. People have found in my work, and it's probably true, that I did things that did relate to the abstract expressionists without necessarily identifying with them. I must have picked it up somehow – it was either 'in the air' or I mimicked their surfaces without knowing it. But the imagery that went on in New York I always felt was kind of shallow. At the time, I thought that De Kooning's 'Women' were relatively shallow representations, and I felt that my pieces had a deeper sense of body-image, of what figures really underwent in our world, what kind of experiences they would have. So I felt I had to push my work. You see, New York is New York, and if certain directions and evolutions are happening in American painting there may not be room for you. So, very early, I had those kinds of awarenesses.

JB *That period, then, goes from the classical narrative relief works, the 'Fallen Warriors' and the 'Burnt Man' series into the 'Gigantomachies'. So, whereas in New York the dominant work was pursuing notions about gesture and the idea of gesture as being the signifier* par excellence *of the artist's authenticity, what you were pursuing was the notion of gesture as in fact being the sign that gave the visible clue to the nature and state of the individual, and an early definition of 'gesture' is 'the employment of bodily movements, attitudes, looks, etc, as a means of giving effect to oratory'.*

LC Rhetorical significance!

JB *Yes, because although we talk about gesture as being the language of the body, there is a way in which it is the rhetoric of the body, and a concern with gesture and the positions of the body had been persistent throughout that period.*

LC Absolutely. In fact, I don't know if even in Greek art you can separate those several definitions of gesture. In other words, the gesturing of the body becomes a kind of civic gesture. If an orator makes a gesture, it's not simply subjective, the gesture carries a lot of weight and is even conventionalised in the understanding of the audience so that they can respond to it properly. It had immediate, verifiable impact upon the audience, giving them certain signals – a kind of language – and it was more of a language then, when rhetoric had more of a public meaning than it has today. The definition of rhetoric has degenerated partly through such ideas as, for example, false consciousness: the orator is thought to have false consciousness. Today the gap in consciousness between who you are, what you're saying, and what is actually going on seems larger – much greater than the gaps that existed in those times.

JB *The scale of the 'Gigantomachies' makes connections with the tradition of history painting. Was there a point at which the production of large public works became something that you wanted to be directly involved in?*

LG Today my figures are roughly twice life-sized in scale. I think of them, though, as being in our scale. In other words, they're actually twice life-size but psychologically they're in the space with us, moving into, and out of, the canvas. They move out, we move in, back and forth, crossing identities along the way. I'm trying to say something about our paradoxical roles where we participate and disclaim responsibility, all at the same time. In the earlier paintings I had a much simpler notion, so the figures are actually bigger even if they are on the same scale – I thought of them in a pedimental sense. In pedimental or frieze-like terms you're distanced and separated from the forms, looking at them from across space so they have a 'god-like' appearance. You can't have intimate connection, for example, with the sculpture of the Parthenon, or any Greek pediment. There's always a big gap, a physical and psychic gap. In the new paintings I try to cross that gap. I like the notion of the gap which is continually infiltrating back and forth. When you look at any of the 'Gigantomachies' you're, in a way, sensing them from a distance, and maybe in some cases somewhat from below.

JB *The work that seems to mark the significant change between those two conceptions of space is the work of the late sixties, the work initially titled* Assassins. *Now they are the size of a cinema screen and because of that scale you read them, scan them, in the way in which you scan a cinema screen, and it was at that point that you also started actually to break into the picture-plane, cutting chunks out so the relationship of the spectator to the image changes and the whole pictorial field alters. This coincided with the point at which the imagery became specific in its reference to current events.*

LG First, it is a gradual process of which part is not even conscious. You have intentions, but those intentions are always being caught in procedures and attitudes which are partly semi-conscious, partly conventionalised. For example, when I was doing the 'Gigantomachies', the Vietnam War was going on and yet I wasn't even commenting on it. So I felt that I had been too generalised and abstracted, despite my intentions, in representing something that was dynamically connected to us, to our lives. And that's when I did *Napalm*, you see. That was an attempt to break the relative stability of the conventionalised screen. I didn't think it was a screen necessarily, but a relatively conventionalised circuit. By putting in those blood-red patches, and by using the scraped-off sludge from the painting and mixing it with colours, it was much thicker. That, in itself, gave a physical tactility to them which interrupted the evenness of the surface – it was physical, material, and that changed the beat of the paint. It changed the tempo, but it didn't change it enough. Finally I got hold of some photographs of guns and soldiers. I started collecting that kind of information and I tried the first painting this way, and at that point I began to cut the paintings. It was almost as if they were bombed-out territory themselves. They're foreign circuits. So, given the kind of art I had, my point of view, it was easy for me to see victims and aggressors. And it wasn't hard for me to realise that you could put yourself in the middle, because we're in the middle of history right now. We are seeing bits and pieces of history all the time on television, interrupted by the soap operas and the advertising, and these bits and pieces are peculiarly disoriented and yet telling, because fragments are very telling. They have a sharp presence. In a way, my tearing of the canvas is symbolic of a thing occurring in the media. The incident itself doesn't diagnose the whole Vietnam War, or even a single campaign. The incident, itself, is so narratively intense that it has a shock value of its own that somehow, for a moment, puts you right in the middle. The scene itself is so sharp that it keeps throwing us, or at us, these bits and pieces, and we're always tripping over them. History is discontinuous, in a certain kind of sense. By taking a fragment you get a curious and intense picture of the whole.

JB *Do you think you were also making a connection with some of the concerns of Modernism? For example, at that time for an artist like Frank Stella, the shape of the canvas and the relationship of image to edge, was fundamental.*

LG I had always delved into that stuff, but I have a totally different definition of 'Modernism'. As far as I'm concerned, Modernism is the art of the modern world. That means that it is a world of relativity, of simultaneity and advanced media transmissions. The world of abstraction, but not the way the abstract artist thought of it, of condensations where essential material comes from all directions and gets condensed in unique formats, like thought clusters. In other words, the big traditions of the past become pierced, porous, infected with other material – accretions are added to them and have their own peculiar condensations. I come to it from the fact that modern communications, habits of thinking, political events, mass societies, force us to have these kinds of conceptualisations. In art, to perceive anything that is going on in the modern world, you can't have a narrow, realistic point of view. You have to be aware how peculiarly opaque and transparent all this material is. It is porous and yet over-determined, all at the same time. So it's from those kinds of logics that I view myself as a modernist.

JB *One of the things that I would argue about your work is the strength of its claim to cognitive status: that is, in one way or another it is about the production of knowledge about the world, although in highly mediated forms. However, we are then thrown back upon the question of the kind of knowledge that art offers that is different, or is additional to knowledge about the world produced by historical or scientific discourses. So, with reference to the subject-matter of your work, if you take what is concretely known about power relations between dominant and oppressed groups, or first and third world countries, what do your representations offer that is extra, or other, to this?*

LG Let's take Renaissance painting. You know, the same thing would apply in the twentieth century if you would give a little twist. In Renaissance painting you get an amazing sensory visualisation of who people were, how they operated, what their sensibilities were, the very way they walked and looked, their introspective attitudes and the way they carried themselves. You cannot always put this into words, maybe, but one gets the sense of the psychic panoply, the self-consciousness that Renaissance man had. If you look at a representative Titian as against a Latin medieval icon, then you realise that the sense of awareness is very different in the two pieces, and so on. So that the very look on their faces tells us something about the way they absorbed information. They look different from modern man and they look different because their awareness of possibility, and their sense of confidence, was considerably different from ours, although, of course, we're very related to them. So that, in a certain way, I think that I am catching those ambiguous, self-conscious looks that modern men have who have, maybe, killed. That might be true for Renaissance man also, but that's indicated a lot less in their paintings – their subjective sense of who they were and how they operated is considerably different from ours. It's like wanting to enter into the psychic constituencies of today. If you were to put a painting of mine, or any other twentieth-century painting, against one from the Renaissance you would receive a very different notion of what the body is, how the body operates upon other bodies and what are the guilt relationships about this. These modern figures are infinitely more self-conscious about their relationship to the spectator, and I think that has to do with how they function today, particularly how mercenaries or the military function, and how we view possibility, not just in military terms, but how we view possibility in general.

JB *In Renaissance painting generally, or in history painting or portraiture up until the eighteenth century, we are confronted with a subject expecting to be viewed in a particular kind of relationship: one which actually places the subject of the representation and the viewer in a relationship of power where, in some respects, the subject is actually dominant. That is, the spectator is in the subservient position because the figures depicted are, mostly, those who have power and they expect to be surveyed. They knew who was going to be observing them and what those relationships were going to be. However, with the nineteenth century and, crucially, the invention of photography, that relationship changes. The distinctions between the spectator and the subjects of representation have started to break down. Now, in your work, the characters seem to me to be expecting to be surveyed, but the ways in which they are being observed and the manner of their observing, is very different indeed.*

LC Absolutely. The whole notion of history and of who they are has been eroded. In fact, the whole notion of who can be shown in a painting, and how they can be shown, has changed considerably. I think, in that sense, European painting is relatively seamless because what you have is a calm sense of purpose which runs through the whole thing, a shared ideology, etc. In my paintings, these guys look so mean because their common sense of purpose doesn't exist, they are lumpen figures. Their self-consciousness is lumpen because, in a certain sense, they are not allowed anything else. And they are aware at some level that they're outlaws. They may enjoy it and they may not – usually they do enjoy it. The thing is that they are outlaws thrown up in a certain kind of society and then used by the society to enforce certain conditions of oppression. Their appearance is in a post-Marxian, post-Freudian world, where different explanations of behaviour operate. Things become much more complex in motivation and they reflect that. They are half aware of themselves.

JB *Marxism displaces the subject in history and questions how that subject is produced. Psychoanalytic theory decentres and fragments the concept of the unified subject. In certain respects, your images are both displaced and decentred. However, an objection that could be made, there is a way in which the real power relations are, in fact, the most hidden. For example, running throughout the work of Foucault is a sense of the infinite productivity of power, making it impossible to follow the tributaries of power to a fixed source. One of the ways in which the real centres of power avoid surveillance, is by actually focusing upon the functionaries. Partly this is because the hegemonic operations of state or corporate or, indeed, cultural power are hard to picture, to represent. Do you think that the concentration in your work upon those functionaries allows power, as it were, to sneak out the back door?*

LC Well, one could take that point of view. I wouldn't say that myself, but I can see that somebody might say that. I think that the representation of power in, say, the Roman era is very direct and immediate. 'You get in the way, we'll knock you down' – that's the Roman notion. It shows in the way they treated the Germans: perfectly straightforward and aboveboard, no complexities involved in it – 'We have sufficient force and we are going to use it' – and no sense of shame or embarrassment or anything else. Simply, that one force is greater than another force and that carries history in its wake. The US also likes to think of itself as using power in as direct a fashion as possible to make its effects felt. However, the transmission has become extremely complex because power needs so many intermediaries – the press, the courts, the legislature, etc. There are all these complex secondary effects, transmission belts, allegiances, etc that are going on all at the same time. Therefore, you get a discrepancy, which is a modem discrepancy, between what is said publicly and what is actually done. It comes from the fact that things that are accelerated are seen differently from things that are slow in transmission. The people, therefore, who are dealing with power, are forced to compensate by acting in more abrupt ways. They have to have a certain simple ideological point and they have to call these guys to get the job done fast, because if it takes too long, the situation can become immeasurably complex. The peculiarly bland look of modem politicians comes, partly, from the grotesquely impossible situation that they are in, where they are themselves the subject of manipulation even while they are manipulating others. It leads them to be arbitrary or simplistic and stereotyped. It leads to the extraordinary kind of irrationality you see in public figures today.

JB *Would you say that there is a strong moral imperative in your work?*

LC Yes, but I would say that you can't easily divorce the moral from the aesthetic, and I don't think you can divorce psychic value. I'm trying to pinpoint who's doing what to whom, so that could be called a moral or ethical act. I want these paintings, if possible, to be open to the types of things that go on today. I want them to be open and porous because porous things absorb in an irregular fashion. I want the canvas surface itself to absorb all sorts of flickering fluctuations in phenomena that inflict themselves upon the surface between the spots and the dashes and the glances.

JB *Would you say that you're more concerned with the representation of politics than the politics of representation?*

LC I'm really interested in both. I think they merge, rather like the issue of moral or aesthetic values. When you say the politics of representation you're actually talking about what representation means, how representation occurs.

JB *How meaning is produced through representation.*

LC I would like to think that the two equal each other – in a certain sense, they reflect off each other all the time. The problem of representation has to be valid because I want the images to look right. That's what I intend by trying to inflect an expression or a gesture so that the painting doesn't fall apart through inaccuracy or false stereotyping, or a mistaken sense of foregrounding. I think of that very seriously because that is the only argument that can really interfere with them, that can deny their validity – that they are essentially false. I have enough self-doubt that I question these images a lot, even while I force them through. I can wonder, myself, to what extent I'm forcing retarded points of view, which would be a serious accusation. I would then try to defend them by showing that they are intrinsically modern in the way that the modern world is composed. Some things correspond to events as we construe them over a period of time and some things approximate better than others. I think a photograph of such an event, say from El Salvador, tells us about things as they occur and, in a sense, gives us a partial construction of what that society is about, and I think my paintings do that too. I think that presupposes a certain relative objectivity, which I think is the best you can get.

Issue 83, February 1985

Richard Deacon

interviewed by Patricia Bickers

Curvilinear v rectilinear

PATRICIA BICKERS *I'd like, if possible, to discuss new directions in your work, but first could you retrace your decision to adopt curvilinear forms instead of rectilinear ones?*

RICHARD DEACON Yes. I found that where one part meets another part in a rectilinear structure became a focus of attention. Whereas in a curvilinear structure the curve as it were rides over those points. There was a period when there was a considerable conflict between a desire to make work which was whole or equal and the tendency to get taken up with part-to-part relationships. One of the advantages of curvilinear as against rectilinear structures is that they are separate from the ground in a way which rectilinear structures aren't. Rectilinear structures seem to be either on or in the ground, they –

PB *Colonise it?*

RD – in a way that a curved structure doesn't. A curved structure has an almost casual relationship to the ground, casual but entirely specific: they are resting on the ground according to themselves, not supported by the ground.

PB *As the scale of your work increases, those considerations of the joins or supports, in order for the structures to tolerate that size, might lead you back into the problem of their having rather more importance than you intend. Also, the casual placing might have to be sacrificed in works meant to be placed outside.*

RD Well, I haven't so far. if one does place work outside, there is a sense in which it does need to be attached to the ground so that –

PB *It won't blow away like tumbleweed?*

RD That has happened to me. The large piece that I made for

Liverpool was disassembled because of its size. This is something I have avoided doing, making work which does disassemble because of precisely the issue you raised, that somehow the joints become focuses of attention. The largest proposal which I had for outside work was for one outside 250 Euston Road. It would have been made in one piece and transported to site and erected as a large piece. Given the nature of the commission that would have been perfectly practicable within the budget.

PB *Why was the project not realised?*

RD The finalists were Michael Sandle and myself. Michael Sandle is re-submitting, so it's still not resolved.

PB *Your use of materials which don't have a natural weight has meant that you will have to secure them, in some way sacrificing that apparent instability or equilibrium in your work.*

RD We're talking slightly speculatively here. With that particular proposal (the Euston Road project) there would have been a small amount of movement with the wind just because of its size and the flexibility the thing has in it. The supports would have been visually clean at the bottom. I felt that this work would have retained the qualities that the other works have. The intention was to make something that was distinct from the built environment around it, that appeared almost in the same way as the flotsam and jetsam in the street so that it was an object, despite its size, which was potentially moveable.

PB *You're really substituting the illusion of movement for actual movement. Of the works made to go outside, it is interesting to note that there are, so far, two wooden ones and two metal ones. In these, as in all your work, the chosen material not only affects form and structural procedure but adds to the layers of meaning in each piece. I suppose I fear that the metal ones will 'take over' because metal is a more durable material.*

RD Well, it's not. Wood is actually very durable.

PB *Would not the laminated layers split apart?*

RD No, the glue is very strong. *For Those Who Have Ears II*, 1983, is in one piece, clearly in one piece. It stood outside on a Welsh hillside in a very isolated spot for 15 months. The two steel ones are virtually flat whereas the two wooden ones have a slight sense of transience: the two steel ones actually function more like markers. In the photograph in the catalogue, there was a fairly deliberate use of the pair of images: *Tell Me No Lies*, 1984, which is a large interior work, is coupled with a distant shot of *Between the Two of Us* in Basel, where it seemed to be very much there as a place-marker, whereas one thinks of some of the others as just having rolled there, to have arrived.

PB Like a Ship *is a very complete work, a very sealed work.*

RD When making a work to go outside, the first thing sculptors tend to think of is making much bigger work to compensate for the loss of scale. I'm not sure that that's necessary. The work I have made to go outside probably arose out of the experience of taking two of the much earlier untitled works: the big 'basket-like' one and the 'loopy' one outside – *Untitled*, 1980 and 1981– and realising that with the first it was entirely counter-productive whereas though the other is largish, it is small relative to the things seen in the outside world yet it actually seemed to grow outside. *For Those Who Have Ears II* somehow derives from that notion that a flatter shape doesn't seem to suffer in the same way that volume does. *Like a Bird*, 1984, is somewhat separate from that; it was an attempt to make a volumetric structure that had some equality of outside to inside using the most minimal of means to define volume without it being a lump. The two steel ones are relatively small, they're not –

PB *Monumental?*

RD – not monumental works. Somehow they're scale-less, as shape they carry enormous distances. They seem to grow the further you get away from them and that, I think, is enormously interesting for making work outside. *Between the Two of Us* uses the same structural language as *Like a Ship*, but is a more complex entity.

PB *There's a return to a certain conflict in the piece, the title indicates that as in: something coming* Between the Two of Us.

RD Yes. On a kind of formal level, that's the state of play at the moment regarding work outside. Four years ago I was very resistant to making works outside. It now seems that I have made some progress. I would very much like to do something on the scale that the Euston Road project entailed but we'll see.

I didn't think it was compromised. The one I did for Liverpool was just strapped across the bottom; it was a large work without any underground structure. In another proposal, it's possible that I will find a way of making something which is stable without being underpinned. There are other factors involved in making work outside which are, I think, potentially far more important. When a work is in an interior situation, one becomes aware of the work as being an envelope or skin between two sorts of volume, an interior and an exterior in an equal balance; in consequence, one has a very intimate relationship with the work. When you place a work outside, the absence of the framing that an interior provides makes that relationship far more difficult to achieve.

PB *What about the possibility of a loss of intimacy? However large your pieces have become, in an interior they have retained an intimacy, an approachability*

RD Right. I think that's a big problem with placing work outside. In the past, on the one occasion that I did take a piece out of the studio and place it outside, I found it so disastrous that I resolved that I wouldn't do it again. Where I was invited to make a work for an outside show, the starting-point, at least, was from the location, from the notion that the work was going outside to a particular place. The pieces of work which have stood outside, *For Those Who Have Ears II*, *Like a Ship*, *Between the Two of Us* and *Like a Bird*, were made, initially, for their locations – the first, which I think was particularly successful, in Margam Park in Wales.

PB *In the catalogue for Edinburgh and Lyons,* For Those Who Have Ears II *doesn't look like a permanent installation. It looks like a set-up for a ravishingly beautiful photograph. The transience of the situation adds to the fragile beauty of it. Did you take that photograph?*

RD No. Most of the other photographs in the catalogue were taken by myself, there may be a difference there between the way in which a photographer pictorialises the work and the way in which I take a photograph. I agree with you, it is a very beautiful photograph but the work also did have, and intentionally, a certain kind of transience to it, as we talked earlier, the reasons for making the transition from rectilinear to curvilinear structures, a certain casualness, in the sense that the juxtapositions of any moment are capable of being changed. So transience does seem to be an issue. The external works, *For Those Who Have Ears II*, *Like a Bird*, *Like a Ship* and *Between the Two of Us*, are all very clear about their relationship to the ground, their being on a curved base, so they seem ready to move off at any time. In photographs it may be that that appears dominant.

Issue 83, February 1985

Stephen Willats

interviewed by Jill Morgan

Counter-consciousness

JILL MORGAN *'Doppelgänger' takes your use of symbols to represent the dominant consciousness and the existence of a creative counter-consciousness to a psychological level. How does this stem from your previous art practice?*

STEPHEN WILLATS I always try to look for symbols that are not only relevant, but give the essence of the period or age that we live in – society at the moment. In previous work I have used tower blocks, I have worked with situations such as offices, housing estates, worked with clubs made by people in the middle of the night. These are all contexts which I see as symbolic of the period at the moment. The glue-sniffing camp in my work *Pat Purdy and the Glue Sniffers Camp*, 1980, was an alienated context that had been made by people as a direct response to the surrounding housing estates. So, with the glue-sniffing camps I had two really important symbols which were in a way directly products of being against each other. With the 'Doppelgänger' work I have been looking for the symbolism between the dominant consciousness, the consciousness of the authoritative institutional kind of society, and symbols that give a kind of counter-consciousness of more social, human-based values, values of community. So, in one sense I see the world of objects in a kind of conflict, eternal struggle with the world of people. With the clubs when I was working with 'Inside the Night' there again was the context of the day and the night, used in a very symbolic way. 'Doppelgänger' came out of this – looking for symbols. I wanted to look for these two states of ideology, two states inside the same person – I thought this was an extremely powerful idea.

JM *Well, I suppose everybody is a* doppelgänger. *How does our personal understanding of the* doppelgänger, *the other self, work in this piece?*

SW As you say, everybody is a *doppelgänger* – well, a little bit. In a sense there is always the eternal struggle between the self having to deal with society, having to socialise, having to exist, having to coexist with a deterministic, authoritative society – a world which one does not determine oneself but nevertheless one has to live within – and then the inner self, the real self say, of privately accepted values and beliefs. Those beliefs that state one's own creativity, one's own personal kind of identity. You get two communities – you get from the second, a community of like-minded persons which you associate with in terms of natural kinds of affinities and so on and then you have the community which is imposed upon you by the society, like at work, having to work or just having to comply. So the idea of 'Doppelgänger' is the idea of two people in parallel inside one person, going forward in parallel, the idea that there is always the other self, so I sit here and the *doppelgänger* is behind me somehow. I was also interested in the mythology of the *doppelgänger* – it's a mythology in the history. So, I thought this was an interesting symbolism, this relationship between day and night and also of the *doppelgänger* between work and the freedom of association with one's real self and with friends. I was looking for the representation of two states of ideology in something the viewers can relate to, as touching on themselves. I made the 'Doppelgänger' work in association with other symbols: the tower block and day and night.

JM *For an artist who has resisted the dominant culture and proposed alternatives to it, are you worried that 'Doppelgänger', with its emphasis on a personal psychological mode, will be appropriated? How do you expect this work to be received by the art world?*

SW Well, I think the artist has a high position in the making of culture. There is art that reinforces the existing view of culture, a descriptive kind of art, art that reinforces the dominant culture, the transmission of the authoritative in the dominant mode – and there is art that instigates different ways of perceiving the dominant culture and manifests the ideology of a counter-consciousness in the dominant culture. Now, you have to deal at the very centre, there is no point dealing undercover, outside the culture – we have to live in parallel, have to kind of exist like everybody else, in one degree or another, with the dominant culture, but the artist has the position of not having to lie back, he/she has to intervene – to go in there and find a way of dealing with it. With the 'Doppelgänger' I was really trying to look for a hook for the audience, which the audience could get on to and hook themselves into the work. The work is structured in such a way as not to legislate to the audience a particular view of the dominant culture or a way of dealing with the determinism of the dominant culture, but to set up disparate references which I use from different mediums, like writing, objects, photography and so on, I create a sort of separation between the references so that the audience can piece it all together themselves. They can home in to the work and go in there. I see it as important to represent this other consciousness right in the middle of the cultural process – to go into the centre and then provide a kind of access through the work into other ways of viewing what surrounds it. This is my strategy, if you like. It's not the only strategy, but it's the strategy that stems from these pieces.

JM *How does the audience's relationship with this work differ from the more confrontational, spontaneous organisation of say, the 'Inside the Night' pieces?*

SW When I came to work with 'Inside the Night' I was interested in confronting the audience with what wasn't normal and a context they couldn't access, or were very unlikely to be able to access – it was aggressive, alienated from the normal and probably alienated from themselves. Through this confrontation I wanted them to re-examine aspects of themselves and of their own reality. Centering the work in the culture within the night, although not giving access to these clubs, did refer to an aesthetic, a sensibility that was in the street – it was familiar though distant. The 'Doppelgänger' and the strategy of the 'Doppelgänger' is a combination of two things really, one the normal self, and normality in society – taking what is familiar on one side of the piece, and then what is not familiar on the other side of the piece; from the familiar you go to what is not familiar – the familiar provides access to the other. Exposure to a single presentation is rarely able to rapidly change somebody's attitudes. What is important is to have a sequence of presentations through time so that gradually a person is able to build up another model of reality, another change of attitude, another set of attitudes. This is what I have tried to do with this work.

There is, as with all my work presented in an institutional context, a social process in the making of the work and in the reception of the work. It is fundamental that it is not work that's developed in isolation from people and society, that it is developed with people directly in a co-operative way. It is through that interaction with that other person that the work itself is formulated. Similarly the audience, in receiving the work, in their recognition of the work, is almost deconstructing it through the same process as we constructed it. I see the work as fundamentally socially based, and to be used by the audience.

JM *The 'Doppelgänger' work is a personal, psychological work. How did you start working with the three individuals in the piece?*

SW These works are very much more intimately made than works I made in the seventies. With all the other works there was an element of, not exactly documentary, but the archival. This is very intimate, and the only way they can be made because it's really somebody's psychology. So I met them all through people I knew from other works – people tend to introduce me to other people – I go round to their place and there's somebody else there and I get chatting to them and they sound interesting and it goes from there. So, I met them all about a couple of years ago and have known them on and off over the past two years. About August, when the ideas for 'Doppelgänger' began to clarify in my head, I had to look through all the people I knew and find three individuals I felt were representative of 'Doppelgänger' in an extreme symbolic way. As you were saying earlier, everybody is like a *doppelgänger*. So here I had to try to find for the audience some extreme contrasts – the stockbroker, the shop manageress and a civil servant – three really stereotyped people in society, representing the deterministic, institutional society.

JM *I remember talking to you when you were in the process of making the work. Going out and working with these people – on the streets with them – it was quite threatening and quite a dangerous kind of process, working with people in this kind of context.*

SW Well, it does certainly involve me going into places that other people wouldn't dream of setting foot in. For instance, once with Amanda we went to an underground garage beneath a tower block in west London which was derelict, we went there at 12 o'clock at night and there was only me and her in the whole place and that was quite frightening. Another time I went with Gary to these tower blocks around Ronan Point at 12 o'clock at night to do this work, because I obviously made the work in the night and there again it was really sort of frightening. Yes, there's always a slight pressure from me I suppose to get in there to take the person you're working with a little bit further in, anyway. But, for instance, when I made the photograph with the stockbroker, he brought along some friends, some punk friends, he was dressed up in his city suit and we went to where he worked in the City, round the NatWest building and he was walking around while I was doing photographs and they got really bored, sort of fooling around with letterboxes and kicking doors and things like that, and there was this really strange group of people with this stockbroker in his city suit and this skinhead, followed by a skinhead, followed by a mohican, followed by myself with the camera, trooping round the City.

JM *In 'Doppelgänger' you are using different techniques with a heightened atmospheric colour, bright crayon pencils, opposed to a tight spatial organisation.*

SW Well it's interesting about the medium – I use crayon because this is a really tacky medium that nobody uses. That's what interested me to start with. The drawings are meant to be sort of ironical in a way. For instance, I am taking the tower block, which is an authoritative structure, and I am setting it up in outer space. I developed a language with the actual medium, enabling me to do certain things. I was interested in the cultural symbolism of authoritative structures – I use buildings mostly – in relationship to people. I can subvert the buildings through changing their visuality into another state of consciousness. In these works, typically, I use the symbolism of the sun with buildings flying around in outer space. What I am trying to do is ironical in a way – divorce the building from its authoritative implications – undermining, subverting its authority. I want similarly to make colour state the difference, and here again I use the device of day and night.

JM *In the 'Doppelgänger' works the use of objects is significantly different from earlier work – the objects are more carefully consciously used.*

SW It is slightly different from earlier works where I would go into somebody's personal environment and, with the participant's co-operation, gather together debris or a lot of objects that symbolised different aspects of their life, or their attitude to life. Here the process is very reductive: one object or two objects which they feel contain or reiterate an important chunk of themselves. These objects were not necessarily objects they had ready to hand or debris, but would involve us going out to find particular objects. These pieces are not archeological. In the piece *Double Cross* made with the civil servant there are two hands: one hand is holding a pen, symbolising the girl at work; the other hand has studs and punk jewellery and is reaching for the cross – the hand at night. But this idea of using the two hands was actually her idea, so we had to find the hands – looking all round London and eventually I found a model's hands – but these still had to be the right hands. The objects were specified and then found.

JM *The texts in these works are also more reductive, more of a slogan for the audience.*

SW The process is similar to earlier works where I made a tape-recording of about half-an-hour and this is transcribed, but instead of using several extracts to form a kind of texture you are just presented with a statement of ten to 12 words – it can still be ambiguous. The one statement we settle on has to be that much more defined – it has to be more effective than, say, six statements.

JM *The Lisson still has the ghostly marks of an anarchy symbol on the wall. You make use of the confrontational language and symbols of the alternative culture. How effective is the language of your participants, which is very direct, in the context of the art world?*

SW The piece, *Every Day, Every Night* from 1984, is made with an anarchist, Marxist skinhead, but he isn't confused, in fact he's very clear – he's from Ronan Point, East London. The violence of his expression is in the fact that it's expressed in a tangential form from most people's expressions. When he says you have to fight to live, fight to survive, he's talking as somebody trapped inside an institutional world within which you are made to feel powerless. But what he's expressing is the will of every person to react against that environment and fight back against that environment and, naturally, it's expressed in strong language, but coherently. I think that what he's said in the piece touches on every person. People would walk into the gallery off the street specifically to look at this work – stop in the street and then come in – the language of the work is the language of the moment. I noticed that when I was making works in the seventies on the housing estates of west London people did change, their language changed, people are more tense, people are more aggressive.

Issue 86, May 1985

Mark Boyle

interviewed by Henry Lydiate

Double negative

HENRY LYDIATE *How did you get involved in making visual work in the first place – where would you pick a point?*

MB It sounds absolutely romantic as hell, but the first night Joan Hills and I met, we sat down and discussed for hours what we were going to do with the rest of our lives, and it's been in all different kinds of media from the way we were working then. But basically we've stuck to what we were trying to do then.

HL *And what were you trying to do?*

MB It was to do with not being exclusive. That sounds like a double negative, but it isn't really. It was this: we're not going to exclude anything from what we make – whatever form it takes. The idea had always been that there is no experience, no sensation, no aspect of reality we would eliminate, and at the same time we had to accept responsibility for what we were doing in our own lives.

HL *How did you find yourself needing, sharing this dialogue with Joan Hills about not excluding experiences? I presume there was a point where you were saying, I need to make visual work?*

MB Well, I wouldn't put it like that, but, yes. You don't realise it's a need until you find that you very rarely think about much else. I was writing poems – had done all my life – very bad ones mostly, but some of them got published thanks to Joan's efforts. But one day I borrowed her paints, because she was a painter, and went out into the sun and painted my first picture. Very soon after that we were both painting frantically together. Then one day we each made an assemblage in the same room. Joan made a whitish one, and I made a blackish one. At the end of that exercise we decided we were going to work together on the same piece from then on, and we have done.

HL *How long is that?*

MB About 23 years.

HL *This was in the sixties. Were there artists, people making visual work, who were important to you at that time, or did you not think about other people? Did you have an education in visual work?*

MB The things that happened to me and us were really so extraordinary that it sounds a bit mad even to talk about. Writing poems and having just produced one picture which wasn't very good, Joan and I went to an exhibition in some town in the north of England which I have never been able to remember since. It was an Arts Council touring exhibition in which there was a painting by Francis Bacon, and I looked at that and I thought, Jesus Christ, that guy is doing in paint what I am trying to do in poems – and he's doing it infinitely better. And the thing that is extraordinary is that what I saw in him was the most total reality I had ever seen in any picture or read in any poem or anything in art before. That was the initial impact and it was the crucial thing that actually pushed me over into working visually. But after a while I began to think, well, nobody else thinks that this guy is a realist. And it is only in the last few years, seeing a programme on television, that I found he'd used the phrase 'the brutality of fact' about his own paintings.

HL *And that was an inspiring thing for you?*

MB Absolutely. One of the most thrilling moments of my life.

HL *What other influences were there on you at this point? Were you influenced by music?*

MB I was influenced by theatre, poetry, music and most of all by Joan – she was gentle, brave and immensely resourceful. Working with her was very challenging. We were absorbed in one another. The influence of painters was enormous – a new influence every week until I got through the entire modern movement.

HL *Did you have worries about making a living, keeping body and soul together, paying the rent?*

MB Not as far as making a living from art was concerned, it never occurred to anyone that we could. We never conceived of that as a possibility.

HL *So how did you get by?*

MB We just would do any job that came up. And didn't see anything demeaning about doing such work.

HL *Were you aware of anyone who was living solely by making work?*

MB I didn't know anybody. It was a different era. You could actually live off fairly tiny wages. I was a head waiter at one pound a week for many years. All the artists we knew were terribly poor. Nobody was selling anything. We all made pictures because it was the most thrilling thing to do.

HL *Why I ask you that is this perennial problem – when will I be able to survive so that I can be making work full-time? It's a serious issue – if I'm not making work full-time, then I might be selling my soul and there's a real danger that I might drift away from what I ought to be doing which is making work. But you're speaking of a different approach.*

MB There was a completely different attitude. Firstly, it wasn't just the sixties. From the time we had an exhibition that was well received by the critics, it was 17 years before we made a profit in any one year. That's not to say we didn't sell pieces, eventually. We did, but we didn't cover our overheads. We just knew that it didn't matter what we did for money, because nothing would stop us making pictures. It may sound severe, but if people fear they might drift away from what they ought to be doing, maybe they ought to be doing something else.

HL *Richard Hamilton once said to me that if someone, from the time they start, is still working 15 years later, they might stand a chance of making some kind of income from it. He said that ten years ago. I believed him then, I know it's true, now.*

MB If you think of yourself as a potential survivor.

HL *Yes, a survivor, not a success.*

MB Joan said this great thing once, about movements. She was doing a lecture and some movement had come up – I think it was kinetic art, which had just arrived on the scene, and I was a bit embarrassed because, like everybody at the time, I had thought how could anyone ever look at anything still again when there was this art that moves all over the place. Joan just said, well, the thing about movements is, they move, and made a gesture sideways. And that's true. The whole thing is in a state of upheaval all the time. People are going to find, even if they are doing quite well, that their lives will fluctuate fairly wildly as each new set of dogmatists arrives, declaring that everyone else is completely irrelevant all of a sudden. And of course it isn't true. The trouble is the public tends to believe anybody that is dogmatic. If the only thing you can be adamant about is the fact that you don't like dogmatism, that you are in state of adamant doubt and so on, then you are going to be a natural victim of people who imagine they have certainties, but I don't actually believe people have certainties.

HL *Nothing could be more certain than if somebody wants to buy a piece of work you've made. But artists I know have problems about that. You made it because it was important to make it, you sell, and then think now should I make another in that style – it's that whole compromise issue – or do I continue to make work because I need to, then if there's a buyer, there's a buyer?*

MB Well, I just see it in terms of empty walls and, if there is an empty wall in the house, it's a great opportunity. It doesn't seem to me that the question of the buyer arises, but I was in the fortunate situation that we didn't really sell much for many, many, many years.

HL *So why were you making?*

MB Everybody raises this as a problem. There are literally hundreds of thousands of poets in this country who write poems on the back of envelopes that they know not only will never get published, but will never even be read by anyone. But no one finds that extraordinary. So why should anyone find it extraordinary if someone should make pictures?

HL *I came across a Scottish artist and I asked him whether he had any problems with galleries. He said, no, not at all. I asked what he did. He said the Scottish coastline is full of wonderful stone, and he just goes on beaches, climbs up rocks, and make these sculptures there. I asked what happened to them, did he take anyone to see them – no – did he photograph them – no – did he write about them – no – did he talk about them – well, sometimes. I then said, so there's no dialogue with anyone else? He said, well, I like to think that maybe someone's child will come across them.*

MB That's great, and some child will come across them and be enchanted. For us, it's been a dialogue between ourselves in one state, and ourselves at a subsequent date in another state. So that it's very easy to see that, in our work, it's possible to be both the person that makes it and an onlooker. I may look at the piece before I start making it and then I am able to come and look at it as an onlooker afterwards and I can be critical of it too in a way that is nothing to do with making it. It's like my daughter Georgia crying in the night once saying I've been having a dream, and I said dreams aren't things to cry about, dreams are wonderful, and she said, well, I haven't liked the ones I've been watching tonight. In the same way it is possible for me to go into the street, walk along and see it like going through a museum – of our own work. It's like strolling through a carousel of wonderful pictures, and all absolutely perfect.

HL *When you were writing, before you were making visual pictures, can you remember why you were writing?*

MB I could give you an answer but I should say I am probably the last person to be able to do so because I think that most people who are producing any kind of art, maybe everyone who is doing anything in life, is unaware of why they are really doing it. You think you know but in fact most of us are directed by our unconscious. And even though nobody probably removes themselves from their work more completely than we have – it's as objective as we can make it – I am very well aware that the whole desire to do it is totally subjective, and what's more almost certainly 99 per cent unconscious. So, all I can say to you is that for as long as I can remember I had a real need to make things, and that first it happened to be poems, then gradually – and it's without motive, no motive that I'm aware of.

HL *Did anybody come along at any stage, saying you're making work I can sell, so can you give me some more?*

MB No one ever came to me and said you're making work I can sell, and that was the crucial phrase I was looking for, the idea of someone who came along and saw – the role of the dealer was to sell pictures. All the dealers we have shown with have been great people. Everyone has the idea that I'm against the gallery system. It just isn't true. It's worked out that we exhibit mostly in museums. That's just the way the breaks went. Without dealers, there wouldn't be the museums, no art world. I'm against awful dealers, of course, but isn't everybody? We had one marvellous bloke turn up who put on a show in his gallery. That was John Dunbar. He was beautiful. He seemed the ideal dealer.

HL *Was it important to you that the work was shown?*

MB We didn't think of it as art. I suppose a lot of people still don't think of it as art. This was after I had stopped working with poems and had become visual, and I suppose to some extent I was still thinking of it as poems. It was inconceivable that anyone would show them.

HL *But when a show occurred, did you then make a link between showing and selling to someone?*

MB Yes. I began to think it was quite definitely effete to have an exhibition without selling something. My attitude was this: I don't need to show; if we are going to show, let's get it quite clear that it is because we intend to sell. I can remember doing a show in Edinburgh, and getting my hands round somebody's throat on the last night, saying how much money do you have in your pocket – the man said eight pounds — and I said, well you've just bought a piece of ours. Because I needed the eight pounds to get the entire exhibition on the train and us down to London again.

HL *Was there a time when you were first asked to speak about your work and you felt, I could do that again? It's quite an odd thing for a maker of visual work suddenly to find himself with a live audience.*

MB I grew up in a family of seven and you had to be able to talk and make yourself heard, and I guess it's never changed. One of the problems is that everyone has become very verbal about art and I don't think that art is something people should be terribly verbal about. It's as if words have taken over from the visual experience. In fact there was a time when that was so, when everyone condemned us because we were still making objective art. At that time you weren't supposed to produce an object. They sold us their photographs and their statements for the same prices people were selling their objects – they somehow managed to differentiate between a photograph and an object. It seemed to me both the photograph and the statement were actually objects. I could never quite work that out. So I never believed in non-objective art.

HL *Talking to people who know I'm not an artist, but that I am involved with artists, they ask me often what I think about certain work which they see as outrageous, and I find myself ill-equipped to explain why I think work is made, what I think it does or how challenging it is to me. My impression is they are frightened by modern work. They see it as difficult, highbrow, avant garde. And most folk have no visual vocabulary, no touchstone at all. The threat is felt because they have no way of understanding.*

MB I have this all the time. It is one of those curious facts that I can put up a piece of mine which is a brick wall, and people will actually stand and like it and comment on it, and so on. Whereas you can have those bricks in the Tate, and people are outraged by them. So I'm constantly having this dilemma, that people are coming to me and complaining about other artists. And I find myself defending artists who – maybe I'm not all that crazy about their work – but I defend them, explain it. And it's amazing how people, if you don't talk to them in a patronising way, just talk to them in ordinary English, and say well this bloke's trying to do this, even if you get it wrong, it's your guess at it – you'd be amazed how people come round. We are out working in the street all the time, talking to those people absolutely endlessly about it. You say people are afraid. I think people are annoyed. If they don't understand it they think someone is trying to treat them as idiots. People writing and talking in an impenetrable way about art makes most of the public feel excluded. It effectively denies them participation in one of the most exciting manifestations of life.

HL *Our conversation has been peppered by references to your family – Joan Hills and your daughter Georgia, your son Sebastian and Joan's son Cameron Hills. How involved is the family in making and exhibiting?*

MB I've already told you about the night Joan and I met. Well, it was just as though two people had come together, two professionals who recognised one another, and decided that we could make a partnership. It wasn't exactly in professional terms, but we decided to work together. We didn't keep it up continuously. There was quite a period when Joan was working as a film editor; but she also went to a couple of galleries to try to get me exhibitions. The first time I went with her I was so outraged by the way those galleries treated her, I said we must never do this again, we just do not ask for shows – it's wrong, we can't allow our personalities to suffer the damage of being treated like that. Then Joan was up in Edinburgh and ran into Jim Haynes and Ricky Demarco. They offered us a show in the Traverse Gallery which was opening at the same time as the theatre. So it was one of those aberrations that, because for a few years Joan was working as a film editor, at the point which was basically the start of our professional career, it got launched under my name. Having started that way, when we got back into working together it was very difficult to make the change because the world actually wanted – maybe still wants – to believe in a single, preferably male, obsessed artist.

HL *So how many are there involved now?*

MB There's Sebastian, Georgia, Joan Hills and myself. Cameron Hills comes in sometimes to work on a specific project, but he has chosen his own career. Sebastian and Georgia have been working with us ever since they were big enough to find a screwdriver, and increasingly as the years went by, became more and more involved in it until they are absolutely full-time and fully committed. At some point everybody has a stage where they become the boss. This has never been formally worked out. So Joan would gravitate towards doing one thing, then take charge of another, and I would be her labourer and just do what I was told – it was relaxing. Similarly, on other bits of it I would be the boss. Now, increasingly, Sebastian and Georgia have got their areas, and they tell me. But, at every stage, from the initial idea right through, all four of us are working on every piece. It's a privilege to work with such lovely friends.

HL *How do you see the future – do you have any special plans, projects or major changes in direction?*

MB I've never really believed in directions. I think a lot of artists need to have a general direction. For me, when the family is totally committed to the next picture, then I think that's the maximum direction you can actually get. I just find myself sometimes not knowing what to comment because I don't have the kind of words which say it right. In some ways you've got to concentrate totally on this next piece – and you're half terrified that you can't actually do it any more – and if you start to think about planning the future, you're not going to be putting everything into the thing you are actually doing at the present.

Issue 101, November 1986

Gerard Hemsworth

interviewed by Andrea Schlieker

All that glitters is not gold

ANDREA SCHLIEKER *How would you describe your move from the early conceptual art works to painting? Why did you start to paint?*

GERARD HEMSWORTH By the mid seventies I was already dealing with notions of representation. I had already produced written works containing surrogates for 'paintings' and it seemed very natural for me to want to undermine 'painting' subliminally by the use of the medium.

AS *How would you differentiate between the use of language in your early works and your current work?*

GH Written language and visual language determine the way in which ideas are presented – also the way in which we apprehend them. Different means of presentation are appropriate for different situations. What's important, to use an old maxim, is the relationship between form and content. Characteristically, language is underlined by time and context which also determine our understanding; meanings can change – for example, I'm more interested in a painting by Pollock nowadays than I was 20 years ago. Then, I felt obliged to look at it as art – today I can look at it as an image of art. Paradoxically my use of language is fundamentally the same now as it was ten years ago, although propositions, as with language, are contingent.

AS *Would you say that you use painting as a tool?*

GH Yes, I see all media as a means to an end, even when the interest is in the medium itself. I have no particular passion for the medium of paint other than its ability to disseminate my concerns.

AS *How would you describe your concept of realism/representation and the imminent destruction of realism in your work?*

GH Reality exists as an idea – pertinent to the individual. Notions and images of reality are constantly being represented and that representation subsequently becomes another notion or image of reality. The interrelation of the various elements/propositions in my work serves to deter the preconceptions and assumptions that one brings to a work of art and allows the work to have its own particular resonance.

AS *When you cover the images with swags of colour, rectangles or seemingly random objects – is that some kind of attempt to destroy the illusion of realism?*

GH The elements are never random, they're a device – they all have a metaphorical reading and are used to make the illusion more apparent.

AS *What significance do you attach to the use of photography in your work?*

GH Its significance lies in the popular notion that anyone can take a photograph which allows me to locate interpretation beyond a purely optical response. Photography itself has its own iconographic references, I see it as a way of mediating an image.

AS *You make iconographical references to various historical works of art, such as Manet's* Olympia *and Van Gogh's* Sunflowers *– why?*

GH I use images of art which have been abused by popular culture. I appropriate them because they are easily recognisable and have already been digested historically. Obviously, some have wider references than others, consequently they are not all used in the same way. Manet's *Olympia* interests me because it challenged accepted notions of representation when it was first exhibited and subsequently has been seen by many as the beginning of Modernism. It is still very much in debate, focusing on voyeurism and sexuality in art along with the dilemma of both the male and female gaze.

AS *You refer to 'gold' in earlier works such as* Ten White Paintings, *1977, and all that glitters is not gold. Can you explain the frequent use of gold in your paintings? Does it still fulfil the same function?*

GH Yes and no – with different works gold has inherent cultural values. It signifies both opulence and power along with merit and quality. I take on board all these associations and more – for me it's a question of undermining the significances that are implied. For example, gold can be read as rather 'tacky', the ambiguities allow me to deconstruct assumptions.

AS *How would you describe the relationship between your paintings and the viewer?*

GH As an artist what I do is parenthesise a concern within the work – by juxtaposing a number of propositions – the relationship of these propositions can be read in different ways by a viewer, who will bring to the work a set of values which I don't necessarily share – the meaning they extrapolate determines my work.

AS *Does that mean the viewer is a constitutive part of the work?*

GH If the pictures are to exist outside the studio, yes. They become part of the manifestation of the work.

AS *What exactly do you mean by a proposition?*

GH Simply that something is proposed for consideration, which allows for both artist and viewer to contribute intellectually and emotionally to the work. I see this in opposition to statements, which seem to limit the work to the artist's concerns.

AS *How would you distinguish between the figuration in your work and that of your contemporaries?*

GH I'm not interested in style in terms of my own artistic signature. The way I render an image is subject to the content and the realisation of the work.

AS *In your work you use a layering technique as well as a particular mixture of abstraction and figuration that urges comparison with other contemporary artists.*

GH The use of layering and different forms of representation are contemporary ploys within picture-making and are used in a variety of different ways, for different reasons and by different artists – it seems only natural to look for comparisons and connections between artists, but it's a pity that one sees those connections in the manner of presentation rather than within the content of the work and its presentation.

AS *Would you identify yourself as a British artist?*

GH Although I feel outside the mainstream of British art – whatever that might be – I think one works within one's own culture, and that manifests itself within the work. I don't believe in internationalism – it reduces everything to the lowest common denominator.

AS *Are there any autobiographical references in your work?*

GH In one sense all art is autobiographical – obviously one's experiences enable one to produce. But if you're asking me, are my works autobiographic, the answer is no – I'm certainly not interested in private mythology or presenting narrative instances from life.

AS *In a number of your works you deal with sexuality. What is your position on sexual politics and your attitude towards feminism?*

GH Sexuality is determined by language – my interest is in readdressing that language. We are all influenced by what is seen as the cultural norm: 'man equals masculine', 'woman equals feminine'; 'men are active', 'women are passive'. Although we all have these qualities we are segregated within a patriarchal society into what is considered the strong and the weak. These prevailing attitudes have been addressed by feminist critiques. Feminism is a contemporary issue which is pertinent to us all.

AS *You often seem to combine the issue of sexuality with a feeling of guilt already in your early work, for example,* Act of Contrition, *1981. Is this a legacy of your Catholic upbringing?*

GH I use guilt ironically – Catholicism provides one with a particular insight on the subject, where sexuality and 'the self' are frowned upon and where religious codes of practice often clash with moral codes. It is only when we readjust moral codes in terms of our own criteria that guilt may become an issue. Ironically, guilt is often needed for satisfaction.

AS *In a lot of your recent paintings there is a striking combination of meticulously rendered realistic representation and wildly gestural abstraction –* Crime of Passion, Rape of Representation, *etc – Could this be interpreted as a result of the desire to counterbalance the neutrality and coolness of the figurative images with a sudden burst of emotional expressionism?*

GH It could be – although my use of both elements is calculating. The overlay of gestural painting can be read directly as obliterating that which is underneath, or it could be read as questioning aesthetic values. They are images of emotional expressionism. My concern here, as with the relationship of other juxtapositions of images, is to undermine preconceptions of them.

AS *Why do you so rigorously adhere to the lifesize as a norm for your paintings?*

GH When I started using visual imagery it seemed natural to make the surface image lifesize. I had no reason to make them any other size – this in turn determined how large or small a work should be.

AS *And how would you explain the recurrent use of diptychs or triptychs?*

GH Simply to give each image its own space. When I use repeated images it enables me to devalue them or assert them as icons.

AS *In your early work, as in your present work, there is a constant play with visual and verbal puns. How important is humour in your work?*

GH Puns are not always humorous – they are a way of suggesting an ambiguity. Humour exists for me as a kind of reflex action, I suppose it allows me to gain some distance from the intrinsic concerns within the work and provides the work with an accessibility on different levels.

AS *Objects and people are the main components of your painting: what is their relationship, for example, in* Boys will be Boys, *1983, and* Professional Foul, *1985?*

GH It's interesting that you should choose those two works as examples. I have only recently seen them together for the first time, and didn't realise that they dealt with identity in opposing ways. The coat-hangers in *Boys will be Boys* become surrogates for the system and its threat to identity in opposing ways. There's a pun on 'support structure', and inevitably as objects they are threatening in that particular work because of the nakedness of the couple. In *Professional Foul* the three men are stripped of their identity – presented as clones, or the same person – the rectangles and the chairs consequently become surrogates for identities, inevitably presenting the threat of an individual characteristic.

AS *Why do you want to make an object into a surrogate for something else?*

GH Because it allows for an interpretation; as with a metaphor it allows one to extend the work. Certain objects have an image value – the image becomes a sign for the object – the object becomes a sign for itself. This enables me to use them as surrogates – as opposed to symbols – which allows for a wider reading.

AS *You use the theme of blindness in two of your recent works – do you want it to be understood as a metaphor for the current state of art criticism? Art appreciation?*

GH Socially and culturally we are programmed and manipulated. We are all blinded by preconceptions. There is a huge difference between looking at art and seeing it.

Issue 101, November 1986

Bill Woodrow

interviewed by Peter Hill

Achtung

PETER HILL *Your exhibition at the Fruitmarket Gallery is your first solo show in Britain for three years. How do you feel about it?*

BILL WOODROW I'm very happy with it. For me it was an exhibition worth waiting for because it includes some large-scale sculptures which haven't been shown in Great Britain before. One of the reasons I waited so long for such a show is because I wanted to show these works in a chronological sequence.

PH *Your most recent work seems to be richer in fantasy, sometimes surreal, sometimes baroque, grander in ambition and more eclectic in materials compared to earlier, simpler and more punning work such as* Hoover Breakdown *of 1979. Is this the direction in which you are moving?*

BW Yes, it has certainly been the direction in which the work has been going, especially with some of the larger-scale pieces. They've become a lot more complex as, over the years, the range of imagery has increased. I don't consciously see them as baroque, but I certainly understand what you mean. I think they are a lot freer by contrast to the earlier works which were quite strict because of their simplicity.

PH *There appears to be a richness of juxtaposition.*

BW I'm more prepared now to try to use an amalgam of image and not just one image with its host material. The original material is often incorporated into the sculpture now, in a very different way to previously. This allows another level of images to come out, in the sense that the car bonnets with the giraffe going through, for example, actually act as architectural bridge-like structures, whereas in some of the earlier work of four or five years ago they would just have been car bonnets with something else attached.

PH *Where does the title* Achtung *come from?*

BW It comes from a label on one of the car bonnets.

PH *In a lot of the recent works you seem to be using the world map in a variety of configurations – is that linked partly to the amount you have been travelling the globe in recent years?*

BW It is due partly to that and partly to the materials I have come across. At one point I found a whole pile of maps which I have used slowly. I used them first two years ago. I have also both used and made globes, and there is one in my most recent work *Self Portrait in a Nuclear Age*.

PH *How important is it that your raw material is 'found', or would you go out and buy something if it was not otherwise available?*

BW I certainly would buy something if I wanted it, I'm not a purist in the sense of having to find materials. Things are found in skips, anywhere.

PH *Given that you are not a purist in that sense, where do you stand in relation to the tools of your trade? I was surprised to read in the catalogue that all the tools you use are hand-held, rather than bench mounted, which contrasts sharply with the consumer goods you employ, such as washing machines, which are the end product of a heavy industrial process.*

BW This is done for convenience, I always go for the easiest way of making something, and if that doesn't work I will then move up to the next most technical way of doing it. As far as I'm concerned I want the quickest, simplest way of bringing two things together or abstracting something. One has more control over the technical side of the creative process, it is more immediate and one does not have to wait a week or two weeks for something to be fabricated, or cast. I like the speed of making something to be as close as possible to the speed of my thoughts and decisions. If it was necessary, though, to use a power saw or oxyacetylene cutter then yes, I would go ahead and use it. But generally all my tools are contained in that small canvas bag over there and I can jump on a plane and get straight to work wherever I land.

PH *So when you arrive in a foreign city, how do you go about collecting material?*

BW Usually I will have a studio arranged, a place in which to work – it might just be a garage – and then I'll get a van or a truck and somebody who knows the city will come with me and we'll spend a couple of days just driving around looking at different places, and to start with I rely to a certain extent upon that person's knowledge. We will go and look at scrap yards, garages, city dumps, those sort of places. I could always find them myself, but it would take a little longer, and sometimes there is a language problem as well.

PH *With the type of work your sculpture has now evolved into, can you trace it back to one original piece?*

BW There was one particular work when I did cut the surface metal of a household appliance, but I can trace it back further than that in a logical sequence which ended at that initial piece. One can pick out that sort of lineage in retrospect quite easily, although you do not realise it at the time.

PH *The first work illustrated in the catalogue,* Untitled *of 1970, consists of a circle of corn in Soho Square, London, being pecked away by a horde of pigeons. You were clearly involved early in conceptual experiments.*

BW Yes, that dates from my time at St Martin's, when I was in second year, I think. Much of my work was in that vein.

PH *How long after this did the original host appliance appear?*

BW Much later. I stopped being a student in 1972, and the appliance didn't arrive until 1979.

PH *So was there a break in the mid seventies when you stopped producing artworks?*

BW Yes, it was a deliberate choice. I had been working as a postgraduate student and this was quickly followed by a show, and some group shows, and then the mechanics of living, so to speak, had to be dealt with – getting a job, finding somewhere to live, not having a studio, having children. All those things took precedence and I made a decision that while sorting all those things out I wouldn't do any work, because I felt it wasn't possible to do the two things well. And it was a good time to stop working anyway. One's ideas are changing and one recognises that it is time for directions to alter. I wasn't satisfied with most of the ideas I had, and I did not have the means to make the other ideas, so it was a whole combination of things.

PH *It sounds quite a healthy thing to do. What did you do during this time?*

BW Well, I was unemployed for a year, which is not as long as graduates are faced with these days, and then I got a job teaching on a foundation course which I did for eight or nine years up to 1980, in Essex. It was a full-time job, very time consuming, but it sorted out the financial side of things.

PH *How did you get back to producing your own work?*

BW There was a middle period, say from 1974 to 1978, when I might produce one or two things a year, just at home, and then I got a studio in 1978 and things started to change.

PH *I imagine even when you were not working, ideas were still being worked out in your head, possibilities considered. Was it a period of gestation?*

BW Not so much in the sense of any particular philosophy, or manifesto, I just knew that I did not want to make work like I had made before. As soon as I had made one piece of work I knew the old way of working was gone, and that was an important moment. I just started making things in a fairly straightforward way as an attempt to get back into the routine of working.

PH *How much contact had you previously had with the other sculptors who are loosely grouped under the umbrella of the Lisson Gallery?*

BW Tony Cragg and I knew each other from our early student days, and Richard Deacon was in the year after me at St Martin's, and from that period onwards we kept in contact and were very close friends. The others I got to know through the gallery.

PH *What really happened at St Martin's, with the succession from Moore to Caro and down to yourselves? Was it a progression or a rebellion?*

BW I think there is always an aspect of rebellion. In a sense that is what makes an art school education interesting, the fact that you can rebel. I remember the times at college when there was no rebellion against the mainstream, what happened was that work produced through mainstream teaching tended to be not particularly interesting.

PH *There is one particular work of yours I would now like to talk about, and it is the only one I have ever seen set in an open landscape. It is* Albero e Uccello, *1983 – why was it set outdoors?*

BW This work in one sense caused me a lot of problems. I took it outside to photograph it purely to make an invitation card for a show in Italy, and it happened to look fantastic in that particular setting – a very beautiful, dramatic landscape. The problem is that the actual structure of the sculpture is not strong enough to withstand being outside for any length of time. So it was just placed outdoors briefly for the photograph. My thinking about it is that I made it, like the rest of my work, for inside and it's caused me problems because a lot of people have approached me about making outdoor work and I have had to disappoint them. I may do in the future, but at the moment I have still to solve the problems this would entail.

PH *Would it be worth taking works intended for the gallery outdoors just to photograph in a variety of landscapes and then returning them to the studio or gallery? The landscape work would only exist as a photograph, in the same way that your corn and pigeons in Soho Square did, but the strength and power of the end would, I believe, justify the means.*

BW There is one other photograph of one of my works outdoors which the owners of it took. It doesn't look too bad, but it still doesn't solve the problem of the work being outdoors permanently. Weather and vandalism are the two main problems.

PH *Over the last two years you have created at least two self-portraits. What moved you into this traditional area?*

BW The first one was made early in 1985 for my second show with Barbara Gladstone in New York. It was just a thing I suddenly decided to do. I'd started making a work which had a hat in it, and as soon as I saw the hat I decided to carry on the figurative notion of the work but without making an actual figure, and I then decided that I would call this a self-portrait. I was very happy with that work, it seemed to express a lot of things about how I was feeling. The figure wasn't there but the clothes suggested a self-portrait. There was the hat, and a canary in a cage at the bottom – though I'm not suggesting I'm a canary in a cage – it all had to do with the connotations of people being restricted within their environment. Since I made that first one I'd always thought about making another. Recently I decided to make one, but with a figurative head which is something I hadn't done before.

PH *It is almost the opposite in that the head is breaking free from the box, as opposed to the canary.*

BW Yes it's this sort of Jack-in-the-box image with the head springing out. People pop out into the world and have to make the most of it at that point. The head that I made for it has this globe inside it, which is visible from the back of the head, like a brain, while the coat is the opposite, it is an exterior image of oneself with the shards of the map pinned to the outside of the coat. I think the work is about the comparison between appearance and ambition – what you are like inside your head, contrasted with the outward manifestation of what you are.

PH *Was there a particular event behind* Car Door, Armchair, and Incident *of 1981?*

BW Yes, that was one of several sculptures which I hoped would have a strong narrative in a literary sort of way. It was a response also to the sort of images I would see through the media, urban images of violence, you know they could be on a very domestic level or much more militarist, or at a street level. The particular one which you mentioned is quite seedy and domestic. I like the narrative to be read by literally following the material from one end to another.

PH *Do you see your work becoming more complex and multilayered in terms of its references?*

BW More multilayered – but I think the idea of complexity in a sculpture is quite a delicate one. The right balance must be found because if it is too complex it can defeat itself. I still like things to be economic.

PH *Do you make sketches or maquettes beforehand?*

BW No. I make drawings as a separate activity and have created a great deal over the last two years.

PH *Do they explore form as one sometimes expects a sculptor's drawings to do?*

BW They are drawings for their own sake and I suppose they do have similarities to the way the sculpture is made. But they are not drawings for sculpture.

PH *In* Still Waters, *1985, where you use three mattresses, have you used paint on the surface of the mattresses, or were the stains already there?*

BW No, I painted those. The mattresses are supposed to represent the waters of a river, and there is a large deer swimming through with its head up, and the paint is round about it to represent the waters being pushed aside.

PH *In a sense you do not question, as Tony Cragg might, where a painting ends and a sculpture begins – but might the addition of paint to your sculptures be a move in this direction?*

BW I have done some work that is more concerned with paint than with sculpture, but I don't necessarily see a barrier between the two. There are two pieces in particular that hang on the wall and are painted, highly painted, images with three-dimensional attachments. There is the screen from *Life on Earth* which is a collage of all the plastics from the chairs, and *Kimono* uses flat images of the bonnets on the wall. After *Hawaiian Punch* I made *Black Magic, White Tricks* and I don't know if you would call that a painting or a sculpture.

PH *Studying the catalogue I became intrigued by one work hanging in a car factory. How did that come about?*

BW I was invited to go and work in the Renault car factory in France, for a month, along with 12 other artists. The factory was celebrating its 25th year, and there were lots of things going on inside it – concerts, poetry, installations. We could, theoretically, use any of the processes and materials in the factory. In reality there were limitations – for example it was impossible to interrupt the conveyor belts. But it was a fantastic project, although I was dubious about it at first because one had to work in the factory the whole time, next to the assembly lines with no privacy at all. It was tough to start with, and there were also language problems, but it grew to be very enjoyable.

It was mainly women in the factory, sewing up car seat covers, and they were very quizzical about the work. What I did was to suspend the two cars side by side on the wall with their doors open and this created a space through the middle of the work in which I hung domestic items like a clothes iron. The women couldn't understand why I would want to use a clothes iron until I explained that life can sometimes seem like a conveyor belt and I had created a conveyor belt through the centre of the cars. The women identified with the iron, and through that came to appreciate the work.

PH *Is privacy important to you, when you are working?*

BW Yes, that is how I work in my studio. My preference is not to have people watching me when I am working. I don't use assistants. That is why the work in France was so strange, but I knew it would give me a great opportunity that I would not get again.

PH *Finally, future projects?*

BW Shows in Munich, London and New York, which all involve lots of travelling, which I enjoy. One of the great things about the last few years is that I have been able to visit cities all over the world, see new landscapes and original artworks that in the past I had only read about and dreamed about. So yes, it has been good.

Issue 102, December-January 1986–87

1987–1991

Joseph Beuys

interviewed by William Furlong

Plight

WILLIAM FURLONG *Joseph,* Plight, *1985, is a work which has involved installing felt around the interior of the Anthony d'Offay Gallery and placing within it a grand piano, a blackboard and a thermometer. Perhaps we could talk about the sources of this particular piece.*

JOSEPH BEUYS It all started as a joke and was related to the difficulties that the gallery was in when the very noisy demolition of the building behind Anthony's wall was taking place. Anthony, who was very despairing, asked me if it would not be better to move. I told him that I did not think that was necessary and I said you have to stand it for a while. The place is good and the connections from this gallery to the other galleries is okay so there is no reason to move just because there is a noise for, say, two years. So then I had the idea of a kind of muffling sculpture with felt and also to make it as a big exposition. Then we forgot about it and didn't speak of it any more until I received a letter from Judy Adam, his assistant, reminding me of it and mentioning that it would be interesting to make an installation with this kind of meaning – insulation from outside influences such as danger, noise, temperature, or whatever. Then I decided to make this piece. I developed this kind of installation. Before that I had been intending to make a work parallel and synchronically with the exhibition of German art in the Royal Academy. I thought it would appear as a stone sculpture, but I found this much more interesting, especially in relationship to the pieces that are at the Royal Academy, since what they are completely missing is one of my main works related to action, performances, environment and to the materials which belong to those actions. There is no fat, there is no felt. This show uses my most beloved and most powerful material – felt – and while those pieces at the Royal Academy are wonderful, they show too little about the theory and scope of what I mean by a wider understanding of art. That was the reason.

WF *There is a recurring theme that one sees in your work. There are ideas to do with survival and to do with the human body and so on. Although* Plight *is concerned with insulating a space from the outside, it seems to me that on walking in there one becomes very aware of one's own body or of one's bodily functions.*

JB Yes, that's another reason for using such materials. I am not interested in staying with the idea of visual art, but in pointing at the necessity to determine an idea of art relevant to us all – to use the senses existing in human beings and even to develop new senses. If they are not there now, they will appear in the future. If people are trained and really interested in art, they could develop more senses. *Plight* is related to the sense of touching as well as to seeing – I am not against vision of course, it's one of the most important senses. You also have a kind of acoustic effect because everything is muffled, and then there is the effect of warmness. As soon as there are more than 20 people in the room the temperature will rise immediately. So this concert hall – I could also call it a concert hall– muffles the sounds almost down to zero. This is expressed by the 'sound actor', the grand piano with a score on it. There are lines, annotations on the blackboard but there are no notes. Instead, a fever thermometer is placed on it to stress that the warmth is the most important quality for me and is a very important criterion for the quality of a sculpture. One person will feel more this kind of accommodation of warmth and other people will find it sucks away the sound. Others might even become oppressed because there is also a negative aspect in the original idea. The negative side is the padded cell which is a kind of torture/isolation thing.

WF *Because one is deprived of a response.*

JB Yes, right, there is no response, because nothing can break through from outside. That's more the oppressive element I would say, and then the positive thing is the warmness and the possibility to protect you from all sides. If you ask me what the work means, I can only repeat the reasons why I have chosen felt during all my attempts to widen the understanding of sculpture to something which is related to humankind's creative structures and senses – and to thought, feeling and the gaining of power. I try to use a material that is transformable into psychological powers within the being who is not aware nowadays of his or her creative potential. Because the period we live in tends to work with a kind of ideology – things like sculpture and paintings are always referred to as visual art – but I think vision is only one aspect, and there are 12 other senses at least implied in looking at an artwork. So I try to change the understanding of art which leads to a wider understanding of art, and that's what I call anthropological art. So this is for me also a series in which anthropological art appears – has to appear – after modern art.

I find the period of modern art ended in Germany with the beginning of the Hitler era. I am not so clear about England but I am almost sure it was the same. I think almost everything which came after the war was a kind of re-reminding of possibilities from within the modern impulse which dates from the turn of the century, and especially now, when people are speaking without any idea of the necessity and logics of the idea of art. They speak once again of 'modern' art but they call it 'postmodern', and this, for me, is a falsification. It is not an organic transformation of the idea of art, it is only a kind of cancer. People don't realise that art should be related to everybody's creativity, and that every future discussion on the changing of the social order will fail if it does not start to base itself on the creative being oriented towards self-determination, self-administration and self-government. This 'transformed' idea of art means a lot, and maybe it appears to be bold, but I think this boldness is necessary if we are to overcome bad positions in the social order.

WF *Why do you cite the Second World War as a point of significance and change?*

JB You could take it ten years later or ten years earlier, but in Germany – and I think it is special in German art – that was the time where modern art disappeared and a kind of revival took place. Some very interesting painters appeared even after the Second World War, but what I think was missing with them was the theory of the thing. What is important for me in modern art is completely independent of whether it happens to be German, Dutch, French, Italian or Russian Modernism.

All those names, like Surrealism and Cubism, developed from single persons so, for me, it is Mondrian, for instance, or Malevich or Tatlin themselves who represent real significance. They suggest a process of 'singularisation' which in future will mean that every person is able to create his own culture completely. By contrast, Egyptian culture, although it was a great and gigantic culture, was not developed by the free individual being. It was a *Kanonenzeit* structure commanded by a Pharaoh presuming to be a representative of all future gods. Culture was therefore determined from the top as a collective art. It is only since the Baroque that, slowly and with some difficulties, we have seen the tendency emerge in which it is given to the free person, as a cultural agent, to develop and determine his or her own idea of the world. So every artist in German art since then, be they expressionist, surrealist, or naturalist shows that they are able to create a world of their own. But although they signalled that this possibility exists in human beings they didn't develop the theory. It is especially interesting to look at a person like Marcel Duchamp who tried to destroy the rule or tradition and hinted towards something else with his *pissoir* piece. In saying this is an artwork only when it is shown in another, special context he missed the point completely. The logic of the statement points to the fact that if this is a work of art which is not done by me but by some Mr Mutt or an anonymous worker in the factory, then the creator is really the worker. So he didn't enlarge this idea into the necessity to study everything in humankind's labour from this point of view. That would have been of great importance since it could have brought together the ideologies of Capitalism and Communism. There is a germ of the right idea but it is let down by Duchamp's practice. He avoided further reflection and so didn't understand his own work completely.

To be very modest I could say that my interest was to make another interpretation of Duchamp and I try to enlarge – or at least to feel – its most important depth which was missing in this work. You know after he stopped doing works and playing chess and such things and he didn't speak any more about art so much, he cultivated this kind of silence in a very old-fashioned form. He wanted to become a hero in silence or in saying nothing or resigning his whole idea of art and this is even of the defenders of the ideology of modern art. Marcel Duchamp is also art. So the silence of Marcel Duchamp is overrated. I will say that during this time when he was silent he could have reflected on his work and come to other conclusions about its meaning, impact and effectiveness. He was really interested in the transformation of art but he did not transform it, he showed some pieces that shocked the middle classes, the bourgeoisie, and so from that point of view he belongs to Dada. I try to go further on over the threshold where modern art ends and anthropological art has to start. In all fields of discussion not only in the art world – be it in medicine, be it in miners' problems, be it in the information of state and constitution, be it in the money system.

WF *If we could finish by perhaps returning then to* Plight. *The meaning of* Plight *is also that of the lot of the individual. One talks, certainly in the English language, of somebody's plight with the implication that perhaps their position isn't all that satisfactory. Presumably this is part of the meaning of the space that you have made.*

JB The English word 'plight' is not only this bad situation, this special bad situation that you are speaking of, it also means betrothal. It means there is love implied, or trust. In English this word has two completely different meanings, one goes in this direction and one goes in the other, so I have used it in both senses within this incinerating environment.

WF *How much do you feel part of what one would call a German identity in terms of recent contemporary art, particularly recent painting? Do you think you share very much with those artists? Is there something one can pin down in your work?*

JB As soon as you try to restrict this question, or to reduce it to works of art which have only recently been done in Germany, I feel very dubious about the connection. But I am completely secure that I belong to German art – there I am completely sure. To give you a real and radical example, I would not be here as an artist if there had not been a personality like Wilhelm Lehmbruck who I admire very much. His existence led me to the decision to become a sculptor and to get interested in sculpture. I didn't even know what sculpture was when I first saw it during the Hitler period. This was when I was relatively young and shortly before I became a soldier. I saw a catalogue which had escaped the book burning activities of the Nazis. It contained pieces by Lehmbruck, and as soon as I saw them I realised that my own ability should lead me to try and show that there is a lot of possibility within the idea of sculpture. Before this I had only been confronted with the social realism of the Nazis which just didn't touch me, didn't give me a feeling of its own necessity. But as soon as I saw some examples of Lehmbruck's work I saw that with sculpture you can change the world. Surely, then, I belong to this tradition.

WF *But can you actually identify anything particularly about your work in terms of its concerns, its underlying theories and its attitudes, of which one could say that it was very much derived from a German consciousness?*

JB People are unwilling to think about what it means to be a German. Their judgements are made only on very banal, foreground things which result from the bad history of the period from the beginning of this century and which includes the First and Second World Wars. This description of German nature has, in reality, nothing to do with German nature. It can appear within German nature because this nature might have some potential to incorporate such things under special conditions. But principally, the German spirit, or, let's say, the task or the idea of being a German, means keeping nothing for themselves and giving everything away to others. Germany's geographical position means it is not possible to see it as a nation in the established sense. The nation idea is easier to realise with a country that is geographically isolated – the splendid isolation of England. Germany on the other hand is surrounded on all sides with different cultures and it was the idealistic poets and philosophers such as Wolfgang von Goethe, Novalis and others who saw Germany as being in this middle position, bridging between extremities. So the German spirit is principally to do with bridging and helping others and not to do with helping themselves, bringing themselves to power and realising themselves as a kind of state. So the function of the German is that he lives in the middle of Europe, he belongs to the middle European countries. This in Germany is a specially hard position.

Germany is now exactly the opposite to a bridge. There is the Berlin Wall so there is no possibility to mediate between extremities which are always coming from the East and from the West, and this is exactly the spiritual position of the German ability. In music, in philosophy, in poetry, in sculpture, in painting and also in their work, so also should their social organisms be constructed after this idea. I insist that everybody will find in the German soul this longing for bridging the difficulties in the world, for finding solutions to any problem, for being a helper, being a mediator and finding the bridge position in the centre of Europe.

Issue 112, December–January 1987–88

Brice Marden

interviewed by William Furlong

Drawing out ideas

WILLIAM FURLONG *I must say the first thing that strikes me is expressed very succinctly in a* New York Times *review of your recent exhibition at Mary Boone. Michael Brenson, who wrote the article, claims that touch and process, which in the past were concealed, are suddenly visible in this series of works. There is almost a sense of a handwriting beginning to emerge in them. How do you feel about that?*

BRICE MARDEN Well, touch and process were also in the other paintings. I always felt it was quite evident if you looked for it. It wasn't self-evident but it was very definitely there. It may be that these paintings reveal more of an underlying emotional state that was existing in the other paintings but which just wasn't coming out. It was coming out in my drawings and that is why I pushed the painting to this extent, to get into it what I was getting into the drawing. They look different but in the long run they won't look that different from the paintings I was doing.

WF *So there was a desire to resolve the dichotomy which existed between the drawings, which reveal a very calligraphic kind of sense, and the panel paintings of the past which tended to be very flat and didn't really reveal much of the process of their making.*

BM I think the older paintings had more nature and my involvement with nature and how it comes through the work. I think in the older paintings there were feelings about nature that were really expressed quite deeply. Observations were expressed on one level and this gives me an opportunity to express them on more levels. Right now I'm involved in a lot of drawing, and drawing out of ideas, and the colour ideas haven't really been applied that much. That is something I want to work on, too. The drawing has been coming much more directly from nature.

WF *I am interested to hear about this notion of the starting point being natural or from nature. Presumably a process of abstraction then takes place?*

BM Well no, it is not a matter of drawing from nature and then making an abstraction. It is like trying to get closer to the basic reaction you have in seeing it. It is not an empathetic response, but is somewhat akin to it. You see something in nature, you draw it and then you want to maintain that kind of energy, you want to get that same energy in to the work that you are doing in the studio. I don't think of it as an abstraction – taking a picture of nature then changing it. It is more searching to be able to depict this energy. It is sort of depicting a life force.

WF *In the catalogue for this exhibition, John Van talks about your approach as an attempt to distil essences – he comments about you recovering something from a deeper past and about how your work searches for ways to transform and to revive languages arising from art history, but stretching back beyond the Renaissance. What you have just been talking about in relation to the way you respond to nature seems to echo this notion of distillation and essence.*

BM Yes, it seems reasonable to me. When you talk about language there is a visual language, a written language, a spoken language. I am involved with the visual language and being able to communicate visually – not depict so much as communicate. It seems to me that the greatest thing you could do would be to make life, and it is a constant attempt to get close to that in painting. I keep thinking I am part of the transformation between the old pictures and the new. I have no expertise in the area, but there is an interesting aspect to oriental calligraphy. They try to get a certain spirit through, an inner spirit, a sort of Zen thing and that is an influence. I don't know what it is, but it's an influence. Also my painting has always really been, I have thought, directly related to the New York School of painting or the abstract expressionists. I have always felt that, no matter how it was classified with Minimalism and this and that, that it really reflected more of those kind of ideas – the possibilities for catharsis, you know, an emotional and expressionist attitude. I think this is sort of coming back. It's not that these paintings are abstract expressionist paintings. They are not, they don't deal with what I can remember.

When I was in school teachers were referring to clichés I was making on Franz Kline, De Kooning and Pollock. These were occurring in the paintings and I was constantly trying to eliminate them, but when I eliminated them I ended up with this minimalist surface.

WF *You are talking about artists that in a way, I guess, helped you to define a sort of context a while ago.*

BM Yes, then you think of Pollock working outside, and getting back to the nature thing. When he was asked about his work in reference to nature, Pollock said, 'I am nature'' I do not feel that when I paint I am nature, there is too much built in – I know too much. But this for me is something to work towards – to get to that point where you are just painting, you know, that sort of magical verb. Other artists that I've been looking at are American Indian artists. I have some pots made by South West American Indians whose surfaces contain, for me, one of the great expressions about landscape in American drawing. Think of the pot as the landscape or as the sky over this landscape, which is identified with the 360 degrees of the horizon rather than 180 degrees. These are the things I think about.

WF *'The rectangle, the plane, the structure, the picture are but sounding boards for a spirit.' This statement of yours has been quoted a lot, but I think it makes your intention clear.*

BM It came from a long time ago but I think it still holds. The artist, you know, just disappears. The artist doesn't have anything to do with it once it is made. It is out in the world and the real meaning of the picture is the person standing in front of it and what they are going to be able to get out of it. I like it when the viewer either works through and can drop all of the 'meaning' and just respond and allow their spirit to respond to what is put forth in the painting. I make it sound as if you have just got to stand in front of the painting and be dumb or something. It is not quite that but it is like opening yourself up to the possibilities of visual experience. I think some painters just manipulate it quite well.

WF *You worked and showed in galleries associated with Conceptual Art throughout the sixties. Looking back on that period I wondered how close you felt to that whole Conceptual Art area.*

BM Oh that is hard. I felt somewhat estranged from it, not a part of it. Somehow I was there and it is like guilt by association – I felt if my work was being read conceptually then it was being misread. I don't disagree with Conceptual Art – that is another possibility. I always had a feeling that with a lot of the Conceptual Art there was a lack of faith in art and I felt that my work was really about faith in art. But then, at the same time I really feel that my work is lacking a certain kind of edge. I think my work is very conservative and it worries me. I don't find Conceptual Art conservative at all, I find it quite daring and progressive. It really is involved with expanding ideas about how you can deal with art and about how you can deal with the whole situation. I like that about it and like being associated with it because of that but I still feel that, in terms of contemporary art, my work is much more conservative. My work is about holding on to values that have been in painting as I see it right from the beginning, and their work isn't.

WF *Would you agree that there has been almost a conscious denial, an attempt not to become too closely identified with the thinking and the activities of the group of artists that must have surrounded you in New York in the sixties?*

BM Well I don't know, give me some names.

WF *I'm thinking of people like Jasper Johns and people that used paint in an expressive manner.*

BM Jasper has influenced me in how he deals with the idea of reality, and painting as a reality rather than depiction. I think he has been a very big influence on that whole generation. I would never in any way consider myself a Pop artist or a Pop-influenced artist. Their's was a reaction to the kind of sloppiness that abstract expressionist ideas had grown into and they tried to clear it all away – it is like my teachers coming in and saying 'get rid of all the clichés'. Frank Stella has been a big influence also with his involvement with reality and what you see in painting. But then the abstract expressionist who was around in the sixties was Barnett Newman. You could see him in the bar and talk to him. It wasn't an everyday occurrence, but he was around and a working influence unlike most of the others. For instance, De Kooning, as I recall, wasn't showing that much in the sixties. He only came back in the seventies, and to appreciate De Kooning in the seventies was almost a form of being obscure. Now we really see it straight and for me, as a student, De Kooning was really the master. He was the one you refer to – the supreme source.

WF *Another artist that has been mentioned in the same context as you is Cy Twombly, and I think the phrase used was 'having an evocative presence' as far as the works were concerned.*

BM It is really hard for me to say. What I like about Cy's works is that they just seemed to me to get more and more beautiful – he is just making incredibly beautiful paintings. I see that as an inspiration and I really enjoy the paintings. I do not really feel that akin. I feel real leaden compared to Twombly. I think he is away out in the air some place and it is just magical. I feel there is a lot of gravity in my stuff that I can't get rid of and that he doesn't need at all. I really like Cy's things but then being an American it is very difficult to see his work.

WF *Although there is one work here whose formal elements you have revised by overpainting, they have surprised me to some extent because of their economy of surface. The paint is stained over the surface of the canvas.*

BM I don't know why but these have all been painted very thin. It may be a reaction to the way I used to paint, layer after layer, which was so involved with refinement. One of the reasons why I wanted to stop making those paintings was that I felt they were too much about refinement and not enough about art-making. With these I think it is much more direct. I put the paint on with a brush and take it off with a knife, so you draw it on and you redraw it as you take it off, trying to keep it as close to the surface as possible. The method of painting came out of the studies I did for the window paintings. I wasn't trying to paint as though they were glass, but there were ideas about light which I got closer to by painting thin rather than by building up the paint.

WF *Perhaps part of their interest is that they confound expectation. Artists such as Anselm Kiefer, Julian Schnabel and so on have made paintings in a fairly lavish matter with heavily encrusted surfaces. By contrast, your pieces seem to have been arrived at in a reductive way rather than through an additive process.*

BM Schnabel's plate things were an obvious sort of reaction – modern art has worked its way right up to the surface and the person who is handling it in the most refined manner now is Robert Ryman. He can still make a thorough and beautiful painting, maintain the plane and have the painting be meaningful, whereas someone like Schnabel has to break the plane or activate it in some way. It becomes collage. The same is true of Kiefer. When you are using collage you use real form and you lose the whole idea of illusion, which I consider to be one of the most important elements in painting. It is about the lack of ability to resolve what you want to say on the plane. It is always resolved on the plane in paintings as far as I can see and these people are breaking it. I just find collage a lesser form because what you use to collage with is a real form and even if does break and refer back it always has that reality which collage, in its worst sense, begins to depend on. With somebody like Robert Rauschenberg it is a different story because that is accepted. He is using real forms and you have to really question what those real forms are all about. But then I don't consider Rauschenberg to be someone you have to consider in terms of painting. But people like Kiefer and Schnabel have to be considered in terms of painting.

WF *Could we go back finally to the works that you have here at the moment. The motifs move across their surfaces in a net-like manner giving a taut, elasticated feel. The source of that imagery is shell-form patterning is it?*

BM Not really. Patterns on shells I more or less think of as patterns of growth sort of petrified. If you say 'I am going to take 20 lines and I will draw this tree', you should be able to tell if it is an olive tree or an almond tree just by the accumulation of lines. These things are really still involved in an awful lot of formal applications. I mean, with these paintings everything still goes out to the edge. I think these newer paintings relate to the rectangle in a very similar way to the one-colour panel paintings, whereas I am beginning to get away from that in some of the drawings. What concerns me now is what I was saying about Kiefer and collage. I don't want to sound like I'm carping or denigrating Kiefer's work. You can't just say it's no good because it is collage. That is just too academic. A lot of his strength comes from his use of these objects, but there also is this disturbing feeling about resolution of the plane. In some paintings I think it works, in others it doesn't, but I find him a very successful painter in terms of what he is doing in his work.

WF *Do you think they become more like illustrations or depictions of the concept and the content rather than the embodiment, which I imagine you are more interested in?*

BM Well, I think his work is about alchemy and my work is about alchemy; one is a realist approach and the other is an abstractionist approach. Kiefer is working with ideas and I find a lot of my ideas are somewhat similar to his. His method is completely different, but at the same time I feel very close. I am much more sympathetic to Kiefer than I am to Schnabel. I don't think Schnabel is really involved with ideas. There are ideas but they are not real subject-matter. It is about look not about meaning, whereas Kiefer is really about meaning. The way they look carries it, and the image carries it a lot but there is a real involvement with meaning which I think is quite moving.

WF *Is there anything else about the new work here that we have touched on but haven't really expanded?*

BM I find if I look at drawings that I made when I first came to New York they are really not too much different from what I am doing now, but they look a lot different. The whole thing is really to keep it from being clichéd even though you can't really change it. As I say, in the long run these are going to look just the same as the old things.

Issue 117, June 1988

Krzysztof Wodiczko

interviewed by William Furlong

I want to be a catalyst

WILLIAM FURLONG *Krzysztof, there seem to be two primary characteristics to your projected works. First, there is the way in which you engage with the specific meanings of a piece of architecture. Second, you present your works outside a visual arts context, so that you are making an intervention into the real world, to put it simply, and people without art knowledge are encountering the works you make. Could you expand on the sorts of relationships that you are interested in with particular reference to the Calton Hill project?*

KRZYSZTOF WODICZKO The structure we are discussing is the skeleton of the front on the unfinished temple which was to be a monument to those who participated in the Napoleonic campaign – one could say the victims of this blood bath of history. In many ways I think it works better being unfinished as it forces visitors to the hill to work to complete their own vision or to project meaning on to an unfinished symbolic structure. This is much more difficult than to project a mental kind of image on to a completed monument. The city is experiencing extremely difficult times of urban crisis visible, at least to those who are interested to see and understand it, in most of the cities in northern England, Scotland and Ireland. They are in some ways similar to what we see in the US or in the third-world countries. This Edinburgh – not the official image of Edinburgh – should somehow become visible. This is not to say that I am capable of transmitting, with any precision, an alternative image containing all the critical issues related to the survival of different groups – the homeless, drug users and addicts, people with the AIDS virus, single parents, all the young in those bed and breakfast hotels, abused groups like women and those who are victims of violence or who are in prisons – but what I can do is at least try to challenge or question the detachment of symbolic structures on this hill from what is happening around. Let us bring a sign or maybe a gesture, an iconic symbol, and juxtapose it with the architecture, with the façade of this unfinished monument. Maybe in some way, in a temporary fashion, complete this unfinished adventure or architectural enterprise through a symbolic act.

WF *So you want to expand the issue beyond the immediate piece of architecture you are working with to the notion of site and of how a site can relate to the resonance of what is around it. The Calton Hill site overlooks the city and in that sense the site is seen to engage with the social, economic, cultural, political and historic issues that are part of the resonance of the city.*

KW It is surrounded by those issues but it is distant. It creates a distant platform, a deck, reflective but distant.

WF *In a way, then, what you are attempting to do is to bring all of those notions together through your work. The work becomes a sort of catalyst for those issues.*

KW Yes, I just want to be a catalyst or to provide an entry. I want people to talk to each other in front of this projection. I would like the representatives of those different groups to whom this hill belongs, including tourists, to start asking questions and maybe some explanations or descriptions could be exchanged. In addition, I hope that some of the groups or some very active individuals who are running alternative programmes – inner city social programmes – will also come and maybe distribute their information and leaflets. I won't mind this. I would actually like this to happen.

WF *In a way the work would set up another sort of map of the city, an authentic one, which is much more concerned with the reality of everyday existence. I suppose what you are really talking about is authenticity in terms of the experience of what a city such as Edinburgh represents.*

KW It is an interruption of the spectacle. Maybe not with a counter spectacle, as it is very hard for me to compete with the Edinburgh Festival – especially the illumination of the city – but the form of disturbance will itself be spectacular in some way. One has to see also that the city already is an event in itself and there are events which project themselves on to those structures without my work. It is just a matter of perhaps helping to concretise them visually and concentrating attention, in maybe a synthetic way, in selected sites. In New

York, for example, the homeless now number 100,000. Their habitat is usually sites and monuments representing, or at least produced to commemorate, acts of individuals or groups to secure liberty, civil liberties, pursuit of happiness, individual freedom, or economic rights for all. The US was formed on the basis of those ideals. Here we have Washington, Lafayette, we have Lincoln – statues surrounded by homeless people who live there and who, even worse, actually look similar to those sculptures. The possibility of connecting frozen gesture and body cracked through changing weather conditions, dirt and pollution with the homeless individual is there. Yet there is a gross contradiction between them – a similarity and contradiction. They should not be together, yet they are bound to exist together. For a project in Boston, then, I projected actual bodies of homeless individuals onto the bodies of those historic figures. The city's Civil War memorial became a memorial to the contemporary civil war. Now I cannot really be as precise on Calton Hill because although it is a fantastic site there are not structures like that. Here I will have to be a little more abstract – more indirect.

WF *Yes I understand what you mean. In a way, by also working out of doors you are using meanings that are already in place. It's as though people are already aware of part of the work but the work itself actually somehow creates a focus for those issues and concerns. It is not as though you are taking something from outside and imposing it. It is very much a part of a set of codes or emblems or myths that we all know about.*

KW It is not like psychoanalytical work on architecture, trying to reveal what it contains. It is really a projection of that new context onto those monuments, forcing them in some ways to speak in new terms or to accept meanings and not only to accept, but also to articulate this meaning. They cannot really be forced to say everything I would like them to speak about. I have to accept the way the bodies are formed and the way their speech is limited. In that sense I have to work seriously with the architectural form, but there is no necessity to include the whole history of meaning of that architecture, although if it could refer to that history it would be even better.

WF *That is interesting, because when we last spoke in 1985 you were using the architecture of Nelson's Column and the Duke of York's monument in London much more specifically than you seem to be doing now. In fact now you have broadened your approach to encompass the notion of the site, its resonances, and the way in which the issues that surround the site can be articulated through the work.*

KW This reflects the transformation of my own work and a shift of focus. But still all the elements of this work are there. It is just as you mentioned, the accent is more placed on what is happening around. More and more, the work is attached to the urban environment as a whole and less to particular architectural sites.

WF *The way you are talking about your current works is as though you are much more concerned with making a social intervention, an engagement.*

KW Yes. Perhaps here I should mention another project which has nothing to do with light and night. It is an attempt to design and manufacture, in a non-mass-scale way, a series of tools which are instruments of survival for the homeless in New York. Design objects function very well as communicative structures, especially in the middle-class consumer culture. The idea is to introduce highly articulate, mobile, functional objects, but ones which articulate things people don't want to see, which confront the attempt, on the part of the non-homeless, to erase the existence of the homeless as living and working individuals, reducing them to the status of rubbish – a part of the architectural environment – a static one, a monumental one. It might be quite effective, especially if the 'functionalism' of those objects was revealed. The condition of an individual who is intelligent and capable, and is using all his abilities to, for example, collect bottles, cans or other objects to sell in order to earn a minimum income, is almost like the lowest degree of enterprise in this highly individualised consumer world. Yet it also provides an opportunity for those homeless to form a collective habitat. Architecture and design cannot liberate anyone but can certainly transmit – if they are critical – the real conditions of existence and maybe help people to survive better. So this symbolic object might be a clue for a different type of aesthetic practice. This is still really the same as an intervention upon an environment.

Issue 120, October 1988

Daniel Buren and Seth Siegelaub

interviewed by Michel Claura and Deke Dusinberre

May '68 and all that

DEKE DUSINBERRE *Would you want to start by talking about personal origin, personal moments of inspiration for art practice?*

SETH SIEGELAUB No, I would want to talk about the larger political context within which I grew up. The context for me during my early working life in the US was the Vietnam War, it was an important factor in my growing up. Whether it was an important factor in the art world as such remains to be seen.

DD *So you suggest we start from those social and political points?*

SS Well that to me, in the US, was a very important background for what was going on in the art world. It was probably so in varying degrees for Larry Poons and everybody else too, but I think it was particularly critical for the kind of art that we're talking about.

DANIEL BUREN I think it's true of all people of my generation. From the time that I was 17 or 18 with the Korean War and then after that the Algerian War there has been a succession of violent and controversial events which have formed the central point for daily actions and thoughts in France. This happened from my youth right through to its peak which, although different, was still political, that is, the events which led up to May 1968. So for people of my generation – even if it has not been totally conscious – I think a lot of our way of thinking, our attitudes, reactions, etc have been framed by those successive colonial wars.

DD *Would you go so far as to make a direct relationship between that cultural/political environment and an art practice such as Conceptual Art?*

DB I am sure it is important although I would not draw a direct line. Personally, I was both very engaged and sceptical about the drawing of that kind of engagement into the production of art. I was strongly critical of those contemporaries of mine in France who brought into art a formal concern with these sorts of problems. For the most part their work consisted of large figurative paintings which described an attitude to the events we have been mentioning. My dissatisfaction with the idea of taking an artwork as a flag for a certain kind of political engagement was that in political terms such a gesture was meaningless. However, there is a strong relation with what I was able to do at the time, if we take into account the kind of consciousness we are talking about. I guess that the bridge was – and this is something which I shared with other people in other places – the question that if one was concerned with the political situation, what would it mean to take the art world itself as a political problem? Is that micro-system a total revelation or reverberation of the general system? If it is not, where does the weight of the political system make itself felt within the art world? I think producers from different cultures and different countries – and I'm thinking particularly of America – shared this total rejection of a practice which put political concern into 'art shapes'. Up until then that had been the only way to deal with issues of this kind. Focusing on something which seemed to have little or nothing to do with this concern allowed us to question where politics was actually feeding into the production of art, its reception, its structure and its context. I guess that, vaguely, under the stupid name of Conceptual Art, a certain mid-sixties sensibility did criss-cross between Europe and America: obviously there were different cultural emphases, but the connections were there.

SS You have to use the term 'politics' in two ways. Daniel is alluding to this although I don't think we've made it quite clear yet. There is 'political' in the superficial sense in which one speaks of the traditional left/right opposition of social forces, and 'political' in the deeper sense which refers to a conscious questioning of what is going on around you, not just in the sense of left/right or imperialist/anti-imperialist, but in terms of the kind of relationships that exist between people, between people and things, between people and institutions. This latter sense calls up in art, as in any other context, a whole range of issues. That moment in the late sixties, particularly in the US in any case, was very full of these kinds of questions. They were *l'air du temps* you might say. A lot of people, even those doing traditional things like Pop Art, were talking about such relationships.

The Vietnam War brought into question a whole range of things – the traditional role of the US, or maybe of France for Daniel and Michel, the role of imperialist power, the wider understanding of world relationships. This also nourished the traditional 'art attitude' which, at least as it has been presented in the twentieth century, is one of contestation too. But that would be the false route – that the artist would naturally be against a power structure is the most superficial kind of trap, and is one that particularly concerns Daniel. As I say, the deeper aspects of this questioning of relationships were of concern to many artists, not just conceptualists, although Conceptual Art was perhaps able to attack these problems more frontally than painting could ever do since it took too much for granted in its very nature.

MICHEL CLAURA *How and when would you make the connection between the political surroundings and the fact that at that time people created, so to speak, a new, dematerialised form of art? You described the context, you described the fact that artists were concerned with that context and politically involved against what was going on, but to what extent is that reflected by this move towards a non-object based form of artwork?*

SS It is not a one-to-one relationship, but there are certain underlying links. For example, the sort of question that could conceivably have been posed at that time was: what could be the connection between a subject like democracy and a kind of art? With reference to this, there is certainly something which is very dear to me about materiality. The process of making a work of art which, although not necessarily less material, certainly in a crude sense, costs less, opens up the possibility of who can make it. It also has to do with how it can be seen, how it can be shown, and a lot of other things which go with that.

DB It was difficult not to be affected by the political situation however hard you tried to avoid it. I think one of the things which links a lot of the people who came to prominence in the mid to late sixties, quite apart from any formal distinction that could be made, is an economic restriction which is seen in the use of poor materials, of no materials at all, in exhibitions outside the gallery, and so on. Remember also that in economic terms those were boom years. It wasn't that artists were simply against the idea of money, they were working in an atmosphere in which one found the widely held belief that the West was set for a future of permanent economic growth. 1968 was the first point at which people realised that this was not true and that we were running towards catastrophe. Unfortunately that has been true of most of the time between then and today. The interesting thing in terms of the art world is that there was a group of people at that time, all of whom were working in a way which had almost nothing to do with aesthetics and which concerned itself with the question of how one can make something from nothing. There were people working with shadows – no cost. People working with words – no cost. People working with bits of wood found lying in the street or hedgerows – no cost, etc, etc. Of course – and perhaps this is something we should discuss elsewhere – a lot of this stuff became chic and expensive, stylish and academic. But if you take it as the emergence of a connection between the sensibilities of people who, in most cases, did not at that time know of each other, it is very interesting to see it in terms of the economy of means.

SS You wouldn't want to rush too quickly to say that that was democracy, but that seemed to me at the time to be an important factor. You can say that of all art movements when they're young – putting bits of wood together in Paris in 1910 was new too – but I think we're talking about something quite, quite different in the late sixties.

DB I would see that in a way as being in the very standard tradition of the Avant Garde. This kind of total contradiction between a society which believed that all was possible, that progress would continue for ever, and a group of artists, not necessarily homogeneous or with shared interests, working on things which were of no cost, usually with no technique, no technology, very fugitive, more or less also against possession – even if that did turn into bullshit for most of them. But if you see the impulse and the opposition it's interesting, it is in the tradition of the Avant Garde, it's a reaction against society as a whole – as opposed to just a form of art. You could say that a lot of avantgardisms have been directed at their immediate predecessors and have developed in relation to, in antithesis to, or in contravention of them. Here was something which didn't have that quality, it dealt with something else. I suppose in terms of generations, the people who came immediately before would be Carl Andre and, as a borderline case, Sol LeWitt – minimal sculptors anyway. Conceptualism wasn't developed in opposition to that and, in fact, there are a lot of people who fall just on the line between the two. Conceptualism was a much more fundamental calling into question of things. That's what is so interesting about it and is probably why we're having this conversation.

DB We also know that, historically, attacking the object – attempting to escape from it – is a twentieth-century phenomenon. It comes in cycles and was not new in the sixties. However, as things get older they can get more radical, and even though it may have been working on family principles it was, for a moment, a more radical questioning of the object than anything which had gone before. From a personal point of view it led to a lot of suspicion. I wrote at the time that although the impulse seemed a good and interesting one, we should be careful not to withdraw the object simply because the object itself was under question. In other words, I was suspicious of the term Conceptual Art because it was easy to place under its umbrella a lot of objects which were much less interesting than a painting. Also because I thought then – and still think – that if the problem of the object is one of the most interesting to challenge, you don't solve that problem by doing no-object work. The idea that something was more interesting simply because there was nothing to see was a ridiculous one, but it was dangerous because, even if it wasn't what most of the artists thought, it was the notion adopted by many observers at the time. Many of the people who championed that view eventually turned back to things which had nothing to do with it. Force of economic obligation and the frustration of the public and the art world have had something to do with this. They are not the only reasons, but they did partly open the door for the production of the most reactionary art that we have seen over the past ten years. I am sure that in a few years' time the art of this period will appear as some of the least interesting and most reactionary of the entire century.

DD *Can you be more specific about the kind of art you mean?*

DB During the past decade we have seen, more or less under the term Postmodernism, the production and acceptance of something which is diametrically opposed – even in ideological terms – to the spirit of the mid sixties. This is not to say that the mid sixties were beautiful, this is bad; I'm more interested personally in what happened in the mid sixties but that's beside the point. What is objective, and not personal, is to say that these two movements are radically separate. What one, with all its mistakes and tentativeness, was trying to say, the other was opposing very loudly, very brilliantly. Expressionistic painting, reactionary sculpture, and so on. Even though the term Conceptual Art is itself ridiculous, it refers to something important. What these people were reacting against was a caricature of Conceptual Art, and what they accomplished in doing so was the erasure of 70 years of art. We have seen the return of the nineteenth-century pompiers in the production of a certain type of painting today – Julian Schnabel, Francesco Clemente, Marcus Lüpertz, I could go on, not forgetting Anselm Kiefer. They show an evident step back, not only compared to conceptualism, but 70 years of art.

SS It's also interesting to note not just the painters but the immediate, art world environment within which they operate. It has changed so dramatically, particularly for me as someone who has not lived the last 20 years in the art world. It has changed in part due to frustrations which may have been potential rather than real, but which existed in the kind of art we started to talk about at the beginning. But also, the nature of the art world in reference to the real world has changed. The art that is produced within it connects to money, to business, to fashion, to the hype which characterises a lot of the advanced capitalist culture today. The relationship is very, very close. There is a very high turnover in every sense of the word, emotionally, artistically and economically. So the art world has changed dramatically, and that change has brought with it a certain kind of art, or it has searched for a kind of art which responds to that kind of hype shit. I'm sure that Conceptual Art corresponded to a certain moment within the art world too, a certain kind of art showing – or lack of it – particularly.

DB We started by saying that everyone was concerned in their own place with these problems. This was true in a personal sense, but it was also true that this was forced upon everyone. Personally, today I have the same kinds of commitments. They are not perhaps so brilliant but they are no worse than they were. What I see, though, is that this commitment is no longer part of the context, and when you dare to say the sort of thing which comes naturally to me about connections which exist between what is happening in the world and what is happening in the art world, you almost look like a zombie. Few people will ever bother to enter into discussion, preferring to think, even if it is not true, that this is an old story all washed up. I'm not talking about myself and a situation in which someone can say to me, look, you said that 20 years ago, forget it. People of all ages who speak of these things from an interesting and new perspective have a very hard time getting themselves understood or even followed. It will change again no doubt, but the present situation I find astonishing.

SS All art movements since the late-nineteenth century have started with a group of people. It is impossible to promote one great artist. Once they have been established by Daniel-Henry Kahnweiler or Leo Castelli or Betty Parsons it is possible for the public to perceive the personality of each individual artist. This process of individualisation of each artist's *troc* becomes more and more the focus of art at the expense of exactly these kinds of social determinants which are not one-to-one. The mechanisms of art promotion do everything to try and avoid the context we are trying to understand here, at the expense of great artists. The business of art history is the valorising of individual artists and the selling of them. Even looking at the problem is difficult because it is so obfuscated and blurred. No one wants to hear that there were 50 people thinking about this kind of thing in the 1960s, they just want to know who the fucking genius was and who they're going to make money with. The kind of questions we are considering are asked by some people of nineteenth-century painting, but to do the same for the period in which we live is very difficult. Everything works against the kind of analysis which attempts to find a commonality.

DB We can go further. This kind of thing, whether it is a fantasy, degenerate, or whatever, did provoke and create a new style. Seth was able to do a show which was a catalogue. It was possible to put on a show simultaneously in Paris, London, New York and New Mexico. It was possible to do a show in a small village. Today, the door has been opened to a new academicism within curatorship. I do not think all that is unconnected to the fact that one can now think that a possible use for the Gare d'Orsay is as a museum. In the sixties there was an explosion – we could show anywhere, and anyone could show. This could be ridiculous, but it was also part of the spirit, everyone was an artist – or could be. Today there is little enthusiasm for the stimulation of production, but a huge enthusiasm for the creation of museums. This increase in the number of art centres is one of the legacies of that period, and it implies a change in the audience, since such centres would not exist without people to attend. People operating in the wider context understood better what to do with those ideas than the artists did. This is a paradox which affects what I do today since as an artist you come after the proposal of a context. I think this is extremely funny, interesting, tricky and dangerous. The effort which this requires from architects, keepers, curators, directors, collectors takes place in a system which has no common measure with the art world of 20 years ago.

MC *Is the question not, in fact, whether Conceptual Art ever existed? Thinking of the fact, for instance, that, perhaps with one or maybe two exceptions, I cannot remember any artist ever accepting himself to be a conceptual artist? Am I right?*

SS I think Joseph (Kosuth) did.

MC *He's the only one to my knowledge. Nonetheless, people have been talking about Conceptual Art for quite a while, including a period of a few years in which they spoke of it as a sort of threat. To some extent because of the combination that existed at the time, which opened up more freedom for exhibitions, I just wonder whether it was because of this that art suddenly became so fashionable. When you say that it opened up this variety of types of exhibition – do it anywhere, by yourself, whenever – does this not have a lot to do with the fact that art has become a real thing in economic terms. It would be paradoxical if, because of something which never existed, one saw the emergence of art as reactionary as you describe. But there is another way of demonstrating that Conceptual Art never existed – it has never achieved power, even within the art world.*

DB The power has been taken from the ends of the artist and transferred to the ends of the curator, museum director, magazine editor, or whoever. There is one example of this which I like because it is so extraordinary. After 1967 even people with totally antagonistic works were able, with somebody's help or on their own, to show anywhere. It was interesting and was difficult and it was totally for a little elite – a bakery is a vitrine for an exhibition, the apartment of a friend is a beautiful place for a show, etc. All of this was put by and almost forgotten as stupidity, or naivety. During the seventies things gradually moved back to the museums, and galleries became more and more important. All of a sudden in 1986 you have a museum by itself which finds a way to get the money and prestige to put on the exhibition '*Chambres d'Amis*'. And what is that exhibition? It isn't one artist in the museum, or two: 70 artists show their work in the private houses of seventy people in the city of Ghent. In 1967–68, several artists with no commitment say, 'We cannot find a gallery, let's show outside.' Twenty years later, the director of a museum makes the ludicrous decision that to show in a private house is more public than to show in a museum – I don't know exactly what that means, but it was stated in the catalogue – he persuades 70 artists, even those of my generation who more or less invented the idea, to show in these houses, and seven months later is given the biggest award to a director for the concept of his exhibition!

DD *Twenty years ago, when people showed in those contexts, what was the relation between the art they showed and the space they used, and was it the same as that which obtained in Ghent?*

DB Each of the people in Ghent was, by force, obliged to do something in relation to that situation and in that, of course, I included the possibility that the relationship could be antagonistic. But no one was doing any oil painting and using the bakery as a vitrine. Everything they did was done for a coherent reason, it wasn't interesting or chic.

SS Another difference is that in this case it is the museum director who is, in effect, the major figure – the artist if you like. Twenty years ago it wasn't like that.

DB Everything you did as an organiser was done more or less through a process of osmosis, but don't forget that you are a perfect example of what is now the cliché. Everyone really has copied you in the worst way, which is to be the chief and the artist of the show.

SS It was my lack of economic means and *l'air du temps* which created the relationship that existed between the kind of shows I did and the artists with whom I was involved. It was an attempt to get away from the gallery because my feeling at the time, as it is now in the case of publishing, is that a space becomes sacralised. The economics of the situation is such that you need to fill a space with eight or ten shows a year, and it is inconceivable that you can do that and remain interested in all of the work you show. You didn't run a gallery, the gallery ran you – it was just another form of alienated work experience. The gallery came to determine the art to the extent that painters would paint paintings to fit the walls of their dealer. I simply took the responsibility of working with the artists whose work was around and bubbling up. Osmosis is probably the best way of describing what went on.

DD *Do you three think, then, that there was such a thing as the Conceptual Art movement or was it a fiction?*

SS I think all art movements are fictions in that sense. They are promotional and, ultimately, economic devices. It's perfectly normal for a group of people to get together in order to work, discuss and help each other, whether to raise crops in 2000 BC or to make art in 1988, but the art world refers to these things as movements for purely economic reasons. It's something that I think Barnett Newman referred to as the hardening of the categories. The world just has to have these little boxes and I hate them. I hate them. It is just an easy way of describing something so that you don't have to deal with it.

DB And I think that, because most of the people at that time were concerned with these issues, it was difficult for them to accept this kind of labelling. All recent movements, from Pop Art onwards, have an image. By contrast, the success of a word like 'conceptualism' lies in the total depreciation of the products which lie behind it.

SS The other thing about categories is they prevent you from seeing the reality. They give you the impression that each generation has one thing going on and that's all. It's all that's happening, they prevent you from looking. It's a formalist and ultimately reactionary way to view the world.

DB Even though the exhibitions at the time drew on a group of 40, 50 or 60 artists, I am sure that history will see conceptualism in terms of the work of four or five artists who work in a particular way.

SS One of the reasons there is an interest in this kind of art is that economically it has not been successful in the way that other art has and in the way that its reputation might suggest. There is, therefore, a romantic side to its image, that of the poor artist.

DD *When did this fictional movement cease even to be a fiction? When did it lose steam?*

DB In a personal sense it decayed very quickly. The first period was 1965–70, and then in the seventies there were a lot of things which followed on. We couldn't call that a second generation, but there were people who were just too young who were influenced by our generation. As a fashion it carried on until the late seventies, and even after that it was still being used as a recommendation and this big wave of painting and sculpture rose up from those who stupidly thought we had tried to erase these things from the planet. The move against conceptualism started earlier though. Conceptualism featured strongly in the 1969 'Prospekt' alongside Arte Povera and some Minimalism, and this was followed by 'When Attitudes Become Form', and a number of other shows. By 1972 or 73, however, 'Prospekt' was full of painting, a gesture which collapsed totally because the general mood was still for questioning art, questioning objects. In 1980, with a very different kind of product, painting came back into consideration.

SS A very important facet of this work was that if you wanted to show it you had to deal with these people. It was never a question of just sending something somewhere. The way the economics worked out, it was cheaper to send the artist than to send the work.

MC *That is also where Conceptual Art became human. People had to be on the spot, but quite often they were there just to be around.*

DB Speaking of the romantic aspect of things, people saw no direct relationship between having a show and selling something. It was absolutely not wrong, not something to feel guilty about, if you had a show and sold nothing at all. It was not wrong to sell either. Travelling meant that it was about human relations. Don't forget the museums deal with objects and in those terms they are pretty good. They know how to classify a thing, how much it weighs, how much it costs, but when you invite somebody, all these things are erased, they have no idea how to proceed.

Issue 122, December–January 1988–89

John Berger

interviewed by Janine Burke

Raising hell and telling stories

JANINE BURKE *The revolutionary quality of your work consists in the demands it makes on the reader to rethink systems previously accepted. To read your work is constantly to be challenged. This is obviously a life process for you and a way of thinking about the world. What is there in your background that challenged you sufficiently to put that process into effect through words and images?*

JOHN BERGER I have two clues about it. One is to do with my very early childhood. Although I lived with my mother and my father, my childhood was rather like that of an orphan. I was alone from a very early age. I had to find out everything for myself. One of the things I lacked was a strong sense of identity which comes principally from the love of one's parents, I mean, the expressed love. It was there but I didn't really experience it. It meant I could identify easily with other people, I could lend myself to them. I felt that I never belonged to one place or one milieu. The second thing is simpler to explain. From a quite early age, from six till 16, I was sent to those totally barbaric English private schools. I wasn't victimised but they were crazy places, mad and vicious. At 16, I ran away. If you take what now obsesses the English, their upper-class spies, all of them went to somewhat similar schools. It's because of the system they found themselves in that they became Soviet spies. Well, I didn't become a Soviet spy, I was a bit younger but I decided that I wanted to get the bloody hell out of that country and never have much to do with it again. Above all, with its ruling class. Because that's what we're talking about, the ruling class.

JBU A Painter of Our Time *was your first novel. You'd trained as a painter, you were already writing art criticism. How did that novel come to be? Was it through the practice of writing criticism or was it due to the abandonment of painting, the act of painting itself?*

JB That book was a kind of farewell to painting. The reason I decided to abandon painting wasn't because I didn't like it. Even now there is nothing that gives me more satisfaction than drawing or painting. Nor was it because I thought I lacked talent, but in the late forties with the issues of war and peace and the threat of nuclear war, particularly before the Soviet Union acquired nuclear parity, it seemed to many of us that the world had only a few years to survive and so the urgency of political statements, political action and propaganda was enormous. Painting seemed a very indirect way of contributing to that whereas words seemed not all that effective but rather more so. This, I rationalised to myself, was why I gave up painting. I threw myself into journalism about art but also about political issues, into political activity, into meetings. Then, as time went on, I became so engaged that the return to painting, although remaining a dream which I still have, became impossible.

JBU *So it didn't hurt?*

JB No, it didn't hurt.

JBU *You certainly raised hell as a young art critic.*

JB Well, it wasn't difficult to raise hell in that polite world.

JBU *In* A Painter of Our Time *you presented Janos, the central character, with a moral dilemma, and you placed him in a milieu, gave him friends which are not usual, not the stereotype of the artist's life.*

JB It so happened that more than half of the artists I knew, mostly older than myself, were refugees from Fascism. Jewish, but not all. People who had left Nazi Germany, Austria, Poland and come to England just before the war. I lived in a circle of refugees and there was a kind of complicity and understanding between us, despite our different experiences. These people had survived because of England, and England, compared to what they'd left, was democracy, freedom. But there was something that distanced them from the English and made them feel foreign. I knew what it was. The English refusal to recognise pain. For the refugees, pain was inevitable, even a spur to creativity. It was what we had in common. Out of that experience came the character of Janos.

JBU *So from a very early age you decided to reject England?*

JB It wasn't only a rejection of England, it was a desire or ambition to become a European. Only now, in terms of my existence as a writer, is this true. I've become a European. I chose France because the men I most admired – Albert Camus, Roland Barthes, Maurice Merleau-Ponty, not to mention artists like Alberto Giacometti – were here. Yet I think that my adopted country, though it had become France, was Europe and I mean both eastern and western Europe.

JBU *That's a big home. It means your life and your writing needs to be complex enough to address a range of different issues, particular to those places.*

JB Becoming a European didn't necessarily mean I had insightful things to say about all those places but it meant I could cut through the local prejudices of countries, of classes, to reveal elements which are quite simple, and not so diverse, but which so much official culture buries.

JBU *In 1972 you won the Booker Prize for* G. *You gave part of the money to the London Black Panthers and criticised Booker-McConnell for its financial interests in the Caribbean. How was that received by the London literary world?*

JB There was a ceremony at the Café Royal in London where several hundred members of the literary world gathered. I got up and made my speech, and when I was about half-way through, and it was clear what tack I was going to take, many of the guests picked up their spoons and began to hit them against their glasses, saying, 'Sit down, shut up, you bugger', exactly like schoolboys and schoolgirls. So I had to wait several minutes even to be heard. Then somebody – some liberal – said, 'Let him have his word.' They were quiet for a while, then at the end they did the same. It was remarkably infantile. Apart from the Booker, *G* also won three other prizes. In a sense, those prizes were decided by the literary establishment so I can't really say that I was considered Enemy Number One. The reaction was profoundly English – which was to forget it. 'We will pretend to forget it though we will never forget it.'

JBU *Like a* faux-pas*?*

JB Exactly.

JBU *G is an anti-hero, isn't he? A transparent character who is acted upon by circumstance. Events drain through him, and he's formed by them rather than having an inner life. Women are the formative agents. G remains a mystery.*

JB It's not that he's an anti-hero, it's rather that he's a myth. The essential quality of a myth is that it has an outward action but no personalised centre. That's why he doesn't have a name. The idea of writing a book about Don Juan came to me when I was writing the book on Picasso because it seemed to me that he was a kind of Don Juan of painting.

JBU *Picasso is a very physical text, as though you're tackling him, wrestling with him. You're as keen to represent the mythology of the Picasso persona as you are to discuss the paintings. It seems logical that you could draw out of this the possibility of a fictional work.*

JB I asked myself, when was the last time one could have a Don Juan as opposed to a Casanova character in European history? There are two preconditions. One is a society that is stagnant, that is not politically or socially mobile. When you have a dynamic society, the energy of a Don Juan would be directed in a different way. He'd fight society, challenge it. He might be a fantastic chaser of skirts but it wouldn't be his principal role. Secondly, he would need a society where women are the property of men. The last period when those two conditions applied was just before the First World War. In Britain today, they could apply, at least in some milieus, despite the feminist movement.

JBU *Does writing come fluently to you? There is a marvellous luminosity to your words, a distillation, an honesty so profound it is almost abstract.*

JB I actually have rather little talent for writing. I have much more talent for drawing, for example. Maybe I have a talent for vision but not for putting it down. Therefore when I write never, to begin with, does it come out any sort of way that I want, I write the same pages six, seven, eight times. That means for every book, I write six or seven. That's why they take so long. Writing and rewriting, so the words come as close as I can get to the original vision or melody. Perhaps a distillation occurs.

JBU *Both the reading of your work and the sense of how you've created it are very physical sensations. That's one of the most arresting qualities of your writing, particularly when you talk about painting. It's literally arresting, it gives the reader pause.*

JB It's true that I'm so physically concentrated that I can't get out of a chair afterwards, I've got cramps in both legs. It's also true that I say the words to myself, out loud. Both of those things are very physical. Perhaps it comes from this lack of facility, this lack of talent in the usual sense of the word. Most creative achievements are like that: they begin with a difficulty.

JBU *Was* Ways of Seeing *made to challenge Kenneth Clark's* Civilisation*?*

JB Mike Dibb, the director, suggested he and I work together and we decided to do several programmes on art. Soon after, Kenneth Clark's series went to air and we thought we were doing the opposite of that, a kind of reply. The BBC didn't believe in our series at all. They gave us a very small budget, they didn't even give us a studio to work in. They gave us a Nissen hut in the suburbs of London which had no soundproofing. It was so close to a main road that every time a lorry went past we had to stop and retake. Then they forgot about us, which was a stroke of incredible luck because we did as we liked. We worked on those programmes for nine months, so we had time to perfect them. When we showed the four programmes to the BBC, they didn't like them at all. So they were shown very late at night but finally, after much discussion, they were rescheduled and became successful.

JBU *The most influential part of that series, and the book, was the critique of women's imagery. It came at a moment in the early seventies when the analysis of women's imagery in art and advertising had just begun. Was this section of* Ways of Seeing *the result of a collective process or your own observations coalesced over a long period of time?*

JB Many of the ideas came from *G*. There are some sentences that are almost the same. But the ideas generated by the women's movement were discussed and, undoubtedly, we owed a great deal to that. There is a group of women who are interviewed at the end of the programme: they viewed the series before it was finished and gave us advice, too. Completely unexpectedly to us, the book and the series became well-known, influential. Now there's a danger, I feel that *Ways of Seeing* has become a kind of holy writ which is the exact opposite of what we were trying to do. We wanted to open up the questions that others would take further. And the feminists have taken it further. We were simply catalysts.

JBU *In* About Looking *you mention Barthes's followers who 'love closed systems'. What are your thoughts on the post-structuralist enterprise? Do you see it as a post-1968 turning away from radical action?*

JB For Barthes I have enormous admiration. I've learnt a great deal from him. My feeling for him has nothing to do with structuralism, it is actually to do with the pain that is in him. This is so well described in *Camera Lucida*. To me, post-structuralism represents two things. One is an acceptance of political closures. Those political closures were there, I don't think the writers made them up out of cowardice though the movement has its academics. Academia always makes its cosy corners. Secondly, it drew attention to a consciousness of the text as artefact. That is quite important because it comes back to an awareness of what storytelling is, an awareness that stories are different from life, and they join life, not simply because they are parallel to life but because they have a certain autonomy while touching life all the time. So on the one hand there is the political quietism but on the other it draws attention to what had been forgotten, a notion of engagement it was necessary to re-find.

JBU *Geoff Dyer's* Ways of Telling, *which deals with the body of your work, does you a great disservice. Will you rectify this balance by writing your autobiography for us?*

JB From time to time I write tiny bits of text that are autobiographical but I can't imagine that I would write an autobiography. The reason for that is linked to the first thing I said: I have such a weak sense of my own identity except when I'm working on something and, of course, that means something other than myself.

JBU *But that's the gift of the storyteller, isn't it?*

JB Maybe the storyteller can never write an autobiography, maybe that's the contradiction. It's been proposed to me, for instance, 'to write about my experiences in those private schools'. But then I think about what's happening in South Africa and I think, who cares what's happening in those schools? It's so small compared to the important things. I can't give my energy to it.

Issue 124, March 1989

Ilya Kabakov

interviewed by William Furlong

The unofficial line

WILLIAM FURLONG *Your installation* The Untalented Artist And Other Characters, *1989, consists of a series of room spaces that have been cordoned off and divided. A lot of other elements are included like the debris from a building site. In the catalogue you talk very vividly of the Soviet apartment. Could you explain what is clearly a very strong relationship that you have with the experience of having lived in Moscow apartments.*

ILYA KABAKOV I don't want to depict the reality of a communal apartment and the details of living in one. The artwork is not intended to represent the real thing. I really want to talk about other things in my work. It is not intended to depict the ethnic quality of what living in a communal apartment is all about, although it does demonstrate some aspects of it. It is more generally a question about closing a person in and about a person having to live in a space of four walls, how he actually communicates and has contact with other people in this situation. In one respect it is a perfect situation for constant exchange and contact through always being surrounded by other people. The individual has to find some way of maintaining his personal self separate from the huge sea of people around him. The communal apartment is more a depiction of how a person mixes and how he protects himself from those around him.

WF *So the apartment is merely being used metaphorically as a way of exploring the human condition within certain situations. The installations here seem to be inhabited by comic characters, on the one hand, and on the other by very tragic ones.*

IK Another important metaphor in the situation of a communal apartment is that nobody chooses their neighbours. They are just thrown together and they have to live with them as they find them. The communal apartment divides into two parts really – the corridor and separate rooms where people live privately or separately in their own area, and the communal kitchen which is a kind of battleground where there is constant exchange and contact. Sadly there isn't a communal kitchen in this particular installation as it doesn't have a part in it. I hope that in New York, in the Ronald Feldman Gallery, I will be able to put together the whole thing with the kitchen and all the rooms and the corridor.

WF *Are these installations, which you base around characters, an attempt to escape from what is an overbearing structure into a more private real world by analysing and making manifest every aspect of one's existence, right down to the debris that we all have and use? For example, the room titled* 'The Man Who Never Threw Anything Away' *seems to me to be a way of substantiating an existence.*

IK This is absolutely true.

WF The Man Who Flew Into Space From His Apartment, *1981–88, is rather like a cell with a seating contraption which looks as if it could launch somebody. There are also various other objects in the room that seem to evoke the presence of a human being. There is a sense of a presence here.*

IK Every room is always, in a way, like a prison, to a person. If you live in a room, to get to the outside world seems to be the ultimate desire. If you want to you can just go out of the room into the corridor to the kitchen to meet other people. The corridor and the kitchen are like the outside world to the occupant and are where he escapes from his inner world. But this outside world of the communal apartment is not adequate for him and he wants to escape the whole of that and to get right out of it. So the cosmos of space that he wants to get out into is for him like some kind of other world, some heaven, some wonderful place or some paradise.

WF *In that respect it opens up those issues to do with the artist's relationship to the state which clearly one has to deal with when looking at the work.*

IK I don't think that is right really. I am not arguing, but it is more about an attempt at trying to get into the other world by your own means and, although this character has tried to get into the other world by this crazy invention, it has a kind of pathos because it is obviously not adequate. It seems to us that it is silly and comic but on the other hand when he flew away nobody found him on the earth afterwards. So it may have been a successful experiment. We had no proof to the contrary. So it is an open question and it may have been successful.

WF *At the Riverside Studios you have a maze-like installation of some of your narratives in book form. One thing that interests me in all this is the relationship between what clearly are autobiographical experiences and the way they are expressed through a third party.*

IK *The Short Man* has three characters in a way that work in it. There is the 'Short Man' who put the thing together and who composed it. There are my drawings in it and there is also another character who thought up the installation as a whole. So there are three characters working all at once and it is not clear who is the main character. Whether it is the artist, whether it is one of the characters that have been invented or whether it is the further character who emerged and created the whole.

WF *You have painted the main section of the gallery with a colour half-way up the wall rather like an institutional building. There are paintings leaning against the wall and through the centre is the paraphernalia of decorating and building. It gives a sense that something has been started that hasn't been finished.*

IK This uncertainty about whether something is in the process of being built or in the process of being taken apart and thrown away is very elemental in the way the communal apartment functions. There is a sense of movement all the time, and of never knowing in which direction you are going. When I actually put this installation together, I never really knew whether it was going to be built any further than it is or whether it was going to be taken down. At what point that feeling begins is also unclear because when you are building something there is always rubbish and when you are taking something away there is always rubbish, and the rubbish is very much a symbol of this uncertainty of movement. The rubbish not only is a symbol of the ruin of destruction and entropy, but it also has a particular potential because all these people's lives are really basically a clutter of things that have been drawn from that rubbish. So rubbish has a capacity to go either way. It is sort of neutral but a symbol of both things, of construction and destruction. There is always the chance that nothing but a lot of rubbish comes out of it.

WF *The composer who combined music with things and images reminds me of one of the stories in the book of a concert in an apartment, or in the corridor of an apartment, and the ensuing complaints that were documented. You spoke of the desire to bring something within this very confined space that had some sort of cultural resonance.*

IK It is about this character who is very upset because people were just interested in doing the washing up and running around without actually thinking of culture or having any cultural part to their lives. He wanted to encourage them to think about something more highbrow and so he got them all together to sing as a choir and bring together this combination of pictures and texts. It was very difficult to stop people rushing about and to get them together so he stopped them by actually putting up stands in the corridor. It was a way to compel them to join in. Terrible rows occurred and fights took place. It is a fable about how people drive one another to their deaths.

WF *I think the work deals through the use of metaphor and symbols with issues such as private spaces as opposed to overwhelming social and political pressures. There is a sense of personal survival being investigated here which I find very interesting.*

IK There was a problem with the installation. It was very difficult to get people to understand what a communal apartment was and why, if it was so awful, people actually lived in it. But there is definitely some consideration of these more general issues there, a very successful metaphor of human life and existence. This can't really be conveyed in something abstract, it has to be portrayed in something that the artist knows as a reality. You have the problem of the two extremes. If you have a really pure metaphor then it loses its bearing on anything real, whereas if you use something that is straight from reality then it will seem too autobiographical and not referring to other things. I hope this installation has somehow fallen between the two.

WF *How would you locate yourself within Soviet art? Would you see yourself as belonging to a tradition or some line of development or area of concern within Soviet art?*

IK We had avant-garde art which suddenly came to an end – there didn't seem to be any direction in which it could go further. Then there was socialist realism which came to its own end as well, and then at the end of the fifties, unofficial art emerged. I see myself as part of the unofficial culture, but some people see this as already coming to an end. These three movements were directly connected one to the other.

WF *If there ceases to be official art what then is the unofficial?*

IK I think it always has existed and always will but will have a different name.

WF *Are there any western artists that have been particularly important to you in the area of installation, of using one's experience and developing it into installations?*

IK It is really hard to say whether western artists have had an influence because we are so isolated and we have only had acquaintance with western art through little cuttings in magazines and bits and pieces. We have had nothing general and only when we came to the West were we able to see these works and have real contact with them. But I feel there may be certain parallels in art because things emerge and things are so universal that they come out of their own accord. It is possible that a similar situation would provoke a similar artwork.

WF *Are there any final remarks you would like to make?*

IK There is just one thing about the installation which I feel hasn't really worked. It is that it is a fragment of something rather than the whole. Another thing is that light forms a particularly important part of it and it is very difficult to recreate the kind of light that you have in a communal apartment. In a clean, nicely laid out gallery it is almost impossible.

Issue 125, April 1989

Ralph Rumney

interviewed by Stewart Home

Situationists in a museum – what a load of rubbish!

STEWART HOME *I'm curious to know how you feel about an exhibition on the Situationist International being held at the Centre Georges Pompidou and the Institute of Contemporary Arts.*

RALPH RUMNEY My feelings are rather mixed. We held protests against the Stedelijk and the Milan Triennale because we wanted to do our own thing. That was a long time ago. What's happened now is that our work has entered the public domain and so we can't really stop museums taking an interest in it. It's there, it's history, it's recuperation – it's whatever you like. At the same time, I thought the title of the exhibition 'On the Passage of a Few Persons Through a Rather Brief Period of Time' was quite nice. I especially liked the subtitle, 'About the Situationist International'. And now that I'm getting older and I want to earn a living, it's nice to see this work doing something for me after all these years.

SH *I notice there's been little support for the show from Michèle Bernstein or Guy Debord.*

RR There wouldn't be. Bernstein because she doesn't need it. It's pointless to her, it's something she did and from which she now more or less dissociates herself. Not that she's ashamed of it, or disagrees with it, but because she's doing other things and that's it. Debord just has to keep up this view of himself as being totally intransigent.

SH *Whereas the Scandinavians, the Situationist Bauhaus and Group Spur would seem more supportive of the exhibition.*

RR They all turned up at the private view and were doing little happenings, which I rather disapproved of. I went to the opening to see the exhibition and because I wanted to meet old friends and learn a few things. There's a lot of work in the show which I'd not seen before.

SH *I think the exhibition is going to surprise a lot of people in London. Situationist theory is considered relatively sophisticated, whereas most of the painting is extremely primitive.*

RR Pinot Gallizio was a total primitive. Asger Jorn was not an unsophisticated painter but he created the Institute for Comparative Vandalism – he was an intellectual primitive. Primitivism had a very strong influence on CoBrA and also on the Germans. I don't know if I'm wrong to make this distinction but I think of myself as a completely different kind of painter. I could never have joined CoBrA.

SH *But it's this type of painting which dominates the exhibition.*

RR Yes, it does, it's very strong painting. The curators asked me to lend paintings and I said no, my paintings aren't anything to do with it. I would have been inclined to lend some of the erotic things, but the dates are wrong.

SH *These are the polaroids and plaster casts that you exhibited at Transmission Gallery in 1985 and which were also included in your recent retrospective at England & Co.*

RR Which I regard as more situationist, more political, than most of my other work.

SH *To return to the situationist exhibition, how do you see the public reacting to it?*

RR I read the visitors' book and that was very interesting. Almost everyone who'd written in it had said this is disgraceful – situationists in a museum, what a load of rubbish! I, however, believe that history should be recorded. I have also come to believe in museums. One of their functions is to make ideas available to people. When we were making our work, the last place we wanted to find it was in a museum. But it's all over now and I don't see why it shouldn't be recorded, catalogued, documented and so on.

SH *One of the good things about the exhibition is to demonstrate that there's postwar work which stands up alongside the achievements of the futurists, dadaists and surrealists. It's as strong as anything they did. What are your feelings about this?*

RR My feelings are somewhat mixed because I regard my painting as very much distinct from Nordic, CoBrA-based, expressionist works. I don't like this type of painting very much. I liked Jorn's work, it's extremely distinguished, I liked Gallizio as a person but I'm not crazy about his work.

SH *I thought his* Anti-Material Cave *of 1959 was the strongest thing in the show.*

RR Of course it was, it's amazing. There's this primitive reality about Gallizio. I think the splits within the movement were due to it containing both intellectuals and these rather marvellous primitives. I'm not convinced that the intellectuals necessarily made the greatest contribution to the group. It was what was actually done that was important, far more important than the theory. Theories are evanescent. Situationist theory was intentionally inspissated to make it difficult to understand and extremely difficult to criticise.

SH *And also to give an impression of complete originality! But what about influences?*

RR The College of 'Pataphysics was an influence on the situationists. Debord hated anything which could be seen as having influenced him. He saw the College of 'Pataphysics as a wretched little coterie. I declined to become a member of the college because of the situationists. I liked their publications, they had a coherence and a persistent line of thought running through them which if you look at the 12 issues of *Internationale Situationiste* is not there. Now then, that may actually be in favour of the Situationist International and say something rather good about it, because where I would criticise Debord is that he wanted to be in charge of the group, he wanted to set up a party line and he wanted everyone to toe it. In fact he never really achieved this and consequently you get this amalgam of divergent ideas which did amalgamate in the first three days of May 1968 and in the punk movement. It's not every little group of 12 that can lay claim 30 years later to having had any influence on two events as important as that.

SH *To return to Debord, what I find interesting about him is this sense that he always needs a collaborator, whether it be Gil J Wolman, Jorn, Raoul Vaneigem or Gianfranco Sanguinetti.*[1]

RR Sanguinetti is where he met his match. He got a collaborator who was smarter than he was. Sanguinetti is absolutely brilliant.

SH *There's a figure who I feel is always lurking in the background of the situationist saga and that's Michèle Bernstein. I get this feeling that she played a key role within the movement, but I can't specify exactly what it was she contributed.*

RR You can't put your finger on it because she won't tell you and she wouldn't thank me if I told you. Since she was my wife, I've got to respect her wishes. I can tell you various little things. She typed all the Potlatchs, all the SI journals and so on. One of the curious things about the SI was that it was extraordinarily anti-feminist in practice. Women were there to type, cook supper and so on. I rather disapproved of this. Michèle had, and has, an extraordinarily powerful and perceptive mind which is shown by the fact that she is among the most important literary critics in France today. A lot of the theory, particularly the political theory, I think originated with Michèle rather than Debord, he just took it over and put his name to it.

SH *Something I found strange about the exhibition was that there was no real acknowledgement of influences. There was very little about the Lettristes or the International Movement For An Imaginist Bauhaus.*

RR That's the fault of the curators. They might have found it very difficult to do in any other way.

SH *The presentation of the exhibition is very low-tech, the books are displayed on weathered boards. How do you feel about this?*

RR I don't feel anything one way or another, they can present it how they like. It's their exhibition. It's not my exhibition, it's the curators' – Beaubourg – they've done the exhibition. Apparently there was a vast shortage of money for the show. On the one hand, Beaubourg's been crying out about this. On the other hand, they're apparently charging the ICA an absolute fortune to have it. It seems extremely odd that they didn't have enough money to do a little bit more. I think the curating was wrong because whatever one says or feels about Jean-Isadore Isou, it should have started with him. That would have made the historical exhibition I'd have liked to see. I feel that the situationists have somehow achieved this trick of commandeering and imposing a version of history, rather than allowing it to be told as it was.

SH *I found the inclusion of Art & Language and NATO rather mystifying.*

RR That's the curators, Peter Wollen and Mark Francis. I met them both and neither of them struck me as a serious expert. They were asking questions about things I'd expect them to know. The English tend to be a bit soft intellectually. You could say they are supermarket intellectuals, anything that'll go in the trolley, let's have it.

1 Wolman played a central role in the Lettriste International (LI), a tiny splinter group which broke with Isou's Lettriste Movement in 1952. He represented the LI at the congress organised by the International Movement For An Imaginist

Bauhaus (IMIB) held in Alba, Italy, in September 1956. This conference laid the groundwork for the unification of the LI and the IMIB the following year. The new organisation was called the Situationist Intemational (SI). Wolman was expelled from the LI shortly before it merged with the IMIB in July 1957. The IMIB consisted of Jorn and whoever else happened to be around. When the SI was founded, Jorn played a leading role in it. He resigned in 1961 but continued to assist in the funding of its publications. Vaneigem joined the SI in 1961. In 1962, there was a split within the organisation, leaving Bernstein, Debord and Vaneigem in control of its political faction. The more culturally orientated faction formed itself into the 2nd Situationist International, centred on the Situationist Bauhaus – a farmhouse in southern Sweden. The Debordists referred to themselves simply as the Situationist International. I use the term the specto-SI to differentiate them from the original International. Vaneigem resigned from this group in November 1970. In 1972 Debord, Martin and Sanguinetti dissolved the specto-SI. Sanguinetti and Debord then jointly wrote *The Veritable Split in the International*, a rambling text in which they denounce the backsliding of their former comrades.

Issue 127, June 1989

Gilbert & George

interviewed by Andrew Wilson

We always say it is what we 'say' that is important

ANDREW WILSON *You are going to be having an exhibition in Moscow opening on April 21. What form will this exhibition take?*

GEORGE It will be pictures from about the last seven years. It won't be a retrospective over the whole of our career.

GILBERT It's much simpler, they will understand our vision much simpler if we limit the selection.

GEORGE In Russia, where they know nothing of our work, they need an actual impression of our living selves. They don't want to see an academic show. It would be too confusing for them.

AW *And how did the exhibition come about?*

GEORGE It is an old dream of ours. Part of our 'Art for All' theory is our work can speak to people of different cultures, so we always liked the idea of showing in a communist country.

GILBERT Three or four years ago we approached the British Council, they told us that they would only be able to do a group show. Then we tried to approach the Russians through Italy – then Fiat, because they have a lot of factories in Russia. And then we told Paul Conran about our dream and he told us that if you want to do a show in Russia you have to speak with James Birch, and that is how it happened.

AW *Has there been any sort of censorship exercised in the choice of images?*

GEORGE In every country, wherever you show, there is always some form of censorship, and we always like to do that in advance. We like to pre-empt any difficulties, we always like to take it up to the line but not over. We don't want our work to be banned. You strike a balance.

GILBERT Our show in Basel was different, because the museum director wanted to shock the audience.

GEORGE In fact he made a special room of the sexual pictures.

AW *With Francis Bacon's exhibition in Moscow there was some censorship of his more pornographic paintings. Are you worried at all by this precedent?*

GEORGE No, we have already made that sort of adjustment in the selection, and the authorities there are perfectly happy. It is not the interesting thing about art to get people running from the museum in horror – that would be very unproductive.

AW *This exhibition is going to be happening at an historically important time with the fall of Communism. How do you feel about that?*

GEORGE We are very excited about that, to be part of that movement, it has always been of interest to us.

AW *And you visited Russia last year?*

GEORGE Just to see the space and meet the people – they were very, very appreciative of our work, I must say that.

AW *What do you think Gorbachev will think of your work? Will he see the exhibition?*

GILBERT We don't believe he should have to have a view about it, only the person who goes to the exhibition can have a view on it. It's like here, we don't want politicians, we don't believe they have to have a view of our work.

GEORGE We believe that culture comes first, and politicians follow that. It has always been the case in history. Whenever the artists arrange a certain culture among the people, they think, 'I want to do this or that because of the paintings I have seen, or the books that my grandmother read', they then vote for a particular type of government. So the politicians are following the culture.

GILBERT The recent revolution in East Germany was started by artistic people.

GEORGE The 'New Forum' was a group of people with paintings in the room and poets.

AW *Do you think the same way about Margaret Thatcher then?*

GEORGE Here it is different because you have the vote, you have freedom in the West. East they do not have the vote. Here it is easy, because the people can vote for what they culturally expect of the government. There are parties representing every single opinion in Britain. There is a Communist Party here you can vote for. People have to vote for what they want.

GILBERT But you can only change the view and the vision of the human person through culture, through different books, through art, pushing forward the frontier of knowledge, making it a much freer society. Tolerance, I think tolerance is the most important thing. If you have tolerance then everybody can have different ideas, and different ideas are very important. A more complicated, richer life.

GEORGE That is why the best role the government plays is like you have here in the West, where they just arrange opportunity. They don't say 'This is a good artist or a bad artist', they arrange a system whereby in the last ten years the number of galleries in London quadrupled and where the number of artists living by their work is ten times more than it was under Labour. More and more.

AW *So, you don't think it is important to worry about what Thatcher's taste in art is, or even if she has a philistinic attitude towards art?*

GILBERT That has nothing to do with it, we don't worry what politicians think, that would be giving them too much power.

AW *But don't they control to a large extent the purse-strings of arts funding?*

GILBERT Not ours. Arts funding, that is very difficult, because we don't believe completely in arts funding ourselves. We believe it is much better that you make your art, you try to sell it, whoever wants it can buy it. But once the state tells you what kind of art they want, and support it in buying it – then we don't like it.

GEORGE That was Mrs Thatcher's greatest achievement in the arts really, wasn't it, privatisation of the artists? Because before this government, the artists were nationalised. As well as doing their paintings you had to work at the Slade for 30 years and for that you were given a funny award and a pension that was enough to drink yourself to death but not enough to rescue your career as an artist. And so they all died unhappy. They had a small memorial show at the back of the Tate, and that was it. Now they are privatised – it is much better.

GILBERT Anyway, that is what we believe, very much. You have to be free. It's not important what each member of the government thinks about art, as long as they arrange a freedom that you can do whatever you want. If they would start to knock on our door and tell us what to do, then I would change my mind.

AW *But take another position. Say Thatcher's attitude to homosexuality and, say, the censorship implicit in Clause 28.*

GEORGE We are not interested to lecture the prime minister on her views on heterosexuality or homosexuality, and anyway we have never heard Margaret Thatcher's view on sexuality. And we don't believe that she is the architect of Clause 28, which was in actual fact from the extreme small bookshop that pushed the case so violently that it was bound to receive the sort of response it did. I mean if you go on the street now from this house with a photograph of two men fucking, and say 'You do agree to this, don't you?' to every single person, I would think that is a rather stupid way of doing it, no? That leaflet that caused the trouble could never be published with public money in any country in the world.

GILBERT We never want to confront – subversive we like to be – never confront, because if you ask too many questions...

GEORGE All the people who have brought about Clause 28 have just made sexuality divisive, which is a very bad thing. We believe that everyone is a sexual person, that is all. After all, you don't need to know the sex of a piece of meat you are eating for dinner, do you? It is just meat. Or flowers, if you send a beautiful bunch of flowers, you don't check which one is spunking off with the next one.

AW *Do you worry about the oppressive attitude towards homosexuality in Russia?*

GEORGE Yes, we heard a good joke about that, but I think the attitude is more oppressive towards sexuality, I am sure that is the case.

GILBERT What was the joke about homosexuality in Russia?

GEORGE Oh yes, this is not actually our joke. One of the organisers was at Marlborough Gallery talking to Bacon's organiser there and she said 'When choosing pictures don't you have to be rather careful? Is homosexuality legal in Russia?' And he said 'Yes, of course. In prison!' What an amazing reply!

AW *How much do you think that your work is appreciated in this country, and do the art critics understand your work?*

GEORGE Yes, we have an enormous following here, not less than any other country and probably more. But a wider range of people, from all classes and walks of life. In a lot of countries only a particular class go to galleries.

GILBERT But critics don't want to look because they are racist.

AW *Racist in what way?*

GEORGE In that they will only attend to art that is from wine-growing countries. The educated bigot in Britain just likes foreign art. Art equals foreign to them. That attitude came about through people like Roger Fry.

AW *You have also expressed your dislike of what you term leftwing liberal critics.*

GILBERT Yes, and sometimes we call them 'Black Shirt Marxists', because that is what they are. They want to dictate taste, and we don't believe in that.

AW *Critics like John Berger also seem to hold similar beliefs to you regarding the death of aesthetic meaning, the use of photography or the redundancy of the artistic gesture.*

GEORGE I wouldn't know what their beliefs are.

GILBERT We have never read John Berger but we heard that he was interested in the force and capacity of the photograph as a means for mass communication. We believe the camera is the best modern brush today – because the artist wants to speak to the world. That is what he has to do, so that is the best form.

AW *You have all these Christopher Dresser pots and so forth around this room and in the rest of your house – do you see Victorian values as corresponding to your own values in any way?*

GEORGE Well, we never think of it in those terms really. What we like is that they were modernists, they were completely new, fresh – when they were alive – totally modern. We could also be interested in art from all sorts of periods or even from before that period. There are always artists who are interested, as we are, in the meaning and the force of culture in all periods. At any stage in history, there is always somebody pushing the barriers of civilisation in the western world forward, and we like to contribute to that. We don't believe it is time to stand still, there is still room for improvement.

GILBERT What we like is a complicated art, that is the kind of art we like to do. We don't believe in having only one view – it is many views we believe very much in. We never believe that the artist has to be good, and doesn't accept bad. We believe in the whole circle with everything in it – the flower and the shit. You can also fit our art into different frames. You could say it looks Japanese, if you want to. It looks medieval, if you want to. It looks like high-tech, if you want to or like computer art. So it fits in on every level. What we are interested in is speaking, having a vision.

AW *In 1967, when you met, at St Martin's, was that what you had against Anthony Caro and the New Generation Sculpture – that it didn't 'speak'?*

GEORGE We were against the elitism of those forms. We realised that with all the discussion around sculpture at that time, they were building up a language that was outside life and which the minute you got onto the Charing Cross Road would not mean a damn thing. It was only within that club. It was too elitist. We say that the picture is there in the museum or the gallery for people to view in the light of their own life, agreement or disagreement is not the crucial thing. If they say: I don't think those artists should have made that picture, and it shouldn't be put on the wall, it doesn't matter, you see. It is too late, they have seen it, and we've got 'em. Bad luck, right? That picture's gone into their heads, it is too late.

GILBERT But we know that there is so little that speaks to viewers, even if they visit the National Gallery they don't understand what it means – these Renaissance artists, or this king going up and down this mountain.

GEORGE Fifty dead Jesuses. Why does every western city have to have another fifty dead Jesuses? Quite crazy. The form of the painting should serve the meaning. The form can be as elaborate as necessary in order to serve the meaning, it should never be the issue. With our pictures nobody ever says, we like the nice bit of red in the corner or the nice line going down the middle.

GILBERT Art is a re-examining of life. That's what it is. Every day we are all the same – we still have the same bloody stupid face, but we are still worried every day, so we re-examine ourselves, you know?

AW *At the time before you became living sculptures, what sort of questions were you asking yourselves?*

GEORGE Oh, we just studied. We used to go to different lectures and experiment, it was a time of experimentation. We are probably the most trained artists in London, I'm sure. We both went to art schools for many many years – 12 years – studied painting, sculpture, drawing, history of art and architecture, psychology. Everything.

GILBERT I think that our biggest invention was on the day that we said 'we are the art and the artist', I think that was the best. We are still doing that, we have never changed from that. We believe that all good artists have to do that. Every artist – even Constable – it is his vision that is important, not the landscape.

GEORGE You still are looking at a 'Constable'. You don't say what a lovely field, you say it is a fantastic Constable. It is him speaking to you. It is the living artist. It is the life of that dear, dead man coming out, not the elm tree.

GILBERT We only believe in the vision. That is why if we could just chuck it on the wall, we'd prefer that. But the vision is important, because that is what changes the world.

GEORGE We always say it is what we 'say' that is important, you see.

AW *Your early works, made with charcoal and oil paint with images which are largely concerned with a reaction to nature, seem to nod towards a traditional concern of the artist.*

GEORGE Yes, but those large pieces were all based on photography, without which they could not have existed. We then developed that language – how to actually make a big one. A lot of people come out of art school, look in a museum, see what it is, and say 'Oh, so I will do something like that'. They start with a box of colours, a box of oil paints. We didn't do that, we started with ourselves. It took us four years to find red, whereas the artist has all the colours there immediately, first thing. We had to go out and buy red. We didn't have all the colours there that the artist normally has. It took us another three years to find yellow.

AW *Does art have a role to play in society?*

GEORGE The very reality that we sit here now is a cultural reality. Everyone wants to say nowadays that it is a political reality that we live in. We don't believe that. We think that we are what we are culturally. Without culture you would just have some crazy army crashing through this window at this very moment with machine guns. In countries where they don't have art, you don't have freedom. You have to have shelves and shelves of books. Culture has enormous power. If you just say the name 'Charles Dickens' to anyone in the street, even if they have never read a book in their whole life, something of the dear man's life will come into their heads and live again. That is the force of culture which must be very important, otherwise they would not lock up poets. In extreme rightwing countries and extreme leftwing countries they lock up all the artists and writers. The Left here would love to lock us up.

GILBERT And the Right – people like Roger Scruton. We always say that, on both sides.

AW *So are you apolitical?*

GILBERT We always say we are boring Conservatives.

GEORGE Normal. Normal.

GILBERT That is what we like to be – normal.

GEORGE Average. Lower class, uneducated Tories!

AW *Do you have political beliefs beyond that?*

GEORGE We are always perfectly amazed that in every other walk of life – except the art world – it is perfectly normal to be either Labour or Conservative, or even something else. Taxi drivers, when they start raving about politics, can be Labour or Tory, some are one and some are the other, it's not such a big problem. 'What gets up my nose is this', he says, it is just a discussion. Whereas in the art world it seems you have to be anti-Tory because it is a big, mad, violent-to-the-death-fight, which is crazy. It is a free country, you can be either, so what is the problem? It is fairly normal to be a Tory, if it wasn't they wouldn't have been in power for so long. It is not so unusual. We always say if artists are supposed to be so original, so creative, how come they have all got the same damn political party? That can't be so original, they should at least have a variety of opinion. American artists all love Communism.

GILBERT We dislike millionaires who want to be communists, it is obviously so hypocritical. But in general party policies are becoming less important – like in Europe – because it's only going to be a kind of middle party.

GEORGE Well, like the Conservatives are, in fact.

AW *Should artists intervene in or reflect society?*

GEORGE We have no interest in reflecting or showing society – we are only interested to be forming it. What we believe tomorrow is what the artists are today. Already we see the world as very, very different from when we started, and we have been a part of that, I am sure. Good writers don't reflect society, they form their tomorrows. D H Lawrence didn't reflect the morality of his time, did he? He forged the morality of the next generation – don't you think? Everyone fucked differently after that book, they actually started shagging differently. There were plenty of writers then who just reflected the status quo – but you don't remember their names, do you?

AW *Yet, how do you react to Prince Charles's intervention in the daily life of society, and his concern for forming a new understanding for architectural standards?*

GEORGE We are very supportive of the monarchy, we should say that first of all, more than any other artist we know. But we don't believe that a person from such a privileged background as Prince Charles is able to have a clear, modern view. He has not had the opportunity to see a wide spectrum of life really. He can only walk along the street surrounded by men with guns in their waistcoats. He cannot 'see' life, and you have to see life, and you have to see life very clearly in order to know where to go on next.

GILBERT And it is very simple – would he understand or like our art or not? He wouldn't. He would be against it because he would say that our images would have to be painted and he is wrong here as he is with architecture. I think that high-tech architecture will never stop. You cannot stop it, it's fantastic. I like it very much. We prefer Prince Albert's views on modern art and architecture.

GEORGE He is a fantastic future king who has been badly advised really. I think that is the case.

AW *It seems to me that your work is founded on, among other things, a concern for the values of the surface. What to you is the nature of reality, and in what way is it your subject-matter?*

GEORGE Our subject-matter is the world. It is the Pain. Pain – just to hear the world turning is Pain, isn't it? Totally, every day, every second.

GILBERT Our inspiration is all those people alive today on the planet – the desert, the jungle, the cities. We are interested in the human person, the complexity of life.

AW *But as far as reality in art is concerned, would you agree with what Wyndham Lewis wrote in* Tarr *that art is life with all the humbug of living taken out? Is art life or a purified version of life?*

GILBERT For us, art is searching for life, a re-examination of life for the new generation. It is artificial, because we don't know what life is all about, so you have to put up a new idea.

AW *Do you agree with Wolf Jahn's interpretation of your work in terms of an ascension analagous to the life of Christ?*

GEORGE That we like very much. We always saw all of life like that.

AW *You don't feel that that is blasphemous at all?*

GEORGE As Christians, not, absolutely not – we are the most Christian artists we know.

GILBERT I don't believe in blasphemy because that is against freedom.

GEORGE Most people who worry about blasphemy are not Christians in any sense. Jesus Christ came on Earth to be a sinner like all of us. I think that is the basis of the Christian inspiration, wouldn't you say?

AW *Critics like Peter Fuller have said that your work is a blasphemous obscenity.*

GEORGE But he is not a Christian by his own admission. I mean, Jesus Christ didn't reflect the life of his time, he formed the tomorrows.

AW *Do you go to church?*

GEORGE We are not churchgoers or religious in the formal sense, no.

GILBERT But that is too limited, saying that it is blasphemy, what does it mean today?

AW *What about drawing a parallel with the Salman Rushdie affair?*

GILBERT But even that, muslims will have to give in, in the end, they cannot kill people for religious intolerance.

GEORGE Blasphemy equals religious intolerance.

AW *Were you involved in the publication by Thames and Hudson of Wolf Jahn's book on you, in a financial sense?*

GEORGE Yes, absolutely. Of course. All our books are helped in some way.

GILBERT Every art magazine has to be funded, even by advertising, that is sponsorship.

GEORGE We are always amazed that art critics sometimes write in newspapers against commercial sponsorship, and on the same page as a whisky advertisement! It is very hypocritical, no newspaper that carries an art column can be published without sponsorhip – it costs £3.70 a copy – without the ads. Sponsorship of art books is very important, because then we can invest in the minds and lives of the future. Go and look in the bookshops: it is 99 per cent Van Gogh. Do you want that? When I was 16, and first became interested in modern art, I couldn't find a book on modern art. And that was wrong. With tennis, which is sponsored, that is different. Oh yes. Every art critic is sponsored.

GILBERT Publishers, they don't believe they can sell books on modern English artists. So why shouldn't the gallery help in creating a book, if they make money out of it, why not?

AW *Judith Collins of the Tate Gallery has cited you and Andy Warhol as great spiritual artists of today. Would you like to see your work as stained-glass windows?*

GEORGE Stained-glass windows is the interpretation of overeducated people. There are vast sections of society that weren't taken to country churches by toffee-nosed parents who just see it as computer art, just as space invader art. That reaction depends on your social background. It is to do with class.

AW *This comparison with Warhol has been made before. Do you admire his work? Are there any artists that you do admire?*

GEORGE There is one big difference between Warhol and ourselves which I think is an important one, and that is his interest in very famous material. He likes very famous film stars and famous politicians, rich superstars, rich film stars. We are not involved in that, we are interested in the human person, regardless of class or background or anything. All the people in our pictures are humanoid – they are devoid of class. They could come from any background, they could be South American or English or Russian or Dutch or Australian. They don't have to be famous, mad, or drugged before they can go into our work, which they have to be to get into Warhol's. We respect all artists because they are all working for a particular purpose and aim, and obviously you have to respect and admire that. But, on the other hand, we are working for something different. One cannot just look at fine art here.

GILBERT I like Dickens.

AW *You read Dickens?*

GILBERT I saw the films like *The Old Curiosity Shop*. I was very impressed. I like the complexity of life, the structure and the morality and all that. And it speaks –

GEORGE – across the history, doesn't it? And across the classes. They seem to stand the test of time very well.

AW *But have you read Dickens?*

GEORGE We are not involved in reading books, we are not from that class really.

GILBERT We like and prefer the raw world in front of us, let's stay naked in front of the world and try to sort it out.

AW *But you have books in your bookshelves over there.*

GEORGE Not so much for reading, they are mostly visual. Lives of the artists, things like that.

GILBERT We became interested in reading about the miserable lives of the artists in the eighteenth century, nineteenth century – they're all the same, we found out – miserable, unhappy.

AW *Are you miserable?*

GILBERT Deeply miserable, yes.

GEORGE We are more miserable than anyone else we know. We think it is very important to be miserable. We don't believe that anyone made any progress through being cheerful. Civilisation is not 'advanced' by people lying on the beach with a gin and tonic. Everything is subservient to the art, in fact, and everything has to fit in around it. We try to clear out our life and empty it. We give all our feelings and thoughts and fears and dreads and hopes straight into our pictures – you cannot be more open than that. There is hardly a subject of life that isn't universal that we haven't discussed in our work.

GILBERT We don't have any other private life – we eat, go to sleep, think about art. When we have an exhibition we get drunk, that's it. That's very simple.

GEORGE Come home, do some more.

AW *You only get drunk when you have an exhibition?*

GEORGE Generally speaking.

GILBERT Generally speaking, yes.

AW *Do you see this rejection of a private life in terms of a sacrifice that you are making?*

GEORGE If you go blindfold into a library, take a book off the shelf and it is about somebody who did something, whether it is in the field of medicine or military or politics or poetry, it has always been done with enormous personal sacrifice, it has always been like that in the history of civilisation. Totally. Nobody has a jolly life for giving. A jolly life for taking, yes, but not a jolly life for giving. Everybody gets beaten up – even if you invent penicillin – you just get smacked in, the first day. They didn't say 'Wonderful, fantastic, brilliant' – they said, 'Get out, banished from the city.'

AW *Why do you think it is necessary that you should do your art together, would you ever make works as individuals?*

GEORGE We never considered that, and that has been one of our greatest strengths in fact – being two. And it is very good because it makes the artist more normal because the whole of the world is more or less divided into two. It is the most common unit – two people. So it makes it a very democratic form, in a way, more normal.

GILBERT We always believe that every artist has to ask another person. He asks, 'Do I like this, or not?' He asks himself like another person.

GEORGE 'Do I do a bit more red here or not?' And back comes this horrible silence. Whereas if there are two, it is very useful.

AW *It is a long time since you made a presentation as 'Living Sculptures' – do you feel you might do it again?*

GILBERT We feel we never stopped, because I think the very big photo pieces are exactly that even if we are not there ourselves.

GEORGE The form is incidental, the meaning in the end is the important thing. We see it as a big continuation, we just changed forms.

GILBERT I mean we like films. We would like to do another film.

AW *And do you watch a lot of television?*

GILBERT No, less and less. There is so little on that is interesting.

It's all the same, mediocre.

GEORGE We just relax sometimes in front of the set.

AW *And the cinema as well?*

GEORGE We never go to the cinema, to the theatre, or concerts – never.

AW *What led you to agree to this interview?*

GILBERT We agree to every interview.

GEORGE It wasn't a big decision really, we like to be democratic. Why should we refuse someone? We are not such toffee-nosed artists, we are not snobbish, we even will do an interview for *Modern Painters*!

Issue 135, April 1990

Anish Kapoor

interviewed by Douglas Maxwell

I am a painter who is a sculptor

DOUGLAS MAXWELL *You were born India in 1954. Can you tell me a little bit about your childhood?*

ANISH KAPOOR It was a marvellous childhood, growing up with a very powerful culture in a context where my parents were both in a sense quite aloof from the culture. My father's Indian and my mother's not, although she grew up in India. My mother's Jewish.

DM *What sort of education did you have?*

AK I went to English-speaking schools. The school that I did my secondary schooling in was rather like a British public school. I was highly anti-authoritarian, I couldn't deal with all that public school authority, so I did not work at all. However, I never failed a class. I managed to survive, but only by the skin of my teeth.

DM *Did you have any interest in art?*

AK I think I could have had, but perhaps because it was all so very structured I didn't really deal with it.

DM *Did you take much interest in art outside of school?*

AK I did. But India wasn't a place to go to exhibitions. Of course there were museums, we did do that. But really the culture and art was all around us.

DM *I've never met anybody who's Indian and also Jewish. Is your Jewishness a strong thing with you?*

AK I think it is. All of these things are avenues into a whole cultural world which is very rich. I wish I could have been Christian and Buddhist as well. That would have been perfect.

DM *You spent two years in Israel. What did you do there?*

AK I thought I wanted to be an engineer so I went to college to study engineering. I lasted six months. I decided it wasn't for me.

DM *What made you want to go into engineering?*

AK I always felt that the thing I enjoyed most was making things with my hands. Since my father was a technical person, it seemed the logical way to go. I stayed for another year and a half on a Kibbutz, and decided then that I was going to be an artist. I never thought about it again. It was a very clear decision. I was about 18. I had been painting when I was in India, abstract painting of some kind, in the style of early Pollock, which I am still fascinated by, Rothko and that period. Early Picasso – when Pollock was very influenced by him. There was quite a tradition in Indian art in this area which I was somehow aware of. There are still some well-known Indian artists who are deeply influenced one way and another by Picasso and the post-cubist mode.

DM *Where did you go to art school?*

AK I decided that I was going to come to England and go to art school. That's one decision I don't know how I arrived at. I went to Hornsey and did a foundation course, and then I did my degree there. I loved it. I felt for the first time that I was really interested in something. My whole personality changed.

DM *What were the early influences on you? Did you go out to galleries and museums that you'd read about?*

AK I did some of that, but I was only a young, naive art student. At that age one doesn't know what to look at, or how to look. It took me quite a long time to realise that there was something specific to look for.

DM *And what was that, when you discovered it?*

AK It's difficult to articulate. It had to do with an attitude to making art. By then I was especially interested in artists who were very much in vogue, like Joseph Beuys, I suppose, Carl Andre and Donald Judd, etc.

DM *What about British artists?*

AK Yes. British artists – it was difficult. I didn't connect with many, other than, perhaps, the ones that were teaching me at art school. There was someone I found very important to me then, Paul Neagu. I think he's extraordinary. He really had a lot to do with the way my growth as a person occurred. He was a foreigner working in that context here, so that had something to do with it. He opened my eyes to the idea that making art wasn't about making more or less beautiful things and that there was some deeper purpose to it. And the fact that maybe there is something fundamentally human, something, for want of a better word, spiritual about making art. I think quite early on at Hornsey I understood that was what I as a human being wanted to try and deal with.

DM *Apart from Neagu, who or what were the other major influences on you?*

AK I was very interested at the time in Paul Thek. He's a sad story but he was a marvellous artist. I never saw one for real then, only in art magazines, but I think what was important about them to me then was that they were deeply ritualised situations. One has got to understand this within the context of performance art, when the object wasn't the issue as it is now.

DM *Did you get involved in performance art?*

AK In a certain way. I took part in some of Neagu's performances. I didn't make specific performance pieces, but I made some performance-related pieces.

DM *At college were you with the stream or against it?*

AK I was aggressive.

DM *Did you want to be successful, is that what it was?*

AK The whole of the department was in one big space which was almost not divided up, so that painting, sculpture, print-making, everything was lumped together in one great room. You had to fight for your space, so I made big things in order to have my space.

DM *What sort of big things?*

AK One artist who was very important to me was Marcel Duchamp. Not the Duchamp of the readymade but the Duchamp of the *Large Glass* and *Étant donnés*, which I came to slightly later on, the Duchamp of alchemy. This was clearly delineated in terms of what I was interested in. The *Large Glass* is about the bride and the bachelors – a perfect kind of oppositeness. So I made quite a lot of work that had to do with this polarity – big situational things. One that comes to mind was a kind of male machine – it had a motor in that made it 'tap' on the floor. It was in front of a ritualised scene with symbolically female things – bowls, pots. All of these things have somehow stayed with me and remain a real part of my investigation.

DM *At college did you think much about the future?*

AK We didn't think much about how to make a living, if that's what you're asking. In a way, I think it's one of the sadnesses about the way people go to art school now, that so much of art school education nowadays seems to be about making it as an artist. Courses in what to do when you leave, and all that stuff. I think this kind of thing is a direct influence of the last ten years of political thinking. The early seventies certainly weren't like that. There was a much more altruistic belief that one did what one did, and if you did it well enough, and you did it with all of yourself, then you'd find a way to make ends meet.

DM *When you finished college, what happened then?*

AK I did four years at Hornsey – a year foundation and a three-year degree course. Then I did a postgraduate year at Chelsea.

DM *Did you go back to India at all?*

AK I couldn't afford to. I had a very curious and increasingly agitated relationship with this part of myself. I was beginning to wonder what kind of a person I was. Was I English? Well, I certainly wasn't English. Was I Indian? I felt like I was but didn't know how to understand that. I didn't have any context for it. And I think that was a deep crisis. It lasted quite a long time. Especially during the early part of the year after I left art school. I left Chelsea with a feeling that I hadn't been to art school for five years in order to do anything else, so I was not going to do anything else. But in order to be an artist I also felt I had to find something that was truly mine. I couldn't carry on working without really knowing what that was for me.

DM *How did you resolve the problem?*

AK By going back to India in 1979.

DM *Was that a way of sorting yourself out?*

AK I thought it might be but I wasn't sure, of course. It was an astonishing kind of revitalisation and an affirmation that all the things I thought might be true were true. It was a real surprise. All those themes I had been working with – about opposition, about fundamental polarities, which seemed elemental – were equally true and elemental in Indian culture. I hadn't realised that the direction I had been working in was there already. I was only there for a month or so, but it was a real affirmation of my being.

DM *Did that come as a relief?*

AK A huge relief. So much of being an artist is about understanding, and having a sense of place, a sense of belonging, a sense of being in the world in some real way.

DM *How did you realise this affinity with India was in your work?*

AK The whole of the Indian outlook on life is about opposite forces. One thing I was fascinated by were the little shrines and temples by the roadside, which are all over India, and are specifically orientated towards this dualistic vision.

DM *Had anybody taken any interest in your work at all from the point of view of buying it?*

AK No. I didn't imagine I could ever sell any of my work. It didn't matter. I was doing a little teaching by then at Wolverhampton Polytechnic. I had to in order to survive and stay in Britain. I did then and still do hold an Indian passport. I had to show the Home Office that I was supporting myself and not living off the dole. I really enjoyed teaching.

DM *Does anybody know how to teach art?*

AK No. In the end I think I learnt much more than I taught. I was passionate about it. I had a tutorial group and I discussed the things that I was interested in. Making art isn't an intellectual or theoretical activity, it's deeply rooted in the psychological – in the self. And there are ways of talking about it or engaging with it which are very specific. In a post-Freudian age the language is there to be had, at one level at least.

DM *Where was your own work going?*

AK When I came back from India I was excited by what I had seen and very soon the first powder pigment things emerged.

DM *How did India influence you in producing that work?*

AK One of the things I saw there was pigment being used in temple rituals and for cosmetic purposes, as well as all sorts of other things in Indian life. I thought it was an incredible material.

DM *When you first worked with raw pigment, how did you feel about it?*

AK As if I was dealing with some kind of personal truth, with something I instinctively knew about. The first pieces I did were all red and white. Red is a very central colour to me. I began to do what I have always done – deal with opposites. Red and white seem to be classic opposites. That seemed clear.

DM *Did you think this moment would last?*

AK I didn't think of it in terms of lasting or not. It was just what I was doing then and that was what mattered. I could only see it growing. I began to leave some of the old influences behind. During that period, 1979, the beginning of 1980, I felt as if I didn't really make any works. It was more to do with discovering a language. I was putting together a vocabulary of form, of colour, that slowly coagulated into words.

DM *Were you leaving behind influences?*

AK I don't think there is such a thing as originality. In the end it's all a question of degree. That time was a time of feeling that I was closer to myself than I had ever been before. The way forward for me then was not by looking at the work of contemporary or modern artists, it was much more a real investigation, for the first time in my life. All the Indian artists I have ever seen – until then anyway – seemed to be making a narrative of Indian culture, using it for its wealth of mythology and all of that kind of thing. But very little, it seems to me, had been done with the phenomena of Indian culture. What I mean by that is the 'stuffness' of it – perhaps the material of it, the real elemental thing that India is. And the medieval nature of its culture, that is to say that even everyday acts have symbolic mythological significance. It was a way of imbuing the materials and colours with which I was working with a real history, a psychological history.

DM *Colour remains immensely important in your work?*

AK I think I am a painter who is a sculptor. My view is that sculpture has always been about presence in the world, a kind of emanating out of the world – physical, here. What I have always been engaged in – which is what I think painters do – is to deal with an illusory presence in the world, one that isn't necessarily here. That's the nature of painting. It's a mindscape or a soulscape, whereas on that level sculpture would be a bodyscape. For me the two things somehow seem to have come together, so that I am making physical things that are all about somewhere else, about this illusory space. Even with the early work, that was very much there. The powder pieces were like islands sitting on the floor, icebergs, partially revealed, partially above the ground. That seemed to be implying that the rest of the object was under the ground or the other side of the wall.

DM *Coming through, emerging.*

AK Exactly.

DM *You had an exhibition in Paris in 1980. Was that the first exhibition, and how did it come about?*

AK Well, when I was teaching in Wolverhampton, there was a man who was teaching there too called Patrice Alexandre and he asked me if I would do a show in his studio in Paris. So I went to Paris and spent about three weeks there – made some work, and showed it. And that was the first time I showed.

DM *What was the response to your work?*

AK Well, one's never sure of that. It never got written about or reviewed or anything like that. But I think a lot of people saw it, and I think it was a surprise.

DM *That was an important moment for you?*

AK It was. Something happened to the work too. Most of the things were made directly out of powder. Some of them were made out of other materials and then covered in powder but I have never seen that as a contradiction. I have always believed that things need to be made only as well as they needed to be made and not any better. But something happened in making that show – the works suddenly looked clearer than ever before. Maybe that's the good thing about doing a show, it's definite. Soon after that I did a show with Simon Cutts in Camberwell which was seen by a lot of people and seemed to get a very good reception.

DM *How were you living at this time?*

AK I wasn't selling anything. I was teaching and that was just about liveable. And I was doing all the things that one did, like applying to the Arts Council for grants. I never got any money from them, but every time you apply for a grant you get a bunch of people come round, and one of the people who once came round was Sandy Nairne. This happened to be about the time that he was putting together the 'Object and Sculpture' show. He didn't give me a grant but he asked me if I would be in the show, which was much better than having a grant. It also put me in touch for the first time with Bill Woodrow and Richard Deacon.

DM *Your first solo exhibition in London was with Nicholas Logsdail at the Lisson Gallery in 1982 – was there anything else apart from group shows up to that point?*

AK One show with Coracle Press, the first 'One Thousand Names' show. It was the first time that I had shown that body of work which started in 1979 – I showed a small part of that early work. It was a beautiful little gallery, and I enjoyed doing the show there.

DM *How did you come to meet Nicholas Logsdail?*

AK He saw the show at the Coracle. Soon after that he asked me if I would go and see him, and we decided we would work together.

DM *Was that a long discussion?*

AK It was fairly quick. I had known his gallery for a long time, had been going there as a student, and thought it was the best thing I could do. So I did it.

DM *And you had a show there – how was that received?*

AK Very well I think. I had two powder pieces and two earth pieces in that show which prompted me to move on from powder pieces. I often think of that time, and wonder if I should have carried on making powder pieces. But I think in the end I am glad I didn't.

DM *Do you think you've got it out of your system?*

AK No, I've still not got it out of my system. The emphasis shifted then. It seemed not necessary for it to be powder any longer. What became important at that moment was colour. I mean more important that it had been before.

DM *Can you describe to me the process you go through to create? Does it start by drawing?*

AK Things evolve out of each other. That is very important. Then, if I am trying to pursue a particular idea, I would probably resist drawing it for a while because it is much more alive in my head than it can ever be in a drawing. When I have enough confidence about it I'll draw it. I've found from experience that if I draw something too soon I end up not making it. So I let it be there for a while. Then I try to concretise it in the way of a drawing – a drawing normally on the wall of the studio – something brief and direct, and indicating very roughly what it might be.

DM *Some of the things you make are pretty damned large and pretty damned heavy. Does the thought: where is this going to end up, bother you?*

AK Pigment pieces are difficult to own and to domesticate. I feel that is quite important.

DM *It's important that they should be difficult?*

AK I think it is important that they should be difficult, yes. Because, especially now, we live in a world where the art object is consumed on such a vast scale, and that simply makes it another commodity. I feel that it is important to resist that. My work used to be too fragile, now it's too heavy. I think that's important.

DM *That's a lovely juxtaposition. Do you feel that you are going to strike a balance by being about the right weight and the right strength?*

AK I hope not.

DM *When did you start working in stone?*

AK Two to three years ago. I had wanted to make work out of stone for a few years, but I had always been terrified of it. It seemed so impossible. It took me a long while to have the courage to make a work in stone. Someone invited me to show in their gallery in Finland – and

I said I would do it if I could work in stone. In Finland they have all this marvellous granite, so of course I chose the most difficult stone to start with, which is typical of my nature. I spent about two months of purgatory there trying to realise this sculpture. I was working on about four or five pieces, which are still unfinished, but I think now I know how to deal with them. I really jumped in the deep end – they are enormous things in really hard stone. But the experience has given me a real feeling for the stuff.

DM *Had you ever tried it before at all, even on a small scale?*

AK Never before. With the pigment pieces, the whole thing was about colour, powder and impermanence – on one level there was this whole engagement with a very ephemeral material. I felt that the magic of the work was taking me towards something that seemed to require me – that's why I'd used earth earlier on too – to work with something which was real.

DM *What was Nicholas Logsdail's view at this time, of you changing to stone?*

AK He has a intimate relationship, I think, with his artists and with the work that is going on in the studio. And at some levels too intimate. He was wary but in the end – I mean what does it matter what Nicholas thinks? In the end one has to do what one has to do.

DM *Recently, Anish, you declined to take part in the Hayward show 'The Other Story'. Can you explain your reasons?*

AK Because I believe that being an artist is more than being an Indian artist. I feel supportive to that kind of endeavour. I feel it needs to happen once. I hope that show is never necessary again. Western artists have been able to look at non-western influence and make it part of western culture in some very energising ways. But it's never happened the other way round. I think we are in a time where it is possible.

DM *Where does the inspiration come from? I suppose that is an awful question.*

AK It is a very big question. I think the whole point is to find out.

DM *Some people say – if I ever found out how I did it, I wouldn't be able to do it anymore.*

AK I think the artwork isn't as important as the artist. It's a question of 'seeing' the process of art-making as being a process of self-discovery. Let's say the work is a kind of reflection of some inner processes out of which the work grows. It also has to do with the feeling that the last work I made is not as important as the work that I am going to make. I think this is crucial. Every time I do a show there is this feeling – can I do this again? In the end it doesn't matter whether it can be done again. What matters is saying 'yes'. How do I keep myself agitated enough in order to keep growing and not stop with what I've done already.

DM *You have been chosen to represent Britain at the Venice Biennale. Was that a terrifying prospect for you?*

AK At first. I haven't a clue about how it happened. I just got a call one day from the British Council telling me that I'd been selected. My first reaction was 'Oh no'. But then I realised that I felt that I could do it. One must treat it as just another show in order to get on with it.

DM *An Indian representing Britain – that's an odd notion.*

AK Yes. It is an odd notion. I think they are amazingly courageous. I think there is a whole attitude that the British Council has towards artists working in this country which is just great. They see artists working in this country as British artists irrespective of where they come from. Now I think that must be applauded.

DM *Has your work ever been shown in India?*

AK No, I've never shown in India.

DM *What has success meant to you as an artist?*

AK One of the most important things that showing does is that it affords opportunity to make the kind of work that you may not have made otherwise, and to work on the kind of scale that I might not have worked on before.

DM *Do you take criticism of your work to heart at all?*

AK Oh, come on. Of course I'm very sensitive to it. Everybody reads what's written about them.

DM *Do you have a favourite piece of your own work?*

AK There are two works that I go back to continually, as measures of what I am doing. One is *White Sand, Red Millet, Many Flowers*, and the other is also a powder piece and is called *Part of the Red*.

Issue 136, May 1990

Richard Hamilton

interviewed by Jonathan Watkins

Reconstructing Duchamp's *Large Glass*

JONATHAN WATKINS *Did you intend your reconstruction of Marcel Duchamp's* Large Glass *to be seen as a work of art, or has it been transformed into a work of art by the way, for example, it has been exhibited at the Tate?*

RICHARD HAMILTON I haven't thought much about such considerations. I did it because I was asked by the Arts Council to organise the Duchamp retrospective which took place at the Tate Gallery in 1966 – and I realised that it wasn't possible to have a meaningful show without some representation of the *Large Glass*, and decided to make one myself. I repeated the studies, and went, in a year, through the process that Duchamp had gone through in 12, but I had the advantage of not having to act creatively. It was simply fulfilling a need of the exhibition.

I had begun to realise, even while I was working on the reconstruction, that Duchamp had quite an interest in this idea of replication and when Duchamp came to London he signed it – he even thought it would be nice to have three *Large Glass*es.

JW *As opposed to two? Two would constitute a self-contained pair.*

RH Yes, it was an idea of multiplicity which was essential to his aesthetic. He often used this theme of three, indeed it is an important motif in the *Glass* itself. He uses the number three as a 'refrain in duration'. The first reconstruction was the *Glass* made in Stockholm by Ulf Linde. I'd seen it in Pasadena in 1963 and had reservations. It was inadequate in that it wasn't of the quality of Duchamp's *Large Glass* largely because Linde had no opportunity to see the original. He worked from photographs, and had to make it quickly – he did a marvellous job considering the time in which it was done and the fact that he hadn't the opportunity to see Duchamp's *Glass* – he still hasn't seen it. No photograph can convey the filigree of lead wire on the mill wheel of Duchamp's *Glass*, so Linde's reconstruction is less refined. For example, the drawing on his *Glass* is not done with round wire, it's made from square section wire cut from sheets of lead. Linde either didn't know the wire was round or couldn't get it. These are inadequacies which I am sure he too would attest. Linde's achievement was in pointing to the need and to the very possibility of remaking the *Glass*.

So there was Linde's *Glass* and mine. Linde wanted to do another one, because he thought he could do it better the second time round, and Duchamp said it would be nice to have three, but then he was forgetting his own *Glass*! Now another has been made in Japan.

JW *Did you think 'I'm making a work of art' while working on your reconstruction – that is to say, were you making an object which you thought could be legitimately acquired and exhibited by a museum – it now stands in a room, accompanied I think by a Matisse, a Picabia and so on – or are you surprised by the way it has been treated?*

RH I had not expected to see it there in the Tate, treated in the way it is – with my name on it beside Duchamp's. I think it's to some extent legitimate. As I explained earlier, I did it because I needed it for the Tate's Duchamp retrospective. I asked the Tate if I could have funding to do it and the only way they could justify the cost would be to have it on permanent exhibition. It wouldn't have made sense for them to spend all that money and then throw it away.

Shortly after the Tate agreed to provide money for the making of the *Glass* I met Roland Penrose, a good friend of mine, casually somewhere and he said, 'Oh, by the way, the trustees were discussing the idea of your making a *Large Glass*, and having it on permanent exhibit, but we cannot because it will be a reproduction, and the Tate isn't allowed by its terms of charter to have reproductions in the permanent collection.' I was rather disappointed because it meant I now had a problem with funding the project. I happened to go to New York on quite other business and saw a friend of mine, Bill Copley, an admirer and friend of Duchamp, a friend of Roland Penrose and very rich. I told him the Tate story and that I couldn't make the *Glass*, not thinking that he would do anything about it. And he said, 'Well I'll have it. What will it cost?' When I came back to England I worked out that it could be done for $5,000 and when I pointed out to Bill Copley,

'It's not my work that you're buying, it's Duchamp's work', suggesting that he might give Duchamp a similar amount, $5,000. Duchamp didn't have that much money at the time, and seemed happy at his bonus.

It is important to remember that at this time I was paid as a member of the art teaching staff at Newcastle University, and had a studio there to work in. $5,000 more or less covered the cost for materials and the expense of sending an assistant, Roger Westwood, to Philadelphia to make detailed photographs. We had to have colour slides, pieces of glass with colour matches taken from various parts of Duchamp's *Glass*. So work began.

Towards the end of making my reconstruction, Ronald Alley of the Tate was in the North and he looked in to see how it was getting on, and afterwards I got a message saying that the Tate had changed their mind – that they didn't regard it as a reproduction – they wanted to take over the financial responsibility and have it permanently. But it wasn't in my hands any longer – the money so far had been paid by Bill Copley, and if they wanted my reconstruction an arrangement had to be made with him to take over further expenses and to repay the costs so far. They agreed to do just that. Bill Copley hadn't seen the *Glass*, he was just paying up as I needed the money. But he agreed to let the Tate have it, and things went on. Then I started asking the Tate for the last production costs, and was told they couldn't pay until the trustees had seen it. I warned them, 'Bill will see it at the same time as the Tate trustees, so you'd better get something done quickly.' So things got a bit tricky, but Bill Copley continued to pay. Then when the exhibition was held, Bill came to the opening and declared, 'It's mine', so the Tate couldn't have it after all. But he did agree that they could have it on indefinite loan after the end of the show.

A few years later a *Glass* was needed for a MoMA exhibition in New York and Bill loaned his. The museum paid the transport costs from England and after the exhibition they erected it in Copley's apartment on the nineteenth floor of a building overlooking Central Park. I thought that was the end of it. Years later I heard that Bill Copley was looking for a buyer for his *Glass* and that it was being hawked around museums in America. I passed the rumour on to Norman Reid, the director of the Tate, who happened to be going to New York – and he went to see Bill Copley. As a result the Tate agreed to buy it – for $50,000. I wrote to Bill Copley, just saying I thought a

500 per cent mark-up was a bit steep, the Tate having to pay $50,000 for something that the British taxpayers had already contributed a good deal to – they paid my salary while I worked on it, they provided me with the studio. The Civil Engineering Department, the Metallurgy Department, all sorts of people at the University had done things. Students had spent many unpaid hours working on the *Glass*. Even local industry – I got things made without payment by local industries because I wanted things to be done as economically as possible. I wrote to Bill Copley thinking that he might reduce his price for the *Glass* in the light of all this, which he probably didn't know about anyway. He sent a letter back to me saying, 'I don't have to take this shit from you', and I haven't seen much of him since then.

JW *And the Tate paid $50,000.*

RH After Bill Copley got my letter he refused to let the Tate have it, even though he'd shaken hands on the deal. I was in trouble then from the Tate, they said I'd fucked up by writing to Bill Copley. So I was getting shit from both Bill and the Tate. Then some years elapsed and Norman Reid, who was wonderfully persistent, rang to say he was happy to tell me that Bill Copley had agreed to lend the *Glass* again on a long-term basis, on condition it was insured for $100,000. So it was shipped back over and reinstalled in the Tate. But because of the insurance value, he got a tax discount on $100,000, which he could have had before. The whole thing was a stupid misunderstanding all the way along.

JW *When was that?*

RH It must have taken ten years for the whole thing to get sorted out.

JW *The fact that your* Large Glass *is installed at the Tate tends to subvert notions of conventional museum practice – as, of course, does every work by Duchamp when it is seen in the context of a museum. His work reminds us that aesthetic quality is neither necessary nor sufficient as a condition for art.*

RH It depends on what you mean by 'aesthetic quality' because some works by Duchamp have tremendous aesthetic quality and feel. I think the *Large Glass* is extraordinarily plastic, exquisite and elegant. Beautifully constructed. We've called my *Glass* a 'reconstruction', but it isn't a reconstruction in a normal sense – it is a replication of the process of construction. It's following procedures rather than reproducing an image. The *Large Glass* is the only work that I know of that you could do this with – a work of that quality – you couldn't reconstruct *Las Meninas* in that way.

JW *It was as if you were following a recipe?*

RH Yes, the recipe is there in the *Green Box*, which I was very familiar with, having made the English version of the notes. I knew the ideas intimately. What was valuable about the exercise, not only for me but for subsequent generations, is that we have an opportunity to see the *Glass* as it was before the accident. Some people think of the breaking of the glass as a kind of contrived possibility, something that was foreseen by Duchamp. I don't think it was. I had a clue from a conversation with Duchamp, when I asked him about the breaking. The *Glass* was found to be broken at a time when he was in Paris. Nobody knew because the box in which it had returned from the Brooklyn exhibition hadn't been opened. Years had passed and Katherine Dreier, who then owned it, found that this great work was wrecked and, as one might think, irrevocably. She didn't write to Marcel. She travelled from New York to Paris and invited him to lunch and at this meal she broke the news as gently as she could.

Marcel told me that Dreier was so distressed when telling him – she was on the verge of tears – that he was more concerned with comforting her than worrying about what she was saying. The exact words he used were 'I am able to accept any malaise'. I realised then that if he used the word *malaise*, he didn't welcome the breaking.

In a way it's right that the accident should have happened, because of the chance elements in the work – the whole aesthetic of chance on which the piece is built – and that it should have happened so beautifully. Duchamp relished the fact that the breaks were symmetrical. There are many misunderstandings about Duchamp. It has been part of the myth that Duchamp spent many months fitting together thousands of slivers of glass, as though it were a jigsaw puzzle. But Marcel told me that what made it possible for him to repair things was that the glass hadn't been displaced. It had been shattered, but most of the glass was held together by the technique of glueing wire over the glass to create the drawing.

JW *So it was like safety glass?*

RH In a way. In the corners, where there is no wire, there might have been a problem but I don't think even loose bits had shifted too much. The two large pieces of glass had been put together face to face, with the wire on the outside, and they broke together which is why, when the faces were opened up, this symmetry of cracks was revealed. And that's what delighted Duchamp. There's a beauty in the way in which it was broken – the *Glass* as it is seen now with its shimmering fractures. It's very beautiful as it catches the light, like an enormous jewel.

JW *A wonderful retinal experience?*

RH Yes, but on the other hand, it is nice to see the *Glass* as it was when young. I think that my reconstruction serves that purpose.

Issue 136, May 1990

1991–1995

Victor Pasmore

interviewed by Mel Gooding and Peter Townsend

The artist's eye

MEL GOODING *You said in 1951 – and I think you were talking about the spiral paintings you made for the Festival of Britain – 'What I have done is not the process of abstraction in front of nature, but a method of construction emanating from within. I have tried to compose as music is composed.' Later you said about the Tate's* Spiral Motif in Green, Violet, Blue and Gold: The Coast of the Inland Sea, *'The coast of the inland sea in this picture is the sea coast of subconscious experience.' Do you feel that still represents to some extent that you're doing in your art?*

VICTOR PASMORE Oh yes. My views are stated quite clearly in that catalogue I wrote for the exhibition at the National Gallery, 'The Artist's Eye'. My theme was the Renaissance and the modern revolution in painting. Well, what I said quite clearly was that the modern revolution is a subjective revolution, as opposed to the Renaissance which was objective. The art of the Renaissance was the first after the Middle Ages to look at nature objectively, to look at nature from the outside and study it scientifically, and painting itself was based on an objective view of nature. The modern revolution, beginning with late Turner who I think is the first modern, and then going on to Van Gogh, is a subjective revolution. So that fits in with my idea of these things as very subjective. You've got to bear in mind that I was brought up in the old tradition. My father had quite a good collection of pictures – he had a Constable you know – that sort of thing, pictures done from the traditional objective view of nature. And so that was my personal education in painting, in the Old Masters. Then at school, I discovered a book on Turner, with a lot of colour pictures of his late works. These excited me enormously, and I went to see them at the Tate Gallery. Here was an entirely new idea of painting, it struck me, the first time. I mean if you look at a Rembrandt, the first thing you see is the portrait and then if you know anything about seeing paintings, you see the thing as an independent painting. First you see the portrait then, afterwards, an independent object. But in these late Turners, the first thing you saw was the painting. And then after you read the title underneath, you saw it was a seascape, and so this was quite the reverse way round, and this excited me enormously. That was my first introduction to modern art. When I came to London in 1927, I was only a weekend painter, I never went to a school of art. I was ten years working, I was earning. I used to go to the evening classes at the Central School, and I somehow found myself mixed up with the Avant Garde. I began to see reproductions – you couldn't see the originals because modern art wasn't in any musuem – but you saw books in Charing Cross Road, little books with cubist paintings. It was late Turner, which I came to quite accidentally and immediately liked, which introduced me to the subjective revolution in modern art. When I came to London and saw reproductions of these cubist paintings, I had no difficulty in immediately recognising them. Then I had about seven or eight years trying to do these various things, imitation Matisses and cubists – I used to do huge Braques. I was working at weekends and in the evenings, and I had never read anything about it, and I didn't know really what it was all about.

MC *Who were you talking to about these things at that time?*

VP Well there was Claude Rogers and William Coldstream. They were doing this kind of thing. Coldstream was doing completely abstract stuff but the point I must make is that one really didn't understand what it was one was doing, and it was all so easy. I mean, it became too subjective. The whole thing had become too free, one wasn't ready for this. I think Coldstream and Rogers felt the same way. One needed something objective, something back.

MC *A call to order?*

VP Not necessarily order. Something objective, outside, and that's not easy to find. So there was no option but to go back to the old-fashioned object, the still-life or the portrait or landscape. So I did that picture, *A Parisian Café*, and, well it was just really going back to some objective standpoint. Coldstream also got fed up with abstraction. He couldn't do it, like I couldn't, and he got a job in the documentary film unit. And so coming out of that, Bill wanted to be completely objective, trying to paint like a mirror and measuring everything. Bill used to say, 'I'm fed up with this film business.' I said, 'Why don't you start painting again?' The problem was, where to start? I said, 'You can't go back to that brushstroke, pure brushstroke! You can't go back to that but you've got to start somewhere.' So I said, 'Let's paint each other's portrait.' I was still in the office then, so it had to be a weekend. We tossed up who would start. Bill won the toss. After a while we decided to have a rest and look at what he was doing. He'd produced a dreadful thing, a sort of third-rate Sargent. Well, we both agreed, there's no future in that. We agreed that we'd try again. Next weekend, Bill turned up with a ruler and plumbline, and instead of starting as one usually does, the classical way – do the outline of the head and shove in the eyes and mouth – he started with the eye and measured the distance between that eye and the next one, and then down to the nose, and marked all this on the thing. A completely sort of objective way of doing it. We had a look at that. We agreed it was a bit grim, but there was something concrete here which you could start on. That was the first Euston Road picture. But I never went as far as that – that was too much for me. Bill simply slammed the door on the whole School of Paris, and there was no means of going back. But of course I left the door open, so there's a world of difference between my *Parisian Café* or that portrait I did at Euston Road, *Girl with a Handbag*, and anything done by Bill. My portrait was quite free and easy, I would invent the thing half-way through, change the expression or everything. I never really closed the door to the subjective.

Then the war came. And Bill and Graham Bell joined up, Bill became a war artist. And the war artist thing was just right for Bill. He was the only chap really who came out of the war-artist business intact, because this was just the job – this sort of photographic documentary art – and I think his best paintings were those he did of bombed buildings. It saved him because it gave him a moral and a social responsibility all in one hat – and he was actually paid for it. But I became a conscientious objector. [Bombed out of his Ebury Street studio, Pasmore went to stay with Bryan Guinness in Hampshire.] Bryan Guinness had a big house down in the country and he had a marvellous library of art books. I helped with the farm there, but other than that I had nothing to do. And so for the first time I started reading books about art. I was reading Cézanne's and Van Gogh's and

Seurat's letters and it suddenly dawned on me that what these chaps were writing was quite different to what they were painting. What they were painting really belongs to the past. Slightly different, more subjective, but there's no fundamental difference between a landscape by Cézanne and a Constable. But what they were writing is something away in the future. What they were writing was the sort of thing that Matisse or Picasso would paint.

And I began to think, I want to paint what they are writing. I thought what one must do is create a language, an objective language created by the artist as, say, music. The language of music has been created by musicians. The musical scale is not a bird twittering in the tree, it is entirely invented by musicians. So I thought, one's got to have a language based on visual sensations. Not just one, but a whole series. All these things, like a circle or a square or a spiral or a triangle, or whatever you like, are not only objective shapes which you see in nature, but they are also basic visual sensations. I thought I'd experiment with these various visual sensations – circles, squares, spirals, and so on. I'll experiment with the lot. That *Snowstorm* is not a snowstorm, never was. I put that title on afterwards to please the Arts Council. It was simply spirals. And I might do triangles, or do a straight line, or divide the canvas in half. It's really a question of producing an objective language.

Just about that time, about 1950, Ceri Richards, whom I used to know very well – we used to have long discussions on art – said, 'Have you seen this book by Charles Biederman? I can't make head nor tail of it.' So I said, 'Lend it to me, and I'll see what I think of it.' Now Biederman was a very conceited sort of chap – his book was mostly illustrated by himself and Leonardo da Vinci – but what struck me about his book was that he was in really much the same position as I was, he was the same age as me, a little older. He was trying to find a standpoint for abstract painting. He had two theories: one, which struck me as rather interesting, was that in ordinary naturalistic painting you've got your surface and you're going back from it – there's a foreground, a middle distance, a distance – you're going back. But of course if you're going to make the painting independent, you've got to come forward. In traditional landscape painting the foreground is rather strong and the sky is rather thin. But Turner paints the sun in impasto and brings the background right into the front, and he puts the foreground into the back, which makes the thing on the surface. The next thing of course is collage – you build the thing forward. The logical next step is to actually make this into a relief, where you bring the whole thing forward, you see. I'd already got to this before. I was doing relief before I saw the Biederman book, because an architect had asked me to do a big mural in a bus garage canteen at Kingston in Surrey. I did the usual rectangles, squares and, looking at this thing, it seemed to be a bit feeble on the wall, it didn't really measure up to the architectural space. I thought if I turn this into a relief this will bring it to life. Which I did, and this brought the whole thing more in relation to the architecture.

This was the first time that I started doing reliefs, low reliefs – and so Biederman's book confirmed what I was doing. I found this was marvellous. He was saying that this was the end of abstract painting. That was going too far, but it encouraged me to continue. This seemed to be a logical development of abstract painting. The other thing, which I didn't agree with, was that he wanted a return to an objective basis in nature. And this is where I quarrelled with Biederman. We had a long correspondence. The objective basis on which Renaissance art was based was the mirror and anatomy. In order to draw the figure really truthfully, you had to learn some anatomy. And also to draw objectively you had to imitate the mirror. What Biederman wanted was an objective basis in the process of nature, not the appearance. In the actual process, the structural process. But when you get down to brass tacks, what on earth does it mean? What are the processes of nature? There are millions, and I couldn't agree with this. What I wanted was an objective artificial language, not some vague thing about the processes of nature. They could be anything. It sounded an extremely attractive idea, but when you get down to it there's no connection between the processes of oil painting and a tree. None whatever.

MG *At a certain point you went back to what one might call a more poetic, lyrical sort of painting. In 1969 you wrote: 'In art the peripheral images of thought and perception reappear as anonymous objects before which is always the question. While reason sleeps, the symbol awakes.' Can you say something about that?*

VP Well, it's again a subjective approach to the problem. The point is that there are two things in painting, there is the sign, the abstract sign as in child art – a circle with two dots stands for a head – a child, drawing you, won't look at you at all. That's a sign. It's not a symbol.

A symbol is something much wider and rather vague. It's more cosmological, absolute, universal – you can't rationalise symbols. You can rationalise signs. And so, for the symbol to come to life as having any new subjective meaning, you've got to get reason to be asleep. And the symbol comes from something intuitive, something which is not reason.

MC *Here you're going back to this very basic, almost surrealist concept of what art might do, which is to let the rational mind go into abeyance, and the unknown to come into play.*

VP Yes, it is a sort of surrealist approach, I quite agree. I try and let the picture do the talking. And the fundamental thing for me is the material of the painting and the tools. Now the classical way of course is to have an idea. I used to have long arguments with Barbara Hepworth about this. She said, 'I have an idea, I dream up an idea of a shape in my mind, and then I simply copy the idea.' Well, that's one way of doing it. But I don't do it that way at all. I've got a flat surface, first of all – I just spray a blob on that. Well, that dictates the image. And you can add to it and it becomes a symbol, which is purely subjective, it has no logical meaning.

MC *You did a portfolio of prints called 'Correspondences', you'll remember, with poetry and graphics, word and image. How important an idea has that been to you?*

VP I've always been trying to find a title for my art – *Simple Living Water*, for instance. That doesn't mean ordinary water, that's a metaphysical title. I'm very interested in opposites, in nature as an interaction of opposites. This is what keeps the thing going around. It's very old, it's a religious thing. But I'm interested in that. *Living Water* is two opposites. I don't mean living water in the sense that it's moving, in the physical sense of the word. Water is a purely physical thing. *Living Water* is an entirely metaphysical title. The picture on the front of the catalogue, that's called *A Harmony of Opposites*. I give the paintings, when I can, a title. When I haven't got a title like that big blue one downstairs – there's no title. They want to call it 'Blue Water'. I'm not interested in that.

PETER TOWNSEND *In retrospect, Victor, how do you rate the Euston Road?*

VP I think Euston Road was the only thing that really tried to make a commitment over this political situation between 1935 and 1940. The Euston Road people – I talk about Bill Coldstream and Graham Bell particularly and William Townsend – really took the thing seriously and they did try and make an artistic commitment to this, and I think that was a terrific thing to do. The point, as I said, was they hadn't got the language to do it. People like myself were still sort of child artists, but were trying to be grown-up.

MG *The basic course that you taught, and that you developed, what were the principles that underlay that?*

VP To try to find an objective language created by the artist not derived from nature but based on visual sensations, not based on visual objects, but based on visual sensation. Colour is a visual sensation. A square or a circle, or a spiral, are both visual objects and also basic visual sensations. I took them as basic visual sensations.

I would think that's absolutely relevant for abstract painting. The trouble is that nobody really understood this. In the art schools it simply became a sort of playground, and was taken up by the education authorities as a sort of first-year course for people to fool around with. But I've told these chaps, I'm still doing this basic course after 50 years, and the idea that it's a first-year course is all nonsense. The big mistake is to make it a basic course for all kinds of art. It's only relevant to abstract art.

Issue 146, May 1991

Alan Charlton

interviewed by Andrew Wilson

For me it has to be done good

ANDREW WILSON *Your recent exhibition in Schafhausen marks a departure for you in that you have created a retrospective 'made new'.*

ALAN CHARLTON That's true. The 14 new paintings go through the different forms and shapes that the paintings have used over the last 20 years. One of the reasons that I could do this without becoming confused myself explains the difference between me and a painter. I always say that I am an artist who makes a grey painting. It is because I think like that, that for me it is no problem to look back on things that I have done 20 years ago. I don't work in a progression, the intentions and the aims are constant, I don't see it as a problem. This was more than just a retrospective of work. For me it was also a time to reflect on what I have been doing. I think that after 20 years you can give yourself that luxury. It was a cleansing process. Having been put in a situation to rethink through things, the need to make further changes actually increases. By working through the different shapes that the paintings had, I was made much more aware of how I have always dealt in using different shapes and this pushed me into trying different shapes again.

AW *In making the Schafhausen retrospective to what extent do you now feel the need to change your work radically?*

AC As time goes by you tend to have very fond memories of paintings and in a way you start to think that they were better than they actually were. When I worked on some of the earlier paintings I thought that actually they were not that good. They were the paintings that were the germ of the idea and that is their importance and really I can stop all these silly memories of how good they were because, actually,

I wouldn't want to make them again.

AW *But have you made them better this time?*

AC Well, that's a curious thing because technically, of course, they were made better but the really strange thing was that all the problems were exactly the same as when I made them the first time, it was really a re-living of the same experiences. I think an artist is always concerned and worried that his recent work is not as good as his earlier work, and I am pleased to have put that all to rest for myself because I feel that what I am doing now is better than what I did before.

AW *How important is the notion of the installation for you?*

AC It is very rare for a painting to be made for a specific space. It is more often about placing and positioning the painting in the space which works best for the painting and the space. It is the space that they are concerned with, they are not architectural features or anything like this. Usually each exhibition is quite literally just the last five or six paintings that I have made, or in some cases a work that keeps the installation in mind, and it is quite possible for them to be shown in other places.

AW *El Lissitzky talks about this notion of 'total context' where meaning can only be found between the placement of works within a room.*

AC I like to think my paintings are a direct act against composition. I would never want composition to act within the paintings, my composition is within the installation. How the paintings are positioned is my act of composition within the space. I also have no hesitation in showing the same painting in a different place even though it will look a completely different painting and that is because making the painting is about activating the space that it is in. My paintings are completely against the framed two-dimensional painting which creates its stage set for you to make believe to go into. The reality of my paintings can be found in the reality of the space.

AW *Artists such as Lissitzky, Aleksandr Rodchenko, Vladimir Tatlin or Laszlo Moholy-Nagy positioned their work within a social dimension and ideology that was reified in their painting. Is it necessary for any ideology to be recognised at work in your paintings and offer another dimension of reality?*

AC The work that those artists did was coming directly out of a literal social response which they were very clear about. For myself it is more unclear, it is there but it doesn't appear in that same literal sense. The first grey paintings were made in 1967–68. When I was making those paintings my intention was just to make a painting, with no other ideology at all. At the end of the 1960s there was a particular need to find an art form that used different traditions and rules from before, and at the end of the 1960s society itself was breaking down and trying to find different standards, and some of the standards and values that I wanted within the paintings were a direct response to that. I don't like to tie the paintings down and have them represent this or that political point of view. My paintings are about equality and the equality sometimes happens within the forms themselves and in the way I think about making the art. So, from the concept of making the painting, to building the painting, to painting the painting, to packing the painting, to seeing to the transport of the painting, to seeing how the layout of the catalogue is, to seeing to the day-to-day activities of the studio – all these qualities for me are completely equal. Everything has the same importance and is totally opposite to the artist who turns up at his studio with a nice white canvas and daubs some paint on it for two hours and then goes away and when it's finished he rings the gallery and says, 'You can collect my works of genius now.' For me it is totally different. Immediately after leaving art school I took the position that I should go to the studio six days a week, working an eight-hour day with the same routine and minimum of fuss as if I did any other job. I wouldn't like to represent a political stance in my work, but at the same time I could say that there are certain artists who represent the Right and I would say that in that sense I represent the Left.

AW *Why choose grey?*

AC The reason was really very direct. I wanted to make a painting out of completely unartistic means, and so the stretchers are made from the cheapest everyday joinery timber that you could buy in a wood yard. In the same way I decided to use a colour which was an urban colour. When I first began to use colours deliberately to be much more unartistic and much more urban some of the first few paintings were black or brown and just by chance also one was grey. I came to realise that the grey itself had something more than this original theory and that it had this special stillness and reflectiveness. I fell in love with the colour, it was as simple as that. Also, and I know it sounds very naive or simplistic to say it, I always wanted people to look and say, 'I've never seen a painting look like that before.' Perhaps the real problem now is that I still see the paintings like that.

AW *Does the use of grey have any negative connotations, a certain indifference being neither black nor white but somewhere in between?*

AC This has become for me an endlessly changing question and in the end it is about the multi-feeling that it has, the static of nothingness. Although I said earlier that everything is equal within the paintings, the fact that they are grey is the crutch and that really does become unquestioning because whatever else happens that is the constant, that is the unchanging realism throughout everything else. But what place does reality have here?

AW *Is there no reality outside the making of the paintings?*

AC Oh, I think reality is there, it is all about reality. That everything is real, everything is about the making of the paintings, to the showing of them to the space – everything is a real sensation. Other than that I can't say what else, there is nothing.

AW *You established the parameters of your vocabulary at Camberwell and the Royal Academy Schools. What was your attitude to your time at art school?*

AC I wanted to be an artist for as long as I can remember and so I automatically went straight to art school in Sheffield, but my ambition was to go to London because just as a concept it had to be the best place to go, it was that lure of the capital. I applied to Camberwell which at that time, and even today I think, was known as the best figurative art school in the country and I had come from a very working-type background and so for me it seemed very logical that you should choose the art school which would learn you your craft. Within the first year at Camberwell I realised that art was not just about an ability to draw or paint but more to do with thinking and ideas. Teachers could always come and tell you that this was right and this was wrong and I thought that art shouldn't be about that. Art should be something much more private, much more personal, where somebody couldn't tell you what to do, and that's when I decided that I had to make up my own rules and that's when the paintings started to change. I found I could make a painting which nobody could tell me was right and nobody could tell me was wrong. It was my painting.

AW *So, why did you go at this stage to the RA Schools?*

AC It was a little bizarre that I should have gone there because I was already making the grey paintings with the small square holes in. It was more a pragmatic choice than anything else. I was married,

I had a three-year-old son. Like many people who leave art school who think they can do some small job and paint in the weekend, so did I. This can never work out. I had been accepted for the Royal Academy on drawings that I had made in my first year at Camberwell and yet I still really didn't plan to go. I had been working in the steelworks for the whole of the summer and when I saw the letter and the money that I would receive as a grant I thought that this was not bad money. I went with the intention of not discussing art with anybody in case their ideas infiltrated. In the evenings I would go to my studio and make the first set of paintings that I made my first exhibition with.

AW *You said that you went to Camberwell to learn a craft and the way you talk about making the paintings is in those terms, almost as an attempt to reinstate certain attitudes towards the making of art which had been lost.*

AC I am not interested in the craft. For me it is more important that I should make the paintings as best as I possibly can out of respect for the idea. If I made the painting quickly, not giving much care to how the woodwork is constructed, how the canvas is straight, how the paint is painted, it would be so disrespectful to the idea. You have to make whatever you do the best you possibly can to give it a chance. I am not impressed by the intricacies of craftsmanship. For me it has to be done good.

AW *In 1973 you took part in an exhibition organised by Michel Claura: 'Une Exposition de Peinture réunissant certains Peintres qui mettraient la Peinture en Question' with Daniel Buren, Robert Ryman, Agnes Martin and Brice Marden. How important was this recognition to you?*

AC It was the first group exhibition that I had been in. At the end of the 1960s there was a spirit that crossed the western world as if certain ideas were raining from the sky and people were picking up on them. There were some artists who had a similar idea about art who didn't necessarily know or speak to each other. I was never directly aware of this and was so immersed in what I was doing I never attempted to put myself into context, and this was the first time that I realised that many of these artists – although the work wouldn't necessarily look the same – took a very similar attitude to what they thought that their art should be. My French is non-existent but I think that the exhibition's title is saying that – 'When is a Painting a Painting?' – and to really take that question itself was a new question.

AW *But each artist was involved in different questions about what painting could be. Marden talking of painting as a 'grand undefinable endeavour' is a long way from –*

AC – yes, and yet each painter was exploring how to make a painting in a different way and to take it literally out of the frame. That was the common situation.

AW *So, two years later in 1975 you were one of 17 artists in the Amsterdam Stedelijk's exhibition 'Fundamental Painting', and then again you were in 'A New Spirit in Painting' in 1981 at the Royal Academy. All three exhibitions celebrated the important nature of the activity of painting as painting – the latter in a very debased sort of way. Did you feel comfortable in these supposedly agenda-setting exhibitions?*

AC By 1981 there had been many changes and 'A New Spirit in Painting' was evidence of this. To make an honest comment I would say that 95 per cent of the artists in that show were absolutely awful and I wouldn't give any credit whatsoever to them, and for the other 5 per cent some were artists I would respect, but on the whole I would characterise most of those artists as the enemy. But I didn't refuse the invitation to be in the exhibition because at that time I thought that the enemy was winning and that the best way to counteract this was by terrorist activity. So, when this other position was being glorified, people walking through the gallery would enter the space where they would see my painting – a large grey painting in seven parts – and they would think 'my God, Charlton is still there, we can't get rid of him'.

AW *Did you feel beleaguered at the time of 'New Spirit', when Neo-Expressionism had the upper hand?*

AC In 1978–79 it was really as if the doors had closed and it was only after 1983 that things started to change again. During those five years I was fortunate that I had some relationships with galleries who continued to support me. It certainly wasn't an easy time. I had my work to do and even if people didn't like it I couldn't stop it. It didn't ever make me re-question what I was doing. However, every single morning I would question whether to continue because at that time I had a family with two children and it was financially very difficult. At the end of the 1970s we had reached a very strange position where the art world was ready for something different, it was really just wanting a fashion to change. This coincided with this very conservative period of people wanting to return to old values, to things that they could understand, all of which seemed to reflect the economy of the time.

AW *So it was very much a market-based change?*

AC Yes, but it also reflected that nervousness everywhere where people wanted to be among things that they understood. It was as if the painting was back in its frame again. The artist was not a politician any more, he wasn't an orator, he was just somebody who painted pictures and everybody including the artist felt happy with this regressive situation. The reason why today, in 1991, the interest in that type of painting is almost zero is that it was shallow because it didn't try to add something new, it only went backwards. None of the artists formulated a new way and – this is an expression you don't often hear now – but I believe in modern art. By that I mean that art is always looking forward and that the next generation, however much they might learn from the past, their intention should always be to add something new.

AW *In that sense I feel that a lot of young artists today don't seem to be adding something new, they have gone back to the past, to something that had some sort of ideological context around it which they could assimilate into the surface of their work as decor. It is very stylish and it can be very beautiful but it just sits there dumbly.*

AC If I was 20 years old now I am not sure what I would be doing. When I first started making my paintings it was all about making a painting which was about trying to break down rules. To shock people so they think 'What is this painting about?' or 'How do I look at it?' is not such a bad thing. This is a danger for many young artists working in a similar way today who often make very beautiful pieces but in a way they are working by rules which were established 20 years ago. For that reason I don't think I would begin doing that now as a 20-year-old, I think that I would still like to try and find a different way. An academy of any sort within art has to be a bad thing.

AW *Those two early group exhibitions had artists asking questions about what the painting could be. To what extent were you asking questions?*

AC I approach each painting as making a statement rather than an experiment. I don't have to question many things that I do. The path is laid and I just have to follow it. From the beginning I knew what I shouldn't do. I knew all the things that I didn't want in the painting. It was by taking all these things away that I could build something positive. Many of my conditions or rules were not just unique to how to make a painting, they were in a sense a foundation for how I was going to live my life and the paintings in a way just followed those foundations. Yet also everything evolved through knowing the right thing to do and when. I had a very theoretical position, but the danger after working for many years is that it is easy to analyse many reasons why the grey. What I want to preserve is the quality of just doing something because it seems the right thing to do at the time. I can say that even with very direct memories of when the paintings have wanted to change. I mean that sounds a very romantic way to put it, but sometimes that has happened – the paintings go and I follow them. The paintings are the dog and they are pulling me along, the questions and the analysis of the reasons why come afterwards. To really question something too much can hinder it because the real idea just flows. I cannot foresee the situation of just sitting down to rack my brains for a new idea. If that happened I would prefer to give up. There is no separation from the idea, the theory, the practical, the attitude that I have to other art, the way that I live my life – it is for me all the same thing. I know myself that if I didn't have these other values within my life the paintings, in a sense, would just fall to pieces, they are part of my reason for living. It is all so intertwined.

AW *So it's a job which you need in order to live?*

AC Well, unfortunately it's more that I need my life to do the job.

AW *The symmetry of your work and its repetition points to a banalisation of originality because in a sense you are doing the same thing each time with slight changes of emphasis.*

AC Yes I would relate to that feeling except you credit me with too much because I think it is a very poetic and powerful position to make the same painting every day but I have never really done that. I have got certain constants that run through the paintings but they are always changing. I would like to feel that I could reach that point. For me it has that same strength as the rhythm of the sea – the sea is always there, always the same but always changing – the changes in my painting happen like that.

AW *This all seems to imply that you are interested in much more than making a painting. This is pointed to by the Giacometti quotation used by you for the 'Fundamental Painting' exhibition: 'The adventure, the great adventure, is to see something unknown appear each day, in the same face. That is greater than any journey round the world which, on the face of it, seems removed from the concerns of your work.'*

AC But it is the same for me as for Giacometti – to make that same grey painting is the adventure because the same grey painting is never the same grey painting, it is always a different grey painting and has the same feeling as searching for the unknown. This adventure is greater than travelling around the world because I think that you can see everything within your own room, I don't think that you have to go to the moon to find out something more about the way that you feel. That is also what the paintings are about. They are about that continual working each day and seeing things in that minute way, and although I only see my job as making paintings I think that they are a part of something which is too big for one person.

AW *So you wouldn't agree with Frank Stella's comment about what you see is all there is. Would you perhaps say that there is something else as well?*

AC I think that it is not about all there is. I think that the physical painting on the wall, that is a vehicle to make you see art. I feel that art in the painting is some abstract view and the way the painting is made, painted and shown, is to try and put that feeling over. The difference is that you see the painting and it is exactly what it is but when you stand in front of it, it is about somebody who has made a painting with a feeling. If you just stood in front of a painting and saw it completely in formal abstract ways I think you'd miss the point.

Issue 149, September 1991

George Segal

interviewed by Andrew Graham-Dixon

Artists will kill each other for a place in history

ANDREW GRAHAM-DIXON *Do you think you're a Pop artist?*

GEORGE SEGAL That depends on your definition of Pop Art. I feel like we're all characters in the Japanese movie *Rashomon* today. I had a strange time last night looking at the show. The joy and delight of art critics is practising critical ranking: you're number one, two, three or 29. My overwhelming reaction last night was – I know everybody or almost everybody, I know certainly all the Americans and my relationship to them, to their ideas – and my mental life for the past 30 years has very little to do with the show, the catalogue and all the critical talk.

AG-D *Do you actually feel as if your work doesn't belong there? Do you feel like an outsider?*

GS No, absolutely not. I'll give you a worm's eye point of view. When I was an art student I was overwhelmed by the look of abstract painting – abstract expressionist painting – which was brand-new in New York. And my father said, 'you bum', I wanted to become a fine artist and he said 'you'll never make a living at it, and I can't support you'. That loving paternal injunction is overwhelming. I was at an art school, trying to learn how to make myself into an art teacher and sneaking in fine art in a clandestine way. I saw an exhibition of what I later discovered to be student derivative imitation Abstract Expressionism and this was being done at New York University and I instantly switched, I fell in love with it. My direct teachers were overwhelming father figures – Tony Smith was one, William Baziotes was another. Smith used to walk down the halls with Rothko paintings under his arm, showing us what the new work looked like and inviting me to go to club meetings.

I started to try to paint abstract expressionist paintings. There was this injunction, there was this terrible pressure on young artists, 'jump on the bandwagon of the history of art with us' and 'we've invented this new thing'. I was told, 'Get a big canvas, go to the hardware store, buy a five-inch house-painter's brush, use black and white.' I said, 'What do I paint?'. I was totally split. I loved the look of the paint. This was NYU, Washington Square, this was late forties, early fifties, right after the war – everybody in art school because they had a GI bill paying tuition. New York City was full of these refugee great European artists and there was a smell, an excitement in the air, there was this competitive challenge, the Americans chauvinistically swaggering after seeing the suffering of these European exiles who were wallowing in a totally strange unfamiliar city. We thought they were demi-gods because we had seen reproductions of this stupendous School of Paris work and it was marvellous. We were going to challenge this supremacy in the same way that, as young art students – forgive me for being peripheral, I'm getting excited about that time – we had discovered jazz and we had the nerve to go up to Harlem because we were young and we could physically take care of ourselves and we would listen to the new jazz by black musicians. In the Apollo sometimes there were these dance contests, they called them cutting contests, 'cutting a rug'. One tap dancer would get up and do a fancy step, the next fellow would get up, repeat that step and do something that would top the first fellow. Then the original fellow would come and repeat the marvellous achievement that went on before and then do something that would top number two. And so on it went. I used to think that was commercial nonsense, I thought that was Hollywood entertainment. Because we were listening to these jazz musicians invent a new way to pour out their passions and we were sympathetic to both the subject-matter of the passion and the incredible new way of saying something that was very sad and very direct with no punches pulled.

I'm faced with Abstract Expressionism. I think it's marvellous, the men are anti-materialist – they talked and sounded like New York cab drivers – and then they're talking James Joyce. Tony Smith would say 'read *Ulysses*' and then next week he would show us cubist paintings by Picasso and say, 'What are the connections between James Joyce and these cubist paintings?' So that the toughness, the brashness, the New York harshness was balanced by this last refuge for idealism. You couldn't expect to make money at it, you were stupid if you did.

You had to – if you wanted to learn about art and practise fine art no matter what the form – you had to find some other way to support yourself. That was bluntly it.

So in that atmosphere, I keep thinking *Rashomon*, like I'm giving you some other side of it. I quarrelled, I loved Smith and Baziotes and I quarrelled with them. They left me no room to grapple with the world I could see and touch with my hand. Everything else was staggeringly admirable. Everything they were talking about – pure form, the expressiveness of the paint, of the colour of the history of art and what could be these enormous possibilities for new art. I floundered around. Number one, I graduated – I got that stupid degree that entitled me to teach art and I knew nothing about it. I went home and, across the road, my father had a chicken farm and I built a chicken farm. This is the stock joke that is comparable to James Rosenquist painting signboards – I became a chicken farmer. I met Allan Kaprow and Kaprow introduced me, not only literally, to Robert Rauschenburg, Jasper Johns and John Cage and Merce Cunningham, but it was to this world of ideas. Kaprow was a strange hybrid: he was teaching art history, he was publishing articles regularly in *Art News* about the new art and it took me ten years to discover that he was a master of esoteric mystery because he knew what Futurism looked like and I had never heard of it at the time. Neo-Dada with the Neo-Surrealism movement, he knew somehow intimately what happened at the Café Voltaire in Zurich. He knew about concrete poetry and things like that. So finally he takes me to a Cage class.

AG-D *When did you meet Kaprow?*

GS I met Kaprow in 1953. I graduated from NYU, I was a licensed art teacher. I couldn't – didn't – want to get a job teaching art and started building a chicken farm. He got a job, accidentally moved in down the road and some mutual friend introduced us and we were going to invent the New Brunswick School of painting in New Brunswick, New Jersey I guess. I became a member of the co-operative gallery that Kaprow belonged to called the Hansa. Now all these people had been students of Hans Hofmann, I was the only exception. They ran a range from Yosten Kevitch who is a child of David Smith, working with street garbage. In anthropomorphic human form, Gene Foulet. Besides Kaprow my other buddy was Jan Muller who was a refugee from Germany, his father had been a socialist and he was a figurative painter and he was painting scenes out of Shakespeare [and] Myron

Stout, black and white abstract paintings that he called the seed pods of the gods – figurative expressionism via Van Gogh. So that New York was a goulash of every kind of painting that was an echo of Abstract Expressionism or in reaction against it.

AG-D *Would you say that there was one Pop Art, if we accept the label for a minute. Looking at the American artists who are in this Pop Art exhibition at the Royal Academy, was there a strong sense of community among you or was it more that there were mini-communities within that. I mean, were you ever particularly close with, let's say, Claes Oldenburg or Roy Lichtenstein?*

CS Yes, I think we all gravitated to each other. I think the common glue was dissatisfaction with Abstract Expressionism. Not, strangely enough, the look of it. The critic Clement Greenberg had made a mighty pronouncement that the history of twentieth-century art was an implacable march towards abstraction and there was this rigorous exorcism of everything figurative in art. I thought that was laughable and I was attracted by, gravitated to the company of artists my own age who also objected to that ordered scenario. There is this rebelliousness – yes I knew Lichtenstein, I knew Oldenburg, Jim Dine, Kaprow, I knew all the people in the Fluxus movement – there was a feeling of community in those early years, we all shared a certain mental life. I loaned my farm once to Kaprow, who organised six Happenings that were international. We knew artists in Europe, especially Paris. Wolf Vostell smashed and destroyed a TV set on my chicken farm. A student of Kaprow scavenged the tubes the next morning which I thought was very good.

AG-D *Did you have six Happenings all in one day?*

CS Oh yes, we had them all in one day. Kaprow did a Happening. He had me order two tons of hay and this formed a barrier. He had an army of people armed with twigs ripped out of the woods – I guess it's Burnham Wood – and then he asked me to order a bulldozer that he was going to drive and he was going to oppose this army armed with twigs. I censored his artwork, I told him 'you never drove a bulldozer before', and he said 'no', and I said 'suppose you slip and kill somebody', and he said 'oh no', I said 'oh, well, I'm censoring your artwork'.

AG-D *You never actually made Happenings yourself did you?*

CS No.

AG-D *But do you think any of that, I mean the idea of a Happening – there's a sense of theatre that's present in your work – do you think there's any relationship there?*

CS I was very close with Kaprow. Initially my jaw dropped at his scholarship, at his familiarity with every wrinkle of the Avant Garde. I'd never heard of Futurism. I thought that Futurism – I'll come to your answer, forgive me – I thought Futurism was a movement that was far more modern than Cubism. Then I discovered that the futurists had made the glaring error of supporting Mussolini. That's one aspect. No, Kaprow did a lot of work on the Happenings, he made a whole string of them. A long list of artists – Oldenburg, Dine, Red Grooms, Bob Whitman – were making Happenings. Every time someone did a new Happening, Kaprow would publish a new article and envelop the personal statement into his grand theory and they used to get very mad at him and object. But it was all this seething building of a new art movement. I objected to the Happenings purely in terms of ephemeral form. I loved the idea of being able to walk into a physical space and walk around it and have it punctuated by severe, austere forms that were bits, pieces, fragments of the real world. For me, it was literal Cubism – I could walk around it and see it from different points of view. But I was more introspective. I wanted to enter it over and over again and I objected to writing a Happening, having it performed six times and then have it exist only as a single typewritten sheet of instructions. I was hungry to make forms with my own hands.

My quarrel with Kaprow – I was always quarrelling with somebody, I don't know why, maybe that is the whole point – my quarrel with Kaprow was that number one, the pleasure of working with your own hands was removed. It became so totally cerebral, the expression depended on it being acted out and the delicate nuances changed from week to week. I suppose I could never become a playwright by that token. I thought Kaprow was wiping out the history of art which has to do primarily with the pleasure of making your own form – if there's any validity to that. I quarrelled with the abstract expressionists because they wanted me to leave out the real world. They had all kinds of noble intentions except everything was couched in pure colour, pure form, thick or thin or marvellous paint. I learned a lot, or I used Duchamp's ideas as a crutch or precedence or justification of, say, the found object. The qualities of a found object, they're anonymous – nobody knows who made them – they are mass-produced in a factory system and they are poignant and full of associations. In spite of themselves, found objects are extraordinarily expressive. I've never pretended to be cool, witty, detached or ironic. I have great admiration for Lichtenstein, he's a close personal friend. I have great admiration for his work. The fact that he's cooler than I am makes no difference but I am a prisoner of my own temperament and I can't apologise for dealing with expressive feeling.

AG-D *When you talked about found objects, in* Woman Shaving Her Leg, *1963, you chose the object, you constructed that, it's not just something that you happened upon, so you've actually made a deliberate choice. There's a difference with Duchamp, isn't there?*

GS Duchamp wrote that in one of my catalogues. Sidney Janis asked him to write a preface to my catalogue and he came up with a single hand-written sentence: 'With Segal, it's not the found object it's the chosen object.'

AG-D *Did you know Duchamp? Did you meet him?*

GS Yes, I met him late on. I felt he was unapproachable. I discovered his fragility and vulnerability and Rosenquist was quite accurate in how he characterised Marcel. I think Marcel's grandness lies in the strength of his ideas. I'd say the same about Cage. Cage is a role model – exemplary life, the consummate philosopher, cool and unflappable – I don't believe that for a second. I don't believe the coolness propaganda at all.

AG-D *Was Cage an influential figure for you? Was he a friend of yours or is he a friend of yours?*

GS Hard to define friend – we know each other, we've seen each other for years and I've been warm with Cage and Cunningham for a long time. I've not been socially friendly, we meet at these public occasions.

AG-D *Did you ever go to a Cage performance – say in the sixties – and think, yeah, he's interested in what I'm interested in, there's a sense of contact, there's a sense of community?*

GS Absolutely. I did go to an original performance, I think David Tudor performed 4'33" of silence. Tudor came in very fussily like a pretentious concert pianist and sat down and he moved his elbows and he arranged things and then nothing happened. Finally people caught on and they started to shuffe and you could hear sounds coming in from the window and it was traffic noise and lights were blinking. I became intensely aware of the space of the room and the quality of the sound because psychologically it was *coitus interruptus*. I was grinning from ear to ear and I was in an absolute state of delight because this was precisely like the poetry of the real world in contradistinction to the rules, regulations, boundaries, restrictions, fences of abstract expressionist painting. It opened up the poetic possibilities of the real world. It's terrible to be a young painter, you're supposed to reinvent the wheel, like every generation is supposed to: number one, become personal. Number two, invent a new grammar, a new way of saying it. You couldn't – you literally couldn't – use Renaissance space, you would be sneered at, they would take your club membership away.

MEMBER OF AUDIENCE *I'd like to ask you about what I perceive as the tragic element in your work which seems to have gotten much more so.*

GS The young lady who spoke, she's noted the tragic elements in my work and I'm glad she noticed. Andrew asked me if I'm a Pop artist. The abstract expressionist artists, who are this grand wall against which we're all throwing pots of paint, had this noble transcendent ambition. In conversation with Barney Newman once, years ago, he explained to me what was for him the personal meaning of this painting which was a zip, a red zip on a blue background. He said, 'That's Abraham. Abraham was a patriot from the Old Testament. It was also the name of my father', and he expected that enormous field of colour and that vertical stripe of contrasting colour to be packed with all the allusions and associations of a lifetime of physical memories of his own father, with all those contradictions and all that richness, coupled with ancient myths. Now, as a statement of ambition, I think that's unparalleled. I think you trapped me. I'm supposed to be a Pop artist I don't, I repeat, I don't pretend to be witty, detached or ironic. I think I'm interested in something like a unified field theory. I'll explain: it has to do with preserving what's best in abstraction, which is the unquestioned power of pure composition to express what is unconscious. Unconscious, that means all those invisible feelings that are trapped inside our body that we all experience, plus some evidence of this materialistic miraculous sometimes brutal real world outside our skin.

We go into a show and we see an enormous group show, and my compliments to Marco Livingstone, he's done an enormously impressive job of pulling together a lot of closely related work. All of us, each of us sees that show from our own point of view, and we bring to it our own history, our own feelings, our own associations. I'm questioning the validity of history since artists will kill each other for a place in history. And possibly there are other things more important.

Issue 151, November 1991

Richard Deacon

interviewed by Patricia Bickers

Between the two of us

PATRICIA BICKERS *The last time we spoke in 1985, (see pp.235–38), you had made your first 'outside' work,* For Those Who Have Ears II, Like a Bird, Like a Ship *and* Between the Two of Us, *and you had just become involved in the Euston Road Project that was eventually aborted. Yet in the catalogue accompanying the unveiling of* Between Fiction and Fact, *at the museum at Villeneuve d'Ascq, the director wrote that, when the idea of commissioning a public sculpture was first discussed, 'Richard Deacon's name leapt to mind'. What transition did you have to make from the concept of outside work to public art?*

RICHARD DEACON The transition really is to do with practice rather than anything else – and interest. So in 1985 I did the work at the Serpentine Gallery (*Blind Deaf and Dumb*) and in 1987 I was in the show 'Skulptur Projekt Münster', in Münster. At the same time in 1987, on the basis of those works, I was invited to make a proposal for Warwick University (*Let's Not be Stupid*) and I was also successful in a competition for the Yonge Square in Toronto (*Between the Eyes*). So Warwick University and Toronto are the first works which really fall into the category of çommissions or into a tight definition of public art. Earlier, in 1986, I'd been to Gateshead to discuss the possibility of making a piece in Gateshead – that was an abortive proposal because the site that I was working with disappeared, although I did subsequently make a work for Gateshead. At this stage I'm unsure how much a sequence of opportunities gave rise to a transition of interest rather than there being a conscious decision that at a certain point I was interested in making public art. The transition between what you've called outside art and the commissioned work is not a clear one.

For Those Who Have Ears II, *Like a Bird* and *Like a Ship* occupied rural – even in Liverpool – greenfield sites, whereas the works in Warwick University and Toronto were urban sites. The transition occurred with *Blind Deaf and Dumb* at the Serpentine Gallery. That's the most important work in this connection and that's the work that bridges the two kinds of work. On a purely practical level that's the first work for which I really used an outside fabricator and could therefore engage with a set of practices which married up, to some extent, with my studio-based practices but which also had a root in building, in making structural steel work. I was able to plug in to an expertise which allowed me to work with a dimension of material which I didn't have access to before.

There's a kind of practical level in which, by a happy accident, I clicked with the fabricators. Also, the work outside was drawn before it was done, which was a radical departure in practice from the studio practice, but by forcing myself to produce a sequence of production drawings, or near-production drawings, I was then able to make a proposition to someone else and say this is what I want to do. It's a *sine qua non* of commissioned work that you're able to do that. So there was a practical route.

A second element would be to do with finding that I did want to make sculpture on a different kind of scale, either smaller or bigger. I remember a conversation with Nicholas Logsdail when I described myself as wanting to make sculpture that was not necessarily framed by the gallery, wasn't defined by gallery possibilities.

The third element I think occurred to me when I was working on the proposal for Münster, where I began to realise that an urban situation had more of an interest than a greenfield site, that I wasn't actually interested in putting an object in a greenfield situation. The problem that I have had with that in the past has always been to do with the inertness of the object in relation to the environment. The two original sites in Münster were two empty corner lots and the sculptures (*Like a Snail A* and *B*) were thought of as being like houses. In a sense the possibility of working in an urban situation did enable some of the inside and outside qualities of my work to be transferred from an interior situation to an outside situation. It's as if there is a possibility of borrowing the interiority from a building and using it outside of it, so that the spectator is able to enter the sculpture in a way that has associations with the way one enters a building but at the same time you're seeing it as shape or form.

I'm not interested in making architecture, I'm interested in making sculpture, but it does seem that the juxtaposition of a volume against a building allows that interior quality, which is part of one's experience of a building, to be applied to the sculpture. That sense of interior, whether it's an imaginative interior or an actual interior, is a part of the spectators' experience.

There is additionally a question which comes up concerning what way that space is different from the space of a gallery or a museum. This is a very complex question about the meaning of 'public', because as a word it has multitudes of meaning, both negative and positive. One of the meanings of 'public' is a social welfare meaning, another has to do with 'freely available to all'; 'public affairs' is 'a matter of concern to us all', while 'public life' is distinct from 'private life'. I would resist the notion of public art as being an act of social welfare and have tended to work on the assumption that making sculpture is itself a public act in the same way that to speak a language is a public act. In order for it to be an expressive medium there has to be some sense in which 'public' is applicable to the idea of making sculpture. In that sense, there is considerable continuity between sculpture which I make for a gallery space and work which I make for an outdoor space. The outdoor works are structured according to site but they don't have the rigid criteria of site specificity that, for example, Richard Serra might envisage, although in practical terms, their movability is distinctly limited. They do belong to the site and, in making the work, or making the proposals for the work, there is considerable investigation into both the geographical and historical conditions of the site and also, through model-making, the actual dimensions of the place. In that sense they are tailored to the space, but they probably don't fit the tight definition of site specificity and, in a certain sense, the notion of separateness is tied in with the way that I think about making sculpture anyway: the notion of the completeness and detachment from floor and, in some senses, detachment from surroundings, is part of the rhetoric, or part of the vocabulary, that I use in making sculpture.

PB *It's actually something we talked about in 1985.*

RD Yes, we talked about the difference between a house and sculpture.

PB *And the idea that your sculpture looked almost casually placed, as if it had just 'arrived'. Of course in public sculpture you can still retain that quality but you do have to secure it, as in the Warwick piece. I was going to ask you about the Toronto piece which rather wittily uses a plinth.*

RD I actually always thought of it as a bench rather than anything else. The site in Toronto is a square in front of a new development. The new buildings occupy two sides of the square, and the other two sides of the square are bounded by streets, one of which runs alongside the Toronto Lake front. The street that runs north from the site is an old logging road and goes all the way from Toronto to Winnipeg, so the geographical position of the plaza is quite specific.

In some ways it's a classic modernist situation: a square into which a man on a horse or whatever was to be placed. I always thought that within that situation, apart from the object, there should be another way of being in the square other than walking through it. I thought that there should be some place to sit down. I did toy with some other configurations of bench until it occurred to me that it could be made into a foot for the sculpture which also, in some senses, echoed the kinds of thoughts I'd had about the site anyway, in the way that the sculpture steps off the plinth the way the road steps off the water. And it seemed to enable you to sit down and to use the plaza as a place to be without having to look at the work.

PB *Going back to what you were saying earlier about your preference for urban sites, it is interesting that in the Warwick project you chose a site that was already there and in fact specifically you said that virtually nothing had to be altered beyond the removal of two concrete flower holders and, of course, some lights were sunk into the site. So, would you balk at the idea of a purpose-built site for a Richard Deacon sculpture?*

RD Well, the Toronto situation is a purpose-built site – brand new. When I first visited the site, there was nothing there. It was a competition and the intention was that the successful artist would collaborate with the architectural partnership in the final design decisions about the plaza and the artist was given some clout to make it possible for that to happen. I must admit that those are the situations that I find the most complex and the most difficult to deal with. I've been far more comfortable with the situation in Warwick or Gateshead or Plymouth, or even in Villeneuve d'Ascq, where there was an existing situation with which I was interfering or with which I was interacting. And I suppose that if I really think about why that might be, it has to do with the ability to retain an independence in the sculpture rather than it being a part of a whole.

PB *It looks more 'other' in that it's an interloper in an existing space.*

RD There are no rules in these things obviously, but that very specific relationship of object to building can very easily lead to the one becoming a sign for the other and that isn't a relationship that I find particularly interesting. I'm not happy about making sculpture that acts like a logo for the site or for the building. I am interested in making sculpture that interferes with the space, not in any particularly aggressive way, and it may very well be that I'm interested in engaging with the spectator and the spectator's perception of the space, but I suppose I'm not interested in making a play park and I'm not interested in making a subservient sculpture, but neither am I interested in making a dominant or an aggressive thing. To take a simple example, I've got no objection to people sitting on the work but I don't want the work to become a bench, much as I like and admire Scott Burton's work.

I would like the sculpture to behave on site in ways not dissimilar from the ways in which I think Brecht thought of using the theatre. The work makes certain demands on the spectator as well as allowing itself to be appropriated in certain ways by the spectator so that there is a relationship between the spectator and the work which isn't only one way. That would be an interesting way to define publicness: as being the capacity for reciprocation rather than as a piece of social engineering. The capacity for reciprocation seems for me to be at the heart of what I think of as 'public'.

PB *What did you mean by 'Art for Other People' and how is it different from 'public' as you've just defined it?*

RD The two aren't exclusive. I always thought of the works in the 'Art for Other People' series as 'letters' and their scale was to do with a sort of domestic utterance, but they were never addressed at specific individuals so in that sense they were addressed publicly. Ostensibly it implies a one-way communication as in 'I write, you read', but in fact before I begin to write I have to know that you can read. There is in fact a reciprocation built into that. It's a thought that has struck me several times, that, in some senses, a lot of the work that I make in the studio is as much made for my own interest and understanding, and as a way of engaging with the world, and that in that sense it's for me, whereas the intention behind the works in the 'Art for Other People' series was always – and with foreknowledge – that they were externally directed. That's were the distinction arises.

The external directedness of the 'Art for Other People' series did marry up quite well with the external directedness of the large-scale work. I also did note that there were much stronger formal connections between the two than there are between the larger sized, but still studio-based, work.

That might have to do with model-making or it might have to do with the notion of objecthood that is employed. The 'Art for Other People' series is much more portable, much more transient in some ways, but their identity remains constant in a variety of situations. One of the sensations that I've wanted to have in the larger-scale works is the sense of their being distinct, in the sense of an object being distinct, and to make use of both the double sense of objecthood and a borrowed interiority as being two of the components that the work has. They're not intended to be lumps, but the notion of the complete thing is an important element that needs to stay in the work, in order to act as a foil or an opposition to other senses: it's one of the core experiences for the way in which you deal with the identity of the work, and that would probably be the link. In relationship to the other work, I've tended to use words like 'envelope' and 'skin' as being the core parameter that the work has, but that doesn't really work in the 'Art for Other People' series because the size of the work mitigates against it. It's something to do with the object being the same scale as yourself, the sense of reading it as a body.

PB *I thought it was very interesting that you introduced, if you like, that third category, because of something that Peter Schjeldahl said on the question of scale which I thought was very good: 'Small, medium and large, they are not for him just different conditions for the same thing but distinct genres corresponding to different orders of rhetorical engagement.'*

RD I thought Peter said that very well.

PB *The next question is obvious; there are 29 works in all in the 'Art for Other People' series, 25 of them were done between 1982 and 1987, but there have been only four more since. Is this merely because you have been occupied in making public sculpture?*

RD I think there's a number of hours in a day, and areas of activity that didn't exist before have arisen. It's also true that – once the parameters of what you're doing become too clearly established – I think it becomes slightly more difficult to make something. The 'Art for Other People' works are made kind of idly.

PB *A species of three-dimensional doodle?*

RD Yes. I think idleness is a much more profitable source of ideas, and source of things that are of interest, than being prodded by necessity. There is a suspicion that the small works are much more marketable than the big works; it may be to do with a certain amount of self-censorship. In fact all these factors seem to be components, one: just time; two: looking for occasions just to be idle and three: not wanting to make items on a market-oriented basis. I mean, there's nothing wrong with working for the market, I don't want to give the impression that I've got any antagonism to it. That doesn't seem to be why I make sculpture. There is a certain amount of orneriness: if people continually ask me why don't you make more small sculpture, then I think I'll tend to make big sculpture. If people continually ask me why don't I make big sculpture then I'll probably make lots of small sculptures.

PB *Finally, do you feel that you are being groomed to be Sir Richard Deacon?*

RD The question is 'Do I feel part of the establishment?' And the answer is that I don't particularly feel part of the establishment and I'm not particularly interested in becoming a part of the establishment. I am a trustee of the Tate and I agreed to become a trustee because I have a great admiration for Nick Serota and what he's done there. That's a much more establishment role than I would have envisaged for myself. I have no other ambitions to become a larger establishment figure. I think you're quite right to point out that broadening critical recognition particularly in relationship to large-scale work in public places has often had a very damaging effect on artists' production. I feel that about Henry Moore and I feel that, to some extent, about Anthony Caro. As a counter-example, I would put an artist like Richard Serra, the critical edge of whose work doesn't seem to be blunted by that kind of public exposure.

Issue 160, October 1992

Richard Serra

interviewed by Patricia Bickers

Weight and Measure

PATRICIA BICKERS *Watching* Weight and Measure *being installed at the Tate Gallery yesterday it looked less like an installation than an assault on the gallery, on the status quo.*

RICHARD SERRA I think that's because you were watching the tonnage being moved in. The only way that you can move that kind of tonnage over a floor which doesn't have a substantial weight load is to span the beams underneath. To span the beams and to make sure that everything's done properly and cautiously, you have to bring in heavy I-beams which act as rails to guide the blocks. I was talking to the engineers yesterday. To make sure that everything is done properly, they've overloaded the space with safety precautions and I think they've used more hardware than they need. It's okay with me, but I think that accounts for the fact that when you go to watch the installation, you may think there's an assault being made on the Tate. After the big steel I-beam rails come out and the piece is set, I don't think the installation process is of concern nor do I think it's of any consequence.

To tell you the truth the nature of installations for me differ with each job or with each site. This isn't the first time that I've had to prop underneath. I did it in Berlin for the *Berlin Block* in 1978. I did it in Bordeaux for a piece there called *Threats of Hell*, 1990. I did it in Eindhoven for a large show. I've done it at the Stedelijk for *Sight Point* in 1971–75, an outside piece, where we hit water and had to drop pylons through the ground. Those are just things that you come up against when you are testing the capacity of a building or a site.

PB *It's part of the mythology that made one think that the installation of the work resembled an assault?*

RS One of the things that I run up against, and it detracts from the consequence of the work, is the focus placed on the how which becomes an excuse to concentrate on the process of building rather than the consequence of the piece as it exists.

PB *What struck me at first was how small the pieces appeared to be until you came up close to them, then they seemed incredibly dense.*

RS They're forged. Forging is the most compressed, compacted way, so to speak, of making a patty-cake. More molecules are pressed into the same space than in casting. If you cast you can often see – whether it's concrete or it's iron – that there are holes where the material breathes due to evaporation. In forged works, you can actually feel the compression and you can see from the markings, particularly in these pieces, that they've cooled from the inside out which gives them the colouration that makes them almost look flamed. They've still got the afterglow of being in the oven. Of the forged pieces I've made in my life, these are the best, but we took particular care and had them in and out of the ovens for about three months, we really hammered them as tight as we could get them. As they were cooling down we flamed them, which means we took all the mill-scale off, so they have the look of meteorites as if pulled out of the earth or out of a volcano. In a sense – this wasn't the intention – they look very old. They already have a kind of, not a patina, but a look of something very old.

PB Fulcrum, *the piece you made for the Broadgate site in 1987, still partially retains the mill-scale 'skin'.*

RS We could have sandblasted that off to begin with but what happens if you do that to works in steel is that after the first rain, or the first four or five rains, they blush very orange. I would just as soon have the mill-scale peel off over six or seven or eight years, then the steel will turn dark amber. With the pieces in the Tate, because they're indoor, we've actually accelerated that process by flaming them continuously. If you flame something that is forged as it cools down, you have a chance of retaining the colouration of the surface, whereas if you sandblast it, it turns grey and it denies the weight, it looks more like aluminium.

PB *Looking again at* Weight and Measure, *I was reminded of* Unequal Elevations, *a piece of 1975 in Count Panza di Biumo's collection, where there's a similar measurement differential between the two rectangular elements. Is there any connection between the two works?*

RS The two elements in *Unequal Elevations* were not forged, they were cut blocks, but I would say that it was probably the germ for this work. It is probably the prime mover in all these pieces but to tell you the truth I'd forgotten about it, it just becomes part of your vocabulary.

PB *You said recently, of Barnett Newman's* Zim Zum, *1969, in the Tate, that it creates 'a one-directional path with a beginning and an end like a corridor' and that the zig-zag walls neither 'hold a volume nor do they define a mass. Space just floats through'. Yet in a way you have created if not a corridor, a sight-line, one that deliberately excludes the octagon.*

RS I think that there's a couple of things about this piece as it relates to Newman, and as it relates to my early work, that we can talk about. I didn't create the sight-line, the architecture creates the sight-line. Basically what I'm trying to do is to not only use the central axis, but to refocus it. My problem with the Newman is that it functions more like architecture in that it doesn't hold the volume of the space between the vertical elements. I've made pieces you walk through and it's always been my concern to try to make the interior of those spaces different in kind and substance and feeling and emotion than you would anticipate. The thing about the Newman piece is that it attempts to do that architecturally. I'm more interested to take a volume and make it resound as content. Now I think in any work of art, whether one's dealing with volume, line, plane, mass, space, colour or balance, it's how one chooses to focus on either one of these aspects that gives the work a particular resonance and differentiates it from other people's work. Not that I don't think that Newman's a great sculptor, it just wasn't his concern. And it may be that his concerns were more visual, less to do with how you feel in the space than how you perceive space.

PB *You've taken control of the space.*

RS Hopefully. I think that in terms of the hierarchies of those spaces, the octagon is the dominant space and it is the space that acts as a pivot or a fulcrum – and it is the most grandiose. At one point we actually had three elements: we had one placed in the octagon and it wasn't until we removed it that the piece came together and was less compositional. I can understand why one would put a work there – a Rodin or a David Smith – it's obvious to me that that is the place that collects people, but you might as well collect the people there and have them see the space rather than collect the work there. But I have to tell you it took me over a year to come to that conclusion.

PB *When I came to the Serpentine to watch the drawings being made, I was struck by the similarity of the dimensions of the* Orozco *and* Siqueiros *drawings in the East and West Galleries, and those of* Weight and Measure. *At first I thought it was deliberate but your canvas drawing installations are usually site-specific.*

RS One of the things that did come up in dealing with these rooms is that even though they are symmetrical in plan, the elevations of the East and West Galleries are not equal – the wall in the East Gallery is 120 inches high and the one in the West Gallery is one 137 inches high. If you divide these end walls in half, one drawing is 60 inches high and the other one is 68½ inches high. I conceived one drawing in two parts for two rooms. The blocks at the Tate are 68 inches and 60 inches high. That's just a coincidence of dealing with the sites in relation to their measure. I did the piece for the Tate for the perception of the viewer over the field, whereas I did this particular drawing in relation to the fixed measure of the walls. We decided to deal with the difference in elevation as a device to create an echo between the drawings. As you enter the room it seems that the far wall is much more telescoped and further away from you. It's also because of the light. In the West Gallery, because the piece is only eight inches higher and also because the wall goes to the ceiling, it seems to pull the wall towards you.

PB *You have said that you were not interested in deconstructing the site in a postmodern, deconstructionist sense, but would work with the 'givens'. Perhaps it's completely fortuitous but when I came yesterday I noticed that the star-shaped rosette in the centre of the ceiling of the North Gallery recalls Islamic decoration, then I discovered that the title of the work is* Two for Rushdie. *Is that just an accidental given?*

RS It's something you noticed that I didn't. But, if other people do, I'll take it.

PB *You have also stated that a drawing installation only works when it alters one's perception of the space. Looking at the titles,* Serpentine Corner *is a contradiction in terms as well as a contradiction in form, and in* Two for Rushdie, *the drawings are asymmetrical in a perfectly symmetrical square space.*

RS It's about four inches off. Perceptually it's a square.

PB Orozco *and* Siqueiros *seem to be slightly different. They are a kind of matching pair.*

RS They're different in elevation, they're different in mass, I think you sense that as being different and I think that if you pay particular attention to the rooms you see that one is light and almost more absolute in a sense and that the other one is more volumetric and upright. I think the drawings expose a small but substantial difference in the rooms.

PB *It struck me that some of the problems presented by the North Gallery were similar to those presented by the octagon of the Duveen Galleries in the Tate, although that's a somewhat more fearsome problem.*

RS That's true. I think it's very difficult to get away from the logic of the container in both instances. The thing about the square room is that it's a very difficult room to deal with in that almost anything you do in the room reinforces the formalness of its disposition, so if you go against the formalness it looks like you're trying to compose. If you go with the formalness of the square and the circle, it looks like you're augmenting a kind of geometry whereby your introduction looks like decor. What we did the first day was just physically move canvas around all day. We had them high and low, we had them in two corners, we had them in left and right corners, we kept doing that until we came to the conclusion that there were two possible installations that were of consequence that made you move around the room and made you organise the room perceptually, and that detracted from the overbearing formalness of the room. We finally arrived at the one in diagonally opposite corners, but they're not mirror reflections of each other. Their placement makes you turn right and turn left and then circle the whole space and watch the movement of the wall and to some degree it diminishes the square in the circle or, at least, the emphasis is on how you move in relation to the corners and how you perceive in relation to the walls, rather than walking to the middle and seeing the co-ordinates of the room.

PB *You said in your 'Notes on Drawing' that a visit in your twenties to Mexico where you saw the work of the Mexican muralists, especially Orozco in Guadalajara and Mexico City, taught you that the context was the issue not the stretcher. You have two works here titled* Orozco *and* Siqueiros, *are the titles intended to reiterate that point for your first drawing installation in Britain?*

RS No, I just think that Orozco and Siqueiros were very informative to me at a young age and they're like ghost figures for me. Everybody has their historical hangovers and maybe you ought to look at them all sceptically, I don't know. They're people that I admire and I think that if you pay some recognition to them with a title, it may make other people look into their work, particularly with the advent of so many wall drawings, a lot of which I think of as applied art or bad decoration. If you look back to Orozco and Siqueiros, they actually distort the walls. To me they seem much more interesting than an extended Vasarely on the wall.

PB *Do you also respect their political engagement? Is that something you would relate to?*

RS Oh certainly, absolutely. Their whole need to develop their language came, I think, from a need to speak out. If you think about those figures within that context, not only isolated from Europe but also having to confront enormous political repression, it's very difficult to imagine they were able to accomplish so much, particularly Orozco's early works which are absolutely, incredibly beautiful. You can imagine: you're 18 years old and you're painting a still-life and looking at Cézanne, you hitchhike to Guadalajara, walk into that Collegio at the hospital and you see those works – and I hadn't really seen Pollock up to that point – they made an enormous impression on me.

PB *What led to your decision to title the works in the North Gallery,* Two for Rushdie*?*

RS I was thinking of the divisiveness that's going on within my own country between the Republican party and the Democratic party, as expressed by Patrick Buchanan. Buchanan has actually come out and said that there is a cultural revolution going on equal to Reagan's economic revolution. It's tearing the country apart. And I was thinking not only of the way that they targeted the GSA and destroyed my work *Tilted Arc* but also of the way they targeted the NEA and attacked Robert Mapplethorpe and Andres Serrano. That kind of censorship isn't just intolerance, it actually leads to repression of the kind that ended up with Salman Rushdie's life being threatened. It's not that artists' lives are being threatened yet in the US but the political right started to attack artists, women and gays, and civil rights have been diminished. If artists want to pursue their work with some modicum of freedom, they ought to stand up and say 'enough'. I don't do that particularly through my work. I make a division between my work and my language. I think that, if you have a voice and you are concerned about the fact that your freedoms and your rights are being suppressed and that censorship is actually forcing a lot of artists to reiterate the ideology of the status quo, one ought to speak out. In America there's enormous solidarity, say, within Hollywood, and within the writing community, but not within the art world. Galleries tend to line artists up like competing horses, and artists haven't been able to come together in the same way writers and filmmakers have. One of the things I find most encouraging about the art world is that women have been in the forefront. Women have been the strongest group politically, other than gays. They are very organised and have led the struggle. Maybe that's because they've been continually repressed. That may not be true in this country, I really don't know.

PB *You said once that your sculptures are not just to be looked at, that they are behavioural spaces. How would you like people to behave?*

RS Anyway they want. It's okay with me. I don't mind what people think, as long as the aggression that they have isn't misdirected and brought to me personally and that the work isn't used as a scapegoat for other agendas. It often happens that work is used as a scapegoat for a political agenda that someone brings to it. I think that that is a disservice to all of art. I think that's what's happened to Rushdie.

PB *What would you say to people who might use your own words about the Duveen gallery about you and say 'overblown, authoritarian and a bit heavy-handed'?*

RS It's partially correct!

Issue 161, November 1992

David Tremlett

interviewed by Cathy Courtney

Flat sculpture

CATHY COURTNEY *When you draw on the walls or ceiling of a room or gallery are the shapes related only to that space or do they have a reference to certain journeys you've made in the past?*

DAVID TREMLETT The drawings from the last ten years have always had a connection to the physical size of a room and with expressing a sense of proportion in it. I have been making what I consider a structural support or form which has clearly an architectural aspect to it in terms of its shape. I have always based my drawing on a type of geometry. By dividing up the wall surfaces in a particular way, the structure and sense of construction changes. I want to draw shape or form in a way which also has a structure, a sense of sculpture, a form with a certain force.

CC *Do you consider yourself a sculptor?*

DT There has been a thread throughout all the work which is sculpture. It's been quite often the thesis of other people that I consider everything that I've made as a form of building or of sculpture. I never painted. I can't remember when I last used a paintbrush. Everything that I make is always about building it up or pushing it out or carving it away. I studied sculpture and therefore thought in a sculptural way. The difference in thinking between painters and sculptors is often a question of the physicality of things. You can sense sculptural thought and you can sense painterly thought. I would say there is a very marked difference between the two. When I make my wall drawings, as in most of the things I do, I always have this sense of 'How do you build it?' I like the contradiction of the work being always very flat. I do it directly to the wall and I'm working with a material, pastel, in a way which is very close to the whole concept of building. Pastel is a fine dust which is modelled by hand and massaged onto the walls. There is a sense of making sculpture every time one is produced. I have no concern if it is specifically three-dimensional or in the round. My concern is that the real structure that I make is solid, it's rigid, that the forms are indicative of this and the way they are made is a very solid, rigid way of production. Yet the work consists of a fragile material which can blow away if not fixed. These contradictions are the magic for me in the process. It's full of ambiguity, the notion of creating a fragile pastel drawing which will support the rest of the room. It's a fiction of real strength and it's also a great reality. It is a flat sculpture, you couldn't get much flatter.

CC *What about your use of borders?*

DT There has always been a white border – the wall in the buildings and the paper in the books – around everything. This for me is the simplest way of creating something flat. The idea of flatness is one of being as pure and as honest as I can to the surface being drawn on. There are never two colours playing against each other, they never touch, one colour never appears to come in front of the other or to recede. There is the sense of two forms having been drawn flatly against a white surface.

CC *Is there somebody whose work is at all comparable to yours who works in a painterly way?*

DT I suppose the form that I use is linked to that which has existed for the last century starting with Constructivism, where a simple geometrical form has emerged and people use it in terms of 'art'. But it's not just our century. I can go back to the Renaissance and see a similar way, for example, of how a fresco is made. The person that comes to my mind is Bramante, an architect who also made extraordinary interiors in churches. He used the quite simple geometric form as an addition to the construction of a church. He would include the circle or a series of lines to fit in with windows or beams or parts of the architecture or to change the colour of a part of the architecture. It is this thinking that I look to. It's the desire of an artist to work within architecture or within a space. Sometimes I have to leave a room almost untouched, with just one or two small structural elements specifically placed. It's always been of importance to be particular about where I work and how to change the space. I've rarely worked on the outside of a building, it's always been inside. There have been rooms I've looked at and known that they would produce more problems than solutions. The rooms need a certain quality, sometimes they are too fussy, too many windows or doors, sometimes they are too magnificent, like churches filled with too many columns. The room has to be simple in the sense that it's possible to add a certain difference in colour and structure to give it another strength. A sensibility about weight and form inside walls, about hidden structure, concepts about why aspects might support others, these are concerns of mine.

CC *Have you ever felt that you've added too much and in some way destroyed something in the room?*

DT I wouldn't dream of touching a wall unless I knew exactly what was going to be done. I consider the project, sometimes without touching a piece of paper, until I have a very clear idea. It's like a carving. You cut away and you have to be very careful about your mistakes because otherwise you can knock off your sculpture's nose. Pastel is a precise material and I cannot afford to make a mistake. It's not possible to draw a pencil line on a fresh wall and rub it out and then put pastel on it because the rubbed line will always come through.

CC *When you travel and draw in ruined, isolated buildings which you happen to come across, do you approach the work differently?*

DT It's approached the same way. For example, I made some drawings on abandoned buildings in Tanzania and my desire, without intruding too much, was to give the building a certain new structure to support the window aperture or whatever part I was using. It's a gesture almost of 'don't fall down any more, let me give you a little more life and hold you up'. It has, maybe, a romantic sound but really it's a love of the place and an addition to it. I add, in a discreet way, something which I hope helps the place. I don't suppose anyone will ever see it, but that's of less concern. My concern is for the building.

CC *Your work has changed slowly over the years?*

DT The earlier work was more linear. For me, a changing pattern is inevitable, I enjoy it, it's the drive that my experience of the world has probably given to me over the years. You push yourself through certain periods and you come out with a certain difference. I've always admired artists who had no fear of change. The good artist for me is always the one who asks questions and moves in a discreet way. I still feel a desire to move. Maybe the taking out of sections from the forms I use is to do with the idea of 'incompletion'. I consider everything

I do to be an incomplete part of something else. It drives me on to something new every time. I'm restless and tend to travel, my motivation is to go and look somewhere else and that's the essence of my way of seeing things. I like to lead the life of my work and I've always loved the artists who really do live their work.

Issue 161, November 1992

Dan Graham

interviewed by Mark Thomson

One-way mirrors

MARK THOMSON *At first glance it seems quite a long way from the text pieces of the sixties to your current work, the glass pavilions. Would you describe it as a process of evolution or one of changing focus?*

DAN GRAHAM Well, I think that the similarity begins with one of the first pieces I did, *Homes for America*, 1966–67, which is basically about the relation of art to an urbanological or suburban scheme. I was always situating things in terms of built vernacular architecture, playgrounds, street plans, model houses and the model pavilions are proposals for things that would be sited in specific suburban and urban contexts. The use of one-way mirror in the pavilions evolved from my original use of glass and mirrors in temporary interior subdivisions of spaces. That work involved the notion of more than one audience, the audience's relationship to itself and another audience, and the spectator in relation to him or herself and his or her own viewing process.

In the early printed-matter pieces, the context was the magazine system with reference to the reader as a kind of spectator, so I'm going from reader as spectator to public audience as spectator. And the one-way mirror comes from its use as a very standard material in high-rise office buildings during the seventies and eighties, just as the use of magazines was the idea of using a medium that was somewhere between art and a public communications area. The models began simply as propaganda to get pieces done, and the first show of models, at the Oxford Museum of Modern Art in 1981, had two groups of works: works that proposed modifications to existing vernacular architecture and work that was half-way between sculpture and the pavilion form, a form which you find in the garden historically from the Renaissance garden through the Enlightenment garden through forms such as bus shelters, telephone booths and also temporary exhibition pavilions such as the Barcelona Pavilion by Mies van der Rohe. So it's really the exhibition pavilion taken outdoors or the kind of urban pavilions that are derived from traditional garden pavilions.

MT *How interested are you in the paradoxical properties of glass, the fact that it transcends itself – it's there in front of you, cool to the touch, yet its whole purpose is to pretend not to be there.*

DG I think that glass is invisible but that also, depending on the lighting, it can be partly visible, and one-way mirror-glass extends that normal property of glass, with its reflectivity changing depending on whether the light is on one side or the other. Glass is both an insulator and it joins you to the outdoor world in a somewhat voyeuristic kind of way. The first time I used this was in an interior pavilion in the Venice Biennale in 1976, where in effect, I took an existing rectangular shape, divided it in half with acoustically insulating glass and had two entrances, so you'd have two audiences. On one side, opposing the glass divider, was a mirror – on the other side, opposing the glass for the other audience, was a normal white wall. So both audiences were able to see a view of themselves on the mirror, viewing the other audience viewing them or, say, the people on the side that had the large mirror could go in very close to the mirror and simply look at themselves looking, or stand further back and see a wider perspective, or they could turn, look in the direction of the acoustically insulating glass and not see an image of themselves in the other direction because they are looking at a blank wall. Although it appeared to be a symmetrical situation for both audiences, in fact it wasn't, because the audience in the room with the mirror has a very different situation of spectatorship to the audience in the other room. In effect, this was the framework for all the one-way mirror outdoor pavilions that came later, except I realised that the flaw of that particular piece was that it was very much the old white cube art gallery architecture idea, and I wondered what would happen if you had an open window on the side where there was the white wall. And that amounted to the first outdoor quasi-architecture, quasi-sculpture piece that I did, *Clinic*, 1977, where I made the white wall the entrance – a transparent glass entrance – to a clinic space.

MT *A clinic for what?*

DG A medical clinic. The first room was the waiting room. The other room with the mirror, which in this case was simultaneously reflecting a view of both audiences and also the sky in the background – the sky becoming a moving, changing wallpaper – would be a consultation room. Downstairs, underneath the structure, would be the medical rooms. After that came the *Alteration To A Suburban House*, 1978, and, at the same time, when I first started using one-way mirror, there were many plans for these sculpture pavilion projects, the first of which was *Two Adjacent Pavilions*, done for Documenta 7 in 1981.

MT *Do you see the pavilion as having a recreational purpose, or is there a psychological approach? These things sound a bit like isolation chambers where you go and look at yourself.*

DG Both. The first use of one-way mirror was actually for surveillance – the way it was used in psychological laboratories was that students could see through the invisible side and observe the doctors or psychologists with their patients on the other side, and the people on the other side would only see a mirror view of themselves. In the contemporary one-way mirror office building you have something very similar: on the outside the building reflective of the sky and the environment becomes equated to the natural environment, and I thought in a way this was an alibi for corporations during the ecologically conscious early seventies through the eighties to equate, in a way, their buildings to the outside environment. What I do in my one-way mirror structures is, I don't make it strictly a one-way situation. Because I have sunlight coming from both sides and because the sky is in flux during the day and during the twilight period, the relationship between people in the environment outside and people in the environment inside is in continuous flux. So the views from the interior and the exterior are both intersubjective in relation to people's gazes from either side, and equally equated to and alienated from the environment at the same time.

MT *The basic principle of these glass buildings, on a social plane at least, seems to be to make the process of capital transfer visible and to be 'open' about the process of work.*

DG This is the system of International Style post-Bauhaus architecture up until the early seventies, in which the productive qualities of the interior environment were made accessible to people on the street. In the business office building, the idea was that people were working and the overt production capabilities of the company inside would be available and visible to people on the outside. Of course, in fact, we would see things only on the ground floor or maybe first and second storeys, where very functional, lower echelon type things were being done, such as the very obvious simple banking tasks. But the people who served at the head of the corporation would actually be at the top and would have an unimpeded view, looking down over everybody else, monitoring the city. So these buildings are very contradictory.

MT *Is your work a kind of parody of that form of architecture? Do you see it in terms of a parody?*

DG I see it as emblematic of the city and the way a lot of the architecture in the city works. In a way the city has become something like a cinematic screen, where you are seeing a mirror view which shows the image of the consumer placed on top of commodities or on top of productive processes, and the whole skin of the city is partly mirror, partly transparent. This began with my work, *Public Space/Two Audiences*, in the Venice Biennale of 1976, for 'Ambiente', a special theme show curated by Germano Celant. My object was to have the outside part of the piece be similar to a showcase type situation, but it would be displaying the spectators, their gazes at themselves, their gazes at other spectators gazing at them, in place of the art object that you would normally see displayed in the Venice Biennale.

So in a way my work is displaying the system of display and also the system of spectatorship inside the display system. There's also, deriving from Laugier's *Primitive Hut* from the beginning of the Enlightenment, a history of architecture which is emblematic of the city or a utopian idea of architecture, being placed as a temporary pavilion or a rustic pavilion, or in Laugier's theorisation as elemental primitive hut in the countryside, in a garden, in relationship to the architecture of the city, where it became a utopian alternative to the city and emblematic of a liberated idea of what the city could be. So my work, when it's in a park or exhibition outdoor setting, relates emblematically in an analogous way to the architecture of the existing power structure in the city. I wouldn't call it a parody of it. I would say that there is a critical dialectical reference to whatever that system is. That system is both an optical system, a power system and also a system of larger urbanism.

MT *For example the* Triangular Insert *piece, 1988, which has a certain apparent critical function.*

DG This was the piece that was done for 'New Urban Landscape', the exhibition inaugurating the World Trade Center – the plaza in front of it became Battery Park City. The piece was situated outside the main new office building by the architect Cesar Pelli, who also did the Canary Wharf buildings, which are based on the same system. I found a niche on the outside of the building, but accessible from the plaza area, where there were many new outdoor collaborations between artists and architects and landscape architects, which could easily be a shelter for homeless people at night and could also be a way that people could look inside through the glass into the lobby but not be seen – because of the function of one-way mirror the people on the inside wouldn't see them. It was also making a comment on that particular type of architecture by altering it or making a slight addition to it, but it turned out to be a temporary situation.

MT *The other day I was looking at the arts sections of Clinton's and Bush's election manifestos. Bush's was three times as long as Clinton's, all sorts of stuff about unAmerican values and so on. Do you think that you are representing unAmerican values?*

DG In an American context, specifically in the piece on the rooftop of the DIA Center, I'm trying to make a relationship with the type of temporary urban artworks that were done in the early to mid seventies and the corporate or foundation-sponsored forms of the eighties. During the eighties the museum and garden situation became attached to an idea of 'public space' which was built and controlled by corporate funding and corporate urban architecture as 'public amenities'. The seventies was a very interesting period in New York, when the city was in a state of depression and ruin, where punk rock began, where alternative spaces were formed from derelict buildings either by artists or by people using leftover derelict buildings such as the Clocktower or schools such as PS1, creating an alternative art culture and also a rock and political and social culture.

That was all changed during the Reagan period. At the same time art became corporatised, many branches of the Whitney became housed in the lobbies of corporate office buildings, you had museums such as the IBM Museum attached to the IBM atrium. The atrium was like a botanical garden, with public amenities – a coffee bar, performing bandshell etc – and then the museum below exhibited essentially art on either the theme of America or related to science and information technology.

A few foundations such as the DIA Center, which had an enormous amount of money behind them, started doing spaces that were essentially designed to show the one great work of art by the genius artist. What I was trying to do was to go outside the interior of the DIA building onto the roof and to do an outdoor park that could easily be used as a performance space, and also contained a videotheque space next to it that would provide shelter during inclement weather conditions, where not only my own videotapes are shown, but also a video archive spanning the late seventies to the early eighties would be available in a space that also had some of the features of the IBM atrium, because it has a coffee bar, a resting lounge etc. In a way I wanted to bridge the gap, particularly on this West Side of New York, from the mid-seventies spaces like the Kitchen and the landfill before Battery Park City was built where a series of shows called 'Art on the Beach' took place, through the late seventies and eighties, which saw the corporatisation of these kinds of art spaces, into the nineties. I think people want to know the history that was eradicated from the recent past.

MT *The DIA piece,* Rooftop Urban Park Project, *1991, has a slightly recreational overtone because of the way it's raised a metre or so off the ground: the flooring is boardwalk material, like Coney Island.*

DG That was done for two reasons: the first reason was that existing on the roof were the tops of skylights that were lighting the exhibition space below, a large air conditioning complex, and many things that were in the way of an unobstructed optical situation. Also there was a need to put railings for safety around the perimeter of the space, and around the skylights so people wouldn't fall into them, so by raising a platform in the centre of the space it meant that you were floating along the edge of the horizon line, that you had a very good view of the Hudson River and the city.

The boardwalk planking was to evoke the idea that it is along the seaside and is partly recreational, in some way relating to Coney Island. The main thing about Coney Island is that it was the first time electric light could be brought outdoors to make a space usable at night, very much equivalent to what was happening inside the city, where electric lighting and electricity made possible the cinema. So it was like a cinematic amusement park, built on the water. There's a very good book about this by the architect Rem Koolhaas called *Delirious New York*, which has been a big influence on me.

I have to admit that the DIA Center was interested in my project developing the roof because their main holding now is the real estate that they've invested in. From my point of view it also meant that I could push the DIA Center away from the idea of the isolated genius artist doing a genius artwork to a more collaborative, open-ended situation, and also connect to a trend that is widespread in the US and Europe for artists to develop park and urban situations, either collaboratively or on their own.

MT *So you are working more with structures with a concentrated spatial sociology, for example the* Skateboard Pavilion.

DG The *Skateboard Pavilion* and *Two-way Mirror and Hedge Labyrinth*, exhibited at the Serpentine recently, were proposals I made for a very large outdoor World Garden Fair that is held every ten years in a different city in Germany, where they redevelop the central park area of the German city by relandscaping it. This particular exhibition is going to be in Stuttgart next year and they wanted artists to design stopping points which would function as resting points, pavilions or modifications to the landscape.

In a way the *Skateboard Pavilion* is based on the fact that many skateboarders have designed their own skateboard rinks. There's a magazine, *Thrasher*, devoted to these designs. There's a canopy above the skateboard rink/bowl which is a four-sided pyramid of one-way mirror, truncated at the top, somewhat in the style of the neoclassical, neo-Ledoux/Boullée imagery that Cesar Pelli was using for the World Trade Center and also for Canary Wharf. As it's one-way mirror, when the skateboarder comes up to the rim at the top of the bowl they're in a position to look up at themselves and they see a kaleidoscopic image of themselves and maybe other skateboarders, and on the other side the sky. Again you have a kind of kaleidoscopic, amusement park, carousel-type look, and the cutaway area is allowing a diamond-shaped pattern of light to fall on this one-way mirror glass and sets up another myriad of reflection and re-reflection. It was definitively rejected – I started with the idea that in parks and playgrounds you always had things for small children, old people, or for family groups, but the teenager isn't served. And I also noticed that a lot of the cement megastructures of buildings and of art galleries and museums from the early seventies, such as the Hayward Gallery in London, have been colonised by skateboarders.

MT *Why was it rejected?*

DG Well, I think because it was something for teenagers. Teenagers always mean trouble in an outdoor situation. The *Two-way Mirror and Hedge Labyrinth* was rejected at a very late moment. I wanted to combine the idea of the Baroque hedge maze with modern materials such as one-way mirror.

MT *Do you view the educational function of the work as an optical education, a psychological education, even a religious education?*

DG There's a history that goes back to the Renaissance: the first gardens were actually based on archaeological excavations of Roman statues and ruins, and other statues, that were related to the ones that were unearthed in that particular area, were found and arranged in displays. Botanical gardens were often quasi-educational: the history of the greenhouse/conservatory, which replaced the meditative outdoor picturesque English and French gardens, was slotted into a public education format. The Parc de La Villette on the outside edge of Paris was based around the Science and Technology Museum and the idea of making available to people in that area, which has always been working class, a complex that would be educational, recreational and also an amusement park, or the emulation of EuroDisney. In the past, parks have been historical – many of the parks I have been interested in deal with the dialectic between the city and the allegorical or utopian garden. The question of the garden in relation to the city and as it relates to the museum begins in the Renaissance and the early Enlightenment. This question becomes part of the aspect of what park design and outdoor art should be about. It should somehow merge present with past history of landscape architecture and pavilion design and existing buildings, it should be recreational and educational at the same time. Specifically what's happening is that the museum, which in the Renaissance period and then in the picturesque landscape English garden period located philosophical, educational and scientific and also political propagandistic ideas outdoors in sometimes public, urban plazas and sometimes private, meditative situations, has now become part of a much more public park design programme.

MT *How do you approach the displacement of having a completed public space project in a gallery, in a showroom situation alongside models, prototypes and r&d work?*

DG In the Lisson Gallery exhibition there were large showcase windows where the outdoor environment, which included the playground area for a school and also a system of landscape hedges, was available, so you had an idea of the urban context for which the models were representing ideas or solutions by looking out the window. Also, most of the models involved one-way mirror reflective glass, so that the outdoor environment was actually reflected onto the glass of the models, and I think that provided a certain kind of context – the show was designed with that idea in mind.

The main contextualisation of the Marian Goodman show is the building across the street, which is a typical one-way mirror office building of the early eighties. If today was a sunny day you'd have reflections from that reflected onto the work in front and vice versa. In fact we are in the area, 57th Street, where a lot of these atrium buildings of the eighties, that definitely had an influence on the development of the new urban corporate park, are located. So although the physical situation of the gallery at this time of year is not ideal, you really should visualise the context of this area of the city and other things that I have done in adjacent areas of the city. The virtue of the Serpentine piece was that it was built in a very large garden situation that was accessible by pedestrians and people in automobiles, and the changing conditions of both the park and the city were reflected in the piece, and changed the way one read and experienced the piece. It also involved hedges, and the park itself uses hedges as boundaries, so it fitted into that kind of situation. It also had the virtue of being both urbanological and park/garden architecture at the same time. It was very costly to put up, and if it's ever relocated, there must be considerable expense involved, even in the models. The models reach a scale where you can put your head or your hands inside and experience the situation perceptually rather than just conceptually, and in that sense I think the larger scale, which makes it just a tiny bit more expensive, helps to visualise real situations. They've paid for themselves, because eventually they seem to be more saleable than outdoor projects, which are very hard to locate and are often one-off.

MT *And they're generally commissioned by a city or are part of a large manifestation in public places, with a fixed budget?*

DG They are occasionally done for private people. In France they tend to be located in museum parks and art spaces built around chateaux in different regions. I don't know if that system's going to continue. I think what's happening in France is that it is now shifting to parks and cities or areas around the edge of cities, and France is getting back into the competition between cities, a situation that is also true in Holland and Germany. I think the system of commission and context is really in flux. In this show there's a project for a swimming pool which was suggested by the husband of my Japanese dealer, who has a construction company and resort by the sea. He suggested that I do a swimming pool which would be in relationship to the surrounding ocean and also to the resort, for his employees. More recently he's decided to buy land adjacent to his resort and to expand the resort, and add to it a restaurant and hotel complex, so the swimming pool would work both for his employees and for people in the hotel/restaurant complex.

MT *Is there a Zen aspect to the work, do you think?*

DG I think the forms are peculiarly Japanese, and that what remains of the Japanese garden has become part of very large, somewhat corporate complexes, and the gardens are almost invariably stone, cement and very rudimentary water, but they are hardly natural. I'm always thinking of suburban contexts, and I think what's interesting about Japan is that the swimming pool and the golf course become extensions of the traditional garden, the Kyoto garden. The swimming pool also mediates between a private residential social situation involving the suburban neighbourhood and the resort hotel/motel complex. So I think it was a good suggestion. One thing I haven't done is a golf course – golf courses developed from the traditional English garden and maybe became models for a business/corporate society. They are meditational and recreational at the same time.

Issue 162, December–January 1992–93

Sophie Calle and Greg Shephard

interviewed by Lynne Cooke

Doubleblind

LYNNE COOKE *Sophie, you don't like to be interviewed, do you?*

SOPHIE CALLE I don't like it, no. I think I have my own way of explaining my work. I only get the urge to answer a question when it involves a very practical point.

LC *It somewhat surprises me because you're a storyteller* par excellence.

SC Storytelling is very different from an interview. I like to tell stories and it's what I do in my work. I'm not going to tell them again when I speak to you. This is not story telling, it's a kind of analysing and this is not the language I like to use. I can understand certain artists need to sit on the side of their work but I don't think I need to.

LC *Do you feel that if you were asked for the reasons or the impulse behind a particular work you could give quite different answers on different days?*

SC I could give you different answers on different days. I could also try to give an answer without reflecting on why I did it at the moment I did it, which sometimes requires much more subtle self-inquiry. I'm not good at analysing myself. It's not my type of thought. I'm clumsy when I try to analyse my impulses.

LC *Do you think, too, that knowing too much can actually be a hindrance, that it can make you too self-conscious?*

SC I'm not in danger of this because I never do it. I never think in those terms.

LC *Does that mean that most of your works are structured intuitively?*

SC Yes. Mostly I can find a reason afterwards, but that's just as a game.

LC *When you say it's a game, is that game any different from the games you might play within a particular work?*

SC It depends on each project. This movie is exactly the game I'm playing in life.

LC *When you set up this project,* Doubleblind, *did you have in mind that it might turn into a film or was it more a way of behaving, a way for the two of you to explore or develop a relationship? The film follows you both driving across the US from New York to San Francisco via a drive-in wedding in Las Vegas.*

SC It started in different ways. First it started because over the years a few people proposed that I do something with a camera. But I always thought film was a very heavy medium. I would rather see myself in my autofocus camera and, also, I preferred doing things without the need for production money, so I never was interested.

Then I met Greg who wants to make movies. My principal thought was that making a movie was a way for me to do something with him that, maybe, could make us closer than we were. So my first impulse to do that movie was one based purely on love. Then I was invited to Mills College in San Francisco to teach. So we decided to cross the country together in the car, which I thought would be an occasion to do something with this notion of filmmaking. But, as I say in the movie, when I arrived in New York two or three days before we were supposed to leave, Greg hadn't done anything to get ready, the car was not ready, he had not bought the cameras, nothing was done. I was hoping for a lot from that trip. I thought that trip would bring us together – movie or no – so for me that trip was very, very important.

Once we started there was no communication between us. We were going to cross the country with two cameras and just make parallel trips. The initial idea was that each of us would take images of what he or she felt like taking and say what he or she thought, not only about each other but also about the people we met or saw. The idea was to have parallel stories because in reality we were not talking to each other at all. But we quickly realised that, in terms of imagery, we had the same ideas. We were shooting the same things, so there would not have been much of a visual contrast between our two stories. In terms of talking, there were three levels of language. First, as a private source – for me this was very easy, because I spoke directly in French to the camera. Greg doesn't understand French. He didn't know what I said. For him it was more complicated. He had to whisper and then he had to redo the text later in the studio, or he had to write notes in a book while driving. In addition, every evening each of us wrote in our books what we had seen that day. The second level is the beginning of conversation between us, the third, the commentaries. Greg doesn't really tell stories, he tells the camera what he thinks, whereas I include storytelling, comments, memos – a little more like an autobiography.

Our approach to imaging grew out of a mistake. Neither of us had ever touched a camera before. We learned in the car how it works. We read the instructions in the car. When we watched the results of the first few days of recording we were desperate, because everything was in movement, jerky, nothing was still except the car, because in the car we were sitting. Everything that was shot in the street, in the hotel, in the motel was impossible to use so we thought the movie was finished. Then we realised that, if we froze the images, we were saved. So, every time we were in the car, we used moving images. Every time we stepped out of the car, it is still shots.

GREG SHEPHARD For two years prior to the time we left I had wanted to do a project with Sophie. The idea of doing it had nothing to do with whether or not we were successful. We had no idea if it would work.

LC *There are a couple of things that establish and keep the momentum going, that keep it rolling, one of which is the seemingly endless way that the car breaks down – the delays, the loss of time, the escalating amounts of money it costs. Sex is the second one. These two subjects seemed to provide the principal leitmotifs.*

GS We had no way of knowing that from the beginning. It just started happening when we chose the storyline. There were in fact other stories that I had going on. I was writing a script in my head, and for a long time I played with the idea of you having access to just my mind, of me writing the script, while Sophie was obsessed with our relationship, and the car's breaking down. But we didn't know, as Sophie said, what we had until we got to California. Then we had to find a story in the 48 hours of tape. This video is structured in three acts: from New York to New Orleans, which is essentially the first act. New Orleans to Las Vegas, which is the second act, that culminates in the climax – the wedding – and the resolution from Las Vegas to San Francisco.

LC *It's a classic, isn't it? A three-stage movement with a climax in the middle. How much did precedents in the genre of the road movie affect you, for example – Jack Kerouac and the whole Beat ethos of crossing the country and of being on the road, or Robert Frank's pictures of America?*

GS Or *Easy Rider*.

LC *Were you thinking of any of these in particular?*

SC No. The only thing I was thinking of in terms of movies, and I think it's what brought us to resolve the mistake, was *La Jetée*, Chris Marker's movie. Because the first time I saw it, years ago, for the only time in my life I was jealous and I wished I had done it. *La Jetée* gave me the right to seek to make my own movie. It was not in my head when we started but I guess it came back when we watched the first few days of recording.

GS For a long time I've wanted to make a movie and this is one way to find out how to do it. We're all walking references of everything that we've ever seen, I don't think we consciously think.

LC *You weren't therefore consciously making dialogue with any existing works?*

GS No. We were dealing on two fronts: we kept the cameras going as much as we could and we dealt with the predicament of our relationship. There were times that we would like to have had the cameras on but we didn't, and other times when we were lucky to have them on and just did what we did. From the 48 hours of footage we used 75 minutes. We left a lot of good things out.

LC *My impression is that, and this seems true in general of going on long drives, that after a while the car becomes a kind of self-contained bubble, and, although you may be looking outside it, nothing is as vivid as what's going on with the person you're driving with. That takes on a life of its own. It becomes much more absorbing than the world you're passing through.*

GS Does that come across in the video?

LC *Yes.*

SC We didn't know that at the beginning. When we started editing, we realised that we were more interested in ourselves, that we were the subject. So many things outside were finally just cut. For example, we thought that the scene in the bar was going to be 20 minutes long. It was to be our main scene yet finally we cut it, and cut it, and cut it.

GS Now three minutes is almost too much.

LC *You also get rid of landmarks. There are very few scenic vistas and very few recognisable landmarks.*

GS I like that part of it. We talked about it a lot. I also like the fact that we don't ever have the radio going. Most of the music is music that we brought on tape, I thought it made us a little more in our own entity, in our own bubble.

SC The more the trip went on the less we were interested in the exterior world. At a certain point, I didn't even want to go out of the car. I didn't want to see anything, I just wanted to drive, to forget and drive. At the beginning of the trip we considered stopping here, stopping there. The more it went on the less we wanted to see anything.

LC *And what one does see tends to be vernacular like the interiors of motel rooms and diners, ubiquitous and interchangeable. At any point it's not clear where you are, because these things are the same all over the country.*

SC It was not easy editing. I've never worked with someone. I'm not used to making concessions so everything was constant compromise. We worked with the editor at San Francisco Artspace, Michael Penhallow, who was perfect for us. Every time we got to a part when neither of us was strong enough to persuade the other, we would follow his choice. What I also wanted to say was that maybe we said things we would not have said to each other if it had not been for the camera between us. It allowed more even in terms of action. I'm not saying that Greg got married because there was a camera or that I asked him because of it, but I think it gave us a kind of licence.

GS Yeah. When we finally did get married, it was like being a part of our own movie in a way, even though we didn't know if we had anything at that point. Being in the movie gave an unreality to it all, and of course being in Las Vegas heightened that.

LC *It's a wonderful moment when we see the back of the car with the two of you in it, and a woman leaning out of an adjacent window apparently reading the wedding service. I thought you couldn't hear anything nor could she hear you.*

GS We had her taped but we decided to let the ambient sounds dominate.

SC I think the movie has also kept us together. We would have split many times during this year if it had not been for the editing. Our private lives may compete with the movie but the movie totally influenced our private lives – it's all very incestuous.

LC *How do you feel about working collaboratively, Sophie? Previously you worked intimately with people but not collaboratively.*

SC I find it exhausting. Every time I do a project alone, I always do what I want but I always play a lot with other people's advice. I need people's advice, maybe to decide that they are wrong. I always need to share projects – I need that exchange. The only difference with the movie is that I could not make the final choice.

GS I'm interested in the way that we kept our thoughts, ideas and feelings at the time separate, and then we came together and collaborated at the end. When we both went into the same pool we found out what each other had said and thought. And, at that point, we had a responsibility to the three-act structure. It results in an interesting mingling of fact and fiction.

SC For me, I was never concerned by the structure. I always thought in terms of my autobiographical story. Greg is always thinking in terms of progression, I never do. We each had our own focus, mine was minute by minute, and Greg's was in terms of the movie as a whole.

GS It has to have some semblance of order. There are some things I'd like – love – changed. I'd love to be less exposed in some areas. At some point, I just jumped in, and I got into thinking, 'How does this character work in relation to Sophie's obsession with him?' I really try to go all the way with that, that's why I'm still a little shaky about it.

LC *Do you feel a bit naked?*

GS I set out to feel naked. I mean, at some point we both got naked. But it's still not easy.

LC *Is that because there's a tendency to assume that artistic truth is the same as autobiographical truth, whereas at some point you adopted a character that would mesh or dialogue with the expectations that you had put in there, one which takes on its own artistic logic and truth, a logic and truth that may be somewhat different from what might have happened if there hadn't been that particular structure within which you were working?*

GS During the making there was no thought except trying to shoot everything. There was no thinking. By contrast, in the editing room, the question was, 'Is it boring?' I had never addressed my work in those terms before, because I was never afraid to be boring. So I guess that this comes from my previous experience of video, of watching video. The decision to cut was not made in terms of artistic choice but of whether it would make it boring. 'Boring' became the main criterion.

LC *Can you work together again or have you discovered so much about each other that –?*

GS Artistically, we could obviously work together. There are personal reasons that might get in the way if we were to work together again.

SC Well, emotionally, it would be difficult. Somebody suggested we should make a Part Two, from San Francisco to New York by the northern route – with a divorce in Reno at the beginning. However, I don't have any ideas right now about working again with videotape. I found it enormously time-consuming. I've never worked longer on anything in my life to result in just a little tape at the end – 11 months non-stop.

Issue 163, February 1993

Sol LeWitt

interviewed by Andrew Wilson

To avoid a rational step, intuition is important

ANDREW WILSON *The earliest drawings in this exhibition date from 1958 and include studies of frescoes at Arezzo by Piero della Francesca. What were you trying to achieve with these works?*

SOL LEWITT When I made these drawings I had reached a low point of my art-life. I had no idea what to do. After art school and the army I had done some work in New York as a graphic designer on the lowest level. I became quickly dissatisfied with this work and wanted to return to making art, but really didn't know where to start. So I dragged out some art books and started making drawings from them. Piero appealed to me for his sense of order, superimposed on which was a sense of passion and ritual. I found that in Velazquez too. I also did drawings from Ingres and Goya.

AW *In your wall drawings and elsewhere you represent solids or structures not through perspective but by isometric projection. Why is this? Is it a distrust of spatial illusion?*

SL I wanted to render form but without space as much as possible. Painting is an activity done on a flat surface. One lesson learnt from the fresco painters of the Quattrocento in Italy was that they had a sense of surface, of flatness, where actual linear perspective was not used but a system of isometric perspective that flattened the forms. I thought that was more powerful in terms of expression and adhered to the sensibility of the idea of the flatness of the wall and the integrity of the picture plane. I have always tried to keep the depth as shallow as possible and the integrity of the wall.

AW *Nevertheless, I was surprised to see the way in which some of your recent wall drawings – like* #652 On three walls, continuous forms with color ink washes superimposed, *or drawings in the exhibition like* Continuous Forms and Color, *1988 – had developed in articulating a play of ambiguous spatial illusion.*

SL They evolved from the renderings of a cube and became more and more complex. I tried to make the forms complex but to keep them as shallow as possible. Not to make a great illusion of space.

AW *Your development from the drawings of 1958 – more or less traditionally figurative and representational – and your structures of 1962 and 1963 is evidence of a radical change in a very short space of time. What sparked this off?*

SL At that time I had a job at the Museum of Modern Art in New York and met other artists such as Dan Flavin, Robert Mangold, Robert Ryman and Scott Burton, and the critic Lucy Lippard who also worked there. Bob Ryman and Lucy Lippard lived in my neighbourhood as did Eva Hesse and Tom Doyle. We had many talks and saw shows at MoMA as well as galleries. The discussions at that time were involved with new ways of making art, trying to reinvent the process, to regain basics, to be as objective as possible. The work of Frank Stella and Jasper Johns, who were in a show at MoMA ('10 Americans') about then, were of particular interest.

My thinking was involved with the problem of painting at the time, the idea of the flat surface and the integrity of the surface. By the end of the fifties Abstract Expressionism had passed, it was played out. Pop Art had a completely different idea. It was more involved with objects. I wasn't really that interested in objects, I was interested in ideas. Also at that time the ideas of Joseph Albers, of colour moving back and forth. While I was working at I M Pei I met Eva Hesse and Robert Slutzky who had studied with Albers. I decided that I would make colour or form recede and proceed in a three-dimensional way. The idea of flatness of plane naturally evolved into three-dimensionality of form which became wall structures, at first made with colour advancing and receding and then with only black and white, and finally as freestanding pieces.

AW *What did you learn from Flavin ?*

SL Flavin's piece, *The Nominative Three*, using a progression of one, one-two, one-two-three, was an important example for me. It was one of the first system pieces I'd seen. Donald Judd's progression pieces of that time were also very important. I began to think of systems that were finite and simple. This was the basic difference between the idea of simplifying form to become less expressive, and the idea that the form was the carrier of ideas.

AW *Immediately before the first structures you made works which used as their source the serial photographs of Muybridge. And yet the drawings you made showed single figures, isolated, caught. Not a sequence.*

SL As with the Piero and Velazquez drawings, I knew that there was something there that was important to me but I didn't know how to use it. The idea of seriality came later – the idea that all of the parts were only the result of the basic idea, but that each individual part was equally important, and that all parts were equal – nothing hierarchical. A man running in Muybridge was the inspiration for making all the transformations of a cube within a cube, a square within a square, cube within a square, etc.

AW *Was it also important that Muybridge used this method as a means of finding out some form of truth, scientific truth, about movement?*

SL That part wasn't as significant to me as the idea that it led to the motion picture which was the great narrative idea of our time. I thought that narration was a means of getting away from formalism – to get away from the idea of form as an end and rather to use form as a means.

AW *You see your serial work as forming a sort of narrative?*

SL That was what I was after, yes. As the Muybridge was a narrative of a man running so the combinations of a serial work function as a narrative also. And also each part encapsulates the entire process and whole idea.

AW *Another result of seriality is the creation of a degree of paradox – where a simple system yields complex results or where logic can beget absurdity – is this something you consciously aim for?*

SL The price that you have to pay for following this logical system is that the more complex and absurd the result became perceptually, the more you would get a forest of trees where it might be almost impossible to discern the original idea. I was very involved in writers like Samuel Beckett who were also interested in the idea of absurdity as a way out of intellectuality. Even a simple idea taken to a logical end can become chaos. So when you go back to the wall drawing of continuous forms, you have the same sort of connection between the simplicity of a cube and the chaotic materialisation of a great deal of form. But one follows from the other, and starting with one you have to end with the other, otherwise you don't do the whole process.

There is always the tension that leads to a certain ambiguity on one hand and absurdity on the other, and some of the wall drawings – the location wall drawings – were made specifically with this in mind. The more information that you give, the crazier it gets, until to construct a very simple form or figure such as a circle you could have three pages of text. In a way it was an extension of the idea that prolixity created simplicity and unity.

Looking back at it now, I think it was in a way also satirising some of the more advanced conceptualists that were abounding at the time. I wasn't really involved in conceptualisation as a movement as such but I was more interested in using abstract or geometric form to generate other kinds of ideas, but not to get into the backwaters of philosophy.

AW *Would you also say that your work is at all concerned with metaphysics?*

SL Obviously a drawing of a person is not a real person, but a drawing of a line is a real line.

AW *In 1970 you also wrote that you preferred an art that was 'smart enough to be dumb'.*

SL It is just that in a way cleverness wasn't an attribute that I admired a great deal. I felt that one should be intelligent enough to know when not to be too intellectual, or to keep things simple when things could get out of hand and be too complex. Perhaps I was talking about some of the more difficult conceptualists. But I admired, for instance, an artist like Hanne Darboven who made a great career out of using numbers and dates. You can also think of On Kawara in the same way.

AW *What led you to write the 'Paragraphs' and 'Sentences on Conceptual Art' for* Artforum, *in the summer of 1967?*

SL Robert Smithson managed to get *Artforum* magazine to offer some pages for artists to express their ideas. I wanted to counter the current notion of Minimal Art. This was being written about by critics, however I thought it missed the point because it regarded this art in a formal way rather than what I believed was more conceptual (for example, Flavin, Stella, Judd, Carl Andre, Mel Bochner, Smithson).

AW *Recent studies of Conceptual Art have prioritised the position of Duchamp's readymade within the formation of Conceptual Art – how important to you was Duchamp's example?*

SL Duchamp was making a different kind of art evolving from Dada and Surrealism. These forms are absolutely conceptual, but I was not interested in them. The use of the term was prior to my own.

AW *Given that one of the major tensions in your work exists between the idea and its embodiment in material form, can an idea that is not realised ever be more important than an idea that is? Do you ever see the making of the final object as unnecessary?*

SL There are always many ideas that are never realised but are important in that they lead to other ideas that may be realised. I've always maintained in my work that there is a double focus and that the idea and the result of the idea are symbiotic and impossible to extract from one another. I never thought that if the thing existed only as an idea, it was a complete idea. I had the idea that the cycle had to be complete to be a work of art.

AW *But you have written before that a blind man can make art, but the visual result is important. It is what you first see.*

SL No, but it came from somewhere. A blind man can make art but a blind man can't see art.

AW *Is there a difference of significance between, say, a wall drawing and a drawing on paper that is for a wall drawing?*

SL They are drawings as an end in themselves, too. It's more than just documentation. Once it has fulfilled its function as a road map for making the wall drawing, it exists in itself as a drawing, as a work on paper. I think of them as being of equal importance. I think that the plan is there to be understood.

AW *Yet earlier you would exhibit the two together which you don't do now.*

SL I use the title instead. Usually the title is the plan and explains the drawing. The title is the clue to the idea of the piece. Whereas previously I used to make drawings or diagrams to show what the idea of the piece was. Now, what I usually do is try to give a clue to the idea of the piece by means of the title.

AW *So when you write that 'the serial artist functions merely as a clerk cataloguing the results of the premise' you make your work seem like a chore. Is it really that?*

SL When an artist decides to make photographs of a man running each frame is a part (a necessary part) but only a part. But making each part could be a chore or not.

AW *You have said that Conceptual Art is good only when the idea is good. So what in your terms leads to a good idea, or a bad idea, or a banal idea?*

SL In the course of your mental meanderings through the day you reject a lot of ideas that come through your mind. You do a lot of your work in the course of ordinary activities during the day and your mind either rejects or selects different ideas. You throw them out as you go along. When you finally come to something that you think is fairly interesting, then you want to do that. Maybe it is a bad or banal idea but at the time it seems good.

AW *Can the following of the instructions by your assistants ever lead to a wrong result? Do you ever see one of these wall drawings and think 'That's been done wrongly'?*

SL No I haven't. Whatever happens wrongly is because my instructions were wrong and not because of the execution being wrong.

AW *Some of your earlier wall drawings – those shown at Konrad Fischer or the Dwan Galleries in 1969 – are isolated on the wall rather than occupying the whole surface. Doesn't that create a sense of hierarchy or frame between the wall and drawing?*

SL *Wall Drawing #3* which I did at Konrad Fischer was a band of pencil lines that was just one metre high and went across the whole wall. I was using the whole wall rather than putting different things on the wall. Which is the idea of the space of the wall, the whole space.

AW *Putting different things on the wall in blocks like* Wall Drawing #2 Drawing Series II(A) (24 Drawings) *is a bit like –*

SL Hanging paintings.

AW *Even a page layout?*

SL Yes.

AW *And the idea for wall drawings was sparked off, wasn't it, from making drawings for a book,* The Xerox Book, *published in 1968?*

SL Yes that was done at the same time. These early wall drawings came from that because that is what I was doing. I had had the idea of doing drawings on walls before that but this was the actual first time. I was working on *The Xerox Book*, or had finished it, and that was just the drawing in my mind. I didn't have the idea of the whole wall, I just had the idea of putting it on the wall.

AW *A book is a prime example of a serial narrative structure because you are turning the pages, but you can go to any page at any time.*

SL Right.

AW *And doesn't the book form provide a much purer, more distilled way of showing a serial progression of a drawing, rather than having it on the wall?*

SL Maybe less so, because having it on the wall meant that you saw the whole thing at once, but with the book you only saw each one individually. That was the reason for doing *The Variations of Incomplete Open Cubes*, 1974, as a book. The book is one part. There is the three-dimensional realisation, plus the drawing, plus the photograph. Then the drawing and the photograph become a book. But when all the drawings and photographs are on the wall you see the whole thing in one view.

AW *The creation of bookworks had been a constant preoccupation. You were, with Lippard and others, a founder of Printed Matter, to make artists' books more easily and freely available.*

SL A lot of the conceptual work actually existed better in a book form than on a wall. It was really difficult to read everything that was written or to see everything that was presented on the wall. It is much easier if you are sitting at home with a book looking at part of it now and part of it tomorrow and so on and so forth.

Also the price of books was much less than a work of art. Everyone could own one and each one was actually a work of art in itself. We had the idea of Printed Matter as a vehicle to get these books into the hands of people. I had been doing books, as other artists had, but they just piled up. Usually dealers did them as part of a show and they would hand them out, but there was no central point of distribution until Printed Matter and some others began to distribute these books.

AW *Do you think that art should have social or moral purpose?*

SL No. I think artists should have a social or moral purpose. But there is some art that I think is very good art that is socially, politically and morally motivated like the work of Hans Haacke, or the work of John Heartfield, for instance. I think that these are very successful artists who use those ideas very well but, also, many such works are very banal even though the politics are correct.

The sixties was one of the most art-generative times, but even though there was a political and social upheaval, the arts represented more of an aesthetic than a political upheaval. There actually wasn't much political art being done at the time. Not nearly as much as now.

AW *So an involvement with the Art Workers' Coalition was more about being politicised yourself, rather than making the work political.*

SL Yes.

AW *Is the element of installation important to you?*

SL In some works.

AW *When you showed the 1966 works* Modular Floor Structure *and* Double Modular Cube *at the Dwan Gallery, you wrote that 'although the space of the gallery was a guide to the size of the work, the pieces did not work absolutely with the space'. What did you mean by this?*

SL I was thinking about the difference between originating a work for a specific space on the one hand, or originating a work in the studio as a thing in itself and then putting it in its space. Or on the other hand, if you do a thing for a specific space it will always work in that space. If you do a thing for itself, it may or may not work in any given space.

AW *Why did you suggest that conceptual artists should be mystics?*

SL I was trying to break out of the whole idea of rationality. At that time there was a great deal of geometric painting that I thought was very boring, and it was very rational. Conceptual artists were intuitive rather than rational. In other words, to discover their idea – the main idea, the instigator of whatever it is – a leap of faith or a leap of aesthetics had to be made otherwise it was just another rational step. To avoid a rational step, intuition is important.

AW *So is the idea synonymous with intuition?*

SL Yes. Eventually one must free oneself from the restraint of dogma – intuition does this.

Issue 164, March 1993

Agnes Martin

interviewed by Irving Sandler

You have to do what you have to do

IRVING SANDLER *To begin with a generalistion, what would you like your pictures to convey?*

AGNES MARTIN I would like them to represent beauty, innocence and happiness – I would like them all to represent that. Exaltation.

IS *You also think of your art as classical, because it is detached from the world, cool and untroubled, and strives for perfection and freedom from whatever drags people down. Do you think of your painting as continuing a classical tradition in the history of art?*

AM No, I just hope I have the classical attitude.

IS *At the same time that you value a detached and cool art, you require that your art express feeling. It is commonly thought that detachment and feeling are antithetical, yet you would like to bring them together.*

AM I think that personal feelings, sentimentality and those sorts of emotions, are not art but that universal emotions like happiness are art. I am particularly interested in the abstract emotions that we feel when we listen to music. All music is absolutely abstract, except for one piece, 'The Flight of the Bumble Bee', which is not abstract! People are not aware of their abstract emotions, which are a big part of their lives, except when they listen to music or look at art. These are the emotions that align with art.

IS *Today, there are many artists who view modern life as a series of disasters – two world wars, the holocaust, rabid nationalism, ecological devastation – and who believe that the future will be no better. These artists attempt to embody this negative outlook in their art. Has this kind of expression a place in art in your view?*

AM I don't respect their negative art, I think it's illustration. I consider exaltation to be the theme of art and life.

IS *Your art is non-objective which, as you have written, is of extreme importance to you.*

AM I think that the abstract emotions of which we are not conscious are tremendously important, especially since they are all positive. I mean they are happy emotions that we only feel when we get away from daily care and turn away from this common life. I don't think human welfare and comfort are the artist's responsibility. I mean every other activity, every other kind of work contributes to human welfare and comfort. But art has no time for that materialistic area. The reason I think that music is the highest form of art is because it manages to represent all our abstract emotions. I don't think that artists should be involved in political life because it's so distracting.

IS *Your ideas seem to owe much to the Bible, to Taoism and Zen Buddhism. Would you comment more specifically on what influence these sources had on you?*

AM What I'm most interested in are the ancient Chinese like Lao Tse and I quote from the Bible because it's so poetic, though I'm not a Christian.

IS *John Cage was a follower of Zen Buddhism, were you friendly with him?*

AM Well, just to speak to. But I don't agree with him.

IS *Why not?*

AM Well for one thing, he wrote a book called *Silence* and in the very first line he said 'there is no such thing as silence'. But I think there is. When you walk into a forest there are all kinds of sounds but you feel as though you have stepped into silence. I believe that is silence. John Cage believed in chance, and I very strongly disagree. Every note Beethoven composed was invested with his whole mind and being. I think that composition depends on accepting what you put down. Our mind asks, 'is this right?' and it answers, 'yes' or 'no'.

IS *But you did remark once that you were no more responsible for your work than a potato farmer is for his crop.*

AM I don't take responsibility for the inspiration. I mean that artists are all required to do exactly what they are told to do. In the morning we get up and we know what we have to do. At night the intellect goes to sleep and gives inspiration a chance. When people have a decision to make, they say they will sleep on it – that is the part of the mind that's responsible for artwork. It's not an intellectual process.

IS *Yet you would consider certain of your pictures successes and abandon others. I believe you once referred to rejected paintings as 'dead paintings'.*

AM Well, inspiration doesn't always turn out because, even if inspiration is the black corn in the bottom 40, the weather has a lot to do with it. There's a lot of failure. I've often said that the ability to recognise failure is the most important talent of an artist.

IS *Another point of disagreement between you and Cage is his belief that art ought to break down all barriers between art and everyday life.*

AM I don't share that opinion.

IS *Two artists that you admire are Mark Rothko, who tried to suggest what he termed 'transcendental experience' in his painting, and Barnett Newman, who preferred the term 'sublime'.*

AM I agree with them. I have great respect for their work and philosophy, their transcendentalism. They gave up so many things. They gave up line, they gave up form, they gave up organic form. They created an undefined space. I think that was so important. The abstract expressionists found that you can have an entirely objective reality that may be totally abstract. That's revolutionary. And they had so many different expressions.

IS *Your paintings are non-objective and yet I want to talk a bit from my own experience because we have something in common in that we both lived on the great plains in Canada. I spent part of my boyhood in Winnipeg and memories of that landscape remain vivid.*

AM Yes, mine too.

IS *I sense that there are references to that nature in your work, for instance, in the horizontal in your grids, or more emphatically, the openness and expansiveness in your work.*

AM A lot of people say my work is like landscape. But the truth is that it isn't, because there are straight lines in my work and there are no straight lines in nature. My work is non-objective, like that of the abstract expressionists. But I want people, when they look at my paintings, to have the same feelings they experience when they look at landscape, so I never protest when they say my work is like landscape. But it's really about the feeling of beauty and freedom that you experience in landscape. My response to nature is really a response to beauty. The water looks beautiful, the trees look beautiful, even the dust looks beautiful. It is beauty that really calls.

IS *You prefer the grid because it exemplifies wholeness, boundlessness and quiet.*

AM And egolessness.

IS *It is also non-hierarchical, no point having more emphasis than another.*

AM That is the point, all the rectangles are the same size. I think that the rhythms are tranquil, don't you? Everything that bothers us is left out. One man couldn't stand that so he painted one of the rectangles!

IS *How did you find out about it?*

AM One of my collectors told me about it. He asked me whether it was right that one of them was painted. I recognised that it wasn't, so they restored it.

IS *You commented once that you adopted the grid because it was universal, yet your lines are handmade, they emphasise touch, which is associated with the personal, the idiosyncratic. Do you see any contradiction in that?*

AM No. I drew them just as perfectly as I could, I didn't think at all about my hand, but in nature it is impossible to make a perfect line, so the lines have that lack of perfection. The composition carries it.

IS *But the sensitivity of the lines is very important, at least in my perception of the work. Indeed, the fluctuations in the line contribute to a sense of atmosphere in the work.*

AM I didn't expect it but I value it. But then the sensitivity is obvious. Of course besides trying to make them all perfect, I have wanted them to illustrate the sensitivity of perfection. When I say that I want perfection, I don't mean a perfect sheet of work. I believe that life is perfect. We have an ego orientation, and so we are far from perfect. But everlasting life is perfect, and it is that perfection, a transcendental perfection, that I want in my painting. We can't have it because we are in nature but you can have a hint of perfection. It's enough to make a painting alive.

IS *In the mid-seventies you moved from the monochromatic grid arrangement to vertical bands of colour. How did that change in structure and colour take place?*

AM Well, I stopped painting for four and a half years and when I started again, I made those vertical line paintings. The paintings in my first show after I started painting again were all vertical. I don't know why, I can't explain the leap that was my inspiration. I had to do everything I'm told. So does everybody else. You have to do what you have to do.

IS *How did you happen to become an artist?*

AM I painted for 20 years without painting a painting that I liked. I never painted a painting I liked until I got to New York, and they were completely non-objective, then I liked them. When I started out painting, I painted everything from landscapes and Indians to flowers and everything. I even taught portrait painting at the University of New Mexico. Gradually, over 20 years, my work became more and more abstract. It was a process.

IS *You moved to New York in 1957. Why did you decide to move there?*

AM Betty Parsons came out here to Taos and I showed her my paintings. She said she wouldn't show them unless I moved to New York. I think she bought five paintings, and that gave me enough money to go to New York. Then she gave me a show.

IS *That would have been in 1958. What was Parsons like as a dealer?*

AM She was a very good dealer from the standpoint of artists. She took so much interest in them and encouraged them. She didn't make so much money as some other dealers. She didn't price up art as high. She was just a real friend.

IS *When you got to New York City, you found a studio in Coenties Slip in Lower Manhattan – in the middle of a remarkable group of artists who lived there: Ellsworth Kelly and Jack Youngerman, Lenore Tawney, James Rosenquist, Robert Indiana and Ann Wilson. Around the corner there were the studios of Rauschenberg and Johns. What was your interaction with these artists?*

AM Well, we were great friends. I wasn't such good friends with Jasper Johns and Rauschenberg. We knew them but they didn't associate with us.

IS *Did you feel that you had anything in common with people like Kelly, Youngerman, Tawney?*

AM I don't think we talked about that. I treated them as friends and kept off the subject. You see we all lived the same kind of life and we all had the same kind of velocity, you might say. We all agreed, and so it was very, very pleasant to be with people when you don't feel the competition or the resistance. There was no resistance, there was no competition. That's a very pleasant association.

IS *It must have been very supportive as well.*

AM Yes. We all had the same problems, too.

IS *I think the reason that I asked what attitudes you shared about art, is that the kind of painting that all of you did seemed different from that of the so-called 'action painters' who congregated on Tenth Street, just north of you, who went to the Cedar Street Tavern and the Club, and who looked to Willem de Kooning, Franz Kline and Philip Guston. That was my group, up on Tenth Street.*

AM I never went to the Tavern – I don't go to taverns.

IS *I imagine you wouldn't have had too much sympathy for that aspect of Abstract Expressionism.*

AM I don't have too much sympathy with De Kooning.

IS *He was the central figure to the Tenth Street artists.*

AM Which group do you think Rothko and Newman belonged with?

IS *Well, they weren't really part of the group around the Cedar Street Tavern and the Club. They'd come occasionally, but our heroes were De Kooning, Kline and Guston. Did you meet Rothko or Newman?*

AM I considered that I was very good friends with Newman, or he was a very good friend to me I should say, because he used to hang my shows for me. He was very good at it. I only had lunch with Rothko once, but I enjoyed it. He talked about the difference between the life of an artist and a layman – very amusingly. That's the only time I met him.

IS *We haven't mentioned Clyfford Still.*

AM I consider Still the father of American art. When Still started out, before he gave up organic form, you could see the effect of light – this might be water, this might be land and all kinds of things. But then I think he was the first to become absolutely non-objective in his work. When the abstract expressionists were giving up defined space, Herbert Read was writing a book called *Positive and Negative Space*. That is what the abstract expressionists gave us, and the tremendous scale of their work.

IS *I think what you say about Still is absolutely true. He's been very much undervalued in the last few years.*

AM He was so stubborn about showing his paintings.

IS *Did you get to meet him at all?*

AM Yes, I met him. He had a show in Buffalo, so I went up to meet him on the last day because I knew he would come to take one last photo. I purposely went up to meet him, but I didn't get to talk to him very much because he was a very worried man, he was worried about his paintings being poorly hung and poorly stretched.

IS *Another artist we haven't talked about that I would be curious about your response to is Ad Reinhardt.*

AM I don't see we have anything in common, but the journalists seem to think there is.

IS *He would have agreed with you.*

AM I was a good friend of Ad's. At least, I hope I was. He was a very generous man, very intelligent.

IS *But you had no sense of any affinity with his work. Would you feel your work is closer to Reinhardt's than to Kline's?*

AM Well, I like Kline's work. But do you think that Reinhardt's would be closer?

IS *I guess because of the all-over quality and the non-objectivity in his work, I would think, yes.*

AM I like Reinhardt's early work better.

IS *In the mid sixties you became identified with a group of artists who were later labelled 'minimalist': Frank Stella, Sol LeWitt, Carl Andre, Donald Judd, Robert Morris and Dan Flavin.*

AM They asked me to show with them, and I was flattered. They were all so young. I considered myself to be an abstract expressionist but they considered me a minimalist. I couldn't do anything about that.

IS *Did you have some sympathy with the work of the minimalists?*

AM Well yes. They also were classical, you could say. They followed perfection in their minds. You can't draw a perfect circle, but in your mind there is a perfect circle, that you can draw towards. You can't be a perfect man, but in your mind you can conceive of a perfect man. That's the Greek ideal. And the minimalists were the same, working towards that perfection in the mind. But they insisted more than I did on being impersonal. They wanted absolutely to escape themselves and wanting to express something. They didn't even allow people to put their names under their pictures. They listed the names at the back with the numbers. They even had to be talked into that.

IS *I remember the shows in which you exhibited with them, your paintings always seemed to separate themselves from theirs. Around 1967, several younger painters emerged who partly came out of Minimal Art. Their work, I think, relates very much to yours and was influenced by yours. I am thinking of artists like Robert Ryman and Brice Marden.*

AM I don't think they were influenced by me.

IS *You left New York in 1967, and you said at one point in your writing that you had retired from painting. After a period spent travelling, you settled in New Mexico. Could you talk about that experience and also why you resumed painting.*

AM Sometimes, nature calls to you and says, 'come and live with me'. So I decided to experiment with the simple life. I think our culture is orientated towards ego, and winning and overcoming and all of that. Our culture is so chaotic and materialistic. So I decided to experiment with simple living. I went up on top of a mesa that is eight miles long and six miles wide and there was nobody up there and the nearest house was six miles away. There was no electricity and no telephones. I stayed up there for years and became as wise as a Chinese hermit. Then I decided that that is not a natural human way of living, to be so isolated, so I came back down. But it is tempting, isn't it, when you get out in nature, just to give way to natural living?

IS *Despite all the turmoil in our world today, over the decades you have held on to a belief in transcendental experience and exultation.*

AM I think that happiness, innocence and beauty are the first concern of everybody. You see, don't think it is just me. I think that everybody is concerned and that, if they don't have any experience of these positive emotions, they really crack up. That's how important I think they are. You see, we are educated in the intellectual and ego side of things – that's the orientation of our culture – and so the other, happiness, innocence and beauty, has to be stressed. I'll tell you the difference between the intellectual response and the artist's response: the intellectual response is about facts and reaching decisions – reduction, classification, logic – everything we've been educated in. That's the intellectual response. And then there's the intuitive response. That's what art is about.

IS *One last question: is there anything you would like to add?*

AM I would like to say that artists should depend on inspiration. Everybody protests that artists are irresponsible, but artists are not concerned with the material world. I would advise them to turn away from this world and go on a picnic or something. Go into the forest and feel the difference. If you are on the beach and you are looking at the shining waters and the flight of birds, and you are tranquillised by it, and somebody comes down to the beach with a transistor radio and turns it on, you are irritated. That's the difference. The artistic attitude is the one on the beach before the world interferes. Artists are intuitive. They wait for inspiration. That's what art is about, the intuitive, not the intellectual. Art about ideas stimulates ideas, but art that comes from inspiration stimulates feelings of happiness, innocence and beauty.

Issue 169, September 1993

Gary Hill

interviewed by Regina Cornwell

Who are you?

REGINA CORNWELL *Tell me about* Tall Ships, *1992, about the title itself and the experience you wanted to create through this installation.*

GARY HILL The title comes from seeing an old photograph taken in Seattle around 1930. The last tall ship is being moved out of Lake Union before the final section of the Aurora Bridge is put into place. The bridge is actually quite high but still would have clipped the ship's masts. I saw this photograph right around the time of recording the people for the piece.

I imagined a sailing ship on the high seas – that frontal view of extreme verticality coming towards you. It has a kind of majestic buoyancy of something very sure of itself – something that will come forth with a kind of terrifying grace no matter what. It's dark, it's very dark but you can see clearly this beautiful thing cutting through the night – a night that isn't referenced by day. To think of a person like this – the human approaching – the notion of 'ships passing in the night' took on a certain poetic space that felt very open. I don't think I was really clear about the piece until I had this title.

RC *What were your production methods? How did you direct the participants and then transcribe the results for the kind of extreme space of a corridor?*

GH I wanted the whole situation to be as unassuming as possible. All the people in *Tall Ships* are family or friends or friends of friends. My daughter, brother, mother and stepfather are all in the piece. From the time of conceiving of it to actual production, I simplified the movement of the people involved so that they only came forward and then returned to a particular place and position of either standing or sitting. There are a few interruptions to that, for instance, after coming forward they would pause and go back or they would come back a second time after starting to return. It was shot in a long dark room – it was a 50-foot walk towards me and the camera. As each came forward, together we would be almost holding an imaginary ball between us. Some would get more and more uncomfortable, others would pass through this threshold of 'how long have I been out there?' In other words, what all the viewers do, I went through with each filmed person. Originally, the figures were to speak to the visitors but, even after I decided to delete the speaking, I considered the sounds important – I imagined filling the space with silence.

I didn't want any theatre or aesthetic. In terms of the piece as a whole, I wanted to avoid it being an experience to do with technology or anything to do with a multicultural agenda. It's simply the idea of a person coming up to you and asking, 'who are you?' by kind of mirroring you and at the same time illuminating a space of possibility for that very question to arise. Basically, I wanted to create an open experience that was deliberate and at the same time would disarm whatever particular constructs one might arrive with, especially in a museum.

I would like to do more work, as I have in *Tall Ships*, that involves stripping down, breaking down to something very close to absence. It was very easy to make. I only shot for two days, then there was a few days' editing. That easiness somehow reassured me about the work. Rather than thinking 'this is so easy, there must be something wrong', this easiness seemed to come out of the work and it became a case of accepting it, going through with it and not saying 'I must do something else'.

RC *Would you say a few words about the child at the end of the corridor? She is the only child among the participants and assumes the central position.*

GH Originally I hadn't intended to have someone there but as we were installing it seeing that blank void suggested too much a sense of the infinite. Without any figure there the others would seem to go on forever like a hall of mirrors. I wanted the space to retain a sense of place somehow. I decided on having the child there which would produce a certain amount of closure but at the same time suggest an openness, a future, the possible.

RC *You mentioned that producing* Tall Ships *was quite easy. Would you say something about the installation's technology?*

GH All the images are on one laser disk, and there are 12 to 16 copies, depending on the number of projections, all of which are linked to one computer. There are things called 'switch runners' under the carpet which trigger the images, and there's a five-foot section for each projection. I've used four-inch black and white monitors with lenses placed on top of them. And the reason that they're angled so much – it becomes somewhat of a compromise but I really don't mind that – was that if you do it that way the viewer can get really close to the wall and not interrupt the projection. In other words, they're projected from about nine feet up, directly down on the wall. To do that extreme angle the whole recording was digitally keystoned to cancel out the distortion. So if you look at the images on a regular monitor the figures are distorted with large heads and small feet.

RC *At Documenta IX I had a sense of anxiety in the space. I couldn't see, it was really dark, but at the same time it was an extraordinary experience.*

GH I think this anxiety is very much a part of the ingress. Once you are in and over your initial trepidation then perhaps some questions arise: 'What kind of a space am I in?', 'How long is it?', 'Who are these figures?', 'How long will they look at me?', 'Am I making them move?', 'Can I talk?' These questions are not so much answered as slowly illuminated both figuratively and literally. As the figures come forth they provide the light in the space. Silhouettes of other viewers begin to appear. In a sense, the 'ships passing in the night' become not only the figures and you, but you and other viewers. You begin to see the shapes and shadows and light cast by the figures on to people's faces. It's very subtle, but the viewers begin to mix with the projections.

RC *Is this a radical departure from other installations?*

GH Well, yes and no. There are technical aspects and to some extent the content is very close to *Beacon (Two Versions of the Imaginary)* from 1990. There are two projections of two different images out through the ends of a tube. The tube rotates very slowly in an equally darkened space and the images continually expand and contract around the room. Technically, the projections of both works were obtained the same way, so the visual quality of the images is very similar. The same kind of 'assemblage' projections are used – very primitive, black and white, with the same monitors and surplus projection lenses. As in *Tall Ships* there are a number of full-figured images along with portrait-like shots. All were recorded with a rotating camera that moved counter to the projections in the installation. This in effect cancelled out the movement so that it looks like a spotlight – or beacon – passing across the people, illuminating them in the space, which also happens to the viewers in the space.

RC *How is this related to* Tall Ships*?*

GH I used a similar approach in recording the people. With the exception of the two readers in *Beacon*, whom much of the time you see reciting the text, the remaining people are seen looking or watching. So in both works the viewers and viewed are intertwined in a number of ways. I hadn't thought of it before but it's interesting to think about the relationship of the metaphors at play in the two pieces – beacons and tall ships.

RC *Given the complexities of the textual layering in most of your work, does the absence of sound in* Tall Ships *point in a new direction?*

GH Suspension of disbelief is silent too, but I think that the silence in *Tall Ships* is more active – it feels present and brings the impending contact with the figures really out in the open. It's as if you are out on 'mind island' with this or that person and you feel there must be something to say. I think this kind of radically stripped down space is also very uncomfortable for some people. Instantly they want to fill it with talking.

The possibility of working with interactive systems has always been in the back of my mind, or a thorn in my side depending on the context I'm thinking in. I wanted the interactivity to be virtually transparent to the point that some people would not even figure it out. I didn't want somebody going in there and, in a sense, playing. I mean 'play' like cause and effect – I'm pushing this and this is happening. I think this is the major problem with interactive work in general. You have to find a way around the mind being told where and when it may make a choice. It has to 'dawn' on the mind.

RC *You have been quoted as saying: 'If I have a position it is to question the privileged place that image or, for that matter, sight holds in our consciousness.' Would you comment on this?*

GH About the image being privileged, even in the most obvious sense, when we say 'seeing is believing' or 'I have to see it', so much of our culture tends to rely on the image. Images are so all-pervasive that in a sense we walk around with our eyes – the given gaze – it's a passive process in a way. Because the image's existence in *Tall Ships* is directly related to the viewer's activity and is always blurring the distinction between lightness and darkness, it resists passivity. The light directly involves the viewer in the space, it becomes something shared by the viewer and the image as an active relationship.

RC *In the light of your strong concern with language, especially in your single-channel tapes, would you comment on this quote: 'Language can be this incredibly forceful material: there's something about it where if you can strip away its history, get to the materiality of it, it can rip into you like claws, whereas images sometimes just slide off the edge of your mind as if you were looking out of a car window.'*

GH Quotes, like anything, have their context. I'm really looking for another way outside the theoretical dualism concerning language and image. I am still very interested in the image being experienced self-consciously rather than merely being a given. I think this comes through particularly in my installation work the way that one has to complete the image or at least negotiate with it in space. At times it's an image on the edge of visibility as in *Tall Ships* and *Beacon* or one that exists for a very brief moment that only becomes 'seen' as part of a 'swarm' of other brief moments making a kind of trace as in *Suspension of Disbelief (for Marine)*, 1992, and *Between 1 & 0*, 1993. But text and all that that implies has also become suspect to me. I'm really interested in the newer possibilities of intermedia, particularly the electronic forms with their inherent feedback attributes. This is why I've continued to work with video and electronic media for so long.

RC *Do you see* Tall Ships *and other recent works as phenomenological, insofar as you are interested in language and thinking about the problem of the mind/body, subject/object split?*

GH When I work, I don't work theoretically. I am not a Heideggerian. I am not a Derridean. I'm not any of these things, although people may assume that I am – I'm more physical. I'm post-historical in the sense that I don't really work much with history. I'm very interested in the way that my body rubs up against the world, the sound of my speech, how we see. I might begin a work on a pinpoint of an idea, but I don't know what will happen. I'm committed to the idea that the event takes place within a process and one has to be open to that event, able to kind of wander in it, see it through until some kind of release feels inevitable.

RC *Are you still making single-channel tapes?*

GH The last tape I made was literally on December 23 1990, commissioned by LA SEPT, for a series called LIVE, in which the artist had to produce a work in real time – no editing – that would be an hour long. This proved to be extremely difficult. Although it's not successful in a number of ways, it renewed my interest in real time.

I'm also interested in making film. It's a different scale. With video, it's so cheap you can shoot as much as you want. In film, real time is replaced by 'you've got to get this, this is the one time'. It's that sort of intensity.

Tape is so far from being something that's about something visual, it's very much a conceptual medium. If you put a camera, a person and a monitor together you have that totality of the loop: a seer being seen and then something that's showing both what is being produced at the same time. That is embedded in the medium, whether you use it literally or not. I'm really talking about feedback, of things folding back on other things – affecting them. Then there's response and interaction which folds back again in a sort of ongoing process of seeing oneself being seen.

RC *Today, while there is more installation work involving media such as video or new technologies, the interest in it is still slight. In terms of a response from the art press, why do you think that it is so minimal and why, when it is there, is it so critically and theoretically underdeveloped?*

GH The object has been revered for so long and is so much a part of the economic base of art that people really have to have an experience that turns their mind and breaks the habit of wanting things. Even Conceptual Art was assimilated more easily into art culture because, in the end, there was still some sort of static object.

Once you ask the viewer to enter time, or tell them that in fact you want their time, there's another kind of expectation. Performance and media art, in their own ways, reside somewhere between theatre and cinema, respectively, and the plastic arts. I think this is what lends them a certain flux – their 'cultures' have more inputs and outputs – by nature they are more interactive and driven by intermedia tendencies.

Most of the time this kind of work falls between the cracks. Either you have theoreticians applying the theories of the likes of Baudrillard and/or stealing from McLuhan – but nevertheless completely missing the point simply because they are not attending to the work itself – or you have the art critic who comes from an historical base of objects and images but doesn't have a clue about technological systems and can't begin to consider epistemological or ontological questions pertaining to art.

RC *For a time you were better known in Europe than in the US, why do you think this was so?*

CH I suppose as far as the art world is concerned that was true. But I really matured as an artist through the media/video community in the US, most notably New York. Maybe in time the art world will see the significance of many things that were done which weren't looked at because video simply wasn't a commodity. Towards the beginning it really functioned as an alternative supported by grants, media arts survived independently of the art world.

My reception in Europe, which really gained momentum in France, was perhaps first due to my concerns with language, in particular the writings of Maurice Blanchot. But I think, too, it had a lot to do with timing. I had been exhibiting a great deal more in Europe at the time and European spaces, whether it was museums, galleries or other spaces, had been quicker to show video installations. Even though I've shown quite a bit in the US – I think I've been in every Whitney Biennial since 1981 – so much of the time the context is compromised. It's still a situation of video being ghettoised, although this seems to be changing both in Europe and the US. Last year at Documenta there were a number of media works, and you could hear curators, critics, museum directors etc saying something to the effect that 'video has finally come of age'. You just felt like saying, 'No, video has not finally come of age, you have finally come of age.'

Issue 170, October 1993

Claes Oldenburg

interviewed by Patricia Bickers

Bottle of Notes

PATRICIA BICKERS *How did the commission for* Bottle of Notes *originate?*

CLAES OLDENBURG It really grew out of contacts with Tony Knipe and Terry Friedman in connection with the exhibition, 'A Bottle of Notes'. The exhibition had been planned for several years in different venues. Originally it was going to be in Germany, but somehow it hadn't been possible to put together the kind of exhibition that Coosje van Bruggen and I wanted, which had to do with the development of large-scale projects out of notes and sketches. Tony and Terry came to New York and with Coosje they assembled the show which eventually opened at the Sunderland Arts Centre, of which Tony was then the director. That was in 1988.

In the course of assembling that exhibition, the idea of large-scale work somewhere in the North came up. I met with Tony and Les Hooper and Peter Davies and talked about sites. One potential site had been in Newcastle, as part of the Gateshead Festival which took place the following year. Then Middlesbrough was suggested to us, that was back in 1986. There were a number of drawings made of the project which were included in the 'Bottle of Notes' exhibition. The idea was to illustrate the whole process, from notes to small studies in three dimensions. This show travelled quite a bit – apart from Sunderland, it went to Leeds, London and Swansea. At the time of the opening, a presentation was made, based on drawings that had been made for the show, to the Middlesbrough City Council in Sunderland. They eventually accepted the sculpture and we drew up a contract and got started.

One of the characteristics of this project has been the amount of change that has happened during the course of the project, not so much to the concept but to the landscape and economy and the state of mind of everybody connected with it. It has taken a long time. In fact, it is probably the second longest project we have been involved with – I think the one in Cleveland, Ohio, was the longest.

PB *Maybe there is a jinx on Cleveland?*

CO It's an interesting coincidence. When the announcements went out in America, everybody thought it was another sculpture in Ohio.

PB *Where was the work fabricated?*

CO We started first in a shipyard in Newcastle, later abandoned. We were told that it would somehow help companies there to build artworks instead of ships. We doubted that, but it was a nice environment, especially to build something that was as nautical in concept as the *Bottle of Notes*. It was a perfect artwork to build in a shipyard.

Though it started out in Newcastle, it has been a long story of moving from factory to factory. One idea was to use the sculpture as part of an apprentice programme, but of course there wasn't enough work and the technology was really gone – quality had fallen to rather a low level. This was about two years into the fabrication.

Coosje and I could see that if this piece was to be realised at all, the technology had to be of a much higher standard because if the piece wasn't very precise it just wouldn't work at all. It had to be very crisp and since it is made out of three-quarter-inch steel it was very difficult to cut. Ideally you would use a laser cutter, but the problem was that laser cutting has to take place on a flat surface, but it would have been difficult to cut the pattern for the bottle out first and then try to fit it into three-dimensional curves. The only solution was to make the whole bottle in steel and then cut it. The problem then was how to get these precise edges. They found the laser technology in Sheffield, where the templates were cut out of masonite. After we had okayed them, they were nailed to the bottle, which had been completed in solid form, and then they had a very expert plasma cutter do the job. This took a long time. During the course of production, other obstacles arose: the company went bankrupt, the company which had taken over the project also went bankrupt, then the next company was forced to close down the factory so that asbestos could be removed.

PB *This saga sounds like a brief history of the decline of Britain as an industrial nation.*

CO Yes. We began to feel that way because every time we went there, we had to have discussions on the current state of affairs, so we felt that this project was really quite integrated into what was going on there. Everybody connected with us wanted to push on and get it done. After it was cut out, it was fairly easy to complete it. A lot of filling was necessary in order to smooth the surfaces and get the edges as crisp as we wanted. Then the 'inside' was fitted into the 'outside' and the *Bottle* was then painted blue and white. Apparently the transport down was very easy because it was all one solid piece.

PB *The site is remarkably close to your original specifications: 'a park situation, preferably with a bit of a slope, perhaps near to some water...'*

CO Yes. It is very close, even if we were thinking of the North Sea!

PB *I had originally imagined a 'rougher', less 'municipal' site.*

CO It was. In the years since the work was first commissioned, they have put up three enormous buildings which weren't there originally, so the surroundings have changed quite a bit. The landscape design already included the trees, the wall and the waterfall, so when we looked at it, we felt that we really had no place to go – it seemed like the whole place had been designed without us. There followed a period of looking at different ways of getting into this landscape scheme. It was really difficult because what we really wanted was the site at the head of the stairs, where it stands now, which meant that we had to remove the existing water fountain. At considerable expense, flag poles were removed, seats and a lamppost – the co-operation from the City Council was exemplary, compared with some of our past experiences. In other words, they changed the landscape to accommodate the sculpture.

PB *If you walk around the corner of the Law Courts you can see the famous Transporter Bridge, also painted blue and white, which acts like a visual 'echo'. It is a pity that it is not visible from the site.*

CO That's true since it was involved in the original iconography but, if the *Bottle* had been placed down at that comer of the Law Courts, it would have been too far out of the range of activities of the area.

PB *But originally that had been in your mind?*

CO That had been considered, yes. The Transporter Bridge was more visible at the beginning. But if they can just complete the west side of the site – I think they have plans for an arts centre, or an extension of the library – I think they will have a rather great complex. I am not crazy about the architecture but I think with the *Bottle* there, it will work as a park. I believe it is in very good scale to the surroundings.

It is just the right height and works well with the church, the tower and the Town Hall and it is also reflected in the water on the other side.

PB *Of course being open in structure, like* Batcolumn, *1977, it doesn't dominate its surroundings.*

CO Right. Actually 12 tons of steel were removed, the present eight-and-a-half tons is what remained after the templates were cut out. One of the things I have always felt about doing sculpture on a large scale is that you have to open it up, have to make it light. Actually, when you look at this sculpture you don't really see the steel, you don't even think of what it is made out of. When the wind is blowing through it, it looks very light against the blue and white sky. Besides the iconography that we bring to a situation, there is the iconography that we hope the sculpture will pick up in the site. For instance, when I walked around the site, I realised that there is quite a bit of blue and white in the buildings surrounding it and that the colour of the buildings behind it is similar to the dark brown of the cork.

PB *That is a change from the ochre colour of the cork in the original drawing.*

CO Yes. The colour was changed because we felt that it would stand out very strongly against the sky.

PB *You once said, in reference to Picasso's Chicago sculpture, that he ignored all the possible inspirations related to the site brought to him by admirers. Your own procedure is very different from that.*

CO Yes, I can think of several sculptures like that, for instance, the Miró, also in Chicago, where the sculptor has simply picked something that he thinks would make a good sculpture enlarged. In the case of Picasso, he didn't have anything to do with the enlargement, it was done by the architects who selected it. Coosje and I feel that that is not the way we want to work. We want to make work directly for the site in terms of materials, iconography and scale. Of course enlarging does come into the process – we start with a certain kind of model, but the model is made in anticipation of the enlarged work so that its scale is part of the thinking from the very beginning. When we came to Middlesbrough we collected what we could with our eyes and from reading and also what people told us: it was an industrial city, a lot of heavy industry, big chemical plants etc with very little sculpture or art in evidence. But it did have Captain Cook – they have a model of his ship in the local mall. We often think about that period in history where western explorers sailed into the Pacific and contaminated paradise. I guess Captain Cook was one of the people who had better motives – he took along artists and scientists and made an attempt to enlarge knowledge and art. Also, he could be related to another 'hero' of mine, Gulliver – also of that time – and to another fictional mariner stranded on an island, Robinson Crusoe, who had inspired an earlier work, the *Crusoe Umbrella* of 1979 in Des Moines. So it's a sort of mythology that appeals to us. The first version of the sculpture was a pocket, a hanging pocket – *Gulliver's Pocket* – full of objects that had been discovered by the Lilliputians. The pocket had to be transparent, so we thought of a cargo net or something like that in which the objects could be contained. We had worked with open structures before – you mentioned *Batcolumn* – in which a very solid object was made more like a rising balloon by letting the air into it. We continued to work with this idea of openness. I can't remember all the steps, but there are some drawings which showed how one day the idea of a note in a bottle expanded to become the bottle itself.

PB *What struck me about the* Bottle of Notes *is that, unlike most of your work which is drawn from a 'lexicon of forms' which has been with you for a very long time, the bottles seem to be a new addition to the lexicon, although I do remember seeing an illustration of a watercolour study of a bottle you did in the late fifties.*

CO That's true, there is a watercolour drawing of a similar shape and there have been bottles in the work but not specifically like this. The bottle has frequently appeared in art but I have never used a bottle before. So it is a new concept, but bottles are certainly part of our household because we drink a lot of Evian so that may have had an influence! The shape of the *Bottle* really comes from bottles with ships in. Bottles are basically containers, they are really not very much in themselves and that's why it has to be a bottle of something.

PB *Unless, perhaps, in the case of a Coca-Cola bottle?*

CO That's true, the Coca-Cola bottle has a particular identity, though I've never used one in my work. *Bottle of Notes* is a kind of a pun in English, it's obviously a bottle that is made out of notes. So the sketches began of a bottle which was made by the thing it contained.

PB *The use of text in this work makes it very different from your earlier work.*

CO We feel that this sculpture has a depth to it, a narrative – you have to find out more about it. The text leads you into other territory.

Whenever I think of French history I think about art but when I think of British history I always think of literature, so for me it is very appropriate that the sculpture should be a 'writing' sculpture.

PB *How did you choose the two texts, the outside text: 'we had every advantage we could desire in observing the whole of the passage of the planet Venus over the sun's disk', and the inside text: 'I like to remember seagulls in full flight gliding over the ring of canals'?*

CO The choice of the outside text was Coosje's. I went out and bought a copy of Cook's journals and Coosje read it and picked this text. In retrospect, it seems the perfect text because it deals with an eclipse and that's what the sculpture is doing constantly: as you walk around it so it appears to move, parts appear to move. The identification of the sun and Venus, with male and female, may not have been part of it originally but that certainly is a part of it now. Somehow, things happen coincidentally – you have known about them without really having known about them. I chose the inside text. Coosje presented me with a number of texts selected from her own writings, and I chose that one. The outside text is in my handwriting, so I am masquerading as Captain Cook, and the inside text is in Coosje's handwriting, which is enlarged from the prose-poem I chose. One of the issues of the sculpture is whether the female text inside is actually trapped by the male text outside, or coexists with it. We like to think that they interrelate. It is like several of the sculptures which we have done which are a direct symbolic statement about collaboration, like the *Spoonbridge and Cherry* for Minneapolis. Of course this sculpture, like all the sculpture, has a personal point otherwise we feel it really wouldn't be art. At the same time, there is a public element and the interrelation between the two. We hope that the public component will develop and that Middlesbrough will develop its own mythology by thinking about what the sculpture means.

PB *How did the collaboration between you begin? Was it gradual or was it a conscious decision for you to collaborate?*

CO It was both in a sense. Our first work together was on *Giant Trowel* which originated in 1971 for Sonsbeek – Coosje was one of the editors of the catalogue. After the exhibition, the piece was placed in the Kröller-Müller Museum. When we got together in 1976, one of the first things we did was to relocate, restore and repaint *Giant Trowel*. Coosje suggested the colour and the site in the garden of the Kröller-Müller Museum. That was our first collaboration and it came about in a very natural way. When we lived in Deventer in 1976–77, we worked together on the *Giant Pool Balls* for Münster. Again it was just a very natural thing to do. When we moved to America in 1978, we became more conscious about it and we decided to devote our time to large-scale projects – that term is Coosje's – rather than to continue working within the gallery system where the works we made disappear and are seen by only a very small audience. *Flashlight*, which was made in 1981 for Las Vegas, was the first piece that we signed together (there were some pieces that we had signed individually). After that we co-signed. We have done about 28 large-scale projects together.

PB *How would you define the difference between the large-scale projects and the earlier 'proposed colossal monuments' of the sixties?*

CO Well, the difference of course is that one is a fantasy and the other is what we call feasible. The difference is to do with scale and gravity – you disregard gravity when you are thinking along fantastic lines. Also, they are not thought through so much. They are more like epiphanies, they are like brief poems about a place. They are not tangible. Whenever they were turned into models they seemed to lose their existence. They were more like ideas. You might say they were like a collective illusion to persuade people that this thing actually existed somewhere in the city – not that anyone would ever be likely to see it. Nowadays everybody travels so much, but my concept was that someone living in India, say, would read about this 300-foot teddy bear in New York and say 'of course it exists!'. They were in the realm of fantasy, which is an important realm for me.

PB *Did it ever happen that someone approached you and said, 'this is possible, I would like to see it realised'?*

CO I think it was Gene Baro who originally challenged me to make one of them. He wrote about the early monuments in 1966 and said 'why don't you try to do something?' but of course it seemed so unreal then. It wasn't until the end of the sixties that I came to believe that these things could actually be built. Building large works in steel is not such an old tradition, even Alexander Calder's works, the really large works, are not very old. *Lipstick* was the first feasible work, made by the Lippincott factory in New Haven in 1969. That opened up a number of possibilities. Then, at about the same time, the NEA began to award grants to sculptors to make civic projects, so the funding came about at about the same time as the fabrication possibilities and, what had seemed totally impossible two years before, suddenly became possible.

PB *Is there an ideal site and an ideal work that you would like to realise?*

CO I don't think so for myself. I think that we are realistic enough with these projects to wait until the site presents itself and we are also very choosy about the projects we decide to undertake, we don't take everything that comes along. We took on this project because we wanted to do something somewhere other than London, in a landscape that we didn't know. We tend to choose something that is interesting and evocative in relation to what we have done before, yet something different. Our last project, the *Matchcover* for Barcelona for instance, is in a totally different environment.

PB *Speaking of London I, for one, regret that none of the 'Proposed Colossal Monuments' for London were realised in the sixties.*

CO They were extravagant though – even the smallest one that I did at that time, which was the 'hat' for Adlai Stevenson, was not realisable. It would have taken up very little space and been very inexpensive. We actually tried to put it up but I guess it didn't pass some kind of regulations. London is a little bit like New York, it is so filled with objects and buildings and people and things that you hesitate to add something to it. At one point we were going to make something for the Broadgate site, but that fell through. Now, of course, there are new sites down by the river in Docklands, so the situation is very different from what it was in 1966. London has changed so much.

PB *Would you now reconsider London as a site for a large-scale project?*

CO Yes, we certainly would.

Issue 171, November 1993

Willie Doherty

interviewed by Iwona Blazwick

The only good one is a dead one

IWONA BLAZWICK The Only Good One is a Dead One, *from this year, features two video projections, one an image taken from a moving car, the other from one which is stationary. One could be the point of view of a surveillance camera, the other of a stalker.*

WILLIE DOHERTY I wanted to try to understand the notion of the terrorist, especially in light of the media ban that exists here and in the Republic of Ireland. This work tries to reinvent that character by suggesting that it's possible for the perpetrator also to be the victim and the victim to be the perpetrator. The first video could be of a person driving alone and feeling insecure or he could also be looking for someone else. Likewise the second video of the car on the street could be about someone watching or could be someone parked there waiting innocently. It attempts to move between those two positions where you have this character, describing the possibility of knocking at someone's door and shooting them and then thinking about a news report of a similar incident and feeling sorry for the victim. I'm interested in whether the victim or the perpetrator is saying that. Attempts to classify these roles, in somewhere like the North, break down very quickly.

IB *The work also articulates another idea about the victim that is more fundamental than merely being a target.*

WD In some ways it's about empowerment rather than about becoming a victim. I mean that in a personal sense as well as in a broader sense. Having made a conscious decision to continue living in Derry I feel compelled to make work that attempts to address that notion of the victim, to find a way to improve our situation and not become entirely victimised.

IB *The cycle of attack followed by retribution – tit for tat – seems to go through your work, the texts swing from passivity to action, victimhood to aggression.*

WD I think that's present because I am aware of both those feelings, of feeling victimised and also understanding the desire for revenge.

IB *I was interested in your use of the road as a metaphor.*

WD It's an image that is familiar through the road-movie genre. A lot of the images that I've been making attempt to play on those clichés – like the road movie or the horror film. When thinking about what it would be like to be shot or to shoot someone, what we know about that kind of situation is mostly cinematic. Even the photojournalist who goes somewhere like the North comes with these pre-existing images, this kind of baggage.

IB *On the one hand the road movie is a metaphor for freedom, a very American thing about frontierism and making a fresh start. On the other hand because your film is shot at night, your view is closed off, focused only on the border of the road, generating a sense of fear, of scenarios of people being kidnapped, bundled into car boots. It has an incredible resonance, which is both ironic and evocative.*

WD Unlike the road movie where we're going somewhere, this driver is going in circles, constantly coming round the same few roads, and the dialogue is also going in circles – it's a situation that's going nowhere. That kind of reference is particular to the state of the current debate and the availability of language to describe Ireland. But it has wider references to feelings of personal insecurity, fears of being abducted, of being watched and the claustrophobia that induces. Again, this may be the experience of cinema, those kinds of fears and sensations are, in some respects, common.

IB *Another significant aspect of the work is that the viewer is in the driver's seat. You're in this privileged position of being inside the driver's head, seeing through his eyes, thinking his thoughts. In a sense you become the driver, potential killer, potential victim.*

WD Again that's a device, using a hand-held camera has historical references to *cinéma-vérité*, to subjectivity. It's a cliché but it works, it does give you that sensation of being there, of immediacy.

IB *The title* The Only Good One is a Dead One *also has its root in the brutal heroics of the Western or the Safari film, the stock one-liner of colonialism.*

WD I try to generate a resonance outside of the particular situation of Ireland, to find different levels at which that linguistic paralysis can be pitched. Trying to find other metaphors and situations is why I've been looking at cinematic language and the wider uses of reportage, scenes of crimes and how they are framed and lit. A lot of images that I've made without text have been in situations like a darkened alleyway, a piece of waste ground lit by flash, the lower deck of a bridge, again fairly dark. So those images have a clichéd familiarity.

IB *There is also a symbolic cliché between the darkness of the unknown and the light of order, authority and the rational. In a sense your use of flash-lit scenes coincides with myths, of primitivism – the primeval, authentic past and the romanticism embodied by the terrorist – both ironically supported by the terrorists themselves.*

WD I think that in the business of trying to visualise the conflict, Sinn Fein and the Northern Ireland Office often end up using the same vocabulary of images.

IB *Another generic aspect of your photographs of landscape is the spillage of the urban into the countryside through strange dysfunctional spaces like motorway verges, half-abandoned development schemes and crumbling housing estates.*

WD The landscape in Ireland is no longer the kind of rural wilderness that we romantically like to think it is. In the same way the pure notion of the Free State or United Ireland is increasingly becoming a non-attainable fantasy. The homogenised and intact notion of that kind of homeland is equally fragmented and now unavailable.

IB *There seems to be a shift in your work from landscape to the figure or more precisely the voice.*

WD Certainly in the installations. I suppose that's because they stem from my desire to participate in the debate about censorship. I've tried very deliberately to give a voice to what has been unspeakable. In some ways that's a directly political act on my part. I'm not so sure how lively that debate is within Britain but in the Irish context the question of censorship and its effectiveness in the resolution of the conflict is one that's very high on the agenda.

IB *It's a self-fulfilling cycle which is that you deny speech and therefore in a sense the censorship itself is suppressed as an issue.*

WD That was the theory but it doesn't work. After the Shankhill bombing, Gerry Adams made a statement which was reported in all the main radio and television news programmes and the voiceover was done by an actor. Now these synchronised voiceovers are becoming virtually indistinguishable from the real thing so the situation has become absurd.

IB *What is the status of that narrative which this man recounts within the installation? It's not* vérité*?*

WD No, it's also not an attempt to create a character but to destroy one, to create two possibilities for a character but have him so fractured that you're not sure which one is which. Or you might be impelled to throw in your own particular bias, if you want, recreate that character or fill in the gaps for yourself.

IB *So he becomes a kind of cypher?*

WD Yes, literally.

IB *There's a banality, an everydayness, about the experiences the voice describes.*

WD I've deliberately tried to retain anecdotal references because that is how we hear these stories on the news, that a man was sitting at home watching television and suddenly gunmen burst in – and it's told in this matter-of-fact way. This is coupled with often very melodramatic accounts and reconstructions from the actual scene. Alongside this, the Northern Ireland Office has released several propaganda films which feature little dramas about the terrorist. What they do in very gory detail is tell us what will happen to us if we don't support the police. The subtext is that unless we collaborate with the police to fight this unknown terrorist element out there, we're dead. It's interesting that the authorities and the people that are concerned with stopping terrorism are involved in the business of dramatising the terrorist, the victim and what it looks like to be shot. These contributions to the culture of terrorism, and to the picturing of the terrorist, are things that have contributed to this body of work.

IB They're All the Same, *a piece you showed in London last year, seems to touch on the same issues.*

WD Again, this was an attempt to give a voice to a face which was that of a 'convicted terrorist'. The work started from seeing the newspaper story about a person who had escaped from Brixton prison. I thought that the face was at odds with that image of the crazed, escaped terrorist. It looked more introspective. I started to look at what motivated someone to become involved in a terrorist campaign. I proposed that motivation through reference to the landscape, the nation or the home. So the more romantic references to the landscape act as clues to his motives, while the more self-referential parts of the text are full of self-doubt. On one hand he describes himself as being ruthless and cruel and on the other as being honest and having integrity. Those are the two extremes of what we understand the terrorist to be, this kind of crazed psychopath and someone who is also driven by conviction. But I think those are both parts of the same understanding, the same cliché. If we fail to understand the political motivation of organisations like the IRA and the UVF then we become completely victimised because we have no means of negotiating with these people. Again, this goes back to the question of censorship and the inability to have this debate. Our only comprehension is that they're a bunch of crazies who happen to come from somewhere called Ireland that seems to be in a state of chaos that is without any apparent resolution. I'm thinking here directly of people in Britain for whom events like the bomb in Warrington become increasingly unfathomable. People don't understand why this happens and have no means of engaging with it in a way that could produce an end to this situation.

IB *Your work seems to be continually examining issues around history and memory and the histories that each group claims for itself.*

WD The work I recently made in Dublin, *30 January 1972*, was in some ways directly about that process of how memory and history work, how events become historicised. I didn't want a direct reference to Bloody Sunday in the title but I wanted to use it as a model, one of many traumatic situations in the recent history of the North, but also as an event after which things were never quite the same. Some political commentators have noted that Bloody Sunday was the single most important event to shape the last 20 years of Irish history and the single biggest recruitment agent for the IRA. For a lot of people in Derry it's unfinished business in that the 13 people who were shot on the day have never been declared innocent by the British government. Until that happens I think Bloody Sunday will continue to get in the way of a resolution between the Irish Nationalists and the British. All those issues have become part of the very distorted picture of the event itself. I was interested in how people who were obviously too young to have been there know about it through various channels, through older relatives, TV documentaries and photographs etc.

IB *This process of myth-making and of making monuments to very recent events, such as the murals painted by all factions on the sides of houses, is also very rapid.*

WD In *30 January 1972* I used two images: one from a television documentary of the event and the other a photograph of one of the places today. I wanted to look at that gap. There is a similar analogy in the soundtrack that accompanies these images which is made up of a kind of a vox pop that I did on one of the streets where Bloody Sunday actually happened. I asked passers-by if they had been there on the day, if there was any particular part of the series of events that they could remember and were prepared to talk about, and if they hadn't been there, if there was a photographic or televised image that they could remember. One of the more rewarding aspects of making this work was that for some people it was the first time they had been asked to contribute to a body of evidence about this event. It's another example of a disenfranchised voice that I was allowing to speak through showing a work.

IB *Underlying these ricocheting narratives lie questions of identity: subjective, mediatised, sectarian, national.*

WD I think the basis of my work is in language where most of these issues are inscribed, those very simple and often overlooked twists of language, those readjustments and definitions which have much wider ramifications. Another watershed in recent Irish history happened in the late seventies when special category status was removed and Republican and Loyalist prisoners were criminalised. At that point it became linguistically possible to refer to both prisoners not as prisoners-of-war but as criminals and terrorists. I think that shift in emphasis is incredibly significant in the current debate about Ireland and how the language we have available to describe that debate has been framed and formed. I'm attempting to renegotiate that kind of framing. That seems to me to be the single most important contribution that I could make. The constructed nature of the language available is all we have at the moment. We don't have the new words yet to describe the other possibilities. So the conclusion is that the other possibilities don't exist. Actually it's just that the words and the pictures are not there – but maybe they can be reinvented.

Issue 172, December-January 1993–94

Jimmie Durham

interviewed by Mark Gisbourne

I want to stay full of rage

MARK GISBOURNE *In a work like* Caliban, *1992, as with others in your ICA exhibition, one notices a sense of deferred identification or personal displacement. Is this what you intended?*

JIMMIE DURHAM In a certain way I did. I did these works specifically for New York last year and I was trying to figure out how I might address a certain situation with what are called minority artists in New York, without anyone knowing that I was doing it unless they wanted to know.

As 'minority artists' we feel a need to use art to search for our identity, which is a strange mindset to me. It seems terribly self-indulgent and goes nowhere, it seems like the most crass way of presenting some fictional sense of self to the public and, if the public believes it, it can somehow come to be understood to be yourself. It is as though you are inventing a human self and hoping to get paid for it. And it worked so well in the beginning – in the late seventies and early eighties, I don't remember – that it became the law whereby all minority artists had to do work that is primarily about our identity.

MG *Are you thinking of people like Jean-Michel Basquiat?*

JD I exclude Basquiat because there was a kind of integration in his work that I don't see much after him. Afterwards we get kind of instructional, kind of confrontational: 'This is to be my identity and it's not yours, ha ha!'

MG *Do you mean a territorial sense of identity and culture?*

JD Yes, that is precisely it.

MG *Caliban, as the half-man, half-beast says, 'You taught me your language and my profit on it is, I know how to curse. The red plague rid you for learning me your language.' Do you feel that contact with the now prevailing white hegemony has done this to Native Americans?*

JD Very much so and at the same time Shakespeare has Caliban kind of liking to say that. There are always two edges to him, that is the way Shakespeare wrote, I suppose.

MC *Though I know that you have retracted much of your famous 1974 essay, 'American Indian Culture', what has remained valid from what you said at that time?*

JD I have to explain a little bit of history about it. I was trying not to be a Marxist but to use what used to be called Marxist thought, and I was doing that because I had just before that moved to Geneva and while there I met a bunch of people who were in Geneva at the UN, activists from the African countries that were just getting free, and they naturally were all Marxists. These people were all my teachers, most of them much younger than me, very many of them had been to Oxford and they had an education that I didn't have. They explained the world to me in a way that I couldn't explain it before. I used to say to them at the time that the problem with Marxism is the 'ism'. You have to believe a set of rules which puts a limit on things and why should we have to live with limits? They would always answer dogmatically that everyone has an ideology and I did not have any argument for that, for I want my ideology to be called 'I hope I don't have an ideology'. At least I can pretend some freedom of thought. But I think what is still important to me from that paper is trying to make an analysis of exactly the way that white English works against us. Because English is not just a language, it is a politics and a form of colonisation – it's really a form of politics.

MC *Has that situation altered much since the seventies?*

JD I think that maybe it will change in the US, but as yet it has not changed. I think what has happened instead is that a language of multiculturalism has been developed as a new way of consuming other cultures more thoroughly than they were consumed before. But there is something more to think about here, for American white kids speak the street slang of American black kids – very artificially, consciously – and they speak it to be hip or with it. That is to say, they consume someone else's attempt to free English for themselves, and the way white kids take it back as though they could somehow own that black English.

MC *In the performance video that accompanies the exhibition you mediate a sense of alienation by interviewing yourself both in the first and second person, the 'I' and the 'you', only to emerge as yet a third person, the 'he' – Jimmie Durham. It reminds me of Max Ernst who invariably referred to himself in the third person. Is there any sort of connection there?*

JD I hadn't thought of it before but I am sure there must be, because artists live with art history whether we want to or not, it becomes assimilated and we forget. I think of Jimmie Durham as a public character, I have another name that is my private name. But I don't really think of myself as that name either and there is in any case a problem of being an artist which is that you do something for a public, and must do it totally privately, and then put it out totally publicly, free of your privacy.

MC *Do you feel that you have to keep your private name as a way of holding something back?*

JD Yes, that's the idea. If someone knows your real name they have a great power over you, they can say bad things about you that become true or more dangerous because they know some reality about you.

MC *If you looked at western art in this century, who would you see yourself identifying with? There are elements that have surrealist and imaginist associations.*

JD It's exactly that they put a value on the imagination and the will to imagine. I also love Marcel Duchamp – I love his love of objects and his love of the sensuality of objects, and the beauty of objects. Though people have explained to me that I have completely misunderstood Duchamp.

MC *Well, maybe you have and maybe you haven't, but I think that you share an interest in the powers most generally described as alchemical, and in notions of transmutation. He's a magus figure in that sense. It is hard to know whether Duchamp loved anything, he is such a strange fish, in a way that Joseph Beuys isn't. And Beuys is someone else I might think of in relation to your work, if not in the materials or objects he uses, but in a sense of a certain view of the imagination. Do you like Beuys's work?*

JD It is often so problematic for me, because it's kind of self-consciously, or Germanically, distancing.

MC *Thinking about the video, does non-linear narrative as white anthropologists called it, or what surrealists called magical thinking, function as a subversive strategy in your work, or is it an extension of your nature and how you see the world?*

JD That's complicated. I imagine I think basically the same as I used to think when I was a child. If you make something right, or with some sort of integrity – in a way I can't quite explain – potentially it can be alive, it can have some sort of power. I do not like to use the word power, it is such a silly word, but such as to be some sort of active power.

MG *Inner life?*

JD Yes, that's it.

MG Coelacanth*, the book that accompanies the exhibition and which centres on a hunt for the now extinct coelacanth, is obviously linked to the idea of a form of cultural extinction as the major export of colonialism. This was a position you certainly held 20 years ago. Do you still believe that?*

JD Probably, but not in the same way. I don't want to imagine that I have gotten softer or wiser, things we seem to get as we get older. I don't want to get older in that sense, I want to stay full of rage.

MG *Yet your work is ironic and witty, whereas before, in your writings, there was a sort of burning anger, a sort of 'in your face' type anger.*

JD I suppose when you stack up a number of years, a whole bunch of experiences, the experiences get to be not so heavy because there are so many they can't possibly maintain their weight. When you see so many of your friends die and certain things didn't get resolved between them there is something very funny about it. But there is also a kind of fineness. There is something about death that is so completely out of the question.

MG *Although you come from a Native American background, I don't feel that your work is particularly totemic or fetishistic in the conventional sense.*

JD I don't think so at all. People read it that way because they have already heard that I am Cherokee. If they had heard that I was German, they would read it with a different set of screens.

MG *Do you feel in any way constrained by the fact that the language that accompanies so much of your work is the language of appropriation, white man's English?*

JD I kind of like it actually. It's fun. I live in Mexico now and I have a great frustration with the Spanish language, because in Spanish there is no etymological dictionary. The Spanish just don't think that way. The most they are willing to say is that this word comes from Greek or that from Latin and nothing more – never that this word comes from Arabic, or this is a Hebrew word, nothing of that. I always need to know the whole life of a language as much as I can.

MG *Is that a compensatory feeling, being a Native American, a displaced person – decentred?*

JD Yes, it could possibly be that.

MG *A yearning for the root of something?*

JD Yes, certainly.

MG *Why have you chosen to live in Mexico?*

JD The first practical reason was that I was living in New York and I could not afford it. I had no place to work and I was getting stupider in the New York sense of always being so busy – you think that being busy amounts to smartness, to a sense of sophistication – and it wasn't. But really I had no more money to live there, I just couldn't do it, and I was not willing to live anywhere else in the US, except New York. What I like about New York is that it hates the US, and the US hates New York, it's like an immigrant ship that pulled in. Manhattan is like a ship that does not want to come into port.

MG *I can understand that, but again New York is very violent.*

JD It's very violent in the sense that it is American, but it is the safest city – it has the lowest crime rate. It's terrible isn't it that Detroit and Houston are competing as the murder capital of the country. And then, I have always loved Mexico and have always felt that there was potentially something that I could do in Mexico, but now I begin to think probably not. But there are so many Indians in Mexico, you shall not deny us there, you cannot even say that you haven't met a good one.

MG *Would you say something about the displacement of Native American culture? Where is it at? Where are the Native Americans now? Are they an extinct people? Are they consigned to history?*

JD This is a point that we are now beginning to think about – that is, myself and a crowd of my friends, but it will I think soon be on the Indian agenda. Firstly, how can we think of ourselves and our history instead of someone else's given narrative? That sounds like just a little first step but over the past ten years we have been talking about 'who we might have been'. Who could we possibly have been before Columbus, before the Pilgrim Fathers and how would we be able to know who we were? We have now come to the conclusion that we were probably pretty much normal human beings, much like other human beings. This is a sort of a revolutionary beginning for us because of this 'noble savage' thing. Going from there, we discuss who are we now – if we were not anyone special at any given point in history, if we are not who they say we are. We refuse to try to be anyone's idea of who we are. How would we then be able to survive as communities and, if we don't want to have a set idea of who we are, then what sort of survival?

MG *How does one get through the layers – three or four hundred years or so of accretion that has lain on you like cement?*

JD I think it might be possible in the same way that I was talking about earlier. You can't always be full of rage because the experiences become increasingly light, because you have so many of them. It might work for us in the same way, for now we begin to joke about how much television we watch on the Reservation. In a few years we might find a way to think about being Indian in the world without any definition, without any given set of things that one does.

MG *I do not see your art as just an exposition of the cultural and historical experience of the Cherokee Nation – there seems something even bigger at stake, that is to say, the nature of 'difference' and 'otherness' itself. How it functions alongside a dominant consumer materialism in our age. It is as if the free imagination itself is also at stake, is that what you feel?*

JD I don't want to do work that has as its purpose the exclusion of someone or something. How might that happen? That is a more complex problem now than we wish it to be, for art always has the signs of art. Even now, especially in places like Los Angeles, there is a new sign of art that is called 'no sign of art here', and it is of course a very recognisable sign of art as the California 'Funky' School. So it's always a kind of a trap.

MG *You mean a kind of anti-art? But that's a position as old as Modernism itself!*

JD Yes, anti-art is just a way in. Is this art? It's always kind of art. How does one do something that is not expected? That's the problem that I work on, how to do something that people do not expect and that I also don't expect.

MG *You installed the works in the ICA space yourself, are you happy with how it has worked out?*

JD Yes, I am very pleased with the look of it, it looks to me like a dispersed Louise Nevelson work. It is a very funny space that looks like it might be a space in Bedlam. In pictures of Bedlam you see a big room full of suffering people who are not doing the right things.

MG *Is it a function of the animistic imagination in your work in the Native*

American sense or is this animistic-cum-animal crossover world intended to be something more in works like Rabbit, *1990,* The Squirrel *and* Armadillo, *both of 1991?*

JD I often think about a division that is the classical division in western philosophy and culture: the physical versus the mental, the ideal versus the material, intellectual versus sensual. What I am trying to work out is my own theory so that I will not feel so stupid, because I always embarrass myself being unable to make the division. Maybe I am trying with my work to challenge the dichotomy that these things are physical and those things are mental, and that you cannot combine the two.

MC *What sort of response would you hope for from the show here? What can we learn in our exclusionary practices of minorities both in the art world and in culture generally?*

JD To look at the work without any expectations. To look at the work sensually and intellectually without the screens and without being so quick to form a conclusion. Everyone today wants to find an answer to the problem and then move on to the next problem.

MC *In a short while after this interview you are going to give a performance, would you talk about what performance means to you?*

JD It came about originally by accident. I started doing theatre work before I started with visual art – that is before I started doing visual art that I defined as visual art. I was making things since I was a child but I didn't think of it as art – just making things. But when I got out into the world I met up with some theatre people and started doing theatre with them. My performances began as theatre-based, but then I started using objects and looking at theatre itself as a kind of public display of something, and as a public display of something – it tends to be communication. I don't intend communication as in conversation. I want to be more complex, more ambiguous, a communication without an answer.

MC *Yet performance remains only in the memory, and/or in the form of documentation of the event, it is therefore the most immaterial of phenomena and perhaps, more imaginative because of it. How would you ideally like your performances to be seen and experienced?*

JD Ideally, I would like people to be something like fascinated, intellectually engaged, emotionally engaged – very much so – and then at the end to be completely puzzled. To say what was that? What happened? What was that about? To go home thinking about it, keeping the ephemeral quality of the performance itself.

MG *My feeling about your work is that of an unarrested imagination, constantly moving backwards and forwards through time. What do you feel about time, as such, and the power of non-linear imagination enabling us to move more freely?*

JD I think there is no time. I think it's a funny invention. There is duration of things. If a piece of history of a people doesn't get resolved, it's not history in the sense of historical conflicts, it's the present. So, when I was growing up I heard stories of The Trail of Tears and our removal as though they were current. When my grandmother told the stories she told them as if they had happened to her and of course they had not, but of course they had happened to her because she felt them.

MG *As part of a people's collective memory?*

JD Yes, exactly. When something gets resolved then it's the past. Until it's resolved then it is the present, it's always in the present.

Issue 173, February 1994

Mark Wallinger

interviewed by Paul Bonaventura

A Real Work of Art

PAUL BONAVENTURA *Over the past five or six years you have tended to work with photography and assemblage, but* Capital, *1990, and* Race, Class, Sex, *1992, exhibited together for the first time at the Saatchi Collection last summer, heralded a return to painting. In the 'History Paintings' of the mid to late eighties, you employed pastiches of English landscape painting to illuminate the nature of political reality under Margaret Thatcher. How has your approach to the medium altered during the intervening years?*

MARK WALLINGER *Capital* began after I had encountered someone sleeping rough in front of the Bank of England, a pretty ironic image. That series of paintings was very much a response to a whole history of measures which had been brought in throughout the previous decade and which had led to this kind of thing becoming commonplace. Thatcher probably lost precious little sleep over it, but the rise in homelessness came about as a direct consequence of the ways in which her government restricted benefits to teenagers and reduced the provision of mental care within the community. *Capital* was developed to function as a stimulus for some kind of debate about how the homeless are represented. With *Race, Class, Sex*, the starting point was far more personal in that horse racing is very much a passion of mine. The work raises questions about why these particular horses have been chosen as subjects and I would be pleased if that started one thinking about bloodlines and patriarchy. But there is not some puzzle to unravel here or some lesson to be learned as there might have been in one or two of the 'History Paintings'.

PB *Unlike* Capital *the political content of* Race, Class, Sex, *and the related* Fathers and Sons, *1993, seems to reside in the space established between the titles and the images rather than in the images themselves.*

MW That's probably true. I could have called these newer works just by the horses' names because they are specific portraits, but I decided to give them a little nudge by providing them with a more loaded superstructure. I have a very ambivalent attitude towards horse racing and I think that goes for most people who become obsessed with the sport. Thoroughbreds are to be admired on so many different levels and yet they are so vulnerable. They wouldn't have existed unless we had chosen to design them that way, manipulating their natural impulses for our own ends. As the playthings of the wealthy they are inextricably bound up with nobility and privilege. They can therefore be seen to function as stand-ins for some kind of commentary on the class structure of British society.

PB *I see little moderation between* Capital, Race, Class, Sex *and* Fathers and Sons *in terms of political intent, but the ways in which that intent has been projected has been tempered. Your approach is more subtle now, more ambiguous, but I still have the impression that you retain a somewhat questioning attitude towards the medium.*

MW That's quite true. I do have this strange and slightly uncomfortable relationship with it. I think that painting probably died in the early sixties, but for some reason we remain in its thrall. To make paintings is a primitivist repudiation of a critique of society as a reified image which sees all of us being sucked in as pixels on a VDU. They are done by hand, they take a certain amount of time to complete, they require a degree of skill, they generate a different kind of attention span. With the 'History Paintings' and, to a lesser extent, with *Capital*, one knew that one was looking at pastiche elements and these were used in ways which weren't a million miles away from the ways in which elements are used in photomontage and assemblage. Pastiche carries with it not just a reference to a particular time or lifestyle, but also the half-lives of aspirations of another age. This generates a certain pathos which is not invoked by *Race, Class, Sex* and *Fathers and Sons*.

PB *It sounds to me as though your relationship to painting is not so far removed from your relationship to horse racing. You are excited by it, but maintain an active scepticism.*

MW I imagine you're right. There's still a bit of magic left in painting and I wouldn't like to overstate my scepticism. I wouldn't be able to paint at all if I was distanced from each single brushstroke.

PB *Most racing art remains essentially naturalistic in style and romantic in its inspiration and has moved far away from the mainstream of Modernism. What is it that attracts you to a subject which few other vanguard artists would think of addressing?*

MW Some of my fondest recollections are of certain horses and certain races. I can recall Arkle's first Cheltenham Gold Cup and in 1986, when Dawn Run won, I had to take myself around to the casualty department of my local hospital with heart palpitations. One day I was looking through this book of stallions and suddenly realised that here was something which would provide me with rich material for work. By then I had begun to think of one or two other ways in which I could tap into the industry because apart from the animals themselves, of course, there's the whole area of bookmaking, representative of the purest expression of capitalism. Money plays a spiritual role in racing representing the possibility of transmutation. In gambling on horses nothing is bought or sold or exchanged other than people's hopes. I knew then that a lot of work would come out of this interest and at no point would it feel artificially generated. It was in me all the while. Plus I could go to racing and actually kid myself that I was doing research.

PB *Even allowing for their seemingly defiant postures, the figures in* Capital *and their counterparts in* Race, Class, Sex *and* Fathers and Sons *have had their wills subdued by politicians in the first instance and by trainers in the second. In* Capital *the figures bear mute testimony to the systematic manner in which certain groups became steadily disenfranchised throughout the 1980s. The canvases in this series function both as portraits of a sort, with your own friends as the models, and as political commentaries on the schizophrenic state of British society. Could the equine series be read in a similar way?*

MW The thing about *Race, Class, Sex* and *Fathers and Sons* is that they are not about prescribing a specific political agenda. One could simply read them as a bloodstock agent might for, after all, the horses are depicted just as they appear in the stud book. Their conformation as athletes can be assumed, but their power as progenitors of athleticism is a matter of conjecture. Their sexuality is not as obvious as it could be. The horses are tethered and all are wearing bridles so there's a fetishistic thing going on there too. I wouldn't want to press anyone reading too strongly.

These animals are clearly under the control of some human agent out of frame, and I like the way in which the lead rein provides a little comment on the figure/ground relationship. But there is none of the moral indignation here which fuelled *Capital*.

PB *The horses which you have chosen to picture come from the highest ranks of the equine nobility and find their echo in the sorts of individuals whose portraits grace the walls of homes up and down the country. In interviews elsewhere, you have commented at length on the British obsession with pedigree and provenance.*

MW After *Race, Class, Sex*, I wanted to do the smaller *Fathers and Sons* because I thought they might be humorous, but I am fascinated by racing's obsession with breeding. Although the area is regarded as a quasi-science, a lot of very well-bred horses aren't particularly good. The qualities of a racehorse are traditionally deemed to derive from its sire, but I'm not so sure that this is always the case. A good mare may keep going for up to 15 seasons, but that only means 15 offspring rather than the hundreds which a stallion is capable of producing over the same period.

PB *So racing's dominant patriarchy might be predicated upon quantity rather than quality?*

MW Yes, and it was for this reason that I chose to illustrate fathers and sons rather than mothers and sons or mothers and daughters. Like *Race, Class, Sex*, the paintings are portraits in the accepted sense of the word and so it is very difficult not to see them both as animals and as emblems of specific emotional and philosophical states. The viewer is invited to compare the similarities and differences between generations. I have stacked the fathers above the sons to indicate lines of succession, and what I find both funny and disturbing about the series is the degree of anthropomorphism with which one invests the subjects. A dumb sort of oedipal psychological interplay is enacted between the father above and the son below. Maybe my unease in all of this stems from the implications of characteristics being handed down and improved upon generation by generation. I am disturbed by the thought that I am a predetermined biological product.

PB *Another series of canvases which you have recently completed began with the registration of your racing colours with the Jockey Club.*

MW The piece is called *Brown's* and depicts the racing colours of 42 people with the surname Brown. Any owner of a racehorse in this country has to register his or her colours with the Jockey Club and there are currently 14,000 on record so it's quite difficult coming up with anything strikingly original. The *Benson & Hedges Book of Racing Colours* shows them all in diagrammatic form and each looks like the costume change for an invisible man. Because jockey silks are referred to as colours there is a nice poetic tie-in with the act of painting. If you mix up all the colours on a palette you end up with brown. I enjoy the idea that the decisions about colour and design have been determined by others and that the flipping back and forth from decoration to denotation is signalled by a single possessive apostrophe. In registering my own colours I have also achieved a more fanatical withdrawal into my own obsession. It took me a long time to choose the colours which would represent me for the rest of my life.

PB *Why then did you choose the green, violet and white of the Suffragette Movement?*

MW I felt that the most subversive act in this rigidly patriarchal world would be to choose colours which were linked historically with the Women's Movement. In 1913 Emily Davison threw herself under and brought down the King's horse in the Epsom Derby. Davison and the King's jockey, Herbert Jones, both lay unconscious on the turf for a while so in a way these colours are an amalgam of those two figures who just happened to coincide at a particular historical moment. While being carried away, Davison was found to be sporting the Suffragette colours. She became a martyr, Jones was largely forgotten and the newspapers of the day led with the steward's enquiry into the result of the race. I visited Tattenham Corner last summer wearing make-up and sporting my own colours in order to acknowledge the significance of that event. The photograph which ensued is called *Self-Portait as Emily Davison*.

PB *Towards the end of last year, your 'fanatical withdrawal' into your own obsession achieved its definitive manifestation when you asked the Newmarket trainer Sir Mark Prescott to purchase a horse for you. The two-year-old filly has been christened* A Real Work of Art *and will have its first run on the flat towards the end of April.*

MW To buy a horse myself and to nominate it as an artwork seemed like the only logical conclusion to everything which had gone before. I like to think of it as a self-inflicted dare. Regardless of its worth as an artwork or as an idea, having *A Real Work of Art* means having the courage of my own convictions.

PB *The cost of the horse was achieved through sales of a commercially produced equestrian figurine depicting* A Real Work of Art *with the jockey in your silks. Its first year's training fees are being met by a consortium of collectors, curators, agencies and gallery owners. Were such partnerships simply expedient or do you welcome the expansion of meaning which comes into play alongside these art-based syndicates?*

MW Things developed as they did in order to get the project off the drawing board, but I do feel that the range of activities represented in the partnerships reflects the kinds of compromises which underpin most dealings in the art world. All I really desire is for my name to appear on the race card, to have my name in brackets after the name of a thoroughbred. That's the thing which fascinates me aesthetically. My greatest hope is that this project will come to take on a life of its own, that it will develop its own discourse through the reactions of the public and the press and through the build-up of the filly's form. The racing papers will ensure that *A Real Work of Art* will come to have significance for thousands of punters up and down the country. Every move this animal makes will be scrutinised in a way which no other artwork could ever hope to be. Her career will produce a burgeoning archive of data and recordings, photographs and videos, all attempting to define her – all paradoxically rendering her as a mediated image, as an abstraction. Her reality will be consumed by the different criteria of meaning which are already in place to receive her.

PB *Are you in any way conscious of trying to increase the popular appeal of contemporary art by choosing to work in an area which can touch upon the lives of so many people?*

MW To make such a large claim would be absurd. What appeals to me about this piece is that it represents the ultimate expression of ideas which have dominated my artistic thinking over the past two years. To have this horse, whose prospects are completely unpredictable and whose activities are totally beyond my control, says something about how far one can go in choosing to annex an object from quotidian reality as a work of art, about how far one can reinvigorate an artistic practice which has such a rich tradition. Racing has an extraordinary aesthetic frisson for me which covers everything from the gambling to the magical identification with the animal on which your money rides to the sheer beauty of the thoroughbred. I find it difficult to separate out these qualities and refuse to think of this project simply in dry conceptual terms.

PB *The decision to pluck a thoroughbred from the world of racing and to confer on it the status attached to a fine art object finds its source in Duchamp.*

MW This work also brings into play the unique status of the thoroughbred. Racehorses are the most documented species on earth and that's not excluding humanity. Records are available right back to the beginning of the breed and what they show is that the thoroughbred occupies this bizarre dimension somewhere between the culturally determined and the natural. In a way, I suppose, thoroughbreds have no natural state at all. In choosing a racehorse as the subject of the piece, I am signalling the fact that the thoroughbred is already an aestheticised thing, its whole purpose being to give pleasure to its owners and followers. By choosing a racehorse, I am presenting something for contemplation which functions as a history of aesthetics in microcosm and this is one of the reasons why I decided on the name.

Along with the idea of the artist denoting something as an artwork, there has always been in my work an investigation into the nature of representation, a disjunction between what a work appears to want to say and what is said. Are we talking about reality here or are we talking about artifice? This filly has become so over-determined by my ideas and by the history of her breed, it's questionable whether she could ever be a good enough representation of herself. As with *Race, Class, Sex* and *Fathers and Sons*, the title obviously plays a crucial role. My action brackets the filly as an artwork without altering her in any other way. It extends Duchamp's gesture by returning the nominated object to its rightful home.

In an earlier work, *Fountain* from 1992, I sought to comment on his legacy and how the most radical of gestures return to the mainstream. A lot of contemporary work claims allegiance to the readymade tradition, but there seems to have been an inversion of power inasmuch as it is the institutions and galleries which sanction and give authority to the objects and activities which come under their aegis. So in fact they become deeply conservative gestures reinforcing the power of institutions which decide the value or quality of the work and in which the public are used as dupes to play the game of outrage. But I hope I have achieved something subversive with *A Real Work of Art*. I like to think of her as an equine mole, like Kim Philby, just waiting to defect across to another world.

Issue 175, April 1994

Thomas Struth

interviewed by Mark Gisbourne

Neutral territory

MARK GISBOURNE *When I first saw your architectural photographs I was reminded of the Renaissance notion of the ideal city. However, your view seems to counter this with the real city as a place of dejection – Utopia turned to dystopia, the imperfect from the perfect.*

THOMAS STRUTH I think that a great deal of my architectural work has been concerned with places representing an identical whole – as ideal compositions – giving them an autonomous identity rather than representing them as if they were the sum of broken or fractured parts.

MG *In that sense then your architectural images, although different in tenor, are somewhat like Renaissance perspective projections, except of course yours are real spaces seen through the monocular 'eye' of the camera.*

TS Perspective was for me a way of restricting myself to a certain method which enabled me to compare the streets more easily with each other and to make the process appear scientific, a sort of systematised neutral position.

MG *Does this 'neutral position' really change your sense of control over subjective content? Does it conspicuously minimise your role as the viewer who is taking the photograph?*

TS What it actually does is allow me, as somebody who lives in the city, to keep it at a distance, to study the object without being overwhelmed by the large number of extraneous, uncontrollable phenomena. When I was studying at the Düsseldorf Academy in the mid seventies, it was important for me to find a way to structure my perceptions of the environment. I think it has to do with the psychology of being within something or standing away and really looking at things.

In many ways it is hard to look at this city in its reality. Maybe it was a way of defending myself from exposure to the postwar history of the environment here, because I clearly felt that by inventing or reinventing, or simply by reinvesting this method (which is an old method), in an urban landscape like that of postwar Germany, I could learn something. It seemed appropriate, and was something that I would not probably have thought about in Paris or London.

MG *It was peculiar at first to your Düsseldorf experience, this preference for a 'cool' as opposed to a 'hot' eye.*

TS Yes I think so. I felt that the architectural perspectives or street scenes were similar to the work of Bernd & Hilla Becher, but that importantly my topic – the streets – was a subject that was in fact what most people were exposed to. I had not known the Bechers' work when I started to photograph the streets, but I became very interested in what they do.

MG *Your architectural spaces appear to deny a cultural or social contract. People are not present, or rather, their presence is pointed to only through their absence.*

TS Yes, of course they are present, indirectly. By not showing people I reveal the urban environment as a place where a community expresses its identity. It stresses for me more, as you might say, a general responsibility we share for the social culture that our cities have.

MG *In many ways this aesthetic is tied to the phenomenological issues of the fifties and sixties.*

TS The theme of perception was very interesting because I came from a background of painting. From 1971 to 1975 I painted reduced street scenes with human figures in them which I had retrieved from photos of New York or other cities. I then wanted to take these pictures myself, so around 1974, I walked the streets of Düsseldorf mostly, photographing people. For three years I made a whole series of photographs of people in the streets or in trams but I found that the series was uninformative because the people in the photographs were very distant. They only signified human beings in general.

MG *They were like cyphers?*

TS Yes, like cyphers, signifying only aspects like the fashion of their clothes but nothing more, nothing that really interested me. Then I decided one day that it was, perhaps, more important and practical to get control of the space first and see in what way that might say something about the people who lived in these sites.

MC *What do you understand, as an artist-photographer, by the notion of the social?*

TS I am very much a person of the sixties which means I was raised not long after the war. My whole idea of working has a lot to do with how humans live. How we live, how I live, how humans live together – human collectivity. That is my core value: what it is to be human. That is everything I believe in. I do not believe in current ideas of post-humanity.

MC *So your answer is that the 'social' is analogous to the 'whole' in your photographs.*

TS For me the most important phenomena are those that bring forth changes in societies or in history. These changes used to be noticeable in the physical world immediately. Today this is not so clear anymore. Today's changes through new computers, sundry inventions in gene technology and new technological systems are not as visible as they once were in the street. If I look at my work from the beginning, it is more the idea of trying to establish a kind of material that one can work with for the future, rather than making nostalgic images to record something that later will become lost. For me, what is also interesting is that in most of the photographs that I took in the seventies or early eighties the spaces still look like that today, there is very little that is past. I guess that in 30 years this will still be so. What fascinates me is the sort of insight and information that I receive from the nature of the space, and this has to be the case before I am able to say anything about this space.

MC *Do you want your photographic images to be non-specific, or at least, relatively anonymous architectural spaces?*

TS These spaces are those of a specific place. The everyday streets are in a funny way more truly monumental as witnesses to the everyday life of people. Also, it makes things much easier to read than if I used images of famous sites like the World Trade Center or the Eiffel Tower.

MC *It's an argument that Benjamin Buchloh brings up about your work, the notion of loss or melancholy that touches upon a sense of the picturesque. Is there a sense of loss or of alienation in your environments? You haven't talked about what these buildings do to people. Your images directly touch on institutional power through urban planning. Are the people who live in these buildings victims of that power?*

TS Yes, in part. But I do not like the idea of victims in society, because

I think that for most of the people there is a degree of freedom to decide or to act, in order not to be such a victim.

MC *In what sense does the idea of a 'healthy alienation' that is found in Walter Benjamin's essay on Eugène Atget's topographical views of Paris around 1900 influence you?*

TS The question interests me very much. I don't have an answer as to why it is so impossible to stop certain developments, like the way social housing is presently organised or the way in which the number of rather stupid TV channels increase, which seems to be an unavoidable development of technology. Through the years I have made a series of photographs of very ugly houses in Geneva, in Chicago and elsewhere because this is still a phenomenon which is too much neglected in public debate. Just now I am wondering about the title for the book and catalogue for my ICA show and I am tempted to entitle it *Silence*. I am interested in how we have filled both our psychological and social space with images and information so that there is very little room left for the self.

Everything is being filled up with mediated information, mediated fantasies, mediated role models, mediated models of society, mediated violence and mediated suggestions for solutions, which are in turn no solutions. There is less and less space for the body, and less and less space for realising what we actually want from society. That is something that gives me deep anxiety. Therefore, in general, my work is less about expanding the possibilities of photography than about reinvesting it with a truer perception of things by returning to a simple method, one that photography has had from the beginning of its existence.

MC *How do you defend yourself against Brecht's criticism that a photograph of a building tells you little about what is going on inside it? You would obviously disagree with that.*

TS Yes I do, very much. For I do believe that in photographs like those of the nineteenth-century English photographers or Atget, you can read the motivation of the person who made the image in them – the psychological, emotional or intellectual scaffolding that the person saw in the environment. And there is the matter of how we can retrieve that or read it from the surface of the image. My belief in the psychology of that situation is very strong.

MC *For the maker as the taker of the photograph? Is a successful photograph a cathartic experience, an image drawn out of you?*

TS Well, right now for example, when I am working with my students at Karlsruhe (we are working with the architecture of Karlsruhe), I believe that if I asked five students to take a photograph of the same street or building in the city, one would be able to see which of them was really interested in the street or building and which was not. Why this happens interests me very much. You forget that by now this is clearly accepted in painting, but in photography this level of sophisticated reading remains under disguise. For what matters is how much of yourself you put into your work. If you have a real relationship with a particular building, landscape or person, as in a portrait, it will show in the picture.

MG *You say that you were doing this type of photography before you studied and worked with Bernd & Hilla Becher, yet you share with them the idea of serialisation, of typology and, to some degree, classificatory practices which rely upon likenesses alone. How does your work differ from theirs?*

TS After seeing their work for the first time, I thought the method was wonderful and that it was very well suited to the photographic medium. But for me, the subject-matter was too exotic, too specialised, too far away. I wanted to apply this method to a subject-matter that was more at one with everyday life, which was nearer to my life.

MG *The Bechers' use of typology is old-fashioned, it is rather an encyclopedic, eighteenth-century way of thinking, as though by putting things together because they look alike we can learn some unifying truth about them. It denies complex social interactions that would differ in relation to the classified types of industrial machinery and gable-ended houses that their simple typologies reproduce. Also, they do not so much photograph loss as the lost. Everything photographed is obsolete as a form, or no longer has utility. The images form a nostalgic archive. This is very unlike your work.*

TS Yes, that is true. They have an inability to alter their method anymore. In the beginning, I was interested in the idea of making a series of works comparing central perspective views, but after two or three years it was no longer interesting to me to simply compare Munich with Paris or somewhere else.

MG *You studied with Gerhard Richter as a painter, what do you retain from this period?*

TS When I stopped painting I realised that what I was really lacking was a theme, and I realised that self-referential forms of thinking were not what fascinated me. To make a painting about painting was something that to me seemed quite obsolete.

MG *Obsolete or self-indulgent?*

TS Yes, for me just not interesting enough. Also, when I am taking a photograph, I am conscious that I am constructing images rather than taking snapshots. Since I do not take rapid photographs it is in this respect like a painting which takes a long time where you are very aware of what you are doing in the process. Exposure is only the final act of making the image as a photograph. Six years ago I was in Naples for three months and spent most of the time looking for locations, for images that would summon up what, after ten weeks, I thought Naples was all about.

MG *Can we talk about your portrait works? You came to them much later.*

TS I started by making a few individual portraits in 1983. My first attempts were of friends, but for some time I had been wondering whether a portrait could be interesting at all. What would there be to say about a person? What was the advantage in making an image of a single person? The first came about when a friend of mine, Bettina Nabbefeld, who liked to knit sweaters, knitted a sweater for me according to my design and, in exchange, I made a portrait. This gave me the freedom to work on a sitter without having to think too much about art. I thought a lot about what she was like.

From the beginning, the portrait method was based very much onthe notion that I would have to be able to read the image of her as a person, and then compare it to the person whom I knew, which is a very old-fashioned attitude. It gave me a reason to go on with portraiture, since for the first time I actually believed in a portrait of mine. I liked it because it revealed a slice of her nature. Then I did a lot more very slowly. I have taken portraits for a number of individuals I like, maybe some 12 or 15 individual portraits, and maybe some 20 or so family portraits.

MG *Are they mostly men or women?*

TS The individual ones are mainly women, the ratio is about three to one.

MG *And how have they changed? I find your family groups are interesting in that none of your photographs are 'physiognomic' in the sense that the photographs of your compatriot Thomas Ruff are. What determines your choice?*

TS Maybe the first two family portraits that I took were made from a very personal incentive, when I was staying with friends in Japan, and then following that, a three-week stay in Scotland. On the last day I took a photograph of the family as a personal memory. Also, the Japan photograph struck me when I saw it on the table. It showed me many things that I had not seen about their faces in relation to their home environment, or about their behaviour as a family group and their body positions in relation to others.

MG *Are you trying to say that they are anthropological, in a sense, rather than physiognomic?*

TS Yes, very much so.

MG *In none of your photography (architectural or portraits) are people doing anything.*

TS Yes. I feel that I can achieve the most in portrait situations when it is a fair encounter between two partners, between two opposites on two sides: me and the camera, and the people being portrayed. I think the tension at that moment is at its highest, as people look at the camera, or at me – the ego in the camera machinery. I therefore like to restrict myself to a certain limitation of process to make it charged and more intense.

MG *Are these figures ever posed?*

TS No. I decide upon the limitations of the frame, then I tell them to pose wherever they like within the frame.

MG *Is it always necessary for you to have a close relationship with people before you photograph them?*

TS Yes, there has to be at least a friendship with one of the group who functions as a door-opener, so as not to make me a foreigner. What I find very interesting when I look at the portrait world of Cartier-Bresson and others is the way they construct, or frame, a certain idea of the sitter: with Malraux it is his writings, with Stravinsky, his music. Their portraits conform to some sort of expression of what they are famed for. You have no idea of a person's status if they are anonymous and not famous.

MG *I notice in portraits you sometimes use colour which you never appear to use in your architectural works. What criteria do you use for choosing colour?*

TS Colour makes space easier to control. With black and white you have to work harder to transform spatial dimensions in more precise ways.

MG *Which comes first, the image or the choice of means?*

TS The image I think!

MG *Do you ever take both black and white and colour shots of the same sitters?*

TS Yes I do. But only with the portraits, for with the portraits, when they are shot in colour the amount of light you have is very low and also the colour film speed is much lower than can be used in black-and-white film. Most of the portrait exposures are for one second and this has a very special implication for the portrait. When you have an exposure of a second and you let people know you are using this exposure, it affects the sitters who consciously feel themselves sitting for a second.

MG *Have you ever been interested in dealing with film, with durational images? There is a sort of limitation in a still image, you do not have the dynamics of movement.*

TS Yes, I feel very attracted to film actually and I want at some point to make a film. I think it is a matter of the story, of the necessity of telling a story in which I can believe at film length.

MG *Are the portraits and the architectural works mutually exclusive? Can you relate the portraits aesthetically to your architectural work, or are they siphoned off in another part of your consciousness?*

TS No, I think that they share the same intensity resulting from looking at society.

MG *Your most recent project has been the museum photograph series.*

TS I made a series of photographs which were intended as large images showing museum rooms of paintings of the human figure in relation to their audience. They are portraits of paintings with human characters telling fairy tales, or human stories precisely shaped by museum curation.

MG *They are of a very different audience to that of a modern or contemporary space. The 'white cube' space convention shows people singly looking at works of art. There is a complex intellectual dynamic working in painting-sized photographs of people looking at paintings in which they themselves are a form of portrait.*

TS Yes, I think that they are a kind of act of remembrance of when art touched directly on the human narrative, as distinct from a Joseph Beuys, Mark Rothko, Mondrian or Gerhard Richter. They are about a sort of human relationship in and to museums. Funnily enough, my museum photographs give the impression that people stop much longer in front of the works than they usually do.

Issue 176, May 1994

Jeff Wall

interviewed by Patricia Bickers

Wall pieces

PATRICIA BICKERS *The epic scale of* Restoration *and* A Sudden Gust of Wind (after Hokusai), *both of 1993 and both included in 'The Epic and the Everyday', recalls that of the great nineteenth-century 'machines', juggernauts of the academic tradition of history painting. It is ironic that through the medium of the photograph, whose status as art the academies opposed even in court, you have revived if not the form then perhaps the ambition of history painting. Was this development influenced, as Thomas Crow has suggested, by your study at the Courtauld Institute which coincided with a period during which art historians, notably TJ Clark, had begun to address the social context of nineteenth-century French art?*

JEFF WALL I studied art history at the Courtauld Institute a year or two after TJ Clark graduated. Since I didn't have any friends in the school, I didn't hear much about him or his ideas directly. But I did read his books on 1848 and Courbet when they came out, and liked them. It was apparent to me around 1971 that deep problems of philosophical aesthetics were posed by staging for oneself the debate between Greenbergian modernism and Ideologiekritik, in one way or another. London and Paris were good places to learn about things like that in the early seventies. I feel that I had a very good education at the Courtauld, even though I almost never went to a class, met an advisor or had a conversation with another student. The school just let me drift along, thinking about whatever I wanted. They probably knew I wasn't serious about being an art historian. I wasn't, but I was serious about art history, which to me wasn't a profession but an aspect of my artistic practice. It was a way for me to reflect on my instinctive admiration for beautiful works of art, something which

I had felt as a child in Vancouver, where there were so few actual works to be seen. Art history helps me to discover objective things in my own intensely pleasurable experiences. So, it wasn't nineteenth-century art in particular that interested me then or now though, of course, I'm quite involved with aspects of it. There were many other things – painting, cinema, photography, literature. I feel that my experience of a work which may be centuries old still takes place here and now, and so to that extent that work is contemporary art. From nineteenth-century art I guess I have taken the notion of the 'painting of modern life', and observed how its shape was changed as it refracted through photography and cinema in this century. That had something to do with the new ways of thinking which were developing in the world of art history in the seventies, as Tom Crow said.

I don't think my pictures are on an epic scale. I think they are always in a pictorial scale. The bigger ones are maybe at the upper reaches of the pictorial mode but, like many people of my generation, I have a phobia about monumentality. So, also, I don't think what I'm doing continues the Salon machine idea any more than the work of Frank Stella or Rebecca Horn, for example, but it may be that the Salon machine is a permanent and even necessary aspect of contemporary art.

PB *In discussing the nature of film, Walter Benjamin contrasted the fragmentary nature of the pictures obtained by a cameraman, which in the final film 'are assembled under a new law', with the totality of the picture produced by a painter. However, it could be said that, since you began to use digital computer imaging in 1991, you have been able to fuse these two aspects of image-making without recourse to the elaborate procedures of nineteenth-century pioneers of 'composite' photographs such as Oscar Rejlander or Henry Peach Robinson.*

JW I thought about my pictures in terms of cinematography, rather than photography proper or maybe art-photography, as it had been defined by the powers that were up until around 1970. My straight or direct photos – ones that don't involve digital technology – seemed to be analogous to the whole cinematographic process but without any editing. Digital technology allows you to put different pieces together after the shooting is finished, so it is something like film editing. Like most people, I gave the early composite photos a passing glance, but didn't see too much of interest in them, for various reasons. It took straight photography and art-photojournalism about 50 years to recreate the concepts of gesture and subject which were not very well handled by the pictorialists – they were too arty, highbrow and sappy.

PB *The seamlessness – the 'totality' – of* Restoration *and* A Sudden Gust of Wind *belies the complexity of their construction. Would you discuss the procedure you adopted in these two works? Are they an advance, in a technical sense, on* Dead Troops Talk (A Vision after an Ambush of a Red Army Patrol, near Moqor, Afghanistan, winter 1986), *one of the most complex of your earliest digitalised works begun in 1991 and completed in 1992?*

JW *A Sudden Gust of Wind* was harder to do than *Dead Troops* but that was mainly because it had to be shot outdoors and not in a studio, where the lighting conditions could be kept exactly the same all the time. I had to shoot only when the cloud cover was at a certain density and only at a certain time of day – otherwise the various pieces wouldn't match. This is difficult in Vancouver in the fall and winter, so in the end it took five months to shoot the 50 or so pieces of film I needed, and then I had to go back to the location about a year later, when the season had come around again, to re-shoot some things that I didn't like. But the computer part of the work was comparable. I don't see any great differences between them, except maybe that it was riskier to try and shoot such pictures outdoors on location. But now I feel I've learned a bit about doing that, and could imagine doing it again.

PB *In the interview for the Lucerne catalogue you said that, paradoxically, the more you use computers in picture-making, the more 'handmade' the picture becomes. Did you mean the more like a painter you become?*

JW A picture-painter can work on one part of the composition in isolation from the whole, to a certain extent. In direct photography everything happens at the instant when the shutter clicks. In a sense photography is determined most of all by the shutter, by the fact that an actual moment is necessary to produce the image of a moment. In painting the illusion of a moment is created, by definition, because paintings take longer to make, so the relationship between any actual passage of time and that which is depicted is purely imaginary or conventional or, rather, some combination of the two. So, putting pieces together in the computer resembles that kind of sectioning-out of the work, and it reminds me of painting because of that. The other aspect of hand-making is that it isn't the hardware or the software that makes the picture, it's the person working with them. Finely crafted montage is very skilled work, and it is difficult and time-consuming to do it properly. My pictures are made by hand using those tools and systems.

PB *It is interesting that Rejlander's most ambitious composite photograph,* The Two Ways of Life *of 1857, and Edouard Castre's Lucerne panorama, represent two of the most important examples of developments which, though they enjoyed a brief vogue, ultimately led nowhere, like 'Sensurround' cinema in the seventies.* Restoration *communicates a pervasive sense of failure that is only partly to do with the subject-matter, General Bourbaki's defeated army, and the decayed state of the panorama as itself. Is there a sense in which you are conscious of the 'failure' of your own chosen medium, for instance, to represent a 360-degree panorama on a two-dimensional surface?*

JW No, media don't fail, they just have boundaries, limitations. I'm modernist enough to think that art derives from the limitations of the medium in which the artist is working. That's what usually attracts me to a subject, genre or technique. Pictorial art exists because of the contradiction of depicting space on a flat surface – so the curved architecture of the panorama seemed to me a particularly interesting situation.

PB *The title of the piece,* Restoration, *and the restoration project itself echoes the nature of Castre's real subject, which is the offer of sanctuary by the Swiss, under the aegis of the newly formed Red Cross, to the defeated French army. It is interesting that 'restorers' actually prefer the term 'conservation' to 'restoration', did you choose your title because of its allegorical resonance?*

JW 'Restoration' is a word with more than one meaning, and I like words like that for my titles. Titles are a kind of literature, very short prose poems, maybe.

PB *Several commentators have drawn analogies between your work and literature, Roger Seamon, for instance, referred to the 'novelistic quality' of some of your images which look like illustrations for a story. Though your work employs narrative devices – gesture, expression and the use of stereotypes – I am reminded of the way pictorial allegory works. This is particularly true in the case of* The Well, *1989, which brings to mind Ingres's famous allegorical nude,* La Source, *and the biblical story of Rebekah at the well, but utterly inverts their meaning.*

JW I think all pictures have a literary aspect, if only because they have to have a subject. To me the question is what, specifically, is that aspect in any particular case. I have thought about the concept of the 'novelistic', too, partly in relation to Mikhail Bakhtin's studies of it, although I think photographs are more like prose poems than any other literary form. *The Well* could be interpreted as a counterpart to something like *La Source*, at least in terms of typology. The iconographic knot connecting women and water is very old and very well tied. It's something real, which traditionally has led to images like Ingres's. I am not in those traditions though I have a certain relation to them. I wanted there to be a kind of suspension of the relation between the woman and the water, which is still absent, still 'not yet'.

PB *The combination of the real and the staged – or rather the staging of the real – in some of your work, recalls the* tableau vivant. *It has been observed that the deliberate staginess has the effect of distancing the viewer and denying any lingering link between the camera and documentary-style truth or objectivity. However, are there other aspects of theatricality that attracted you, like the sense of drama – of something being about to happen?*

JW My interest in stagecraft has less to do with ideas about the problems of documentation than with my wish to be able to get closer into situations which usually happen in the absence of a photographer rather than in his presence. That's why the cinematographic model is so interesting and productive – it is about making things visible rather than seeing, somehow, what is already visible. Photography as an art form evolves in the interplay between these two conditions, I think. There is no complete or absolute spontaneity and, of course, no absolute staginess.

PB The Crooked Path, *1991, appears the least staged of the works in the Hayward show perhaps because there are no people in it. The piece of scrubland at the urban periphery in which the industry of the bees in their makeshift hives is juxtaposed with that of 'Tom Yee Produce Inc', and where the eponymous 'crooked path' contrasts with the rectilinearity of the factory that dominates the horizon all look as if they were casually chanced upon, your intervention being to extract just that section of the scene in order to bring those contrasts to our attention.*

JW *The Crooked Path* is just a landscape photograph. I make them from time to time, when I can. I did nothing to the scene except find it and see it that way. However, I was looking to make a picture called 'The Crooked Path' for a while, and that's how I got to that spot.

PB *You said at the beginning that you thought of your pictures in terms of cinematography rather than photography. Could you imagine yourself ever making a film?*

JW There's only one problem with the cinema – too much movement.

Issue 179, September 1994

Hanne Darboven

interviewed by Mark Gisbourne

Time and time again

MARK GISBOURNE *What is the work that is being installed at the Goethe Institute in London?*

HANNE DARBOVEN It is dedicated to Frederick II (Friedrich Zwei), the great Prussian king, to Sans Souci, his palace, and to his dogs. It is a written daily work begun in 1986. For each day there is a page, plus an index and quotes referring to Frederick II.

MG *Will it include your usual use of numbers?*

HD Of course, the daily numbers that I have always used ever since I began.

MG *Do you consider your work as some sort of archival undertaking?*

HD This I don't understand. It is related to my work today, to my pet goat, Mamma Micki, to my house and garden, to the time I spend here – all that I have that you can see. It is dedicated to an open mind and to philosophy, since Frederick II was around at the time of the Enlightenment along with others like G E Lessing and Rousseau.

MG *Does it deal then with the theme of Romanticism?*

HD Absolutely not! It is not Romantic but refers to a period or time before Romanticism, which came in the following century. Romanticism was a disaster and for Germany particularly so. It was seen in the First World War, and more especially the Second World War, but yet a disaster for the whole world as I see it.

MG *Lessing, as I remember, was the first to separate the arts of space from the arts of time.*

HD Yes, but his idea of artistic space was one of communication with people and it never actually worked out as he wanted it to. And then followed the big disaster, though not in the nineteenth century which retained things from the Enlightenment but in the twentieth. The twentieth century is the disaster of Romanticism. Now you understand why my dedication to Frederick II is so well rounded off.

MG *Referring to your Goethe work installed at the Museum für Moderner Kunst at Frankfurt, was Goethe not a Romantic?*

HD No, Goethe was in no way a Romantic.

MG *He stood on the bridge between the Enlightenment and Romanticism, perhaps, even more so than Diderot in France.*

HD Yes, in a way, but what is important is that in his time a whole series of social elements began to wake up and become more humanist. So the lot of his life was that he lived between these two forces.

MG *Your music fits in very well with your Frederick of Prussia project.*

HD Yes, he did compose a little but I have done it steadily since 1979. I used to play many instruments but now I just compose.

MG *You always seem to dedicate your works to famous people. Why is that?*

HD To be historically famous there must be something of worth otherwise you never achieve lasting fame. I know from my own experience that to become famous requires a certain sort of being honest about something. Beyond that it is nothing but a silly joke, just a glimmer of glory and nothing of any worth happens afterwards. But being really famous means something.

MG *Means something symbolically?*

HD It might become symbolic, this I cannot say, but it is based on the deeper workings of consciousness and honesty. As a German person with a history of the First World War, when Prussia was destroyed forever – it simply disappeared – and for me especially, as it was in my lifetime, of the Second World War, this becomes just an honest work of art history in this century.

MG *Yet you also choose French philosophers like Sartre.*

HD Absolutely! I did a huge work for Sartre and at the time that I did it, in 1975, it was a most delicate time to be writing a work for Jean-Paul Sartre, especially in Germany. So I felt that I had to get his personal signature and approval for it in order to show it at Leo Castelli's Gallery in New York. I got it via Giselle Freunde and Simone de Beauvoir. These things today are totally unknown, that is what it meant at the time of the Cold War.

MG *Are you saying that a work is at its most powerful at the time it is made?*

HD It can be just as powerful today, because it is now a form of history. It does for that time and for now. You must be aware that it was

still the time of the Cold War – what I have called the time after Hitler. We did, after all, have this Cold War for 40 years – 40 years!
And, if you are honest with yourself, it has to worry you every day, otherwise you become uncaring and unconscious of others. My friends and myself took our experiences personally and severely. We felt that there was barely a space left for existence given the circumstances of the Cold War.

I remember as a child all the bombs falling on Hamburg in the Second World War. After the Hitler regime we had to live with the terrible consequences and these have always been with me and are present in my work. I don't need to tell you that war is totally terrible. The First World War was crazy and the Second World War sheer ideology and idolatry, then came the Cold War between East and West.

MG *Would you say that you are a sort of historiographer?*

HD Yes, of course. From 1975 to 1980 I wrote a huge work called *Writing Time* (*Schreibzeit*) including lots of programming. Then in 1983, I completed *East-West Democracy*, but no more. I do not want to do any more historiographical writings now because I did such a lot and for a long time. Now I want to do my free work, that which I conceptually built up in New York in the 1960s. I feel I have fulfilled the responsibilities that I had to myself and to society.

MG *You seem to be trying to treat recent German history as something like a bubble, setting the stability of Frederick's time against the enormous distortion that took place in the interim.*

HD Yes, my historical work is an attempt to reconcile the past with the present. I won't say that the nineteenth-century Romantics were wrong but that they got misused in the twentieth century. They could not have foreseen what would happen, so I won't blame them totally for being misused in our time. Now, all things may be used to liberate each other from the disasters and the 40 years we have been through.

MG *Coming here today from the railway station I saw chanting football hooligans being escorted away by the police.*

HD You have them in England. You know, football is just a game and you can't deny it to the people who behave in a fascist way as a result. One does need a small portion of Fascism, and if it expends itself in a game then so be it. I won't deny that it is a sad reality, but for Lessing and the Enlightenment thinkers this represents a form of tolerance.

MG *Do you see yourself as a particularly German artist in your desire for reconciliation?*

HD Not at all. When I went to New York in 1966 and spent three years there, coming back at the time of the death of my father, I did it honestly. I just see myself as an artist in this world but not a specifically German one. If my art, which I make for myself, seems German I can hardly be blamed. I have made it in all honesty and nothing more. In any event, I am half Danish from my mother's side and I have always lived in the two countries of Germany and Denmark.

MC *So your work is not about redeeming German history as such in works like the Goethe and Bismarck projects.*

HD It is not a matter of redemption.

MC *I used to think the constant references to the funereal, to records, requiem titles, etc, meant that your work was about death. Now I see it is all about life.*

HD Exactly, it is all about life.

MC *You seem to use a lot of the scholar's media in your work: documents, photographs, pen and ink. Do you see yourself as a type of conceptual visual scholar?*

HD I see myself as a writer, which I am, regardless of what other visual materials I may use. I am a writer first and a visual artist second.

MC *Do you do any other writings other than the work for your installations?*

HD Yes, much more, for my diary which I have kept for 30 years and other personal writings.

MC *How does memory fit into that?*

HD Daily, in the case of criticism, of myself to myself – that's memory.

MC *When do you decide a work is finished? Do you ever make any changes through the process of making?*

HD Never. It is conceptualised and then it just takes the set time to execute it. For example, *Frederick II* is one year or 365 days, and that's how long it takes. It's totally conceptual and in my head, and the works take whatever – one, two to five years – to be completed. I also did a work dealing with a century (*0–99*, 1971) and *Requiem*.

MC *You use a lot of numbering systems in your work. What do they mean to you?*

HD Numbers are the most neutral way of talking about things – no names, no objects, just the counting of numbers and the use of dates.

MC *You seem fascinated with them, in the same way as On Kawara.*

HD But he writes the date on the tableau or picture. I write in sentences and I then write in a series of sentences. This is totally different.

MC *Do numbers have a visual meaning for you?*

HD They can have in my case as well. On the wall, all these numbers – seriously written down – do have a visual context, no doubt about it. They can also have the same visual significance for me when they are placed in a book. They even have their own internal systems – but I don't want to talk about them here.

MC *Do your systems work largely one number after another?*

HD No, it is completely unliteral, completely *unliterarisch*.

MC *Your use of numbers never allows you to fall upon a specific number as you might do a page in a book.*

HD No, they are not intended to be read that way, they are completely conceptual and they flow like duration.

MC *You never privilege given aspects of the work either. There is no sense of a rise and fall of emotions.*

HD There are no emotions. This is what led to our Romantic disaster that I spoke of earlier. Absolutely not. I will not do it, I will not permit it. Some English artists do, Richard Long for instance, as in Land Art. But being English he can do it, you see.

MC *Because of German history?*

HD Yes.

MC *It still seems very strange to me that you never appear to let emotion affect you. It seems cold.*

HD It is not cold. Clarity is very necessary. We have had far too much emotion and confusion, don't you think?

MC *What is coming across is the idea that your work is very lucid and in a strange way uncomplicated. Yet it is always presented as dense and complex. Do you think that it is the way in which it is presented that makes it appear difficult?*

HD Yes, of course it's very clear, lucid and very simple. People construct complicated ideas about my work. It is they who complicate it for themselves.

MC *To be frank, some people are frightened off by your work.*

HD Well, that must be their problem. Young people don't think that way. When I was young I had to make myself become aware and develop clarity about that awareness as well. If they are young they have to find out for themselves, get it sorted out and clear for themselves.

MC *You include a number of photographs in your work. What part do they play?*

HD Yes. I choose them quite specifically. They serve as documentation and nothing more. I don't photograph things as pictures as such, rather as just a document of a given time. They are all owned by me. I would never go to a library, it is not a research project. They are all here in my house. I document them here with my co-workers and they are rephotographed by Bernhard Berz.

MG *Do you install your work yourself?*

HD Yes, by writing my work. I always write the instructions for its installation because you must remember, as you have seen where I work, I never see my work as a whole. I have it done in my head, conceived, constructed and written down – even to the point of installation.

MG *Will you be coming to London?*

HD I have given them the plan, I don't have to come. The plan exists and it is followed. I don't go to openings very often, why should I want to go there?

MG *How are people supposed to read the work?*

HD As they want to, it is obvious how to read it. And if not they can just look.

MG *I mean is one expected to start at a given point and move around in a sequence?*

HD There is always a start and an end but you don't have to follow it. You can follow the signatures if you want to but you don't have to. It is totally open.

MG *They are puzzling though, full of apparent hermeticism and closure. Some might even say elitist.*

HD There is never any sense of writing for others, everything is written for myself alone. There is the concept and the period of its execution. I feel that I don't have to defend myself – 'never apologise and never explain'. This is not my saying, I took it from Carl Andre in the seventies but now I repeat it daily which is a good thing – never, never explain.

Issue 181, November 1994

1995–1998

John Baldessari

interviewed by Liam Gillick

I will not make any more boring art

LIAM GILLICK *The trouble with trying to talk to you is that you have an idea of what you've done and a peculiar idea of history that may bear no relation to reality. One received idea about your work is that you have tried to remain mobile and flexible. Is it possible that the broad scope of work in Manchester and the forthcoming Serpentine show is indicative of this position? It indicates the negotiable status of meaning in your projects across 30 years of production.*

JOHN BALDESSARI Somebody recently asked me if I keep work and I said no, because it is the investigation that is of interest to me. To see if I can do something, to see what's on my mind. So in one way I have some *a priori* ideas and in another way I don't. It's like that answer sometimes given to why people take photographs, 'So that they can see what they're looking at'. You're firing retro-rockets, correcting your course all the time.

LC *I think I am working among a group of artists who have often referred to certain ideas that you have played around with. Time is one of the issues.*

JB I could address this by saying that at the start, when I was a painter, time was an issue in the sense that I didn't have enough of it to give to painting. Working on canvas takes up a lot of time and I realised that photography was faster. It's even faster if you get someone else to do your own work. It might be that you could make a whole argument for Conceptual Art occurring because people sort of ran out of time. They had to find ways to do the same things more quickly. You revert to a shorthand in order to get to the essentials.

I also got tired of static work and started exploring film and video and, as a result of that, I think my films and videos began to look like still images and my static work began to look like movies. Now I sort of miss time, because there are so many demands on me that I don't have the chance to play as much as I used to. I would like to think that I am purely a strategist. You figure out how to do something and that's that. The doing of it is not very interesting because you have already done it in your head.

Unfortunately that's not good enough for most people and you have to come up with some hard cash on the line. So you have to do something. Things change, and the idea that seemed terrific turns out to be not so terrific at all. The whole process is a point of departure, as you work something else begins to happen.

LC *It seems that there were points when you felt it necessary to puncture the more pompous proclamations around Conceptual Art, the rather more fixed positions. How did you feel about the context within which you were working at the beginning?*

JB I don't think that there are any progenitors of Conceptual or Minimal Art or anything else for that matter. There is a kind of *zeitgeist*. We all read similar books, magazines and watch TV or go to the movies. So a person of reasonable intelligence could come up with similar ideas to someone else in another part of the world. I have always had a strong resistance to being told what to do – a pragmatism. What does it matter how the job is done as long as it gets done?

One thing that used to bother me on forays into New York would be the sense that things had to fit into history or they weren't viable and my attitude was always 'don't be a slave to history'. I think what I miss a lot lately is the sense of permission to fail – things have to be right from the start. Sometimes I have the feeling that artists are not doing what they really want to do. I know that people interact with their culture but it's often a case of the tail wagging the dog.

LC *I remember seeing the new pieces that combine painted and photographic elements and being a little taken aback. Was that an example of you doing something that people aren't supposed to do at the moment?*

JB I think a lot of my teaching is connected to nudging people. That affects your own life too. So if you make the statement 'I will not make any boring art' in a teaching context, then you have to make sure you try that too. So I have always thought that teaching was giving permission and maybe I still try and do that with my art. Give permission to myself, say 'It's okay you can do this'. I remember years ago at some comprehensive Picasso exhibit, these two people stopped in front of a work. Picasso had indicated a painting within the painting with a broad sweep of the brush, and with a pencil he had marked out a Baroque frame. One of the people pointed at it and said 'I didn't know you could do that.' The other replied, 'What?' And she said: ' – use a pencil in a painting.' I think we all labour within certain parameters, but occasionally someone makes a breakthrough.

LC *But are there cut-off points for you?*

JB Yes, sure there are some things you don't have time to explore properly. I would still like to be conducting chemistry experiments in my father's garage. But you narrow the scope of your search a little. Lately, it seems that I am following a multiple track, because compartmentalisation still annoys me. I would love it if all that artists did was to make museums implode. You couldn't have departments any more because there would be no reason to have departments. It seems like such a tired and old fight but it's still there. It's one thing that interests me about photography. How photography sees the world. How it's used compared with other mark-making devices. There are other ways of recording the world, but if I can explore one kind of artmaking in parallel to another kind of artmaking, then certain stuff opens up for me that I haven't seen before.

LC *It's funny that you talk so much about photography because even now some people try and drag that 'art v photography' non-problem out into the open. But was there a time when the use of photography in an art context really affected the way in which work was read. Where people would say 'Fine, but all you've done is to take a funny photograph'.*

JB Yes, and that's why I did it, because I thought 'What an interesting terrain'. People tend to rebel against current art practice and I wondered what would happen if you gave people what they wanted – text and photography. That was certainly around them, in advertising and magazines. The curious thing was there wasn't any text and photography in the art galleries and museums. So it was a perfect set-up. And to get that kind of stuff through the front door I would print onto canvas, but even then you would get a lot of resistance. I remember the time I first put some straight photographs in a gallery, in a group show, and they were sold. Everyone was dumbstruck. I gave up using text some time ago because I thought that the battle had been won to a certain extent. Photography on the other hand continues to interest me. We live in a very visually literate society, especially when you consider things like MTV and condensed books. All you have to do is shift the attention a little bit and people can read your work. I don't have a feeling of 'them and us', but I do recognise different levels of engagement. Hybrid situations really interest me. But Roy Lichtenstein once said something like, 'There's as big an audience for art as there is for chemistry', and maybe he's right.

LC *I was surprised to hear you talking recently about process and materials.*

JB I seldom get concerned about materials. When you're a student at art school you often use what's cheap. I didn't know what acid-free paper was until I was about 40. And even now I am not certain about some of the materials that I use. I use a particular type of photographic paper because I like the way it looks – kind of bland. I tend to avoid anything that has too much of an artful look about it.

LC *Some people we both know used to drive around with a bag in their car that had 'Learn to draw' printed on it. Where did that come from?*

JB It was from a rubber stamp that I had made during the heyday of Conceptual Art. You would get all these proposals and invitations to participate in complex projects. At a certain point you could get a headache from reading all these things so I just stamped 'Learn to draw' on them and sent them back. And I had these bags with the same phrase on them made up for a few friends. I had another stamp that said 'Born to paint' and a friend of mine in the Hells Angels designed an embroidered patch for me with a skull, palette and crossed paint brushes. Brice Marden has one of them.

LC *Did you have one of those childhoods where people would say 'Oh, John, he's an artist'.*

JB No, I didn't. Both my parents were European but if I expressed any interest in art I was steered away from it, the implication being that I wasn't going to make any money. But in school you seem to get that tag. If there's a mural to be done about Christopher Columbus discovering America, you're the one that gets to do it.

LC *But are you an art fan, someone with a broad interest in other people's art?*

JB I think so. I go to as many shows as I can. It's part social and part doing homework. Seeing if there are ideas I can steal from anybody. In that way it is just like a doctor keeping informed of a new procedure. I think it's pretty important.

LC *One of the first book works of yours I got was* Ingres and Other Parables *and there's something about the way that book is written that avoids the legalistic tone that is so familiar in other conceptual work. It was funny that you were saying that some people in America used to see you as something of a European artist, maybe it is because you are so clearly implicated in some of those earlier pieces.*

JB I think that anything I say for anyone else has to involve me too.

LG *I tried to ask that question the other night about the way in which your use of film stills suddenly mined a rich source of visual material right at the point when people were saying it is the end of this or that, the end of painting or the end of art.*

JB The use of film stills came about rather gradually. They were widely available and ten cents a piece. In fact, not all of them were film stills, some were publicity shots and newspaper material. But then I realised that these images contained certain recurring subject-matter. So guns and kisses were the first files, and the first works covered those areas. I have a whole file of people falling off horses – not necessarily from Westerns – just people falling off horses. You can use this material metaphorically. Allowing certain things to click in the brain.

LG *It is one thing to use a photo for a straightforward documentary reason and another thing to start altering the image with circles, crops and colour. A conceptual orthodoxy seemed to emerge very rapidly and you broke that down once more.*

JB There are ways of making people look elsewhere. And then there's the issue of creating another surface. In the case of a second surface of colour and shapes you often don't know where to look anymore.

LG *There's something about the way you can get really high consuming photographic images.*

JB Sometimes I sweat over an image and it still doesn't work. But I keep going because I know there is something in the photo. The amount of sifting and winnowing I do is incredible – there must be 500 images for each piece that is out in the world. There are 20 pieces in the latest show at Margo Leavin but there must be at least 200 maquettes, and just to get to the maquette stage involved a lot of choices.

LG *But did you always work that way?*

JB That's always been the way. But the rapidity of consuming photographic information is something that I try and slow down.

LG *The contemporary cliché is that people have a two-second attention span.*

JB I still abide by that. You've got about ten seconds to prove yourself.

LG *There's this idea that some of your work is funny – and it is funny – but it's quite hard to be funny with an artwork. There's witty art and ironic art but to actually be funny is something else altogether.*

JB You feel very vulnerable and stupid with certain pieces. It's also about having enough belief in your art to be able to say something. I never set out to be funny. When you see something that is apart from the norm you tend to laugh. My work comes from trying to see the world differently because I am tired of seeing the world the way it is presented. Our environment doesn't come to us with instructions.

Issue 187, June 1995

Anya Gallaccio

interviewed by Patricia Bickers

Meltdown

PATRICIA BICKERS *In the pages of* Art Monthly *recently you have been both accused and excused for claiming to be one of Thatcher's children. What did you mean when you said that?*

ANYA GALLACCIO In the sense that I am a product of that era – she came to power just before my 16th birthday. I think I'm more of a reaction to her. I had a very privileged childhood, very middle class, liberal parents and a belief in the future. I had high expectations and a lot of questions – I felt that I could make a difference. Now that I'm teaching I am shocked that students don't question their situation, they expect me to offer them a service, to give them the answers. Damien Hirst organised 'Freeze' during his second year at college – he'd been planning it for most of that year. It was a conversation, a dialogue, not a *fait accompli*. We weren't polite graduates who were content to wait around to be discovered. We took control of the situation. We did not wait to be invited in. I guess you could say that that is a Thatcherite idea.

PB *Do you think it's also part of the legacy of 'Freeze' that students today are more self-conscious in a way that you weren't?*

AG It is amazing how 'Freeze' has been cemented into art history. Hardly anyone saw it and most people don't even know what it is they are acknowledging – in a way they are not even interested in finding out – it is not the show that was important but the energy, the spirit of enterprise. 'Modern Medicine', 'Next phase', Damien's 'Butterflies' – wherever the space – the emphasis was on being professional not 'alternative'. The mainstream spaces weren't available to us so we found our own.

A lot of students now take for granted that they will be taken up when they leave college and that they are going to be famous but there is already a backlash against that kind of professionalism. A lot of work being produced at art schools now is really boring because people are trying to be 'professional', making art that looks like art. The original energy of 'Freeze' was not cynical. It was a genuine enthusiasm to make work and get it seen. I don't think anyone at the time realised quite how much was at stake.

PB *On the other hand that's not really surprising because dealers and collectors are scouting for talent at degree shows in a way they weren't in 1988.*

AC No, they weren't. That is a reaction to the situation – dealers trying to harness that energy, to appropriate it. But they are destroying it.

PB *Why was the lead piece that you showed in 'Freeze' called* Waterloo*?*

AC It was my Waterloo. It would either make or break me. My degree show had been a disaster. 'Freeze' was a challenge, an opportunity to pick myself up and get on with it. It was the first time that a lot of things fell into place and made sense for me.

PB *You once referred to the 'danger and beauty of molten lead'. For you it was actually very dangerous, wasn't it?*

AC I burnt my foot very badly and had to go to hospital. I had made half the piece myself but the others had to finish it – with me on crutches directing. It was kind of taken out of my control, the men wanted to do it all very quickly, in a much more efficient way. I resisted that. To me it was very important that I did it, so that meant that it had to be done in small amounts that I could lift.

PB *The obvious question is how aware were you of Richard Serra's work with lead such as* Splashing *or* Casting *of 1969?*

AC I wasn't aware of it at first – but I found out about it fairly quickly afterwards. For me, *Waterloo* was a transitional work. Before that stage, at college, I'd made objects using real materials – shells, clothes – not really changing them, just compressing them in blocks. *Waterloo* included an object, a child's cardigan, cast in bronze in the lost-wax technique. I liked the idea that I was destroying the very object that I was trying to preserve. The rectangle of lead was supposed to be in relation to this very tiny object. I felt that if I just had this beautiful rectangle of lead people would think that I was this really cool sophisticated minimal sculptor and that wasn't my intention.

In the piece that I did six months later at the Anderson O'Day

Gallery, *fret*, I focused much more on the lead. Something else had come out of the process of making *Waterloo* which I was very excited about, I enjoyed the fact that the actual process of making this piece was incredibly dynamic and noisy – there were all these furnaces and flames – it was hot and there was this kind of energy. It was quite terrifying. Yet the end result was very peaceful, elegant, beautiful and poetic.

PB *The copper piece,* in spite of it all, *that you made in Broadgate, is sited within spitting distance of Serra's* Fulcrum. *Did you see your work as being in some way a counterpoint to his?*

AC I was much more conscious of Serra's work at that time. I liked looking at his work and the work of Carl Andre. I enjoyed the tension between the way I made work and the way that they would probably make work. It's kind of a dirty word but I think I'm a very romantic artist, and there is a lot of poetry in the work I do, and that possibly is very English.

I'm treading a very fine line between what is acceptable and not acceptable. For a woman to work with flowers, for instance, is a really crazy thing to do, at least if you want to be taken seriously. To me that's exciting. Obviously when I was working with lead and with copper, people took my work much more seriously – initially – because I was using serious sculptural materials. At the same time there was this kind of feminine, intimate quality about the work which I just pushed further.

PB *Subsequently, your approach to materials, and to the theme of mortality, has been more elegiac.* prestige *of 1990, the installation comprising 24 screaming kettles at Wapping Pumping Station, was another transitional piece. It remains unique in your work.*

AC To me it's one of the most successful pieces I've ever made and very few people ever saw it. It's also a piece I haven't been able to reshow because I have really guarded its context. I wanted to show it in the 'British Art Show' but I couldn't find a place for it. It is the only piece of my work that I have really protected.

It was actually made before my brother's death and that is really, really important to me. Obviously it became much more poignant because he died just two days before the private view, but he had helped me with it. I think that sense of longing and loss was always in my work, in a clumsy sort of way – that idea of an object that you can't possess, something that's quite intangible – but that was the first piece that clearly articulated it. I was really shocked by it myself.

PB *Did the context come first?*

AC The context always comes first. In a way I deal with clichés. The starting point is often very obvious: the kettle piece was made in the tower that housed the steam from the pumping station which produced the energy that was like the life force of the building. The building itself had enormous presence, there was no way that I could make a physical impression on the place. It was like a ghost place – a perfect place for me – so loaded that I thought mine had to be a really slight intervention.

Initially I had wanted to fill the space with steam, and I had actually spoken to Richard Wilson to get him to help me, but about three or four weeks before there was a water shortage so I couldn't do it – it was one of the luckiest things that could have happened. People said the kettles were steaming but in fact they were linked to a compressor and the air whistled through holes drilled in them, but it was cold air. It was all show, an empty hollow, which is what Wapping has become. The sound travelled an immense distance and as you came nearer it grew louder and louder but as you left the tower it went back to being this low kind of noise that you were aware of subliminally, it was very mournful and sad, tugging at you in a way that you couldn't ignore. I hadn't anticipated this. I had thought that the piece would be aggressive – angry, even. It was impossible to document. Photographs don't even begin to describe it.

PB *The sound was an audio equivalent for the visual and olfactory traces left by your other work. Would you work with sound again?*

AC I thought about doing a lot of things with it afterwards, but they just seemed crass in comparison. I did make a piece in 'Sweet Home' using sound, but it wasn't the same. I worked until fairly recently with an opera company in order to support myself and I was very interested in the emotional resonance of opera and of music, but I think the time has passed now.

PB *How conscious were you of the influence of Arte Povera in making the work?*

AC I was deliberately acknowledging that tradition. When I was at college, Jon Thompson was very important to me, and a lot of the work that he was interested in was European. Most of my contemporaries were looking at American work. The work I looked at was that of Pistoletto, Kounellis and Broodthaers, so when I made *recover* in

1992 for the Centro Luigi Pecci in Prato, for me it was a challenge to be on their territory and using a material that was very heavily associated with Arte Povera, the rags.

PB *How did you come to work with flowers?*

AC The first flower piece was a photographic project, *fleur*, which I did for the book *Technique Anglaise* in 1991. I thought I could cheat and fake a whole 'room' of flowers. I painstakingly ripped up this gypsophila – only two or three millimetres across – and arranged it all on a piece of paper. To me it was like a maquette. I never imagined that I would ever be able to afford to do anything so extravagant. Then I was asked to show the piece at the 1991 Art Fair at Olympia. Until that point, all the shows that I had done had been in derelict spaces where you didn't have to worry about the carpet. Often I had a space all to myself so it was quite easy to frame the work in that you were working within a rectangle. *Fleur* was a very quiet piece and I didn't see how I could have that kind of quality in the context of the Art Fair. Eventually, I reduced it down to some 9,000 narcissi, pressed between two panes of glass. *Preserve 'Cheerfulness'* was the first piece I did like that.

Basically I needed some kind of framing device and it is a convention to put precious things behind glass to protect them, including pictures. All I was doing was presenting flowers between glass. I liked the fact, especially in the sunflower piece *Preserve 'Sunflower'*, 1991 – the next piece I did – that as in the lost-wax process, the glass which was supposed to protect and preserve the flowers actually accelerated their decomposition.

PB *But the glass is also a 'mediator', something between you and the immediate experience of the work that is so important to you.*

AC Yes, but I enjoyed that, too, because in a dumb way it referred back to the history of painting. The surface of the glass worked as a kind of painting in one sense, in that if you say that painting is dealing with surface and with the illusion of three-dimensionality, then you had that dialogue going on. That was incidental, it wasn't my intention. In other works I investigated that.

PB *You deliberately gave your works painterly titles like* red on green, *1992, for the ICA piece with 10,000 red roses, and* red on white, *1992, for the piece using blood and soil that you made in Los Angeles.*

AC To me they were like paintings in space. I have a terror of painting and drawing – art with a big 'A'. Yet a lot of the work I like looking at is painting: thirteenth-century Sienese paintings – they are very flat with very bright colour – also, Barnett Newman, Mark Rothko and Yves Klein — that intense blue and gold.

PB *Is it to do with the experience offered by the paintings of Rothko and Klein?*

AC Yes, it is to do with a kind of response. I began to feel more and more frustrated with having to use glass, in the way that if you want to do a painting you need a support for the paint. Instead of just being a framing device, it was beginning to assume too much importance and I was trying to think of a way of getting rid of it when I was struck with the idea of the daisy chain. I'd toyed with the idea for about a year before I dared to do it – but to me it was really liberating. It actually gave me much more leeway to use the space, in a way making a drawing in the space. And the whole thing goes in the bin at the end of it.

Another factor was that I have been asked more and more to do shows in commercial spaces which have to be kept clean and tidy. Also, there is the question of cost – flowers don't go very far for your money – so the notion of the daisy chain meant, coincidentally, that I could halve the number of flowers and still fill the whole space.

PB *Is there a danger that you are increasingly seen as the 'flower girl'?*

AC Yes, totally. I'm sick of travelling around the world and installing them because they're not surprising me anymore.

PB *And whose responsibility is that, yours or the curators'?*

AC It's difficult. It is Catch-22. In the case of 'Brilliant!' and the 'British Art Show', they weren't commissioning new work which means that I had to reinterpret a previous work, not necessarily in ideal circumstances, and that is really problematic for me because my work is site specific, it depends on the space even if it's in a very superficial way.

In the case of the 'British Art Show', the space in Manchester wasn't right for the chocolate room. I thought it was important that I was represented in the show because I feel that my work is quite separate from my contemporaries', but having said that, I haven't been particularly well represented. The audience of course is going to assume that I chose that space and that I chose to do that work. I can't put that responsibility on anyone else.

I've made a lot of my mistakes very publicly, more so than other, studio-based artists. So I feel that sometimes I should be given a bit of leeway. On the other hand, why should I be?

PB *This dilemma is particularly acute in your case because in a sense the work ceases to exist at the end of each show. On the other hand, you don't wish the work to be recorded – and marketed – in the form of photographs.*

AG To me the whole thing about the work is the emotional response to the physical presence of the work, so although my work, especially the flower pieces, is very photogenic, you cannot capture it in a photograph. People have suggested that I should do beautiful, big, framed photographs *à la* Richard Long to sell but I think that by doing that I would be saying you don't have to go and look at the work, and for me the most important thing is to see the work – to be physically with the work.

PB *You have, of course, worked with photographs, for instance, in 'Broken English' in which photo-booth snaps were floated in a container full of water, as though in a developing tray, and in the piece,* tense II *– for the Museum of Installation show – in which you placed unfixed photographs of flowers on the floor of the building, directly under the skylight, which gradually faded. In both works you treated photographs as unstable material, as mutable as any other you have used.*

AG Yes. It is not a new idea – photographs don't tell the truth. However, I do document all the work I make anyway because, and this is a ridiculous contradiction, the only way I continue to get shows is by showing curators photographs of my work.

PB *This refusal to leave a permanent record – in the form of a photograph or other trace – seems to go beyond the decision to abandon the object in your work.*

AG My work is very much tied to me and I've always had a terror of feeling possessed. I think a lot of the work came out of that and also the whole thing of being part of the art world and the art market. Your work is a commodity, there is no way of separating yourself from the system and successfully negotiating a career. You can't escape it. You have to engage with it.

I'm a quite demanding person and so, in a sense, the work is. If you ask me to do an exhibition or buy a piece of my work, that is not going to be a cushy option. It's not like some nice crate is going to turn up from England. I'm going to turn up!

PB *So what takes place is not just a financial exchange. The curator or the collector must not merely accommodate the work, they must live with it and care for it.*

AG It's about relationships and it's about not being taken for granted.

PB *So, in a sense, the work is a surrogate for you?*

AC Yes.

PB *What was it like for you to return to the Pumping Station in Wapping?*

AC It seemed really important to me. I didn't seek it out, but I felt I was ready to confront that space. It felt like coming home. I think the work in the last year has changed anyway, and become much more celebratory.

PB *What was the genesis of* intensities and surfaces *this year?*

AC It was an obvious extension of working with glass. I had been thinking about working with ice for about a year and a half. The space that I chose to use was the boiler house. It would have been – it's all very literal – the hottest place in the building with a lot of water running through. Ice seemed a perfect kind of metaphor – it melts, it thaws – it's like the building is coming back to life. I wanted you to come across it in a very theatrical kind of way, in the way that in horror films you discover Frankenstein's workshop.

It's a very big statement to make and I could only do it once. It had to be constructed in one day. I didn't see it properly until the afternoon of the opening. That is quite terrifying. There are all these contradictions: it is totally solid – the ice weighs 34 tonnes, each block weighs 200 kilos – and yet it looks hollow at the centre. It was very important to me that it was solid, that we didn't cheat. The salt inside the ice was like putting a time bomb in the piece, something totally unpredictable. I imagined the salt would dissolve and work its way down vertically, leaving a kind of void.

PB *Again, like the lost-wax process.*

AC Yes. As the ice melts and becomes more transparent, you can see an organic shape, it was like having a cancer or a heart – one destroys and the other makes things live – inside this elegant, formal block.

PB *Was the light primarily an aesthetic element?*

AC Yes. I didn't really want any light outside the object. I wanted it to emanate light, as though it had a life. The ice itself actually sucks up any traces of natural light and colour. It's incredible. I imagined that the light at the bottom would make it glow, but actually it often makes it look hollow. It makes it look less substantial. I like the fact that this thing – to make dumb associations again – looks so ethereal yet it's extremely dangerous. One of those blocks could kill you if it shifted.

There was a lot of discussion about whether we were going to be allowed to give the public access but I felt that it was very important for people to be able to approach the block, the way you need to be close to a Newman or a Rothko, you want to be enveloped. It's the same with Damien's shark piece – from a distance it's not scary.

PB *Have you any unrealised projects that you would like to see through?*

AC I want to make a cast of a whole oak tree, a felled oak tree in glass. Again, I would be destroying the object, the tree, by making the mould. Also glass itself is organic, it's made from sand and seashells, so again there are these traces of past life in the physical properties of the glass. I have since discovered that Giuseppe Penone has plans to cast a whole tree. I don't know if that means that I can't do it because I imagine that Penone's tree would be very different from my tree.

PB *It is obviously important to you that you would be destroying an age-old metaphor for longevity – an oak tree – in order to make something so fragile.*

AC Yes. I'm sure the thing itself would look indestructible but in reality it is not. The metaphor still stands. Life is not certain. The future is not certain.

PB *Lately you have been considering a garden project. In your terms, gardening is a process that would not compromise you in that it is ever-changing, mutable and needs tending – a metaphor for life?*

AC I've been working with the Public Art Development Trust on a proposal for King's Cross, a planting scheme for a council estate. I have a big problem with public art but the context of this project is very interesting to me because it is a very public space and at the same time it is a very private, domestic space. I have been looking at plants symbolically and thinking of ways of reclaiming some of those spaces.

PB *England is a garden, every square inch is or has been cultivated. In a sense the urban and the rural form a continuum.*

AC Yes. The piece with the carpet last year, *Forest Floor*, is sited in a Forestry Commission forest just outside Oxford. It looks natural, it looks wild, but actually, it is very structured – it is a factory and a wood. The carpet is a flowery-patterned Axminster – a representation of nature – fitted to an area of trees in the middle of a bluebell wood, about seven metres square, which is as big as I could afford to make it. It is now hidden in the undergrowth.

PB *You don't make it easy for people to see your work.*

AC But if you bother to engage with it, you will get something back. I like to think the work is generous in that way.

PB *Is an Anya Gallaccio retrospective a contradiction in terms because you are always working in the present?*

AC I think so. When I die, there will be all these instructions and if someone is mad enough to want to do it, they could – if they make it in the spirit in which I intend it.

PB *How can you control the way it which it is made?*

AC I can't. When Sol LeWitt first did his wall drawings, the intention, I believe, was that the person who bought them could do them themselves. The reality is that a team of experts go around and install his work and, if there are any modifications to be made, they can make those kind of decisions on the spot. I haven't quite worked it all out yet but I'm determined to.

PB *Otherwise there is no Gallaccio legacy.*

AC To me that really doesn't matter. I want acknowledgement now. I am not interested in making some huge monument to myself to prove that I was on this planet.

Issue 195, April 1996

Steve McQueen

interviewed by Patricia Bickers

Let's get physical

PATRICIA BICKERS *Why did you want to go to film school in New York on leaving Goldsmiths?*

STEVE MCQUEEN Well, I wanted to go to New York University because I wanted to make feature films. I had had it with art and I wanted to go off and make films so I went to America where I quickly discovered that film school was not the place I wanted to be. I just wanted to just get on with it. At NYU, everybody wanted to be Scorsese or Spielberg, whereas what I wanted to do was throw a camera up in the air and catch it but no one was letting me do that. So I came back to London and started to make films. I was making art films rather than feature films, though I don't see any differences as such. Obviously there is a difference between showing film in a cinema rather than an art gallery, but I was interested in the gallery as a space.

PB *What did you do before you came to film?*

SMQ I always answer this question by saying that the first thing you get when you're a kid is a crayon, and then if you're lucky you get a paintbrush, and then if you're lucky... For me it was very much an evolutionary thing and in the end I got a camera to play with. I was painting at Goldsmiths and then I stopped at the end of my first year and just stuck with the camera. I already knew that I wanted to be involved in filmmaking. It was the whole idea of working with people that was interesting. Also the fact that film moves – physically as well as emotionally. It was much more dynamic than other art forms.

PB *When you say that you like working with people, do you mean in a collaborative sense?*

SMQ Definitely. You're living with people for a week, a month, or six months – sometimes even a year, to make a film. So it's a relationship-building thing, at the same time you're making work. The best thing about making films is the time spent making them. When I see works that I've made, I always think what a great time I had making them. The films remind me of that time.

PB *Despite the time spent on making them, the films themselves are short and tightly structured. Do you edit them down, selecting the best takes?*

SMQ There are only one, two or maybe three takes of something. Usually one shot leads to another shot which leads to another. It is almost like building something until it's high enough and then stopping just before it falls over. It is just having some kind of sense of where you put one brick on top of the other.

PB *Do you have any sort of shooting script or story board to start with?*

SMQ I always draw scenes and stuff like that but no editing usually. I just communicate a lot directly with the cinematographer or whoever I'm working with.

PB *So there is an improvisatory element in your work?*

SMQ When people come into the situation it becomes much more direct. I want people to do what they want to do because when they feel comfortable it seems to translate better on screen. It is when you put people in a straitjacket that it doesn't seem to translate very well at all. The individuals I work with are usually people I know.

PB *You said earlier that you were interested in the gallery as a space in which to show your films, yet the way in which you present them is very cinematic. Is this deliberate?*

SMQ Very much so. I try to get away from this kind of 'popcorn mentality', as I call it. Projecting the film on to the back wall of the gallery space so that it completely fills it from ceiling to floor, and from side to side, gives it this kind of blanket effect. You are very much involved with what is going on. You are a participant, not a passive viewer. The whole idea of making it a silent experience is so that when people walk into the space they become very much aware of themselves, of their own breathing. Unlike silent movies, which weren't really silent because there was always a musical accompaniment in the background, it is real silence. I find it difficult to breathe when I'm in the space. There seems to be no oxygen. I want to put people into a situation where they're sensitive to themselves watching the piece.

PB *Is that why the camera angles are often dizzying and unexpected?*

SMQ The thing is I don't see the angles as being odd at all. I think basically you can put the camera anywhere. There is no right or wrong angle for something. The idea of putting the camera in an unfamiliar position is simply to do with film language. Sometimes it is spectacular, sometimes it is ugly, sometimes it is uninteresting. But it has to do with looking at things in a different way. Cinema is a narrative form and by putting the camera at a different angle – on the ceiling or under a glass table – we are questioning that narrative as well as the way we are looking at things. It is also a very physical thing. It makes you very aware of your own presence and of your own body.

PB *That is certainly true of the moment in* Five Easy Pieces *when the man apparently pisses into the audience/camera lens. I was reminded of the opening sequence of* Sunset Boulevard, *where the camera looks up at the body of William Holden floating in the pool above. Billy Wilder has said that what appears to be a straightforward shot was in fact a highly complex set-up.*

SMQ I remember that film. That was a great shot by Billy Wilder. Wonderful. And the photographers flashing, taking photographs – really wonderful. I wanted a situation where I was peeing while people – the audience – would be under me, as it were – the dynamics of that situation.

PB *Was it complex to set up?*

SMQ No, not at all. It was extremely simple. We made a glass container, put it in between two tables, got the camera underneath the table, and shot it. It was very straightforward, very simple.

I think you can be very effective with very simple means. I don't like to put too much effort into things. I find that once you get involved with special effects it is no longer about what is happening in front of the camera and I really want to concentrate on what is happening in front of the camera, like the man apparently peeing on the surface of the screen.

PB *And like the way that the two wrestlers in* Bear *keep blocking out the light above and which at times blocks them out, like the photographers' flashes in* Sunset Boulevard.

SMQ Yes. The whole idea is that they're blocking out the light, the camera isn't doing anything. My main interest is in the movement of the two people on screen.

PB *In all your work one is very conscious of the protagonists moving into and out of the frame. For instance in* Five Easy Pieces, *you first see only the fringe of the tightrope-walker's skirt coming into the frame from the left. Inevitably, one thinks about what is metaphorically off-screen, on the margin – our fears, our erotic desires, issues of black and white, of taboos for instance in* Stage.

SMQ I don't deal with black and white, I don't deal with taboos. I think it is all to do with passing through, like at the beginning of *Five Easy Pieces* when the tightrope dips down into the black screen and then disappears out of the screen. I used to really like road movies and the whole idea of passing through, and as you pass through everything changes. It is also to do with the structure of the whole set-up, the idea of breaking up the frame. The idea of something going on other than what you see, of what is going on beyond the frame like in *Stage* when the hand claws back the frame.

PB *Does the title,* Five Easy Pieces, *refer to the movie?*

SMQ It was a definite reference to the movie though I didn't see it till I'd finished making the piece but I knew the scenario. It is a very minimal film because nothing much happens, it is just about passing through. I used to be a big fan of Jim Jarmusch – *Stranger than Paradise* – and obviously Wim Wenders – *Alice in the Cities* and *The Goalkeeper's Fear of the Penalty*.

PB *You have referred to* Bear, Five Easy Pieces *and* Stage *as a trilogy. All three seem very much connected at a level of both expressed and unexpressed desire. There is a strong erotic thread joining all three.*

SMQ Yes, frustration, in some ways. Frustration and release – very literally in the peeing shot, when the guy is holding on to his penis and 'pissing it out'. I wanted to deal visually with situations which were to do with flirtation, to do with aggression, with sensitivity – the whole emotional rollercoaster. I wanted to deal with the whole gamut in my own limited vocabulary.

PB *The hula-hooping sequences filmed in close-up in* Five Easy Pieces *are overtly sexual.*

SMQ Well, for me, when I first did it it was to do with whirling dervishes and the whole idea of spinning to get closer to God. But the hip-thrusting hula-hooping is just like fucking, wanking or masturbating – five guys doing it together. Maybe no one gets closer to God by masturbating – I don't know.

PB *The tightrope-walker above appears to be essentially feminine – would it have worked as well if it had been a man?*

SMQ No, I think you're quite right. It is painful walking the tightrope back and forth. Your feet hurt. It is very much like she's making love

– the expression on her face, her breathing. I wanted her to be out of the way of this boy's stuff below. I wanted her to be up there somewhere, doing her own thing while the boys could just get on with what the boys were doing. There's a lot of distance between the two.

PB *The camera angles exaggerate the distance.*

SMQ Yes, the idea is that she is walking over the guys' heads. Also there is the symmetry of the shot, the partition of her hair and the partition of her spine, together with the position of her arms which breaks up the frame quite beautifully.

PB *You take that much further in* Stage *in which you employed a split screen, literally dividing the frame. Having avoided, in your other work, the danger of binary opposites – apart from the obvious one of black-and-white film – here you court it, the risk being that it will be read literally in terms of black and white.*

SMQ The problem with these issues – a white woman and a black guy – is that they are heavy things to deal with. They aren't what I was concerned with at all. I wasn't being naive about them, but a black man and a white woman is such a cliché whereas *Bear* didn't seem to be clichéd at all. Maybe the situation is too concrete, an *Othello* kind of situation. There are some very good moments in there, but it is like a ball and chain with me, this film.

PB *Perhaps confronting the problem head on, by splitting the screen as you did, is a strength.*

SMQ In some ways it has been a good experience because it is pushing me to do other things.

PB Just Above my Head *is something of a departure although there are lots of continuities. Most obviously it deals with questions of visibility. The fact that you are black, and that you are both the artist and the subject of the film, inevitably gives it an extra edge.*

SMQ When I walk out into the street or go to the toilet, I don't think of myself as being black. Of course, other people think of me as black when I walk into a pub. Obviously being black is a part of me like being a woman is part of you. I just want to make work. People try to contain things by putting them into categories. I don't.

PB *A lot of contemporary women artists find that they cannot relate to the kinds of issues that exercised feminists in the seventies. They, too, say that they just want to make work. They are feminists – yes – but they are not fighting the same battles. For an older generation of black or female artists, visibility was a fundamental issue – Rasheed Araeen, for instance, called his book,* Making Myself Visible, *for him it was everything to do with his being black. In* Just Above My Head, *on the other hand, we gasp as your head disappears out of the bottom of the frame, briefly lost from view, precisely because we are able to identify with the subject regardless of race, colour or gender.*

SMQ I'm in the position I am because of what other people have done and I'm grateful, for sure. But at the same time, I am black, yes. I'm British as well. But as Miles Davis said, 'So what?' I don't say that flippantly but like anyone else I deal with certain things in my work because of who I am. I make work in order to make people think.

PB *In* Just Above My Head *there is almost a moment of epiphany, the moment when the tree looms out of the sky behind your head, a soaring, even transcendental image for both the subject and the viewer – that is the very opposite of the fearful moment when your head disappears from view.*

SMQ For me that whole thing was to do with gravity. All along, all you've seen is empty sky, just whiteness, with this head bobbing along. Then we see these tree branches spread across the screen and it's like 'Oh, we've landed. Thank God!'. It is like something to hang on to where before there was nothing else apart from white sky.

PB *When I first saw this piece, it struck me as the counterpart to the tightrope sequence from* Five Easy Pieces. *To reverse my earlier question, was it essential that the protagonist in* Just Above my Head *is a man?*

SMQ It had to be me – the reason being that I'm a person who likes to work, I mean physically work. It was a case of 'I'm going to walk!'.

PB *You use both real time and slowed-down time in your films. What dictates your decision to alter the time?*

SMQ I generally use 50 frames per second – it's not slow motion (25 frames per second is the normal speed that film goes through the projector). It is a very subtle thing – I don't want to romanticise things. It is almost like that feeling when you're sleeping but you're awake. It is to do with that. Funnily enough, both the situations in which I have used slow motion have been to do with feet: the tightrope sequence in *Five Easy Pieces* and the sequence when I am crawling in *Stage*. All the rest have been fragments slowed down frame by frame.

PB *I wasn't really aware of the tightrope sequence being slowed down because the tension of the moment was such that it seemed like real time, just as in real life, in moments of high tension or drama, time seems to slow down. In that sense, you have manipulated a natural reaction in the viewer.*

SMQ I like to make films in which people can almost pick up gravel in their hands and rub it but at the same time, I like the film to be like a wet piece of soap – it slips out of your grasp. You have to physically move around, you have to readjust your position in relation to it, so that it dictates to you rather than you to it.

PB *You are working on a new project with a professional cinematographer. How will this affect your approach?*

SMQ It is like working against someone in some ways, which I quite like. It is about making a relationship as well. There's a lot of grip there. A lot of things to hang on to.

PB *So it is a behind-the-scenes collaboration like that between you and the other protagonist in front of the camera in* Bear.

SMQ Exactly. It is exactly that in fact. It is a journey. I didn't know what was going to happen in that film. I had one idea – these two guys clashing – and from that things just developed, scene by scene, looking at rushes, changing things around.

PB *Is this new collaboration with a professional cinematographer a way of getting back to your original ambition of making feature films?*

SMQ Yes, definitely. I will do it. When you make a film it is like a journey. It is basically therapy. For me, the only way to work on an idea is to get a camera and develop things as I go along.

PB *How would you handle sound, in particular dialogue?*

SMQ That's difficult. I have difficulty putting words in people's mouths. The best dialogue is very, very thin dialogue – you let people improvise and then basically you record what they've improvised and then write it down. Sound itself, though, is not a problem, you just press 'record' and 'play'.

PB *Can you conceive of a time when you would use colour?*

SMQ Yes. The reason I have avoided it up till now was because I thought it was a bit distracting. What I was trying to be was direct. But now I think 'Yes, I'll get there', but with the right project.

Issue 202, December–January 1996–97

John McCracken

interviewed by Patricia Bickers

UFO technology

PATRICIA BICKERS *Some of the earliest sculptures in this exhibition have been made for the first time from drawings and projects you made in 1965.*

JOHN MCCRACKEN Yes. In those years I kept a sketch book and put down every idea I had. There were some 500 ideas and I made only 25 sculptures out of those. Recently it became possible to make some so I pulled some ideas from the sketches, made plans and had them fabricated.

PB *How did you make the transition from painting to sculpture, beginning with the slotted reliefs?*

JMC In a sense the slotted pieces just came out of the blue. But on the other hand, when I had occasion to look at my slides two or three years later I saw that the paintings that I had started out doing had seemed to evolve into sculptures. Some of my paintings started to get hard-edged and to get bigger and turned into symbol paintings – Xs, crosses, circles and arrows. Then they physically changed so that some surfaces were hard, polished lacquer, then they became completely hard-surfaced on the front and sides, sometimes with insets, then there was actually a slot in the face of the painting and this turned out to be a painting version of the sculptures that came immediately afterwards. So it was almost as if the paintings themselves had in mind where they were going and, when they got to this slotted relief stage, all they had to do was jump off the wall and become sculpture in the round.

PB *Were you aware at the time of Donald Judd's article, 'Specific Objects', published in* Arts *magazine, and of his contention that the most interesting work being made was neither painting nor sculpture, but what he referred to as three-dimensional work. Were you aware of similar work to your own being made elsewhere at the same time?*

JMC I was, at least, to an extent. I think that mostly I was intuitively aware of that kind of thing. While in school I had done sculptures that were more or less traditional, kind of like abstract expressionist sculptures but, later on, the use of colour in more abstract forms and industrial techniques naturally led to new things. Judd's term, 'specific object', was an apt term. To my mind what that is about is making new objects that are just themselves. You don't ask what they depict, or what they represent, they have their own primary being.

PB *Your concern with colour and surface, not merely in terms of finish, suggests a continuing relationship with painting. The objects function simultaneously as sculptures and as paintings.*

JMC Yes. Sometimes I think that my sculptures are in a way paintings of sculptures. If you look at them formally they are paint, or coloured material, on canvas or cloth, on wood supports. So they use traditional painting elements to make a three-dimensional form. And illusion is involved too because, for example, the blue slotted piece – *Yarmuk*, 1965 – appears as if it is solid, made of blue material with a slot cut out, whereas in fact it is hollow, so it represents a solid piece.

PB *In Judd's terms, of course, illusion was outlawed yet you wilfully persist in it despite being linked with Minimalism from the beginning. Indeed, you were included in the seminal exhibition, 'Primary Structures', in New York in 1966. You have never objected to being described as a minimalist.*

JMC No. I didn't mind the minimalist tag. Even before I had heard of Minimalism I was consciously on a reducing track. I wanted to see how pared down I could make a thing and still have presence. I had been affected by seeing Barnett Newman's work, among others. He seemed to pare everything down to a minimum and still have something strong. As for illusion, although I was using it, on the other hand I was presenting a real form with no tricks. I didn't want to make objects in exaggerated perspective or things that were blithering to the senses. I wanted the work to be straightforward so that the effects that you see are believable, natural phenomena that occur with real objects.

PB *Peter Schjeldahl once wrote that the first time he saw Carl Andre's piece,* Lever, *he felt an utter 'rightness' about it. That is exactly how I felt the first time I saw one of your plank pieces. How did you arrive at that point?*

JMC After the slotted pieces I made blocks and slabs. One day I was sitting in my studio, pondering the question of how to make the work simpler still, and I looked over to one of the walls where I had sheets and parts of sheets of plywood leaning against a wall that I had used to make the rectangular shapes and I thought to myself, I guess that's it, I will just make a board. So I made two boards which I decided to call 'planks'. Again trying to use a factual description. They were one-foot wide and an inch thick and eight-feet long, which in the US is a standard basic size.

PB *In retrospect it is a perfect resolution of the relationship between painting and sculpture in your work.*

JMC Yes. It is obvious, really, because the 'plank' stands on the floor close enough to lean against the wall and so it touches the physical world that we walk around in – the sculptural world – and at the same time it touches the wall, or the world of painting, which to my mind represents mental space. It is sort of bridge between the two worlds. I think the 'planks' are both paintings and sculptures, but formally they are sculptures because they are objects in space, whereas paintings are flat, two-dimensional planes that are usually coincident with walls or shown on walls.

PB *In 1974 you made a work,* Five Black Paintings V, *that treated painting as an object, or a relief.*

JMC Yes. That was number five in a series of five paintings in which the surface and the sides of the painting were finished in polished black, so that it was a sculpture of a painting, really.

PB *Even in your earliest works, your use of colour was extremely daring. I was particularly struck by* Think Pink, *1967, and the lavender-coloured* The Case for Fakery in Beauty, *1967. Where did those colours and titles come from?*

JMC At the time, I was leafing through women's fashion magazines because, as a matter of fact, there were even articles on art in them. One, for instance, by John Coplans, called 'Art Bloom', appeared in an issue of *Vogue* magazine – it mentioned my work among others.

PB *Dan Graham did many magazine projects at that time, including a piece called* Figurative *for* Harper's Bazaar, *in 1965. There is currently a resurgence of interest here in contemporary art among fashion magazine editors and among artists in magazine projects.*

JMC It seemed then that those magazines were almost like art magazines. I drew colour and title ideas from them like *Room in Paris*, *Think Pink* and *Live it up in Lilac.*

PB *One of the things that I think is currently very attractive about your work is its accessibility. It is not just the seductive surfaces but something to do with their relationship to the camera.* Think Pink, *for instance, is an invitation to the viewer to participate. There are none of the embargoes that Judd placed, at least theoretically, upon the viewer in any encounter with his work.*

JMC Yes, Judd's work is very severe by comparison, very serious.

PB *It doesn't make your work less serious, but you are more permissive. Is this a West Coast/East Coast thing I wonder?*

JMC I think so. There was an acceptance of sensuousness and more obvious beauty. I don't quite know why. In a way, you would think the West Coast, being close to Asia, to Japan, would have a lot of severity and Zen-inspired art. I wanted pieces to exist in – and speak with – pure form, but at the same time I wanted them to be approachable, to be interesting and sensuous enough so that one would bother to look at them in the first place. A form has to be made out of something, so why should it be made out of boring material? I was trying to marry all the elements, the form, the colour and the surface, so that they became singular entities that one could perceive and contemplate.

PB *You have referred to your sculptures as 'beings'.*

JMC Yes, I tend to think of all my works as beings, in a sense – even the paintings – but especially the sculptures. Any sculptor needs presence and that can be defined as personality almost, or beingness. A highly developed human has a body and a mind and a soul so I try to make sculptures that have the same attributes, not just physical objects only concerned with physical being but objects that also have a metaphysical dimension, or an interior, or mental dimension. So a material object that at times seems to dematerialise and become a non-material image was to me something that I wanted my objects to do because that's what humans do, or are capable of doing.

PB *The work of Brancusi comes to mind, one reason being that he, too, was unafraid of the term beauty, but also because although his forms were organic and referential while yours are purely abstract he, too, thought of his sculptures as in some ways transcending their material nature. Looking at the black polished surface of the eight-foot high piece,* Cephren, *from 1988, it is easy to believe, as many people do, that you designed the monolith in* 2001: A Space Odyssey. *The quality of 'beingness' that you strive for in your work could be said to be exactly what the monolith appears to embody. Is there something in that?*

JMC Yes. That is an interesting way to put it. People did think that I designed that monolith at the time, which I did not. It is easily possible that whoever did design it, in 1968, had seen my work. But the most interesting thing is that there is a relationship between the meaning and use of that monolith and my own work. It is a kind of mysterious message from some other race of beings. I often think in metaphorical terms of making sculptures that appear to have been left here by a UFO, by beings from another and more developed dimension or world, or place in time.

I was interested to read in a book about the making of *2001* that they first intended to use a pyramid form – since architecturally the Egyptian pyramid is one of the most mysterious and powerful things on earth – but they found that, for the purposes of the movie, it wasn't strong enough, and that a monolith form – a rectangular, shaft-like column – was stronger. This shows that form itself speaks or communicates – just form, aside even from scale, although scale is part of it. I have always considered that my work primarily uses pure form to speak with. At the same time you have to make form out of something so I use colour. And, since I want sensuousness, and touchability – mentally speaking – in my work, I also use the polished surface. The polished surfaces, I don't know if I knew this when I first used them, give a seeming transparency and illusoriness, a not-thereness, to the work.

PB *You have experimented with pyramidal forms yourself recently, using computer technology.*

JMC It is difficult to extract actual dimensions and measurements from a two-dimensional sketch of complex compound angles so I began using a computer with a three-dimensional drawing programme to make pieces like the blue faceted piece, *Runway*, 1990. I also began to use the computer to make pieces that I didn't necessarily need a computer for – to brainstorm – because I had learned to use the computer as a visualising tool, just like one uses paper and pencil.

PB *Have you considered making virtual works?*

JMC Yes, I am actually beginning to work on doing just that. I would like to be able to make pieces that are as clear visually as a photograph so that the work really does seem to exist in 3-D, even if it is only in pixels. Beyond that, the idea of making a sort of animation, so to speak, so that you could move around it, the viewpoint moving dynamically around such a form would be interesting. Or what you seem to suggest, which I hadn't thought of, to watch a form develop from nothing to something.

PB *It seemed a logical extension of what you were saying about work being both there and not there.*

JMC Yes. I am fascinated by the computer but at the same time I try to keep in mind that it is only a tool and use it as something that is supposed to produce results. For one thing, it enabled me to produce more work and to make the work more accessible in more ways. Not that I want to make it so that nobody wants to come to a physical real-world opening!

PB *Paradoxically, your work will always have to be seen precisely because of the way in which the sculptures elude our perceptual grasp, particularly when they are as large as* Column, *1986 or* Cephren, *so that you can't verify the shape from the template at the top so that at one moment* Cephren *appears to be square in section, the next, a pyramid.* Column *is the colour equivalent of* Cephren *– is it black, or is it blue? The exact shade eludes me.*

JMC It is true of anything sculptural, there is a whole dimension, a kind of sensing-in-the-round as you look at it. *Cephren* is actually an extremely dark blue, so dark that you might just think it is black.

PB *In the light of everything you have said about the dematerialisation of form, the question that comes to mind in looking at the polished metal pieces begun in 1988 is why didn't you make them before that date?*

JMC I had wanted to make stainless steel sculptures for several years before I actually made them. I just had to get the idea firmly in my mind and also it had to become physically and monetarily possible to make them. They are welded together from plates of stainless steel and then ground down and polished.

PB *What special qualities do they add do you think, being completely reflective?*

JMC Again, I was thinking that I would like to have pieces made that seemed to have been made by UFO technology – something extreme – the polished steel seemed like that. There was also one made along with these that was polished bronze. It was beautiful but it had flaws in it from the welding, and every time they fixed them others would appear, so the fabricator never finished that piece. I was always sorry that I didn't just keep it anyway and keep it in a flawed condition because it was just gorgeous.

PB *A mirror would be apparently flawless. Is perfection, supposing it were obtainable, actually undesirable?*

JMC That kind of crafting, where everything is kind of flattened out and has an extreme flawlessness, would be to my mind unnatural. I do not try to get flaws in my work but I accept them if they are not distracting. The thing really is the idea, or it is the non-physical image that is the idea, or that conveys the idea.

PB *You have exhibited for the first time here a set of ten new paintings that look very different from previous paintings. They are very gestural but the kaleidoscopic brushstrokes appear to float freely, an illusion that is increased by the use of very deep three-inch supports that appear to lift the surfaces free of the wall.*

JMC Yes, I have done something different with these paintings. I have always painted, off and on, and have even tried mixing painting with sculpture a number of times, but I have always been bothered by the edge. If you come in over the edge with a brushstroke, the loaded brush hits the edge of the canvas and splatters paint all over the place. You can go off the edge okay, like an aeroplane taking off from an aircraft carrier, but coming in, the aeroplane hits the end of the landing deck and crashes. What I did with these, then, was attach four extensions that were clamped to the sides of the paintings, extending the surface out about eight inches, so that I could land outside the painting area and then cruise in over the edge, and also sweep out over the edge more freely. I wanted to keep that exterior space beyond the rectangle active. I think of the edge as the border between the physical and the mental, and I think to an extent that what is visible implies what is invisible. I am trying to isolate and present a two-dimensional plane of activity. I don't want the painting to go around the edge of the canvas at all. I want it to appear as if it had been cut out from a larger surface or plane.

PB *They seem alive, like biological cultures under glass, an analogy that comes to mind particularly with the resin paintings.*

JMC I am trying to make fields of energy that do seem to move or that can be perceived in multiple ways. A certain amount has to come from the painting, as much as possible, but the viewer might see through one of these works, and maybe even see things that are not really strictly speaking in the painting. I think of these works as being instruments or devices that are to be used. Like looking at configurations in trees or clouds in the sky.

PB *You have said this about your sculptures that you almost want people to look through them to another dimension. They too are devices in this sense.*

JMC Right. I think people are sometimes puzzled about my paintings, and I have been, too, but when I conceived these works I found that for me they actually clarified in my mind what all my work is about which is the whole business of perceiving the two worlds, the physical and the mental, or spiritual – or the multiplicity of worlds – and of enlarging our usual frame of reference and sense of being.

Issue 204, March 1997

1998–2007

Gustav Metzger

interviewed by Andrew Wilson

A terrible beauty

ANDREW WILSON *Is there a continuity between your auto-destructive art of the sixties and your recent 'Historical Photographs'?*

GUSTAV METZGER To me there is a continuity and it is in the need to interact with society, admit to major social problems and face up to history – the past, the present and the future. However, the technique has changed. Then I was interested in technology and now I am not. I wanted to be as close to the machine as possible. I didn't want to become a machine, but to feel the machine in me, to intuitively grasp the meaning and the potential of electronics, cybernetics, even atomic power. I lived it and dreamt it, day and night. Now I am more aware than ever before of its dangers.

AW *Is aesthetics important to you?*

GM Yes, indeed. I think this will probably shock you but I am concerned with beauty, perhaps more than with anything else even though there were times in my life when I was so obsessed with politics and agitating against the art world that I wouldn't consider aesthetics and I certainly wouldn't have used the term beauty. Auto-destructive art is deeply concerned with beauty, with a terrible beauty. Adorno questioned beauty: what do we do after these calamities behind us and also facing us now? How do we respond? I responded with auto-destructive art and I say that it is beautiful. It is tinged with horror, threat and beauty. That is my feeling about the work I am doing now as well. An aesthetics which goes beyond beauty is at the centre of my work.

AW *What is the 'aesthetic of revulsion'?*

GM The aesthetic of revulsion is the artist introducing materials and activities and images which most people don't want to know about and don't want to see but the artist says, 'Look, I'm giving it to you in your face. Take it. This is a reflection of a horrible world.'

You can go right back to the most primitive activities and the most basic human activities and people will find it revolting and won't want to talk about or publicise it. The work of the Viennese Actionists is an example of artists exercising their right to produce the aesthetic of revulsion in its most extreme form and being punished for doing so. People don't want to see that kind of aesthetic activity. When you see Jesus Christ with the wounds and the blood dripping it is not a nice thing to see, and that is the aesthetic of revulsion. In the fifties an artist like Alberto Burri tore sacking apart – well, it's not a nice thing to do.

In auto-destructive art I followed this trend, tearing things apart not with my hands but with chemicals. I was fairly sophisticated. A sheet of nylon can itself be very beautiful and then you take material that will destroy it within seconds – tearing it to tatters which fall onto the floor. Well it's rather revolting isn't it? It's not what normal people do, it's only lunatics who might do it. And you cannot touch the pieces of nylon that have fallen to the floor – they are acid, you would burn yourself – you shrink from the smell of acid. The rust project was meant to fall apart within ten years by rust – it would have been a real mess – but that was what I wanted. This was my aesthetic of revulsion which I tried to force on to society and they said, politely, 'No thank you'.

AW *How do you find beauty and revulsion in the same image?*

GM I always knew, deep down, that the work I was doing in auto-destructive art would contain beauty and revulsion. That is my answer. The aesthetic of revulsion necessarily includes beauty. If you look at a Goya, there is horror and there is beauty. Falling material, an opening up, is beautiful. The result of a cut, take Lucio Fontana's cut, is beautiful. You could go on and on. There are sadists who manipulate and cut the skin – a gentle cut on the skin can be beautiful. In love a slap on the face can stimulate an orgasm, or someone might hang themselves from the ceiling and risk death because it is a beautiful experience. Throughout life we have these extreme interactions. There is no direct answer. One shouldn't look for direct answers, they wouldn't be interesting.

The aesthetic of revulsion – the presentation of extreme states whether they are psychological or physiological or where the material itself is repulsive – is embedded in my work. What do we do? We live in a world that is revolting. We live in a world that is falling apart. Inevitably artists mirror reality, artists have always done that and the worse that reality gets, the more you will have this kind of art from people.

AW *Do you see yourself as an iconoclast?*

GM No not at all, but it is part of it. I am not a Luddite. I don't destroy. I create ideas that can go beyond the present chaos. I have always seen auto-destructive art as a constructive force, I still do.

AW *What are your aims behind the 'Historic Photographs'?*

GM Behind the concept of the 'Historic Photographs' a door opens in which photography can be reconsidered. The photographs are so distorted by their particular presentation to the viewer that they are able to spend a long time thinking about them but once you start thinking about any individual photograph you inevitably think about photography. What is the truth of the photograph? The truth of the photograph is when you look at it and say 'I have seen it', and I can sit back and take notes of what I have seen, and I can describe it. By doing what I have done to these photographs you can perhaps see the photograph very clearly, only for it to disappear from sight – but the disappeared photograph is still that photograph. I am offering the public a new range of reflections on the photograph, and every picture I have chosen has a great and exceptional meaning when contemplated within its historic context.

In Oxford, as in Paris at 'Life/Live', I have placed the work showing the massacre on the Mount in Jerusalem, *To Walk Into*, near to the work showing Nazis forcing the Jews to wash the pavement in Vienna in 1938, *To Crawl Into*. There has been an intense public debate for decades in Israel about the mistreatment of the Arabs. The discussion goes along the lines that because the Jews had been persecuted by the Nazis this forces them to retaliate, forces them to relive the Holocaust by inflicting the Holocaust on somebody else under their domination.

When I experienced the horror of this catastrophe of Jews killing unarmed Arabs and wounding hundreds on that day in 1990, the revulsion in me became so strong that it opened up the door to the whole project of the 'Historic Photographs'. I decided to show works where Jews dominate and mistreat Arabs. There are the Nazis, and there you, the Israelis, are and I accuse you: 'You shouldn't do this. They, the Nazis, shouldn't have done it, but you shouldn't do it.' It is my duty as a Jew to say this to Jews. 'Don't do it, I warn you, don't repeat the Nazis.' That is why these works are placed in direct confrontation with each other. And that is also about the aesthetic of revulsion. I am revolted by each image, by each historical reality and I want to warn people and how can I warn them as an artist? – by bringing them as close as possible to that pictorial reality by saying 'Go in, crawl in on your knees, pray that this may never happen again. Walk in so that you touch both the Jewish police and the poor Arabs and feel your way through this reality – don't just look at it.' By making it as difficult as I do, I expose people more to the deepest parts of this reality than if I had just said 'look at this picture'. Everybody looks at pictures to saturation point and then they turn away, but I am hoping that people will physically penetrate and be physically moved by penetrating this scene of terror in Jerusalem, the holiest of cities in the world.

The 'Historic Photographs' are not just about images but history. With these works I also want maximum tension and this is the key to the installation. Spaces are minimal and tight so that people will feel oppressed, pushed and manipulated. When you are in you can't move away without being close to feeling trapped. The 'Historic Photographs' show an aggression towards nature and an aggression towards humanity.

AW *Would you disagree with the idea that after Auschwitz there can be no more poetry?*

GM No, I don't disagree with it. It is such a fundamental question. It is of such incredible ungraspable importance, that I would not dare say that I don't believe in it. All I can say, modestly and hesitantly, is that I do now want to work. There were many years when I didn't want to work, when I rejected the invitation to work.

AW *In the seventies during the 'three years without art' you announced a shift from production of art to theoretical activity. How would you compare your activity to that of conceptual artists who had adopted a similar strategy?*

GM Well the quickest answer is that my position was more radical. I never produced a single object for the gallery wall in that period. I never identified the thinking I was doing with any art object and it never occurred to me to do so, whereas they were continuously and progressively muddying the waters between philosophy, thinking, research and actual production – increasingly so, to the point at which Art & Language became 'wall artists' toured around the world.

AW *What was the form of theoretical activity that you undertook at that time?*

GM As you know, from the beginning of 1965 the centre of my concern was the obsession with trying to understand the development of science and technology. This led to my contact, since its formation in 1969, with the Society for Social Responsibility in Science, and with scientists who were researching new ways of understanding and developing science. I was the only artist who was involved enough to get close to these people on the edge of radical thinking on science and the history and philosophy of science. This was the cutting edge of my work – the understanding and reflection on the dangers of science and the challenge to create a science that is not destructive.

From 1974 the concern moved to the fields of architecture and design. I was aware that there were gaps in my knowledge, and these fields presented a challenge. The organisation of the AGUN symposium – Art in Germany Under National Socialism – with Cordula Frowein in September 1976 fitted well, as it included architecture, town planning and design.

AW *One aspect of auto-destructive art is the way it refuses the marketplace.*

GM This has certainly been a key drive and achieved its culmination in the 1974 exhibition 'Art into Society/Society into Art', at which time I called for the 'three years without art' (1977–80). With the auto-destructive work I was against the marketplace and only concerned with public monuments which they didn't let me build, so the energy ebbed away. The acid paintings were a form of performance, and were never meant to be preserved. With the protest against commercialisation I was again helpless because nobody took any notice. The artists laughed at it, nobody talked to me about it. Now I am involved with the potential of the 'Historic Photographs' but there is a difference, the 'Historic Photographs' will be sold if anyone wants to buy them. I was asked recently by a friend if I had sold out. What do you think?

AW *Do you feel you have sold out?*

GM No, I don't, but who am I to judge?

AW *But if a commercial gallery wanted to represent you?*

GM The answer would be 'No'. Why should I say 'Yes'? Here I am, having survived. I am intact. I am as healthy as I have been at any stage for the last 30 or 40 years. I am full of optimism and believe in the work that I am doing. I am not dependent on handouts or commissions from the art world. If I did otherwise I would be going against all that I have fought for. What would be the point? It would be retrograde in every sense.

AW *You have said that the images of the 'Historic Photographs' were not disposable images. You are always surrounded by newspapers and yet the images in newspapers live only for the moment, they are disposable by their very nature.*

GM There is no contradiction. When you say that the newspaper is discarded and the 'Historic Photographs' recycle what has been discarded, that is exactly what makes it so relevant. You could say it is always the same newspaper and it is always the same image. In that sense it is eternal. Every image is significant and always has the same significance. It is reality. There is nothing more real than reality and newspapers come as close as anything to it.

The other reason I am interested in newspapers is that it is information which I can use in my work and life. I need this sort of information in order to survive – biologically, economically and socially. It is through newspapers that issues are discussed. You cannot escape. We are now trapped in newspapers, we could dispense with television but we could not dispense with newspapers. You pick up and unravel reality and lies together.

AW *Do you see the piles of newspapers around us here in this room in any way as 'batteries' in the Beuysian sense?*

GM Yes, indeed there is a warmth. Physically it warms the room, you can sleep on it or near it – that is part of it. It is sculptural, it is tactile.

AW *How would you describe your own politics?*

GM First of all and the simplest answer: I don't belong to political parties and my distrust of politics in England is increasing. But politics is important and relevant. There must be a deep and sudden change where art again deeply engages with the world – the globalised world – that is changing so rapidly, or we will go under. I said this before in another way in 1974: let us stop work in order to break this situation down. In my old age I am no longer so radical. I am not saying 'Stop it', I am now saying, 'Change it, please. But if you don't you have had it.'

I always thought of myself as an artist who wanted to affect people. Asked what art is about I would say it is about society. It is for other people. Auto-destructive art was a solution to the question of how

I could get my art involved with society. The idea of creating auto-destructive art was my role as a political animal. What more could I do as an artist in politics than create these monuments which would deeply affect and change society?

I feel a certain gap and a lack in people today. By and large young artists are not politically engaged and I can't see them engaging unless they change. This situation relates to Thatcher and to a period when an attack was made on the Left, a concerted attack and a successful one – and the reverberations of that attack are with us and are in the young in that they don't question or talk about society. They don't bring up any radical ideas, they just potter away in their studios and then the British Council and the Arts Council come along and they help them along like little babies: 'Out into the world you go. South America, never mind where, never mind how repressive the regimes might be, never mind that people have been killed there, so long as we can produce and push you out "babies out you go".'

Nevertheless I admit that I am fascinated by a lot of the work being made by young artists in Britain today. I got a lot of pleasure from walking several times through the 'Sensation' exhibition. I'm glad that the work is there and I do believe that London is a hotspot. I also believe that London is going to produce significant work and I am very, very confident about this. I do believe that deep down there are artists now who are working on important social issues, who are thinking very deeply. It's just a question of stimulating them and then hopefully the work will come out. I am quite confident that it will – another generation, another drive – I hope so, there is a good chance.

AW *Between 1944, when you left the anarchist commune you had been living in up to that point, and 1957 you appear to have been uninvolved in political activity. Did you think that the two activities – art and politics – were mutually exclusive?*

CM In the early forties I planned to be a full-time revolutionary who would move around like they did in Russia. I really meant this and was preparing myself for a kind of martyrdom – possibly even death by firing squad. And then I was trying to be an artist who would be a revolutionary in and through art. The key to this was Wilhelm Reich and I tested the possibility of creating an art that would represent Reichian ideas – liberation and fulfilment through biological, sexual, psychological activity – and it failed. I couldn't do it. This was the crisis of my youth, for a time I gave up being a revolutionary, it didn't work out. I regarded myself as a failure for a certain number of years, and I was a failure and I suffered.

In my youth I was torn between two directions in art – the extremes, the warmth and the sensuous or a facing-up to pain and agony. This is reflected in this exhibition. You have the warmth and freedom of the liquid crystal environment and the coldness of the 'Historic Photographs'. Here I am fulfilling a life's work – the two poles are actually present.

Issue 222, December–January 1998–99

Hans Haacke

interviewed by Patricia Bickers

Mixed messages

PATRICIA BICKERS *In the catalogue for 'Viewing Matters: Upstairs', the exhibition at the Museum Boijmans Van Beuningen, Rotterdam that you curated in 1996 – that was a precursor of this present exhibition – you cited Marcel Duchamp's observation that the spectator 'adds something to the work that the artist never thought of, he not only adds, but also deforms, in his own way'. The importance of the active viewer has since become the trope of much contemporary art practice, or at least of discourse about it, but it has been a central concern of your own work at least since the kinetic work of the 1960s.*

HANS HAACKE In the sixties I wanted to get the viewers physically involved with my work. It was to break down the barrier between the viewer and the object and lead to a shift in attitude towards the art object. When viewers are allowed or even asked to handle an object, its institutional sanctity is no longer intact. It is off the altar. The work I did for this show – I call it a work – is another attempt to get the viewers involved. It is to remind them that, in effect, they are the ones who produce the meaning of an artefact: it is a social product. In the normal museum exhibition the focus is chiefly on the discrete object which, presumably, acts as an autonomous signifier, independent of the social roles it has played in the past and those it performs today, as if it were endowed with inherent universal qualities. In this show I have tried to demonstrate that normal perceptions of an object – I am using the term 'perception' here both in the optical as well as in the figurative sense of the word – are not normal at all. The meaning an object has for us depends on the context in which we encounter it and, while its physical qualities guide us to a certain degree, we, in fact, generate its meaning.

PB *In recent years the ideology of museum display has shifted away from the chronological, overtly didactic hang towards an ahistorical, thematic and contextual approach – I am thinking of the recent displays at the Pompidou Centre, the Museum of Modern Art, New York and Tate Modern. In the latter sense, the museum sector could be said to be catching up with you. What are your views on this development?*

HH I can speak only about the three-part sequel 'Modern Starts' at MoMA. In its first instalment, 'People, Places, Things', I was pleasantly surprised to see paintings and sculptures together with items that are generally not seen as belonging to the so-called fine arts among them, reportage photographs, including Atget's, that gave a sense of the period in which the paintings and sculptures had been produced. The odd effect was that many avant-garde paintings, particularly those from Paris, looked a bit staid and smelled of the well-appointed drawing room. That was surprising. Since the artworks were not arranged according to school or style, but rather following thematic categories, I got a better sense of the different approaches to traditional themes. Many of my friends were very critical of the show. On the whole, this first instalment intrigued me. I missed the second instalment because I didn't want to cross the picket line of the museum staff who were on strike at the time. The part of the last instalment that I did get to see (I didn't manage to see the whole) was disappointing, in particular the presentation of the works of the sixties and early seventies that had been made with a deliberate political intention. All the sharp edges were rounded off. It looked very polite, as if made for the collector's home. People who had not been around at the time could not get a sense that these works had been offensive to what was then called the establishment, that they played a role in the cultural and political turmoil of the period, and that the Museum of Modern Art itself had been under attack. The Vietnam War, racial conflict in the US, the cultural if not political revolutions that swept most of the countries of the western world – all these conflicts that deeply affected my generation – had effectively been sanitised.

PB *Is this not an inevitable consequence of institutionalisation?*

HH It is, of course, inevitable that everything loses its freshness and urgency with time, not only such socially and politically intentioned works. If things survive, not only physically but also in the sense that people pay attention to them, they cannot possibly continue playing the role they did at the time when they were made. I do believe, however, that one could present them in such a way that the viewer can understand the context in which they were produced, the raw nerves that they touched, and so get a better sense of their 'performance'. They were not made for the white cube. I have seen exhibitions that do accomplish this.

PB *Is there a sense in which you, and your critique of such institutions, are being co-opted, in this case by the V&A and the Serpentine, in the same way that once-offensive work can become sanitised in the context of a museum?*

HH Thanks to a variety of pressures, including decades of institutional critique and other critical approaches to the role of museums in our society, there is now a certain willingness by some to look at the ways they function. After all, there are curators and administrators today who participated in the cultural revolution of the sixties and read the same books as we did. Of course, there are limits to how far they are ready to expose themselves in front of the world. Like their predecessors they are dependent on the goodwill of governmental, and now corporate, forces and need to consider the interests of their trustees. But to the more adventurous among them it is not as problematic as it once was to extend an invitation to me. In turn, I do not consider myself automatically as being co-opted when that happens. Some people, who have looked at earlier works of mine, are wondering whether I have mellowed. Maybe so. But perhaps they have a somewhat one-dimensional view of me. In the show at the Museum Boijmans Van Beuningen and also in this work here at the Serpentine, I am not primarily interested in looking at today's power structures in and behind the institutions – not that this is no longer of interest to me. Instead I am focusing on the artefacts in the collection, their presentation, the institution of the museum and the institution of art history. The production of meaning intrigues me as much as looking at who funds the institution and what they get in return. To a degree, of course, they are linked.

PB *Sometimes the softer, more mellow, approach can work on the consciousness in slower, more telling ways. For me the juxtaposition, in Rotterdam, of images from Goya's 'Disasters of War' series, with Duchamp's late drawings from 'The Lovers' series, made at the time that he was secretly working on* Étant donnés *– itself a highly ambiguous work in terms of both its violence and eroticism – was especially arresting.*

By means of this 'exhibition of exhibition', as you have called it, you make this process of manipulation obvious to the viewer.

HH I apparently enjoy 'manipulating'. In effect, everyone who presents something to the public engages in manipulation, whether they are aware of it or not. Every selection, and every arrangement of such a selection, inevitably gives the material a spin. I hope I succeeded in making the viewer aware of my manipulation so that I am not suspected of having pulled a fast one. This approach is not political in the immediate sense, but it may lead people to recognise why or how they respond to images and that this has ideological implications and by extension also political consequences.

PB *In the past you faced constant institutional opposition from MoMA, the Whitney Museum of American Art and so on, but today doors are more likely to open for you. You were able, for instance, partially to destroy the German Pavilion for the Venice Biennale in 1993 – it even won the Leone d'Oro prize – and to see through your Reichstag project in Berlin. It has been a long hard battle, but is your present status an advantage or is it in some ways a hindrance to your work?*

HH Surviving these troubles, thanks to the help of a lot of courageous and enterprising people, has given me a thick skin. And, as you say, my status as a veteran has indeed created opportunities I would not have had otherwise. But there are many institutions that would rather not deal with me. Name recognition has its downside. Some among the older museum people in the Netherlands were aghast at what I did in Rotterdam. Particularly after my 'Sanitation' of the Whitney Museum last year, I seem to have regained the status of an untouchable in some quarters of New York. The work in Berlin is still controversial today. But if doors do open it would be hypocritical to pretend they are closed. One should go through them and use the situation for whatever it is worth.

PB *You can certainly be said to have opened doors for other artists. In fact, your work seems especially pertinent to us now in Britain because many artists, as well as critics and curators, look to you and to the art of the sixties and seventies with a kind of nostalgia for some kind of golden age of direct political engagement. Have the rules of – political – engagement changed for you since the sixties?*

HH As the political scene in general has changed so have the 'rules of engagement'. More specifically, in Europe, the quasi takeover of public institutions by private interests has advanced tremendously. It began in the seventies. The US served as an example to emulate. As the East used to look to Moscow, so the Europeans looked to the US for guidance. In both cases, it amounted to a sell-out. In Britain this process accelerated during the Thatcher years. Labour did not stop it. In fact, practically all social democratic parties in Europe embraced the notion that cuts in cultural funding are necessary and that they could be offset by funds from corporate sponsors. Neither the politicians nor the press, nor a generally uninformed public, thought much about the consequences of this de facto privatisation of institutions whose budget nevertheless continues to be underwritten by the taxpayers. In this neo-liberal hall of mirrors, people seem to think they can get something for nothing which, of course, is rarely the case. Train wrecks are no longer recognised as such. It may take an economic or political catastrophe to change currently prevailing attitudes – I don't hope for such catastrophes to happen.

PB *In 1978 you wrote that formalism had rendered art a 'socially irrelevant phenomenon', a situation your own practice has always sought to redress. In the same article you argued for the contingent, or relative, nature of aesthetic value in contradistinction to the liberal myth of the ideological neutrality of beauty. Your rearrangement of museum collections directly addresses both these issues.*

HH One of the journalists I spoke to at the Serpentine was surprised that I used the word 'beautiful' with a positive connotation. In Rotterdam and also in London I included artefacts I personally consider beautiful, next to others that I think are silly, ugly or even despicable because of what they stand for. These value judgements reveal my 'habitus', that is my background, my acculturation, and how the world I live in – personally, professionally as well as a political being – has shaped me. I may share some or even many of these views with visitors to the show, who happen to come from a similar mould. Through strategic arrangements and the scrambling of categories I tried to promote an awareness of this contingency. At the V&A a crucifix is neatly separated from Buddha statues, and so are Islamic prayer rugs from Jewish religious artefacts like a Torah mantle. In the central gallery of the Serpentine they are brought together and face each other. And, depending on how one looks at this constellation, they surround with empathy or could have reason to be challenged by the presence of a huge male nude in their midst – a plaster cast of Michelangelo's *Dying Slave* in the Louvre. Even though the young man appears to be in his death throes, at least according to the title and its original destination (the tomb of Pope Julius II, the posture of his body and the expression on his face could also be understood as conveying religious – or erotic – ecstasy, a tangle of 'mixed messages'.

PB *You have cited, among others, Duchamp and Lautréamont as precursors of your critique of the museum and of aesthetic value – the latter's proposed encounter between a sewing machine and an umbrella on an operating table having as much logic apparently as some of your own juxtapositions – while the potted palms at the entrance to 'Mixed Messages' at the Serpentine Gallery deftly reference Marcel Broodthaers's own 'museum' project. However, the display as a whole, with its witty reference to the Great Exhibition of 1851 in the form of the two rather vulgar vases depicting Victoria and Albert, unambiguously signals the exhibition's underlying theme: the legacies of empire. You have literally, and metaphorically, held up a mirror to the viewer. Was it inevitable, this being the centenary year of Victoria's death, that this would be your central theme?*

HH I was not aware of this anniversary. As you know, the V&A was founded under Victoria's reign, with Albert's express support. The museum has its roots in the Great Exhibition. I was told that the vases – on their backs are images of the Crystal Palace – were the first items in the museum's collection. Established at the height of empire, many of the non-European objects in the collection originate in those parts of the world that belonged to the empire. The imagery of a good number of them is a testimony specifically to the formerly British, or generally western, domination of the world. In the same vein, in the Rotterdam collection, I came across many traces of the Dutch West and East India companies which were powerful rivals of Britain's colonial ambitions.

PB *Which, of all the exhibits you encountered at the V&A, was for you the most telling?*

HH There were many. Just to speak of one: when I saw the aquatints from Calcutta (after James Baille Fraser, 1826), I was struck by the oppressive presence of an enormous triumphal arch, imperial palaces and massive steepled churches in the middle of what amounted to an Indian village. Indigenous labourers are seen scurrying through unpaved streets, diligently stepping aside when a horse-drawn carriage of their colonial masters passes. I juxtaposed these images with a large painting by Henry Courtney Selous, celebrating the opening of the Great Exhibition. Victoria and Albert and the royal entourage occupy the centre. They are surrounded by representatives of the Church of England, the British aristocracy and delegations of European potentates. Behind the royal company we see the iconic palm tree. To round out this ensemble, in front of the official state painting I positioned a sculpture, made in 1990 by Viet-Hong Lieu, a ten-year-old Vietnamese boy in London. I found it in the Museum of Childhood in Bethnal Green, a branch of the V&A. Out of wood he had made two brightly painted cut-out figures – a white child with a lollipop in his hand, crying bitterly and, standing behind him, an older boy with darker skin and black hair. The older boy is throwing up his hands in horror at the turd the screaming kid had deposited behind himself.

PB *Extraordinary! Was there one exhibit that you would like to have included that you were unable to, for whatever reason?*

HH Yes, a beautiful eighteenth-century Indian chintz with images of Indians and Dutch traders. I found it on display in the Indian galleries. The textile conservators considered it too fragile for a move up the road to Kensington Gardens. As a replacement, I was offered an Indian petticoat piecegoods fabric, also of the eighteenth century. Along its borders are Indian depictions of Europeans having tea. But that was also eventually nixed. It could only be displayed in a case. Aside from the problem that the budget did not allow for a case, I was opposed to putting it into a glass coffin. It would not have been possible to see it with all the reflections, and would have been robbed of all its sensuality and tactile qualities. It also could not have served as a backdrop, as intended, for a silver epergne with palm trees, the proverbial Indian elephant and exotic figures commissioned in Bengal by a British client.

PB *This is one of the effects of institutionalisation that you referred to earlier and it is the subject of Louise Lawler's* Glass Cage, *1991–93, a black-and-white photograph of Degas's sculpture,* The Little Dancer Aged Fourteen, *that you included in 'Viewing Matters'.*

HH Yes. I was very happy not to have been obliged to put her in a glass cage as seen on Lawler's photo from the Boston Museum. In Rotterdam she was resolutely holding her own, exposed, with both feet on the ground, and facing Rodin's amputated *Man Walking*. Had the conservators of the Boijmans been as squeamish as their colleagues at the V&A, this confrontation would not have been possible.

PB *It must be a tremendous responsibility, taking on these institutions on the one hand, but also working not only with the work of other artists from the past, but with that of contemporary artists.*

HH I hope my colleagues understand it as a tribute to their works rather than as misuse. Putting the whole thing together was extremely exhausting, with long stretches of frustration and anxiety, but also of great joy working with these 'readymades'. Originally, I was to have prepared a solo show of my own works. I was not really in the mood for that, particularly since I had already had a show at the Tate Gallery in the eighties. It was a fortunate coincidence that Lisa Corrin, the curator, and Julia Peyton-Jones, the director of the Serpentine, had already opened a dialogue with the V&A regarding a collaborative project inside the museum. My venture expanded that collaboration in the other direction, up Exhibition Road into Kensington Gardens, where exactly 150 years earlier the Great Exhibition had been held.

Issue 244, March 2001

Ed Ruscha

interviewed by Patricia Bickers

No man's land

PATRICIA BICKERS *In an interview in 1978, you used an expression that could have been the title of one of your works – 'no man's land' – to characterise the territory between a work and its interpretation, specifically between your first book* Twentysix Gasoline Stations, *1963, and one interpretation of it by Eleanor Antin as an autobiographical 'travelogue' since it apparently tracks gas stations on the route between Los Angeles, where you live, and Oklahoma City, where you grew up.*

ED RUSCHA I did make a work called *No Man's Land* about 15 years ago but I think that I destroyed that work. It was a painting of a map of the State of Oklahoma before it was a state, when it was known as Indian Territory. People read things that are sometimes not intended by the artist. I am constantly surprised by interpretations of my work that are amusing to me and I almost want to say 'Yes! Maybe there is some truth to that.' The critic, Dave Hickey, once said something like: 'He paints Standard Stations and he paints Norms... Oh, I see, he's painting "norms and standards"', but it never occurred to me and I consider myself very open-minded to my own work and yet that never dropped into place! So interpretation is a no man's land.

PB *Why did you destroy the work?*

ER Because it seemed a distraction at the time. I destroy very few works – either they are outright mistakes or the execution is badly done and irreversible.

PB *You seem very relaxed about the matter of interpretation. Do you feel that to some extent a work is completed, in a Duchampian sense, by the viewer or is there a limit to the degree of interpretation that you can accept?*

ER There are no hard rules. I am not the kind of artist that does something that needs to be received in a direct, understood way. It is like alchemy – you bring these odd things together to make some kind of statement which, I suppose, is the artist's style. I constantly find myself putting little signifiers into my work but I don't do it for clearer communication, I'm doing it for the power of the work. I think that people overinterpret Duchamp's work. I understand why they do, it is because they are fascinated by it – as I am – but I don't really ask myself what it is about. What can you really say about a chocolate grinder? I just find it an extremely powerful picture, even if you didn't know what it was – they could have called it a pepper grinder and I wouldn't know the difference – and I'm not sure that it is that important to know. Maybe it had nothing to do with his art but he just saw that thing and the visual impact of it inspired him to make the work. I find myself in a parallel mode with him in this respect. I remember first seeing his work and being stumped and very intrigued in the same breath. Similarly, I saw this reproduction of a Jasper Johns painting, *Target with Four Faces*, 1955, when I was at art school, and I was just thrown by this work. I actually took it to art school with me and said 'tell me about this, what is it?'. They said: 'It's symmetrical – you can't make symmetrical art!' It's just a mode of thinking that you can't make work like that. That idea of teaching art, of helping you along the path of understanding, is secondary to just walking up to a piece of art and just seeing it and having it be powerful to you. I've always followed my instinct on things, I think it is important to respond to things intuitively as an artist.

PB *Yet you have said that working in a very 'premeditated' way on the books, for instance, was a very 'liberating' experience, while at the same time you emphasise the importance of intuition and have referred in the past to 'working with the accident' in a way that is even reminiscent of Jackson Pollock.*

ER I really wish sometimes that I took more advantage of accidents because I know they can lead you down very interesting paths. Sometimes I make materials 'accidents' or something will happen that is jarring to the thinking process. Sometimes I picture myself as being somebody who is very conservative and linear in their thinking and yet I don't want to be. Sometimes I should just lighten up and let the accident happen.

PB *One of the most 'painterly' paintings in this exhibition is* Ace *of 1962, which is painted in thick impasto, yet you have always said that you are not a painter, that you 'use' painting. In fact you have even said that you actively dislike paint – so much so that you temporarily gave up painting in 1969 – painting* Ace *must have been torture for you.*

ER As I recall, the painting was a bit tongue-in-cheek – the issues were being pushed to a comical extreme – I was making the painting appear as though the paint was so thick that it was actually scraping up more paint and piling it up against the edges of the letters. I guess that was the crazy dance that I was doing with this work. I knew that I was going to get beyond this but I liked the painterly aspect of it to begin with but gradually I moved out of that and got down to flat painting.

PB *In an interview published in* Studio International *in 1970 you said, 'I'm terrified to think that I'll be painting at 60.' Do you remember saying that?*

ER I do remember saying that. Maybe I had misgivings or doubts about continuing, but I always kept going. I knew I wasn't going to stop being an artist when I stopped painting, I knew there was going to be some other avenue for me. Then when I did resume painting, it was with the stain works, the organic works.

PB *Yes, at the time of that interview you were making a series of silk-screen prints for Editions Alecto in London which led to the related painting series of the early seventies such as the exquisitely painful sounding* Sand in the Vaseline (Equalised egg yolk on satin) *and the apparently dead-pan* Various Cruelties (Blueberry extract on rayon crepe)*, both of 1974.*

ER I didn't start out wanting to make those prints using organic materials but I'd done the stains book before and somehow one thing led to the next and I began to experiment. I've always felt that that was a very successful venture for me – more successful than a lot of my things – but nobody really looked at them, they were never very successful.

PB *Was the series made in response to finding yourself in a different context? In that same interview you talked about your first impressions of London and, in fact, the titles of the works in the series:* News, Mews, Pews, Brews, Stews *and* Dues, *set in Old English type, are very redolent of old London.*

ER I was intent on invoking symbols of Great Britain: News = England being a tabloid-minded country. Mews = little alley streets; Pews = Westminster Abbey, Church of England; Brews = stouts, ales, bitters; Stews = local cuisines; Dues = Robin Hood, unfair taxation.

PB *The title of this print series brings to mind an equally evocative later work, one of the 'dark' paintings from 1988 entitled* 17th Century *in which the sky rains words – 'war!' 'taxes!' 'alchemy!' 'plague!' 'damsels!' 'melancholia!' and 'firewood!'– in Gothic script. In fact, it reminds me of Albrecht Dürer's apocalyptic drawing of the sky apparently raining blood.*

ER That was not really part of my thinking but there is something slightly apocalyptic that gets into my work. I don't know where it comes from – maybe the Catholic Church – I don't know.

PB *In the black spray-paintings of the late eighties, which have also been referred to as the 'silhouette paintings' or the 'nocturnes', the words are 'blanked out' altogether.*

ER It was the bang of the black and white together that I was into at that time. The censor strips – I am always trying to think of a better word for them – are almost like little private thoughts, they add a mysterious dimension to the painting.

PB *Andy Warhol once commented that there are no people in your work.*

ER That is when I first met Andy. I gave him a copy of that book [*Twentysix Gasoline Stations*] and he said, 'Oh Gosh, I like it – there are no people.' I never really thought about it but that's when somebody else comes to you and tells you something about your own work that you didn't dream of – like 'norms and standards'.

PB *At the time you also avoided using cars in your work, an otherwise obvious subject perhaps, saying that it would be hard 'to make a statement about cars without flavouring it too heavily'. On the other hand, although you have emphasised that your subjects are chosen because they are 'more-or-less neutral', at the same time you added: 'Now that I think about it, all these subjects lead you back to people.'*

ER Maybe the people are implied. There is a tradition, especially in British art – a great, deep, heart-pounding tradition – of figurative painting. You have to have some reference to the human body – or you have to have gone through that – even if you're an abstract painter. But I have never felt compelled to paint pictures of people. I have painted a picture of a magazine cover with a dead man but it was like a painting of an illustration on the cover of a magazine. I took somebody else's illustration of a dead man and repainted it, so I'm not really painting people, I'm painting a magazine cover. I am surprised that there are so many people – so many artists – who really, sincerely still believe that the human figure – the human body – is essential to our understanding of the universe.

PB *You once said that had you lived in New York your career would have been very different. Here too, while Britain looks to Washington politically, it is tied to New York aesthetically. LA art, and West Coast art in general, have tended to be perceived in Britain, at least until recently, as not being serious – and not just because of its humour, though despite our much-vaunted British sense of humour, we don't seem to like it in art. Was there a similar perception of LA art in New York?*

ER Oh yes. Not just artists but writers and very intelligent people feel that unless you have somehow checked into Manhattan, or lived in Manhattan at some point or another, or at least have a PO box there, you're destined for territorial purgatory. New York is undoubtedly an extremely dynamic city and the most vital place on earth for the creation of art, but it is a mistake to think it is the only place in which to make art.

PB *In recent years, though, there has been a great deal of interest in West Coast art, in your work and that of contemporaries such as John Baldessari and Bruce Nauman, while Ann Goldstein and Anne Rorimer's show, 'Reconsidering the Object of Art', recouped the work of many marginalised West Coast artists – including that of a number of women artists – who had been left out of an essentially East Coast story of Conceptual Art. Today there is a perception of great energy coming from West Coast America, particularly LA.*

ER It makes a better argument to use not territorial distinctions but gender distinctions. In some ways women had a better deal back in the fifties than they did in the seventies. So you could have that gripe if you wanted to, and likewise you could have that regionalist gripe, too. Things are changing, communication is changing so fast that people can live in Kansas, or anywhere in England, and make a statement as an artist, they can know everything that's going on in London and New York, but still they are kind of lost because they are not in the 'scene'.

PB *Any discussion about LA, or about your work, inevitably leads to the subject of Hollywood. You once admitted that, 'like everyone else I'm a frustrated film director' and you have made two short movies so far:* Miracle *in 1975, which features both a car and a person – a mechanic – and* Crackers *which exists in a movie version from 1970 entitled* Premium. *However, you have never used video in a work.*

ER No. They wanted me to show my two films on video here, but then I'd become a video artist and I don't want that association, not because I don't like video but because I still like the idea of film. It's an old cranky medium, and it is going to be out the window very soon, but still I'd like to stay with it, firstly because you can project it as big as some academy-sized screen but also because film is very fine-grained and you can get some very good pictures with it.

PB *Could you see yourself ever using video?*

ER Actually I recently got a video camera but I use it to document things. For instance I used a video camera to shoot the ongoing *Sunset Strip* series for the last two years.

PB *Is that as a substitute for taking conventional photographs with a camera or are you using both at the same time?*

ER No. I would not be abandoning any technique that I was always in love with, but I do love photographs. I love photographs that come from negatives. I don't like digital photographs – they look like digital photographs – and I still like silver gelatin prints.

PB *You wouldn't use video to make a work as such?*

ER I might use a video camera because of the usefulness of it, and because of the directness of it. I love doing film, but it can be so laborious. For instance, you might say about this room here, 'Hey, what's wrong with this room? This is perfect light, absolutely perfect light', but if you want to shoot a movie like this, and you want it to look this way, you can't do it – you have to re-light the room so that it looks like it does right now.

PB *And this gets in the way of making work, it sidetracks you?*

ER It does sidetrack you. My son showed me a feature of this new video camera: we went into a dark room and closed the windows and shut off the lights and you could see people and everything that was going on in the room with this little night-time enhancer and so you could actually shoot a movie with no light whatsoever using the night-vision enhancer. I couldn't believe it – I mean that's staggering.

So I don't know, there might be something I could do with video but I don't like video projections. I'm sick of going into galleries and seeing video projections, they become so standard that they become numbing and the medium suffers for that. I always liked Bill Wegman's videos, and Bruce Nauman's, though – well there are a lot of people that make good videos – but with film you have a captive audience, but in a gallery situation people just walk in and out of them.

PB *It's a mode of viewing akin to what supermarket supervisors call 'grazing'.*

ER Grazing? Yes. You don't have the time containment that you do with a film.

PB *Throughout your work you have kept all these elements – the word, the backdrop – as you have referred to the landscapes in your paintings – and narrative – in a state of tension, never quite surrendering to the demands of any one element or medium, be it film, photography or painting. Perhaps if you made a full-blown feature film that tension would be lost?*

ER Well, yes. I try every so often to look back on my work and in doing so I discover things – for example, I could have taken one of those gas stations and just blown the thing up and printed it on the canvas and let that be my art, and yet that is something that I would consciously reject. I can't tell you why, but I just don't think it has a place with me.

Issue 252, December–January 2001–02

Michael Snow

interviewed by Michael O'Pray

In synch

MICHAEL O'PRAY *This is the first major show of your work here which has gone beyond your film work. How did the show come about?*

MICHAEL SNOW Catsou Roberts had discussed with me her ideas for an exhibition of my work, several years before she became a curator at the Arnolfini. When such a show became possible, we thought it would be good to do something that was partly retrospective and would attempt to show my work from various periods and in several media in addition to photography and film. We decided to show work that had a 'vision' emphasis, that was camera-related or photography- and film-related, but was gallery work. Films were shown in the auditorium. The book *Michael Snow almost Cover to Cover* which appeared with the Arnolfini show discusses these themes very well.

MO'P *Were you happy with the results?*

MS While inevitably it was only possible to show one or very few examples of a particular area of work, I was very happy with the final selections.

MO'P *I was struck by the conceptual coherence across the media.*

MS The premises for the exhibition go back to the sixties. The show starts with several mutually supportive but distinctive 'Walking Women' works. All my work between 1961 and 1967, including my 1964 film *New York Eye and Ear Control*, used the same outline of a side view of a walking woman. The 1962 *Four to Five* is my first photo-work: black-and-white photographs of a black silhouette walking woman in different urban settings. *Test Focus Field Figure* made in 1965 is a painting which uses the 'projection' of spray enamels to make three simultaneous different-sized 'projections' of the same figure. *Morningside*

Heights, made in the same year, is a sculpture and painting and, for the first time in my work, uses a transparency. *Hawaii*, 1964, in a sense edits four images including a picture of sound.

MO'P *You've worked in so many different media – films, photography, books, holography, sculpture, video – can you say more in a general way why this has been so?*

MS No. Put too simply – of course – I started playing music professionally in high school, kept playing when I was at art school, drawing, painting and sculpting. I made my first film in 1956. Offand on, for several years, I would think that it was wrong to work in so many media but I gradually realised that I was mediumistically amoral. Different media posit different experiences.

MO'P *I wanted to ask you about the differences between the gallery space and the cinema-theatre type space. They suggest movement and stasis, and different kinds of 'looking'. Can you say something generally about this?*

MS While it is possible temporarily to stop gallery-goers in their tracks, a 'picture-gallery' situation – think of it as a comic strip – is a stroll. The ambulatory spectator trucks, dollys and pans, so to speak.

MO'P *You've always had an interest in new technologies.*

MS During 1984 and 1985 I made many holographic works from which *Egg* was included in the show, partly because it belongs also to another family of works: those that contain the image of the artist. I used Polaroids, for example, in *Authorization*, 1969, and *Venetian Blind*, 1970, which are not self-portraits but images which contain the imprint of the maker. There are lots of photographic works, each like my films, trying to foreground a particular possibility, particular forms and contents of the medium. For example, *Field*, 1974, is a pure light and shade work composed of 99 snapshot-sized photograms and two positive and negative photographs.

MO'P *You're also known for using sequences.*

MS There are several sequential works – *Digest* involves the spectator in looking at the photo series manually. But there are also timed, looped, colour-light projection carousel slide pieces.

MO'P *The idea of the world filmed as a stubborn resistant reality reduced to light on a screen and worked over by camera movement, filters and so on seemed crucial to your early film work:* Wavelength, *1967,* Back and Forth, *1969,* La Région Centrale, *1971, etc?*

MS Any physical subject is 'reduced' to light when filmed.

The experience of that particular transformation is one of the points of my work. That transformation is a factor in the carousel slide pieces like *Slidelength* (which came out of my film *Wavelength*) and *Sink*, both made in 1969. For each of the 80 shots in *Sink* I used different colour transparencies on the lamps illuminating my filthy studio sink, consciously colouring the illuminating light in order to make a work of projected colour-light.

MO'P *Transparency is a continuing device and concept in your work.*

MS *Recombinant* made in 1992 is also a carousel slide piece but in it the slides are projected on a kind of bas-relief which was constructed for the work. This 'screen' remains a visible factor as the 80 different images appear on it. *VUEEEUV*, 1998, is a transparent photo-image on cloth, suspended so you can walk around it. It shows the naked truth about transparencies – they're the same on both sides – the image of the rear view of a nude woman is a rear view of a nude women on the other side.

MO'P *You have a reputation as a filmmaker here, but when did you start getting involved with video?*

MS I made *De La* in 1972 and that was one of the first real-time gallery uses of video. I also used video manipulation in the 'lecture' scene in my film *Rameau's Nephew* shot in 1973 and 1974. There are other video installation works such as *Intérêts*, presented in 1983 in a history of video art exhibition in Charleroi, Belgium. For the opening scene of the film *Presents*, 1981, I wanted to stretch and squeeze the image in a controlled way, and trying to find the way to do it I came across and finally used a 'Quantel' process that was being used at the time for television 'wipes'.

MO'P *What about recent work?*

MS There are two recent video installations: *Sheep* and the much more complex *That/Dela/Dat* which is a three-screen in-synch video installation. It's a looped continuous projection gallery work made for an ambulatory audience whose parent, so to speak, is my 1982 film *So Is This* which was made for a seated audience in a cinema theatre. I'm adding a new video installation, tentatively called *Video Fields*, for the John Hansard Gallery show. I've also included in the show *Flash 20:49 15/6/2001* which is the essence of the flashbulb!

MO'P *There seems to have been a slowing down of your film work since the early eighties. Does this signal an interest in other media or what?*

MS I don't think there's been a slowing down. I've never been exclusively a filmmaker and the pauses even between the earlier films are when I'm working on other stuff and planning the next film. In 1978–79 I worked on a big sculpture commission *Flight Stop* and in 1984–85 I was almost totally involved in holographic works. Then in 1988–89 there was the huge outdoor sculpture commission, *The Audience*.

There is a significant time lag between seeing what was done in the first scene of *Presents* which started 15 years of notation of ideas for a film of shape-changing based on elongation and compression. I didn't, couldn't start actually making it until some of the ideas I had could be realised and until I could find the money. I was finally able to start work on this stretching and squeezing film in 1997, when I shot the staged 'realistic' footage. After 15 years the film was finally finished in December 2001.

MO'P *What has been the effect of digitalisation on your view of filmmaking?*

MS This new film *Corpus Callosum* was shot on digital Beta tape and with various animators who know how to use a software called Houdini that was developed in Toronto. The film is 93 minutes long and premiered recently at the Rotterdam Film Festival and was also shown at the Berlin Film Festival. The new film was done digitally because – no question of it – computers offer previously impossible shape-changing possibilities. Video has an inherent instability that can be consciously used and its digital alterability is one aspect of that.

MO'P *Your work is intrinsically experimental in the real sense. You're always exploring a very precisely thought out optical idea usually deriving from the nature of the medium you're using.*

MS I always start from ideas, then see if they can be done or how they could be done. For me, the use of digital tools to make *Corpus Callosum* is related to my conceiving of and having built the camera-activating machine to make my film *La Région Centrale* in 1970.

MO'P *Tell me about that side of* La Région Centrale.

MS I wanted to make a 'landscape film' and I imagined a camera moving in all arcs of a spherical space, at controlled speeds but without photographing its tripod. A lot of wonderful machines existed around 1968-69 to move cameras – extraordinary cranes and dollies and so on – but there was nothing that at some point in the possible movements wouldn't photograph its mount, that was moving it. I knew what I wanted to do with the camera but I'm not a technician. I was lucky eventually to meet Pierre Abeloos, a Montreal technician, who solved how to do it and built the machine.

MO'P *Your reputation in this country rests on your films, which in the seventies had a huge influence on the British film Avant Garde, and what came to be known as the structural school of film. How far did you ever identify with these kinds of movements?*

MS Those filmmakers – all people I know – who were identified in 1969 by the American critic P Adams Sitney as 'structuralists' were surprised. None of us knew that we were a 'movement'. Sitney was right. We were/are.

MO'P *What do you think is the future of film?*

MS Photo-emulsion film may eventually be replaced by video but not yet. Film still has its special and incomparable qualities. I've been thinking that there is something left to discover in single-frame shooting that can't be done on video, and that may be my next film.

Issue 256, May 2002

Douglas Gordon

interviewed by Jean Wainwright

Mirror images

JEAN WAINWRIGHT *I'd like to begin by talking about your reinstallation of* 24 Hour Psycho, *1993, at the Hayward Gallery in exactly the same position as it occupied in 'Spellbound' in 1996.*

DOUGLAS GORDON This is the first time I have had the opportunity to do this, to revisit a space – to reinstall something, playing with the idea not entirely of an instant recall but some kind of a recollection. Often when artists come into a space like this they have to almost think of it as some kind of a battle to be able to take it on. My idea was that *24 Hour Psycho* has always been here, it just so happened that maybe it had to move out of the way but only temporarily – this is the permanent thing. There is definitely something tongue-in-cheek going on here – but if people didn't see the work six years ago that doesn't really matter. The people who did maybe will get the humour and conceit of it – but again it's changed – because of this huge mirrored wall so that just as you begin to think 'I've seen this before' the rug is pulled from under you. It makes it difficult to orient yourself around the space – just by including a mirror or two. It will be interesting to see how the viewer will look at the work – whether through the mirror or the real thing – and what is the difference between that anyway? For myself when I walk down the other mirrored corridor I find it easier to look at *Between Darkness and Light (After William Blake)*, 1997, in the mirror because it seems to be safer than looking at the real thing – because I am terrified of that piece. I have never watched *The Exorcist* in my life, it's a lot for me to take. Also to me a lot of work seems to be very high-tech these days which is not something that I am very interested in. I started off my practice – or the practice that is known – with *24 Hour Psycho* which is very DIY.

My original idea was that somebody could go down to Virgin or Tower video and buy *Psycho* and watch it that way – they didn't have to have my authorisation for it.

JW *What first triggered your interest in the mirror image?*

DG Maybe a lot to do with fear and a mixture of superstition which probably grew into teenage voyeurism which probably evolved into a middle-aged sadism or something – wanting to see but also not wanting to necessarily get involved. There is an implication of some kind of trauma all through the exhibition. If you take the idea of your memory of a traumatic event it often happens in slow motion which leads you back to something like *Psycho*. The text on the mirror, 'I've changed, You've changed', relentlessly repeated, could be used in real life as an excuse or a comfort, it's almost like a mantra. Everybody has heard it and everybody has probably used it and when you look in the mirror you probably don't know the difference between the 'I' and the 'You' any more.

JW *Can we talk about curiosity, your experimentation with slowing time to see what happens?*

DG A lot of this comes out of the performance work that I used to do as a student when I was very influenced by Alastair MacLennan. I remember at the Riverside doing the National Review of Live Art where I performed with two friends from Glasgow and we were upstairs moving very slowly and Alastair was downstairs moving even slower. The great thing was that very simple dual speed thing – which I was more conscious of when viewing his work than when I was performing. Most films attempt to represent the speed at which we live – and we all live in relative speed to one another unless one is in a narcotic state where that doesn't happen, which is equally interesting. With Alastair's performance you became very conscious of the difference between the two speeds and the way that is going to affect your cognitive process, your physical interaction with objects. I think this is one of the things that probably was behind *24 Hour Psycho*, the way people behave in space with an image that is moving that fast.

JW *If we talk about* Between Darkness and Light (After William Blake), *you have edited and combined two films:* The Exorcist *on one side of the screen and* The Song of Bernadette *on the other. Each has its distinctive soundtrack combined with a forceful struggle between good and evil.*

DG Again that has been an interesting thing in this installation which hasn't happened in other places. The soundtrack of *Between Darkness and Light...* becomes the soundtrack for a lot of other pieces in the show and makes you interested in the fact that *Fog*, the hand pieces, the text works and *24 Hour Psycho* are all resolutely silent. So for me this was interesting and genuinely experimental. I didn't know what would happen once we let the sound penetrate.

JW *With your installation* Something between your mouth and my ear, *1994, sound is also very important.*

DG The genesis of the work was that I started to rethink the idea of reading – that maybe reading was more about hearing and that related to Umberto Eco and Gianni Celati and when you read a word off the page you hear a voice in your head. I started to think that the first things I read might have been the first things I heard – and the first things I heard might have been the things my mother heard.

JW *Quite Lacanian.*

DG I never checked this out with my mother. I wanted to get close but not too close...

JW *It might have been a disturbing experience.*

DG It may have been more of Sandy Shaw than I would have liked to have admitted to. Because of the nature of the space it's difficult to see where people might end up. Having gone through so many bleak and anxiety-inducing installations in this exhibition you end up in what is apparently a welcoming situation with what could be seen to be quite a warm conceptual work. It is the only space where filtered daylight penetrates so it is as dark as it is outside – take that as a metaphor if you like. The implication of course – and these works are all models for other things – is that if these are things that I may have heard, I may have heard others too and therefore not just me but everybody else. So even the most welcoming work in the show should manage to twist itself round in someone's head and become something a bit more ambiguous.

JW *Two of your other self-portraits also have a twist.* Self Portrait (Kissing with Scopolamine), *1994, where you kiss your negative image in the mirror and* Kissing with Sodium Pentothal, *1994, your multi-slide projection. Did the people you were kissing in that work know you were drugged?*

DG Some of them knew. The idea was that I told some of them and not others. Pentothal is a so-called truth drug, you know how in some B-movies where they are trying to beat a confession out of someone they'll inject them with sodium pentothal.

JW *When you see the piece it is detached and silent so all the things you might have said are left hanging.*

DG I suppose the missing part of that is what you can only imagine, but there are missing parts in everything, even the text pieces which seem to be finite. In the list of fears in *From God to Nothing*, 1996, there are for sure some that are missing.

JW *You wrote down 147 fears in the form of a stream of consciousness?*

DG It was a stream of consciousness over a period of days. Some of it came out of homeopathy which I grew up with. Part of the idea is a self-diagnosis – so you would respond to prompts from the manual – a lot of it was to do with looking at your fears so that you could help yourself. I see *From God to Nothing* as a very positive piece, it's not paranoid at all. I think by listing your fears you recognise what they are. Usually the work is installed horizontally so that it is difficult to find a beginning or an end, but here it is vertical so there is an implied hierarchy because of the physical situation.

JW *Narrative is important to you, your two works* Fog, *2002, and* Black Star, *2002, both relate to the James Hogg novel* The Private Memoirs and Confessions of a Justified Sinner, *1824. Can we talk about the way that these two works relate to each other?*

DG *Black Star* is in an absolutely pitch-black space. You have the black light which people associate with a club or disco with all its positive/negative ideas and heightened I think because obviously in a club there are a lot of surfaces that that light can reflect off, but here there is nothing apart from the person. It almost gets to the point where you feel you are being x-rayed – not a real situation but the metaphor. Part of the work is my narration of Hogg's book. The first idea was to mirror what was happening in the novel. Even though the novel has a very straightforward narrative, when you are actually inside it the simplicity disappears. In *Black Star* you are standing inside a very simple shape – a star – but it is actually incredibly difficult to see what the shape is. The other reason for a star is a much more populist idea that Satan is supposed to be conjured up in the middle of one. The trick or joke for me is that people could be standing in the middle of it without realising, because I believe that is what happens in life anyway. There is also a lot going on in Hogg's text – you don't know if it is a fake, it is close enough to the truth but not quite. You don't know whether the manifestations of evil or the excuses are in Robert Wringhim's head or whether they actually happened – so there is doubt. My voice could be a comfort to people but then when you start listening it is not telling you exactly what you wanted to hear which is always good.

JW *What is* Black Star*'s relationship to* Fog*?*

DG *Fog*, I really should stress, is based on, not an illustration of, the scene with the protagonist's brother. For people who know the book they may get the idea that you are watching someone who is about to die, but for people who don't it shouldn't really make that much difference. What I tried to do in terms of the editing – and this projection could be seen to be a universal idea of someone trying to think outside of themselves – was to induce the fear that someone has of losing their own shadow, of having two shadows or of sharing a shadow with someone else. It plays on all the mythology of vampirism and the usual satanic stuff. The guy who played the role is the godfather to my kid, which I think is a nice bit of mythology to hang around the work. It doesn't have to be stated but in time that might become a more interesting idea. Just as an aside to this we shot *Fog* in New York on a sound stage which turned out to be the same stage used for *Fatal Attraction* – the fight scene between Glenn Close and Michael Douglas – which I thought was kind of great – the idea that when the fog comes down we will see the other set.

JW *As well as references to Hitchcock stylistically you also reference Warhol.*

DG I did a version of *Empire*, which was called *Bootleg Empire*, it is almost like the amateur version of the auteur masterpiece – it's very shakily done. I lived in Berlin for a while and I went to see Warhol's *Empire* and I thought 'I may never get to see this again', so I filmed it for an hour, went to the pub and then came back and filmed it for the last hour. So mine only lasts for two hours – so it's like 'the best of' or something. But quite often my version is seen with his films in exhibitions, which is kind of funny as mine is slightly more dramatic as it is shaky and there are shadows of people walking in front of the camera. But equally Barnett Newman was a very big influence on making the cinematic pieces. When I was 16 I came down to London from Glasgow and went to the Tate Gallery where I saw one of Newman's paintings. I had never seen anything of that size before and rather than look at it I timed how long it would take to walk from one end to the other. This was my first realisation that time and art had a very close connection. The fact is that you can't ignore it and it takes you ten seconds to walk the length – I just thought that was incredible. But I think I was also overwhelmed by the physical fact that if your eyes are being drenched you carry away a retinal imprint of the work and if it's physically affecting you then it must be psychologically affecting you too. Then years and years later to remember Newman and then read in one of the Warhol diaries that everybody thought that Andy was the party guy but Andy said 'no way I can't compete with Barnett Newman' the fact that they were occupying the same space at the same time. I also remember the Warhol show at the Hayward, but it was equally influential to be in a toilet at a party in Glasgow in 1992 watching *My Hustler* and pretending to be still in the toilet so that I could see a little bit more. It was very 'factory'. That was cool.

JW *Many of your works show a fragmented body such as* Left Dead and Dead Right *or* Hand and Foot.

DG They are not so much about the fragmentation of the body in terms of psychology – not that the psychoanalytical reading is irrelevant – nor are they about the fragmentation of the body in a pornographic sense in order to be able to look at something distanced from the body. I was more interested in some ways in what happens away from what you can see: if this is happening to the hand and foot let's imagine what's happening elsewhere. So it is that reverse fetishisation idea, you are not fetishising the thing you are looking at but what you don't have access to. Again this is a little like the mirror idea – by seeing it through the mirror maybe you are not as culpable as being involved in it in real life. You can look at something which is fairly innocent – which is the only thing you can see – rather than something that is actually happening which is far more dramatic off-screen. For me the idea of the off-screen is as interesting if not more so than what is happening right in front of you.

JW *What about appropriation and authorship? If I didn't know you had made* Fog *I would think it part of a B-movie that I was unfamiliar with.*

DG Good, this is perfect – because for me the pieces that have been 'kidnapped' will not in time occupy so much of a different status from the works that I have allegedly filmed. The multiple and contradictory mythology around the work is as important for me as the work itself. In the video installation, *Pretty much every film and video work from about 1992 until now. To be seen on monitors, some with headphones, others run silently, and all simultaneously*, 2002, there are a couple of films of flies dying. When we showed it at the Pompidou Centre one story was that I had found these films in a college or medical school that had been doing experiments – partly because it was more believable if it wasn't an artist who had made it. It would be more interesting to get away from the idea of the gesture of art and into so-called real life. But then we put another story out that of course it was me that had made it. It was more interesting for me to have contradictory stories around the work.

JW *In that context can we talk about your body tattoos 'always', which is in mirror writing, 'forever', 'everyday' and 'trust me'? When you made them were they artworks?*

DG This was where art came in handy. Because of the background I come from, a tattoo was a very taboo thing to have in my family. That indelible mark on the body – which of course is why you like it when you get it done – but I could say, 'this is done as an artwork' and then when you are out of the art gallery it is no longer an artwork.

JW *There is a connection to* Three inches (black), *1997, here.*

DG What was interesting to me was that the black tattooed finger became like a story-telling object in itself. It is the left digit, the left-hand side and all that sinister mythology as well as the significance of three inches. It was photographed immediately after the tattoo was made. This guy and I had a relationship to make this thing, he allowed me to take the photographs of it and I gave him the finger to take away. Unfortunately he couldn't be at the opening.

JW *There is often an ambiguity in your work, as though you don't want to fix people's relationship with it.*

DG It is interesting that you put it like that. I'm coming from the other side of that, where my idea was that things are fixed so let's jeopardise them. I like jeopardy. I like the idea that having had an exhibition at the Hayward I can now disappear. In the same way that I never wanted to occupy one particular field of art practice, I think there shouldn't be an onus on the artist to maintain a position in the world. I think that it is very important that I should give myself the option of saying 'no' as often as possible, for there to be an option that you can suddenly shift and leave the artist out of it. In a way, although there is a biographical/autobiographical theme to the show, the way Fiona Bradley, the exhibition's curator, and I spoke about this when we were installing and planning it was that it should almost be done and look as if I wasn't here for whatever reason. So it is clearly not a retrospective, but it is an overview of an aspect of a practice.

Issue 262, December–January 2002–03

Mike Nelson

interviewed by Patricia Bickers

Triple bluff

PATRICIA BICKERS *The opening sentence of the preface to your book,* A Forgotten Kingdom, *published to coincide with your ICA show in 2001, defines the term 'baroque' as 'that style which deliberately exhausts (or tries to exhaust) all its possibilities and which borders on parody'. Although the passage in fact comes from Borges's 1954 edition of* A Universal History of Infamy, *does it in part define your own practice?*

MIKE NELSON That definition formed the basis for the ICA show, 'Nothing is True, Everything is Permitted'. The parody downstairs was of the institution itself, while the parody upstairs was of the artist and the artist-run space. Also, 'Gallery Lago' was named after the town in *High Plains Drifter*, the first Malpaso Western Clint Eastwood directed in 1973, in which, in a nod to his own history, he knowingly parodied the genre of the Spaghetti Westerns of Sergio Leone. That sense of exhausting one's own genre very much interested me, particularly at that point, in terms of my own work. Having run the gauntlet of very intense exhibitions following *The Coral Reef* at Matt's in 2000, there was a sense of exhaustion but also of excess in the construction.

PB *In America in the fifties, B-movies, particularly Westerns, offered Hollywood directors such as Fred Zinnemann, who of course directed* High Noon, *an opportunity to tackle political issues covertly while remaining faithful to the genre. You also use genre and offer people different entry points (sometimes literally) to your work, 'permitting' us to engage with it on different levels.*

MN That has been the pretext for structuring my work for a long time. It came from an interest in Soviet science fiction which functioned in a very similar manner to the way American Westerns did, though perhaps in a more obviously political way. When I was at college in the nineties I was very interested in Ilya Kabakov, and work that was coming out of the former Eastern Bloc, but I was also very interested in American West Coast art, in particular that of Ed Kienholz, which I looked at partly for what not to do. I liked his awkward, maverick, status within the art world, and the way he ignored the conventions and niceties of art. I saw his huge retrospective in Düsseldorf in 1988 and I'd never seen anything like it before. His large, expanded environments might look slightly tame now, but at the time they were amazing. His work has been quite overlooked.

PB *Yes, he and George Segal, whose 'environments' or tableaux Rothko referred to as 'walk-in Hoppers', were both misfits. Oddly enough, when I realised coming here that the living room-cum-workspace-cum studio installation in* Triple Bluff Canyon *was a recreation of your own, I was reminded of Kienholz's* Barney's Beanery *of 1965, a recreation of his favourite LA eatery for which he ripped out one wall of his own house.*

MN You see those missing doors over there? Well, don't tell my landlord! In a sense Kienholz's working practice was similar to mine – take for example the proposal pieces from the mid sixties: find the site, raise the money, make the piece or it just stays as a proposal. There is an interesting relationship between the bus piece which I made in San Francisco last year, *The Pumpkin Palace*, and a sketch piece of a homemade wheelchair that I made out of junk. I picked up an old chair, some wheels, and an antiquated golf cart which became a neck brace at the back – which was very Kienholz-like, very like *John Doe*, which he made in 1959.

PB *The world – or worlds – that you create are overwhelmingly, even tragically masculine. In these male territories women are absent, or are represented, for instance, by porn magazines left lying around in sleazy hotel lobbies, bars or locker rooms – places where women are either excluded or where they would be unsafe.*

MN Places where men go, yes. In the mid nineties I made a body of work about a fictional all-male motorcycle gang called *The Amnesiacs*. For me the piece was about loss, the sudden death of a friend in the week that I began work on the piece. I invented another fictional world structured around a New English Library kind of biker genre from late sixties, early seventies in which the complications of loss and absence were dealt with in a deliberately clichéd way. A lot of my work draws on genre and on clichés, but you can use those structures to articulate something in an elegant and unexpected way. The title, which came later, was taken from the Hal Hartley film.

PB *In effect you created a kind of fictional support system.* The Coral Reef, *on the other hand, was made up of a constellation of isolated yet interconnected cells where there is no suggestion of a supportive infrastructure.*

MN *The Coral Reef* was bound up with a collection of complex, fragile belief structures trying to gain a foothold under the prevalent ideology's surface. Men seem to be more easily seduced by ideology and by power structures than women, perhaps. The work used the literary structure of introductions to non-existent books, or reviews of, for instance, *A Perfect Vacuum* by Stanislaw Lem, the first chapter of which 'reviews' itself while arguing for its status as only another short story within the anthology. In the case of *The Coral Reef* the faked reception to the 'Art Gallery' was a visual equivalent of this literary device. The work invited you to lose yourself among these lost people who would be seen almost exclusively as male.

PB Trading Station Alpha CMa, *shown at Matt's Gallery in 1996, seemed to represent an important departure, leading directly to* The Coral Reef *as well as to* The Deliverance and The Patience, *2001, in Venice. The gallery became a warehouse with shelves stacked with materials in the midst of which was this hut-like structure with signs of habitation by a Unabomber-type loner or some half-human, half-animal creature.*

MN I've always liked the idea of Robinson Crusoe. In this case this was a figure that had been isolated by difference rather than geography. The idea of the dog with the human mind picked up on the gallery's namesake, Matt E Mulsion, but then mixed in with this were references to British science fiction such as that of Olaf Stapledon, and Soviet social allegory – Mikhail Bulgakov – as well as elements of Kafka, to create a work which occupied the space between two films and their literary references: Andrei Tarkovsky's *Stalker* and Arkady & Boris Strugatsky's *Roadside Picnic*, Francis Coppola's *Apocalypse Now* and Joseph Conrad's *Heart of Darkness*. Structurally the work anticipates the later work in that the first reading is only on a formal level. It's not until one reaches the central living section that it is possible to re-read the work backwards, from the inside out, with the voice (or imagery) of the narrator in one's head.

PB *There are parallels with your own practice, perhaps: you inhabit the white space of the gallery filling it with the grubby detritus of others' secret lives that brushes against us, literally and metaphorically. It reminds me of a description of one of the earliest 'Happenings' in the sixties as being like a ghost-train ride. This is very different from the experience of a Kabakov installation.*

MN I think the experience I am interested in evoking is more akin to H P Lovecraft's way of writing about the supernatural in literature. Rather than writing a clear narrative or adhering to a linear structure, he runs one story into another, creating an atmosphere that conjures up the sense of a narrative unfolding. Perhaps a good example of a filmmaker who works in such a way is Dario Argento. Kabakov's work is more distanced, and the narrative structure is much clearer. He creates sets that are often quite unconvincingly built – deliberately so – that can be looked at and 'read'.

PB *Arguably resistance to narrative structure represents the last bastion of Modernism to fall, yet you have fearlessly used narrative, genre and even allegory to address political and social, as well as aesthetic issues. How conscious were you of the baggage of Modernism?*

MN I think my interest in narrative comes out of the fact that I found it very difficult to absorb theory at college but after I left I would find those same ideas articulated in some lowbrow piece of fiction – it was like going straight to the source.

PB *In fact,* A Forgotten Kingdom *is impeccably postmodern in that it creates a narrative out of other, pre-existing narratives.*

MN Exactly. Like all my work it could be used as an example of a postmodernist practice rather than as an illustration of it. When I talk about the work, I do so in a very structural way in terms of the reference points, ideas and situations that I was thinking about at the time. At the same time I am always aware of talking around the work – giving clues, yes, but always talking at one level above or below the actual or potential meanings. I think there is a kind of warmth in the work I make, it probably communicates to most people on a phenomenological and emotional, rather than on a deconstructive level. I try to achieve something that somehow enters your psyche or subconscious and comes back to enrich or aggravate you.

PB *Both* The Coral Reef *and* The Deliverance and The Patience *tapped into something absolutely fundamental about the human psyche. The labyrinth of rooms, the narrow corridors, the banging doors recall every nightmare featuring a room that you are afraid or forbidden to enter for fear of what you may find, like Bluebeard's castle. Form and content seemed to come together seamlessly in both works.*

MN Yes. It is a form that seems quite obvious, yet I had certainly not seen it used in quite that way. I am also interested in the geometry of it: early works such as *A Staging of the Reconstruction of the Southern Palace of Babylon*, 1993, a series of half-built or ruined walls creating rooms set on compass points like a maze, or the work made for the Economist Building in 1993, which referenced the geometric patterns of Islamic reliefs within a 'modernist' mosque in Baghdad that was contemporary with it. Similarly *The Coral Reef* was intended to disorientate you – it was built in the form of a swastika, and constantly turned back in on itself. There was little symbolic meaning in the choice of form, I had used it before. It just worked.

PB *The viewer might not necessarily be aware of the form, but if they were, it would add another –*

MN – level, yes. It was made apparent in the 2001 Turner Prize piece, though – *The Cosmic Legend of the Uroboros Serpent* – not that anybody realised!

PB *Yes. You and Martin Creed directly addressed the context in which you were showing – the Turner Prize and Tate Britain – in Creed's case by drawing attention to the space, in yours by apparently withdrawing from it. You used the Tate as a warehouse in which to 'store' a work for which you had been nominated, namely* The Coral Reef.

MN Yes, I thought we worked really nicely together. I liked the fact that you walked through Martin's *The Lights Going On and Off* before getting to *The Cosmic Legend of the Uroboros Serpent*.

PB Triple Bluff Canyon *works very differently from the installations that preceded it. As in* The Deliverance and The Patience, *you have chosen to reveal the artifice behind some of its construction, but in this case, the characteristic 'transit space' of the foyer only leads us back into the gallery. Instead of the immersive experience of the earlier work, there are three separate but connected elements.*

MN Yes, it kind of forces you to stay outside it. This piece came on the back of *Magazin* for the Istanbul Biennale and *The Pumpkin Palace* for Capp St Projects in San Francisco. In a way I was very aware that I'd not shown in Britain since 2001, so there would be certain expectations. Also I was working within the constraints of a museum – although they were very generous with time, I was given six weeks to construct the piece. My original idea for the piece was to build a multiplex cinema featuring the foyer downstairs but with locked doors. You'd then have had to turn back and work your way up the staircase to the back of the cinema where you would have found all these theatres, projection rooms and receptions, each with their own identities and narratives going on. There would also have been a sequence of films running so that in a sense it would have been a narrative or journey with a jump cut of space aggravated by a jump cut of film, so there would have been a doubling of the narrative. I would still like to build this cinema one day and people will enter the foyer and perhaps experience a sense of *déjà vu*. In the present installation the foyer functions almost like a trailer, intended to build up the suspense, the sense of expectation, yet you step outside it into the empty space of the gallery, and I am sure that after raising so much expectation a lot of people were disappointed. I will build sequential rooms again one day, but it is nice to stop that in its tracks just now.

PB Triple Bluff Canyon *is also more overtly autobiographical. You not only show your hand more but of course the workroom-cum-studio is based on your own.*

MN So I claimed, anyway – the *Independent* seemed to think it was a nutter's den! I'm a convincing nutter, then. I must admit though, the people in the street for years must have thought 'what the hell goes on in this room?' as they walk past. I hope that one might just stray into the museum by chance once and espy this room and think, 'Fucking hell, look at that – it's that room from our street, where that nutter lives!'

PB *The identification of the artist with the obsessive is perhaps not so surprising when the installation includes Jordan Maxwell's 'Basic Slide Presentation' demonstrating his paranoid vision of the world 'bounced off and distorted through a convex mirror', as you put it, and projected on to the gallery wall.*

MN For me *Triple Bluff Canyon* came about partly through an interest in magic and alchemy that I have referred to in other works. The studio desk and shelf, for instance, had earlier been replicated in 1998 for a piece entitled *The Black Art Barbecue, San Antonio, August 1961*, based on Dürer's *St Jerome in his Study*. The idea of replacing the replica with the real complemented the cyclical structure of the Robert Smithson rebuild and the short story that Brian Aldiss wrote for the catalogue, and added to the alchemy that turned an earthwork into politicised icon, and finally into a repoliticised artwork.

PB *That represents another sense in which* Triple Bluff Canyon *is a departure in that it directly references the work of another artist.*

MN The reference to Smithson was not meant to be a homage. Although I knew of *Partially Buried Woodshed*, which he made for Kent State University, Ohio, in 1970, I'd never fixated upon it till I found a copy of the 1978 *Arts* magazine special Smithson issue, with a photo of the work on the cover, in a pile of magazines I bought for $10. As an image on a magazine cover it somehow became more distanced, yet more tangible. I don't know if that sounds odd, but it almost became the reason, the most absurd and banal reason, to rebuild it. Also, I kept coming back to the final scenes in *Stalker*, and to *Roadside Picnic*, which has been a constant reference point in my work over the years. The strange, almost desert-like terrain kept coming back to me and that, combined with the references to magic, alchemy and geometry, especially in the form of the foyer, together with Land Art reference, represented the three different trains of thought that went into the building of the show. There are also references to the work of artists I'd been interested in as a student like Walter de Maria, most obviously to *Earth Room*, 1968, but also to the geometry of pieces such as *Broken Kilometer*, 1979. These, combined with J G Ballard's *The Crystal World*, a seminal text for Smithson – with its shifting planes of perception in the fractured crystalline forms of the jewelled jungle – underpinned the idea rearticulating *Partially Buried Woodshed*.

PB *Whether or not Nancy Holt is correct in believing that Smithson's intentions were partly political, following the killing by the National Guard of four students and the wounding of nine others during the campus protest some months later, the work did take on an 'iconic status'. You, on the other hand, include overt political references, not least in the substitution of sand for earth and by the inclusion of oil drums, one of which is labelled 'Texaco'.*

MN Which takes us back to Jordan Maxwell.

PB *And to George W Bush.*

MN Yes. I like that sense of a work being politicised after the event. And now I am making it overtly political. It is like a mirror image of *Partially Buried Woodshed*, somewhat like the Aldiss short story. While I was making it, it was quite hard to stand back to look at it, at that mass of sand, it was quite incredible – although I shouldn't use that word. On the opening night, Aldiss overheard someone say, 'Look at that, it's incredible!' but he said, 'Don't be ridiculous, it's not incredible. It might be marvellous but it's not incredible, look, there it is!'

Issue 278, July–August 2004

Tacita Dean

interviewed by Maria Walsh

Lost in translation

MARIA WALSH *In your writing on* Girl Stowaway, *1994, you document how real events in your life become interwoven with the story of the stowaway. This dialogue between the real and the fictional is an intriguing aspect of your work in general.*

TACITA DEAN That was particularly true of *Girl Stowaway*, although what you might think is the fictional is probably the real and vice versa. That work, more than a lot of the others, was about the fine line between fact and fiction. The photograph of the stowaway was found in the book, *The Last of the Windjammers* – it just said *Girl Stowaway in the Herzogin Cecilie*. So I bought the book and what made it into the beginning of a work was the fact that it disappeared in my bag in the x-ray machine at Heathrow airport, which was not a story, it was true. That whole work was so much to do with coincidence and things that were invited and things that weren't that it was actually very difficult to write up because when you explain a coincidence you often kill it. It is like explaining a dream.

MW *What is the relationship between the texts that you write and the films?*

TD It is quite important for me that they sit next to each other, that they are independent yet connected, and that neither one explains the other. My writing is very anecdotal. Also, when I give talks they are always very anecdotal because I don't want to explain the work. Now people are always asking me to write and I've managed to bring it into what I do so it has a legitimate status as something that stands by itself. For example, one of the books in the Musée d'art moderne de la Ville de Paris catalogue is just a text by me, the W G Sebald one. It is a dedication to Sebald in a way.

MW *In this text you write of discovering that the judge who sentenced Sir Roger Casement to be executed was your great-great-uncle, Sir Rufus Isaacs.*

TD Yes, that was quite shocking to discover because funnily enough I've always been very impassioned about the injustices meted out to Casement, but there again he was caught trying to buy arms from the Germans in the First World War for the Easter Uprising. It is a most appalling act of treason from the British point of view, but yet, if you read everything around it, he was caught between a test of his own Irish nationalism and his moral sense of right and wrong. He was really a great man in terms of what he did before in the Congo, drawing attention to the appalling treatment of black workers/slaves by mostly Belgian imperialists. In South America, too, he was an extremely brave spokesman. Sebald writes about him with great sensitivity in *The Rings of Saturn*.

MW *You are very interested in history and heroes, or anti-heroes.*

TD I never consciously pursue them, but I can see I have an incredible attraction to failure, even public failure to some extent. I've just recently filmed my uncles talking about their fathers, one is my uncle through blood, my father's brother, and the other is my uncle through marriage, my mother's sister's husband. My grandfather, Basil Dean, effectively started Ealing Studios but it failed to make money and so the father of my uncle, Michael Balcon, then made it a great success, making all the Ealing comedies. Because I'm connected to both of them, I was really determined to document this in some way or other. So I've just made this 77-minute film, *The Uncles*, 2004. What came across so strongly was the social and historical failure of the Dean father, despite being innovative and his importance at the time, as opposed to the Balcon father who is actually a success story. And the poignancy around the failure and arrogance of Dean, and the repercussions it has had on his family, as opposed to Balcon who was knighted and venerated, was very interesting.

MW *I wasn't aware of this film, but when I heard the sound piece you did for BBC Radio 3,* Berlin Project, *2002, it struck me that, while your work has always been very personal, it seems to be becoming more autobiographical, though not in a literal way.*

TD Yes, I've noticed that too. *Berlin Project* was the most personal work I had ever done up to that point. I think the reason why I am getting a bit more autobiographical, and *The Uncles* is totally autobiographical, is because I've moved to Berlin and suddenly it has given me permission to make work about England, because prior to that I would travel the world for my subject-matter. It is something that I hadn't noticed – the autobiography in *Boots*, 2003, is subliminal when you encounter the work, but when you read my texts you then see the connection and Boots's association to my family. *Berlin Project* includes Boots – I interviewed him about his father's life in Berlin – basically Boots had this legacy of being the son of a minor traitor. He was born in London but lived in Munich and Berlin as a boy during the whole Nazi period. His father was a British silent movie star working in Germany who ended up being forced to act in English language radio plays which were broadcast out of Berlin as Nazi propaganda, alongside the likes of Lord Haw-Haw, only to a much, much lesser degree. Boots told me he tried to walk to Switzerland with his brother to escape but couldn't because of his leg – he had a bone disease as a boy, which meant that his leg just stopped growing so that was why he had his boot and why he was called Boots – although, and this is interesting, we've always known him as Boots and presumed it was because of his boot but when he read my text he was quite upset that I had thought that. He said he'd had that nickname before his accident, which I think is very extraordinary because it means it is horribly ironic. I think it is not true. I think it is a mis-memory.

MW *The notion in myth of one's name prefiguring one's destiny is a theme that recurs in your work. I'm thinking especially of* Blind Pan, *2004, the set of prints based on Oedipus.*

TD I'm very interested in 'the naming of' and in how that has had an effect on me. Again, not necessarily very consciously. *Berlin Project* led to Boots. Then in some primal moment – it was in an interview with someone – I remembered I'd done this drawing at the Slade in 1991 called *Oedipus, Byron, Bootsy*. I found it and it is just three boots, each bearing a name. Byron had a clubfoot. Oedipus means 'swollen foot' because his feet were bound so he was always lame, and Bootsy is Boots. I've had this project that I've long wanted to make but maybe never will because I'm making it in so many different ways – *Blind Pan* and *Boots* are all steps towards making it – which is this unscripted journey between the end of Sophocles's *Oedipus Rex* and the beginning of *Oedipus at Colonus* when Antigone guides her blind lame father into the wilderness until something is resolved in him so that he can die. You don't know how many years they are in exile, so it is a very powerful thing between the father, the blind disempowered king and his daughter. I actually had glandular fever at the beginning of the year and I was really unwell when I made *Blind Pan*. It was a really unconscious work somehow. I can't even remember what I wrote on it. I found this very old photograph that has a beautiful patina to it and I took this tiny section of it. I tried to use a device like Botticelli used with *Dante and Virgil in Hell* where the two protagonists appear in each of the five images so it gives a sense of their journey. The photograph is actually overlapped so that at the beginning of each one you get a bit of the end of the previous one. The last one is this epiphany at Colonus. But the Oedipus/Antigone thing is there in *Boots* because Boots was Antigone's godfather, my sister's godfather – my sister's name is Antigone – and he is lame and blind in one eye.

MW *It is like a family romance in the psychoanalytic sense, which is of course so related to myth.*

TD Boots was mythologised in our household. I knew, or I've known the man all my life. He was so perfect because he was such a conflicted person and it comes across in Boots. I didn't script him at all.

MW *So it was spontaneous on his part?*

TD He had just two pages about the history of the villa. He decided that he'd had an affair with the real mistress of the house, evidently a beautiful but sad French woman called Blanche. I brutally edited him down of course because there was a lot of rubbish. He was actually an architect and my idea was that he would play the architect of this villa in Porto. But as soon as he arrived, this villa that everyone thinks is wonderful in a postmodern way because of its clash of styles, he thought was appalling because he was a deep modernist.

MW *I saw Boots in Paris at the Musée d'art moderne de la Ville de Paris. How is it set up at RIBA?*

TD The RIBA room that we have has three doors so it absolutely invites Boots. Also the building is so much like Casa de Serralves, that same period. It is from the thirties and a bit fascist in a way so it is a perfect venue. I wanted to show it here at Frith Street as it is the principal work I've made in the last year but it needed more space.

MW *Why are there three versions of* Boots*?*

TD I wanted to use Boots's perfect dated urbanity, that in some ways he carried in his body that period of western culture when many were polyglot and somehow Europe was less divided in a strange sense even though now we have the European Community. Then, people would freely move between cultures and be multilingual.

MW *People of a certain class, perhaps?*

TD Yes, people of a certain class. In that period in the thirties his father was mixing with the likes of Marlene Dietrich and Greta Garbo and people like that, so Boots was a true cosmopolitan. We don't really have so many people like that any more and that quality in him made it very difficult to place him in time, which was very important to me. That and choreographing the silence of the building with the particular sound of his walking. Boots is bilingual in German and English and spoke French. When I filmed him I didn't have such a strict plan. I wanted to film him in all these different languages without knowing I was going to do three versions. I'm always very chaotic when I film. It is later when I am editing that I am extremely disciplined. What I imposed on it was obviously the language separation but also that he would take a different walk around the villa for each version. So in the English version he goes into the study, in the French, the dining room, in the German, the library and then they all go upstairs to the pink bathroom. What it meant was that I really had to go through hell, particularly for the French version, because, in the room I had designated, he only said one French word, '*toutes*', in the whole take, so I had to do it all with cutaways and artifice. It also meant I had to lose a lot of wonderful stuff because he was talking in the wrong room but I was determined to stick to the three versions. The problem was that in the bathroom he would start in English and then, without even a breath, go into German and then French, which was my poor directing of course, but to choreograph him around his speech was a huge challenge. What I love is that he changes with the language, which is so beautiful. In the German version, he is a bit fascist in a way, isn't he? Whereas the French version is much more romantic, the English is very wistful.

MW *Boots's character doesn't take over the building in the way that a character usually dominates place in mainstream fictional narratives.*

TD They both have parallel stories. An empty house of that beauty is poignant anyway and Boots becomes an empty house also to some extent. I realised later he is the equivalent of the Bubble House. I find they are very valedictory. And then he dies afterwards – unexpectedly – like Mario.

MW *I'm sorry to hear that. I remember reading that you filmed* Mario Merz, *2002, just before he died.*

TD Neither of them was expected to die. I think Mario gave himself to the film. Who knows what goes on in the heads of old men?

MW *I imagine they would be thinking about death?*

TD It is something I live in deep fear of in relation to my father. Maybe being away from home brings these things to the fore most probably. Maybe I'm trying to prepare myself the whole time in making all these works.

MW *I'd like to ask you about the position sound has in your work. For instance, in* Foley Artist, *1996, the minimal narrative fragments scripted on the dubbing chart evoked an absent film.*

TD People's perception of sound is extraordinary. It is so muted by image. With *Foley Artist*, it was absolutely pivotal that people perceived the sound. The sound was so central. But all my soundtracks are incredibly laboured over. I don't think people have a clue about how much I labour over the sound and actually with 16mm it is always a tragedy because you lose a lot by going onto optical. So as a result of my tenacity in sticking to film because of the image and other reasons, I do lose some of the work I do on the sound. Every dog in *Boots*, every motorbike, every passing car – everything – I put in. That particular melancholy that you get during the end of the three films is to do with those sounds – you don't notice them because you think they are there. Like in *Sound Mirrors*, 1999, I remember putting in the sound of that moped going round and round, a sound which is so specific to that south-east England seaside melancholy. I'm so attentive and careful about things like that. It is the same with *Banewl*, 1999. I put in everything. I always record sound live and collect sound while I am in the location, so most of it is recorded in situ but was just placed differently. It is another ingredient that adds to the visual because of course image in 16mm is recorded mute. And that for me is one of the primal separations between video, digital media and film – the muteness of film, of cinema, and that everything has to be added.

MW *There is a fascinating kind of muteness or blankness in your films.*

TD I'm sure that comes from its roots in silence. And also by creating a soundtrack you are making something that is much more deliberate and simple in a way. One of the reasons why I just can't relinquish my hold on film is the sound thing. The other thing is the fact that I can work alone in such a concentrated and laborious way. I have my own little Steenbeck now in Berlin. With digital editing, you can nip to any scene you want, whereas I have to spend hours waiting for it to spool to the beginning or the end in order to check something or even just to sync it. It is such a nightmare but somehow this is the process with which I have to work because the slowness of it impacts on the final result. It is such a prolonged and difficult process that I think I must be one of the few people still left in the world doing it.

MW *But maybe the process puts you in a very particular kind of space?*

TD Yes, I lose time in the most extraordinary way.

MW *I'm interested in how this notion of losing time and the laborious nature of the editing process relates to how a viewer might respond to your work. There are different kinds of time. The one we usually inhabit is the time of measurement, one has to do things on time, be on time, etc. Various philosophers discuss another kind of time, almost like a geological time, a time that the human being cannot apprehend because it is outside of one's life span.*

TD Did you read Simon Crowhurst's text in the Tate catalogue? It is such a beautiful text. It is all about geological time – he is a geologist – in relation to his father's notions of time. I love that text. It talks of how the minutiae of our own time relates to this other time.

MW *I've always felt that the time outside of the human life span and human time were somehow intermingled in the experience of watching your work, especially* Disappearance at Sea, *1996,* Banewl *in different ways, and also* Boots. *I think this is related to the slowing down and the sense of losing time.*

TD With *Banewl* that was quite explicit in a way because you are dealing with our human time and natural – but natural sounds too wide – the cows' time in relation to this cosmic thing that is too big for our brains. With *Boots* you have it in an historical time in a way. I'm absolutely fascinated with time. I've always been so in awe and rather terrified by the relation between local time and universal time and how that relates to death, the localness of your own death in relation to this absolutely universal thing.

Issue 281, November 2004

Simon Patterson

interviewed by Ian Hunt

Mexican stand-off

IAN HUNT *I want to ask about* General Assembly, *shown again this year at Fruitmarket, 11 years after the Bosnian war that was its immediate context.*

SIMON PATTERSON There was a discussion about whether to update it. It was shown in Japan about six years ago and I didn't update it then, it was just changed to fit the space. Although it's historical in that they're all past Secretaries General, it still feels quite current, especially with the more recent prominence of Hans Blix and the role of the UN weapons inspectors, and the Second Gulf War.

IH *When I first saw it I was working more as a journalist and doing digests of the unfolding situation in Bosnia. And the UN was screwing up.*

SP I listened to the radio a lot during the civil war in Bosnia. But the work did not begin there. I was wondering what to do for Chisenhale and felt it had to be a three-dimensional work. I had in mind the scene from *Bombay Talkie*, the Merchant-Ivory-Jhabvala film, where the actors are dancing on a big typewriter. I saw the keyboard coming out of the wall – just the keyboard not the typewriter. And I was learning to type at the time. Putting in the references to Swift's *Gulliver's Travels*, the place names of some of the lands that he'd visited, followed on. The title was an unconscious connection. I read the book as a boy, but didn't remember that there was a General Assembly in it until after making the work.

IH *It's the Parliament of the Houyhnhms, the reasoning horses.*

SP Swift thought their shit smelt sweetest of all.

IH *What struck me was the positioning of the viewer in this large-scale work as a potential participant – who couldn't in the end take part. As a hand-wringing journalist, that struck home.*

SP I knew it had to be on that Claes Oldenburg scale. I took something the size of your finger, a key, and changed it into a seat, keeping within the realm of human scale, which even fits with that Swiftian scatology – a move between your finger and your bottom. But then you are surrounded by it and can't really sit anywhere. And notionally you type out the surrounding text, the quick brown fox jumps over the lazy dog...

IH *But it mixes real nations with fictional lands, and this was when Clinton was urging Americans to get their atlases out to locate Yugoslavia, and newsreaders were struggling with Serbo-Croat.*

SP In an obvious way that's there. The permanent members are represented, the great powers, post Second World War – of Britain, France, the US, China and Russia. And then you've got Luggnagg, Glubbdubdrib. I had wanted this interest in language to extend to the catalogue, which was meant to include the essay in Esperanto as an extension of the work. That was only realised this year.

IH *Esperanto, with the Bretton Woods institutions, being part of that ambition for universal solutions.*

SP A universal solution and an idea of failure. Stalin, I was reading somewhere, was apparently a brilliant linguist, and when he was a young revolutionary in 1905, he tried to learn Esperanto.

IH *Works based on stunt doubles pick up on that wish to put the viewer in a physical experience.*

SP The cable car piece made in Bregenz does that (*Where Doubles Dare*, 1998). That had to be for an outside space and I was stuck on the problem of how to compete with the landscape. I went up the mountain in one of these modern gondolas, wondering what to do. Back in the hotel room I switched on the TV and *Where Eagles Dare* was on. There's the scene in it where Richard Burton makes the jump from one car to another. It seemed too good to be true. The father of a friend of mine at school was a stunt player, I think he was in some of the long shots when you see the cable going into the wheel at the top. I bought a dictionary of stunt players and tried to find him but he wasn't listed for that film.

IH *A dictionary of stunt players?*

SP For the industry. Incredible names: Enos 'Yakima' Canutt, speciality chariot racing, credits include *Ben Hur*. Screaming Mad George, speciality being set alight. The names often seem appropriate:

A J 'Alf' Joint, speciality falling down stairs. But getting back to Bregenz, I put Richard Burton and Clint Eastwood on the cable cars in Nazi script – in fire engine red – so you could see it a mile off. It's about the frisson of being on the cable car and wanting to make that leap, the moment your stomach goes. I like anything on high or to do with flying.

IH *The piece I was thinking about was the installation from a couple of years ago using dazzle-ship painted walls and stunt players' names.*

SP That was called *Ladies from Shanghai*. The dazzle-ship painting in white, black and grey was all around a kind of square corridor. It took kilometres of masking tape. On one wall were the names of the stunt players, and on the facing wall was the mirror image of that name, the name flipped. It might be the character they played, or the guy who was in the King Kong suit when they weren't using models. *All About Eve* was in it, with Anne Baxter and Bette Davis mirroring each other. In that film Anne Baxter starts off as a double for the Bette Davis character and then becomes more famous than she is. It was a labyrinth, with these disorientating zig-zags.

IH *It felt like a place of potential action.*

SP It's really about re-enactments. When I was making *Enter the Dragon* the first time in 1999, again in Bregenz, it felt too cold, just the mirrors from the climactic fight scene and the big red letters of Bruce Lee's name spelt out at his sort of height. But when I played the Lalo Schifrin soundtrack, a kind of Chinese funk, it worked. People began striking poses, it became more of a pavilion. This interest in stunt players and re-enactments is about how, as an artist, you can't compete with film. Stunt players provide some kind of way in, because they are sort of real people. They're the people who are really doing it: on fire, falling out of planes. And yet they're stand-ins, surrogates, and totally anonymous. Unless you're a complete nerd you don't read the credits that far down. You're on your way out to catch the bus home.

IH *For me there's an ability to start playing with the viewer, intriguing with them, but to retain a formality of presentation. You can't enter these works completely even if they surround you, and so they differ from some modes of working where real life experiences are queasily nominated as art.*

SP Going back to this thing about people being stand-ins, standing in for something – but that's avoiding your question.

IH *I suppose I'm talking about a sort of theatricality that can't know itself as theatricality. You hold back from that. There's often an invitation in terms of your movement around the piece, the viewer is never just an eye, but it's from a version of minimalist thinking.*

SP I've always felt there's some connection there, but it's not something that, as an artist, you want to bang on about. Part of this is that from the start I wanted to work with material that was familiar – film, football and so on – but not just to borrow its familiarity, to do something else with it.

IH *We can notice areas you return to: Westerns, action films, politics, history. But we don't attribute to you as an artist omniscient knowledge of all this material, we understand that the activity is to encounter our own areas of greyness.*

SP With something like *The Great Bear* from 1992 – the tube map – which wasn't an absolute list of anything, it was the footballers you got questioned about, not the philosophers going round the Circle Line, who were obviously taken from Bertrand Russell's basic reader in western philosophy. No one ticked me off for the choice of sinologues.

IH *To come to* Ur, *the wall drawing you made this year at Fruitmarket. The equivalent area of greyness is in those Iraqi, or are they Sumerian, rulers. It is easier to locate ourselves among the American names, the presidents and vice-presidents, because it is simpler to add to an existing set than to start building a new one.*

SP There is a vice-president called George Clinton. I couldn't resist including him. But *Ur* is, in a way, like *jp233 in CSO Blue,* the rejigged airline map. These wall drawings look controlled but aren't, they're much more emblematic, almost agitprop. The *Ur* wall drawing was quite organic, content was added while I was doing it. I wanted to do something that was quite literal and when I looked at wiring diagrams they looked like plans of ancient cities or temple complexes, like satellite images. *Allahu Akbar* was made in 1991, and was about making a bridge of words, a suspension bridge of names between East and West. *jp233 in CSO Blue* was made after it in 1992. Both were explicit commentaries on the Gulf War. The title was a clear signal: it's the bomb dropped on airfields. It sounds like a made-up code for something but it isn't. And then CSO blue is the Chromakey colour that is used for superimposure in films and TV. The whole war was mediated by that: dropping petrol bombs at night to make it look more spectacular. The *Ur* wall drawing is a revisiting of all that. It sets up a siege –

the armies are massed outside the city walls for an absurd battle, like something from a bad Ridley Scott film.

IH *A land war as opposed to an air war?*

SP I'm unsure where it goes beyond that.

IH *There are areas of non-communication. Diametrically opposed worlds that position the liberal viewer in well-meaning ignorance.*

SP But there's also a question about how relevant this knowledge is. There are chunks missing from the king lists in Iraqi history. Missing figures, and ones who couldn't have lived that long, who are almost mythical.

IH *But names like Halliburton or Falluja aren't included. And it's questionable what reiterating them could say in an artwork. If you're concerned that it's agitprop, does that mean you are presuming agreement about the war? Such agreement isn't unreasonable, it's whether art can do something within it.*

SP The *Ur* drawing has Semper Fe in it – always faithful – the Marine motto that was sprayed in red on the side of the mud bricks of Ur. That motto sits with the vice-presidents, arranged in their divisions, facing the Iraqi kings. The arrangement itself comes from the field of battle at Waterloo. Which isn't the key to unlock the work, it's just another layer of absurdity. It isn't agitprop in a strong way but it's obvious enough, I hope.

IH *Quite often the sense-making we attempt with your work produces the comedy of categories clashing. The* Ur *drawing is more solemn in that respect.*

SP It is more solemn. The circuitry started out as a TV diagram, though it's much mucked about with. It couldn't possibly transmit an image.

IH *I want to ask about the works on colour and colour matching. An announcer's voice links a set of football club names to a score, and to standardised Pantone® numbers or HTML codes, that can supposedly be made anywhere the same way. Sarat Maharaj has a swipe at the Pantone® system in his Documenta XI essay. What's your interest in it?*

SP There are three versions of *Colour Match*, for England, Scotland and France. The colour attributed to a certain team is arbitrary, it's just a result of where the list falls in the continuous visual spectrum. And in the first aural version, it's completely for the mind's eye. You were given clues because I added things like 'warm red' to the Pantone® number. Then I brought back the visual element in the

Scottish and French versions, with the projection of the colour. In one it's the sine wave that goes from light to dark, in the other it's more continuous. But simply put it's to do with that disjuncture between perception of colour and how it has been described. When you hear the word the colour has already shifted.

IH *You're looking for glitches of perception within this administration of colour.*

SP It pretends to be a reasonably absolute system, but as usual it's an approximation, there's always accident. And the teams are ordered aphabetically, which in a way is no order at all, but a state of flux. It's all the teams that have ever played in the football league. Some of those teams have since gone bust, Wimbledon has gone to Milton Keynes, and so on. And some names, like Middlesbrough Ironopolis, are evocative of another age, a former industrial past, handlebar moustaches and centre partings. Football first came in with the *Last Supper* pieces. I wanted to make something to compete with that level of spectacle. Football is spectacular and sensational and it's hard to compete with that when you make art, with that visceral level of enjoyment – or displeasure, depending on what's happening.

IH *Do you think the voices that you've selected and their familiarity, combined with the evocativeness of the names, are a richer system than quantified colour?*

SP Sound is incredibly unpredictable. But about the voice for that first piece: before I met Tim Gudgin I was incredibly nervous. It was just about meeting someone who was so familiar in a certain way. If I read the names they sound as dull as dishwater, but his voice finished the work. If you make a video piece and manage to put loads of stars in it, that's never enough. It's like in *Ed Wood,* where they're talking about getting Bela Lugosi. What do you get if you take a horror film or a science fiction film that's like shit, and put a star in it? 'Shit with a star in it.' It wasn't enough that it is Tim Gudgin, except that he did complete it as a work. People in TV talk about actors as movable props, which I think is incredibly cruel. But in a way there is a kind of thinking about things as components, materials. You make the same kind of choice of a voice that you would about another object, and that can also be absolutely the right reason to use that material, that voice.

IH *Thinking of actors as movable components gets near the heart of your concerns. What happens when square pegs meet round holes, the incommensurate that is produced when two things meet in an inappropriate comparison. That brings me to* Escape Routine, *the video you made in 2002 around one of your obsessions, Harry Houdini, which combines air safety instruction with escapology. How did it come about?*

SP I was coming back from a show in Zürich on Swissair and got the idea of the cabin crew doing magic tricks and performance. The universal language of air safety is in fact varied. Each country, each airline has its own way of doing it. What they had was an animation and the crew had almost become redundant. Again, looking at things that are being made redundant and trying to find a new function for them. After various conversations with Swissair, it became clear it couldn't happen in flight.

IH *But your first instinct was for in-flight performances?*

SP Yes, so it would have been whoever got on the plane who saw it. As you can imagine that did not go down too well. We haven't even managed to get the video screened as part of the in-flight entertainment. The performers are stand-ins for me. Because I'm not good enough, courageous enough to be a performer. It's the nearest I've come to making a performance, except for getting out of a straitjacket on the Gateshead Millennium bridge in Newcastle. It's funny but *Escape Routine* has a kind of coldness running through it, which is odd as all the people involved were couples: the flight attendants and Shahid Malik the escapologist and his wife Lisa.

IH *The coldness that is in the work is appropriate because the experience of air travel is of becoming a human parcel, confined to a seat and an agreed mode of behaviour. Your subjectivity, will, wish to move about, are given over to the agreement to share the transport with others. And there is a remainder in these smoothly functioning systems. That's an area you get at. The wish within rather bland or standardising experience is to protest. By using these areas of impersonal modern experience you're getting at our wish to find a bit of freedom, in a social contract that can be chilly.*

SP One of the cabin crew said she was always catching people having sex in the toilets. 'Disgusting, filthy places, I don't know why they do it!'

IH *But that's a small, not entirely futile act of escape isn't it? One of the ways in which people like to break the rules, that proves how well regulated things tend to be. Maybe I could ask you more about escapology and Houdini, this figure who set himself before the public to get out of things that he himself had designed. Does he function as some kind of emblem for a modern artist?*

SP He was a creation of the theatre and made films, but he's a bridge to the nineteenth century too – strangely old-fashioned but completely knowing about modern techniques and promotion. I've been interested in him since I was a student.

IH *I'm edging my way to the awkward psychological question about why you are interested in an escape artist.*

SP It is about the potential for failure. The risks an artist takes aren't physical, usually, unless you're Marina Abramovic. They are a different kind. I envy that sort of catharsis you get from performance.
I don't have the physical courage to perform. That is where the work stands in for you.

IH *This year you've gone on to make a sex film with pocket watches,* Time Piece.

SP The sexual content is intended but the viewer brings that with them. It's the sound of athletes exercising, a woman and a man, and two swinging watches, gold and silver, male and female, going in and out of phase, left and right channel – and all the edits are mapped on the three killings from *High Noon*. It's very short, but we threw everything including the kitchen sink at it and did it in 35mm. It is going to be shown as a filler in a cinema in Birmingham, with the ads, so it has been cleared for certification. Even I was blushing at the first recording session – people would come into the sound booth and wonder what kind of film we were making. It's a weird work, I don't know if that's just because it's new. Jon Bewley of Locus+ called it visceral, which is not a word I'd normally claim in relation to my work, but it's more visceral than anything else I have done.

Issue 288, July–August 2005

Angela Bulloch

interviewed by Maria Walsh

The light fantastic

MARIA WALSH *In recent years you have mostly been exhibiting outside of Britain. Can you tell me about your exhibition at Modern Art Oxford?*

ANGELA BULLOCH It is primarily work since 2000. Three works from the early nineties are included, but it is not a retrospective. It is formulated by certain thematics, which run through some of the work – the use of film and referencing within that. Two of the early works, *Solaris 1993*, 1993, and *King of Comedy*, 1991, use a specific direct reference to existing films. That was a good departure point to show other kinds of works like *Z-Point*, 2001, in which the handling of film is part of its theme.

MW *What attracts you to the particular films you reference such as Tarkovsky's* Solaris, *1972?*

AB In the case of *Solaris* it was the dynamics between two characters in a narrative. The way that I've arranged my re-editing or appropriation of Tarkovsky's film has to do with particular actions of the characters, so there are all sorts of pieces missing. The edited selection deals only with when the male character falls asleep and the female character is imagined by him. The female character is just a figment of his imagination and so she either comes to life or she dies. I've organised my editing according to her existence and her death. There is also a question of my presentation of the film directly opposite two pairs of spheres which come on and slowly dim away. The programming of the behaviour of those lights is also relevant to the action of the characters and my editing of the script.

MW *Antonioni's* Zabriskie Point, *1970, is a particular iconic film from cinema history and you've chosen to appropriate the moment of the explosion. Could you talk about your attraction to that moment and the translation process into the modular sculptural object?*

AB That piece is the same proportion, 3:4, as a 35mm film but it is really an object because they are all physical cubes in a large arrangement. The film itself shows the end sequence of *Zabriskie Point* where there is an exploding house. The house explodes in the mind of the woman looking at it. One doesn't necessarily know in the film whether it really happened or whether she just imagined it. There is that tension. It is perhaps just what she felt, she was angry and imagined that is what she would like to see happen. I chose that film because I was interested in this question of reality and viewpoint: did it really happen or was it her imagination? As in *Solaris*, the female character is really imaginary – a figment of the man's imagination that he is projecting on to the sea of Solaris.

MW *As a viewer, you are also uncertain at times because you respond as if she is a real character. I mean obviously it is all fiction but, within the fiction, there is a strange play between the real and the fictional.*

AB That's right. That is very interesting to me and it is very specific to my choice of films. In the case of *King of Comedy*, I chose the moment where he is practising telling his jokes to an imagined audience and imagining that they are all loving him and finding it all great. But the way I have arranged my work puts the viewer in the position of being the person standing in front of a very satisfied happy crowd which appears to think you are really funny. So with that work it is a case of putting the viewer into the psychological dimension of the character's imagining.

MW Fundamental Discord: 16, *2005, refers to Akira Kurosawa's* Ran, *1985. Your use and translation of this film seem different again.*

AB *Ran* is based on an interpretation of *King Lear* set in a seventeenth-century Japanese context with endless wars going on. The battle scenes are highly choreographed in the film. They used different banners and colours – the reds, yellows and blues – in an endless almighty massacre in the struggles and the conflicts between three factions, the brothers and their despotic father. It is a test of love and power, which is like *King Lear* except in *Lear*, it is his daughters who are tested.

MW *Have you used the colours as a base for* Fundamental Discord: 16*?*

AB I have a filmic base which is totally abstract and I've made a programme which is overlaid onto the filmic one. That programme which I've made uses white, red, yellow and blue characters, and their movement – the choreography – follows the different struggles and events that occur in the film but using graphical dimensions. The characters become colours in my work. The objects themselves don't move, it is the colours that move, but I conceived the piece as a singular image – as if it would be stacked up – which is then distributed across the floor in a very formal grid arrangement, each cube being actually a metre apart in each direction.

MW *In the gallery installation, there seems to be a kind of dialogue between the light effects of* Z-Point, Fundamental Discord: 16, *and* Chain, *2005, which is partly due to the resonance of* Z-Point*'s soundtrack throughout the space.*

AB It is difficult handling sound. I spent most of the summer experimenting with speakers and sound systems. It is not physically possible to control sound in only one place but you can do an awful lot, so there is a sweet spot for the sound directly in front of *Z-Point*. You can hear the music in other places, but that speaker system is chosen because it acts somewhat like headphones without having to put any on physically. The way you experience the sound is to do with your own movements. You become aware of your ears, or the physical nature of where you are located.

MW *The notion of scale and perspective is interesting in relation to the viewer. The light effects of work such as* RGB Rhythm Boxes: So You Want to Be (A Rock 'n' Roll Star): Patti Smith *and* So You Want to Be (A Rock 'n' Roll Star): The Byrds, *both of 2005, seem to be playing simultaneously with both distance and proximity, whereas with* Z-Point *you are engulfed by the largeness of the object, the wall of pixelated images creating an almost sublime effect of pure colour and light.*

AB I imagined putting a work like *Z-Point* on the top of a building, within the cityscape, so that it would offer a very different kind of perspective or distance from it. That is what I was first thinking but that project didn't work out. The further away you can get from images like *Z-Point*, the better you can read them. It is all a question of distance and where you are located in relation to the image.

MW *Reading suggests a point from which you can determine the image as a spatial configuration, a perspective often denied us in an information society. Your work insists on a physical intensity within the flux of information, for example, the perceptual aspects of* RGB Spheres I–IV, *2004–05, seem to incorporate the whole body in a sense.*

AB They make a kind of physical engagement with the viewer and with your eyes, which is not only retinal. It is more than that because they really are objects and one is in that space and the space has been organised and framed by the work in some cases. For instance, the middle gallery is an awkward space to work in because it has a ramp and pillars and to put objects into such a room is quite complicated so I did a different piece there, quite a subtle piece. It is called *The Repressed Room*, 2005, and it takes the form of a mirroring of all the light sources within the room. There is a mirrored bulb and the windows have been mirrored so you don't see outside or through them. It is a work but it is not an object. It is just an action on the light sources in that room, and so the room turned in on itself.

MW *Again that reminds me of some of your early works like* The Laughing Crowd Room, *1990, and* Before and After Follow Each Other, *1989, which literally depend on the viewer to bring the work into being. In effect you have used the gallery space as an extended object.*

AB Yes, but the space also effects a not necessarily conscious action on the part of the person seeing it.

MW RGB Spheres I–IV *appropriates Bridget Riley's 1964 painting* White Disks*?*

AB It is *White Disks I* actually. There are a couple of different versions of that painting, which is a seemingly random arrangement of black painted circles on a white background. I used the formal arrangement of the painting for my work. *RGB Spheres I–IV* are arranged so that if you split the grid of Riley's painting into four, the top left section is *RGB Spheres I*, *RGB Spheres II* is the top right-hand configuration. Basically, if you brought all those walls together you would get a large version of the arrangement of the whole painting and, in fact, the holes on the front panel of the small wooden cubes of *RGB Rhythm Boxes* is the compete arrangement after the Riley painting.

MW *The viewer has to move in a particular way to access the whole.*

AB Yes and I'm also lining up where the holes allow light to pass through and that makes a projection which is only visible when you have something to project onto which is the wall. These two projections also cause an interference with each other in much the same way as the two music tracks do. The programmes for the projections are calibrated to the tempo of the song, the pop version of 'So You Want to Be A Rock 'n' Roll Star' by The Byrds which is a shorter unit than the extended form for the later version by Patti Smith.

The differences between The Byrds' version from 1967 and Patti Smith's version from 1979 are interesting in the same way that *Solaris 1993*, the work I made in 1993, is different from Tarkovsky's original from the seventies. What is important is the shift between this and that time and a different way of producing something, the means of production.

MW *Many contemporary artists use cinema as a kind of memory bank that refers to particular moments in history.*

AB And music works that way.

MW *How would you see your recontextualisation of cinema relating to history and memory?*

AB All of the references I've chosen have something to do with my experience of them in time. They have all been produced within my lifetime and my recontextualisation is specifically from my view on them. It would be different if I was using a reference from a thirties film. I have not experienced those times literally but that doesn't mean to say that I don't know about them. I live in Berlin and I know many films that refer to certain historical events and places so you can walk through the city and try to imagine Bertolt Brecht there. It can make something seem to come alive when you actually experience the place where something is created or, particularly with fiction, walking through the actual places is interesting, but I don't use those kinds of references in my work. I'm interested in them but I didn't experience that time.

MW *This sense of experienced time seems to connect back to your interest in particular imaginary moments, the fiction within the fiction –*

AB – as well as creating objects within a space which people perceive and experience at an actual physical level. What is interesting in relation to what you've just said is that, after spending much time producing *Z-Point*, I actually decided to go to the place where it was originally shot in California. I worked with a camera person and we set about specifically making films with a view to showing them within my modular structure, which is a very different and complicated way of trying to imagine how something would look in that form yet starting with another form like producing a video. I'm working with a digital format but trying to imagine how the images will change is very difficult. You have to be able to shoot in a way that you know will give you the right end result. Shooting something which doesn't look how it is going to end up was a very interesting process.

MW *Is that the piece you showed at the Institute of Visual Culture in Cambridge?*

AB Yes, *Horizontal Technicolor*, 2002. I used a CinemaScope format so there is a black gap on the bottom and top so the image seems to be floating. If you showed it on a television, the negative areas would be visible on the screen. I created it to produce the negative space as well. Physically going to the place was important. In Death Valley near Zabriskie Point, there is a place called The Artist's Palette. It is a sort of circular road that takes you past all these different types of mining chemicals in the ore of the desert, which make spectacular colours in the landscape. It is all rather poisonous, yet it is a beautiful landscape with this kind of psychedelic colourful view.

MW *Not unlike the light effects in your pixel boxes. How do you go about choreographing these works?*

AB It is tremendously laborious to make these works. I work directly with one person only to make these programmes. For example, there are 48 cubes in *Z-Point* and in each one of those cubes are three lamps, three channels, and if you think about the duration – it is eight minutes 13 seconds looped, that makes 493 seconds – so for each of those seconds, there are 48 × 3 changes or shifts in value made – 144 × 493 = 70992 different values in this piece. On a human scale, it is hard to imagine so many changes of values simultaneously, but on the other hand it is also very exciting when somebody discovers or finds a new prime number, a tremendously abstract but wonderful thing. It happened recently, a doctor found the next prime number. It is beautiful.

Issue 292, December–January 2005–06

Aernout Mik

interviewed by Hester R Westley

Crossroads

HESTER R WESTLEY *How much does your early sculptural training feed into your current work?*

AERNOUT MIK I trained as a sculptor and when I started out, I worked as a sculptor. At some point in the early nineties, the sculptures started to develop into installations or situations. Then I found myself working with live elements, either animals or people, who came to inhabit these situations and consequently I became more interested in the sculptural presence of action and with live elements in a space. From there it was a short step towards video. But what I really wanted to do was to bring video back into space as a physical element. I used to call myself a sculptor as a provocative gesture – now, who cares? I am a video artist but I have no interest in film or filmmaking. When I started working with video, I focused on small groups of people and the work was relationship-based. It came out of a sculptural attitude – simple gestures or very simple situations that held a certain kind of tension. Then my work became more about public spaces and started to develop on a larger scale, moving towards things that have a socio-political meaning. But in place of a scenario, I focus on relationships, the balance between different elements or between incidents. For me the most important thing is the tone and that comes about through the relationship between a crisis and its resolution, or action and non-action. It's a much more static thing than a narrative or scenario.

HRW Training Ground, *2006, confronts the viewer on two long low screens which stretch diagonally across the floor. The viewer's physical apprehension of your work is obviously very important to you?*

AM The screens are really interruptions in space. When they are set into a wall they become architectural elements in themselves. They affect your sense of stability and that is a very important aspect of my work – to connect the visual with the tactile. I want my work to interfere with your own sense of body in space. Therefore I seek to control every aspect of the environment. In the next gallery *Scapegoats*, 2006, is on a Plexiglass screen that is sunk into the floor so it becomes a free element, like a monolith in space, like a hallucination.

HRW Scapegoats *is the first work in the exhibition which plays with the presence of the viewer. This is taken further in* Vacuum Room *which offers multiple viewing positions – it's almost as though you're implicating the viewer in what is going on on screen.*

AM *Vacuum Room* is a six-screen installation. I constructed the set and was outside the space during filming. Of the six security cameras, there was one that I could look through and talk to the players in the space through a microphone. This was for practical purposes only. I wanted to shoot 360 degrees so I couldn't have a cameraman in that space. For the viewer there is a choice between cushions and chairs. If you sit on a chair, your body becomes intermingled with what is going on on the screens. There is a power relation between someone sitting on the floor and someone sitting on a chair. There is consequently a mirroring of the power relations that are being played out in the piece. The whole infrastructure of the piece is set up for visitors. Again it becomes an installation rather than a film. You are in the space with me.

HRW *To what extent do you direct the participants in your films?*

AM I don't have a scenario and I give the players minimal information. If they have too much information, they start to act. In this way, they are unsure about what is going on which gives a sense of uncertainty and insecurity to the proceedings. I give them a little bit of information but not enough that they are able to become characters. I don't like the word improvise in this context but the action is not planned. It is important to me that something real is going on during the shoot but this is not *Big Brother*. I am directing events. But there is so much going on that everything gets messed up. There are the actors and there is the real situation.

HRW *Do you feel that video is the most appropriate art form for a media-dominated age?*

AM I think as an art form video connects in the most straightforward way. But I'm not offering a story that you can assimilate like you might expect to find in a film. I'm offering an experience of space and time that is related to the speed of the images. This is why my work always involves action but it's action that doesn't lead anywhere. There is a simulation of events but there's no narrative. It's more like patterns of eternally different variations. So although there is action going on, there's also a sense of stretching time. You can spend time with my work and try to reposition yourself in relation to the imagery.

HRW *The lack of chronology in your films, the way they loop, creates the contradictory experience of being both intimate with time and estranged from it.*

AM The way I construct my pieces has to do with memory. If you have a critical moment in your life, you have to live it over and over, you can never really grasp it. It's a process but a static process. You are constantly trying to reconstruct that moment, whether it was a happy moment or a tragic one. The more you try to catch it, the more it eludes you and therefore it becomes a process, a continuous action.

HRW *Your camerawork and the way you film would appear to be as important as what you film.*

AM My imagery refuses to focus on psychological images or on specific people. The focus is always on the mass in the space, it is always an accumulation of small events, no one event is more important than the other. I try to work in a way that a human presence has the same value or the same significance as any other random object. I don't seek to make any moral commentary. What I offer appeals to a sense of ambiguity, an elusiveness which is balancing – it is more a description of how our experiences are organised, how we experience the world at this moment. I seek to render the normal abnormal and this brings about a sense of detachment. This is a correction to how we consume images. My work is not directly about political crises but about the crisis of how we relate that information to our personal lives. I think, at the moment, there is a sense that things are falling apart. In Holland we have gone through enormous changes over the past five or six years, both politically and on the street, and immigration is a major part of that. There are problems with second and third generation immigrants and this leads to tensions in the cities. Many people respond to those tensions with fear and that fuels populist reactions. The country I grew up in no longer exists. But this is not confined to Holland, it is happening all over Europe and the fear is accompanied by issues of security and all that kind of crap. There is a feeling of disquiet but we are not able to put our finger on it and this affects our sense of reality.

HRW *To what extent do you draw on images that you know we can all relate to? For example, could* Scapegoats *be portraying TV scenes from the aftermath of New Orleans?*

AM It is reminiscent of New Orleans but that is only a minor element of that piece. What is important in my work is the way images have a relation to the images of your daily life. What contributes to the feeling of ambiguity in my work is that it is always at the crossroads of situations that we feel familiar with. The images never fully develop in that direction but there are moments, flashes of recognition. In a similar manner to filmmakers such as Gus Van Sant, I am creating an area that is an accumulation of moments – they don't make a narrative, but it is a crossroads. *Vacuum Room* is a kind of political arena. It could refer to somewhere in eastern Europe but it's not eastern Europe. Sometimes the geography seems reminiscent of somewhere and could be applicable to certain situations, but you cannot pin those situations down historically. Images in the films have potential. In this sense they are archetypal images.

HRW *In this exhibition some of the pieces almost seem to be in dialogue with each other, especially* Raw Footage *and* Training Ground.

AM *Raw Footage* and *Training Ground* were conceived at around the same time but they are not directly related. But seen at the same time, they pose questions about what is staged and what is not, our ability to distinguish reality from fantasy. I was involved in a project in Utrecht last year about war and for a long time I'd been interested in seeing what we hadn't seen. Obviously what we see of war is highly selective. If you focus on one event through the camera, there is always something else going on beside the camera – a non-event if you like – but which is always there and part of a different reality.

HRW *Is your work a criticism of our image-obsessed society?*

AM I think my work comes about as a response to a saturation of images, which has had a numbing effect. The work has no moral direction, it has no critique, but that doesn't mean it doesn't contain moments which are not critical or that it cannot have an effect that is critical. If you are looking for a straightforward critical action it is not there, but the result of the work maybe goes in that direction.

Issue 305, April 2007

Index

Copyright Notices

This edition published in 2013 by
Ridinghouse

Ridinghouse
5–8 Lower John Street
Golden Square
London W1F 9DR
United Kingdom
www.ridinghouse.co.uk

Distributed in the UK and Europe by
Cornerhouse
70 Oxford Street
Manchester M1 5NH
United Kingdom
www.cornerhouse.org

Distributed in the US by
RAM Publications
2525 Michigan Avenue Building A2
Santa Monica, CA 90404
United States
www.rampub.com

British Library Cataloguing-in-Publication Data
A catalogue record of this book is available from the British Library

ISBN 978 1 905464 56 2

Art Monthly co-ordinator:
Frederika Whitehead
Ridinghouse co-ordinator:
Rosalind Horne

For this edition:
Ridinghouse Publisher: Doro Globus
Editorial Assistant: Louisa Green
Proofreader: Eileen Daly
Designed and produced by
Mark Thomson
Assisted by Rob Payne
Set in OT Arnhem
Printed by Samhwa Printing Company,
South Korea

Acknowledgements
The editors would like to offer sincere thanks to all of the artists and their interviewers who have enabled us to create this book, as well as to *Art Monthly*'s publisher Jack Wendler, and Frederika Whitehead, Letty Mooring and Penny Williams of *Art Monthly*, Karsten Schubert, Rosalind Horne, Doro Globus and Louisa Green of Ridinghouse, Eileen Daly, and the designer of this book and former deputy editor of *Art Monthly* Mark Thomson. All of this could not have happened without the assistance of Arts Council England and the Henry Moore Foundation.

Supported by
ARTS COUNCIL
ENGLAND

The Henry Moore
Foundation